Guarantees the strong and the weak limited freedom.

Guerrilla war

Low-intensity conflict

Limited conventional war

Conventional war

War of limited mass destruction

War of unlimited mass destruction

State of Nature

Conflict destroys
the Civil State and
returns to the State
of Nature.

Clausewitz

War

Determine the level and type of conflict.

Accordingly, the Civil State always experiences conflict.
It is never "at peace." The moral duty of agents of the state
is to identify the type of conflict and reduce it to the lowest
possible level with the least amount of force. See pages
232–233 for further explanation.

TERRORISM AND HOMELAND SECURITY

Fifth Edition

Jonathan R. White
Grand Valley State University

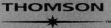
THOMSON

WADSWORTH

™ Australia • Brazil • Canada • Mexico • Singapore • Spain • United Kingdom • United States

THOMSON

WADSWORTH

Terrorism and Homeland Security, **Fifth Edition**
Jonathan R. White

Senior Acquisitions Editor, Criminal Justice:
  Carolyn Henderson Meier
Development Editor: Elise Smith
Assistant Editor: Jana Davis
Editorial Assistant: Rebecca Johnson
Technology Project Manager: Susan DeVanna
Marketing Manager: Terra Schultz
Marketing Assistant: Gregory Hughes
Marketing Communications Manager: Stacey Purviance
Project Manager, Editorial Production: Jennie Redwitz
Art Director: Vernon Boes
Print Buyer: Doreen Suruki

Permissions Editor: Stephanie Lee
Production Service: Jamie Armstrong, G&S Book Services
Text Designer: Jeanne Calabrese
Photo Researcher: Sarah Evertson
Copy Editor: Jessie Dolch
Illustrator: G&S Book Services
Cover Designer: Yvo
Cover Images: Explosion: The Stocktrek Corp./Getty Images;
  dynamite and timer: David Glick/Getty Images
Cover Printer: Phoenix Color Corp
Compositor: G&S Book Services
Printer: R.R. Donnelley/Crawfordsville

Library of Congress Control Number: 2005923897

ISBN 0-534-64381-7

Thomson Higher Education
10 Davis Drive
Belmont, CA 94002-3098
USA

For more information about our products, contact us at:
Thomson Learning Academic Resource Center
1-800-423-0563
For permission to use material from this text or
product, submit a request online at
http://www.thomsonrights.com.
Any additional questions about permissions can be
submitted by email to **thomsonrights@thomson.com.**

To the Counterterrorists of SLATT
"These dawgs will hunt."—Art Van Dorn

About the Author

Jonathan White is professor of criminal justice and executive director of the Homeland Defense Initiative at Grand Valley State University, Grand Rapids, Michigan. The former dean of social sciences and founding director of the School of Criminal Justice, White was seconded to manage the State and Local Anti-Terrorism Training program under the Bureau of Justice Assistance after the attacks of September 11, 2001. He returned to Grand Valley State in 2005. Before his career in academics, he worked as a patrol officer, undercover investigator, and assistant administrator in the Jackson Police Department in Jackson, Michigan, and as a training specialist with the Michigan State Police. He holds a doctorate in criminal justice and criminology from Michigan State University, a master of divinity from Western Theological Seminary, and master's and bachelor's degrees in military history from Western Michigan University. White maintains an active role in domestic and international antiterrorism training and teaches counterterrorism at the FBI Academy.

Brief Contents

Contents

Preface

Terrorism began receiving increased attention on university and college campuses as the number of American casualties grew from terrorist violence in the 1990s. Community colleges and lower-division university courses have been added to the new array of offerings as a result. While numerous colleges have used both *Terrorism: An Introduction* and *Defending the Homeland* in these courses, several instructors have asked for a text more suited to introductory classes for freshmen and sophomores. They have also asked that the book present the issues involved in homeland security. *Terrorism and Homeland Security* was written to address their requests.

This book introduces criminal justice and other social science students to the field of terrorism. It is designed for students who have little or no understanding of the world of terrorism, and the purpose is to provide basic knowledge as a foundation for further understanding. It reviews major theories in the field; definitions and motivations for terrorism; religious, ideological, nationalistic, and ethnic terrorism; domestic and international terrorist movements; technological, cyber, nuclear, biological, and chemical terrorism; terrorist financing; Jihadist networks; the organization and function of homeland security; the protection of constitutional rights and civil liberties; and the effect of the media on terrorism.

Three things are particularly important in this book. First, it is designed for student comprehension. Terrorism is extremely complex, especially when students explore it for the first time, and this text provides a base for student understanding. Second, the world of terrorism constantly changes. In fact, terrorist groups must change to survive, and this text contains timely information to capture the changing nature of terrorism. Finally, the book combines summaries of major scholarly works, practical and scholarly research findings, and results from investigative journalism. This information is assembled in such a way as to provide an easy-to-understand and comprehensive picture of its subject.

Issues in terrorism are emotionally charged; therefore, the information is presented from various positions. Although it is generally written for those who will counter terrorism, the purpose is to explain many points of view without taking sides. This is true whether examining issues like the Israeli-Palestinian conflict or the controversy surrounding the USA Patriot Act. It is hoped that the text presents information that will allow students to make informed decisions and to engage in critical thinking. The topics are designed to stimulate classroom discussions, individual reflection, and student research.

Terrorism and security issues are also complex, so each chapter includes references for further research, along with suggested websites. Thomson Wadsworth has also developed a website for students and instructors who want to seek greater depth. References to this site appear throughout the text, and the website contains extensive introductory details for everyone who seeks more information. By the same token, anyone wishing to approach complexity needs to be introduced to the topic. *Terrorism and Homeland Security* attempts to provide the base and the tools for going further.

A Note on the Revision

In some ways, this book is a revised edition. At times, instructors who have used *Terrorism: An Introduction* and *Defending the Homeland* will recognize familiar passages or approaches. There are two important differences, however. Much of the detail in the earlier works has been replaced with more focused and simplified explanations of current issues. This should enhance student understanding. Second, *Terrorism and Homeland Security* explores dozens of new topics. For example, there are discussions of the Hawala system, drugs and terrorism, models of suicide bombings, the al Aqsa Intifada, terrorist financial networks, and activities in Central and Southeast Asia. In this regard, the book is more akin to a new product than a revision of earlier texts.

Distinctive Features

This textbook is designed for teaching and learning; therefore, a variety of distinctive teaching and learning aids designed to simplify issues and enhance student understanding have been added to this edition. These include the following features:

Chapter Objectives   Each chapter begins with objectives that will help the student know what they are to understand as they approach the chapter.

Key Points and Questions   Each section begins with a set of questions that will help guide students through the material and tell them what the important points are in the paragraphs that follow. Furthermore, as students answer and think about the *Key Points and Questions*, they will be encouraged to analyze issues and form opinions. This will enhance their understanding of the material. Instructors can also use the *Key Points and Questions* to stimulate classroom discussions.

Summary of Main Ideas   To further help students understand the objectives, each chapter ends with a summary of main ideas presented in the chapter.

Key Terms   Each chapter also includes a list of key terms appearing in the chapter. As students prepare for papers and examinations, these key terms will help them master concepts. A glossary for key terms appears at the end of the text.

Suggested Readings   Additional readings are presented at the end of every chapter. The first suggestion contains a synopsis of one or more of the best-known scholarly works on the subject of the chapter. This is followed by a sentence or two describing some of the better-known popular and scholarly works.

Web Resources   Internet references are provided after the suggested readings. These references will help students prepare class projects, research papers, and/or in-depth studies.

With these chapter features, students can have a ready-made test review by combining the Chapter Objectives, Key Points and Questions, Key Terms, and Summary of Main Ideas.

In addition to the chapter features, there are a variety of in-text resources that students and instructors can use to learn additional concepts, think critically, and better understand the changing nature of terrorism. **Expanding the Concept** boxes take a deeper look at an issue presented in the narrative. They range from explaining points of view among experts to summarizing complex concepts. **Tables** summarize information to illustrate points in the narrative. **Another Perspective** boxes explain the terms associated with a topic, often providing varying definitions and explanations for major concepts. For example, it is very difficult for students to encounter the Middle East for the first time. Therefore, Chapter 9, the background chapter on the Middle East, contains a glossary of "Important Terms, Concepts, and People in the Middle East" to guide students through peace treaties, political conflicts, people, and historical events. **Maps** have been added and expanded throughout the new edition to illustrate the geographic locations where terrorism began, has developed, and continues to grow.

The Companion Website

The editorial staff at Thomson Wadsworth surveyed criminal justice and social science instructors to determine the type of textbook they would like to see developed for a course in terrorism. Instructors overwhelmingly asked for a simple introduction to terrorism. In addition, several instructors asked me to write a more basic text in the wake of the terrorist attacks of September 11. While *Terrorism and Homeland Security* is the outcome of these requests, many instructors and students enjoyed the depth of *Terrorism: An Introduction* and *Defending the Homeland.*

For instructors who would like a basic text but still want the depth of the previous works, the editorial staff developed a solution. Several points in the book refer students to the Thomson Wadsworth Companion Website (http://cj.wadsworth.com/white_terrorism5e) where instructors and students will find in-depth discussions of theory, history, models, and campaigns. For example, the site contains information on the Spectrum of Conflict; the tactical typology of terrorism; detailed histories of terrorism in Ireland, the Middle East, and other regions; detailed summaries of works on several scholarly positions about terrorism; discussions of campaigns and specific attacks; and theoretical models of terrorism. It also includes homeland security issues, discussions on the transformation of war, law enforcement activities and intelligence gathering, and examinations of security policy.

Instructors may use this website to take their classes to new levels. Many of the historical, political, and sociological issues raised in earlier publications are now provided at no charge on the Thomson Wadsworth website. By using the text and these tools, instructors can help students move to their highest level of understanding. *Terrorism and Homeland Security* is designed to give students a place to stand; the website provides steps beyond that base. The website also contains a rich array of teaching and learning resources that you won't find anywhere else. It features chapter outlines, chapter reviews, chapter-by-chapter web links, flash cards, and more.

Ancillary Material

In addition to the rich website and the main text of the book, the following supplements are available to instructors. (Available to qualified adopters. Please consult your local sales representative for details.)

Instructor's Resource Manual   This helpful resource for instructors contains everything you need to prepare for your lectures and exams: Chapter Objectives, Detailed Chapter Outlines, Chapter Summaries, Key Terms, Classroom Exercises and Discussion Questions, and a Test Bank with multiple choice, true/false, fill-in-the-blank, short answer, and essay questions, with a full answer key.

Current Perspectives: Readings from InfoTrac® College Edition: Terrorism and Homeland Security   Edited and introduced by Dr. Dipak K. Gupta (San Diego State University), the sixteen articles in this reader offer a representative selection that helps you introduce students to important issues in terrorism and homeland security. It includes FREE access to **InfoTrac College Edition,** and can also be bundled with the text for free.

America's New War: CNN Looks at Terrorism, **Volumes I and II**   These two videos feature CNN clips with in-depth coverage of recent terrorist attacks and events on the international stage. Volume I covers anthrax and biological warfare, new security measures, al Qaeda, homeland defense, renewed patriotism, and more. Volume II examines the case of Jose Padilla, Guantanamo Bay detainees, the train bombings in Spain, the capture of Saddam Hussein, the search for weapons of mass destruction, recent incidents of domestic terrorism, and more. Your Thomson Wadsworth representative will be happy to explain our policy of videos by adoption size and help you to obtain the videos of your choice in accordance with this policy.

Wadsworth Criminal Justice Video Resource Center   Visit cj.wadsworth.com/videos to view Wadsworth's video policy and see a full list of Wadsworth's video offerings, including titles such as *Waging War against the New Terrorism, The Bombers,* and *Stopping the Money: An Economic Approach to Counterterrorism.* Clip lists and video descriptions are also available to download or print.

Acknowledgments

No book is written in a vacuum, and few writers can produce a finished product without support. Many people assisted by taking time for interviews, listening to concepts, critiquing ideas, or simply being around at the end of a long day.

Friends in the academic world were invaluable. Thank you to President Mark Murray, Provost Gayle Davis, Trustee Emeritus Karen Henry Stokes, Dr. Terry Fisk, Dr. Erika King, and Dr. Rodney Mulder of Grand Valley State University for their enthusiastic support. For sharing information and critiquing ideas, thanks go to Dr. David Carter, Michigan State University; Dr. Richard Holden, Director of SLATT; Dr. Robert Taylor, University of North Texas; Dr. Brent Smith, University of Arkansas; Dr. James Hendricks, Dr. Taiping Ho, and Dr. Stephen Brodt, Ball State University; Dr. Randy Borum, University of South Florida; and Dr. Richard Ward, Sam Houston State University. I would also like to thank the reviewers whose comments helped shape this revision: David L. Andersen, Minnesota State Community and Technical College; Dr. David Baker, University of Toledo; Mark H. Beaudry, Northeastern University; Edward Berger, Pima Community College; Bob Bidwell, Isothermal Community College; Joseph Byrnes, Florida International University; Dr. Victoria DeRosia, Castleton State College; Captain Michael M. Eagen (ret.), Webster University–Luke Air Force Base; Dr. Stephen Ellsworth, Saint Leo University; W. Ralph Garris, University of South Carolina–Lancaster; Dr. Mark Gasiorowski, Louisiana State University; Dr. Robert E. Grubb, Marshall University; Dr. Richard Hill, University of Houston; Dr. Lynette Knight, Webster University–Luke Air Force Base; Michael Levinson (J.D.), Loyola University; Dr. Jane D. Matheson, Northeastern University; Dr. Mark Mullenbach, University of Central Arkansas; Dr. Thomas R. O'Connor, North Carolina Wesleyan College; Dr. Benn Prybutok, Montgomery County Community College; Paul Rivas, University of Wisconsin–Milwaukee; Dr. Jonathan Schachter, Northwestern University; Todd Scott, Schoolcraft College–Radcliff Center; Dr. Judy Van Wyk, University of Rhode Island; and Major Dennis White (ret.), Lamar Institute of Technology. Your ideas improved the book. The faults are mine; the improvements belong to you.

Many people in the federal government deserve my gratitude. To Domingo Herraiz, the director of the Bureau of Justice Assistance, and Eileen Garry, deputy director of BJA, thank you for laughter, encouragement, endless meetings, and your unfailing support of SLATT. To the FBI: Thank you Deputy Director John Pistole for letting me sit in on IACP terrorism meetings, listening to ideas, and sharing information; Acting Assistant Director Patrick Peterson for saying it was worthwhile; SSA David Crane (ret.) and SSA William McCormick for being comrades in counterterrorism; SSA Paul George for being the real thing; SSA Kate Kilham for criticism that challenged and produced a better product; and the staff and students of the FBI National Academy for your continuing enthusiasm and desire to learn.

To Dale Watson, Paul Pillar, and Stephen Simon, thank you for allowing me to sit on panels with you, for answering questions, and for your service to our country.

I am also grateful to Senator Carl Levin for his interest in the field and the help of his staff. Gratitude goes to Congressman Michael Rogers for taking time for a critical review, and to Congressman Peter Hoekstra, chair of the House Select Committee on Intelligence, for discussions in the dark days after September 11, frequent airport encounters, and examining models of terrorism sketched on napkins.

There is not enough room to list all of the U.S. attorneys who shared material and kept me in several different cities each week with dozens of different law enforcement agencies. So, please let me say thank you to the chief prosecutors from the Department of Justice. You are appreciated.

I must thank Chief Edward Lohn of the Cleveland Police Department and Chief Roger Bragdon of the Spokane Police Department for their enthusiastic support. I hope this new effort lives up to your standards. Thanks also to Kevin Zucatto and Stephanie Taylor of the Australian Federal Police. To my friend Deputy Chief Constable Peter Howse (ret.) of the Norfolk Constabulary, United Kingdom, thank you, as always, for making me part of the U.K. team.

The editorial staff at Thomson Wadsworth was wonderful. Elise Smith, you deserved your promotion and you handle frantic authors very well. Eve Howard, you took the time to make sure this would work. Good luck Sabra Horne in your new endeavor. Finally, to my editor Carolyn Henderson Meier and editorial assistant Rebecca Johnson, thank you from the bottom of my heart. Your tolerance and support meant more than you know.

The Institute of Intergovernmental Research is on the cutting edge of several issues in criminal justice, including terrorism. Gratitude goes to Emory Williams, Doug Bodrero, Viola Bodrero, Jennifer Turner, Brandon McGahee, Gina Hartsfield, Karli O'Neil, Stephanie Roeser, Charlene White, Scot Tedcastle, Eric Arillo, Jonathan Morse, and Regina Schimpf. The book is dedicated to the other IIR group, fellow members of the million mile club. Thanks SLATT team. *Si vis pacem, para bellum.*

Finally, thank you Marcia for three and one half decades of art, joy, and love.

Disclaimer

Much of the work for this book was completed while I was on leave from Grand Valley State University serving as the director of the State and Local Anti-Terrorism Training (SLATT) program. SLATT is a Bureau of Justice Assistance (BJA) program managed by the Institute of Intergovernmental Research (IIR) and the Federal Bureau of Investigation (FBI). The material in this book does not necessarily represent the positions of BJA, IIR, or the FBI.

Part One THE CRIMINOLOGY AND CONTROVERSY OF TERRORISM

Chapter 1

Definitions, Tactics, and Behavior

© EPA/Robin Townsend/Landov

Skinheads offer a salute in Spain. Can such activity evolve into terrorism?

Although the word *terrorism* has many different meanings, September 11, 2001, changed the way Americans use the term. Before that date, few Americans paid much attention to terrorism. Afterward, many of them accepted the idea that America was at war with terrorism. Most people project their own meanings onto the word, so it is not surprising to find that governments, journalists, lawyers, and professors have many different things in mind when they say "terrorism." Meanings also change over time. Violent activity in one period may be called terrorism, while the same action may be deemed war, liberation, or crime at another time in history. The behavior of terrorists changes when the meaning changes. It is difficult to define the term and place the behavior of terrorists in a particular category.

Chapter Objectives

After reading this chapter, you should be able to:

1. Explain the importance of defining terrorism.
2. Summarize definitions of terrorism by leading experts in the field.
3. Explain official definitions of terrorism.
4. Discuss the implied meaning of declaring "war" on terrorism.
5. Summarize the tactics terrorists use.
6. Define force multipliers.
7. Explain the ways terrorists seek to justify violent behavior.
8. Summarize the thesis of the book *Warrior Dreams*.
9. Explain the differences between the behavior of terrorists and ordinary criminals.
10. List and define three points of view regarding terrorist profiling.

Why Definitions Are Important

Key Points and Questions:

1. Why do people argue about the meaning of terrorism?
2. Why is any definition of terrorism pejorative?
3. Give some examples of different definitions of terrorism from various interest groups.

Many arguments may arise when anyone tries to define terrorism. Instead of agreeing on the definition of terrorism, social scientists, policymakers, lawyers, and security specialists often argue about the meaning of the term. Walter Laqueur (1999, pp. 8–10) says it is difficult to define because the meaning changes through history. Alex Schmid (1983, pp. 77–103; and 1988, 2004) says terrorism cannot be defined because it is a concept, not a physical object. H. H. A. Cooper (1978, 2001) summarizes the difficulty with the phrase "a problem in the problem definition." Terrorism is hard to define because it means different things at different times. We can agree that terrorism is a problem, but we cannot agree on what terrorism is.

There are several reasons for confusion. First, terrorism is difficult to define because it has a pejorative connotation. A person is politically and socially degraded when labeled a terrorist, and the same thing happens when an organization is called a terrorist group. Routine crimes assume greater social importance when they are described as terrorism, and political movements can be hampered when their followers are believed to be terrorists.

Further confusion arises when people intertwine the terms terror and terrorism. The object of military force, for example, is to strike terror into the heart of the enemy, and **systematic terror** has been a basic weapon in conflicts throughout history. Some people argue that there is no difference between military force and terrorism. Many members of the antinuclear movement have extended this argument by claiming that ready-to-use nuclear weapons are an extension of terrorism. Others use the same logic when claiming that street gangs and criminals terrorize neighborhoods. If you think that anything that creates terror is terrorism, the scope of potential definitions becomes limitless.

The definition of terrorism usually fluctuates according to the interest of the group defining the term. Law enforcement agencies define it with criminal codes. Governments call violent opponents terrorists. People advocating the redistribution of wealth claim that repressive governments are terrorists. Some people believe the target matters. When groups target military forces, it is not terrorism, but when they attack civilians, it is. Militant pro-life supporters call doctors who perform abortions terrorists, whereas pro-choice advocates use the same term to describe their opponents. Many Palestinians believe that Hezbollah is a legitimate military organization, but Israel calls it a terrorist group. Like crime, terrorism is defined in many different ways, and the meaning changes when differing groups use the term.

Definitions of Terrorism

Key Points and Questions:

1. Summarize Jenkins' and Laqueur's simple definitions of terrorism.
2. Why does Laqueur believe it is pointless to move beyond simple definitions?
3. What are the strengths and weaknesses of simple definitions of terrorism?
4. How does Crenshaw define terrorism?
5. Does Herman's argument shift the focus of the discussion?
6. Summarize terrorism using Schmid's method.

The most widely used definition of terrorism in criminal justice, military, and security circles is a rather simple view fostered by Brian Jenkins of the RAND Corporation and Walter Laqueur, a leading authority from Georgetown University. They defined terrorism separately but arrived at remarkably similar conclusions.

Jenkins (1984) calls terrorism the use or threatened use of force designed to bring about a political change (see Another Perspective: Two Ways of Looking at Terrorism). In a **simple definition** closely related to that of Jenkins, Laqueur (1987, p. 72) says terrorism constitutes the illegitimate use of force to achieve a political objective by targeting innocent people. He adds that attempts to move beyond the simple definition are fruitless because the term is so controversial. Volumes can be written on the definition of terrorism, Laqueur writes in a footnote, but they will not add one iota to our understanding of the topic. In a later work, Laqueur (1999, pp. 8–10) again promotes a simple definition, reminding readers that terrorism means different things at different points in history.

Both Jenkins and Laqueur freely admit problems with their simple approach. An uncomplicated definition does not describe the topic, and there is no meaningful way to apply a simple definition to specific acts of terrorism. Simple definitions also leave academicians, policymakers, and social scientists frustrated. In short, simplicity does not solve the problem presented by Cooper; that is, there is a problem in defining the problem.

But definitions hardly stop with pragmatic simplicity. Germany, the United Kingdom, and Spain outlawed terrorism more than a decade ago, and America has examined the idea of a **legal definition** (Mullendore and White, 1996). The beauty of legal definitions is they give governments specific crimes that they can use to take action against terrorist activities, but there is also a downside. Legal definitions contain internal contradictions. Under the legal guidelines of the United States, for example, sometimes U.S. foreign policy seems to be supporting terrorism.

Martha Crenshaw (1983) says terrorism cannot be defined unless the act, target, and possibility of success are analyzed. Under this approach, freedom fighters use legitimate military methods to attack legitimate political targets. Their actions are further legitimized when they have some possibility of winning the conflict. Freedom fighters become terrorists when they abandon military methods and military targets, or when they fight with no chance of winning.

A different definition comes from Edward Herman (1983), who says terrorism should be defined in terms of state repression. Citing corrupt Latin American governments, Herman argues that repressive policies have resulted in more misery for more people than any other form of state-sponsored terror. In another publication, Michael Stohl (1988, pp. 20–28) sounds a sympathetic note, claiming that governments most frequently use terrorism to maintain power.

Walter Laqueur (1987, p. 6) says such conclusions are correct, and one would be foolish to deny that state repression has caused less suffering than modern terrorism. Yet, Laqueur argues, governmental repression is a long-term political problem, separate from modern terrorism. To include it in the discussion confuses the issue and does little to enhance our understanding of terrorism.

In an effort to solve the definitional dilemma, Alex Schmid (1983, pp. 70–111) tries to synthesize various positions. He concludes there is no true or correct definition because terrorism is an abstract concept with no real presence. A single definition cannot possibly account for all the potential uses of the term. Still, Schmid says, a number of elements are common to leading definitions, and most definitions have two characteristics: Someone is terrorized, and the meaning of the term is derived from the targets and victims of terrorists.

Schmid also offers a conglomerated definition of terrorism, or an **academic consensus definition**. His empirical analysis finds twenty-two elements common to most definitions, and he develops a definition containing thirteen of those elements. Schmid sees terrorism as a method of combat in which the victims serve as symbolic targets. Violent actors are able to produce a chronic state of fear by using violence

Another Perspective

Two Ways of Looking at Terrorism

JENKINS'S DEFINITION
Brian Jenkins says that:

1. Terrorism is violence or the threat of violence.
2. It may be a crime, but criminals are not terrorists.
3. The victims are of secondary importance.
4. Terrorism is designed to create drama.
5. The drama is for a target audience.
6. These factors separate terrorism from other forms of conflict.

PILLAR'S DEFINITION
CIA executive Paul Pillar says there are four elements to terrorism:

1. It is planned in advance rather than being an impulsive act of rage.
2. It is a political activity.
3. It is aimed at civilians.
4. It is carried out by subnational groups.

Sources: Jenkins (2004b); Council on Foreign Relations (2004).

Official Definitions of Terrorism

State Department   From title 22 of the U.S. Code section 2656f(d): "The term 'terrorism' means premeditated, politically motivated violence perpetrated against noncombatant targets by sub-national groups or clandestine agents, usually intended to influence an audience. The term 'international terrorism' means terrorism involving citizens or the territory of more than one country. The term 'terrorist group' means any group practicing, or that has significant subgroups that practice, international terrorism."

Source: U.S. Department of State (1999).

FBI   The FBI defines terrorism as "the unlawful use of force or violence against persons or property to intimidate or coerce a government, the civilian population, or any segment thereof, in furtherance of political or social objectives." The FBI further describes terrorism as either domestic or international, depending on the origin, base, and objectives of the terrorist organization.

Source: Federal Bureau of Investigation (1999).

Vice President's Task Force   Terrorism is the unlawful use or threat of violence against persons or property to further political or social objectives. It is usually intended to intimidate or coerce a government, individuals or groups, or to modify their behavior or politics.

Source: Vice President's Task Force (1986).

United Nations   A TERRORIST is any person who, acting independently of the specific recognition of a country, or as a single person, or as part of a group not recognized as an official part or division of a nation, acts to destroy or to injure civilians or destroy or damage property belonging to civilians or to governments in order to effect some political goal. TERRORISM is the act of destroying or injuring civilian lives or the act of destroying or damaging civilian or government property without the expressly chartered permission of a specific government, thus, by individuals or groups acting independently or governments on their own accord and belief, in the attempt to effect some political goal.

Source: Weinberg, Pedahzur, and Hirsch-Hoefler (2004).

Defense Department   Terrorism is the unlawful use or threatened use of force or violence against individuals or property to coerce or intimidate governments or societies, often to achieve political, religious, or ideological objectives.

Source: http://www.periscope.usni.com/demo/terms/t0000282.html.

Defense Intelligence Agency   Terrorism is premeditated, political violence perpetrated against noncombatant targets by subnational groups or clandestine state agents, usually to influence an audience.

Source: http://www.periscope.usni.com/demo/terms/t0000282.html.

outside the realm of normative behavior. This produces an audience beyond the immediate victim and results in a change of public attitudes and actions.

Some scholars believe Schmid has solved the definitional dilemma by combining definitions. Others think he has refined the indefinable. While analysts wrestle with the problem, most of them end up doing one of three things: Some follow the lead of Crenshaw and Thomas Thorton (1964, p. 73) and look for illegitimate violence instead of political revolution. Others follow the lead of Schmid, either synthesizing definitions or using those of others. Finally, some people ignore the problem altogether; they talk about terrorism and assume everybody knows what they mean.

The best way to define terrorism is to move toward simplicity. Terrorism is a method of fighting. Thomas P. M. Barnett (2004, pp. 43–46) explains that the rules of conflict changed at the end of the Cold War. Nations existing in a secure economic structure are prepared to fight within the rules of state-to-state war. Terrorists, on the other hand, do not have a vested interest in maintaining economic and political structures because they do not benefit from them. Therefore, *they fight outside the rules.*

The simple definition of terrorism is consistent with **Barnett's logic.** Terrorism occurs outside the "rules" of warfare and criminal activity. Terrorism uses violence or threatened violence against innocent people to achieve a social or political goal. Terrorism is a method of fighting somewhat greater than civil disorders and somewhat less than guerilla warfare.

Go to **http://cj.wadsworth.com/white _terrorism5e** and click on Web Links for an in-depth discussion of terrorism as a mode a conflict.

The Meaning of the War on Terrorism

Key Points and Questions:

1. Is it possible to declare war on terrorism?
2. Describe Friedman's view of three wars against democracy.
3. How do Blank, Cohen, and Hill reflect government policy by describing a war on terrorism?
4. Why does Howard believe the war metaphor should not be used?

Shortly after the attacks of September 11, 2001, President George W. Bush addressed the nation, stating that America and its allies were in a war with terrorism. This was a rhetorical reaction to a tragic day. Nearly thirty years earlier, President Lyndon

Expanding the Concept

What's in a Name? Declaring War on Terror Expands Governmental Power

Not everyone thinks the United States should declare war on terrorism. James Bovard offers a scathing analysis of the idea, arguing that the government uses the word "war" to trample freedom. Rather than protecting America's borders, Bovard says, the government uses the rhetoric of war to increase its own power at the expense of individual rights. This process started during the Reagan presidency and continues today. Bovard calls the war on terrorism a "political growth industry."

Source: Bovard (2003).

Johnson declared war on poverty. During the 1990s both Republican and Democratic presidents declared a war on drugs. Like President Bush's comments in the wake of September 11, these were symbolic calls. In reality, Congress probably does not have the Constitutional power to declare war on a concept.

Many people accept the idea of a **war on terrorism,** even though no one seems to be able to define the term. Thomas Friedman (2004), a columnist for the *New York Times*, believes the United States is at war with terrorism. Friedman calls the fighting after September 11 democracy's third great struggle against totalitarianism in the past one hundred years. The first came against the Nazis (1939–1945), and the next struggle involved the West against the East during the Cold War (1945–1991). Today's enemy, Friedman says, are militant groups who hate America more than they love life.

Stephen Blank (2003) of the U.S. Army War College also accepts the metaphor of war. Like Friedman, he believes that this new war differs from conflicts of the past. Blank contends that America's best weapon is to assist legitimate governments faced with armed insurgencies. Terrorism is caused by different radical groups driven by localized economic, social, and political pressures. They can be countered, Blank says, by providing military assistance to legitimate governments and pressuring repressive governments to reform.

Ariel Cohen (2003) also believes the United States is in a war with terrorism. Examining Central Asia, Cohen believes the United States must project military power in the face of terrorist groups. He argues that it is necessary to position military forces in Central Asia so they may be used in Afghanistan and elsewhere. He warns, however, that American military forces should not associate with repressive governments. Fiona Hill (2003) of the Brookings Institution agrees. To conduct the war on terrorism, she says, it is necessary to identify militant groups and select the proper tactics that will destroy them. Cohen and Hill see no problem with a war on terrorism as long as political leaders understand that the war will require innovative weapons.

Not surprisingly, the federal government claims the United States is at war with terrorism. In an official statement on the second anniversary of September 11, the White House (2003) lumped domestic and international terrorists together, stating that the central front of the struggle was in Iraq. The weapons America would use in the war on terrorism would be the Homeland Security Act of 2002 and the USA Patriot Act of 2001, the press release stated (see Expanding the Concept: What's in a Name? Declaring War on Terror Expands Governmental Power).

Military historian Michael Howard (2002) has not been so quick to join the bandwagon. He believes that terrorism is an emergency situation best handled by intelligence and law enforcement services. Military forces may be used, but they serve as reinforcements for law enforcement or as special operations units for intelligence organizations. Counterterrorist work is sometimes a matter for criminal courts and is at other times best left to ruthless secret actions of intelligence units. Counterterrorism involves tedious investigations and information gathering operations. When counterterrorism is called a war, it evokes images of battles, sophisticated weapons, and lightning strikes against a well-defined enemy. This is not the nature of terrorism, nor does it indicate the methods used to combat it.

The Tactics of Terrorism

 Key Points and Questions:

1. Describe terrorism as a method of fighting.
2. What is the most common terrorist weapon?
3. According to Jenkins, what are the most common terrorist tactics?
4. What are force multipliers?
5. List and describe the force multipliers that terrorists use.

Although it is difficult to define terrorism, it is not difficult to summarize terrorist tactics. To begin, Ian Lesser (1999, pp. 8–10) suggests that terrorism is defined by a situation, and it changes with each new situation. If he is correct, then terrorism can be seen as a method of fighting. Tactics change in terrorism just like they change in war. Groups change structures and goals, and terrorists learn from the past and their previous successes and mistakes. Terrorists change tactics continually. This means security forces must be willing to change the way they respond to terrorists.

Jenkins (1984) says there are six **tactics of terrorism**: bombing, hijacking, arson, assault, kidnapping, and hostage taking (see Expanding the Concept: The Most Common Tactic of Terrorism). Recently, the arsenal of terrorism has changed to include potential threats from **weapons of mass destruction** (Jenkins, 1987; Brackett, 1996, p. 45; White, 1986, 2000). Technology has also modified bombing. In the age of information and electronics, disruption of services through electronic hacking and logic bombs have also become tactics of terrorism.

Jenkins says the six tactics can be enhanced by **force multipliers** (see Another Perspective: Force Multipliers). In military terms, a force multiplier increases striking power without increasing the

Expanding the Concept

The Most Common Tactic of Terrorism

Although terrorist tactics change through time, the most common weapon of terrorism has been and is still the bomb. In 1848 anarchists talked about the "philosophy of the bomb, meaning that the only way to communicate with the social order was to destroy it. In the late 1800s, militants used bombs to attack governments and businesses. The Irish Republican Army (IRA) found the bomb to be their most important weapon after 1969, and by 1985 the organization was deploying extremely sophisticated ones. Groups in the Middle East, Sri Lanka, and eventually throughout the world found that bombs could be delivered by suicide attackers. Hijackers first used bombs to take over planes, and then, on September 11, 2001, terrorists turned civilian airliners into bombs.

Another Perspective

Force Multipliers

Transnational support   Increases the ability of terrorist groups to move and hide.

Technology   Allows a small group to launch a deadly attack.

Media coverage   Can make a minor group appear to be politically important.

Religion   Transcends normative political and social boundaries, increasing violence and decreasing opportunities for negotiation.

strength of a unit. Terrorists routinely use force multipliers because they add to their aura. All political terrorists want to give the illusion that they can fight on another level.

Four force multipliers give terrorists more striking power. Christine Ketcham and Harvey McGeorge (1986, pp. 25–33) conclude that technology can enhance a terrorist group's ability to strike (see Expanding the Concept: Enhancing Conventional Explosives). Jeffrey Goldberg's (2002) research on the Tri-Border Region in South America (see Chapter 5) demonstrates that transnational support networks multiply the striking power of terrorists. Daniel Benjamin and Steven Simon (2002, pp. 365–382) demonstrate that media coverage and interpretation of terrorist events often serve as force multipliers. One incident can be converted into a "campaign" as live electronic media scramble to break the latest news. A frightening new force multiplier, according to Bruce Hoffman (1995), has been the introduction of religious fanaticism in terrorist activities.

How Terrorist Groups Justify Behavior

Key Points and Questions:

1. Why do people justify participating in violence?
2. From what sources do terrorists seek justification?
3. Summarize Post's motivational theories.
4. Identify and explain Stern's view on group cohesion.
5. Does the research of Berlet and Lyons support Stern?

Killing and maiming people for a belief is not an easy task, even when people are deeply committed to that belief. Terrorists, like soldiers and police officers, need to feel justified when they use force. Executioners cannot spend much time crossexamining themselves if they want to do their job. Warriors need to feel they are serving the greater good. This is one of the reasons governments use their most sacred symbols to acknowledge sacrifices in war. Terrorists have the same need for social approval, but they are routinely condemned by the population at large; therefore, terrorists must look to themselves for approval. They must find a **justification for violence** (see Expanding the Concept: Seeking Group Approval for Murder).

The **terrorist group** becomes the primary source of social reality for an individual terrorist. It provides social recognition and reinforcement for its members. Like soldiers, who undergo a similar bonding process during basic training, po-

Go to **http://cj.wadsworth.com/white_terrorism5e** and click on Web Links for an analysis of Uruguay's urban guerilla group Tupamaros and an in-depth discussion of the need for terrorists to portray themselves as representatives of "the good."

tential terrorists join groups for varied reasons: They may be sympathetic to the cause, or they may simply be social misfits. The terrorist group reshapes identities and can provide a ticket to social acceptance.

Jerrold Post (1987) examines the way terrorists justify their behavior by measuring the effect of retaliation on group cohesion. Some politicians have argued that terrorists can be stopped only when they know they will be repaid harshly for every act of violence. This argument is politically popular and similar to the insistence by one criminological school that swift and sure punishment deters crime. Post is not convinced such an argument is applicable to modern terrorism.

Post believes there is no single terrorist personality but that terrorists follow similar behavioral patterns. The individuals who are attracted to terrorist groups are social outcasts. According to Post, terrorists are usually people who have been rejected by mainstream society and who fall in with likeminded individuals. The social misfits in terrorist groups reinforce each other. Mutual support inside the organization is more important than retaliation. Post believes groups create a mentality of "Us-against-Them," and terrorists expect to be pounded by their adversaries.

The constant reinforcement of antisocial behavior in terrorist groups produces conforming behavior inside the organizations, with the exception of strong leaders who may splinter the group. When an individual rejects mainstream society, that individual's only hope for social acceptance lies in the group that rewards his or her behavior. If the group rewards antisocial behavior, the individual is further motivated to attack the norm. According to Post, the rejection of external authority results in the acceptance of internal authority because behavior must be reinforced somewhere.

Jessica Stern (2003b, pp. 159–160), believes that several factors must be in place for group cohesion to be effective. First, the group must identify an enemy and create an atmosphere in daily life of "Us-against-Them." Second, the group must have "a story," almost a mythological element, that inspires and guides its membership. Third, the group needs its own language or symbolic words to demonize the enemy.

Chip Berlet and Matthew Lyons (2000, pp. 323–344) complement Stern's research in this area. They say that groups first look for conspiracies and then blame (or scapegoat) a particular group for the conspiracy. Eventually, they demonize the scapegoats for being the primary cause of social injustice. Stern concludes (2003b, p. 157) that leaders must be able to inspire members to action and constantly search for more demonized enemies. Terrorists and their leaders reinforce each other in the process.

Warrior Dreams

Key Points and Questions:

1. According to Gibson, what is the basis of American paramilitary culture?
2. What is the social background of the "warrior culture"?
3. What is the goal of the individual warrior?
4. Who or what is the paramilitary rogue warrior's enemy?

James William Gibson (1994) offers an interesting psychological analysis of violent rhetoric and political activity in the United States. He maintains that the American extremist political right seeks an *outlet* for social frustration in a paramilitary culture. In his book *Warrior Dreams*, Gibson says extreme conservatives have suffered an identity crisis since the Vietnam War. Living in a culture that values guns, violent confrontation, and victory, a number of extremists, Gibson says, have submerged themselves in a paramilitary culture. This lifestyle involves an almost cultlike attraction to paramilitary activities, including paintball war games, paramilitary religions, war films, war books, and a mercenary culture. He draws parallels to extremist movements in Nazi Germany to illustrate his thesis. Gibson argues that "warriors" are social outcasts whose life is centered on violence. They can be close to no other person except other warriors. Family, sexuality, individual personality, and normative social relations are suppressed in a warrior environment. **Warrior dreams** is the term Gibson uses to describe the aspirations of this paramilitary culture.

The target of warriors is worth noting. Gibson says that warriors are in conflict with an enemy who lacks all standards of human decency. The enemy's name changes—he or she may be a Communist, dope dealer, Mafioso, criminal, academic, or liberal—but the enemy's mission is always the same: to destroy American society and culture. The warrior responds, not by joining regular police or military forces, but by becoming a lone wolf, an eternal soldier in search of a war.

The lone warrior has shunned the shackles of society. Even the rogue warrior cultures of SWAT teams and special commando units have no place in the lone warrior's life. These units reflect organized military values, and the warrior rejects them. He (and the dream warriors mean *he*) is at war with the status quo. In essence, the paramilitary culture of the extremist right justifies the actions of militias, groups like a right-wing American group called The Order, and neo-Nazis. It provides a formula for justifying terrorism.

Terrorist Profiles: Three Views

Key Points and Questions:

1. List Hacker's three types of terrorists.
2. Can Hacker's typology be updated?
3. Why does Laqueur argue that all terrorist profiles will eventually fail?
4. Does Ross's model contradict Laqueur's argument?
5. List and define the factors involved in Ross's model.

The late Frederick J. Hacker (1976), a physician who developed expertise in terrorism and hostage negotiation, was one of the first to engage in **terrorist profiling**. He found that terrorists seek reinforcement based on their orientation to life and defined three types of terrorists: criminals, crazies, and crusaders. The categories are not mutually exclusive; any terrorist group might contain any or all of these personality types.

In Hacker's typology, criminals join terrorist groups because they want some type of monetary payoff or because they seek vengeance. Crazies become terrorists for the thrill of the terrorist lifestyle. Crusaders are people who believe deeply in a cause. They join terrorists groups to achieve an ideological goal.

Updated practical classification systems have expanded Hacker's original view, which critics have maintained is too simplistic. Many law enforcement agencies try to determine whether terrorist actions are the result of criminal or political activity. They also evaluate the personality of individual terrorists and try to group them in similar categories using a variety of psychological assessment techniques to gage terrorist behavior (Turvey, Tamlyn, and Chisum, 1999). Agencies also attempt to assess the level of potential threats and the behavior of violent political extremists. The FBI's Behavioral Science Unit is an example of a law enforcement organization engaged in sophisticated psychological assessment (see Another Perspective: Terrorists and Ordinary Criminals).

A practical example of such classification systems comes from the United Kingdom. Police officials there make practical decisions on the basis of terrorist profiles and the classification of each incident of terror. When faced with an act of terrorism, the local ranking police official assesses the event. If it is classified as criminal activity or the result of a mentally deranged individual, the local police commander handles the incident. If the commander deems the action to be the result of political terrorism, the central government is informed, and the incident is handled at the level of the prime minister. In addition, if the level of the threat is sufficiently high, the matter may be referred to the national government.

Although such terrorist profiling has practical applications in law enforcement, the larger question remains: Is it possible to profile the terrorist personality? Some critics say "no."

Walter Laqueur (1999, pp. 79–104) says that no one can develop a composite picture of a terrorist because no such picture exists. **Laqueur's views of terrorist profiling** are defined by his notion that terrorism fluctuates over time and the profile of terrorism changes with circumstances. Therefore, there can be no terrorist mosaic because there are different types of terrorism. Laqueur says we can be sure that most

Another Perspective

Terrorists and Ordinary Criminals

Terrorists behave differently from ordinary criminals. Consider the following:

1. Criminals are unfocused. Terrorists focus their actions toward a goal.
2. Criminals may live in a criminal underworld, but they are not devoted to crime as a philosophy. Terrorists are dedicated to a cause.
3. Criminals will make deals to avoid punishment. Terrorists rarely cooperate with officials because they do not wish to betray their cause.
4. Criminals usually run when confronted with force. Terrorists tend to attack.
5. Criminals strike when the opportunity to do so is present. Terrorists strike against symbols after careful planning.
6. Criminals rarely train for crime. Terrorists prepare for and rehearse their operations.

Source: Bodrero (2002).

terrorists are young, but their actions and psychological makeup vary according to social and cultural conditions.

Laqueur believes that other group characteristics can be discerned through the type of terrorist movement. Nationalistic and separatist groups are aggressive, and their actions are often horribly violent. Such violence may or may not be the result of psychological inadequacies of the individuals involved. In democracies, Laqueur says, terrorists tend to be elitists; nationalist movements produce terrorists from the lower classes; and religious terrorists come from all classes. Individual and group profiles are the result of political and social conditions.

In the final analysis, Laqueur believes it is impossible to profile a terrorist personality because terrorism is not the subject of criminology. In the past, he says, perfectly "normal" individuals have opted to engage in terrorism as a rational political statement. Terrorism is a political phenomenon different from ordinary crime or psychopathology.

Jeffrey Ian Ross (1999, pp. 169–192) offers an alternative view. Rather than attempting to delineate an individual profile, Ross tries to conceptualize terrorism by combining social structure and group psychology. He believes such a model is necessary for policymakers to develop better counterterrorist responses.

Go to **http://cj.wadsworth.com/white_terrorism5e** and click on Web Links for a detailed summary of Ross's research.

Ross defines five interconnected processes involved in terrorism: joining the group, forming the activity, remaining in the campaign, leading the organization, and engaging in acts of terrorism. He says many analysts have tried to explain terrorism on the basis of these processes, but they fall short because there is no overall model of terrorism. Rather than simply profiling the typical terrorist, Ross explains how social and psychological processes produce terrorism.

Two factors are involved in the rise of terrorism at any point in history. The first centers around social structure. Structural factors include the way a society is organized, its political and economic systems, its historical and cultural conditions, the number of grievances citizens have and their mechanisms for addressing grievances, the availability of weapons, and the effectiveness of counterterrorist forces. Ross says that modernization, democracy, and social unrest create the structural conditions that facilitate terrorism. In Ross's analysis, urban areas produce the greatest potential for unrest and the greatest availability of weapons. When governments fail to address social pressures in such areas, the likelihood of terrorism increases. When counterterrorist intervention fails, the amount of terrorism is likely to increase.

Ross believes that structural factors interact with the psychological makeup of potentially violent people to produce terrorism. Several schools of psychology can be used to explain violence, but none is adequate to explain terrorism. Although Ross's (1999) ideas do not provide a typical profile of a terrorist personality, they help explain the transformation of terrorism through history and provide social and psychological indicators of terrorism. Ross believes certain psychological factors interact with social factors to create a climate conducive to terrorism. Laqueur (1999) says a profile cannot be made because terrorism is a political activity. Ross counters by arguing it is possible to measure political activities and develop behavioral models on the basis of such measurements.

Summary of Main Points

1. Definitions of terrorism are important because they have social and political consequences.

2. *Terrorism* can be defined in many ways. Alex Schmid developed a comprehensive academic definition. Walter Laqueur and Brian Jenkins use simple definitions.

3. Even official definitions of terrorism differ. In the United States, law enforcement, intelligence, military, and other government organizations define terrorism differently.

4. The "war on terrorism" is a nebulous idea because it is not possible to declare war on a concept.

5. Terrorists tend to use simple tactics, and the most common is the use of bombs.

6. Force multipliers increase striking power. Terrorists use the media, international connections, technology, and religion as force multipliers.

7. Like all people, terrorists must be able to justify their behavior socially and psychologically.

8. *Warrior Dreams* is a sociological analysis of behavior among Americans with a paramilitary attitude.

9. Experts disagree on whether terrorists, terrorist groups, and terrorist behavior can be profiled and defined.

Key Terms

Make sure you can define, explain, or identify the following people, ideas, organizations, or terms:

systematic terror   3
simple definition [of terrorism]   4
legal definition [of terrorism]   5
academic consensus definition
   [of terrorism]   5
Barnett's logic   7
war on terrorism   8
tactics of terrorism   9

weapons of mass destruction   9
force multipliers   9
justification for violence   10
terrorist group   10
warrior dreams   12
terrorist profiling   13
Laqueur's views of terrorist
   profiling   13

Suggested Readings

Now that you've been introduced to this topic, you can learn more by reading:

Bruce Hoffman's *Inside Terrorism* takes readers into the heart of modern terrorism, examining various campaigns and the politics behind the violence. He offers explanations of violent behavior and the internal works of terrorists groups.

You may also want to read:

Walter Laqueur, *The New Terrorism*, an intricate historical and political analysis of modern terrorism.

Ian Lesser, *Countering the New Terrorism*, a collection of essays from RAND experts with a marvelous introduction by Brian Jenkins.

Alex Schmid, *Political Terrorism*, a book that may seem a bit dated until you delve into the material.

Web Resources

Go to *http://cj.wadsworth.com/white_terrorism5e* and click on Web Links to find:

- The Council of Foreign Relations' *Terrorism: An Introduction*
- The RAND paper on terrorism as a mode of conflict (Cragin and Daly, 2004)
- Thomas Barnett's explanations of terrorism and conflict

The Companion Website for *Terrorism and Homeland Security*, Fifth Edition

http://cj.wadsworth.com/white_terrorism5e

At the Book Companion Website you can review chapter outlines, use the flash cards to test your terrorism vocabulary, and check out the many other study aids you'll find there. You'll find valuable data and resources at your fingertips to help you study for that big exam or write that important paper.

Terrorism Updates

http://www.wadsworth.com/criminaljustice_d/special_features/ext/terrorism _site090802/index.html

Visit the *Terrorism: An Interdisciplinary Perspective* website to find the most current information about the fields of terrorism and homeland security. With a focus on domestic and international issues, this site explores the scope of terrorism in our world today. You'll find essays on important topics in terrorism and homeland security, critical thinking web activities, and InfoTrac College Edition keywords. Most importantly, the website is updated weekly with current news and research articles on domestic and international terrorism. You are invited to use these web resources to supplement your understanding of the topics covered in this chapter.

Current Perspectives: Readings from InfoTrac College Edition
Terrorism and Homeland Security

The sixteen articles in this reader offer a representative selection that helps you understand the important issues about terrorism and homeland security. It includes FREE access to InfoTrac College Edition and can also be bundled with the text for free.

Chapter 2

The Origins of Modern Terrorism

British troops stand guard after capturing Dublin in the 1916 Easter Rebellion. The Irish Republican Army took its ideas from revolutionaries in Russia and France. IRA tactics served to mold terrorist campaigns in the twentieth century.

© Bettmann /Corbis

Many Americans became acutely aware of modern terrorism after the first World Trade Center bombing in 1993 and the bombing of the federal building in Oklahoma City in 1995. Yet, modern terrorism began decades, even centuries, before these recent activities in the United States. The modern concept of terrorism grew from the French Revolution (1789–1799), and the word was originally used to describe the actions of a government, not a band of revolutionaries. As Walter Laqueur observes, the meaning changed with the flow of historical circumstances. The development of modern terrorism can be traced through (1) the birth of **revolutionary terrorism**, (2) revolutionary actions in Russia, and (3) conflicts in Ireland. Current domestic and international terrorism grew from these three roots.

Chapter Objectives

After reading this chapter, you should be able to:

1. Outline the impact of Western history on the origins of terrorism.
2. Describe the evolution of the term *terrorism.*
3. Define the forms of radical democracy.
4. Identify the major proponents of radical democracy.
5. Summarize the effect of the Russian Revolution on terrorism.
6. Explain the origins of nationalistic terrorism.
7. Outline the history of terrorism in modern Ireland.
8. List the practical benefits of understanding the history of modern terrorism.

Modern Democracies and the Birth of Terrorism in the West

Key Points and Questions:

1. When was the term *terrorism* first used?
2. How did the meaning of the term *terrorism* change?
3. Who were the radical democrats?
4. Why did many people in the upper classes associate the radicals with terrorism?

Democracy evolved in Great Britain, and it came with revolutions in the United States (1775–1783) and in France (1789–1799). The American Revolution transferred power from the British upper classes to American upper classes (see Phillips, 1999, pp. 79–232). In the French Revolution, power was transferred *between* classes. The middle class wrestled power from the nobility, and the power struggle was extremely bloody. France provided the first **revolution** in the modern sense of the word, that is, power was transferred from one class to another. The term *terrorism* also appeared during this period (see Hibbert, 1999; Accampo, 2002, pp. 93–95).

Edmond Burke, a noted British political philosopher of the eighteenth century, was in Paris during the French Revolution. He referred to the violence there as the **Reign of Terror** and used the word *terrorism* to describe the actions of the new government. Terrorism in this sense referred to the French government's slaughter of French nobles, their families, and sympathizers (for a comprehensive history, see LeFebre, 1967). But the meaning of terrorism would change within fifty years.

The reason for this change in Western minds was due to struggles to bring democracy to other European countries. The European democrats of the early 1800s were not united. Some of them wanted constitutional monarchies, and others wanted to eliminate the power of the upper classes. These democrats were called "radicals," and many of them engaged in violent, fiery rhetoric. After **radical democrats** were involved in several revolutions in 1848, governments and the press began to refer to the radicals as "terrorists" (Jensen, 2004) (see Timeline 2.1).

The radical democrats working for the redistribution of wealth became known as socialists. They maintained that all institutions, as well as ownership and con-

Timeline 2.1

How Modern Terrorism Evolved

Event	Effect
French Revolution, 1789	The government's Reign of Terror
European street revolutions, 1848	Conservatives call radicals "terrorists"
People's Will in Russia, 1878	Revolutionaries use terrorist tactics
Russian Revolutions of 1917	Leaders endorse terrorism
Black and Tan War, Ireland, 1919–1921	Irish win with Russian tactics
Modern terrorism since 1945	Groups study past terrorist tactics

trol of industrial production, should be democratic. Wealth was not a private matter; wealth belonged to everybody. The radical democrats believed political power should be held in common. Their concept of **socialism** was especially popular among some groups of displaced workers. Unfortunately, the upper and middle classes frequently believed terrorism and socialism were the same things (Roberts, 8-27-02).

When the revolutionaries of 1848 were suppressed, radical democrats took control of the revolutionary movement. They tried to continue revolution through covert violence and assassination. Although they could not successfully confront armies and police forces in Paris, Vienna, or Berlin, they could plant bombs and set factories aflame. A campaign of subversive revolutionary violence followed. The term *terrorism* was increasingly used to describe this kind of violence.

Terrorism and the Anarchists

Key Points and Questions:

1. How did the terms *socialism* and *anarchy* come to be related?
2. Who was the founder of modern anarchy?
3. How did Proudhon disagree with Marx?
4. List some of the major leaders of the anarchist movement.

By the 1850s, the radical democrats divided into two streams: militant socialists and more peaceful socialists. Both groups began to refer to their movement as **anarchism**. The term *anarchy* was not new. It originated several hundred years earlier when Greek philosophers spoke of eliminating governments, but the new anarchists were also concerned with the distribution of wealth. This frightened the upper classes, which already associated socialism with terrorism.

Pierre Joseph Proudhon (1809–1865) was one of the advocates of modern anarchism. His political activities eventually landed him in a French prison, but Proudhon was not a man of violence. He called for the extension of democracy to all classes, to be accomplished through the elimination of property and government.

Property was to be commonly held, and families living in extended communes were to replace centralized government.

Proudhon disagreed with **Karl Marx**, the leader of the Communists, and other socialists about the role of government. Most socialists saw centralized government as a necessary evil. Like the democrats, the socialists believed government had to exist to protect the individual rights of citizens. Proudhon, on the other hand, believed all government was evil. Proudhon had revolutionary ideals, but he was a man of peace. He believed that anarchy would develop peacefully as people learned about the structure of governments and the capitalist economy. Not all of Proudhon's disciples followed this call. A number of anarchists believed society had to be violently destroyed. Upper classes, governments, and businesspeople called these anarchists terrorists; the anarchists even called themselves terrorists.

Richard Jensen (2004) believes that the initial calls for revolution in history cannot be associated with terrorism. Even though anarchists disagreed about the path for creating a new society, they avoided violence. Those who advocated violence usually did so only rhetorically. But this changed in the 1880s as anarchists began assassinating heads of state. They also started using Alfred Nobel's new invention, dynamite. The media sensationalized anarchist events, leading people to conclude that anarchism was a vast international conspiracy of terror (see Expanding the Concept: Anarchism, Socialism, Communism, and Terrorism).

Several important people emerged from the ranks of the anarchists. **Mikhail Bakunin** (1814–1876) was a Russian revolutionary who fought against the Tsar. He was joined in revolutionary activities by Sergey Nechaev. Later Russian terrorists formed an anarchist organization called the **People's Will (Narodnaya Volya)**, which operated from 1878 to 1881 (discussed more below). The primary spokesperson of the People's Will was **Nikolai Morozov**, and the organization's main tactic was to assassinate Russian government officials. Russian anarchists killed several officials, including Tsar Alexander II.

Karl Heinzen (1809–1880), a radical German democratic who embraced anarchy, came to the United States after the 1848 revolutions failed in Europe. Benjamin Grob-Fitzgibbon (2004) believes that Heinzen sat at a pivotal point where modern terrorism can be directly related to the past. Grob-Fitzgibbon criticizes theories that state terrorism was linked to the anarchists and other radical democrats. They were assassins at worst, he argues, not the forerunners of modern terrorism, with its in-

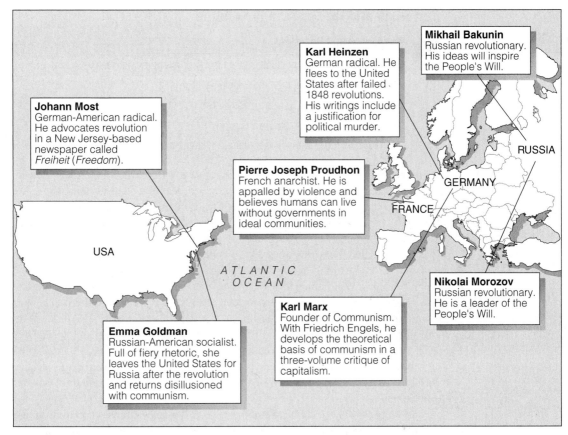

Figure 2.1
Revolutionaries and Peaceful Theorists

discriminate killing. Heinzen was different because he advocated political murder—murder that could be arbitrarily distributed through society. Heinzen's theories were relatively insignificant until **Johann Most** starting publishing Heinzen's writings in a radical newspaper. Most was born in 1846 and immigrated to the United States. He advocated terrorism from his New Jersey–based newspaper and called for "propaganda by the deed" and the "philosophy of the bomb." Violent action—**propaganda by the deed**—was the best form of propaganda. The **philosophy of the bomb** was the method for communicating such propaganda, according to Most. Grob-Fitzgibbon believes these two concepts represent the beginning of modern terrorism.

Although anarchism was an international movement and violent anarchists assassinated leaders from several countries, including President William McKinley in 1901, it was hardly a conspiracy. Anarchists were united mostly in spirit. Indeed, an international organization of anarchists would have been contradictory, as they inherently opposed large organizations. Regardless, the fear of conspiracy grew, and many people came to believe that anarchists were internationally organized (see Figure 2.1). They pointed to revolutionary forces in Imperial Russia to prove this belief.

Terrorism and the Russian Revolution

Key Points and Questions:

1. Describe social conditions in late nineteenth-century Russia.
2. Outline the campaign of the People's Will.
3. Why did the lower classes revolt in 1905?
4. Describe the Russian Revolutions of 1917.
5. How did the Communists transform anarchism into a revolutionary theory?

Late nineteenth-century Russia differed significantly from the other great powers of Europe. Class distinctions between nobles and peasants were virtually the same as they had been before the French Revolution, and Russian peasants were extremely poor. Industry had come to some of Russia's cities, but Russia's economic and governmental systems were not sufficiently geared to handle the changes. Tsar Alexander II (who ruled from 1856 to 1881) vowed to make changes in the system. When he tried to do so, he found himself in the midst of revolutionary terrorism.

The People's Will launched a campaign of revolutionary terrorism in the late 1870s, seeking to terrorize the government, the Orthodox Church, the police, and the military into submission. According to Laqueur (1999, pp. 15–16), they were motivated by anarchist revolutionary theory. Mikhail Bakunin and Sergey Nechaev met in the 1860s and formed an intellectual union. Both spoke of revolt against the Tsar, and both endorsed violence as the means to do it. Yet Bakunin and Nechaev basically stuck to rhetoric. Laqueur says their significance was their influence on later revolutionaries.

The People's Will murdered the police chief of Moscow and went on a campaign of bombing and murder. In May 1881, they succeeded in striking their ultimate target—they killed Tsar Alexander II. Alexander III (who ruled from 1881 to 1894) was infuriated at his father's murder and launched a period of national repression. Leaders of the People's Will were either killed or arrested, and the remaining revolutionaries went underground. But they resurfaced to confront Nicholas II (1894–1917) in the 1905 Russian Revolution, a failed attempt to topple the Tsar.

In 1905 Russia had lost a war to Japan and was consumed with economic problems and bureaucratic inefficiency. A group of unemployed workers began demonstrations in St. Petersburg, while some enlisted men in the Russian Navy mutinied. Their actions were brutally repressed, but the spirit of revolution burned below the surface. Russian revolutionaries needed another national disaster to create the atmosphere for victory, and it came in 1914 when Russia entered World War I.

By 1917, the Russian people were tired of their economic woes and their Tsar. In February, a general strike in St. Petersburg turned into the first of two revolutions that year. Unlike in 1905, the Russian Army joined the workers, and a new Russian government was formed. The Russians assured their allies that they would remain in the international war, and they envisioned a period of capitalist economic expansion to save the beleaguered Russian economy. Workers' councils (*soviets*) were established in major Russian cities.

The primary mistake of the February revolutionaries, or Mensheviks, was that they kept Russia in an unpopular war. This had two immediate ramifications: It

Synopsis of Revolutionary Russia

1840–1870	Some revolutionary theorists embrace terrorism as a tool for accomplishing their political and social goals
1878	The People's Will begins a bombing campaign in Moscow
1905	A revolt begins in St. Petersburg and spreads throughout Russia. The Tsar makes many concessions to the revolutionaries and is able to remain in power.
1917	Bolsheviks topple the government and silence their opponents

created unrest at home, and it inspired the Germans to seek a way to remove Russia from World War I. The Germans found help for this from Vladimir Ilich Lenin. Lenin promised to take Russia out of the war if the Germans would then help him obtain power. The German High Command liked the idea and smuggled Lenin across Germany and Poland into Russia. He gained control of the Bolsheviks (the Communist revolutionaries who opposed the Mensheviks), orchestrating a second revolution in October 1917 and removing Russia from the war.

The October revolutionaries used terrorism in a new manner: They used revolutionary terrorist violence as an instrument to gain power and repressive terrorism to maintain it. Lenin and one of his lieutenants, **Leon Trotsky**, believed terrorism should be used as an instrument for overthrowing middle-class, or bourgeois, governments. The philosophy of the bomb toppled governments, they found. Then once power was achieved, they advocated terrorism as a means of controlling internal enemies and coping with international strife. The Bolshevik leadership introduced the **Red Terror**, rounding up real and potential opponents and executing them without trial. Suspected supporters of the old regime were slaughtered when Red Army units moved into a new area. The Communists also spoke of exporting revolutionary terrorism to frighten the foreign states intervening in the civil war. Russia was very weak after the revolutions of 1917. It faced foreign intervention and was torn by civil war. Lenin and Trotsky hoped to keep their enemies, primarily Western Europe and the United States, at bay.

Go to **http://cj.wadsworth.com/white _terrorism5e** and click on Web Links for an in-depth discussion of the role of revolutionary Russia and the former Soviet Union in terrorism.

Nationalistic Revolutionaries

Key Points and Questions:

1. What was the main goal of nationalist organizations?
2. Compare nationalistic terrorism and anarchism.
3. Cite examples from Bell and Clutterbuck to support your answer.

Ironically, nationalistic trends accompanied anarchist violence in the West. At the same time anarchists were calling for an end to government, a number of organizations were born that demanded a right to self-government. The 1800s witnessed the growth of both anarchism *and* nationalism. Many nationalists who found themselves under foreign control adopted the tactics of the anarchists in order to fight foreign powers occupying their lands. **Nationalist terrorism** had a different purpose, however. The main goal of nationalistic forces was to use terrorism to wrestle control of the government from other nationalities or ethnic groups. If anarchists fought to impose an ideology on government, nationalists fought to govern.

Despite the difference, some scholars believe the growth of nationalistic terrorism and anarchism are related. Grant Wardlaw (1982, pp. 18–24) sees a historical continuation from anarchism to nationalist terrorism. Richard Rubenstein (1987, pp. 122–125) agrees when examining contemporary anarchist and nationalist groups. Rubenstein says both anarchists and nationalists go through similar stages of development as they learn and then use terrorist tactics. In addition, both groups tend to use the same type of justifications for violence, claiming that it is morally necessary for their particular group to govern society. Even though their goals seem to be different, anarchist and nationalist terrorism is essentially the same.

J. Bowyer Bell (1976) gives an example of the links between the anarchistic and nationalistic traditions by examining the **Irish Republican Army (IRA)**. Since 1916, the IRA has been inundated with socialist revolutionaries and nationalists who reject some aspects of socialism. Even though the two sides have frequently been at odds, both groups are heir to the same tradition. Modern nationalistic terrorism has its roots in anarchism. Both traditions formed the framework of modern European terrorism, and Ireland serves as the best example.

Not everyone agrees that the link between anarchy and nationalistic terror is so clear. Lindsay Clutterbuck (2004) argues that nationalistic terrorism in Ireland is extremely important because its innovations ushered in the practice of modern terrorism. Unlike many analysts, Clutterbuck believes terrorism did not develop as a logical step from anarchist violence to modern practice. Irish nationalists invented new strategies and tactics. Ireland, not Russia, set the stage for modern international terrorist operations, and they have not changed for the past one hundred years, Clutterbuck says.

Irish History and the Growth of Modern Terrorism

 Key Points and Questions:

1. Why was Ireland ripe for terrorism when the IRA was created?
2. Explain the birth of the IRA and the importance of Michael Collins.
3. How did the actions of the British Army revitalize the IRA?
4. Outline the tactics of the IRA.

The struggle for Irish independence lasted for centuries, but the past one hundred years of violence in Ireland parallel the rise of modern terrorism. The beginnings of the IRA can be traced to an attempted revolution in Dublin in 1916, although the conditions fostering terrorism in Ireland had been cultivated long before. (See Chapter 11 for further discussion of the situation in Ireland.) Ireland was ripe for terrorism before the current round of violence began in 1969.

The Irish lost control of their kingdoms after the Vikings invaded about A.D. 800 (Costigan, 1980). The English came shortly after the Vikings left in the twelfth century, and English nobles increased their holdings in Ireland for four centuries. When Protestantism took hold in England in 1540, the English nobles attempted to impose their religion on Catholic Ireland. Waves of Protestant settlers displaced the Catholic Irish in the north, and after a few generations they became as Irish as the native Irish. In 1803 the British voted to place Ireland in a United Kingdom. The northern Protestant Irish embraced the idea, but Catholics in the south and north did not.

Modern expressions of nationalistic revolt grew from the 1500s. When the English established a large Protestant colony in the north called the Plantation of Ulster in 1590, the Irish revolted. Violence continued through every generation. During the Napoleonic Wars (1795–1815), the Irish tried to join the French in the fight against the British. But the Protestant north and its English allies always remained in control. Further disaster struck in 1845 when a famine hit Ireland. Facing starvation, Irish immigrants moved to Canada, Australia, New Zealand, and the United States (Woodham-Smith, 1962).

One group of immigrants formed the Irish Republican Brotherhood in New York City in 1857. After the American Civil War (1861–1865) many Irish soldiers who fought for the north turned their attention to their native land. Unable to fight the English directly, they joined with other Irish people in an underground campaign to create a republic of Ireland free from British control. In 1916 several of these Republican groups tried to take control of Dublin. Patrick Pearse, one of the prominent leaders, called his group the Irish Republican Army. Fighting lasted for a week, and the British ruthlessly tried to destroy Republicanism.

Modern terrorism came to Ireland in 1919 when **Michael Collins** took command of the IRA and waged a fierce campaign against the British. He had studied the tactics of the Russian revolutionaries from the 1880s to the Russian Revolution and felt their tactics would drive the British from Ireland. His followers used bombs, murder, ambushes, and other terrorist tactics to fight the loyalist Protestant police force and the British Army. The loyalists and the British responded with their own campaign of terrorism.

The British yielded to Collins and granted Ireland independence in 1921. When they opted to keep the north to protect Irish loyalists, Collins was infuriated and sent his IRA terrorists into the north. He was killed in 1922 by former revolutionaries who opposed peace with the British.

This is an important period in the history of terrorism. The Russian revolutionaries took the philosophy of the bomb from the discussion table to the street. Michael Collins brought the philosophy into the modern world. Terrorists throughout the twentieth century studied Collins and mimicked his tactics (Clutterbuck, 2004).

After Collins's death, the Republic of Ireland outlawed the IRA. Although it split into differing factions, it remained alive underground for nearly fifty years. When violence grew in Northern Ireland after a failed Catholic civil rights movement, the

British sent the army to stop the rioting. Young soldiers saw loyalists waving the British flag and Irish Catholics waving the flag of the Irish Republic. They sided with the loyalists against the Republicans and brutally repressed the Catholics. Ironically, this caused the rebirth of the IRA.

From 1970 to 1990 the IRA used bombing as its primary tactic, supporting the bombings with murder and kidnapping. They also raised money through charities and organized criminal activity (see Chapter 5 for more on how terrorism is financed). IRA terrorists would frequently establish roadblocks, killing their adversaries after stopping their cars. They also assassinated government officials, enemy terrorists from loyalist organizations, Catholics who worked for compromise, and police officers and soldiers.

Some splinter groups in the IRA became master bombers. They began by planting bombs in buildings and cars. As their expertise grew, they infiltrated secure areas to plant time bombs in government buildings and vehicles. They moved to civilian targets in the United Kingdom, trying to murder British citizens indiscriminately. They developed sophisticated radio-controlled bombs to attack police and military forces. Many of the bombing tactics terrorists use today have been copied from the IRA.

Go to **http://cj.wadsworth.com/white_terrorism5e** and click on Web Links for an in-depth discussion of terrorism in Ireland over the past century.

The Influence of Past Experience

Key Points and Questions:

1. Summarize Dyson's conclusions about terrorist behavior.
2. Describe the influence of Vladimir Lenin and Michael Collins on terrorist thought.
3. Are current terrorist networks based in these traditions?

William Dyson is a retired FBI agent who worked in counterterrorism for thirty years. Assigned to the Chicago division, he worked with local police officers to establish the first Joint Terrorism Task Force in the United States before the concept was popularized in New York City. Dyson (2000) says that unlike criminals, terrorists study the history of past campaigns and the theory that motivates them (see Expanding the Concept: Why a History Lesson?). Counterterrorism, he concludes, starts with understanding the roots of terrorism.

In 2000 the History Channel ran a four-part series on the origins of modern terrorism. The series combined the ideas of some of the world's leading scholars and concluded that three issues helped to shape modern terrorism. First, the ideology of modern terrorism emerged from nineteenth-century revolutionary thought. Second, such thought spawned ideological revolutions in Russia and caused Michael Collins to believe that the same tactics would work in a nationalistic revolt. Finally, terrorists in the twentieth century studied Michael Collins and improvised from the IRA tactics. Clutterbuck (2004) does not give as much credit to the Russian revolutionaries, but she clearly comes to the same conclusions about the IRA. Modern terrorism is a product of the recent past.

Why a History Lesson?

Imagine this scenario: Tony Soprano, a fictional organized crime boss on a popular television series, is sitting around a table with his criminal gang. He puts down a cigar and orders his compatriots to begin a detailed study of organized crime history in America. He tells them this will make them better criminals. Do you think Tony will be disappointed with his crew's response?

Now imagine this scenario: Members of al Qaeda want to bomb embassies in Nairobi and Dar es Salaam. They learn to attack buildings by studying the history of Hezbollah. Hezbollah learned the tactic by studying earlier Palestinian militant groups. Palestinian terrorists learned to attack buildings by studying Jewish terrorist groups from 1936 to 1948. Menachim Begin, a former prime minister of Israel and leader of one of the Jewish terrorist groups, studied the tactics of Michael Collins and the IRA from 1919 to 1921. Collins got his ideas from studying the campaign of the People's Will in Russia.

Unlike the first scenario, the second really happened.

History is important when examining terrorism for a simple reason: Terrorists study the past to learn their trade.

Source: The History Channel (2000) and Goldberg (2002).

Today, terrorism is dominated by religion, ideologies that seem to serve as surrogate religions, and racial and ethnic divisions. Much of the world is aflame with self-proclaimed religious terrorists who would refer to Collins and Lenin as devils. Ironically, their roots are in these traditions.

Summary of Main Points

1. Modern terrorism has ideological and practical roots in Western history.

2. The term *terrorism* was used to describe the revolutionary government in France, but it came to be associated with radical democrats.

3. Radical democracy took several forms, including socialism, Communism, and anarchy.

4. Many analysts believe that modern terrorism was rooted in the Russian People's Will and the revolutions of 1905 and 1917.

5. Nationalistic revolutionaries applied the tactics of violent anarchists and expanded on them.

6. After a failed rebellion in 1916, modern terrorism came to Ireland with the Irish Republican Army. IRA tactics have served as the basis for modern terrorist tactics.

7. Unlike criminals, terrorists study the past. It is possible to gain an understanding of current terrorist operations by studying recent history.

Key Terms

Make sure you can define, explain, or identify the following people, ideas, organizations, or terms:

revolutionary terrorism   17
revolution   18
Reign of Terror   18
radical democrats   18
socialism   19
anarchism   19
Pierre Joseph Proudhon   19
Karl Marx   20
Mikhail Bakunin   20
People's Will (Narodnaya Volya)   20

Nikolai Morozov   20
Karl Heinzen   20
Johann Most   21
propaganda by the deed   21
philosophy of the bomb   21
Leon Trotsky   23
Red Terror   23
nationalist terrorism   24
Irish Republican Army (IRA)   24
Michael Collins   25

Suggested Readings

Now that you've been introduced to this topic, you can learn more by reading:

Walter Laqueur's *The New Terrorism* is one of the best books analyzing the historical development of terrorism. Laqueur takes readers through the history of terrorism and demonstrates its current transformation into religious fanaticism.

You may also want to read:

James Joll's *The Anarchists* explores anarchists and their theories.

J. Bowyer Bell's *The Secret Army* is a history of the Irish Republican Army.

Grant Wardlaw's *Political Terrorism* is dated, but the examination of historical development and theory remains excellent.

Yonah Alexander and Walter Laqueur reproduced the original writings of many terrorists in *The Terrorism Reader*.

Richard Bach Jensen, Benjamin Grob-Fitzgibbon, and Lindsay Clutterbuck produced three articles on historical influences on terrorism in the Spring 2004 issue of *Terrorism and Political Violence*.

The History Channel's four-part series "100 Years of Terror" is also worthwhile.

Web Resources

Go to **http://cj.wadsworth.com/white_terrorism5e** and click on Web Links to find:

■ An article on the sociology of terrorism by Mathieu Deflem
■ The Anarchy Archives, an online research center on the history and theory of anarchism
■ A discussion of the changing role of terrorism since the French Revolution by Robert Adams

The Companion Website for *Terrorism and Homeland Security,* **Fifth Edition**
http://cj.wadsworth.com/white_terrorism5e

At the Book Companion Website you can review chapter outlines, use the flash cards to test your terrorism vocabulary, and check out the many other study aids you'll find there. You'll find valuable data and resources at your fingertips to help you study for that big exam or write that important paper.

Terrorism Updates

**http://www.wadsworth.com/criminaljustice_d/special_features/ext/terrorism
_site090802/index.html**

Visit the *Terrorism: An Interdisciplinary Perspective* website to find the most current information about the fields of terrorism and homeland security. With a focus on domestic and international issues, this site explores the scope of terrorism in our world today. You'll find essays on important topics in terrorism and homeland security, critical thinking web activities, and InfoTrac College Edition keywords. Most importantly, the website is updated weekly with current news and research articles on domestic and international terrorism. You are invited to use these web resources to supplement your understanding of the topics covered in this chapter.

Current Perspectives: Readings from InfoTrac College Edition
Terrorism and Homeland Security

The sixteen articles in this reader offer a representative selection that helps you understand the important issues about terrorism and homeland security. It includes FREE access to InfoTrac College Edition and can also be bundled with the text for free.

Chapter 3

Changing Group Structures and the Metamorphosis of Terrorism

AP/Wide World Photos

Terrorist groups transform their images routinely and must keep their numbers high in order to carry on sustained fighting. Here a group of soldiers from the Liberation Tigers of Tamil Eelam march through the jungles of Sri Lanka. The Tigers call themselves guerrillas, fighting to represent the Tamil population of the country, but their adversaries call them terrorists.

I f psychopathic killers are excluded from the equation, modern terrorism is usually a group activity. Most terrorist groups are socially organized, managed, and maintained, and successful groups must be structured according to the same principles as any other organization. Labor must be divided in particular ways, and each subunit must complete its assigned specialty to complement the work of other units. Even though its goals are more difficult to accomplish because the work must be completed with extreme secrecy, a terrorist group must be organized and managed for success. Yet, an alarming trend has developed during the past few years: Individual terrorists have been taking action on their own or with the support of a very small group. This chapter discusses the recent evolution of terrorist structures.

Chapter Objectives

After reading this chapter you should be able to:

1. Explain the failure of the New World Liberation front (NWLF).
2. Summarize Gurr's research on terrorist campaigns.
3. Explain the relationship between group size and effectiveness.
4. Describe a basic pyramid organization.
5. Define the concept of an umbrella organization.
6. Describe other models of terrorist organization.
7. Outline the management problems terrorist groups face.
8. Summarize the factors involved in individual terrorism.
9. Define "leaderless resistance."

Trying to Walk the Walk

Key Points and Questions:

1. What was the New World Liberation Front (NWLF)?
2. How did the NWLF's attempt to expand affect its operations?
3. Why did the NWLF form an alliance with the Tribal Thumb?
4. Can a typical terrorist group develop mass appeal?
5. How does popular appeal affect group size?

It is helpful to examine a small, ineffective American terrorist group to introduce the organizational problems terrorist groups face. In 1970, a small group of radicals formed the **New World Liberation Front (NWLF)** in San Francisco. According to John Wolf (1981, pp. 63–64), the NWLF was responsible for thirty bombings over the next seven years. The NWLF claimed to be a "moral" revolutionary group, and it attacked only "legitimate" targets symbolized by corporate capitalism. Utility companies were a favorite, although they also bombed two sheriff's vehicles in the San Francisco area. They were at war with the establishment.

As the NWLF tried to expand its operations, its leadership may have come to see the irony of its campaign. Even though the group had hoped to be the vanguard of a revolutionary movement, few people were willing to join the revolution. In an attempt to compensate, the NWLF "expanded" its operations by forming a number of revolutionary brigades. In reality, these brigades represented nothing more than the same few radicals operating under a variety of new names (U.S. Marshals Service, 1988).

In frustration, the NWLF turned to a final ploy to obtain support. Linking up with another small band of militants, the group joined the prison reform movement and allied itself with a group of militant ex-convicts called the Tribal Thumb. This sealed the fate of the NWLF. Whatever chance it had had to obtain even the slightest political support was lost through the alliance because this association with violent felons cemented public opinion against the group. The NWLF was denounced and alienated. Aside from encouraging corporations to improve their security and law enforcement their investigative techniques, the NWLF was a dismal failure.

The experience of the NWLF is an example of how many modern terrorist groups fail. To have a major effect, a terrorist group must have the resources to launch and maintain a campaign of terrorism. Technological weapons and industrial sabotage are starting points, but they do not provide the basis for extended operations. Groups have to be large—at least larger than a few social misfits armed with bombs. To become large, the group has to generate popular political appeal through a cause that is acceptable to a large segment of the public.

Most terrorist groups do not have this appeal. They are organized like the NWLF, developing ornate organizational schemes and grandiose plots but lacking the ability to carry out a meaningful campaign. Small groups generally sponsor small amounts of violence. Individual acts may gain the public's attention through media exposure, but they lack the ability to maintain steady pressure on their opponents.

Group Size and Campaign Length

Key Points and Questions:

1. What was the purpose of Gurr's study?
2. Characterize a typical terrorist campaign.
3. Why is a terrorist campaign usually short?
4. Do Gurr's findings affect policy?

Ted Robert Gurr (Stohl, 1988, pp. 23–50) conducted an empirical analysis of terrorist groups operating during the 1960s in an attempt to identify some of their operational characteristics. His work remains an important study of their organizational structures. In the past, many people assumed terrorism was the result of revolutionary activities, just as many today assume it is state-sponsored or a product of a few misguided zealots. Gurr's data question such simplistic notions.

Gurr's analysis produced some interesting conclusions. First, most terrorist actions involve only a few people who generate more noise than injury. Second, although it is popularly believed that political revolutionaries dominate terrorist groups, the majority of successful groups embrace other doctrines, such as nationalism or religion. Third, in most instances only a **large group** achieves results by mounting campaigns of terrorism; a **small group** cannot do so. Gurr concludes that there are diverse causes for terrorist violence and many remain to be identified. No matter what the cause, however, most terrorist campaigns end within eighteen months of the initial outburst of violence.

Terrorism is short-lived because it seldom generates support. Although violent radicals envision success, many terrorist activities remain isolated because they lack support structures. As a result, terrorists seldom challenge authority. Political revolutionary and radical groups do not generate the popular appeal needed to gain support for their activities. Gurr believes large groups become large because they embrace popular political issues. Only a few groups have been able to adopt popular positions since 1945.

A policy implication may be drawn from Gurr's study: If his conclusions are correct, they imply that most terrorist organizations are small, short-lived operations. Small groups are a law enforcement problem. Although terrorism is waged to gain political ends, the scope of most terrorist activities is too restricted to pose a serious threat to the state. The level of most terrorist activity would seem to dictate a police response. Small groups are not able to alter the political environment substantially. As in the case of the NWLF, standard investigative procedures can be used to stop small terrorist movements. Weapons of mass destruction may change these assumptions, but the analysis seems correct for conventional terrorism.

There is another implication of Gurr's work. If terrorism is the result of a popular social issue, sympathizers can enhance the power of the group. The number of terrorists need not be large if a sufficient number of supporters is available to assist the group. For example, the Basque Nation and Liberty (ETA) has a relatively small number of operatives, but it enjoys sympathy in the Basque region of Spain. In Central Asia the Islamic Movement of Uzbekistan (IMU) gains support because it has joined the ranks of militant Islam and capitalizes on ethnic differences in the region. Strong support for a group is more important than the actual number of operatives; therefore, counterterrorist policy cannot be limited to targeting a group and its leaders.

Group Size Is Important

Key Points and Questions:

1. Did the size of Italian terrorist groups affect their capabilities?
2. Why could Hezbollah and the Liberation Tigers of Tamil Elaam operate over a long period?
3. How do resources affect a group's ability to operate?
4. Why can large groups conduct campaigns?
5. What could terrorists do to attract a political base?
6. Can terrorist groups compromise their values to create a large base of support?

Vittorfranco Pisano (1987, pp. 24–31) illustrates the importance of group size with an analysis of terrorism in Italy from 1975 to 1985. There were a tremendous number of terrorist actions in Italy during the ten years of Pisano's study, along with the relatively large number of groups responsible for the attacks. The reason for the plethora of groups, according to Pisano, was that most terrorist organizations were not capable of mounting a long-term campaign against the government. They could strike only a few times before their resources ran out or they were captured. Large Italian terrorist groups took advantage of this situation, using many different names in an attempt to confuse authorities. Yet, investigators came to realize that only large groups were involved in sustained actions, or a **terrorist campaign**. Everyone else became **single-incident terrorists**; that is, they could mount only one operation.

Hezbollah serves as an example of a large successful group (see Chapter 8). Dilip Hiro (1987) and Robin Wright (1986, 1989) both find that Hezbollah began as a political movement inside revolutionary Iran. In 1982, Hezbollah moved to the Bekaa Valley in Lebanon in response to an Israeli invasion. The Israeli Foreign Ministry

(1998) claims that Hezbollah's movement to Lebanon allowed it to grow. Utilizing local support and continued financial backing from Iran, Hezbollah has emerged as a strong, semiautonomous structure. Its size allows the group to conduct extensive terrorist attacks against Arabs who disagree with its objectives as well as against Israel. Hezbollah is large enough to maintain a campaign, and religion provides a common base among its members. Supporters believe Hezbollah conducts military operations against Israel. Opponents, like the United States and Israel, define Hezbollah's activities as terrorism.

Nationalism and ethnic identity can also serve to bind a group together. The Liberation Tigers of Tamil Eelam (LTTE) is an example. The LTTE began fighting the Sri Lankan government in 1976, claiming to represent the Tamil minority on the island nation of Sri Lanka. Because Sri Lanka has an extensive Tamil population, the LTTE has been able to recruit an extensive fighting force. O. N. Mehrota (2000), writing for the Institute of Defense Studies in India, estimates that the group may have up to ten thousand members. Not only has the LTTE mounted an extensive terrorist campaign, including a track record of successful suicide bombings, but it also crossed the threshold into guerrilla warfare in 1983. Size is the crucial factor in LTTE operations.

As terrorist groups become larger, however, governments increase their response to violence. This means that terrorist groups must be able to increase their activities when security is tightened. They frequently do this through the use of force multipliers and increasing the drama of violence. Christopher Hewitt (1984) says most groups are too small to use force multipliers and spectacular violence over a long period of time. Like Gurr, Hewitt concludes that small groups do not have the resources to damage an opponent over an extended length of time: They cannot launch a campaign. Terrorists have political impact, according to Hewitt, when they are large enough to maintain a campaign of terrorism.

Hewitt argues that terrorist campaigns became important after World War II for two primary reasons. First, the campaigns of large terrorist organizations accounted for the majority of terrorism around the world. Small, isolated terrorist organizations failed to match their larger counterparts. Second, large terrorist organizations have prompted governments to employ macropolicies. Large terrorist organizations can actually bring about a change in government political response because they represent a problem far beyond the means of local law enforcement. Therefore, large groups represent political threats.

Yet, extremists rarely attract a political base—except among other extremists. In general, people do not readily flock to small terrorist organizations. Large groups like the ETA and the Irish Republican Army (IRA) have gained support because their causes are popular among national and ethnic groups. Islamic radicals, increasingly known by the term *Jihadists* because they do not represent Islam, maintain a large loosely connected affiliation through a common religious theme. Many small groups recognize this and try to follow the examples of the larger groups. By rhetorically abandoning their extremist positions and taking on a more popular political cause, small groups hope to broaden their appeal. They usually fail in this attempt because small groups are seldom attractive to ethnic, nationalistic, or religious populations. Like the NWLF, most small groups fade to insignificance.

Since they want to appeal to a broad base, most terrorists try to hide their most radical positions and sensationalistic violence in nationalistic and religious messages. Murder and theft are disguised as patriotic acts. For example, in an anonymous tract titled "Wenn alle Bruder Schweigen," a romanticized account of The Order (a right-wing terrorist group engaged in a number of crimes in the mid-1980s), the writer claims the terrorists to be nothing more than American patriots fighting for their constitutional rights. Posse Comitatus, a white supremacy group formed in the United States in the 1970s, reflected the same sentiments in "The Last Letter of Gordon Kahl," the story of a man who shot it out with police officers instead of paying taxes (Sapp, 1985). American militias maintain this tradition, and the left-wing German Red Army faction made similar claims from the opposite side of the political spectrum.

Despite attempts to expand and develop a broader political following, most terrorist groups fail miserably when they try to increase their size. Walter Laqueur (1987, p. 9) says this is because they are composed of fanatics. Such people do well converting other fanatics, but they have virtually no appeal in mainstream society. Terrorist groups remain small because they cannot see beyond their immediate agendas.

Creating Terrorist Organizations

Key Points and Questions:

1. Describe various patterns in terrorist organizations.
2. What type of activities take place in a pyramid organization?
3. What are the functions of each level in the pyramid?
4. What organizational innovations can a large group introduce to the pyramid structure?
5. What functions do cells and columns play in an organization?

James Fraser, a former counterterrorist specialist in the U.S. Army, discusses the organization of terrorist groups by analyzing two factors: the structure of the organization and its support. According to Fraser and Ian Fulton (1984, pp. 7–9), terrorist groups are necessarily designed to hide their operations from security forces, and so analysis is difficult. Still, certain organizational principles are common to all terrorist groups. Groups employ variations of command and control structures, but they are frequently organized along the same pattern no matter what causes they endorse.

The typical organization is arranged in a **pyramid** (see Figure 3.1). It takes many more people to support terrorist operations than to carry them out; therefore, the majority of people who work in terrorist organizations serve to keep terrorists in the field. The most common job in terrorist groups is support, not combat.

According to Fraser and Fulton (1984), the hierarchical structure of terrorist groups is divided into four levels. The smallest group is at the top and is responsible for command. As in military circles, leadership makes policy and plans while providing general direction. Other researchers have often pointed out that the command

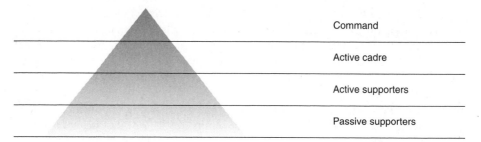

Figure 3.1
A Pyramid Organization

Source: Fraser and Fulton (1984).

structure is not as effective as in legitimate organizations because of the demand for secrecy. The command structure in a terrorist organization is not free to communicate openly with its membership; therefore, it cannot exercise day-to-day operational control.

The second level of Fraser and Fulton's hierarchy is the **active cadre**, or the people responsible for carrying out the mission of the organization. (*Cadre* is a military term; these are the same people most of us call "terrorists.") Depending on the organization's size, each terrorist in the cadre may have one or more specialties. Other terrorists support each specialty, but the active cadre is the striking arm of the terrorist group. After the command structure, the cadre of active terrorists is the smallest organization in most terrorist structures.

Under the active cadre is the second largest and the most important level of a terrorist organization: the **active supporters**. These people are critical to terrorist campaigns. Any group can carry out a bombing or kidnapping, but maintaining a campaign of bombings and kidnappings takes support. Active supporters keep the terrorists in the field. They maintain communication channels, provide safe houses, gather intelligence, and ensure that all other logistical needs are met. This is the largest internal group in the organization.

The last and largest category is the organization's **passive supporters**. This group is extremely difficult to identify and characterize because passive supporters do not readily join terrorist groups; they simply represent a favorable element of the political climate. When a terrorist group can muster political support, it will have a relatively large number of passive supporters. When its cause alienates the mainstream, passive support dwindles. Passive support complements active support.

Most terrorist groups number fewer than fifty people as active supporters, cadre, and command and are incapable of mounting a long-term campaign. Under the command of only a few people, the group is divided according to specific tasks. Intelligence sections are responsible for assessing targets and planning operations. Support sections provide the means necessary to carry out an assault, and the tactical units are responsible for the actual terrorist action.

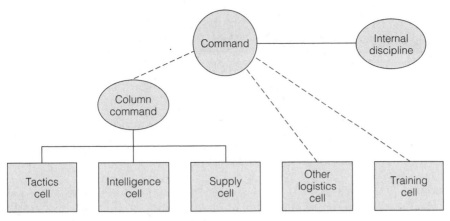

Figure 3.2
Terrorist Group Organization

Source: Fraser and Fulton (1984).

Larger groups are guided by the same organizational principles, but they have major subunits capable of carrying out extensive operations. In particularly large groups, subunits have the ability to act autonomously. Large groups have the tactical units and the support sections to conduct terrorist campaigns (see Figure 3.2).

Anthony Burton (1976, pp. 70–72) describes the basic structure of subunits. Terrorist organizations have two primary types of subunits: the cell and the column. The **cell** is the most basic. Composed of four to six people, the cell usually has a specialty; it may be a tactical unit or an intelligence section. In some organizations, the duties of tactical cells vary with the assignment. Other cells are designed to support the operations.

Groups of cells create **columns**, which are semiautonomous conglomerations of cells with a variety of specialties and a single command structure. As combat units, columns have questionable effectiveness. They are too cumbersome to be used in major operations, and the secrecy demanded by terrorism prevents effective intercolumn cooperation. Their primary function is combat support because elements in a column can be arranged to support the tactical operations of cells.

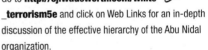

Go to **http://cj.wadsworth.com/white
_terrorism5e** and click on Web Links for an in-depth discussion of the effective hierarchy of the Abu Nidal organization.

While both Fraser and Fulton's work and Burton's analyses appear to be dated, the structures they outlined are still applicable to terrorist groups. Patrick Seale (1992) finds the same type of structure when examining the Abu Nidal group, which was sponsored by many states in the Middle East and Europe. Reuven Paz (2000b) sees similarities with the organization of the Islamic resistance movement Hamas. Religious terrorists, such as Aum Shinrikyo in Japan, also copy the group model (Brackett, 1996). The only terrorists who do not follow typical organizational models are individual terrorists who operate without a group.

New Models for a New Day

Key Points and Questions:

1. Describe an umbrella organization.
2. Name one group that has used the umbrella model.
3. How might terrorists copy the umbrella of piracy?
4. What models did the RAND Corporation develop when examining the dynamics of group change?
5. What impact do new organizations have on terrorism?

Around 1982, new types of organizational styles developed from the pyramid, and organizational transformations continue today. The first change came with the birth of the **umbrella organization** (see Figure 3.3). In this style of organization, several small pyramids gather under a sheltering group that manages supplies, obtains resources, creates support structures, and gathers intelligence. It also will not become directly involved with terrorism, claiming to be a legitimate organization representing a political cause. The sheltering group convenes periodic meetings with sympathizers, suppliers, and terrorist leaders, thus allowing terrorists to resupply, select targets, and plan. The sheltering umbrella disassociates its activities from violence, casting a blind eye when the semiautonomous pyramid groups take action.

The actions of Unionists and Republicans in Northern Ireland illustrate the operation of the umbrella. Both sides maintain legitimate political organizations to campaign either for continued relations with the United Kingdom or unity with the Republic of Ireland. Paul Dixon (2004) argues that much political activity is conducted as a public drama to hide other activities. A number of researchers claim that violent paramilitary groups have operated under the umbrella of legitimate organizations for decades, while the respective political party—the umbrella—continually denies any connection to terrorist violence (see Hastings, 1970, pp. 40–56; Winchester, 1974, pp. 171–180; Lee 1983, pp. 59–97; Dunn and Morgan, 1995). Legitimate groups form umbrellas under which terrorist groups could operate.

Gal Luft and Anne Korin (2004) worry that such practices may soon take place on the high seas. Arguing that most people incorrectly assume that piracy is an activity of the past, they note that incidents have doubled in the past decade. Today's pirates are armed with global positioning systems, satellite phones, machine guns, rockets, and grenades. Most of them currently work for organized crime syndicates, but Luft and Korin fear that international terrorists will take note of the recent rise and success of piracy. If their thesis is correct, organized crime provides an ideal model for terrorists: a seemingly legitimate business (the sheltering organization) provides cover for pirates (the pyramid organization) while denying all connection with illegal activities. Today's piracy is already conducted under an umbrella. In reality, the legitimate business is the front for an organized crime group. The business group, in turn, denies any affiliation with crime, and it shelters the pirate groups operating under its shield. Terrorists need merely to copy the model.

Researchers from the RAND Corporation (Arquilla, Ronfeldt, and Zanini, 1999) identify several other types of new organizational styles that emerged in the 1990s

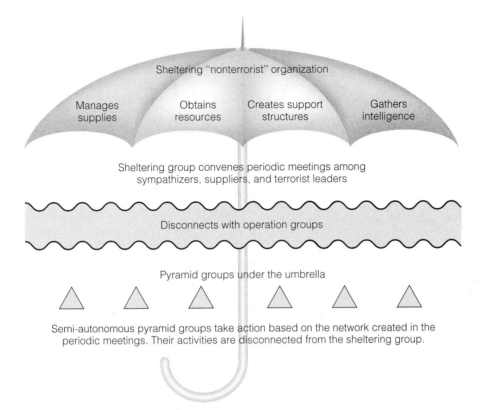

Figure 3.3
The Umbrella Organization

(see Figure 3.4). **Virtual organizations** were created through computer and information networks. **Chain organizations** linked separate groups with like-minded philosophies or religions without creating a hierarchy. **Centralized hubs** developed to manage or support individual cells. Other groups gathered under the banner of **leaderless resistance**. These groups or individuals simply operate on their own.

Three critical factors can be derived from the RAND project. First, as organizations change, the network gives them strength. As Ian Lesser (1999, pp. 1–5) says, the old-style pyramids have given way to virtual, chain, and hub organizations. As in the case of umbrella organizations, this allows more amateurs to engage in terrorism. A makeshift group may spawn only a single incident, but it does so within the context of the network. This activity results in a **de facto campaign**: The amateur group creates a random act, while the supporting network conducts a campaign of single random acts.

The second observation is that the network is supported by a larger nonviolent following motivated by nationalistic, ethnic, or religious concerns. The organization gains strength in a time-tested manner. To paraphrase a Chinese revolutionary leader, the terrorist organization swims in a sea of nonviolent supporters. As Bruce

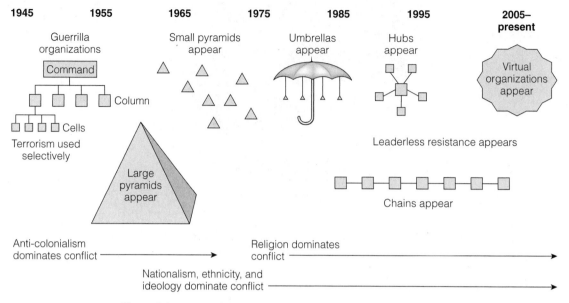

Figure 3.4
Timeline of Organizational Styles

Hoffman (1995) and Walter Laqueur (1999) argue, the dominating force in contemporary terrorism is religion. Today, the most violent terrorist networks swim in a sea of theology. (This process is discussed in Chapter 4.)

Finally, the role of force multipliers dominates terrorism. Terrorists use the electronic media, especially the Internet, to their advantage. Careful use of the media creates an aura around an incident, keeps a potential threat alive, and provides propaganda for supporters. Technology provides the means for killing more victims in a single incident, and transnational support comes from the nature of the network. Sadly, religion is often the force multiplier that binds the process together.

The Problems of Managing Organizations

 Key Points and Questions:

1. Where do management and structure intersect in terrorism?
2. Why is secrecy a managerial problem?
3. Are small groups relatively autonomous in any style of terrorist organization?
4. Why are terrorist groups decentralized?
5. How do leaders cope with problems?

Whether groups organize in a traditional pyramid, an umbrella, a hub, or even a virtual organization, it is possible to chart the structure of even the most secretive groups. The reason is plain. Terrorists need to organize like any other group. You

could probably make a fairly accurate diagram of most terrorist groups after taking an Introduction to Management class. Terrorist leaders face operational problems and seek to solve them with the same strategies you would learn in such a management class. Terrorist leaders also have special organizational problems.

The first problem is the need for secrecy. This dominates the operational aspects of terrorism and leads to a variety of problems that open organizations do not encounter. Ironically, although secrecy is the greatest strength of the terrorist organization, it also reveals its greatest weakness. Sometimes a terrorist group's work is so secret that even the members do not know what they are doing. Terrorism demands secrecy, and secrecy prevents effective communication.

Because the necessity for secrecy is so great in any style of terrorist organization, subgroups are usually allowed a relatively high degree of autonomy. Terrorism is a decentralized affair, and the larger the group, the greater the degree of decentralization. This is not the most desirable kind of organization, but it is an operational necessity. Terrorists know a centralized structure is easily infiltrated and destroyed by security forces. One well-placed informant can destroy an entire organization.

Decentralization offers relative security: Very few people know many other members of the organization. This approach affords great protection but difficult administration. The organization of the Provisional IRA can be used to illustrate the problem. The IRA is organized like most large terrorist groups. It is governed by a Supreme Council whose members are drawn from IRA battalion or column commanders. Column commanders are responsible for a number of cells, which in the IRA are frequently called by military names such as platoons, squadrons, and companies. The command of the IRA, however, has problems that emanate from secrecy and decentralization.

On paper, the organizational chart looks extremely logical. In practice, that logic is modified by the need for each unit to be protected from discovery. This means members of various cells and columns usually have no idea who the other members of the IRA are and what they are doing. They get their orders from one person, and that person supposedly represents the Supreme Council. This paves the way for potential splintering or, at the least, misunderstandings. It is easy to see why the IRA is difficult to manage.

To prevent factionalism and excessive autonomy, terrorist commanders turn to internal discipline for control. In essence, what the commanders continually threaten to do is to terrorize the terrorist organization. Factionalism and autonomy are controlled through fear of retribution.

Ironically, internal discipline can become a major stumbling block in the terrorist organization. There are two opposing dynamics at work, one pulling for cohesion and cooperation through fear and the other pulling for autonomy through decentralization and secrecy. Sometimes, attempts at discipline backfire. For example, when leaders try to punish errant members by assassination, they may find themselves the target of disgruntled followers. As a result, large terrorist organizations frequently find themselves splitting.

Another problem of terrorist management is gaining immediate tactical support for operations. As Fraser and Fulton (1984) suggest, the most important element of a terrorist campaign is the number and structure of active supporters. Without active supporters, launching a campaign is impossible. Although the press has frequently

Go to **http://cj.wadsworth.com/white_terrorism5e** and click on Web Links for an in-depth discussion of urban and guerrilla models developed by Carlos Marighella and Ernesto "Che" Guevara.

pictured terrorist leaders as secretive plotters controlling hidden armies of true believers, in reality terrorist leadership must exert itself to develop and maintain active support. The majority of time is spent creating networks of active supporters, not launching headline-grabbing operations.

Yoseff Bodansky (1986b) illustrates this point in his analysis of state-sponsored terrorism. According to Bodansky, the logistics of mounting a terrorist campaign are massive. To maintain political pressure on an established government through the use of terrorism, a vast infrastructure of active supporters must be created. Bodansky outlines the types of activities that accompany terrorist campaigns. At a minimum, terrorists need three basic operational supports. *Intelligence* is necessary to plan and carry out an attack. This includes everything from the selection and observation of the target to the forging of documents and travel papers. A *direct logistical network* must be established to supply terrorists with weapons; this is complicated because terrorists must use elaborate security procedures to protect logistical networks while security forces use various methods to detect them. Finally, a *support network* for safe houses, transportation, food sources, and medical supplies has to be arranged. Bodansky concludes that it takes thirty-five to fifty support people to keep a single terrorist in the field. Bodansky's (1999) subsequent work reinforces these initial findings.

Training is another need that complicates the business of terrorism. True believers may have the political motivation to engage the enemy, but they frequently lack the practical skills to do so. Terrorists must maintain bases to prepare for such tactical necessities as target practice and bomb making. True believers are easy to find, but trained fanatics are not. Terrorist groups must have both facilities and resources to support training activities.

Managing a terrorist campaign is also a complicated matter. It is conducted in secrecy, and yet the demands on the terrorist command structure are as great as the demands on the leaders of any organization. To compensate for the difficulty, some large international organizations have routinized their approach to terrorism by developing large bureaucratic organizations to manage their affairs. This is an alternative to allowing a state sponsor to dominate the internal affairs of the group.

Brian Jenkins (1987) believes that the bureaucratization of terrorist groups complicates terrorism in many ways. Jenkins says some large terrorist organizations unintentionally developed into bureaucratic structures to meet the rigorous organizational demands of a terrorist campaign. Other organizations established such structures on purpose. Once the bureaucracies were in place, a new set of problems developed,

essentially resulting from a standard bureaucratic problem: Once formalized, these structures must produce reasons to justify their existence.

All terrorists face management problems, and the issues involved in launching attacks are not simple. Terrorist attacks require political support, planning, organization, and resources. Every terrorist group, regardless of size, must take these factors into account. The resources must come from somewhere. Some analysts have argued that attempts should be made to uncover the resources behind the organizations. They believe that too much time has been spent on examining the organizational structure of terrorist groups and not enough energy has been devoted to understanding and uncovering the support networks behind the structures.

The Individual: The Ultimate Small Group

Key Points and Questions:

1. What two ways can technology be used to enhance the destructive power of a single person?

2. What is the new disturbing trend in terrorism?

3. Who is Louis Beam and what did he mean by "leaderless resistance"?

4. How can leaderless resistance be related to a lone terrorist?

5. Describe the thesis of the novel *Hunter*.

6. Cite an example of lone wolf terrorism.

7. Compare the terms *lone wolf* and *berserker*. Which term do you think best describes individual terrorism?

The technology of modern society has produced an interesting paradox: It can serve humankind, but it can also be used destructively. A technological structure, such as a power grid, fuel distribution system, or computer network, can be changed into a weapon if attacked. Weapons of mass destruction can throw a social system into chaos. This has had an important impact on the size of terrorist groups. For the first time in history, a single individual can become a lone force of significant destruction.

Jessica Stern (2003b, pp. 141–145) points to a disturbing trend in terrorist organizations. Religiously motivated terrorists are gathering in loose groupings with no leaders. Stern says that many such groups are virtual organizations held together by ideology and information. The Internet becomes a critical aspect for recruiting, keeping the ideology alive, and inspiring members. The most successful leaderless groups contain a variety of different actors: professional terrorists, those motivated solely by the cause, members relying on the group for financial support, freelancers, commanders, and "lone wolf" avengers.

Louis Beam, a right-wing extremist leader involved in the Ku Klux Klan and Aryan Nations, was one of the first to understand the situation. Group organization, infrastructure, and financing were the weakest links in the chain. Law enforcement officials had figured out methods for infiltrating extremist cells, and they placed informants and undercover agents inside violent organizations. When these methods failed, the police followed the money. These tactics threatened all but the most stable terrorist groups. Beam proposed a solution. According to Mark Pitcavage (1999a), Beam believed that a group, no matter how secret, simply could not evade law enforcement. As a result, Beam called for the elimination of organizations. In the extreme, this could even mean eliminating terrorist groups.

Beam talked about "leaderless resistance," saying that extremist groups did not need to have extensive organizations; it was only necessary to take action. Resistance in any form was acceptable. There was no need to coordinate activities. Resistance was enough. Several movements followed the idea. Hans-Josef Horchem (1986) points to subversive Green Party extremists in Germany, who do everything from telephoning in bomb threats to placing glue in locked doors. The Animal Liberation Front (2000) advocates such tactics on its Web page. Timothy McVeigh's bombing of the Oklahoma City federal building in 1995 illustrates the extreme violent end of the trend. It is difficult to gather intelligence on a group when there is essentially no group.

Another trend in leaderless resistance is the notion of the **lone wolf**. This concept can be found in the right-wing fantasy novel *Hunter* (Pierce, 1989). The protagonist represents the ultimate small group, the individual, and the novel describes how an individual extremist can murder people of color and Jews in the name of white supremacy. William Pierce, the extremist author of the novel, says the police cannot infiltrate a mind.

Eric Rudolph is an example of a lone wolf. Charged in connection with four bombings, ranging from a 1996 attack that drew international attention at the Atlanta Olympics to a 1998 abortion clinic bombing that killed a police officer, Rudolph is almost a real-life parody of Pierce's Hunter. Unlike Hunter, however, Rudolph spent most of the time on the run. He had good reason to hide. Marlon Manuel (2000) of the *Atlanta Journal-Constitution* says local, state, and federal governments spent millions of dollars trying to catch Rudolph. Federal agents, however, did not capture their suspect. In May 2003 an observant deputy sheriff arrested Rudolph for loitering. Most lone wolves tend to be single-incident terrorists, but Eric Rudolph allegedly has been able to plot four incidents: the bombing at the Olympics, two abortion clinic bombings, and an attack at a gay nightclub that wounded 110 people. In addition, his actions have become the legends of right-wing folklore.

I have argued that another term, **berserker**, can be used to describe some individual terrorists (White, 2000). The term lone wolf suggests that a person suddenly pops up out of nowhere, performs a sinister act, and vanishes. Mark Pitcavage (1999a, 2000) says that in reality this does not usually happen. Most lone wolves are true believers who are well-known for their associations with violent extremist circles. Some lone wolves are better viewed as true believing extremists who go off the deep end. The term glorifies their actions and should not be used. This is why I also use the term *berserker*. It is more than an academic term and has investigative consequences.

In old Norse and British warfare, a berserker was a warrior who went crazy in the midst of battle. Bernard Cornwell (1997), the gifted author of the series *Sharpe's Rifles*, provides a frightful description of such a warrior in a set of books about King Arthur. In *The Winter King*, one of the young medieval heroes of the book, Dervel, is in a shield wall facing an army of Arthur's enemies. The shield wall is crucial. As long as the warriors have their shields locked together in front of them, the enemy will have a difficult time breaking through and winning. Young Dervel feels relatively safe behind this wall of shields.

Unfortunately, to Dervel's horror, two warriors step out of the enemy shield line and strip themselves. They dance naked, consumed by battle madness and mead, and are ready to charge Dervel's shield wall and accept certain death. They are drunk, they are naked, and they are removed from the world of common logic. They are also dangerous. Dervel's friends must lower their shields to strike the crazed berserkers. In so doing, they will expose themselves to the enemy army. These naked madmen are not lone wolves. They are crazed, frightened, true believers.

The concept of the berserker may capture some individual extremist violence better than the term lone wolf. This is important for investigators. Berserkers can leave a trail of clues before they "charge a shield wall." For example, Buford Furrow, a right-wing extremist who attacked a Jewish center in Los Angeles, broadcasted his extremist involvement long before the attack. Benjamin Smith, another extremist who went on a murder spree in Chicago, was a public advocate of Creatorism. In practice, many lone wolves do not materialize from thin air. They are berserkers who take violent, irrational actions. When extremists perpetually advocate violence and murder, they may produce a crazed individual who will go on a rampage.

Summary of Main Points

1. Small groups like the NWLF failed because they lacked the ability to expand and support operations.

2. Gurr suggests that only large groups are able to conduct a terrorist campaign.

3. To be effective, terrorist groups must have the ability to create a large base of support. The actual number of terrorists may be limited, but any group needs supporters.

4. A pyramid organization is a four-level hierarchy that can be used to model functions in a terrorist group.

5. An umbrella organization is formed when a sheltering group gathers smaller groups under its protection.

6. Arquilla and RAND researchers modeled several other types of terrorist organizational styles.

7. Terrorists face the same managerial problems as other organizations except that terrorist operations are more difficult because they must be secret.

8. Individuals can take terrorist actions without functioning within a group. Although they may terrorize the public, it is difficult for them to mount a sustained campaign of terrorism.

9. *Leaderless resistance* refers to autonomous groups or individuals acting on their own without centralized leadership.

Key Terms

Make sure you can define, explain, or identify the following people, ideas, organizations, or terms:

New World Liberation Front (NWLF)   31
large group [of terrorists]   32
small group [of terrorists]   32
terrorist campaign   33
single-incident terrorists   33
pyramid   35
active cadre   36
active supporters   36
passive supporters   36
cell   37

column   37
umbrella organization   38
virtual organizations   39
chain organizations   39
centralized hubs   39
leaderless resistance   39
de facto campaign   39
Louis Beam   43
lone wolf   44
berserker   44

Suggested Readings

Now that you've been introduced to this topic, you can learn more by reading:

Ian Lesser and colleagues from the RAND Corporation have assembled an excellent overview of terrorist structures in *Countering the New Terrorism*. John Arquilla's article shapes most of the current discourse on understanding terrorist organizations.

You may also want to read:

Sean Hill and Richard Ward, *Extremist Groups*, is the definitive guide to terrorist organizations around the world and an invaluable resource.

Aaron Mannes, *Profiles in Terror*, is a guide to Middle Eastern terrorist groups.

Sean O'Callaghan has an insider's look at terrorism in *The Informer*.

Web Resources

Go to *http://cj.wadsworth.com/white_terrorism5e* and click on Web Links to find:

- Profiles of terrorist groups from the International Policy Institute for Counter-Terrorism
- An analysis of the changing structure of terrorism by L. Paul Bremer
- The complete RAND report *Countering the New Terrorism* on new terrorist structures

The Companion Website for *Terrorism and Homeland Security*, Fifth Edition

http://cj.wadsworth.com/white_terrorism5e

At the Book Companion Website you can review chapter outlines, use the flash cards to test your terrorism vocabulary, and check out the many other study aids you'll find there. You'll find valuable data and resources at your fingertips to help you study for that big exam or write that important paper.

Terrorism Updates

**http://www.wadsworth.com/criminaljustice_d/special_features/ext/terrorism
_site090802/index.html**

Visit the *Terrorism: An Interdisciplinary Perspective* website to find the most current information about the fields of terrorism and homeland security. With a focus on domestic and international issues, this site explores the scope of terrorism in our world today. You'll find essays on important topics in terrorism and homeland security, critical thinking web activities, and InfoTrac College Edition keywords. Most importantly, the website is updated weekly with current news and research articles on domestic and international terrorism. You are invited to use these web resources to supplement your understanding of the topics covered in this chapter.

Current Perspectives: Readings from InfoTrac College Edition

Terrorism and Homeland Security

The sixteen articles in this reader offer a representative selection that helps you understand the important issues about terrorism and homeland security. It includes FREE access to InfoTrac College Edition and can also be bundled with the text for free.

Chapter 4

The Advent of Religious Terrorism

©EPA/Christian Hartmann/Landov

A man walks near vandalized Muslim gravestones at Haguenau's military cemetery in eastern France, June 2004. Religious terrorists see themselves as the sole representatives of God, and they justify violence and hatred of their enemies in the name of religion.

Religion is one of the factors dominating terrorism today. Bruce Hoffman was among the first scholars to discuss the implications of this trend, and Mark Juergensmeyer and Jessica Stern also analyze terrorism from a variety of religious traditions. A central question from their investigations is, Are there common social and psychological factors among terrorists who are motivated by religious belief? Their answer is yes, and it is given greater weight when the theological implications of violence are examined. Samuel Huntington argues that religious terrorism is a symptom of a greater clash of civilizations. Others, such as Princeton's John Esposito, disagree with Huntington, seeking another model to explain religious violence. This chapter will focus on the issues surrounding religion and terrorism.

Chapter Objectives

After reading this chapter, you should be able to:

1. Explain the difference between religious and political terrorism.
2. Discuss the trends in religious terrorism.
3. Summarize the way religious terrorists use sacred stories and literature.
4. Describe the process of *demonization*.
5. Summarize the social characteristics of religious terrorists.
6. Explain the impact of religion on the way terrorists organize groups.
7. Explain the logic of religious terrorism.
8. Describe the "clash of civilizations" and responses to the idea.
9. Define the role of eschatology in religious terrorism.
10. Summarize two views regarding the relation of Islam to terrorism.

Analysis of Religious Terrorism

Key Points and Questions:

1. Why are experts like Hoffman and Laqueur concerned about the combination of violent religious fanaticism and technology?
2. List the differences between political and religious terrorists.
3. How can religious sacred literature be used to support violence?
4. How does theater relate to religious terrorism?
5. What are two dangerous trends in religious terrorism?

Bruce Hoffman (1995), one of the first analysts to explore the meaning of modern religious terrorism, believes we are witnessing a resurgence and proliferation of terrorist groups motivated by religion. He says this phenomenon is changing the face of terrorism. Laqueur (1999) points out that religious terrorism is nothing new, but the appearance of apocalyptic groups is dangerous in a technological age. Why are experts like Hoffman and Laqueur concerned? The answer is that as terrorists behave differently from regular criminals, religious terrorists behave differently from political terrorists (see Table 4.1). In short, religious terrorists are not constrained by the same factors that inhibit other types of terrorists.

Hoffman says terrorists motivated by religious imperatives differ from political terrorists in several ways. **Holy terror**, another term for religious terrorism, contains a value system that stands in opposition to **secular terror**. Hoffman says secular terrorists operate within a dominant political and cultural framework. They want to win, to beat the political system that is oppressing them. Their goal may be to destroy social structure, but they want to put something in its place. Secular terrorists would rather make allies than indiscriminately kill their enemies. Holy terrorists, however, are under no such constraints. They see the world as a battlefield between the forces of light and darkness. Winning is not described in political terms. The enemy must be

Table 4.1

Differences between Political and Religious Terrorists

Criminal, Political, and Ethnic Terrorists	Holy Warriors as Terrorists
World is a political culture	World is separated into good and evil
Killing is a sad necessity	Killing is a sacramental act
Violence is limited by values	Violence is indiscriminate
Speak for the group	Speak for God
Influence the wider audience	Have no wider audience
Greatest good for greatest number	Greatest good for self
Enemies degraded	Enemies demonized

Source: Hoffman (1995).

destroyed. For political terrorists, killing is the outcome of an operation. For religious terrorists, killing *is* the operation.

Hoffman says holy terrorists see killing as a sacramental act. Pointing to Islamic terrorism as an example, Hoffman says the purpose of the terrorist acts is to kill the enemies of God or convert them to Islam. Certainly, the vast majority of Islamic theologians would disagree with this and they point to many examples in the Koran where Muslims are obligated to avoid forced conversions. Muslim scholars are also offended by the use of the term "Islamic terrorism." Militants in any religion, however, convert faith to their own radical interpretations. This is the nature of both religious violence and terrorism in any religion.

To illustrate Hoffman's point, refer to a Hebrew Bible or Christian Old Testament and turn to Joshua 8, the story of the battle of Ai. In this story, God tells Joshua to trap the warriors of the city, kill all of them, and then turn on the city. Nothing in Ai is to be spared, including unarmed civilian survivors. Today, no mainstream Jewish or Christian theologian argues that God would order such destruction. Most of them say that these stories were written by people who conquered Canaan and then looked back to place a theological spin on their violent actions (Bright, 1981, pp. 144–161). Violent religious extremists in the United States, however, read such stories and believe they are directed to kill Jews and nonwhites. This is what Hoffman is illustrating. Violent extremism can become Islamic, Jewish, or Christian terrorism. Violent extremists take theological issues out of context.

Since they take actions out of context, religious terrorists have no social limitations on violence. They are **true believers**, so consumed with their own concepts that they dismiss the religious views of others (see Another Perspective: True Believers, Islamicists, and Jihadists). As a result, they kill indiscriminately, doing so because they believe they are killing the enemies of a deity. Religious belief is a ready-made source for justifying terrorism because it can sanctify a terrorist. When a person becomes a true believer and a religious doctrine sanctions the use of violence, **deified terrorism** results, that is, the act of terrorism itself is made sacred and holy. Religious terrorists are no longer working for mere mortals; they are on a mission from God.

Hoffman (1995) says religious terrorists believe they speak for the divine. Religion embodies a sacred ideology. When performing acts in the name of a deity, a religious person feels justified and righteous. This is true whether the cause is love or war, and it is not limited to socially illegitimate forms of violence. Governments frequently call on citizens to "praise the Lord and pass the ammunition." True-believing terrorists have done little more than mimic mainstream social patterns. They use the established social paths of religion and ideology to justify their actions.

Hoffman says that in political terrorism, terrorists attempt to create a theater. Their actions are symbolically designed to influence a wider audience. Religious terrorists again differ in this area: They have no wider audience, playing only to God and therefore having no reason to constrain themselves.

There are two other dangerous trends in holy terror, according to Hoffman. First, religious terrorists are not **utilitarian**; that is, they are not a person seeking the greatest amount of good for the greatest number of people. Religious terrorists seek the greatest good for themselves. Second, they demonize their enemies. All terrorists degrade their opponents, thereby making it easier to murder people. But religious terrorists take the process a step farther, into **demonization**. They equate their enemies with the ultimate source of evil. Enemies are devilish and demonic, in league with dark forces. It is not enough to beat them. The enemies must be eradicated from the cosmos.

Hoffman says these traits in religious terrorism create an environment conducive to the use of weapons of mass destruction. He extends this concern to Islamic terrorist groups, the Christian white supremacy movement, Jewish messianic terrorists in Israel, and the Sikh movements in India. Fringe elements of true believers substitute the concept of universal love with love for a selected group of believers. In this sense, the type of religion is almost immaterial, and this is the reason terrorist analysts use terms such as Christian, Jewish, Islamic, Hindu, or Buddhist terrorism.

The Social Characteristics of Terrorists: Juergensmeyer's Terror in God's Mind

Key Points and Questions:

1. How do holy warriors tend to divide the world?
2. What are the results of this division?
3. Show practical examples that support Juergensmeyer's thesis.

Mark Juergensmeyer (1988, 2000) spent many years examining the issues surrounding religious terrorism (see Expanding the Concept: Juergensmeyer's Qualities of

Religious Terrorists). According to one of his earlier works (Juergensmeyer, 1988), believers must identify with a deity and think they are participating in a struggle to change history. And this struggle must be a **cosmic struggle**; that is, the outcome of the struggle will lead to a new relationship between good and evil. When they feel the struggle has reached the critical stage, violence may be endorsed and terrorism may result.

In a later work, *Terror in the Mind of God*, Juergensmeyer (2000) examines the uncompromising attitude of such philosophy. The call to violence, Juergensmeyer argues, is a call to purify the world from the nonbeliever and the incorrect interpreters of tradition in a holy war. The lines of battle are clear. Those people who do not stand with the holy warrior are evil, and such a war allows only one way of thinking. If the holy warrior falls in a losing cause, the warrior becomes a martyr for hope. If the warrior is successful, it is a victory for the deity. There is no middle ground and no compromise. Victory is the only course of action.

Juergensmeyer examines holy warriors from several different faith traditions and finds commonalities. It is interesting to apply his logic by comparing the al Qaeda Manual (al Qaeda, n.d.) with the defense manual of the American extremist right-wing group known as the Covenant, the Sword, and the Arm of the Lord (1982). Both begin with theological passages claiming their interpretations of God's word are correct. They both quote U.S. Army manuals (al Qaeda does a better job), interspersing tactical directions with scriptural quotes. Juergensmeyer argues that such actions can be explained by the mind of the holy warrior. The language remains the same across religions and across cultures.

Religions That Kill: Stern's Terror in God's Mind

Key Points and Questions:

1. How do terrorists use myths?
2. Why does Stern believe people are returning to their sacred stories?
3. List the ways religion changes the structure of terrorist organizations.
4. How do professional terrorists function in religious organizations?
5. Is leadership affected by changing terrorist structures?
6. Explain why religion impacts "lone wolf avengers."

The famed psychologist Carl Jung devoted much of his work to the study of sacred stories. Most religious scholars call these sacred stories *myths*. This does not mean that myth means untruth. A **myth** is a sacred story that conveys deep-seated truths. In this sense, a myth is not a lie or half-truth; it explains the basis of belief.

Mircea Eliade (1961) and Joseph Campbell (1985) spent their lives discussing the power of mythological traditions in culture. Terrorists are no different from other people, and they, too, need their own sacred stories. Jessica Stern (2003b) examines the religious basis of these stories and explains how they are incorporated into the mythological structure of holy terror, or as Stern calls it, **sacred terrorism**. Terrorists use myths as a story to explain a religious struggle, and Stern believes the **sacred stories** of a terrorist group serve as an important source of motivation.

Stern (2003b) believes people around the world are returning to their religious roots as a means to escape the complexity of modern life. People have too many choices, she states. All of the choices bring confusion, and most people want to escape confusion. Returning to old established patterns of earlier generations, frequently the truths of their traditional religions, people confused with modern complexity seek to ground their lives. Unfortunately, old truths in one society may collide with the truths of another society. This is especially true when one group believes it is under attack. When mythological truths compete, violence often results.

People use stories to explain deep truth beyond the immediate world, and terrorist groups build their own mythologies to justify their actions through a story. Stern believes stories change the nature of terrorist organizations, and they help to produce a number of different group organizations and styles (see Chapter 3). Some organizations center on rigid structures. Other groups grow when a number of insecure people gather around a strong personality. Some groups are informal, and everybody has a leadership function. Some loners loosely affiliate with a group but tend to act on their own. Criminals flock to other associations. Stern says the most successful groups operate with a variety of different styles of subgroups.

Individuals come to a group, according to Stern, because they believe they have been called to the story of an entire people. They join a cosmic struggle, a holy cause. New recruits take a number of paths to terrorism, but they are usually motivated by the organization's sacred story. Most sacred stories emphasize self-sacrifice and even death. As a result, many new terrorists seek a path of martyrdom, sometimes facing grave dangers and other times intentionally committing suicide to destroy cosmic enemies. Another path involves developing some type of specialty, and many are motivated to become mighty warriors. If you think of ancient heroic stories like those about the mythic ancient Greek Hercules, you can see Stern's point. Hercules was half human and half god, and he had strength far beyond that of any mortal. Upon his death, Zeus, the king of the gods, placed Hercules in the heavens as a constellation. This type of myth serves as a model for the ultimate warrior. In a similar way, stories about warriors who sacrifice themselves can be used to justify self-sacrifice or suicide.

Many times people become disillusioned and leave the group. They may still be sympathetic to the cause, but they become disillusioned with leaders who fail to live up to mythical standards. Stern says leaders originally join a group because they believe in the myth, but after a time the lifestyle produces the need for "professional behavior," and the group must face **professionalization of the leadership**, that is, the emergence of a **professional terrorist**. In other words, the power of the myth becomes less important and the day-to-day job of terrorism grows. Terror for the sake of terror becomes a way of life, and peace threatens the leader's livelihood.

To maintain the power formally given by the sacred story, leaders develop internal enforcement mechanisms. Rewards are given and withheld to encourage correct behavior within the group. When ideology breaks down, leaders may find themselves in alliances with enemies. At this point, the behavioral patterns of religious terrorists cease to matter. They eventually become long-term professional leaders who know only one kind of work. They are professional terrorists for sale to the highest bidder.

Stern also believes that religion helps to produce the "lone wolf avenger," or the berserker described in Chapter 3. An individual lone wolf avenger needs to find some type of justification for his or her actions, and religion provides the perfect path. Stern says lone wolf avengers have a special, narcissistic relationship with their deities. In essence, they create a god in their own image. They become the ultimate loners, and Stern demonstrates that they present the most difficult targets to deter or detain.

The Logic of Religious Terrorism

Key Points and Questions:

1. How do nonkilling religions evolve into militant ideologies?

2. Describe Eliade's two spheres of human experience.

3. What purpose do symbols and myth serve?

4. Summarize Tillich's view of literalizing myths and symbols.

5. How could you use the idea of "the Promised Land" to illustrate Tillich's point?

6. Use the Balkan Peninsula and *The Turner Diaries* as examples to demonstrate Campbell's thesis.

Anthropologist Marvin Harris (1990, pp. 437–453) believes human beings have experienced two types of religions: killing and nonkilling religions. **Killing religions** developed during the food-gathering cycles of pre-agrarian and early agricultural societies, and they were based on the premise that a deity would help the community in times of crisis. In the killing religions, gods slaughtered enemies. Harris says these beliefs gave way to the nonkilling religions because the older, killing religions did not, in fact, protect early villages from the ravages of war and natural disasters. The **nonkilling religions** embraced enemies and developed elaborate theologies to justify violence as a last resort. The nonkilling religions appeared in order to try to transcend everyday experience. Harris says the irony of the human experience is that nonkilling transcendence is often transformed into a militant ideology designed to protect a state or some other social group by this rationalizing of the use of violence as a last resort. Why does this happen?

Many years ago, the scholar Mircea Eliade (1961) provided an answer. Eliade says the world of human experience is divided into two spheres: the **ordinary and extraordinary worlds**. We use language and logical concepts to describe the ordinary or everyday world, but we use symbols and myths to talk about the extraordinary or spiritual world.

The ideas of Joseph Campbell (1949, 1985) complement Eliade's thesis. Campbell says we express our spiritual nature in symbols and myths, but we are limited when we try to talk about them. Music, art, drama, and poetry can convey mythological meanings, but it is difficult to put extraordinary events into words. We are forced to talk about mystical experiences using everyday language. Since we have no words to describe the spiritual world in spiritual terms, we can only talk about these experiences the same way we talk about the common issues of life.

The late Protestant theologian Paul Tillich (1957) says this can be dangerous because it can allow us to "literalize" symbols. This means the symbol no longer represents the sacred experience, but it *becomes* the experience. When this occurs, the symbol displaces the myth and becomes an object of worship. The **literalization of myth** occurs, and the symbol no longer points to the sacred. It has taken the place of the sacred.

Consider the following illustration of this process. Joseph Campbell (1985) argues that in the sacred stories of the Israelites, God promises the Hebrews a land flowing with milk and honey. In Campbell's analysis, God pledges "sacred space," a place where God and humanity can commune. Campbell says, however, that because the story is told in everyday language, the purpose of the sacred story is transformed. Rather than pointing to a sacred place of divine communication, the everyday language of the story makes it look as though God promises the Israelites a geographical location. In other words, the story is misinterpreted as "God promised Abraham the state of Israel." When the sacred story is interpreted in this manner, the liberating effect of the myth is subordinated to ethnic identity and nationalism.

Taking away abstract anthropological and theological concepts, let us look at two practical examples. Since 1991, parts of the Balkan Peninsula—the area of Europe containing Serbia, Croatia, Slovenia, Bosnia, Yugoslavia, Kosovo, Montenegro, Bulgaria, Albania, Romania, and Greece—has been devastated, first by a civil war and then by seemingly endless fighting among several groups. A closer look at the issues surrounding the Balkans reveals the logic of religion and violence.

Ferdinand Schevill (1922) completed a definitive study of the Balkan Peninsula about eighty years ago. Although much happened in the twentieth century, including the formation of Yugoslavia after World War I (1914–1918) and the partition of the entire region into several countries in the 1990s, the fundamental reason for conflict in the region did not change. It is based on three interpretations of religion.

Through the course of history, the Balkan Peninsula became the area where Christendom violently encountered Islam in the eighth century. As Christian kingdoms began fighting Islamic kingdoms, the transcendent nature of both Christianity and Islam was subordinated to the political needs of each kingdom. The situation took another turn in 1054 when the Western Christian Roman Catholics and the Eastern Christian Orthodox Church split over theological matters. Soon, Catholics and Orthodox Christians were slaughtering one another in the name of religion. Members of all three religions attacked one another with zeal, despite the fact that both Jesus and Mohammed taught peace, and the Koran recognizes that Christians and Muslims worship the same God.

This situation continued for the next one thousand years, with each side politically dominating the area at times in history and repressing the other two religions when gaining control. The symbols of nonkilling religions, the peace of Jesus and the teachings of Mohammed, were transformed into deadly elements of political expression. When Yugoslavia was created after World War I, ethnic and religious animosities did not disappear. Indeed, they surfaced again during World War II as each religious group fought the other two. The Communist leader Joseph Tito (1892–1980) was able to create a coalition government that maintained a delicate peace after the war. Following his death and later the collapse of the Soviet Union, however, ethnic religious leaders reemerged, resulting in a religious bloodbath in the area at the end of the twentieth century.

Another practical example of this process comes from the extremist right in the United States. In *The Turner Diaries*, a fictional work by white supremacist William Pierce, the main protagonist has a religious experience. Earl Turner, the novel's hero, has been committing small-time acts of violence against Jews and nonwhite races when he is invited to join a white terrorist group known as The Order. (An actual white supremacist group that operated in the American West in the 1980s took its name from this story; see Chapter 14.) As Turner is inducted into the terrorist group, he has the first religious experience of his life.

The fictional Turner describes himself as someone who is not religious, but an official of The Order gives Turner "The Book," a "holy" work describing God's plan to create a racially pure world in the face of Jews and people of color. Turner is taken aback. He admits to having a transcendent experience, but he says he does not know how to describe it. He can only respond by killing racial and ethnic "inferiors." (Note how this matches the theories of Eliade, Campbell, and Tillich. The concepts—Eliade's extraordinary language, Campbell's transfer of a mystical symbol to a geographical place, and Tillich's conversion of the symbol to a literal object—are transformed into everyday reality. One group is permitted to enter the ordinary reality, and outsiders are to be destroyed.) Turner cannot express his thoughts in ordinary language, and he comes to realize he can only experience the extraordinary by doing something spectacular. So he goes on a killing spree. Terrorism and religion are fictionally united, and *The Turner Diaries* inadvertently illustrates the "logic" of religious violence.

History is filled with stories of people who have literalized myths, taken sacred stories out of context, terrorized in the name of their deity, and expressed spirituality through violent actions. The process is constant. When people transform a nonkilling religious call for universal love into a mandate to love only those who look, act, and believe like them, they introduce a formula for religious violence. The process is completed when symbols and myths are literalized. Unfortunately, this is a part of terrorism.

Huntington's Clash of Civilizations and Esposito's Response

Key Points and Questions:

1. Define the epochs of modern history.

2. According to Huntington, what is the most important factor in current international conflict?

3. Define the civilizations in Huntington's scheme.

4. What are torn countries and fault lines?

5. How do Esposito and Pipes respond to this classification system?

6. How does Barnett modify the clash of civilizations?

In 1993, Harvard professor Samuel P. Huntington (1996) introduced a theory of conflict for the twenty-first century. Huntington maintains that past epochs were dominated by particular types of conflict. Medieval Europe from the Reformation (1517) to the Thirty Years' War (1618–1648) could be characterized by religious wars. After the Peace of Westphalia (1648), dynastic rights and territorial needs dominated international conflict. This gave way to nationalistic wars after the French Revolution (1789–1799). Nationalism dominated global wars until 1918, the end of World War I, when ideology moved to the forefront. The age of ideological conflict climaxed when capitalism and Communism threatened the world with the nuclear standoff between the United States and the Soviet Union. When the Soviet Union collapsed in 1991, Huntington says, the world changed.

Huntington uses the term **clash of civilizations** to describe conflict in the post–Cold War era. He believes cultures clash with other cultures and religion is one of the most important concepts in defining a culture or civilization. At the beginning of the twenty-first century, the United States stands alone as the world's only superpower, and the struggles that threaten world peace will no longer focus on nationalism or ideology. Most wars will result from volatile regions where cultural confrontations threaten to spread violence.

Huntington argues that there are eight primary cultural paradigms or civilizations dominating the modern world: (1) Western, (2) Confucian, (3) Japanese, (4) Islamic, (5) Hindu, (6) Slavic-Orthodox, (7) Latin American, and (8) African. Each cultural region corresponds to a particular geographical area where people hold similar beliefs, values, and attitudes (see Table 4.2).

Huntington believes that international peace will be threatened in "torn countries." These are regions where more than one civilization exists within an area. The Balkan Peninsula, discussed above, is a classic example of Huntington's thesis. Three

Table 4.2

Huntington's View of Civilizations

Western	United States, Canada, Western Europe, Australia
Confucian	China, parts of Siberia, Southeast Asia
Japanese	Japan
Islamic	Middle East, Turkey, Southwest Asia, parts of Southeast Asia, North Africa, Balkans
Hindu	India
Slavic-Orthodox	Russia and Eastern Europe
Latin American	Mexico, Central and South America
African	Africa

Source: Huntington (1996).

civilizations, Western, Slavic-Orthodox, and Islamic, dominate the region. There is a tremendous amount of violence as these civilizations clash, and the potential for war in ongoing. Huntington believes that hot spots will continue to produce violence and the United States must be careful to avoid intervening in these areas of cultural and religious conflict in the coming decades. The main conflict will be between Islamic and Christian civilizations.

Not everyone agrees with this assessment. In fact, two scholars who frequently disagree with each other offer separate arguments against Huntington. John Esposito (1999, pp. 238–242) disagrees with Huntington's thesis on two levels. First, Esposito says that culture or civilization is defined by much more than religion. He argues that history, language, geography, social structure, and ethnic factors also influence civilization. Esposito's second point focuses on Huntington's claim that Western Christianity is confronting Islamic civilization. There is no Islamic civilization, Esposito claims. The world of Islam is politically and socially diverse; it is not a single civilization.

Daniel Pipes (2003, pp. 248–251) disagrees with the majority of Esposito's approach to research, but he joins Esposito in rejecting Huntington's belief in a clash of civilizations. When looking at Islam, for example, Pipes says the major clash is not *between* civilizations, but rather *within* Islamic civilization. Pipes believes that moderate Muslims are attempting to engage modernity, and they are forced to fight violent fanatics who are trying to reinterpret the religion. The primary fight is between Muslims, but it spills over when fanatics practice terrorism around the world. Pipes urges the United States to embrace moderate Islamic governments and assist them in this global struggle.

Thomas Barnett (2004) provides another context for the clash of civilizations. He believes that a global economy can be developed to lift the world from poverty and create a new international political and economic order. He calls this "a future worth creating." Admitting that he was influenced by Huntington, Barnett nonetheless draws a different map, dividing the world between a functioning economic core and an excluded, nonintegrating gap that is not included in the global economy. The clashes that happen within the functioning core are handled by civil authorities, mutually defined rules, and law enforcement. The gap is another matter.

Terrorism comes from the nonintegrating gap, Barnett says, because true believers within the gap understand the threat economic development means to their narrow way of life. He does not believe that countries are Americanized when they enter the global economy; they are bombarded with a multitude of differing cultures. Economically developed countries accept a variety of lifestyles and traditions because their citizens profit by doing so. Religious terrorists know that a successful economy that lifts the planet's poor from an economic gap will destroy the structure of their world. Barnett believes that Huntington's clash comes between economic rather than cultural civilizations.

Huntington's thesis has been widely debated in foreign policy circles, but his conclusions have much to do with the concept of religion and terrorism. Each cultural paradigm or civilization has religious zealots who seek to impose their views on everyone else. Each religion contains true believers who have literalized symbols and myths and subjugated them to ethnic and nationalistic aims. Regardless of one's evaluation of Huntington's thesis, one point is clear: Terrorism is currently dominated by religious violence. Whether you agree that it is a clash of civilizations (Huntington), a clash within civilizations (Esposito and Pipes), or a clash between economic systems (Barnett), the clash is real. True believing terrorists literalize their symbols and kill for the things they represent.

Role of Eschatology

Key Points and Questions:

1. Define *eschatology*.

2. List Crossan's forms of eschatology.

3. What happens when political and eschatological beliefs are combined?

4. Do eschatological expectations cause violent behavior?

In my own research (White, 2001) I argue that apocalyptic thinking and terrorism have become dangerous allies. When applied to terrorism, apocalyptic thinking invites terrorists to fight as holy warriors in a period of fanatic zeal when a deity is about to bring creation to an end. They believe God's reign is almost on us, and they are facing their last opportunity to purify creation before God's reign. The Greek-rooted word *apocalypse* means "revelation," but a better term to use is *eschatology* (see Another Perspective: Eschatology).

Eschatology derives from the Greek word *eschatos*, a concept dealing with the end of all material and purpose in time and space. In the Greek version of the Hebrew Bible, eschatology usually is interpreted as the "day of Yahweh"—that is, a final judgment and the realization of God's purpose for creation. This Jewish idea influenced early Christian writers, but the meaning of God's final presence fluctuated in early Christian dogma (Kittel, 1964, p. 697).

Christians have expected God's final judgment for two thousand years. Yet, they have not agreed on the form it will take. John Dominic Crossan (1999, pp. 257–287) describes four commonly held eschatological frameworks: ascetic, apocalyptic, ethical, and political. **Ascetic eschatology** refers to the process of self-denial, while the **apocalyptic** version envisions God's destruction of the existing order. According to Crossan, **ethical eschatology** is quite different. It calls for followers to embrace radically moral behavior in recognition of God's imminent reign. Crossan says **political eschatology** is frequently ignored today because it combines expectations of religious judgment with political action. People fear political eschatology.

Another Perspective

Eschatology

Eschatology (ES-ka-TOL-ogy) is the theological study of the end of time. It deals with divine judgment. Religions that emphasize a final judgment believe that the end of time is in a deity's hands. This means that their concept of divinity controls the outcome of creation. Many militants, however, believe they must participate in the end of time. They feel they are responsible for ushering in the divine kingdom. When terrorists use such religious arguments to justify violence, they combine terrorism and eschatology.

Daniel Pipes (2003, p. 72) says that traditional Islam is concerned with political morality, not an eschatological final judgment. Although Muslims, like Christians and Jews, believe God will stand in final judgment, Pipes does not feel this reflects an eschatological perspective. Militant Muslims, however, have replaced traditional theology with a political utopian ideal that human beings, not God, must implement. Pipes's analysis makes Crossan's emphasis on political eschatology even more crucial. If one is expecting apocalyptic or ascetic eschatology, there is no need to worry. God is in control and will make the final judgment. On the other hand, some forms of ethical and almost all forms of political eschatology rely on the actions of human beings. In other words, the Osama bin Ladens of the world have displaced God with their own political view of creation (see Pipes, 2003, pp. 39, 71–76; Qutb, 1990, p. 138).

Gunther Lewy (1974, p. 40) also emphasizes political eschatology, arguing that linking political beliefs with an end-of-time theology is a prescription for violence. Given the variety of meanings attached to eschatological expectations, it is not surprising to find that various terrorist groups have developed their own "end-of-the-age" philosophy in apocalyptic theologies. As Lewy implies, some of these theologies are indeed quite dangerous. Some people would like to violently usher in the new age, and an eschatological philosophy is tailor-made for individual terrorists who have rejected both the material world and the norms of social behavior. It provides a cosmic battlefield where forces for good are called to fight an unspeakable evil.

The consequences of eschatological terrorism are dramatic. Indeed, they are cosmic in proportion. All deterrents to violence are rendered meaningless by the promise of a new age. When violent eschatology is politicized on a cosmic battlefield, Armageddon's warriors need no further justification to bear arms. They fight for a holy cause, and all actions are justified. As Bruce Hoffman (1995) says, there are no constraints for those in their final hours.

Two Views of Islam and Terrorism

Key Points and Questions:

1. How does Pipes view political Islam?
2. Why do people explore possible relationships between Islam and terrorism?
3. Summarize the view stating that fundamentalism is related to violence. Offer a critique of this argument.
4. How does Pipes respond?
5. Counter Pipes's view with Esposito's conclusions.

The view that some Americans have of Islam has been influenced by various presentations of Islamic extremism in the media and by popular misconceptions and stereotypes. Daniel Pipes (1983) wrote a theological and political analysis of Islam more than twenty years ago, demonstrating that many Western attitudes are incorrect. Islam is a legalistic religion more closely related to traditional Judaism than Pauline Christianity, that is, the theology of the Christian apostle Paul, who emphasized grace and forgiveness instead of the sterner characteristics of religious law. In a more recent publication, Pipes (2003) argues that Islamic militants, frequently called **Islamicists** (see Another Perspective: True Believers, Islamicists, and Jihadists on p. 51), are fighting a political battle to gain control over Islam.

The idea of "Islamic terrorism" offends most Muslims. They argue that terrorism has nothing to do with Islam, and they complain that the Western press does not refer to, for instance, Christian terrorism, Buddhist terrorism, or Jewish terrorism. Unfortunately, when terrorists take action in the name of religion, it is quite natural to expect some discussion of the topic. Violent Islamicists and **Jihadists** (see Another Perspective: True Believers, Islamicists, and Jihadists on p. 51) continually call upon God in their struggle, and this has resulted in two positions about Islam and terrorism.

Reuven Paz (1998) summarizes one position, but it can also be found in journalistic examinations by Robin Wright (1986, 1989), Dilip Hiro (1987), and Amir Taheri (1987). This view states that Islamic fundamentalism is related to political violence. Paz pursues this further by asking the question, Is there an Islamic terrorism? His answer is yes.

Paz argues that Islam sees itself in a global war with the West. This is exacerbated by socioeconomic differences. Islamicists divide the world into the realm of Islam (*dar al-Islam*) and the realm of heresy (*dar al-Harb*). Islamic radicals have relegated the West to the realm of heresy. Paz says success against heresy is measured in the popular support of terrorist groups. Since Muslims in general see themselves in a struggle with the West for social and political reasons, Paz concludes that popular support of militant Islam indicates that an "Islamic terrorism" exists. He says the West should not debate its existence; it should defend itself against Islamic terrorism.

Others are not so quick to accept such logic. David Kibble (1996) argues that Islamic fundamentalism seems to be a threat at face value. Radical groups of Islamicists in Egypt, Saudi Arabia, Iran, and other areas appear to have declared war on the United States and its allies. Indeed, Secretary of Defense Donald Rumsfeld stated that Islamic fundamentalism is the greatest threat to American security since Communism. Kibble believes such fears are unfounded.

Kibble says there are pockets of Islamic extremism in the Middle East that sustain terrorism. He argues, however, that these segments are isolated and divided. A broad spectrum of religious and political beliefs exists in Islam that rejects violence. Kibble believes that when fundamentalists take power, it may be the first step toward democracy. He urges caution in labeling Middle Eastern violence as "Islamic terrorism."

Clarence Bouchat (1996) agrees. He says American fears and misunderstandings of Islam make it appear as if fundamentalists were united and threatening to gather the Middle East in a war against the West. This is not the case. Fundamentalists are a divided lot, just as religious fundamentalists in the United States are divided. The history of the West and the Middle East involves centuries of religious wars. Bouchat says more is to be gained by examining the religious similarities between the two regions than by using such terms as "Islamic terrorism."

Daniel Pipes (2003, p. 45) has very little sympathy for arguments like those of Kibble and Bouchat. He states that American political leaders have had bad advice from academic experts who told the West not to worry about militant Islam. Militants have "Westernized" Islamic theology by making it a utopian dream, very similar to Marxist economic theory. They believe that by forcing Islamic law, or *sharia*, on the world, they will usher in a new golden age. No longer relying on rogue states or the interests of competing nations, these terrorist groups have emerged as a cause unto themselves. Religion is the basis of their calling, and they attract violent followers throughout the world.

John Esposito (1999, pp. 207–211) offers a different view. There are a variety of Islamic political groups, he argues, and most of them see violence as counterproductive. The varied nature of political movements means that each one must be examined within a specific historical and political context. When political groups speak of sharia, it means many different things, and it is impossible to discern the meaning apart from the way it is used in a particular country. Just as there are many schools of thought in other religions, Islam is diverse and divided. There are some violent Muslims, but most of them seek change through the political and social transformation of society. It is not possible to rely on stereotypes or classify Islam as a violent religion. Interestingly, both Pipes and Esposito point out that Jihadists have killed more of their fellow Muslims than any other group they have targeted.

Summary of Main Points

1. The behavior of political terrorists differs from the actions of religious terrorists.

2. When religion is introduced in a terrorist conflict the amount of violence and the number of victims tend to increase.

3. Religious terrorists use sacred stories to create a cosmic battlefield. This allows them to fight on the side of their deity and to demonize all the people who do not support them.

4. Religious terrorists separate the world between good and evil. They do not negotiate or compromise because they feel that God can never compromise with evil.

5. The logic of religious terrorism can be explained by its cosmic nature. Religious terrorists are convinced that their actions take place at a critical junction in history where the fate of all creation hangs in the balance.

6. Many of the new styles of organization described in Chapter 3 can be explained by the effect of religion on terrorism.

7. Huntington claims modern conflict will be defined by confrontations between different civilizations. He believes religion is the dominant factor in a civilization.

8. Eschatology refers to the theological end of time. When people combine politics with eschatology, they believe they are responsible for creating the correct circumstances for the end of time. Religious terrorists combine violence with political eschatology.

9. Muslims resent implications that their religion is frequently linked with terrorism. Islamic radicals, called Islamicists or Jihadists, claim they are acting in the name of God.

Key Terms

Make sure you can define, explain, or identify the following people, ideas, organizations, or terms:

holy terror   49

secular terror   49

true believers   50

deified terrorism   50

utilitarian   51

demonization   51

cosmic struggle   52

myth   52

sacred terrorism   53

sacred story   53

professionalization of the
   leadership   53

professional terrorist   53

killing religions   54

nonkilling religions   54

ordinary and extraordinary
   worlds   54

literalization of myth   55

clash of civilizations   57

eschatology   59

apocalyptic eschatology   59

ascetic eschatology   59

ethical eschatology   59

political eschatology   59

Islamicists   61

Jihadists   61

Suggested Readings

Now that you've been introduced to this topic, you can learn more by reading:

Mark Juergensmeyer's *Terror in the Mind of God* contains interviews with religious extremists. It analyzes the social world of religious terrorism and presents models based on Juergensmeyer's research experience.

You may also want to read:

Jessica Stern, *Terror in the Name of God*, examines the world of religious violence.

Samuel Huntington, *The Clash of Civilizations and the Remaking of World Order*, combines politics and history into a thorough, albeit controversial, examination of conflict in the modern world.

John Esposito, *The Islamic Threat: Myth of Reality*, does not present a favorable review of Huntington, but Esposito takes his readers through the political world of Islam around the globe.

Daniel Pipes, *Militant Islam Reaches America*, criticizes both Huntington and Esposito, but it examines the ideology of Jihadists. It also contains one of the few analyses of the Muslim movement in the United States.

Discussions of militancy in religion are volatile, especially when they cross cultures. Here are some recommendations for scholarly discussions of the place of violence in Islam:

Abdullah Saeed and Hassan Saeed offer a view of Islamic theology in the modern world in *Freedom of Religion, Apostasy, and Islam.*

John Esposito offers a critique of terror in the name of Islam in *Unholy War*, and a theological summary of the religion in *Islam: The Straight Path.*

John Kelsay summarizes jihad theology in *Islam and War.*

The Wahhabi Myth by Haneef James Oliver contains a defense of the Salafi purification movement and argues that Osama bin Laden and other Jihadists are Qutbists.

Reuven Firestone's *Jihad* is a theological examination of the meaning of jihad in the Koran.

Web Resources

Go to *http://cj.wadsworth.com/white_terrorism5e* and click on Web Links to find:

- An article by Bruce Hoffman called "Old Madness, New Methods" about how the revival of religious terrorism demands a broader U.S. policy
- "Explaining Religious Terrorism Part 2: Politics, Religion, and the Suspension of the Ethical," by Mark Burgess
- "Building Peace to Combat Religious Terror," an article by R. Scott Appleby, codirector of the Fundamentalism Project

The Companion Website for *Terrorism and Homeland Security*, Fifth Edition

http://cj.wadsworth.com/white_terrorism5e

At the Book Companion Website you can review chapter outlines, use the flash cards to test your terrorism vocabulary, and check out the many other study aids you'll find there. You'll find valuable data and resources at your fingertips to help you study for that big exam or write that important paper.

Terrorism Updates

http://www.wadsworth.com/criminaljustice_d/special_features/ext/terrorism _site090802/index.html

Visit the *Terrorism: An Interdisciplinary Perspective* website to find the most current information about the fields of terrorism and homeland security. With a focus on domestic and international issues, this site explores the scope of terrorism in our world today. You'll find essays on important topics in terrorism and homeland security, critical thinking web activities, and InfoTrac College Edition keywords. Most importantly, the website is updated weekly with current news and research articles on domestic and international terrorism. You are invited to use these web resources to supplement your understanding of the topics covered in this chapter.

Current Perspectives: Readings from InfoTrac College Edition
Terrorism and Homeland Security

The sixteen articles in this reader offer a representative selection that helps you understand the important issues about terrorism and homeland security. It includes FREE access to InfoTrac College Edition and can also be bundled with the text for free.

Chapter 5

Financing Terrorism

Suspected drug traffickers are led past seized packages of cocaine in Cali, Colombia. Some policymakers believe that illegal drugs are used to finance terrorism.

AP / Wide World Photos

The seventeenth-century Hapsburg General Raimondo Montecuccoli once said a nation needed three things to make war: money, money, and more money. This saying is applicable to terrorism. Spontaneous violence can occur without planning or resources, but organized political violence requires financial backing. It takes money to fund organizations, and resources to support operations. Some new forms of terrorism even require salaries to pay professional terrorists. The families of suicide bombers receive compensation in the Middle East, and other terrorist organizations have found they can take advantage of existing criminal networks to raise money. Terrorists need money to run an operation.

Chapter Objectives

After reading this chapter you should be able to:

1. Summarize some of the methods used to finance large politically motivated terrorist organizations.

2. Describe the relationship between terrorism and crime.

3. Explain the Hawala system.

4. Describe several methods for fundraising using underground networks and fraud schemes.

5. List and define legitimate methods terrorist groups use for raising funds.

6. Outline methods for terrorist financing in different parts of the world.

7. Explain terrorism financing from a macroeconomic perspective.

8. Summarize the two sides in the narcoterrorism debate.

The Importance of Funding

Key Points and Questions:

1. James Adams wanted what type of specialized unit to combat terrorism?

2. What is the thesis of *The Financing of Terror*?

3. Why does Adams believe that some analysts missed the meaning of modern terrorism?

4. What functions did Samed serve?

5. How did the IRA raise money?

6. What was the "Capone discovery"?

7. Do the findings of Kushner and Bodansky support Adams's findings?

As world leaders and law enforcement officials began to examine modern terrorism in the 1980s, a correspondent from the London *Times* developed an interesting thesis. James Adams (1986), then the defense editor for the *Times*, looked at all the efforts Western governments were developing to counter terrorism. While he saw the need for hostage rescue units, specialized police forces, and bomb squads, he believed there was another method for attacking terrorism. Governments needed to stop the flow of money.

Adams's thesis in *The Financing of Terror* (1986) is that terrorism changed between the 1960s and the 1980s and most Western defense policies failed to account for the change. Led by the United States, defense policy has been aimed at uncovering state-sponsored terrorism. Adams says this has resulted in a fundamental misunderstanding of the function and nature of terrorism. Major terrorist organizations are independent of states, and they have created independent financial support networks to stay in business. Adams concludes the best way to attack terrorism is to attack the financial structures that support independent terrorist organizations.

Adams believes modern terrorism developed from revolutionary violence in the 1960s. As violence grew, he writes, the West developed two schools of thought to approach the problem. One school saw increased terrorism as a state-sponsored activity, used to support national military functions. The other school thought terrorism could be eliminated only when the political causes of terrorism, such as injustices, were uncovered and eliminated. Adams believes both groups had a point but missed a central issue.

Modern terrorism is distinct from violence in the 1960s. It grew, was transformed, and came to possess a dynamic of its own. Nation-states became involved in sponsoring terrorism in both the West and East, but not in the manner envisioned by American defense policymakers: States do not play a major role in terrorism.

Adams examines a number of large terrorist groups to find his answer. To obtain autonomy in the struggle for Palestine, the PLO established an economic wing called **Samed** in 1970. Samed became an important financial unit within the PLO. It served as a bank and provided funding for many PLO projects. Adams writes that Samed developed into a rational business structure to support the PLO. It used modern organizational theories providing economic benefits, salaries, and incentives to the fedayeen (warriors who sacrifice). Although Samed's headquarters were destroyed in the 1982 Israeli invasion of Lebanon, operations moved to Tunisia, Algeria, and Syria. Samed ran farms and factories, and it intends to become a strong economic force in the Middle East during the twenty-first century.

Adams also focuses his attention on the Provisional IRA. He states it is popular to believe the Provisional IRA gets most of its money from the United States. America, however, was not the prime source of IRA income from 1968 to 1986. The Provisional IRA maintained its coffers by running an organized crime network in Northern Ireland. This transformation, from revolutionaries to underground gangsters, proved to be the best method of financing terrorism.

In what Adams calls its **Capone discovery**, the Provisional IRA found it could raise vast sums of money by frightening shopkeepers and business owners into paying protection money. He chose the term Capone discovery because the IRA ran operations that looked more like the organized crime gangs of Al Capone's Chicago than activities associated with terrorism. The IRA's protection racket had two results for a typical shopkeeper. It guaranteed Provisional IRA protection for the business in case of trouble, but this was not the prime motivation for the payment. The major purpose was to keep the Provisional IRA from attacking the owner's property or family. The Provisional IRA took so much cash from its protection racket that it was forced to launch a money-laundering scheme.

In 1972, the Provisional IRA found another way to finance terrorism when it entered the legitimate business world by purchasing a taxi company. The endeavor succeeded, and the Provisional IRA soon realized it could make even more money if it forced other companies out of business. Terrorism was used to dominate the market. The technique worked so well the Provisional IRA has set up other front businesses. Crime pays in Northern Ireland.

Adams believes tracing the financial resources of terrorism is important for a single reason. In its battle against terrorism, the West has been focusing on the wrong target. Adams says counterterrorism should concentrate on cutting off the financial sources of terrorism. Terrorist campaigns are not waged in a vacuum; they require organization and resources. In the final analysis, this means they must be financed. Adams concludes that behind the structure of every large terrorist group lies a financial network. A terrorist campaign can be stopped by undermining a group's economic ability to wage a campaign.

Although terrorist organizations have changed since Adams's analysis, they still need money. Harvey Kushner and Benjamin Jacobson (1998) demonstrate this with the underground economic activities that support Middle Eastern terrorism in the United States. Bodansky's (1999) detailed analysis of the financial network that supports Osama bin Laden shows the same type of infrastructure. Since Adams's study, several new developments have taken place in the world of terrorism finance. The underground economic structure that supports terrorism has grown in recent years.

Crime Pays

Key Points and Questions:

1. Why have links between terrorism and crime increased in the past two decades?
2. What is the financial contradiction in terrorism?
3. What factors force terrorists into an underground economy?
4. How do terrorists operate in underground economies?
5. What is the Hawala system and how does it work?
6. List and define money-generating operations.
7. How do charities become involved in terrorism?

As Adams's early study indicated, terrorists need money. In the past two decades the links between criminal networks and terrorist organizations have increased all over the globe. Middle Eastern terrorists engage in smuggling and **document fraud**. Document fraud raises money for terrorist organizations and provides terrorists with false identification. In Central Asia terrorist organizations trade illegal arms, launder money, and distribute drugs. Latin American terrorism is tied to drug production and public corruption. In the United States domestic terrorists engage in fraud schemes and robberies to finance political violence. Why have the links between terrorism and crime grown? The answer is simple: Crime pays.

On the surface, terrorist financing seems to contain a contradiction. Terrorist operations do not cost a lot of money, but the overall budget is quite high. For an example, *The Economist* (2003) reports that terrorism is cost effective in terms of the causalities and destruction terrorist events cause. Events like the 1995 Oklahoma City bombing or the multiple bomb attack of trains in Madrid in 2004 only cost a few thousand dollars. Yet, terrorism remains expensive. Neil Livingstone and David Halevy (1988) explain this seeming contradiction. Individual operations are inexpensive, but organizations are costly. In other words, it does not take much money to set off a bomb, but it takes a lot of cash to run a terrorist group.

The costs of terrorism pose a problem for terrorist groups. Although it takes financial backing to run an organization, terrorists find it difficult to participate in the economic system. This forces them to join an **underground economy**. The FBI estimates the underground economy produces $500 billion per year. An underground economy requires secret institutions, and terrorists have found that a number of enterprises are available for hiding money (Maier, 2003).

The Hawala System

Many international terrorist groups move money through an ancient trading network called the Hawala system. The system originated several hundred years ago in China under the name of *Feng Chin*, or flying money. Today, it is primarily based in Pakistan and India, but there are Hawala dealers around the world.

The system works like this: A group in country A wants to buy weapons from a group in country B, and neither group wants to have a financial record of the exchange. A leader from the group in country A goes to a Hawala dealer and gives the dealers $1 million. He may receive a theater ticket stub, a torn piece of newspaper, or some other receipt to show that the money has been deposited. The leader mails this receipt to a Hawala dealer in country B. The Hawala dealer subtracts a fee for services and gives an arms dealer in country B the remaining money. The arms dealer ships the weapons to the terrorist group in country A. A $1 million illegal arms deal has taken place and no money has exchanged hands between the two countries making the deal.

The advantages of the Hawala system are:

- Money moves with no record
- Money crosses international borders with ease
- It is based on trust, and long-term trusting relationships are in place
- Money can easily be bartered for contraband
- No tax records exist

Sources: Shah (2001) and Schramm and Taube (2002).

Rachel Ehrenfeld (2003, pp. 10–30) says that terrorists run banks and create phony companies to launder or hide their funds. They also engage in secret transactions and form alliances with organized crime. The **Hawala system** (see Expanding the Concept: The Hawala System and Fig. 5.1) is one method used to transfer money from one person to another without leaving a record of the transaction. A Hawala dealer accepts a credit promise from a dealer in another country and delivers money to a client on the basis of the promise. If police forces can follow the money through an organization, however, they can eventually take an organization apart. Frederich Schneider (2002) says the underground economy and its ties to crime are so important to terrorists because all the transactions remain hidden. Organized criminal and smuggling networks have long had the means of hiding money through seemingly legal transactions. Terrorists take advantage of these networks. Schneider believes that terrorism has become a big business.

Terrorists not only move funds, they smuggle stolen goods and contraband. They also forge documents. The *Wall Street Journal* (Simpson, Crawford, and Johnson, 4-14-04) reports that European police agencies uncovered a lucrative underground railroad running from Central Asia through Europe in the spring of 2004. Ansar al Islam, a group formed by ethnic Kurds, and al Tahwid, an allied group headed by Abu Musab al Zarqawi, generate phony documents and sell them to immigrants.

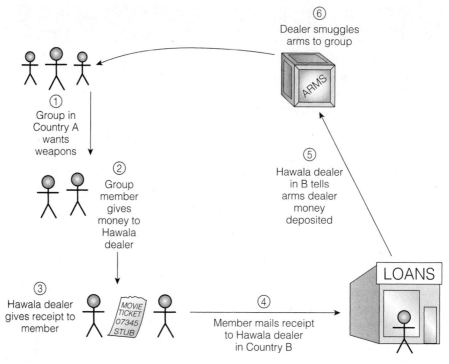

Figure 5.1
The Hawala System

They also use forged passports to move their operatives through Europe and move contraband through the same avenues. These efforts help to keep Ansar al Islam and al Tahwid operational.

According to several researchers (Emerson, 2002, pp. 183–219; Ehrenfeld, 2003, pp. 21–22; Napoleoni, 2003, pp. 111–179) charities have been involved in funding terrorism. Data from national and international law enforcement sources agree with these findings (Scott-Joynt, 10-15-03; Isikoff and Hosenball, 3-12-04; U.S. Department of State, 2004b). Many people who contribute to charities do not know they are supporting terrorist organizations. Others believe the efforts they are supporting are not terrorist operations but legitimate military operations. Zachary Abuza (2003b, p. 93) writes that terrorists often set up a phony charity or skim the proceeds from legitimate organizations. Either way, charitable funds are frequently diverted to terrorist groups.

Domestic violent political extremists use small markets to raise cash. Some violent right-wing extremists sell videos, propaganda, and firearms at gun shows. When I attended a Posse Comitatus, the front of the room was filled with students studying Christian Identity, a White-supremacist religion, and the back was filled with all types of items for sale. The objects ranged from "secret books" of the Bible to primary source material that "proved" space aliens had colonized the earth for white people.

One of the vendors informed me that she regularly traveled the lecture and gun show circuits to sell these items. A founding member of the militia movement lectured and sold videotapes of militia propaganda, and another opened his store for special deals after maneuvers. Right-wing political meetings are enhanced by marketing.

Mark Pitcavage (1999a) points out that the extremist right loves to engage in counterfeiting and fraud. They are especially good at defrauding their own Christian patriots. In one scheme (Pitcavage, 1999b, 11-8-99), a patriot claimed that the U.S. government went bankrupt after abandoning the gold standard in 1933. The patriot, however, found out about the bankruptcy and sued the government for issuing Federal Reserve Notes. The Supreme Court sympathized with the patriot and awarded him $600 trillion in gold. Delta Force went abroad to gather the world's gold to pay off the debt, and now, every American was entitled to $20 million to $40 million. All a person had to do to file a claim was to give the patriot $300 to fill out a claim form.

You might think that no one would be gullible enough to fall for such a story. But Pitcavage found that the patriot presented this scenario at various places around the country and cleared millions of dollars at $300 per victim. Residents of Colorado paid $385,000 for their share of the gold, and Oklahomans shelled out $400,000. People in Michigan and Iowa were the most gullible, paying nearly $2 million.

Domestic extremists are not the only violent fanatics who raise funds in the United States; international terrorists also engage in fraudulent activities in America. From approximately 1981 to 1986 the Abu Nidal organization engaged in different criminal activities in Tennessee and the St. Louis metropolitan area to generate funds, according to a confidential source. Hezbollah ran cigarettes from North Carolina to Michigan and used some of the profits to fund operations in Lebanon. There are a variety of schemes utilizing baby formula across the country. American baby formula is treasured throughout the world because of its nutritional value. Terrorists sometimes steal formula and use illegal distribution networks to raise money (see Another Perspective: Baby Formula Schemes). In Cincinnati, law enforcement officers broke a ring of convenience stores that were selling stolen goods to finance terrorist organizations. Police in Dearborn, Michigan, arrested two men for making false identification for Middle Eastern groups. In the Virgin Islands, two would-be financiers were arrested before obtaining $60 million for international terrorists (WorldNet Daily, 10-6-05).

Terrorism is also linked to organized crime throughout the world, and in some cases it is almost impossible to distinguish between terrorist and criminal activity. Tamara Makarenko (2002) says that Russian organized-crime groups trade weapons for drugs in Colombia. She also finds that both terrorists and criminals take advantage of political instability in regions like Central Asia and the **Tri-Border Region** in South America (the point where Argentina, Brazil, and Paraguay share a common

Another Perspective

Baby Formula Schemes

Terrorists have used baby formula in various ways to raise money in the United States:

1. Buying formula in a state where the price is subsidized and selling it for a higher price in a nonsubsidized state.
2. Highjacking trucks with baby formula.
3. Repackaging baby formula after cutting it with flour and selling it overseas.
4. Repacking expired formula.
5. Selling stolen formula.

Profits are sent to various terrorist organizations.

Source: IIR (2004).

Figure 5.2
Tri-Border Region

The Tri-Border Region is the area in South America where Paraguay, Brazil, and Argentina share a common border. Quite a bit of criminal activity take places in the region, and the Paraguayan city Ciudad del Este is particularly known for its lawlessness. The region is also home to more than twenty thousand Middle Eastern immigrants. Hamas, Hezbollah, and other terrorist groups have been known to frequent the area.

border) (see Figure 5.2). In the Middle East and Southeast Asia terrorists and criminals kidnap for profit. She believes that terrorist and criminal organizations have grown into global enterprises.

The globalization of crime and terrorism has created opportunities for vast profits in the diamond trade. African diamonds, or "conflict diamonds," are obtained illegally and sold in an underground network. According to a British human rights organization (Global Witness, 2003), al Qaeda spent ten years moving into unregulated diamond trading in Western Africa. In the early 1990s it infiltrated legitimate trading centers to establish a base. After success in mainstream trading, al Qaeda slowly and quietly switched from legitimate trading centers to underground criminal networks. Then, taking advantage of weak governments and regulations in Africa, it established its own international trading network. The new system allowed al Qaeda and allied Jihadist groups to make tremendous profits while providing a ready-made network to hide and launder money. It should be noted that the 9-11 Commission (2004, p. 171) examined claims about al Qaeda's involvement in the diamond trade, and members came to a different conclusion. The commission found no evidence that diamonds were used to support al Qaeda. Global Watch disagrees and believes it has presented evidence of al Qaeda's activities.

Terrorists have also been willing to use extortion and **protection rackets** to raise money. Protection rackets work in the same manner as the IRA's Capone discovery. Terrorist organizations force legitimate businesses or other people to make payoffs to avoid being attacked. Loretta Napoleoni (2003, pp. 27–28) reports that the Shining Path of Peru taxed farmers for protection. Rebels and death squads in Colombia did the same thing. Zachary Abuza (2003b) says similar tactics are used in Southeast Asia (see Expanding the Concept: Seven Methods for Funding Jihadist Networks in Southeast Asia). In essence, Abuza concludes, terrorists use the same fundraising techniques that criminals have used for years in addition to their unique methods of gathering money.

Expanding the Concept

Seven Methods for Funding Jihadist Networks in Southeast Asia

1. Cash brought into a host country
2. Funds skimmed from religious charities
3. Phony businesses designed to gather or hide money
4. Proceeds from the Hawala system
5. Direct contributions
6. Investments
7. Street crimes (robbery, theft, fraud, extortion, smuggling, kidnapping)

Source: Abuza (2003b).

A Macroeconomic Theory of the New Terrorist Economy

Key Points and Questions:

1. How did the fall of the USSR and economic globalism affect terrorism?
2. What is the new economy of terror?
3. Where and how did it originate?
4. What terrorist groups participated in the changing terror economy?
5. What crimes are involved in the terrorist economy?
6. Do militant Islamic groups participate in this economy?
7. How might criminologists view the macroeconomic theory of terrorism?

The financial aspects of terrorism have influenced the changing nature of the international economy. After the collapse of the former Soviet Union in 1991, the United States became the world's only superpower. Promoting an economic system that emphasized international production, trade, and consumption, American economic policies focused on reducing the trade barriers between nation-states. Some countries prospered under the international philosophy, called **globalism** or the global economy, but other countries grew weaker and poorer. Globalism is based on the belief that international trade barriers should be removed so that commerce and industry can develop in an international free market. Terrorism took hold in some of the areas left behind in the rush toward globalism, and this changed the nature of terrorist financing (see Barber, 1996, pp. 48–49).

The Economic Terms of Terror

Economists use a variety of terms to convey meanings. For example, *markets* refer to the places where goods are purchased and sold; a *consumer* is a person who buys goods in a market. The following definitions may help you understand the thesis of Loretta Napoleoni (2003) about the new economy of terrorism:

Microeconomics literally means a small economic system. It refers to the everyday transactions taking place in a market.

Macroeconomics means a large economic system. If microeconomics discusses the way things happen in a market, macroeconomics focuses on the way the entire market or economic system functions. When Napoleoni studies terrorism, she is examining the way the terrorist economy operates—a macroeconomic way of approaching the subject.

Globalism or *the global economy* is the economic system that has dominated the world since the fall of the Soviet Union. Proponents believe in eliminating all economic barriers between countries; opponents believe in keeping barriers to protect local economies, jobs, or the environment.

The new economy of terrorism is a technical term Napoleoni uses to describe the macroeconomic structure of modern terrorism. She believes major terrorist groups have globalized an underground criminal economy. This method of financing has changed the shape of modern terrorism. The new economy of terrorism is rampant with *failed states* and *shell states*. A failed state is a nation that does not have the power to govern all of its territory, and a shell state refers to organizations that establish their own area of control in a failed state.

Source: Napoleoni (2003).

Loretta Napoleoni (2003) examines this process while formulating a new theory about the financing of terrorism. Agreeing with Adams's early findings and other studies that found links between organized crime networks and terrorism, Napoleoni goes far beyond a summary of the immediate circumstances. In *Modern Jihad* she argues that terrorism has evolved as an economic entity. The fall of the Soviet Union and subsequent globalism have produced what she calls the **new economy of terrorism** (see Another Perspective: The Economic Terms of Terror).

Napoleoni says that the origins of the new economy of terrorism grew from the Cold War (1945–1991). As Bruce Hoffman (1998, pp. 43–65) says, colonial revolts began at the end of World War II (1939–1945). Napoleoni (2003, pp. 11–28) sees this as the beginning of a macroeconomic shift. Western nations began to use underground methods to found their struggles in the colonies, while revolutionaries sought to find their own sources of money. The origins of the new economy of terrorism can be traced to anticolonial revolts.

To demonstrate the birth of this new economy, Napoleoni turns to France. At the end of World War II France was a colonial power in charge of many foreign countries. Nationalists revolted against French rule all over the world. In Vietnam (then known as Indochina), the revolutionary nationalists were called the Viet Minh after their leader Ho Chi Minh. Although they had Communist backing, the Viet Minh needed money. They muscled their way into opium production, sold the drugs, and used the profits to keep their guerrillas in the field.

Ironically, France tried the same concept. When the war against the Viet Minh became politically unpopular, the French government found it difficult to finance military operations. Napoleoni says the French took over opium profits and used them to finance the war. As a result, drug trafficking became one of the primary methods governments used to finance activities during the Cold War.

Napoleoni says that as the Cold War developed, the Soviet Union and the United States fought each other by proxy, that is, they did not fight each other directly. The Soviets used their allies to attack countries loyal to the United States, and the United States used its friends to attack Soviet-backed countries. Napoleoni believes that modern terrorist groups evolved from these surrogate conflicts, and they looked for ways to become independent from both superpowers. The desire for autonomy led terrorist groups to join criminals in an underground economy.

Napoleoni cites several examples to support this idea. She says a radical Marxist group in Peru, the Shining Path, turned to the drug trade in northern Peru, regulating drug production to fund their activities. The Popular Armed Forces of Colombia (FARC) went a step farther and joined the Colombian drug trade. Militant Palestinians went in another direction, using robbery and extortion to raise funds. The IRA started diverting funds from American charities before turning to organized crime. Napoleoni says these sources of financing fueled most of the terrorist activities of the 1970s and early 1980s.

The Basque Nation and Liberty (ETA), a revolutionary terrorist group in northern Spain and southern France, changed the structure of terrorist finance. Instead of seeking links to an underground economy, the ETA tried to gain control of the economy. They forced Spanish businesses out of the Basque areas of northern Spain and weakened the entire state. The Basque region became a failed state, a place where Spain could no longer exert power. When this happened, the ETA established an illegitimate economy in a shell state (see "Another Perspective: The Economic Terms of Terror" for the definitions of **failed state** and **shell state**). It paid salaries to terrorists, provided for the families of fallen warriors, and even ran a pension system for retired terrorists. The ETA was successful because the Spanish economy failed in the Basque region, leaving the area in a hopeless political mess. The ETA was strong enough to assert stability.

The new terrorist economy can be understood from the example of the ETA. Napoleoni believes that globalization has created pockets in the world where failed or weak states are left to govern with little economic and political power. Terrorists and criminal groups grow in such places, running their own underground economies and providing some form of political stability because they are strong enough to resist the state. Illegitimate groups form a shell state, an organization that acts like a government in a place where the government is not strong enough to act.

As globalization increased, according to Napoleoni, it not only created economic vacuums where shell states could form, it also fueled the growth of a global underground economy. In other words, it provided illegal trade routes for drugs, arms smugglers, contraband dealers, and human traffic. Terrorist groups funded themselves through these activities, and they could not exist without them.

Napoleoni believes that modern terrorism is an international force supported by groups in shell states that continually change both their organizational structures and political goals to maintain income from an international underground economy. They hide their economic views with religious rhetoric or patriotic slogans, but their most important objective is to raise funds. Without funding, a terrorist group cannot exist. The prime goal of a group, then, is to maintain its finances. Powerful groups even become strong enough to invest in legitimate markets, and in some instances they move so much money that they affect the global economy.

Complementing Napoleoni's work is a model developed by Mario Ferrero (2002), who argues that modern radical Islamic groups use violent activity as a means of providing economic stability. Jihadist groups cannot keep outsiders away or fire slackers for being unproductive. Numerous recruits flock to training camps and meetings, including people who are less than totally motivated. The slackers threaten stability by using a group's limited resources. To control this, Jihadists increase rhetoric and violence to drive all but the most loyal members away from the group. This leaves enough resources to support the true believers.

If these macroeconomic theories of terrorism are correct, they have meaning for the nature of counterterrorism. Criminologists frequently believe that crime can be reduced when potential deviant groups have a vested interest in the economic structure of society. **Macroeconomic theory** suggests that counterterrorism policies should be aimed at providing the world's people with economic stability, opportunity, and participation in the mainstream economy (see Barnett, 2004, p. 49). Economic policies to counter terrorism would involve supporting states in threat of failure, providing opportunities for people to participate and benefit from economic systems, and eliminating underground economic networks. When a state fails and a terrorist group creates its own shell state, the group has no incentive to participate in legitimate economic enterprises. As Benjamin Barber (1996, p. 299) says, when economic globalization threatens the ability of ordinary people to meet their needs, they will find other ways to survive. Indeed, this reflects Napoleoni's thesis. Poverty does not cause terrorism, but economic and political failures may result in a shell state where terrorism can be organized and funded.

The Narcoterrorism Debate

 Key Points and Questions:

1. What is narcoterrorism?
2. Does everyone agree with the idea?
3. What are the two positions of the DEA about narcoterrorism?
4. What role does the Tri-Border Region play in narcoterrorism?
5. What arguments do supporters of the concept of narcoterrorism use?

One of the heated issues surrounding the discussion of terrorist financing is the relationship between terrorism and drugs. The term **narcoterrorism** refers to terrorists using either terrorist tactics to support drug operations or drug trade profits to finance terrorism. Rachel Ehrenfeld championed the idea of narcoterrorism in her early works, and she recently expanded upon the idea (Ehrenfeld, 2003). According to her research, terrorists are involved in the international production and distribution of drugs; indeed, she believes, the narcotics trade is one of their primary sources of money. The United States government tends to accept this position, but it is nonetheless extremely controversial.

Steven Casteel (5-20-03), an executive with the Drug Enforcement Administration (DEA), told a U.S. Senate committee that terrorism and the drug trade are intertwined (see Expanding the Concept: The Two Faces of Narcoterrorism). Organized criminals, smugglers, and drug dealers naturally linked with terrorist groups, he says, because all these organizations move in the same circles. Like Napoleoni, he believes that globalization has intensified this relationship. In another report (DEA, 9-03), he says that the relationship between drugs and terrorism has been in place throughout history.

David Adams (2003), reporting for the *St. Petersburg Times*, says that Hezbollah and Hamas use the Latin American drug trade to raise funds. He writes that U.S. military units have tracked their activities in South America, and the military is concerned about the large amount of money involved. According to the U.S. Central Command, hundreds of millions of dollars have been raised in Latin America. The military's prime concerns are the Tri-Border Region, the Venezuelan island of Margarita, and the areas controlled by FARC in Colombia. The DEA (9-03) agrees with this assessment. An official from the U.S. Department of State says it succinctly: Whether it is Latin America or elsewhere, he claims, terrorist groups are financed through drugs. This is demonstrable, not debatable (Walter, 5-2-02).

Other nations also believe that terrorism and drugs are linked. The French Ministry of Defense issued a report stating that drugs are the primary currency used to finance international terrorism. The French government points to the Shining Path and FARC to show the influence of cocaine. The Ministry of Defense claims that radical Islamic groups get most of their money through the drug trade in Central and Southeast Asia. Afghanistan is the primary source of heroin in Europe, and the profits from these drug sales fund all international Islamic terrorist groups (Chouvy, 3-25-04). Officials in India believe that Lashkar-y-Tayyiba and al Qaeda smuggled drugs and other contraband through Africa, Central Asia, and Eastern Europe (*Times of India*, 11-19-03). According to many in the Indian government, militant Islamic groups are funded by drugs.

Joshua Kransa (1997) takes the argument to another level. He says that if people are willing to expand the definition of national security beyond the framework of military defense, drugs pose a security problem. Defining security as social safety, Krasna

Expanding the Concept

The Two Faces of Narcoterrorism

According to the Drug Enforcement Administration, terrorism and drugs are linked.

METHOD 1: DRUG TRAFFICKERS

International drug dealers have found they can use terrorist tactics to increase profits. When using this method drug dealers form alliances with terrorist groups or use terrorist tactics against rivals and the government to create opportunities to produce, ship, and distribute drugs.

METHOD 2: TERRORIST DRUG TRAFFICKING

Terrorists use drugs to finance their operations. In this method, terrorists become drug dealers to raise funds for their organizations or for an operation. Unlike drug traffickers, they use profits for their cause. Drug traffickers, conversely, keep the money for themselves.

Source: Casteel (5-20-03).

says that the drug trade threatens political and economic stability while disrupting society. The drug trade limits the ability of legitimate governments and increases the power of insurgent and terrorist groups. Terrorists, for their part, not only use drugs to exploit the social safety of their enemies, they use them to fund terrorist activities.

Narcoterrorism: Another View

Key Points and Questions:

1. Why do some people reject the idea of narcoterrorism?
2. Do terrorists use other methods aside from drug sales to finance activities?
3. Summarize the arguments used by critics of the concept of narcoterrorism.
4. Are drug traffickers terrorists?

Not everyone accepts the link between drugs and terror. Some people argue that terrorists may use drugs as a source of income, but they also use several other illegal activities to raise money. Selling drugs is only one method, and the drug problem is not caused by terrorism. Other people believe that the use of the term "narcoterrorism" is an attempt to take political advantage of the fear of terrorism. If drugs and terrorism come to mean the same thing, it will be easier to take actions against drug dealers. Critics believe that combining the drug problem with terrorism confuses two different issues.

The 9-11 Commission (2004, pp. 171–172) dismisses the idea that drugs were linked to al Qaeda's attack on New York and Washington, D.C. There is no evidence, the commission writes, that indicates bin Laden used underground drug networks or narcotics trafficking to support the September 11 attacks. The Taliban used narcotics trafficking to support Afghanistan, but bin Laden used a network of donors based in Saudi Arabia and the Gulf states.

In the same article in which he explains narcoterrorism, David Adams (2003) acknowledges critics. First, he points to skepticism about the military and DEA assessment of Latin America. Many critics believe these organizations have overstated the problem. Other people point to misunderstandings. Terrorists are not necessarily linked to the drug trade even when they appear to be involved with drugs. Many Arabs live in the Tri-Border Region, and they support Hamas and Hezbollah. Just because drug traders flourish in this region does not mean that either the Arabs or the terrorist groups are associated with drugs.

David Kaplan (12-15-03) says the financing of militant Islamic groups has very little to do with the drug trade. Based on a five-month study for *U.S. News and World Report*, Kaplan blames Saudi Arabia for funding the spread of an intolerant form of Islam. Violent intolerance, he says, spawned the rise of terrorist groups, and the sect most sympathetic to an intolerant version of Islam comes from Saudi Arabia. Charities are responsible for the bulk of terrorist financing, he believes, and money is gathered through radical mosques, militant schools, and violent Islamic centers. Saudi money can be traced to violence in Algeria, Bosnia, Kashmir, the West Bank, Gaza, Indonesia, Somalia, and Chechnya. The spread of militant Islam is not about drugs.

Pierre-Arnaud Chouvy (3-25-04) does not agree with the position of the French military. He argues that the term narcoterrorism is too vague to describe either drug traffickers or terrorists, and it does not help to address either problem. The problem with drugs involves supply and demand. Western Europe and North America provide ready markets for drug use. Typical Afghan farmers fight to survive. They produce opium, the base for heroin, because it is a cash crop. Western Europe has the demand, Chouvy says, and Afghanistan has the supply. Opium production has nothing to do with terrorism. Narcoterrorism is a convenient term for the French government to use, appealing to public emotions and giving the police more power.

Civil libertarians are especially critical of attempts to link terrorism and drugs (TalkLeft, 8-20-03). Agreeing with Chouvy, civil libertarians see the attempt to link narcotics and terrorism as a ploy by states. If terrorism were to disappear, the drug trade would remain. But if governments link drugs with terrorism, they can reinvent the meaning of crime. Drug dealers will become terrorists, and a frightened public will grant the government expanded powers to combat drugs. In addition, courts more readily grant search warrants and wiretaps against terrorists. Civil libertarians often believe governments want to define drug pushers as "Narcoterrorist Kingpins" in an effort to increase their own power.

Summary of Main Points

1. A number of methods and forms of crime are used to finance terrorist operations.

2. The link between terrorism and organized crime is growing. Terrorists use existing networks to communicate, transport goods, exchange money, and move personnel.

3. The Hawala system is an old method merchants use to exchange money without risking transporting actual cash. Today, some terrorists use this system to fund operations.

4. Terrorists frequently use charities and legitimate business enterprises to gain funds.

5. There are different ways to fund terrorist operations in different parts of the world. Asian networks frequently involve smuggling, drugs, and human trafficking. American and European networks are often involved with fraud schemes and false charities. Africa is heavily involved in illegal diamond trading, and South American terrorists are involved in drug trading.

6. The macroeconomic theory of terrorism is based on the premise that terrorist groups create shell states within failed states. They finance operations using methods from the Cold War.

7. The idea of narcoterrorism in controversial. Proponents believe that terrorists use drugs to finance operations; opponents argue that governments use the term to increase their own power.

Key Terms

Make sure you can define, explain, or identify the following people, ideas, organizations, or terms:

Samed   67

Capone discovery   67

document fraud   68

underground economy   68

Hawala system   69

Tri-Border Region   71

protection rackets   73

globalism   73

new economy of terrorism   74

failed state   75

shell state   75

macroeconomic theory

[of terrorism]   76

narcoterrorism   76

Suggested Readings

Now that you've been introduced to this topic, you can learn more by reading:

Loretta Napoleoni, *Modern Jihad*. Napoleoni explains complex economic theories in a way that people who are not economists can easily understand. She introduces a theory of terrorist financing and a macro analysis of the global network.

You may also want to read:

Rachel Ehrenfeld, *Funding Evil*, an account of terrorist financing, with an analysis of narco-terrorism.

James Adams, *The Financing of Terror*, is still applicable today.

Richard Labeviere, *Dollars for Terror*, compiles news reports from all over the world to create a picture of the funding of militant Islam.

Benjamin Barber, *Jihad vs. McWorld*, is about the global economy, not terrorism, but his work illustrates the risks and challenges of globalism and the potential for political violence.

Web Resources

Go to *http://cj.wadsworth.com/white_terrorism5e* and click on Web Links to find:

- The State Department's analysis of Saudi-based charities financing terrorism
- The report of the Financial Action Task Force on Money Laundering, which includes a comprehensive view on international efforts to control terrorist financing
- The official DEA position on narcoterrorism
- A detailed description of the Hawala system (Cheema, 10-3-01)

The Companion Website for *Terrorism and Homeland Security*, Fifth Edition

http://cj.wadsworth.com/white_terrorism5e

At the Book Companion Website you can review chapter outlines, use the flash cards to test your terrorism vocabulary, and check out the many other study aids you'll find there. You'll find valuable data and resources at your fingertips to help you study for that big exam or write that important paper.

Terrorism Updates

**http://www.wadsworth.com/criminaljustice_d/special_features/ext/terrorism
_site090802/index.html**

Visit the *Terrorism: An Interdisciplinary Perspective* website to find the most current information about the fields of terrorism and homeland security. With a focus on domestic and international issues, this site explores the scope of terrorism in our world today. You'll find essays on important topics in terrorism and homeland security, critical thinking web activities, and InfoTrac College Edition keywords. Most importantly, the website is updated weekly with current news and research articles on domestic and international terrorism. You are invited to use these web resources to supplement your understanding of the topics covered in this chapter.

Current Perspectives: Readings from InfoTrac College Edition

Terrorism and Homeland Security

The sixteen articles in this reader offer a representative selection that helps you understand the important issues about terrorism and homeland security. It includes FREE access to InfoTrac College Edition and can also be bundled with the text for free.

Chapter 6

Types of Modern Terrorism

© Reuters/Ihlas News Agency/Landov

HAZIRLANMIŞ CANLI BOMBA YELEĞİ

A suicide bomber vest with homemade bombs and other explosives is displayed on a mannequin in the city's police department after they were seized in Istanbul. Suicide terrorism is one of the frightening new types of terrorism.

Terrorism has changed in recent years not only because of social and ideological factors, but because technology has had a decisive impact on the various forms of terrorism. When terrorists struck governments in Europe and the United States in the 1880s, they used Alfred Nobel's recently invented dynamite. Today, terrorists have a vast arsenal of technological weapons. Cyberterrorists may attack through the computer infrastructure, and other traditional terrorists may resort to weapons of mass destruction. Modern religious terrorists began using suicide bombers in 1983, and secular groups followed suit. The tactics and types of modern terrorists differ from methods of the past because of the influence of technology and other social factors. This chapter discusses these new types of terrorism.

Chapter Objectives

After finishing this chapter, you should be able to:

1. Summarize what cyberterrorism and cybersecurity mean.
2. Explain both sides of the debate about cyberterrorism.
3. Describe the factors that gave rise to modern suicide bombing.
4. Summarize suicide bombings in the Middle East, Sri Lanka, Turkey, the United States, and Chechnya.
5. Discuss the effectiveness of suicide bombing.
6. List the ways biological agents might be used as weapons of mass destruction.
7. Explain the manner in which terrorists might use chemical and radiological weapons.

Cyberterrorism

Key Points and Questions:

1. Define cyberterrorism.
2. What are the three areas of a cyberterrorist attack?
3. List some potential targets of cyberterrorism.
4. Does cyberterrorism really exist?
5. Summarize differing opinions about the potential effect of cyberterrorism.

The National Conference of State Legislatures (2003) defines **cyberterrorism** as the use of information technology by terrorists for the purpose of promoting a political agenda. Barry Collin (2004), who coined the term in the early 1990s, believes it involves disrupting points where the virtual electronic reality of computer networks and programs intersects with the physical world. Former FBI counterterrorism specialist William Dyson (2000) argues that cyberterrorism is not a separate type of terrorism, but terrorists may use computers during the commission of terrorist acts (see Another Perspective: Definitions of Cyber Attacks). Miami attorney Mark Grossman (1999) disagrees, arguing that the threat of cyberterrorism is real and international legal systems are not prepared to deal with it. Cyberterrorism is computer hacking with a body count, according to Grossman.

The Council on Foreign Relations (2004) defines cyberterrorism by the ways terrorists might use computers and information networks. There are **targets for cyberterrorism**: computers, computer networks, and information storage and retrieval systems. Terrorists differ from hackers, the council argues, because their purpose is to launch a systematic attack for political purposes. The most common tactic to date has been the defacement of websites. David Carter (2003) essentially agrees with the council's definition of the three targets, but he takes scenarios a bit further, tracing computer crime and potential terrorist acts and describing the international appeal of cyberterrorism. It is cheap and it can be accomplished from a distance, according to Carter.

Definitions of Cyber Attacks

Experts suggest a number of ways that terrorists could use computers:

- To gain control of machinery
- To disrupt the Internet
- To destroy computer networks
- To disrupt communication
- To interrupt transportation
- To close financial institutions
- To control media outlets
- To raise funds
- To deny computer services
- To erase data
- To create an electromagnetic pulse that would destroy electrical equipment
- To steal files
- To alter existing data
- To change the content of websites

Sources: Carter (2003); Council on Foreign Relations (2004).

There are many potential targets for cyberterrorists. Yael Shahar (1997) envisions scenarios where a **computer virus**—a program that typically copies itself and moves through a computer system in order to disrupt a computer or computer network (see Timeline 6.1)—is implanted in an enemy's computer. He predicts the use of "logic bombs" that lie dormant for years until they are instructed to overwhelm a computer system. Shahar also believes that bogus chips can be sold to sabotage an enemy's computer network. Trojan horses, or malicious programs that seem to be harmless, can contain malevolent code that can destroy a system, while "back doors" in computer systems can allow terrorists to enter systems thought to be secure. Furthermore, Shahar believes that conventional attacks, such as overloading an electrical system, threaten computer security.

Michael Whine (1999) agrees with Shahar's conclusions, claiming that computer technology is attractive to terrorists for several reasons. Computers allow terrorist groups to remain connected, providing covert discussions and anonymity. Computer networks are also much less expensive and work intensive than the secretive infrastructures necessary to maintain terrorist groups. Computers allow terrorists to reach their audiences with little effort. Whine concludes that computers are a force multiplier for terrorist groups. Research by Charles Tilby (2003) of the Eugene Police Department in Oregon complements Whine's findings in the practical world. Tilby finds evidence of violent groups using the Internet as a tool for planning and striking.

Bowers and Keys (1998) believe cyberterrorism appears to be a threat because of the nature of modern society. More and more, modern Western society needs information and the flow of information to function, so cyberterrorists threaten to interrupt or confuse that flow of information. This leads Tiffany Danitz and Warren Strobel (1999) to remind policymakers that violent political activists also use the Internet as a command-and-control mechanism. They say there is no doubt that computers are vulnerable to crime, and terrorists do use and will continue to use them.

Some research points to attacks that have already occurred rather than focusing on potential targets. A group from the Center for Strategic and International Studies (2004) examined attacks on America's cybersystems. Chaired by the former director of the FBI and CIA, William Webster, the group states that there has been a sharp rise in such attacks, with the Internet providing the vehicle for launching most of the strikes. His group was especially concerned with documented attacks on the National Security Agency, the Pentagon, and a nuclear weapons laboratory. Operations were disrupted in all of these cases.

Despite discussions about potential and actual targets, there is a heated debate about whether cyberterrorism is a real problem. Barry Collin (2004) has no doubt

Timeline 6.1

Points in the History of Computer Viruses

1949	Theories about computer viruses, or self-replicating programs, are first developed at the Institute for Advanced Study in Princeton, New Jersey.
1981	First computer viruses appear at Texas A&M University.
1986	A self-replicating virus is placed on floppy disks.
1987	The Lehigh virus affects command files.
1988	The Jerusalem virus is released and affects files run every Friday the 13th.
1990	Norton AntiVirus by Symantec goes on the market.
1991	The first "polymorphic" virus—that is, a virus that changes its appearance with each infection—is found.
1992	There are thirteen hundred known computer viruses, a 420 percent increase from only December 1990.
1994	E-mail virus hoaxes begin.
1995	Viruses expand, some mutate existing viruses.
1998	Persian Gulf military deployments disrupted by two hackers.
1999	The Melissa virus spreads by e-mail faster than any earlier virus.
2000	"Denial-of-service" attacks knock major Internet websites offline.
2001	The BadTrans virus captures passwords and credit card numbers.
2002	Bugbear, a complicated worm, appears and has many ways to enter computer systems.
2004	MyDoom worm appears on e-mail, moving faster than any previous virus or worm.

Source: Computer Virus Timeline, http://www.infoplease.com/ipa/A0872842.html.

about the existence of cyberterrorism. He says cyberterrorism is the place where the physical matter of everyday life intersects with the electronic virtual domain of computers. All forms of cyberterrorism are designed to strike at one or more of three areas: the place where information is accessed, the place where data is controlled, and the points where information is mined. The purpose of terrorism is either to destroy, alter, or acquire information. Collin concludes that the future is grim for those who think they are safe behind firewalls, passwords, and encryption.

Journalist Joshua Green (2002) does not agree, pointing out that although terrorists kill people in many ways, they do not use computers to do so. Green agrees that computer security and hacking are real problems, but he is not quite convinced that cyberterrorism is much of a threat. Terrorists cannot use hacking to any great advantage, he says. Although it is not difficult to attack a system, Green argues it is very difficult to control a system in a lethal way once a hacker has entered. The actual dangers of cyber attacks are merely economic. According to Green, the real problems in computer security are hackers and criminals. The government is fairly well protected from them, but businesses are not. Green believes that lax government regulation makes business information systems more vulnerable than those of the military or intelligence services. He urges the government to impose regulations and bring business security up to government standards.

The U.S. government's response to cyberterrorism differs from Green's assessment. Before the Homeland Security Act of 2002, computer networks were under the protection of the FBI's Infrastructure Protection Center. After the Department of Homeland Security (DHS) came into being, cybersecurity moved. DHS now controls computer security through the Information Analysis and Infrastructure Protection (IAIP) directorate. In January 2004, DHS unveiled a new program, the **National Cyber Alert System**, designed to detect and destroy cyber attacks and cyberterrorism. In addition, DHS runs the "Cybernotes" website to distribute security weekly downloads. Collin (2004) advocates this type of aggressive attitude. Sitting behind security systems will not protect the infrastructure, Collin says. Like DHS, he believes in using aggressive countertactics before a potential strike. (See Another Perspective: Countering Cyberterrorism in State and Local Government.)

Suicide Terrorism

Key Points and Questions:

1. What is suicide terrorism?
2. Why is the phrase "homicide bomber" sometimes used?
3. Why has suicide terrorism become popular?
4. Summarize five models of suicide bombing.
5. List some groups that use suicide terrorism.
6. How might suicide terrorism continue in the future?

Suicide terrorism involves the intentional sacrifice of an attacker's life for the purpose of inflicting damage on an enemy. The attacker intends to die during the attack. Suicide terrorists most frequently use a bomb, and the phrase **suicide bomber** generally means the same thing as suicidal terrorism in the popular press. Although suicide terrorism seems to be a relatively new tactic in modern terrorism, it has been used in military operations for centuries. For example, in Europe in the eighteenth century soldiers who were chosen to be in the first group to storm a breech in a fortress were aptly called the "Forlorn Hope." During World War II some Japanese pilots chose or were forced to fly their aircraft into U.S. ships. Modern suicide terrorism began with the advent of religious terrorism in the early 1980s, but suicide operations are part of military history.

Some people use the phrase **homicide bomber** to describe suicide terrorism, arguing that it places the emphasis on the victims and blames the attacker for political murder. Conversely, organizations supporting suicide terrorism often call their attacks "martyrdom operations" to keep people focused on the cause. Regardless, suicide terrorism is a terrorist attack that depends on the perpetrator's death for success (Cronin, 2003, p. 2).

Suicide attacks are popular for a variety of reasons. Early research (Post, 1987) found attacks to be popular because they virtually guaranteed some type of delivery and they served as cheap "guided missiles." More recently, B. Raman (11-22-03, 12-3-04) says terrorists favor suicide attacks because they are so intimidating. Like Post, he points out that suicide bombers can penetrate secure targets with a good chance of success. They are also difficult to stop.

Audrey Cronin (2003, pp. 9–11) gives several reasons for the popularity of suicide attacks. They generate high casualties as well as publicity for the attacking group. The nature of the attack strikes fear into an enemy, and the attacks are effective against superior forces and weapons. Suicide bombers give terrorist groups maximum control over the attack. Again following the pioneering findings of Post, she notes that the attacks are cheap and virtually impossible to stop.

Rohan Gunaratna (2000) suggests it may be possible to model some aspects of suicide bombings. After examining suicide attacks between 1983 and 2000, Gunaratna sees three things that all attacks have in common: secrecy, reconnaissance, and rehearsal. He believes that local groups operate in secret to prepare the bomber and the target area. Since locals can blend in to the surroundings, they provide supplies and information. They also conduct the initial scouting or reconnaissance of the target. A support group far away from the target can rehearse the attack in secrecy. The better the rehearsal, the greater the chance of success. The bomber usually conducts the final reconnaissance during the operation, but he or she can detonate the bomb in case of discovery. This ensures some measure of success.

Cronin (2003, pp. 6–8) believes political geography has had an effect on suicide terrorism. She says different styles of bombings emerged from different places. The Hamas model, patterned after the actions of Hezbollah, involved a professional group to plan and execute the attack and a support group to prepare the attacker. For many years researchers believed this was the only model for suicide bombing (Institute for Counter-Terrorism, 2001). Cronin found, however, that different models emerged over time. The Liberation Tigers of Tamil Eelam (LTTE) trained suicide bombers from an early age. The Kurdish Workers' Party coerced victims into suicide bombings. The September 11 suicide attacks defied the previous models, while bombings in Chechnya represent a different combination of social and psychological factors. Cronin finds no single model for suicide bombing. (See Expanding the Concept: Suicide Attacks Are Deadly and Timeline 6.2: Chechnyan Suicide Attacks on p. 89.)

While looking at patterns of bombings, researchers from the Institute of Intergovernmental Research (IIR) found five general methods for preparing bombers, although they see new patterns evolving (see Expanding the Concept: Historical Methods of Suicide Bombings) (Cid, 2004; White, 2004; Taylor, 2004). Of course, there are many exceptions for every general pattern. Suicide bombings can change from

Suicide Attacks Are Deadly

From 1980 to 2001 suicide attacks accounted for only 3 percent of all terrorist attacks, but they accounted for 48 percent of all deaths by terrorism. In Palestine from 2000 to 2002, suicide attacks accounted for 1 percent of all terrorist attacks but 44 percent of all deaths.

Source: Cronin (2003, p. 9).

operation to operation, and the manner of assault is only limited by the attacker's imagination. The preliminary patterns from the IIR are, therefore, incomplete.

Research by the RAND Corporation (Hoffman, 6-1-03) reiterates Cronin's point. At one time, suicide bombers could be profiled. They tended to be young, economically disadvantaged, and hopeless. The situation has changed in recent years. With more than two-thirds of the world's suicide bombings occurring in the past five years, the previous profile no longer applies. More than 40 percent of suicide bombers are older than forty. In addition, women and the wealthy have joined the ranks of suicide bombers (Israeli, 2004). In the case of LTTE suicide missions, re-

Expanding the Concept

Historical Methods of Suicide Bombings

Military Method   Hezbollah and Hamas (and subsequently, secular Palestinian groups). The classic model of modern suicide bombings. A military wing prepares the target while a psychological wing prepares the bomber. The two units join just before the attack.

Socialization Method   Liberation Tigers of Tamil Eelam. A second-generation approach. Rather than relying on a psychological wing, terrorists teach children to aspire to suicide bombing from an early age. This long-term socialization allows the bomber to remain motivated even when separated from the group. The LTTE used more female bombers than any other group in modern history.

Coercion Method   Kurdish Workers' Party. Although most suicide bombings in Turkey have followed the military model of Hezbollah and Hamas, the PKK found it could sometimes coerce people into suicide by threatening family members. The victim would die under any circumstance, but she or he could save loved ones by carrying out the operation. The PKK frequently used female bombers.

Self-Contained Method   Al Qaeda. Al Qaeda found that it could create small self-contained groups to provide both military planning and the suicide operation. They used the tactic effectively by bombing the U.S. embassies in Nairobi and Dar es Salaam and again with the attack on the USS *Cole*. September 11 was the best example of this tactic. In 2003 al Qaeda took the idea a step further when terrorists fought their way into a compound in Riyadh, Saudi Arabia, and then detonated suicide bombs.

Grief Method   Chechnyan Black Widows. Chechnyan militants found they could use a combination of psychological tactics to prepare female suicide bombers. Frequently targeting women who had suffered losses at the hands of the Russians, the militants encouraged suicide bombers to follow the path of martyrdom. In some cases, they appeared to ply their victims with drugs before the operation.

Source: Cid (2004), Taylor (2004), White (2004).

Timeline 6.2

Chechnyan Suicide Attacks: The Black Widows

In the twenty-first century, the Chechnyan Black Widows have become a terrorist force in Russia. They get their name from the fact that many of them are widows of Chechnyan fighters.

June 2000	Suicide car bomb against Russian troops.
November 2001	A single attacker kills herself and a Russian officer with a hand grenade.
October 10–26, 2002	Forty-one rebels with female suicide bombers take hostages in a Moscow theater. One hundred twenty-nine people die when Russian forces attack.
May 12, 2003	Two females explode a truck at a Russian checkpoint.
May 14, 2003	Two females explode body bombs at religious service.
June 2002	A single bomber kills herself on a bus loaded with Russian pilots.
July 5, 2003	Two females attack a rock festival in Moscow.
July 10, 2003	A bomb carried by a single bomber accidentally explodes as the bomber is en route to a Moscow target.
July 27, 2003	A single bomber kills herself and a security guard when she's stopped for an inspection.
December 5, 2003	Three females kill 44 people on a commuter train. More than 150 are injured.
December 9, 2003	A single bomber attacks the National Hotel in Moscow.

Source: Saradzhyan (2-4-04).

search shows that the most experienced warriors, rather than the hopeless, volunteer for them. Hoffman (1998, 6-1-03) concludes that previous models of suicide bombers are inapplicable.

Several groups throughout the world use suicide attacks. Rohan Gunaratna (2000) lists Hezbollah, Hamas, Egyptian Islamic Jihad, the Egyptian Islamic Group, the Armed Islamic Group of Algeria, Barbar Khalsa in India, the Kurdish Workers' Party, the LTTE, and al Qaeda. He believes the phenomenon originated in Lebanon with Hezbollah and grew to international dimensions as terrorists around the world copied Hezbollah's tactics. RAND studies indicate that 350 suicide attacks have occurred in twenty-four countries in the past two decades. At first the attacks were motivated by religion, but secular groups began to use the tactic (Hoffman et al., forthcoming). Both secular and religious groups resisting the war in Iraq have used suicide bombers with deadly effects. Gunaratna (2000) also notes that simple devices are effective. Roadside bombs and booby traps require sophistication, but detonation by suicide relieves terrorists from the problem of building complicated devices.

Trends indicate that the popularity of suicide bombing is rising. Gunaratna (2000) believes that security measures can reduce these trends but suicide attacks will continue in the near future. Raman (12-3-04) agrees with this assessment because suicide attacks are so effective. Hoffman and colleagues (forthcoming) see suicide attacks as the wave of the future. They are increasing, these researchers say, because they are cheap and effective. The only hope of reducing suicide attacks is to increase the capabilities of law enforcement officers, they conclude. Regardless of countertactics, most analysts believe that suicide terrorism will continue (Pape, 2003).

Weapons of Mass Destruction: Biological Agents

Key Points and Concepts:

1. Are biological weapons new?
2. Define the difference between bacterial and viral agents.
3. Is the public health system prepared for a biological terrorist attack?
4. What are the four types of biological agents?
5. Describe America's first experience with a biological attack.
6. How did the second attack differ?
7. Why is weaponized anthrax dangerous?
8. List basic facts about smallpox and anthrax.

Biological weapons have been used for centuries. Modern arsenals contain bacterial and viral weapons, with microbes cultured and refined, or **weaponized**, to increase their ability to kill. When people are victims of a bacterial attack, antibiotics may be an effective treatment. Antibiotics are not usually effective against viruses, however, although some vaccines issued before the use of viral weapons are effective (see Hinton, 1999; Young and Collier, 2002). Since bacterial agents are susceptible to antibiotics, nations with bacterial weapons programs have created strains of bacterial microbes resistant to such drugs. Viral agents are produced in the same manner, and they are usually more powerful than bacterial agents. Biological agents are difficult to control but relatively easy to produce. Terrorists may find them to be effective weapons.

Epidemiologists from the Centers for Disease Control and Prevention (CDC) continually scan disease patterns in the United States to determine whether an outbreak is occurring, but there are serious weaknesses in the system. Osterholm and Schwartz (2000) emphatically argue that the public health system is not designed to handle massive casualties produced by a biological attack.

The profit motive behind America's public health structure precludes planning for a worst-case scenario in the case of biological attack. Hospitals are designed to work at maximum cost effectiveness, and physicians are monitored by the amount of patient time they bill. Most physicians are not trained to recognize diseases such as anthrax (see Expanding the Concept: A Look at Anthrax), smallpox, and plague, and there is no economic incentive for them to gain necessary training. The public health structure does not provide economic incentives to produce hundreds of beds

Expanding the Concept

A Look at Anthrax

- Anthrax is an acute infectious disease caused by the spore-forming bacterium *Bacillus anthracis*.
- Anthrax most commonly occurs in hoofed mammals and can also infect humans.
- Symptoms of disease vary depending on how the disease was contracted, but they usually occur within seven days after exposure.
- The serious forms of human anthrax are inhalation anthrax, cutaneous anthrax, and intestinal anthrax.
- Initial symptoms of inhalation anthrax infection may resemble a common cold. After several days, the symptoms may progress to severe breathing problems and shock. Inhalation anthrax is often fatal.
- The intestinal form of anthrax may follow the consumption of contaminated food and is characterized by an acute inflammation of the intestinal tract. Initial signs of nausea, loss of appetite, vomiting, and fever are followed by abdominal pain, vomiting of blood, and severe diarrhea.
- Direct person-to-person spread of anthrax is extremely unlikely, if it occurs at all; therefore, there is no need to immunize or treat contacts of people ill with anthrax.
- In people exposed to anthrax, infection can be prevented with antibiotic treatment. Anthrax usually is susceptible to penicillin, doxycycline, and fluoroquinolones.
- Early antibiotic treatment of anthrax is essential; delay lessens the chances of survival.
- An anthrax vaccine also can prevent infection; however, vaccination against anthrax is not recommended for the general public and is not available.

Source: Centers for Disease Control and Prevention (2001a).

and trained medical personnel who can respond to a biological disaster involving an exotic or rare disease (Cilluffo, Cardash, and Lederman, 2001; Office of Homeland Security, 2002, pp. 43–44).

There are four types of biological agents: (1) natural poisons, or toxins that occur without human modification, (2) viruses, (3) bacteria, and (4) plagues. The CDC classifies the most threatening agents as smallpox, anthrax, plague, botulism, tularemia, and hemorrhagic fever. Michael Osterholm and John Schwartz (2000, pp. 14–23) summarize the effect of each. **Smallpox** is a deadly contagious virus (see Expanding the Concept: Smallpox). Many people were vaccinated against smallpox in the 1960s, but these old vaccinations are no longer effective against the disease. **Anthrax** is a noncontagious bacterial infection, while **plague** is transmitted by insects. **Botulism** is a kind of food-borne illness, and other bacteria can be modified to serve as weapons. **Hemorrhagic fevers** are caused by viruses. One of the most widely known hemorrhagic fevers is the Ebola virus.

America has experienced two notable biological attacks since 1980, and the weakness of the health system was exposed both times. Judith Miller, Stephen Engelberg, and William Broad (2001, pp. 13–33) outline the first modern use of biological terrorism in the United States. Engineered by followers of the Bhagwan Shree Rajneesh in Oregon, the attack occurred in September 1984 when **Rajneeshees**, as they were called, contaminated salad bars at restaurants in The Dalles, Oregon, with the bacterium *Salmonella*. The attack resulted in more than seven hundred people becoming ill with food poisoning. It also indicated that American police agencies were ill-prepared to take action with regards to a biological incident. The police and Oregon's public health system both scrambled to deal with the massive outbreak of food poisoning, which overwhelmed local hospitals. It took a full year for authorities to show that the outbreak was the result of a deliberate action. Even though citizens had long suspected the Rajneeshees, police lacked the technical ability to investigate the crime, and health officials lacked the skills to conduct a criminal investigation. In short, the police could detect neither the microbes nor the patterns of illness necessary to prove a criminal case, and health officials could isolate the bacteria but could not locate their source.

The second bioterrorism attack came in the wake of the terrorist attacks of September 11, 2001 (see Timeline 6.3). It began in Florida when two tabloid writers were

Timeline 6.3

The Anthrax Attacks, October to November 2001

The *Wall Street Journal* summarized the nation's deadly encounter with anthrax and focused on the difficulty of the police investigation. Reporters Mark Schoof and Gary Fields pointed to the following events:

October 4	A photographer is infected in Florida and dies the next day.
October 8	A second infection is discovered in the same newspaper office.
October 12	NBC receives anthrax through the mail.
October 15	Anthrax arrives in Senator Tom Daschle's office by mail.
October 18–23	Anthrax is discovered in mail facilities in New Jersey and Washington, D.C.
October 31	A hospital worker is infected and dies in New York City.
November 21	An elderly woman in Connecticut is infected and dies.

Source: Schoof and Fields (3-25-02).

infected by anthrax through the mail. One of the victims died. In the following days anthrax appeared again as NBC evening news received spores in the mail. Just as in the attacks by the Rajneeshees, there was an initial breakdown of communication between law enforcement and public health personnel. Police and private security officers did not know how to respond, and local public health officials frequently did not know what to advise local residents.

The situation grew worse in October. The office of Senate Majority Leader Thomas Daschle received its regular mail delivery after lunch on Friday, October 12. Fortunately, staff members were in a class that afternoon, learning how to recognize suspicious packages. When staffers returned to work on Monday, they opened Friday's mail and someone noticed a white powdery substance in a letter. Alerted by information from Friday's class, the staffer took immediate action, perhaps saving many lives. The powder contained anthrax spores.

According to reporter Laura Parker (1-23-02), Senator Daschle's office workers were exposed to the highest level of anthrax ever recorded. The dosage ranged from several hundred to three thousand times higher than the amount needed to kill a human being. On the day after the attack, nasal cultures indicated the infection was spreading rapidly; it eventually infected seventy-five people, including a pizza delivery person who happened to be present when the letter was opened.

Physicians at Bethesda Naval Hospital reserved a number of extra beds in preparation for more infections, but they differed on the way the attack should be treated. They settled on a ninety-day regimen of administering antibiotics and vaccines. Some spores contaminated mail facilities, and two postal workers died after being infected in the government's mail distribution center in Brentwood. The Dirkson Office Building remained closed for three months and cost $14 million to clean up.

Osterholm and Schwartz (2000, pp. 19–20) say anthrax is a particularly effective killer. It is a natural bacterial toxin that has been enhanced by weapons programs. People can be infected by eating contaminated food (gastrointestinal anthrax), being exposed through the skin (cutaneous anthrax), and inhaling spores (inhalation anthrax). Inhalation anthrax is the most deadly form, but natural spores are so large that the body's natural defense provides quite a bit of protection.

Miller, Engelberg, and Broad (2001, pp. 40–44) point to the history of bacterial weapons to show how the effectiveness of anthrax has been increased. Weaponized anthrax microbes are smaller than natural anthrax, and the outside shell is "hardened" so that it can exist in a variety of environments. When the microbes enter a friendly environment, such as the moist tissues of the respiratory system, spores open and begin to multiply.

A Canadian study demonstrated that one-tenth of a gram of anthrax can infect a ten-by-eight-foot room in ten minutes, entering the respiratory system with an amount 180 times greater than a lethal dose (Parker, 1-23-02). A suspected hot zone, or infected area, must be contained, and all people in the zone, including responders, need to be treated. The zone can remain contaminated for weeks unless properly decontaminated.

Biological agents present practical problems for terrorists. When an agent is released, it is very difficult to control the spread of the disease. For example, if smallpox were released in an urban area, few safeguards could keep it from spreading wildly, even around the world. The target area is difficult to control. Several scenarios involving biological weapons envision a massive release of anthrax or a disease like smallpox. If this were to occur, there is no reason to believe that attackers would be immune from the effects. Despite this limitation, biological agents have been used in public attacks. It would not be prudent to believe that this threat will simply disappear.

Weapons of Mass Destruction: Chemical and Radiological Agents

Key Points and Concepts:

1. Explain the similarity of chemical and radiological attacks.
2. What are the four categories of chemical weapons?
3. How does radiation poisoning occur?
4. Describe the ways people can become contaminated by chemical and radiological agents.
5. What are the health effects of chemicals and radiation?
6. What are the advantages and disadvantages of chemical weapons?
7. Who holds the monopoly of knowledge on nuclear weapons?
8. How does Ballard describe the nuclear transportation problem?
9. What does Wolf mean by the fear of fear?

The massive power and heat from atomic bombs place nuclear weapons in a class of their own, but chemical and radiological attacks are basically similar. Radiological poisoning and "dirty" radioactive devices are forms of chemical alterations. Chemi-

Table 6.1

Chemical and Radiological Agents and Their Effects

Agent	Common Entry	Effect
Nerve	Food, water, air, skin contact	Convulsions, flood of body fluids
Blistering	Skin contact, air	Burns, choking, respiratory failure
Blood/Choking	Breathing, skin contact	Failure of body functions
Radiological	Food, air, water	Burns, long-term skin contact illness

Sources: Organization for the Prohibition of Chemical Weapons (2000); U.S. Congress, Office of Technology Assessment (1995).

cals are usually easier to deliver than biological weapons, and they are fast-acting. Radiological devices are slower than most chemicals, but their poison lasts longer and they can be spread like chemicals. Radioactive materials are also more resistant to heat than chemicals, so bombs or other heat-producing devices can be used to scatter them.

There are four types of **chemical agents**: nerve agents, blood agents, choking agents, and blistering agents (see Table 6.1). Nerve agents enter the body through ingestion, respiration, or contact. Blood and choking agents are usually absorbed through the respiratory system, and blistering agents burn the skin and internal tissue areas upon contact (Organization for the Prohibition of Chemical Weapons, 2000). Radiological weapons would produce short-term burns and long-term contamination and health problems. Radiological poisoning takes place when a contaminated material comes in contact with any source that conducts radiation. The new material, such as contaminated food, water, or metal, becomes an object that could poison humans. Small contaminated pieces of matter can also become a means of spreading radiation through the air (U.S. Congress, Office of Technology Assessment, 1995).

Chemicals present an attractive weapon for terrorists because they are easy to control, and, unlike biological weapons, the users can avoid the area they attack. Nonetheless, chemical weapons present three problems. First, terrorists must have a delivery mechanism; that is, they need some way to spread the chemical. Second, it takes a lot of chemicals to present a threat. Finally, weather patterns, air, and water can neutralize a chemical threat. Chemical weapons are most effective when used in a confined space.

Because of these difficulties, many experts believe that terrorists will use chemicals or radioactive material in a **dirty bomb**. This means that a conventional explosive would be used to spread a chemical or radioactive agent around a large area. This technique has one major drawback: The heat produced by the explosion may destroy the chemicals attached to the bomb. This does not happen in the case of radiation; therefore, most dirty bomb scenarios are based on the premise that a radiological agent will be used with a conventional explosive.

One of the most fearful types of radiological weapons of mass destruction are nuclear weapons. A stolen nuclear bomb or atomic weapons conjure the worst images of mass destruction. If nuclear terrorism happens, authorities will most likely respond with military support. The United States has plans for dealing with a nuclear disaster; military forces have the monopoly on knowledge in this area.

Reuters (2-8-04) reports that nuclear weapons are available on the black market from sources in the former Soviet Union. Jason Burke (1-18-04) says terrorists have placed instructions online for building a nuclear device. Nonetheless, it is still difficult to obtain and detonate nuclear weapons. It is much easier for terrorists to use a conventional weapon to spread either chemicals or nuclear materials than for them to build a nuclear weapon.

James David Ballard (2003) looks at the problem of nuclear terrorism another way. Congress has designated a site in Nevada as the repository for all the radioactive waste used in America's nuclear power plants, and all this material must be shipped across the country. Ballard wonders what would happen if terrorists seized some of this material? He points out that nuclear waste is a ready-made dirty bomb.

Ballard's point has spurred some federal action, and it illustrates another problem. Terrorists may never use weapons of mass destruction, but the threat that they might is effective in another way. Terrorists can simply *say* they have a dirty bomb or they have released smallpox or they have poisoned the food supply with radiation, and the public may well panic. Fear is a real problem. Several years ago John Wolf (1981) pointed out that the fear of fear is one of the greatest problems associated with terrorism.

Summary of Main Points

1. *Cyberterrorism* refers either attacking cybersystems or using computer networks as a force multiplier.

2. Not all analysts believe that cyberterrorism is a separate form of terrorism.

3. Suicide bombing was reintroduced by religious terrorists, and it has been copied by secular terrorists.

4. There are no standard psychological or social profiles of suicide bombers.

5. Historical patterns of suicide bombings can be observed, but patterns are always changing.

6. Suicide bombing is effective because it is cheap, it enhances terror, and it provides a method for striking back at superior firepower.

7. Biological agents may be used as weapons of mass destruction, but they are difficult to control because they may contaminate their users.

8. The United States has experienced two biological attacks: a food-poisoning attack by the Rajneeshees in Oregon and the anthrax attack after September 11.

9. Chemical and radiological agents are easier to control than biological weapons.

10. The heat of an explosion may destroy a chemical agent, but a "dirty bomb" may be used to spread radiological agents.

11. Radioactive wastes provide a tempting potential agent of destruction for terrorists.

Key Terms

Make sure you can define, explain, or identify the following people, ideas, organizations, or terms:

cyberterrorism   83

targets for cyberterrorism   83

computer virus   84

National Cyber Alert System   86

suicide terrorism   86

suicide bomber   86

homicide bomber   87

biological weapons   90

weaponized   90

smallpox   91

anthrax   91

plague   91

botulism   91

hemorrhagic fever   91

Rajneeshees   92

chemical agents   95

dirty bomb   95

nuclear weapons   95

Suggested Readings

Now that you've been introduced to this topic, you can learn more by reading:

Judith Miller and her colleagues Stephen Engelberg and William Broad explain the threat of weaponized germs and viruses and present a history of biological warfare in *Germs: Biological Weapons and America's Secret War.*

You may also want to read:

Michael Osterholm and John Schwartz, in *Living Terrors*, present a view of potential disasters with a scientific base.

A technical examination of the deadly aspects of chemical and biological agents used in military and terrorist situations comes from Eric Taylor in *Lethal Mists.*

Computer threats are analyzed in the publication *Cybercrime, Cyberterrorism, and Cyberwarfare* from the Center for Strategic and International Studies.

The Institute of Counter-Terrorism conducts a survey of one style of suicide bombing in *Countering Suicide Terrorism.*

Web Resources

Go to *http://cj.wadsworth.com/white_terrorism5e* and click on Web Links to find:

- A list of articles about the hazards of nuclear waste
- "Suicide Terrorism, an Overview," by Boaz Ganor, the executive director of the International Policy Institute for Counter-Terrorism
- A variety of information regarding weapons of mass destruction
- Information about first response and emergency management from the School of Criminal Justice at Michigan State University

The Companion Website for *Terrorism and Homeland Security*, Fifth Edition

http://cj.wadsworth.com/white_terrorism5e

At the Book Companion Website you can review chapter outlines, use the flash cards to test your terrorism vocabulary, and check out the many other study aids you'll find there. You'll find valuable data and resources at your fingertips to help you study for that big exam or write that important paper.

Terrorism Updates

http://www.wadsworth.com/criminaljustice_d/special_features/ext/terrorism _site090802/index.html

Visit the *Terrorism: An Interdisciplinary Perspective* website to find the most current information about the fields of terrorism and homeland security. With a focus on domestic and international issues, this site explores the scope of terrorism in our world today. You'll find essays on important topics in terrorism and homeland security, critical thinking web activities, and InfoTrac College Edition keywords. Most importantly, the website is updated weekly with current news and research articles on domestic and international terrorism. You are invited to use these web resources to supplement your understanding of the topics covered in this chapter.

Current Perspectives: Readings from InfoTrac College Edition
Terrorism and Homeland Security

The sixteen articles in this reader offer a representative selection that helps you understand the important issues about terrorism and homeland security. It includes FREE access to InfoTrac College Edition and can also be bundled with the text for free.

Part Two INTERNATIONAL
TERRORISM

Chapter 7

The Evolution of Jihadist Networks

Two of the world's most infamous Jihadists are Ayman al Zawahiri (left) and Osama bin Laden. The Jihadist movement is rooted in militant traditions developed long before the birth of al Qaeda.

© UPI/HO/Landov

A t the end of the Cold War, the former Soviet Union could have told the world about a group of irregular self-appointed holy warriors. The Soviets encountered these people in the disastrous ten-year Soviet-Afghan War (1979–1989), and the rest of the world would meet them later: in the attacks on the United States on September 11, 2001; in a violent attack in Bali in October 2002; and when these self-styled holy warriors, or *Jihadists*, bombed a train in Madrid in March 2004, killing nearly two hundred people. The Jihadist movement is rooted in violent religious extremism, colonialism, and the Cold War. Ironically, the United States, the United Kingdom, and France were instrumental in developing the **Jihadist network**, or international connections among various Jihadist groups. And everyone is paying the price today.

Chapter Objectives

After reading this chapter you should be able to:

1. Discuss the influence of militant religion on recent developments in international terrorism.
2. Define Jihadist and Jihadist terrorist networks.
3. Explain the origins of the Jihadist movement.
4. Explain two militant theories supporting the Jihadists.
5. Describe the emergence and history of al Qaeda.
6. Summarize al Qaeda's campaign until September 11, 2001.
7. Explain the organizational style of al Qaeda.
8. Discuss differing opinions about U.S. actions in Afghanistan and Iraq.

Religion and Militant Religion

Key Concepts and Questions:

1. What do analysts mean when they use the phrase "Jihadist network"?
2. Why do religious people become upset when other people speak of religious terrorists?
3. List some of the reasons defenders claim that Jihadists do not reflect the values of Islam.
4. What factors complicate efforts to understand the relationship between Islam and Christianity?

In May 2004 the ABC news service reported that the terrorist organization al Qaeda, operated by Osama bin Laden, had eighteen thousand fighters poised throughout the world and the group was ready to strike Western interests (ABC News, 5-25-04). The report centered on the United Kingdom's Institute for Strategic Studies, and it originated with the Reuters news service. Various news agencies around the world ran their own versions of the Reuters story. Aside from reporting the threat, many of the versions had two interesting characteristics. First, they suggested that a particular terrorist group, al Qaeda, was capable of running an organized international operation even though it had been surrounded and pounded by U.S. military forces in Afghanistan. Second, many media reports referred to al Qaeda members as **fighters**, not terrorists. Did this mean that some forms of terrorism are merely "fights"? Neither Reuters nor any other media service answered this question, but they increasingly used the term fighters.

Al Qaeda was born in the last stages of the Soviet-Afghan War, and it grew until the U.S. offensive in Afghanistan in October 2001 when U.S. forces struck the al Qaeda and Taliban forces there. (The **Taliban** was the Islamicist group governing Afghanistan from 1996 to 2001. Led by Mullah Omar, the group was composed of Islamic students who wanted to bring order to Afghanistan through the forced imposition of Islamic law.) As Peter Bergen (2001, pp. 195–235) says, al Qaeda then transformed. It became what he calls **al Qaeda 2.0**, a group he believes to be a decentralized alliance of al Qaeda terrorists spread throughout the world. Yet, al Qaeda is simply one manifestation of the Jihadist movement, and the movement has millions of supporters and sympathizers.

As al Qaeda transformed, its symbolic name came to mean more than its actual power (Windrem and Gubash, 3-11-04). Several groups sympathetic to al Qaeda claimed to be part of a vast network, but sometimes they had no direct relationship with each other. **Jihadist ideology** held these groups together. In short, the Jihadist ideology contends that Islam has become corrupt and needs to be purified. Although they blame heretical Islamic leaders, Jihadists believe much of the corruption is due to the values and economic power of the West, especially the United States. They feel called to destroy this evil influence, but they are not necessarily affiliated and certainly not controlled by al Qaeda. They are independents bound by common ideas. (See Another Perspective: Fundamentalists, Islamicists, and Jihadists.)

Since Jihadists make religious claims, many Muslims become upset when their faith is portrayed in terms of violent terrorism (see Chapter 4). Many Christians feel similarly, for instance, when the fighting in Ireland is described as a "religious war." They believe that even though militant thugs invoke either Protestantism or Catholicism, Irish violence is a violation of Christian principles. Mainstream Muslims feel the same way. In fact, Magnus Ranstorp (1998) says the Jihadists are doomed to failure within their own culture because their theology of violence does not convey the meaning of Islam.

Many Muslims agree with Ranstorp's conclusion. Feisal Rauf (2004, pp. 41–77) responds with a popular theological treatise explaining the strengths of Islam. **Islam** is a religion, Rauf says, that values peace and toleration. There are violent passages in the Koran, but there are violent passages in the writings of all major religions, including Judaism and Christianity. Islam teaches universal human love, submission to God's will, and a life of morality preparing for the final judgment of God. He calls Muslims to embrace the roots of their faith and the commonalities among Muslims, Jews, and Christians.

Former congressman Paul Findlay (2001), who is Christian, is enraged by stereotypic attacks on Muslims. Findlay recounts stories and actions of friends who have embraced the Islamic faith. He tells of personal travels to Islamic lands to demonstrate his belief in a simple fact: People are people everywhere. The religion of Islam, he concludes, does not foster militancy.

Others point to violent sects in Islam. Steven Emerson (2002, pp. 221–233) says Islam has always been associated with political expansion and that militancy is a product of the twentieth century. His research shows that many seemingly legitimate Islamic organizations support the Jihadists and directly or indirectly fund radical Muslim terrorist groups. Missionaries from intolerant sects within Islam travel to the West by the hundreds, Emerson says, and millions of dollars from such sects build mosques in Europe and the United States.

Confusion about mainstream Islam complicates attempts to understand Jihadists. Misunderstandings increase when Jihadists use religious rhetoric and language. For example, Catholic IRA terrorists do not publicize their operations in the name of God. Jihadists do. In addition, some Islamic schools (*madrasas*) in many areas of the world glamorize violence and inspire young people to join terrorist organizations (Stern, 2003b, pp. 258–259). Samuel Huntington (1996, p. 176) points out that Christians, Hindus, and Buddhists do not create international associations of nation-states that are based on religion. Muslims do. Such religious and cultural issues are factors that complicate attempts to understand the nature of Jihadist networks.

The Origins of Jihadist Networks

Key Points and Questions:

1. Who claimed that *jihad* was the sixth pillar of Islam?
2. Name three reform movements and their locations.
3. What are the goals of the militants inspired by ibn Taymiyyah?
4. How did the Cold War influence Jihadist ideology?
5. Did the Soviet invasion of Afghanistan increase or decrease this influence?

The origins of the Jihadist groups stretch back to religious interpretation and reform movements within Islam. Western Crusaders began waging war against the Muslims in the eleventh century, and Mongol invaders struck the Arab lands one hundred years later. Hundreds of thousands of Muslims were killed in each invasion. **Taqi al Din ibn Taymiyyah**, an Islamic scholar (see Another Perspective: Ibn Taymiyyah and Sayyid Qutb: Jihadist Philosophers), was appalled by the slaughter and sought to find an answer in his faith. He believed that Muslims had fallen away from the truth and must therefore internally purify themselves. He called for the destruction of heretics and invaders, calling **jihad** (struggle or effort) the sixth pillar of Islam.

Ibn Taymiyyah's shift is important. Islam is frequently described as a monotheistic religion based on five "pillars": (1) a confession of faith in God and acceptance of Mohammed as God's last and greatest prophet, (2) ritual prayers with the community, (3) giving alms, (4) fasting, especially during holy periods, and (5) making a pilgrimage to Mohammed's birthplace, Mecca (Farah, 2000, pp. 132–148). Jihad has a place in this system, and different Islamic scholars (*ulema*) interpret jihad in various ways. Western interpreters also assign differing meanings to jihad.

Although jihad is frequently translated as "holy war," holy war is a European term. In traditional Arabic, jihad derives from the world *jahada*, which is defined as a struggle or effort against some type of power, usually depicted as a visible enemy, the devil, or one's inner desires. There are many types of jihads that have nothing to do with warfare, such as a jihad of the heart when a person struggles against sin or a jihad of the tongue when one speaks for the good against evil. Traditionally, many *ulema* believed that the original meaning of jihad focused on internal struggles, but it assumed a more military meaning when the early Muslim community faced threats from non-Muslims. Further research suggests that the early Muslim community was divided on the use of the term, and the meaning of jihad evolved from a variety of differing notions (Firestone, 1999, pp. 14–18, 50, 91).

The Arab empire based on Islam expanded after Mohammed's death (C.E. 632), and his successors gradually used the term jihad to refer to the conquest of new territory (Ruthven, 2000, p. 70). As the religion split in various sects, jihad also referred to eradicating opposing theological views. Sometimes, such notions of jihad involved murder, assassination, and open warfare (Armstrong, 2000, pp. 118–130). When Muslims faced invasions from the crusaders and the Mongols, jihad came to be viewed as a call to defend against foreign incursion. Ibn Taymiyyah took the issue a step further, claiming that jihad was not merely a duty, it was the sixth pillar of the faith (Ruthven, 2000, p. 171). He also called for the destruction of heretics and invaders, saying that all Muslims were required to fight for their faith. Jihadists frequently cite ibn Taymiyyah as their source of inspiration (Benjamin and Simon, 2002, pp. 45–52).

John Esposito (1999, pp. 6–10) says that reform movements are common throughout the history of Islam. Two recent movements became important to the Jihadists. In the late eighteenth century a purification movement started by **Mohammed ibn Abdul Wahhab**, who was influenced by ibn Taymiyyah, took root in Arabia. Wahhab preached a puritanical strain of Islam that sought to rid the religion of practices added after the first few decades following Mohammed's death. This doctrine deeply influenced the Saud family as they fought to gain control of Arabia, and it

Ibn Taymiyyah and Sayyid Qutb: Jihadist Philosophers

Taqi al Din ibn Taymiyyah (ca. 1269–1328) was an Islamic scholar who was forced to flee Baghdad in the face of invading Mongols. He believed that the Crusaders and Mongols defeated Islamic armies because Muslims had fallen away from the true practice of Islam. Emphasizing *tawhid*, or the oneness of God, ibn Taymiyyah attacked anything that threatened to come between humanity and God. He forbade prayers at gravesites, belief in saints, and other practices that had worked their way into Islam. He was especially harsh on the mystical Sufis, who believed in love for all humanity apart from Islam. Individual members pledged allegiance to various Sufi masters. These beliefs, according to ibn Taymiyyah, violated tawhid by placing humans and human practices above the Koran. He also condemned governments when leaders failed to practice pure Islam. Ibn Taymiyyah preached that jihad, or holy war, should be waged against all people who threatened the faith. His targets included Muslims and non-Muslims. His ideas deeply affected Mohammed ibn Abdul Wahhab, who led a purification movement in Saudi Arabia in the eighteenth century.

Sayyid Qutb (1906–1966) was an Egyptian teacher and journalist who was initially employed by the Ministry of Education. He traveled to the United States and lived as an exchange professor in Greeley, Colorado, from 1948 to 1950. Qutb's experience in America soured his opinion of Western civilization. He returned to Egypt and became an active member of the Muslim Brotherhood. Qutb was arrested in 1954 after the Brotherhood tried to overthrow the Egyptian government, but he was released in 1964 because of health problems. He published his most famous work, *Milestones*, in 1965. The book outlines the theology and ideology of Jihadist revolution, and its militant tone led to Qutb's second arrest and subsequent hanging in 1966. His books and articles popularized many militant ideas, and they continue to influence Jihadists today. Qutb believed that the Islamic world descended into darkness (*jahaliyya*) shortly after the death of Mohammed (A.D. 632). The so-called Islamic governments of the Arab empires were really corrupt nonreligious regimes. As a result, pure Islam was lost, but a few people, such as ibn Taymiyyah, Mohammed ibn Abdul Wahhab, and Abdullah Mawdudi (1903–1979), kept the faith alive. Qutb rejected the West and called on Muslims to overthrow their corrupt governments. He argued that rulers should impose Islamic law on their subjects, and when pure Islamic states were created, they should confront the world. In *Milestones* Qutb (1990 (reprinted), pp. 112–134) argued that Muslims were in a cosmic battle with the forces of darkness. Whereas Mohammed mandated tolerance of those who would not embrace Islam, Qutb called for the destruction of all enemies. The forces of darkness could not be tolerated, he wrote, and although God was ultimately responsible for the destruction of darkness, Muslims were called to fight it. Qutb's writings were banned in many Islamic countries, and they infuriated the Egyptian government under Gamal Nasser. Qutb was arrested and sent to prison after he returned from the United States. The al Qaeda Manual (al Qaeda, n.d.) cites Qutb as a source of inspiration.

Source: Palmer and Palmer (2004).

dominates the theology of Saudi Arabia and the Gulf states today. Militant application of Wahhab's puritanical principles spread to India and other parts of Asia. Strict Muslims who follow the practices of Wahhab argue that they are trying to rid the religion of superstition and return it to the state envisioned by Mohammed and his first followers (Oliver, 2002, pp. 10–11). Militants, however, force their puritanical views on those who disagree with them (Farah, 2000, p. 230).

One hundred years after Wahhab a reform movement named after the elders of Islam, **Salafiyya**, grew from North Africa. It gave rise to the **Muslim Brotherhood** in Egypt in 1928. Founded by Hasan al Banna, the Brotherhood preached a message of purification similar to that of Wahhab. The Brothers were not militant, believing that Islamic purity would evolve, but militancy gradually crept into the movement. By 1950 a violent wing of the Brotherhood fell under the influence of **Sayyid Qutb**, a radical Muslim who called for the imposition of Islamic law. Qutb argued that most Muslims were religious in name only. In reality, they were heretics, taking Islam down a sinful path. Infidels (non-Muslims) posed another threat to Islam, and both heretics and infidels needed to be converted or destroyed. Qutb was influenced by the writings of ibn Taymiyyah (Oliver, 2002, p. 27).

Militant Muslims embrace the reforming doctrines of Wahhab, the Salafiyya, and the Muslim Brotherhood while departing from the path of Islam and endorsing violence. They see jihad as a duty and means for imposing their strict form of Islam on others. Their goal is to unite the world in a pure Islamic state through the force of arms. Most Muslims reject these ideas, even though they distrust the policies of the United States and dislike America in general (Palmer and Palmer, 2004, pp. 9–34).

John Cooley (2002, pp. 64–104) believes the foundation of modern Jihadist power grew from the Cold War, and he blames the West for incubating the network. The idea of using militant reformers against the USSR was born in France. The French intelligence community knew that Islamic militants hated the Communists for several reasons and therefore suggested to intelligence counterparts in Washington and London that militant Islamic reformers might be used against Communist countries. America, Great Britain, and France soon began to seek alliances with militant Islamic radicals. Using ties with oil-rich Muslim states, especially Saudi Arabia and Kuwait, the Western allies channeled support to both militant and nonviolent purification movements within Islam.

Western efforts to support Islamic reformers came to fruition in 1979. In December of that year the Soviet Union invaded Afghanistan to bolster a failing Communist regime. According to Cooley, this was the chance the West had been waiting for. President Jimmy Carter's State Department encouraged Arab and other Islamic allies to send money and religious puritans to fight the Soviets in a guerrilla war. The puritans were called **mujahadeen**, or holy warriors. The United States formed an alliance with Pakistan, and the Pakistani **Interservice Intelligence Agency (ISI)** began to train and equip the mujahadeen. When Ronald Reagan became president in 1980, American efforts against the Soviets increased.

Several researchers have looked at the relationship between the United States and the mujahadeen during the Soviet-Afghan War (see, for example, Benjamin and Simon, 2002, pp. 98–102; Cooley, 2002, pp. 64–75; Gunaratna, 2002, p. 18; Kepel,

2002, pp. 136–150; Ruthven, 2000, p. 365). In essence, their research points to several important conclusions. First, the United States helped Saudi Arabia develop a funding mechanism and underground arms network to supply the mujahadeen. Second, the United States agreed to give most of the weapons and supplies to the ISI, while the ISI built mujahadeen groups with little American participation. Third, Islamic charities flourished in the United States, and their donations supported the mujahadeen. Finally, when the Soviets left Afghanistan in 1989, the United States rejoiced and abandoned war-torn Afghanistan.

The mujahadeen were not united at the end of the Soviet-Afghan War. Up to thirty-one different groups fought the Soviets, with six major mujahadeen guerrilla armies controlling most operations. The power that held the many groups together was a mutual hatred of the Soviets (Shay, 2002, pp. 108–109). When the Soviets finally retreated, the Afghan mujahadeen believed the power of God had prevailed over Satan. The major leaders wanted to turn their efforts against the other enemies of God: apostate Islamic governments, Israel, and the West. Some mujahadeen returned to their homes to spread holy war, but others had grander schemes. Although virtually ignored by the United States, the Jihadist movement grew, and terrorism grew with it.

Jihad Continues in Afghanistan

Key Points and Questions:

1. What actions did Jihadists take after the Soviet-Afghan War?
2. How did oil influence America's response to the situation in Afghanistan?
3. How did the Soviet-Afghan War benefit Osama bin Laden?

As the Soviets began leaving Afghanistan in April 1988, the United States celebrated a vicarious victory. The Soviets were on the run and in full retreat from the battlefields of the Cold War. The defeat was so devastating that the USSR began to crumble, and by 1991 it had dissolved. The Cold War was over, and it appeared that a new world of peace was at hand. As the world stepped back from the brink of nuclear annihilation, America's leaders and people paid very little attention to events in far-off Afghanistan.

But the fighting was not over in Afghanistan. Saul Shay (2002, pp. 76–81) writes that the mujahadeen groups continued to fight for control of the country. Al Qaeda was one of many paramilitary organizations to join the fray, and the United States failed to recognize the problem on two levels. Cooley (2002, p. 122) and Napoleoni (2003, pp. 189–191) say that American oil companies sought alliances with some groups in hopes of building an oil pipeline from Central Asia to the Indian Ocean. The oil would run through Afghanistan. Americans paid more attention to potential profits than the political problems brewing in Afghanistan. On another level, the United States simply ignored issues. As the Afghan groups continued to build and strengthen, Americans celebrated the end of the Cold War and the "peace dividend"—the money the United States diverted from military spending.

Osama bin Laden was a large part of America's blissful ignorance. The 9-11 Commission Report (2004, pp. 53–54) notes that bin Laden's reputation began to grow as the mujahadeen searched for a continuing jihad. When international terrorist violence increased in Africa and Asia during the 1990s, bin Laden emerged as a symbol of Islamic discontent. Oil-rich Muslim countries were faced with a growing population of young men who had technical educations with no broad understanding of humanities, social sciences, and the larger world. They also faced unemployment due to the distribution of wealth. Bin Laden emerged as a spokesman for the discontented, and his own movement began to take form.

The Rise of Osama bin Laden

Key Points and Questions:

1. How did the Qutb's philosophy influence bin Laden to join the mujahadeen?
2. What influence did Azzam have on bin Laden?
3. How did Pakistan's ISI fit into the development of Azzam's group?
4. Why did Azzam break with the ISI?
5. How did bin Laden take over al Qaeda?
6. What was the impact of Operation Desert Storm on al Qaeda?

Rohan Gunaratna (2002) documents the origins and actions of al Qaeda from the end of the Soviet-Afghan War until the attacks of September 11, 2001. Yoseff Bodansky (1999) offers a biography of bin Laden that predates the September 11 attacks. The 9-11 Commission Report (2004, pp. 47–70) also documents the growth of al Qaeda. All three works point to the importance of the personality of **Osama bin Laden**. After the Soviet-Afghan War, he returned to Saudi Arabia while his agents began making real estate purchases in Sudan.

Yoseff Bodansky (1999) writes that bin Laden was one of fifty-one children born to a rich Saudi Arabian construction magnate in 1957. Bin Laden was raised in the Saudi royal court, and his tutor, Mohammed Qutb, was the brother of the Egyptian radical Sayyid Qutb. Bin Laden was influenced by Sayyid Qutb's thought (see Another Perspective: Ibn Taymiyyah and Sayyid Qutb: Jihadist Philosophers). While attending university studies, bin Laden left the nonviolent Wahhabism of the Saudi royal family and turned toward Qutb's philosophy (see Oliver, 2002, pp. 10–38). Eventually, bin Laden dropped out of college to join the Soviet-Afghan War. At first, he lent his support to the mujahadeen, but later he formed his own guerrilla unit.

While in Afghanistan, bin Laden fell under the influence of **Abdullah Azzam**, a doctor of Islamic law. Azzam was a Palestinian scholar who was influenced by Qutb's writings. He came to believe that a purified form of Islam was the answer to questions of poverty and the loss of political power. He had been working for the Palestinians in the mid-1970s, but he became disillusioned with their nationalism and emphasis on politics over religion. Azzam believed Islam should be the guiding force for war, and he would not abandon religious principles for the sake of a political victory. He left the Palestinians for a Saudi university to teach Islamic law, later joining the Afghan jihad.

According to Azzam, the realm of Islam had been dominated by foreign powers for too long. It was time for all Muslims to rise up and strike Satan. He saw the Soviet-Afghan War as just the beginning of a holy war against all things foreign to Islam. At first, bin Laden found the theology of Azzam to his liking and the answer to his prayers for a path to holy war.

According to the 9-11 Commission Report (2004, p. 58), bin Laden and Azzam "established what they called a base or foundation (al Qaeda) as a potential general headquarters for future jihad." Bin Laden was its leader, and the organization included an intelligence component, a military committee, a financial committee, a political committee, and a committee in charge of media affairs and propaganda.

Bodansky (1999) points out that the United States would hardly have considered funding such a group of rebels, but the Pakistani ISI intervened. The 9-11 Commission (2004, pp. 55–56) writes that the ISI was concerned with the growing threat of the Soviet Union, but it had its own agenda for national security. Pakistan offered to act as the surrogate for the United States and Saudi Arabia, as both nations poured money into the war against the Soviets. The ISI, however, did not tell either America or Saudi Arabia how the money was being spent, nor was the ISI truthful when anti-Soviet hostilities ended in Afghanistan. Various mujahadeen groups struggled to gain power in Afghanistan, and the ISI backed its favorite allies. It also hoped to use groups like al Qaeda in Kashmir, a province in northern India that Pakistan claims to own. In essence, the ISI developed the structure that would support al Qaeda with U.S. and Saudi funds during the Soviet-Afghan War.

Training in Pakistan and Afghanistan under Azzam's spiritual mentoring, bin Laden financed mujahadeen operations and taught the guerrillas how to build field fortifications. By 1986, he left the training field for the battlefield. Enraged with the Soviets for their wholesale slaughter of Afghan villagers and use of poison gas, bin Laden joined the front ranks of the mujahadeen. Allied with hundreds of radical militants throughout the world, Osama bin Laden became a battlefield hero. (When interviewed by John Miller for *ABC News* [1998], bin Laden would not discuss these exploits. He simply stated that all Muslims are required to fight in the jihad.) After taking part in the war, bin Laden returned to Pakistan and joined Azzam in a new venture: to register all the foreign Jihadists in a single computer base.

Things did go well for Azzam, however. When the Soviets prepared to withdraw from Afghanistan in 1988, the ISI created its own Afghan guerrilla force and used it to take control of major areas of the country. Azzam believed the United States was behind this action, and he broke with the ISI. According to a U.S. federal agent who asked to remain anonymous, Azzam called five mujahadeen leaders, including bin Laden and **Ayman al Zawahiri**, a leader of the Egyptian Islamic Jihad, together in an attempt to unite the Jihadist movement. But the meeting ended in shambles, with each leader declaring the other four heretics. Bin Laden and al Zawahiri left, disillusioned and angry with Azzam. At this point, al Zawahiri began sketching out a grand model for al Qaeda, proposing a structure like the umbrella organization of the Egyptian Islamic Jihad.

According to Gunaratna (2002, p. 25), al Zawahiri became the brains behind a new operation. Using bin Laden's notoriety and charisma among the Afghan mujahadeen, he transformed the organization. Al Zawahiri knew from experience that an umbrella-styled organization was difficult to penetrate. In Egypt he had witnessed the effectiveness of Egyptian Islamic Jihad, which had terrorized the country with a small centralized organization supplying logistical support and advice to a set of semiautonomous groups. Al Zawahiri persuaded bin Laden that this was the type of organization to take control of Afghanistan and spread the new Islamic empire.

With al Zawahiri's ideas, Osama bin Laden took advantage of America's inattention and Azzam's waning power. He began to recruit into al Qaeda the mujahadeen registered in his computer base, while al Zawahiri organized training camps and cells. He also expressed a willingness to work with the Shi'ite terrorist organization Hezbollah (Waxman, 1998a; Goldberg, 2002). Yael Shahar (1998) says bin Laden saw the Soviet collapse in Afghanistan as a sign of God's victory. Islamic law was to be imposed on the world, and bin Laden believed al Qaeda to be the organization that could do it.

The only problem was Azzam, who resisted bin Laden and al Zawahiri's takeover. But in November 1989, Azzam was killed by a remote-controlled car bomb. Whether the assassination was due to Egyptian radicals or perhaps bin Laden himself, the result was that bin Laden and al Zawahiri became the undisputed leaders of al Qaeda. Following the philosophy of Sayyid Qutb, their enemies were the United States, the West, Israel, and Muslims who refused to accept Jihadist theology.

Bin Laden's first cause was the Saudi government and its "corrupt" royal family. As bin Laden's mujahadeen fighters, or "Afghans," as he called them, either went home to their native lands to wage jihad or stayed in Afghanistan to train and fight, bin Laden returned to Saudi Arabia, enjoying warm relations with the ISI. But the Saudi Arabian government, which does not tolerate diverse opinions and dissension, was not happy to see him return. When bin Laden brought several of his Afghans into his Arabian construction business, the Saudis watched carefully. While they looked on, bin Laden became independently wealthy.

The situation changed in 1990 when Iraq invaded Kuwait. The United States joined Saudi Arabia in a large international coalition, and bin Laden was infuriated. The cities of Mecca and Medina, two of the most holy shrines in Islam, are in Saudi Arabia. Millions of Muslims, including bin Laden, believe that these sacred sites must be protected. As thousands of non-Muslim troops arrived in Saudi Arabia, radical Muslims were appalled to find Muslims fighting Muslims under U.S. leadership. The U.S.-led coalition called this military buildup **Desert Shield**, and it became **Desert Storm** in February 1991 when American, British, and other allied forces poured into Iraq and Kuwait. For bin Laden, however, it was a desert apostasy.

After Desert Storm the Saudi government allowed U.S. troops to be stationed in Saudi Arabia. This was too much for bin Laden, who now thought of declaring his own war on the Saudi royal family and the United States. By April, he was training and financing terrorist groups and calling for the overthrow of unsympathetic Muslim governments.

Declaring War on the United States

Key Concepts and Questions:

1. Why did bin Laden move to Sudan?
2. What impact did the American intervention in Mogadishu have on bin Laden?
3. What impact did bin Laden's wealth and power have on al Qaeda?
4. Trace al Qaeda's campaign from 1992 to the present.
5. How is the Jihadist network organized under the umbrella or the hub of al Qaeda?
6. Has the U.S. offensive in Afghanistan been effective?
7. What are two views of the effectiveness of Operation Iraqi Freedom?
8. Explain America's dilemma regarding international support.

The PBS television show *Frontline* (2002) noted that bin Laden's protests against Desert Storm brought a Saudi crackdown on his operations, and he was forced to flee the country. Bin Laden found friends in Sudan's radical government formed under the influence of **Hasan al Turabi**. Turabi was the intellectual leader of the Jihadist cause and connected to radical and mainstream Muslims throughout the world. He could provide respectability to Jihadist philosophy, and bin Laden and Turabi formed a helpful alliance. Turabi served as the philosopher while bin Laden provided organizational skills. Bin Laden brought five hundred Afghan veterans to Sudan and built a network of businesses and other enterprises. By the end of 1992 bin Laden employed Afghan-hardened mujahadeen in Sudan. He also began to internationalize, creating multinational corporations, false charities, and front companies. Al Qaeda became stronger with each economic expansion (Bergen, 2001, pp. 76–91; for further discussion, see Reeve, 1999, pp. 45–134; Gunaratna, 2002, pp. 1–15; 9-11 Commission Report, 2004, pp. 63–70, 108–143; Randal, 2004, pp. 115–162, 201–221; Palmer and Palmer, 2004, pp. 100–105).

While bin Laden's fortunes increased, Americans were on the move in Somalia. President George H. W. Bush sent U.S. forces to Mogadishu to end a humanitarian crisis there, and they were joined by other armies, including Muslim forces. The people of Somalia were threatened with mass starvation due to continual struggles among several rival warlords. President Bush hoped peacekeeping efforts could open the area for food distribution. When the Democrats came to power in 1992, President Clinton continued the effort. Most of the world saw the multinational peacekeeping force as a method for feeding the starving Somalis, but not bin Laden. He believed it was another U.S.-led assault on a Muslim nation.

In December 1992, a bomb exploded in a hotel in Yemen that had been housing American troops. According to *Frontline* (1999), U.S. intelligence linked the attack to bin Laden. It was the opening shot in bin Laden's war against the United States and an international campaign of terror (see Timeline 7.1).

In the 1980s, terrorism was frequently associated with a particular state. Bin Laden, however, transcended the state and operated on his own, with the wealth of

Timeline 7.1

Al Qaeda's Campaign of Terror

12-29-92	Aden, Yemen	Hotel bombing
2-26-93	New York City	First World Trade Center bombing
10-3-93	Mogadishu, Somalia	Firefight with U.S. Army Rangers
Late 1994	Manila, Philippines	Operation Bojinka
12-26-95	Addis Abada, Ethiopia	Attempted assassination of Hosni Mubarak
11-13-95	Riyadh, Saudi Arabia	Car bombing of U.S. military personnel*
6-25-96	Dhahran, Saudi Arabia	Truck bombing of U.S. Air Force base*
8-7-98	Dar es Salaam, Tanzania	U.S. embassy bombing
8-7-98	Nairobi, Kenya	U.S. embassy bombing
12-4-99	Port Angeles, Washington	Foiled bombing plot
December 1999	Amman, Jordan	Foiled bombing plot
10-12-00	Aden, Yemen	Ship-bombing of USS *Cole*
12-25-00	Strasbourg, France	Foiled bombing plot
9-11-01	New York City	World Trade Center attacks
9-11-01	Washington, D.C.	Pentagon attack
9-11-01	Shanksville, Pennsylvania	Attack foiled by hijack victims
9-13-01	Paris, France	Foiled bombing plot
9-13-01	Brussels, Belgium	Foiled bombing plot
9-19-01	Detroit, Michigan	Sleeper cell closed
10-8-01	Sarajevo, Bosnia	Foiled attack
October 2001	Madrid, Spain	Sleeper cell closed
Early 2002	Singapore	Three sleeper cells closed

Sources: *Time* magazine; PBS, *Frontline*; *Detroit Free Press*; *New York Times*.
*The FBI has not established links between al Qaeda and this attack.

his construction empire providing financial backing. Yael Shahar (1998) argues that bin Laden's entrepreneurial efforts gave him the freedom to finance and command the al Qaeda terror network. His connections with the Afghan mujahadeen and his reputation as a warrior gave him legitimacy. Bin Laden did not need a government to support his operations. He had the money, personnel, material, and infrastructure necessary to maintain a campaign of terrorism. The 9-11 Commission Report (2004, pp. 185–186) disagrees with Shahar (see Another Perspective: The 9-11 Commission's Analysis of Counterterrorism on pp. 113–114). The commission believes bin

The 9-11 Commission's Analysis of Counterterrorism

Chapter 3 of the 9-11 Commission Report summarizes some of the mistakes government agencies made as al Qaeda was growing.

1. The Department of Justice (DOJ) was geared to gather evidence, prosecute, and convict. It was not designed to look into additional intelligence after a verdict was rendered.
2. The FBI measured success by crime rates, arrests, and crime clearances. It did an outstanding job when investigating terrorist incidents, but the bureau did not emphasize the role of intelligence gathering and analysis.
   a. It did not place resources in intelligence gathering.
   b. The division established to analyze intelligence faltered.
   c. The bureau did not have an effective intelligence gathering system.
3. A series of rulings by the attorney general and mandates from Congress limited the FBI's ability to collect domestic intelligence.
   a. DOJ officials were confused about the relationship between criminal investigations and intelligence operations.
   b. The Foreign Intelligence Surveillance Act of 1978 (FISA) was misinterpreted by DOJ, the FBI, and the FISA court. (The FISA court approves warrants for surveillance under FISA.)
   c. Misinterpretations of FISA prevented intelligence agencies from sharing relevant information with FBI criminal investigators.
4. The Immigration and Naturalization Service focused on the southwestern U.S. border and did not have enough personnel to deal with terrorism.
5. The Federal Aviation Administration (FAA) had a layered defense that gathered intelligence, singled out suspected terrorists, screened passengers, and provided in-flight procedures for emergencies.
   a. The FAA intelligence division was not adequately staffed.
   b. The "no-fly" lists did not contain the names of terrorists known to other government agencies.
   c. Airport security screening performed poorly.
   d. The FAA rejected a ban on small knives, fearing screeners could not find them and searches would create congestion at screening areas.
   e. Procedures for in-flight emergencies did not include plans to counter suicide hijackers.
   f. In defense of the FAA, the 9-11 Commission notes that hijackings had diminished for a decade, and they did not seem to be an immediate threat.
6. Intelligence agencies in general were not prepared to deal with terrorism.
   a. The intelligence community remained geared to fight the Cold War.
   b. There was no overall director of intelligence.
   c. Intelligence operations were hampered by reduced resources.
   d. American universities did not produce scholars with in-depth knowledge of Jihadist issues and appropriate foreign language capabilities.
7. The Department of State had lost much of its ability to establish foreign policy.
   a. Foreign policy planning had been shifting to the National Security Council and the Department of Defense since 1960. (*continued on page 114*)

Laden was and remains funded by wealthy sympathizers. Financial operations in Sudan covered only day-to-day expenses, and many of the companies were not profitable. Regardless, bin Laden had financing and did not need the support of a rogue nation. He only needed a place to hide.

According to *Frontline*, bin Laden went on the offensive in 1993. Using his contacts in Sudan, he began searching for weapons of mass destruction. His Afghans sought to purchase nuclear weapons from underground sources in the Russian Federation, and he began work on a chemical munitions plant in Sudan. Bodansky says he also sent terrorists to fight in other parts of the world, including Algeria, Egypt, Bosnia, Pakistan, Somalia, Kashmir, and Chechnya. U.S. intelligence sources also believe bin Laden's Afghans came to the United States.

Bin Laden was active in Somalia when U.S. troops joined the forces trying to get food to the area. In October 1993, a U.S. Army Black Hawk helicopter was downed while on patrol in Mogadishu. U.S. Army Rangers went to the rescue, and a two-day battle ensued in which eighteen Americans died. In an interview with John Miller of ABC News (1998), bin Laden claimed he trained and supported the troops that struck the Americans.

Bin Laden was also involved in assassination attempts. In 1993, his Afghans tried to murder Prince Abdullah (now King Abdullah) of Jordan. In 1995, U.S. intelligence sources believe he was behind the attempted assassination of Egyptian president Hosni Mubarak. According to *Frontline*, bin Laden called for a guerrilla campaign against Americans in Saudi Arabia in 1995.

Bin Laden's campaign of terror continued in other areas. Like most other terrorist groups, al Qaeda's primary tactic was bombing. In 1993 a group of Jihadists tried to destroy the World Trade Center in New York City with a massive car bomb, and a year later a blind Egyptian cleric inspired a group to attempt several other attacks in New York City. In 1995 Ramzi Youseff tried to attack the United States by planning to down airliners over the Pacific during a thirty-one-hour period. These actions illustrate the evolving nature of the al Qaeda campaign. It was not the result of a mastermind terrorist pulling strings from a secretive lair. It was a loose confederation of like-minded people who had limited interactions. Abdel Rahman, the blind cleric, was a member of the Egyptian Islamic Jihad, and Ramzi Youseff had trained in Afghanistan. Youseff was linked to Khalid Sheikh Mohammed, a bin Laden operative and master planner of the September 11 attacks, but he took no orders from bin Laden. In addition, Khalid Sheikh Mohammed admired bin Laden, but he did not officially join al Qaeda until 1999. Individual Jihadist operators took actions within the aura of al Qaeda (Reeve, 1999, pp. 186–189).

In 1995, bin Laden's Afghans killed five U.S. service personnel and two Indian soldiers with a truck bomb in Riyadh, Saudi Arabia. In 1996, he helped to strike in Dharan, killing nineteen Americans with another truck bomb.

Bin Laden was forced from the Sudan in 1996 by international pressure, and al Zawahiri fled Egypt when security forces began cracking down on the Jihadists. Both men went to Afghanistan, where many displaced Jihadists joined them. Bin Laden consolidated power and absorbed the new Jihadists in his ranks. And then he made a most unusual declaration. Seated in front of a camera with al Zawahiri and al Qaeda's security director, Mohammed Atef, bin Laden declared war on the United States in 1996. He followed this by two religious rulings, called **fatwa**, in 1998.

Magnus Ranstorp (1998) argues that these writings reveal much about the nature of al Qaeda and bin Laden. First, bin Laden represents a new phase in Middle Eastern terrorism. He is intent on spreading the realm of Islam with a transnational group. Second, he uses Islam to call for religious violence. Bin Laden is a self-trained religious fanatic ready to kill in the name of God. Finally, bin Laden wants to cause death. Whether with conventional weapons or weapons of mass destruction, bin Laden's purpose is to kill. In his fatwas of February 1998, he calls for the killing of any American anywhere in the world.

In August 1998, bin Laden's terrorists bombed the U.S. embassies in Nairobi, Kenya, and Dar es Salaam, Tanzania. The Nairobi bomb killed 213 people and injured 4,500; the Dar es Salaam explosion killed 12 and wounded 85. These attacks signaled a new phase in al Qaeda terrorism. While the loose network of Jihadists dominated the scene, the Nairobi and Dar es Salaam bombs demonstrated how al Qaeda had matured. For the first time, the group could operate a cell planted in a country hundreds of miles away from al Qaeda training camps. It used sophisticated bombs and demonstrated complicated planning. Then came the attack on the USS *Cole* in 2000, a failed millennium plot, and the attacks of September 11, 2001. After the United States and allied forces struck al Qaeda bases in Afghanistan in October 2001, the structured operations gave way to the loose network.

Al Qaeda affiliates struck other areas, including in Bali (October 2002) and U.S. compounds in Riyadh (May 2003), Morocco (August 2003), and Madrid (March

2004). Jihadists have also specialized in beheading hostages in front of international audiences, and they have mastered roadside bombs, suicide attacks, and mass murders in Iraq. Many times these groups claim to be the local version of al Qaeda or they operate by their own name.

Far from being a single large organization, as Gunaratna (2002, pp. 148–200) explains, al Qaeda forged relationships with other terrorist organizations throughout the world. Gunaratna says that al Qaeda formed loose alliances with Jihadists in Bosnia, the Caucuses, North Africa, the Middle East, and Central Asia. Southeast Asia, especially Indonesia and the Philippines, became an attractive area for alliances. Bin Laden also tried to form relations with Hamas and Hezbollah. Brian Jenkins (2004) demonstrates that this network strengthened al Qaeda, in that it became a network of differing organizations rather than a single organization (see Figure 7.1). And these loose affiliations of Jihadist organizations added flexibility to the Jihadist network.

Michael Doran (2002) points out that even though the network provided motivations for the various Jihadists, it would be a mistake to think the groups presented a united front. They were fueled by local issues and diverse goals. The different Jihadist organizations say they all believe in the same thing, Doran says, but when local situations are examined, Jihadist causes are varied. Bin Laden's strength came from trying to focus Islamic rage on the United States. In the words of Brian Jenkins (2002), Jihadists see a holy war against the United States as a method for uniting political Islam. It is one of the few issues holding the Jihadists together. Doran agrees.

Bin Laden's use of Zawahiri's umbrella or hub organization also brings cohesion to Jihadists with differing causes (Arquilla, Ronfeldt, and Zanini, 1999, p. 50; Gunaratna, 2002, pp. 75–84). Before the U.S. offensive in Afghanistan in October 2001, al Qaeda existed with a leadership group in Afghanistan and semiautonomous **sleeper cells**—or cells designed to "sleep," or to stay hidden, until the time they were called to action—placed in various countries throughout the world. The sleeper cells could either strike individually or operate in conjunction with the leadership in Afghanistan. When cells operated under the Afghan umbrella, they were extremely effective. The bombing of the U.S. embassies in Dar es Salaam and Nairobi, the strike on the USS *Cole*, and the attacks of September 11, were the result of combined operations. When cells operated on their own, the results were mixed. Potential attacks in France and Italy were thwarted in 2001 and 2002 through the ineptitude of the terrorists. The March 2004 train bombing in Madrid, however, was deadly.

The United States responded to al Qaeda with military actions. In October 2001 American forces began striking al Qaeda and Taliban strongholds in Afghanistan. Critics bemoaned the difficulty of fighting in the mountainous territory and claimed the United States had stepped into a quagmire. Military professionals had other ideas. Within sixty days, al Qaeda and their Taliban allies were forced into the mountains of eastern Afghanistan and western Pakistan. American and allied forces captured or killed a number of al Qaeda operatives, but bin Laden and al Zawahiri managed to escape (see Joyner Library, 2004).

President George W. Bush claimed that the Afghan operation was part of a general war on terrorism—a war that took many paths. In some instances, intelligence services provided crucial information to deter terrorism. At other times, law enforce-

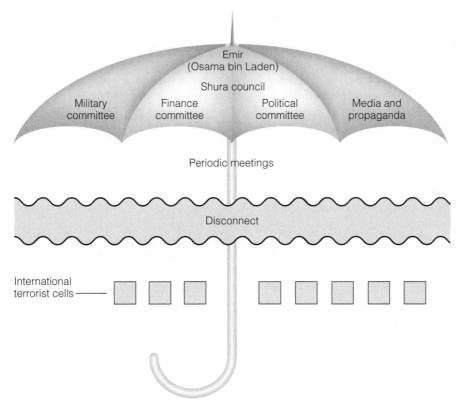

Figure 7.1
Al Qaeda's Umbrella, 1996–2001

Source: 9-11 Commission Report (2004, p. 56).

ment agencies made headline-grabbing arrests. The results of counterterrorist efforts have been mixed. Irm Haleem (2004) says that U.S. operations in Afghanistan caused al Qaeda to completely decentralize. When their Afghan base was rendered inoperable, al Qaeda reformed from an umbrella or hub into a series of autonomous organizations driven by local concerns. John Arquilla and colleagues (1999, p. 50) calls this a *chain organization*, and as such, al Qaeda serves as more of an inspiration than a hub. Numerous groups around the world take action in al Qaeda's name.

The dispersion of the al Qaeda organization in Afghanistan also created new forms of terrorism. Bin Laden and al Zawahiri, or cleverly disguised substitutes, began releasing audiotapes claiming that actions were imminent or claiming credit for attacks in other areas of the world. Jessica Stern (2003b) concludes that by decentralizing to a chain organization, supporting terrorist allies, and maintaining the ability to threaten the world, al Qaeda was more dangerous than ever. This was ironic, given its quick defeat in Afghanistan.

James Rubin (2003) points to another problem. On September 11, 2001, the United States had the sympathy and support of the world. When it launched its offensive in Afghanistan, it again had international allies and support. As U.S. law enforcement took action, it received support from police forces in Southeast Asia, the Middle East, Africa, and Europe. But Rubin points out that when President G. W. Bush shifted his attention from al Qaeda to Iraq, America lost the support it had enjoyed after September 11.

On March 19, 2003, President Bush ordered U.S. forces to attack Saddam Hussein, the longtime authoritarian president of Iraq. Officially dubbed **Operation Iraqi Freedom**, the invasion intended to preempt Hussein from launching a terrorist attack on the United States. Two suppositions by the Bush administration supported the invasion: that Iraq was holding weapons of mass destruction and that Hussein had established ties with al Qaeda. The Bush administration feared that Hussein would put weapons of mass destruction in the hands of bin Laden.

As of this writing, neither the link to al Qaeda nor the presence of weapons of mass destruction in Iraq has been verified except in the minds of diehard ideologues. Ironically, the loose confederation of international terrorist groups found a common cause on their home turf. As President Bush declared an end to major combat operations in Iraq, the real battle with the Jihadists was just beginning. With their common enemy so close to home, various Jihadist groups and individuals made their way to Afghanistan to attack the United States. One group of people believes that Iraq has presented the battleground for America to strike and defeat international terrorists (Wolfowitz, 2004). Regardless, Jihadists around the world, including Osama bin Laden, ideologically embraced insurgents in Iraq.

Robert Kagan (2004) argues that whether or not the decision to go to war in Iraq was correct, the long-range issue should focus on building international political hegemony there. Kagan also points out that the Jihadist network takes strength from two main factors: the dynamic nature of the network and its ability to create so much hatred for the United States that differences between Jihadists disappear. When America cooperates with other nations, terrorist networks are disrupted. When Jihadists are able to take sanctuary in countries that oppose the United States, it is another story. The United States needs international support, Kagan says, but other nations may not give it. This would be a tragedy, he says, because America is less dangerous than Jihadists and other terrorists.

Another opinion regarding the U.S. role in Iraq suggests that the United States has alienated the Arab world and many millions of Muslims for launching the wrong war against the wrong target (Lynch, 2003; Albright, 2003). Former secretary of state Madeleine Albright champions this reasoning and emphasizes that the United States must take its place among nations. Under President George W. Bush, America has taken many actions unilaterally or with minimal international support. Secretary Albright and others argue that the United States must act in conjunction with other nations, especially Islamic countries. This argument maintains that the United States needs to fight terrorism by allying with the international community and alienating terrorists from potential support.

Summary of Main Points

1. Militant forms of religion have made it appear as though there is a conflict between Christianity and Islam. Although this is not the case, confusion arises because militants frequently take action in the name of all of Islam.

2. *Jihadist* is a term used to describe an Islamicist who resorts to terrorism. Jihadist networks are arranged as different groups of terrorist groups.

3. The idea of *jihad* grew from early Islamic experiences, and scholars argue that it has had many meanings. Modern militants, inspired by ibn Taymiyyah, believe that jihad calls them to convert the world to their narrow belief system and to destroy people who refuse to follow.

4. Jihadists tend to look for inspiration from the writings of Sayyid Qutb. Ibn Taymiyyah is frequently viewed as one of the original scholars who developed the idea of militant purification.

5. Al Qaeda began as a means to register mujahadeen during the Soviet-Afghan War, and it evolved into a mujahadeen operation funded by the ISI. Bin Laden rebuilt al Qaeda in Sudan under the influence of Hasan al Turabi, and he returned to Afghanistan in 1996.

6. Al Qaeda is actually a loosely confederated movement of like-minded groups.

7. Most of the world's nations supported the United States when it attacked al Qaeda and the Taliban in Afghanistan. International opinion has been divided, however, over U.S. actions in Iraq.

Key Terms

Make sure you can define, explain, or identify the following people, ideas, organizations, or terms:

Jihadist network   100
fighters   101
Taliban   101
al Qaeda 2.0   102
Jihadist ideology   102
Islam   103
Taqi al Din ibn Taymiyyah   104
jihad   104
Mohammed ibn Abdul Wahhab   104
Salafiyya   106
Muslim Brotherhood   106
Sayyid Qutb   106

mujahadeen   106
Interservice Intelligence Agency
   (ISI)   106
Osama bin Laden   108
Abdullah Azzam   108
Ayman al Zawahiri   109
Desert Shield   110
Desert Storm   110
Hasan al Turabi   111
fatwa   115
sleeper cell   116
Operation Iraqi Freedom   118

Suggested Readings

Now that you've been introduced to this topic, you can learn more by reading:

Rohan Gunaratna's *Inside al Qaeda* is a thorough examination of the birth of the Jihadist network. It summarizes history, structure, and operations in several areas of the world.

You may also want to read:

Peter Bergen, in *Holy War, Inc.*, combines the story of al Qaeda with the author's reporting history and his interview with Osama bin Laden.

John Miller, Michael Stone, and Chris Mitchell, in *The Cell: Inside the 9/11 Plot, and Why the FBI and CIA Failed to Stop It*, give an account of the sleeper cells associated with September 11. The authors also interviewed bin Laden.

Aukai Collins's book *My Jihad* is an account of an American Jihadist. However, one high-ranking retired FBI counterterrorist executive was dubious of its accuracy.

The 9-11 Commission Report has a section on the history of al Qaeda. It is available in print (2004) or online at *http://www.9-11commission.gov/report/911Report.pdf*.

Yoseff Bodansky, in *Bin Laden: The Man Who Declared War on America*, provides a detailed biography of Osama bin Laden researched from public documents.

Jonathan Randal's *Osama: The Making of a Terrorist* is another biography, combining public records with Randal's experience as a reporter.

Web Resources

Go to *http://cj.wadsworth.com/white_terrorism5e* and click on Web Links to find:

▌ Many links regarding "The War on Terrorism" at East Carolina University's Joyner Library
▌ The PBS website "Hunting bin Laden," which includes John Miller's interview with Osama bin Laden

The Companion Website for *Terrorism and Homeland Security,* Fifth Edition

http://cj.wadsworth.com/white_terrorism5e

At the Book Companion Website you can review chapter outlines, use the flash cards to test your terrorism vocabulary, and check out the many other study aids you'll find there. You'll find valuable data and resources at your fingertips to help you study for that big exam or write that important paper.

Terrorism Updates

http://www.wadsworth.com/criminaljustice_d/special_features/ext/terrorism _site090802/index.html

Visit the *Terrorism: An Interdisciplinary Perspective* website to find the most current information about the fields of terrorism and homeland security. With a focus on domestic and international issues, this site explores the scope of terrorism in our world today. You'll find essays on important topics in terrorism and homeland security, critical thinking web activities, and InfoTrac College Edition keywords. Most importantly, the website is updated weekly with current news and research articles on domestic and international terrorism. You are invited to use these web resources to supplement your understanding of the topics covered in this chapter.

Current Perspectives: Readings from InfoTrac College Edition
Terrorism and Homeland Security

The sixteen articles in this reader offer a representative selection that helps you understand the important issues about terrorism and homeland security. It includes FREE access to InfoTrac College Edition and can also be bundled with the text for free.

Chapter 8

The Umbrella Effect

AP/Wide World Photos

Police officers inspect the ruins of a nightclub destroyed by an explosion in Denpasar, Bali, Indonesia, Oct. 13, 2002. Semiautonomous groups operate under a Jihadist umbrella all over the world.

Small terrorist groups began to spread under the shield of al Qaeda's umbrella at the end of the Soviet-Afghan War, and their spread increased after the American offensive in Afghanistan in 2001. Some of them maintained close relations with al Qaeda, while others became fully autonomous. Regardless of their status, they kept one thing in common: The myriad groups were part of the Jihadist movement. In this chapter we will examine the spread of the Jihadists from Afghanistan to the rest of the world, and then we will take a more historical point of view. Al Qaeda was not the first international Jihadist group. The first such organization evolved from the Syrian- and Iranian-backed Shi'ite group Hezbollah, or the Party of God. Over the years, Hezbollah has evolved. Today, supporters claim it is a political organization with a military arm, while detractors believe it to be one of the deadliest international terrorist groups in the world. Before al Qaeda's September 11 attacks, it was responsible for more American deaths than any other terrorist group. Today's Jihadists are assembled under two international umbrellas: one inspired by al Qaeda and the other by Hezbollah.

Chapter Objectives

After reading this chapter you should be able to:

1. Trace the spread of the Jihadists to South, Central, and Southeast Asia.

2. Explain the movement of groups to Africa and the West.

3. Sketch the tactics of the international Jihadists.

4. List the ways Muslims are victimized by Jihadists.

5. Describe the metamorphosis of Hezbollah in Lebanon and beyond.

6. Explain the current status of Hezbollah.

7. Summarize both a sympathetic and critical view of Hezbollah.

Jihad Moves to Central and Southeast Asia

Key Points and Questions:

1. What impact did the collapse of the Soviet Union have on Central Asia?

2. Name three groups that grew in Central Asia after 1991.

3. How did the Jihadists move into India?

4. What effects did the Jihadist movement have in Southeast Asia?

The jihad grew beyond Afghanistan, but it was affected by a variety of local concerns in various regions. In Central Asia five former Communist states—Turkmenistan, Uzbekistan, Tajikistan, Kyrgyzstan, and Kazakhstan (or the "**Stans**")—moved from the Soviet orbit into self-government. Islamicists emerged in these states, and some of them grew militant. India and Pakistan squabbled over ownership of Jammu and Kashmir, and Jihadists moved into the arena as well. Both countries also faced internal jihad movements. Indonesia became the breeding ground for several Jihadist organizations, and one of them, Jamaat Islamiyya, spread to Thailand, Singapore, and Myanmar. The Philippines faced its own rebellions. The Jihadists in Asia linked themselves in a loose network.

Ahmed Rashid (2002, pp. 46–56) describes the growth of terrorism in Central Asia, noting that as the new Russian Federation formed after the 1991 break up of the Soviet Union, the Russians wanted little to do with their old possessions in Central Asia. The five Stans, which lay north of Pakistan and Afghanistan (see Figure 8.1), struggled for political existence as Jihadist organizations joined resurgent Islamic movements. The new governments ended up with authoritarian regimes far removed from the common people. Rashid believes this led to unrest across the region, and the climate became ripe for religious radicals to gain influence.

Rashid argues that the situation after 1991 gave rise to three movements. The Hezb-ul-Tahir, a Palestinian organization, moved to Central Asia to preach conversion to Islam. The group saw this area as a fertile ground for Islamic converts. A second group, the Islamic Movement of Uzbekistan (IMU), proposed a violent jihad against Islam Karimov, the dictator of Uzbekistan. Disillusioned Hezb-ul-Tahir followers gravitated toward the IMU, and the IMU gained strength in the Fergana

Figure 8.1
Central Asia, the "Stans," and Xinjiang

Valley, a rich agricultural area serving Tajikistan, Uzbekistan, and Kyrgyzstan that is important for any political group that wishes to have control of the southern Stans. A third group of Jihadists appears with little attachment to the Stans. Rashid says ethnic Uighars from western China organized to revive an eighteenth-century state in China's Xing Xian (New Frontier) province. Using Kyrgyzstan and Kazakhstan as a base, they began operations in China.

India was unable to avoid increasing violence, and much of its terrorist problem centered on **Jammu and Kashmir** (see Figure 8.2), a disputed piece of territory along the Indian and Pakistani border. Shay (2002, pp. 107–108) says the Pakistani Interservice Intelligence Agency (ISI) took control of several mujahadeen groups at the end of the Soviet-Afghan War. Using its influence within the groups, the ISI sponsored new intolerant religious schools and brought new recruits into Jammu and Kashmir. Violence escalated on both sides, and the death toll soared into the thousands. It also brought India and Pakistan to the brink of nuclear war in the spring of 2002.

The two countries also faced internal problems. B. Raman (3-10-02) says India was concerned with growing terrorism fostered by Pakistani groups, its own internal Jihadists, and Sikh terrorists. (The **Sikhs** are a religious group combining monotheism with precepts of Islam, Hinduism, and Buddhism.) As India and Pakistan backed away from potential nuclear devastation, the Pakistani government removed some of the more prominent ISI leaders who had supported Jihadist groups. It was in Pakistan's interest to do so because the Jihadists soon targeted the Pakistani government when it supported the United States against al Qaeda.

Jihad also grew in Southeast Asia. Zachary Abuza (2003b, pp. 121–187), in an analysis of terrorism in that region, says that Jihadist groups began forming in Indo-

Figure 8.2
India, Pakistan, and
Jammu and Kashmir

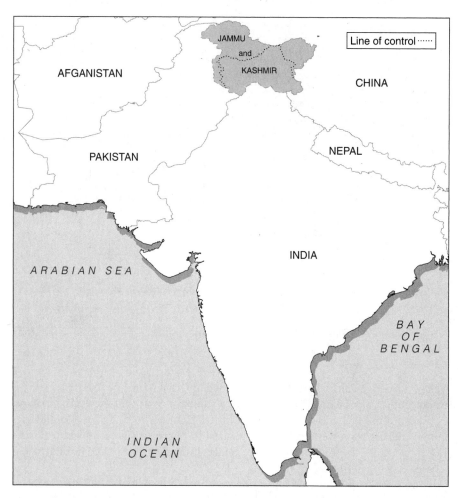

Figure 8.3
Indonesia

nesia (see Figure 8.3) in the early 1990s. The International Crisis Group (2002) says
these movements had their origins after World War II when Indonesia gained its
independence from the Netherlands. Islamic associations became part of the political process, but they were suppressed by the government and the army in the name
of nationalism. Abuza notes that new leadership gained power in 1998, and Islamic

Figure 8.4
Philippine Islands

groups blossomed, asserting their independence. In 1999 fighting broke out between Christians and Muslims in the eastern islands, and militant Islamic groups grew.

The political situation in Indonesia provided a climate for the growth of Jihadist groups. According to Abuza, many of the members of Jihadist movements had been trained in the mujahadeen camps of Afghanistan. **Lashkar Jihad** formed to fight Christians in the east. A more sinister group, **Jamaat Islamiyya**, formed with the purpose of placing Indonesia under strict Islamic law. Both groups had contacts with al Qaeda (Gunaratna, 2002, pp. 174–203; Abuza, 2003b, pp. 138–142), although leaders of both groups claimed to be independent of Osama bin Laden (Stern, 2003b, pp. 75–76).

The Philippines (see Figure 8.4) also experienced Jihadist violence. Historically, the relationship between the Christian islands in the north and a few Muslim islands in the south has been marked by strife. The U.S. Army fought Muslim rebels after the Spanish-American War (1898), and the Philippine government faced both Muslim and Communist rebellions in the 1950s. Religious and ideological rebellions were repeated themes for the Philippines during the twentieth century.

Abuza (2003b, pp. 89–120) outlines the formation of three recent terrorist groups in the Philippines. The Moro National Liberation Front (MNLF) is a continuation of the old religious struggle. Having proposed negotiations with the Philippine government, the MNLF seeks an independent Islamic state. Breaking away from the MNLF is the more radical Moro Islamic Liberation Front (MILF). It has ties with Jihadist movements and seeks to create an Islamic state under strict interpretations of Islamic law. A third group, Abu Sayyuf, claims to be part of the Jihadist movement, but it is most closely associated with criminal activity and seems more interested in money than religion.

Ideology is also active in the Philippines (Hill and Ward, 2002, pp. 281–291). The New Peoples Army (NPA) operates throughout the Philippines. Originally established to fight both the government and its American allies, the NPA hopes to turn the Philippines into a Communist state. The group has been responsible for a number of murders, including those of U.S. military personnel.

Groups in Asia have made their presence felt in a religious-ethnic struggle in the Russian Federation. Reporter Felix Corley (3-4-04) covers the struggle between ethnic Chechnyans and Russians as Chechnyans sought independence after the collapse of the Soviet Union in 1991 (see Figure 8.5). Their dispute dates back to the Communist era when Joseph Stalin (ruled 1922–1953) imposed Soviet power in the region. The Russians and Chechnyans fought two conventional wars, and then some Chechnyans turned to the weapons of terrorism, especially bombing and suicide bombings. They took the war north with terrorist attacks in Moscow and surrounding areas (see Expanding the Concept: Learning to Be Ruthless in Chechnya).

The U.S. Department of State (8-4-04) says that Chechnyan rebels should not be lumped with other Jihadist movements. According to the U.S. ambassador to Russia, Chechnyans are engaged in a legitimate war of independence and are not like other Jihadist terrorists (Turks.US, 2-29-04). Al Qaeda has tried to claim the Chechnyan / Russian conflict, the ambassador said, but Chechnya has been seeking independence for many years, and the struggle predates the Jihadist movement by two hundred years. Others believe Jihadists influence the violent nature of the independence movement. Chechnya thrives on support from Jihadist groups and imports Jihadist

Figure 8.5
Chechnya and Dagestan

Learning to Be Ruthless in Chechnya

Of the many suicide operations carried out by Chechnyans, two gained the most attention in the United States: the October 2002 attack on a Moscow theater and the September 2004 attack on a school in Breslan. Both attacks were suicide missions designed to produce massive casualties. A comparison of the two attacks demonstrates the way Jihadists learned and corrected previous mistakes.

MOSCOW DUBROVKA HOUSE OF CULTURE: OCTOBER 2002

What went as planned:

1. Terrorists took over a theater and isolated it.
2. Terrorists segregated hostages in small groups.
3. Terrorists planted enough bombs to kill most of the people in the theater.
4. Terrorists drew international attention to their cause.

What went wrong:

1. Terrorists formed partial bonds/relationships with some hostages.
2. Female terrorists took orders from males; therefore, when Russian Special Forces attacked, females waited for instructions to detonate bombs. But the males were busy fighting and could not give them.
3. Some hostages kept and used cell phones.

What the terrorists learned:

1. Ruthlessness, including random executions, keeps human bonds from forming.
2. Bombers should be readily prepared to detonate explosives at the first sign of an assault.
3. Cell phones must be destroyed.

THE BRESLAN MIDDLE SCHOOL NUMBER 1 ATTACK: SEPTEMBER 2004

Jihadists learned lessons from the Dubrovka attack. To eliminate bonding and maintain control they

1. Publicly executed hostages at the beginning of the incident.
2. Destroyed cell phones.
3. Executed a terrorist who stated he never intended to attack a school.
4. Humiliated and intimidated the children taken hostage.
5. Played psychological games to keep parents in fear.
6. Denied food and water to hostages.
7. Bayoneted a young boy when he cried for a drink of water.
8. Gave selected females leading roles.
9. Placed bombs to detonate upon any counterattack without orders.

Sources: Spechard et al. (2004); Ostovsky, Beliakov, and Franchetti (9-29-04).

Tactics of International Jihadists

Terrorists follow the tactics described by Brian Jenkins in Chapter 1: bombing, kidnapping, assassination, hijacking, assault, and hostage-taking. Jihadists have not invented new tactics; they merely apply old methods in frightening, new ways.

Bombing   Jihadists introduced the suicide bomber. The practice started in southern Lebanon and spread around the world. Even secular groups have copied this tactic.

Kidnapping and Hostage-Taking   Jihadists kidnap for economic gain and other political purposes. But in 2002, they began murdering their kidnap victims.

Assassination   Jihadists use selective and random assassinations to influence political behavior. In September 2001 they used two suicide bombers to kill the leader of the Northern Alliance in Afghanistan. In March 2004 they bombed a train in Madrid, killing people indiscriminately to influence the Spanish elections. The mere threat of Jihadist assassinations was designed to influence the U.S. presidential election in 2004.

Assault   Jihadist assaults are particularly violent. In Saudi Arabia, for example, one group in 2003 fought its way into an area containing American and British citizens and then executed several of them. In another instance, Jihadists attacked a secure residential compound and drove in bomb-laden trucks for suicide bombings.

tactics (see Expanding the Concept: Tactics of International Jihadists). Ayman al Zawahiri went to Chechnya to recruit and fight with new mujahadeen groups after the Soviet-Afghan War. The Russians even jailed him, although through an oversight, they released him (Sud, 1-26-04).

Sunni Jihad from Africa to the West

Key Points and Questions:

1. What caused the Algerian Civil War?
2. How did Jihadists expand into North Africa?
3. Did Jihadist ideas exist in Africa before the Soviet-Afghan War?
4. How did violence in Africa lead to attacks in the West?

In 1992 an Islamic party won the national election in Algeria. This frightened the West, especially France and the United States, who were afraid that narrow-minded Islamicist governments would spread through the region (see Kepel, 2002, pp. 159–176). When the Algerian military took control of the government and voided the elections, several Western nations breathed a sigh of relief. North Africa was too close to Europe for comfort; the West was not eager to see a government based on strict Islamic law so close to its southern door (see Figure 8.6). Unfortunately, the military coup resulted in the deadly **Algerian Civil War**, during which more than one hundred thousand people died between 1992 and 2002.

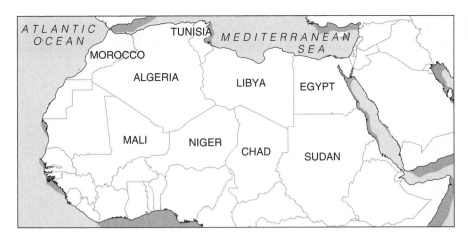

Figure 8.6
North Africa

The Algerian Armed Islamic Group (GIA) grew to resist the military (see Kepel 2002, p. 169; and Esposito, 1999, p. 187). The GIA consisted of new Algerian recruits as well as several Jihadists who had fought in the Soviet-Afghan War. By 1995 new Jihadist groups were springing up in Algeria, and the war became a bloodbath. Violence and other Jihadist groups spread throughout North Africa. Egypt found itself in the midst of a war with three of them; Libyan leaders were threatened for criticizing Jihadists; Tunisia started to move toward a more strict form of Islam; and Morocco, one of the West's closest allies in the region, spawned its own Jihadist movements.

The path of the Jihadist groups is interesting and ironic. The **Muslim Brotherhood** started in 1928 in Cairo under the leadership of Hassan al Banna. The goal of the Brothers was to bring purity back to Islam by reforming government. By 1951, after al Banna's assassination, the movement grew violent, partly because of the influence of Sayyid Qutb (see Chapter 7). After the Egyptian government repressed the Brothers and executed Qutb in 1966, the Muslim Brotherhood returned to its original mission of peaceful reform. More radical groups, however, embraced Qutb's militancy and began a campaign of terror. Afghan Jihadists allied with these militant groups, and when al Qaeda moved to Sudan in 1992, it found willing partners in the north.

Press reports tended to present the Jihadist movements in North Africa as an expansion of al Qaeda, but this interpretation is incorrect. In some cases Jihadist groups shared training and members with al Qaeda, but they had been emerging on their own before the Soviet-Afghan War. For example, one such group was responsible for the assassination of Anwar Sadat in 1981. They murdered foreigners, threatened secular leaders, and attacked Christians. Sometimes their attacks were spectacular, such as the **Luxor massacre** in 1997 (see Expanding the Concept: The Luxor Massacre). At other times the attacks were more localized. Many African and Middle Eastern governments welcomed the call for mujahadeen in the Afghan jihad so they could export their militant Jihadists. The only problem was that the Jihadists came back after the war.

Revolutionary events catapulted the Jihadists into the international arena. Qutb (1990) advocated for revolutionary reform inside government, but he argued it was necessary to confront and defeat infidel governments not under the rule of Islamic

Expanding the Concept

The Luxor Massacre

At the time it seemed like an isolated event. On November 17, 1997, four Egyptian Jihadists dressed in police uniforms approached a group of fifty-eight tourists visiting the Pyramids. Most of the tourists were Swiss. As the tourists disembarked from a bus, the Jihadists attacked. They shot more than fifty tourists. In a gruesome act, they pulled out small knives and worked their way among the dead and wounded. Wounded victims were mutilated and decapitated to increase the drama of the attack. The Jihadists were later killed by Egyptian security forces.

Source: Plet (5-13-99).

law. Muslims believe that Islam cannot and should not be imposed on others, but the Jihadists ignored this belief. They were at war with "infidels" and "heretics," and they sought to impose Islamic law on the world. As a result, the Jihadists used Africa as a springboard to the West. It was not good enough to hit Westerners in Islamic lands; the Jihadists dreamed of making an attack on Western soil.

While the Sunni Jihadists drew inspiration from Qutb, a Shi'ite group provided the model for jihad under an umbrella. **Hezbollah**, or the Party of God, was spawned in Lebanon after the **Iranian Revolution** (1978–1979), which culminated in the overthrow of the secular shah of Iran. Hezbollah's purpose is to spread the Islamic law of Shi'ite Islam. Although it is most frequently associated with violence in Lebanon and Israel (see Chapters 9 and 10), Hezbollah has an international Jihadist wing. It also created the organizational style that groups like the Egyptian Islamic Group, Ansar al Islam, the Egyptian Islamic Jihad, the GIA, the Palestinian Islamic Jihad, and al Qaeda would use. Therefore, it is appropriate to consider Hezbollah apart from the localized groups of Palestine and Israel and their neighbors.

The Metamorphosis of Hezbollah

 Key Concepts and Questions:

1. How did the 1982 Israeli invasion of Lebanon affect Iran and Syria?
2. How did Hezbollah's interpretation of Shi'aism influence its development?
3. Summarize the four phases of Hezbollah from 1982 to the present.
4. How did Hezbollah become an international terrorist group?

Hezbollah is a product of the 1978–1979 Iranian Revolution and the struggle between Israel and its neighbors. Shi'ite scholars, known as *ayatollahs*, gained control of the revolution through the **Revolutionary Guards,** a group of young fanatic Shi'ites who evolved into a paramilitary arm of the revolution. The **Shi'ite** sect of Islam dominates Iran, southern Iraq, southern Lebanon, and portions of Afghanistan and Pakistan. While **Sunnis,** another Islamic sect, believe that Mohammed and the entire Muslim community are equal before God and that everybody will be judged equally at the end of time, Shi'ites believe that one of Mohammed's descendents must return before God judges humanity. They also believe that Mohammed's power flowed through his heirs. Most Shi'ites believe that Mohammed had twelve direct heirs, or *imams*, and that the last imam was taken directly into heaven. He will return as a prelude to final judgment, and until that time ayatollahs are given some of the characteristics of the Twelfth Imam. (See Another Perspective: Karbala and the Martyrdom of Ibn Ali

Another Perspective

Karbala and the Martyrdom of Ibn Ali Hussein

The main difference separating Sunni and Shi'ite Muslims focuses on the person who should be selected to run the community (*umma*) of Muslims. Sunnis believe that the community supersedes all relations and should therefore select its leader. Shi'ites believe leadership belongs in Mohammed's family, the Heshimites. Shi'ites also believe that the direct descendents of Mohammed received part of Mohammed's prophetic call. Most Shi'ites believe Mohammed had twelve such descendents, called *imams*. According to Shi'ite theology, the Twelfth Imam was taken directly to heaven without dying. Before judgment day, he will return to earth to call true Muslims to the faith. Sunnis dismiss this theology, arguing that it is a heresy.

When Mohammed died in C.E. 632, the community split. The group eventually becoming the Sunnis elected Abu Bakr as Mohammed's successor. Two years later they elected Omar, and upon Omar's death, Uthman.

Another group of Muslims believed that Mohammed's male heir, Ali, should become the leader, or Caliph, of the umma. (Ali was married to Mohammed's oldest daughter, Fatima. Mohammed had no sons.) When Uthman was assassinated, Ali finally became Caliph. He stepped aside when he saw that his election would bring about a civil war, but he was assassinated by a radical follower.

Ali's son, Ibn Ali Hussein (literally "the son of Ali, Hussein") led a group of followers to reclaim the Caliphate. His followers, the Shiat Ali (the followers of Ali, or Shi'ites) marched to Karbala to fight the governor of Damascus. Warned in a dream that he would be killed, Hussein dismissed all but seventy-two of his followers. The seventy-two composed the vanguard of the original Party of God. They were killed at Karbala, but their deaths ensured the continuation of Ali followers.

The followers of Ali (Shi'ites) believe they are the true Muslims. The followers of the Four Rightly Guided Caliphs (Abu Bakr, Omar, Uthman, and Ali), or the Sunnis, believe *they* follow the straight path of Islam. Regardless, the name Party of God originated with the Shi'ites and was entombed in a shrine at Karbala in C.E. 680.

Sources: Armstrong (2000), Farrah (2000), Ruthven (2000).

Hussein for further discussion about the split between Shi'ite and Sunni Muslims.) In 1979 the ayatollahs ruled Iran, and the Grand **Ayatollah Khomeini** commanded the Revolutionary Guards.

Go to **http://cj.wadsworth.com/white_terrorism5e** and click on Web Links for a detailed description of the Iranian Revolution and the influence of the Shi'ite sect.

The Iranian Revolution made many Sunni Muslims nervous because the Revolutionary Guards vowed to create revolutionary Shi'ite governments throughout the Muslim world. An eight-year war with Iraq, however, seemed to block Khomeini's plans for revolution, and his Revolutionary Guards spent less time spreading ideals and more time keeping Iran's ayatollahs in power during the first year of the Iran-Iraq War (1980–1988). The situation changed in 1982 when Israel invaded Lebanon.

Judith Harik (2004, pp. 29–39) explains the complicated factors that moved Shi'ite revolutionaries from Iran to Lebanon, giving birth to Hezbollah. Secular Syrian Ba'athists wanted to establish power in Lebanon to regain control of the Golan Heights, an area taken by Israel in the 1967 Six-Day War (see Chapter 9). (The Ba'athist movement was a pan-Arabic socialist party designed to create a secular Arab renaissance.) At the same time, Lebanon was locked in a multifaceted civil war that began in 1975 and would last fifteen years. Secular Palestinians in the Palestine Liberation Organization (PLO) moved into the Shi'ite areas of southern Lebanon after they were expelled from Jordan in 1970. The Syrians backed the southern Shi'ites in the civil war, and this pitted the Shi'ites and Syrians against the PLO. The PLO also used its bases in southern Lebanon to attack Israel. The Israelis, incensed, wanted to strike the PLO and invaded Lebanon in 1982 to drive the PLO from the south.

The Israeli invasion of Lebanon created an unlikely alliance among Iran's Revolutionary Guards, secular Syrian Ba'athists, and southern Lebanese Shi'ites. Iran's foreign policy under the Ayatollah Khomeini's Revolutionary Guards was designed to spread religious revolutionary thought throughout the Muslim world. On the surface, the fervently religious Khomeini had little in common with the secular socialists in Syria, but the Syrians were supporting Shi'ites in southern Lebanon. When Israeli tanks rolled through southern Lebanon, they rolled through Shi'ite villages, and the Revolutionary Guards begged the Ayatollah Khomeini for a chance to protect their fellow believers in Lebanon. Secular Syria and religious Iran now had a common enemy.

Harik points out that both nations needed a surrogate to fight the Israelis. If Iran openly intervened in the **Lebanese Civil War** (1975–1990), Israel or the United States might attack Iran. Syria also needed a proxy because its troops were no match for the Israeli Defense Force (IDF), and like Iran, it feared the United States. As Shi'ite militias resisted the Israeli invasion, one group began to form in the shadows of the civil war. It centered around a **nonorganization**, that is, a governing council to share ideas, plans, and money but designed to disappear and leave autonomous groups to carry out attacks under a variety of names. They called themselves Hezbollah, or the Party of God, and their shadowy nature was ideal for the plans of Syria and Iran (see Figure 8.7).

Iranian officials made contact with the Syrians in 1982. Promising reduced oil prices to Syria, the Iranians asked for permission to move Revolutionary Guards across Syrian territory to eastern Lebanon. Syria agreed to let one thousand Revolutionary Guards cross its borders and move to the Bekaa Valley in Lebanon (see Figure 8.8).

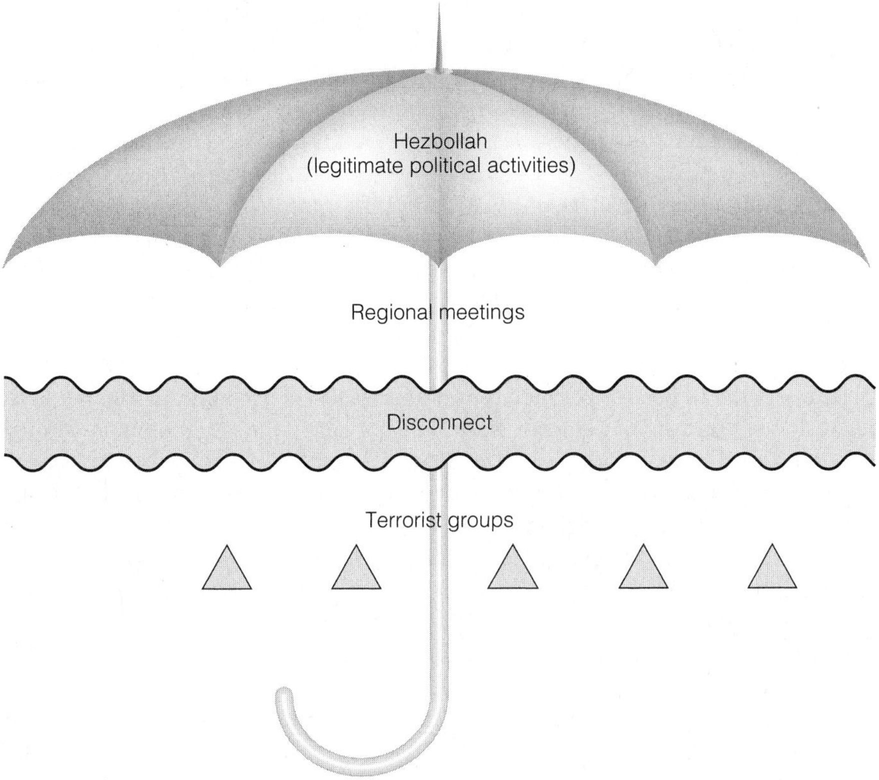

Figure 8.7
Hezbollah Umbrella,
circa 1985

Hezbollah
(legitimate political activities)

Regional meetings

Disconnect

Terrorist groups

The Revolutionary Guards made links with the emerging Hezbollah and provided the Lebanese Shi'ite group with money, weapons, and training. Yet, both Syria and Iran wanted to maintain their distance, and the religious leaders of Hezbollah wanted to deny any affiliation with military action. As a result, Hezbollah became a terrorist organization like no one had yet seen (Hiro, 1987, pp. 113–181, 240–243; Taheri, 1987; Kurz, 1994; Wege, 1994; Ranstorp 1994, 1996).

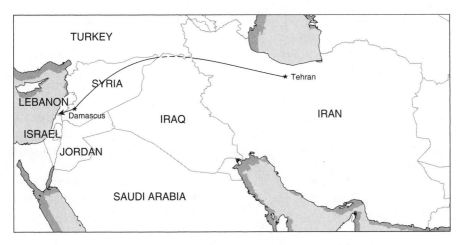

Figure 8.8
The Movement of the
Revolutionary Guards
through Syria to
Lebanon, 1982

Hezbollah grew from a council of Shi'ite scholars who claimed to be part of a spiritual movement. In essence, this council became a large umbrella. Overhead, Syrian and Iranian money and supplies poured into the movement, but Hezbollah denied any direct connection. Below the umbrella, several Shi'ite cells operated autonomously and received money, weapons, and ideas through hidden channels linked with the spiritual leaders. The leadership also formed alliances with two Lebanese Shi'ite groups, Al Dawa and Islamic Amal, while claiming to be a religious movement designed to support Lebanon's Shi'ite community (Gambill and Abdelnour, 2002).

During the first few years of its existence, Hezbollah acted more or less like a terrorist clearinghouse (Reuters, 4-12-96). Following orders from Iran, Hezbollah met as an independent organization, always willing to deny its Iranian connections. According to Israeli intelligence (Israeli Foreign Ministry, 1996), Hezbollah developed under the leadership of three central figures: Sheik Mohammed **Hassan Fadlallah**, **Abus Musawi**, and **Hassan Nasrallah**. Fadlallah, the target of an attempted U.S.-sponsored assassination, was a charismatic spiritual leader. Musawi provided the loose connections to Iran. Nasrallah was a practical militarist, leaving the Islamic Amal militia to organize Hezbollah into a regional force.

In phase one of the development of Hezbollah, from 1982 to 1985 (see Timeline 8.1), the Hezbollah umbrella covered many terrorist groups, including a shadowy organization known as Islamic Jihad. According to Amir Taheri (1987), Hezbollah leaders met in the city of Baalbek in Lebanon's Bekaa Valley and issued nebulous "suggestions" to Islamic Jihad. They also provided financial and logistical support for terrorist operations but kept themselves out of the day-to-day affairs of the terrorist group. By keeping their distance, Hezbollah's leaders were able to claim they had no direct knowledge of Islamic Jihad, and more importantly, they kept Iran from being directly linked to Islamic Jihad's terrorist campaign against Israel and the West. The tactic was successful, and other groups formed under the umbrella.

After 1985 Hezbollah began to change. As part of an organization designed to spread the Shi'ite revolution, Hezbollah was not content to act only as an umbrella group to support terrorism (Enteshami, 1995; Reuters, 4-21-96). Its leaders wanted to develop a revolutionary movement similar to that which gripped Iran in 1978 and 1979. Lebanon was inundated with several militias fighting for control of the government, and Nasrallah saw an opportunity. By following the pattern of the Amal militia, he began changing the structure of Hezbollah. In 1985, he established regional centers, transforming them to operational bases between 1987 and 1989.

Hezbollah literally went on the warpath. After introducing suicide bombers in its initial phase, Hezbollah struck U.S. Marines and the French Army in October 1983, forcing a withdrawal of a multinational peacekeeping force. The marine barracks bombing resulted in the deaths of two hundred marines, while a second suicide bomber killed fifty French soldiers. In its second phase, Hezbollah's leadership launched a kidnapping campaign in Beirut. Westerners, especially Americans, were taken hostage, but Hezbollah always denied any affiliation with the group conducting the operation.

Tactics were extremely effective in the first two phases. Suicide actions and other bombings disrupted Lebanon. The U.S. embassy was targeted for a bomb attack, and Hezbollah managed to kill the top six CIA operatives in the Middle East. Two of Hezbollah's kidnappings were simply designed to murder the victims. Hezbollah kidnapped, tortured, and murdered the CIA station chief in Beirut, as well as a marine

Timeline 8.1

Phases of Hezbollah

1982–1985, Organizing	Different groups carry out attacks under a variety of names.
1985–1990, Kidnapping and Bombing	A terrorist organization is created.
1990–2000, Legitimacy	The group organizes social services, a political party, and a military wing.
2000–Present, Coalition	Hezbollah forms temporary alliances with others in the September 2000 Palestinian uprising against Israel (the al Aqsa Intifada).

colonel working for the United Nations. Judith Harik (2004, p. 37) points out that no evidence directly linked Hezbollah to these actions, and the group denied links to terrorism, denouncing terrorism as a tactic. This strategy made the group extremely effective.

The third phase of Hezbollah's metamorphosis came in 1990. Taking over the organization after the death of Musawi, Nasrallah created a regional militia by 1990. In 1991, many of Lebanon's roving paramilitary groups signed a peace treaty, but Hezbollah retained its weapons and revolutionary philosophy and became the primary paramilitary force in southern Lebanon (U.S. Department of State, 1996; Reuters, 4-21-96). It claimed to be a legitimate guerrilla force, resisting the Israeli occupation of the area. Hezbollah's militia, however, soon found itself in trouble. Squabbling broke out among various groups, and Hezbollah was forced to fight Syria and Islamic Amal. Diplomatic pressure increased for the release of hostages. Nasrallah took bold steps in response. He sought peace with the Syrians, and with Syrian approval, Western hostages were gradually released. Far from claiming responsibility for the hostages, both Hezbollah and Syria claimed credit for gaining their freedom. Hezbollah's militia began to operate in the open, and it stepped up its campaign against the Israelis in Lebanon. This made the organization popular among Lebanese citizens and gave the group the appearance of a guerrilla unit.

Nasrallah had one more trump card. With the blessing of fellow council members, Hezbollah joined the Lebanese political process. Hezbollah's fourth phase brought the organization from the shadows. Its militia, while operating as a guerrilla

Another Perspective

Nasrallah's Management of Image

What is Hezbollah? Judith Harik (2004) says the answer to this question depends on the audience. Hassan Nasrallah has four different answers for different audiences. For the four groups below, he has four different answers.

1. Jihadists: He uses militant language and speaks of holy war.
2. Nationalists: He avoids jihad analogies and calls on Sunnis, Shi'ites, Christians, and secularists to fight for Lebanon.
3. Pan-Arabic: He points to Israel as a colony of the West and denounces Europe's imperial past.
4. International: He cites United Nations resolutions and claims that Israel violates international law.

Harik concludes that this is not the pattern of an intolerant religious fanatic. Instead, this ability to compromise for various purposes demonstrates Nasrallah's political skills.

Source: Harik (2004).

force, repeatedly struck the Israelis in Lebanon. The success of this action brought political payoffs, and by 1995 Hezbollah developed strong political bases of support in parts of Beirut, the Bekaa Valley, and its stronghold in southern Lebanon. It created a vast organization of social services, including schools, hospitals, and public works. This final change worked. In 1998 Hezbollah won a number of seats in Beirut while maintaining control of the south. When Palestinians rose against the Israelis in 2000, Hezbollah embraced their cause, and its transformation was complete. It was a nationalistic group with a military wing, and its stated goals were to eliminate Israel and to establish an Islamic government in Lebanon.

Daniel Byman (2003) says Hezbollah managed to do something else in its last transition. It emerged as an international group. Watching the success of al Qaeda, Hezbollah spread its umbrella throughout the world. It established links in Asia, Africa, and the Tri-Border Region of South America (see Chapter 5, page 72). It also created a presence in Europe and the United States. According to Deputy Secretary of State Richard Armitage, Hezbollah is the "A-Team" among terrorist groups. Al Qaeda, Armitage says, is only the "B-Team."

The Current State of Hezbollah

 Key Concepts and Questions:

1. Describe Hezbollah's organizational structure.
2. How does Hezbollah use its military wing?
3. What is Hezbollah International?
4. Who is Imad Mugniyah?
5. Why is the Tri-Border Region important?

Magnus Ranstorp (1994) finds Hezbollah to be one of the strongest non-state groups in the Middle East. Its leaders, who are called *clerics* in the Western press but *ulema*, or Islamic scholars, by Muslims, are associated with the Shi'ite seminary in Najaf, Iraq. It is organized in three directorates: a political wing, a social services wing, and a security wing (see Figure 8.9). A separate international group in the security wing, **Hezbollah International**, is managed by master international terrorist Imad Mugniyah (Goldberg, 2002). In the wake of the weakness of Lebanon's government, Hezbollah maintains strongholds in southern Lebanon, the Bekaa Valley, and central pockets in Beirut. Each directorate is subservient to a Supreme Council, currently headed by Hassan Nasrallah.

Most of Hezbollah's activities deal with the politics of Lebanon and the vast social service network it maintains in the south. The security wing is based in Lebanon and is responsible for training guerrillas and terrorists. (Supporters of Hezbollah do not make a distinction between *guerrillas* and *terrorists*.) Guerrillas are assigned to militias that operate along Israel's northern border, especially in the Sha'ba farm region. These paramilitary fighters frequently conduct operations in the open, and they engage in conventional military confrontations with the IDF. Hezbollah can maintain all of these operations because it receives funding from Iran.

Figure 8.9
Hezbollah, circa
2004

```
                    Supreme
                    council
                       │
                    Shura
                    council
                       │
   ┌───────────┬───────────┬───────────┐ - - - - - - ┐
   │           │           │           │             │
Security    Political    Social      Finance    Hezbollah
                        services                International
   │           │           │           │
Military    Regional    Schools,    Local and
           political    hospitals,  international
           activities   and other   operations
                        services
```

Terrorists also operate along the border with and sometimes in Israel, engaging in murder and kidnapping. Although Israel is their acknowledged enemy, Hezbollah terrorists have targeted Lebanese Christians and other Arabs not sympathetic to their cause. The primary terrorist tactic is bombing, and Hezbollah has mastered two forms: suicide bombing and radio-controlled bombs for ambushes.

Hezbollah International is a shadowy group, and the Supreme Council denies its existence (Goldberg, 2002). The international section has cells in several different countries, including the United States, and maintains an extensive international finance ring partially based on smuggling, drugs, and other crimes. Imad Mugniyah keeps close ties with operatives in the Tri-Border Region and Ciudad del Este and also runs a terrorist training camp off the coast of Venezuela. Mugniyah met with al Qaeda, possibly Osama bin Laden, in the mid-1990s and allegedly taught al Qaeda terrorists methods for attacking buildings.

A Sympathetic View of Hezbollah

Key Concepts and Questions:

1. List the ways Hezbollah can be described as a self-defense force.
2. What is the main focus of Hezbollah?
3. How do most Arabs view Hezbollah?
4. Why did Hezbollah enter politics?
5. What is Hezbollah's position on Palestinians living in Lebanon?
6. Describe Hassan Fadlallah's response to al Qaeda's attacks on September 11.

Many voices in Lebanon and elsewhere claim that Hezbollah is a legitimate self-defense force. Hala Jaber (1997, pp. 38–39) summarizes this view in a journalistic examination of Hezbollah. Although Western analysts date the origin of Hezbollah to 1982, the organization claims it was formed in 1985. Members say they had nothing to do with the suicide bombings of U.S. Marines and the French Army in 1983, and they deny they were behind the kidnappings of Westerners in Beirut from 1983 to 1990. Instead, they claim that Hezbollah grew from the Lebanese Civil War.

According to Jaber's research, supporters claim that Hezbollah had no intention of spreading the Iranian Revolution; they merely wanted to defend their community. Although they began to fight against the Israeli invaders in 1985, they also fought the Syrians and the Amal militia in 1988. Supporters claim they are a religious and political organization supporting a guerrilla army, and the purpose of the army is to defeat Israel.

According to Jaber (1997, pp. 207–212), Hezbollah members maintain that it is not a crime to resist the Israelis. In fact, many Hezbollah guerrillas simply refer to themselves as the "**Islamic resistance**." The military wing is a small part of the organization. The main focus is social service in the form of education, health services, and social security. Jessica Stern (2003b, p. 47) says that Hezbollah guerrillas know they cannot confront the Israeli Defense Force (IDF) in a conventional war so they use guerrilla tactics, and Hezbollah guerrillas believe that fighting the Israelis is not an act of terrorism.

Research by the Council on Foreign Relations (2004) concludes that most Arabs find Hezbollah to be a source of inspiration. While no Arab nation has ever beaten the Israelis or the West, Hezbollah has a track record of success. If one dates the origin of the group to 1982 and credits Hezbollah with the October 1983 suicide bombings, Arabs believe that Hezbollah forced the French and Americans to withdraw from Lebanon. No Arab nation had ever defeated the West, but Hezbollah did. In 1985 the IDF retreated from central Lebanon, and it abandoned the south in 1990. Once again, Arabs never saw their governments beat the Israelis, but the IDF fled from the power of Hezbollah. Far from being viewed as a terrorist organization, Hezbollah has achieved heroic status in the eyes of many Arabs.

Gary Gambill and Ziad Abdelnour (2002) say that Hezbollah's entry into politics further legitimized its activities. Mohammed Fneish, a Hezbollah representative in the Lebanese parliament, told journalist Tim Cavanaugh (3-11-04) that Hezbollah has the right to resist Israeli aggression after Israel invaded Lebanon. Even after the Israelis left, Fneish claims, the Israelis continued to strike against targets in Lebanon and to occupy Palestinian lands. Fneish says Hezbollah is a political and social service organization, but it will resist Israel. He says there is no relation with Iraqi Shi'ites, but the Iraqi Arabs are inspired by Hezbollah's example.

Alasdair Soussi (6-14-04) writes that most Hezbollah members reflect Fneish's feelings, pointing to Hezbollah's large-scale health care and education systems as evidence that their emphasis is primarily humanitarian. They also claim that the group's goal is to assist the four hundred thousand Palestinians living in Lebanon. Hezbollah supporters believe the organization is nothing more than a resistance movement against Israel and that it soldiers are guerrillas and commandos stationed along the border. Supporters point to the fact that Hassan Fadlallah, Hezbollah's spiritual leader, condemned the September 11 attacks as un-Islamic, refusing to call the hijackers "martyrs" and maintaining they committed suicide while murdering innocent people (Council on Foreign Relations, 2004).

A Critical View of Hezbollah

Key Concepts and Questions:

1. How does the State Department view Hezbollah?
2. List the reasons the Council on Foreign Relations describes Hezbollah as a terrorist group.
3. What are the two purposes of Hezbollah's existence?
4. Describe Hezbollah's terrorist record.
5. What type of threats might develop from Hezbollah International?
6. Why has the Lebanese segment of Hezbollah formed alliances with Palestinian groups?

Despite the above arguments, many people in the world consider Hezbollah to be a terrorist organization. The U.S. Department of State (2004b) summarizes this point of view in its 2004 revised report on terrorism: Hezbollah is a deadly international terrorist organization that has developed international links and uses international crime to finance operations. Its primary sponsor is Iran, and it receives secondary support from Syria, nations that are listed as state sponsors of terrorism. In addition to its murders of Israelis, Hezbollah has killed U.S. citizens and kidnapped and tortured Americans. The State Department sees Hezbollah as a group of international murderers.

The Council on Foreign Relations (2004) reflects the State Department's view. Hezbollah is a terrorist organization because of the suicide attacks it carried out against civilian and peacekeeping forces and because of its kidnapping rampage from 1983 to 1990. It was also involved in the 1985 hijacking of a TWA flight, during which an American was murdered, and two bombings in Argentina in 1992 and 1994. It has been responsible for a campaign of suicide bombings, the murders of Lebanese Christians, international arms smuggling, and a host of international criminal activity, including crimes in the United States.

Critics also point to Hezbollah's uncompromising political stand, saying that it exists for only two reasons: to impose a Shi'ite government on Lebanon and to destroy the state of Israel. Hezbollah parliamentary representative Mohammed Fneish says that Hezbollah will not force Lebanon to become an Islamic republic like Iran, but his party will campaign for it. After Hezbollah is elected, it can take the necessary steps of consolidating power. As far as the elimination of Israel goes, Fneish says Israel was created illegally by Europeans and Americans who felt guilty about the Nazi death camps. They created Israel, he says, as a way of apologizing. Hezbollah does not recognize Israel's right to exist, and it must be eliminated (Cavanaugh, 3-11-04).

Other researchers also condemn Hezbollah. Alasdair Soussi (6-14-04) says Hezbollah exports its revolutionary ideals, claiming that contacts exist between Hezbollah and the Iraqi resistance movement. Maqtada al Sadr, the Shi'ite leader of the Mahdi Army in Iraq, is linked to Hezbollah's Hassan Nasrallah. Daniel Byman (2003), a professor in security studies at Georgetown University, says there is no question about the terrorist agenda of Hezbollah. It might have credibility in the Islamic world, but its record of bloodshed and hostility speaks for itself. It is not a question of whether the United States should stop Hezbollah, Byman writes, it is a question of how.

Jessica Stern (2003b) points out that Hezbollah interacts with other terrorist groups around the world. Rather than standing alone as a terrorist group, it is part of a network of groups that range from Jihadists to traffickers in narcotics. Jeffery Goldberg (2002) says that the director of Imad Mugniyah of Hezbollah International is the primary culprit behind these links. Both Stern and Goldberg believe the network blends Hezbollah with al Qaeda. The existence of the international aspect of Hezbollah, according to such research, proves that the organization is part of an international Jihadist struggle that uses crime and state support to wage a campaign of terror.

Jaber (1997, p. 1) characterizes the practical outcome of Hezbollah in the lives of everyday people in the opening scene of her book. In her scenario, a boy named Mohammed Ghandour and his younger sister watch a video showing a car laden with explosives driving into an Israeli convoy. When the car explodes, Mohammed exclaims, "There's my daddy." In her moving portrait of the Ghandour family, Jaber describes the differing views of the Israelis and the Lebanese.

Hezbollah is part of the Jihadist network, but its origins and reasons for existing are found in the struggle over Palestine. It has reluctantly formed alliances with many of the non-Jihadist groups such as the Palestinian Islamic Jihad, Hamas, the Popular Front for the Liberation of Palestine, and the al Aqsa Martyrs Brigades. Since the start of the al Aqsa Intifada, a Palestinian uprising starting in September 2000, the distinction among many of the pro-Palestinian groups has blurred. Daniel Byman (2003) concludes that the international operations of Hezbollah could potentially be neutralized if the United States were to repair its relationship with Syria and Iran.

Hezbollah provided a model for the formation of an international umbrella of terrorist organizations. The international section remains a conglomeration of like-minded semiautonomous groups. The model inspired the formation of other networks, and none was as important as the groups related to al Qaeda. As Osama bin Laden and Ayman al Zawahiri modified the Hezbollah model within al Qaeda, a plethora of terrorist groups exploded from the Afghan jihad. The allied and semiautonomous groups give an aura to the al Qaeda mystique, and the Jihadist network strengthens al Qaeda's striking power.

Summary of Main Points

1. When al Qaeda moved back to Afghanistan in 1996, a number of allied Jihadist groups were operating in Central, South, and Southeast Asia.

2. Terrorist groups in North Africa predated al Qaeda, but many allied with the Jihadist movement. North Africa became a springboard for attacking the West.

3. Jihadists use the tactics other terrorists have used, but they combine them in new ways.

4. Iranian Revolutionary Guards went to Lebanon through Syria in 1982 and created Hezbollah.

5. Hezbollah has changed several times during its existence. It maintains links with Iran and Syria.

6. In Lebanon, Hezbollah is organized around three main branches: a political wing, a social services wing, and a security wing. Much of the organization's activities center on running for political offices and providing social services.

7. Hezbollah has an international organization outside Lebanon with branches throughout the world. Hezbollah International often works in conjunction with organized crime, drug traffickers, and other terrorists.

8. Supporters of Hezbollah claim that it is a legitimate organization designed to fight Israel.

9. Critics claim that Hezbollah is a terrorist organization that engages in bombing, murder, kidnapping, torture, and other crimes.

10. Hezbollah is part of the Jihadist network, but it is also deeply immersed in the Israeli-Palestinian conflict.

Key Terms

Make sure you can define, explain, or identify the following people, ideas, organizations, or terms:

the "Stans"   122

Jammu and Kashmir   123

Sikhs   123

Lashkar Jihad   125

Jamaat Islamiyya   125

Algerian Civil War   128

Muslim Brotherhood   129

Luxor massacre   129

Hezbollah   130

Iranian Revolution   130

Revolutionary Guards   131

Shi'ite   131

Sunni   131

Ayatollah Khomeini   132

Lebanese Civil War   132

nonorganization   132

Hassan Fadlallah   134

Abus Musawi   134

Hassan Nasrallah   134

Hezbollah International   136

"Islamic resistance"   138

Suggested Readings

Now that you've been introduced to this topic, you can learn more by reading:

Ahmad Rashid's *Jihad: The Rise of Militant Islam in Central Asia* provides an in-depth look at the politics surrounding terrorism in Central Asia.

Zachary Abuza's *Militant Islam in Southeast Asia* details a comprehensive picture of the region.

Judith Palmer Harik's *Hezbollah: The Changing Face of Terrorism* describes the way Hezbollah changed throughout its history and the manner it blends with international terrorism.

Magnus Ranstorp's *Hizb'Allah in Lebanon* is an analysis of the hostage crisis during the period when Hezbollah actively kidnapped Westerners.

You may also want to read:

Hala Jaber, *Hezbollah*, looks at the organization through the eyes of an experienced journalist.

Jonathan Randal's *Going All the Way* is an account of the 1982 Israeli invasion of Lebanon.

Amal Saad-Ghorayeb, in *Hizbu'llah*, examines the political and religious struggles Hezbollah has faced during its turbulent history.

Web Resources

Go to *http://cj.wadsworth.com/white_terrorism5e* and click on Web Links to find:

- A background article about Hezbollah by Gary C. Gambill and Ziad Abdelnour
- Articles on terrorism and political violence, including one by Magnus Ranstorp
- Recent reports and briefings from the International Crisis Group, a group that works to prevent and resolve conflict around the world

The Companion Website for *Terrorism and Homeland Security*, Fifth Edition
http://cj.wadsworth.com/white_terrorism5e

At the Book Companion Website you can review chapter outlines, use the flash cards to test your terrorism vocabulary, and check out the many other study aids you'll find there. You'll find valuable data and resources at your fingertips to help you study for that big exam or write that important paper.

Terrorism Updates
http://www.wadsworth.com/criminaljustice_d/special_features/ext/terrorism_site090802/index.html

Visit the *Terrorism: An Interdisciplinary Perspective* website to find the most current information about the fields of terrorism and homeland security. With a focus on domestic and international issues, this site explores the scope of terrorism in our world today. You'll find essays on important topics in terrorism and homeland security, critical thinking web activities, and InfoTrac College Edition keywords. Most importantly, the website is updated weekly with current news and research articles on domestic and international terrorism. You are invited to use these web resources to supplement your understanding of the topics covered in this chapter.

Current Perspectives: Readings from InfoTrac College Edition
Terrorism and Homeland Security

The sixteen articles in this reader offer a representative selection that helps you understand the important issues about terrorism and homeland security. It includes FREE access to InfoTrac College Edition and can also be bundled with the text for free.

Chapter 9

The Question of Israel and Palestine

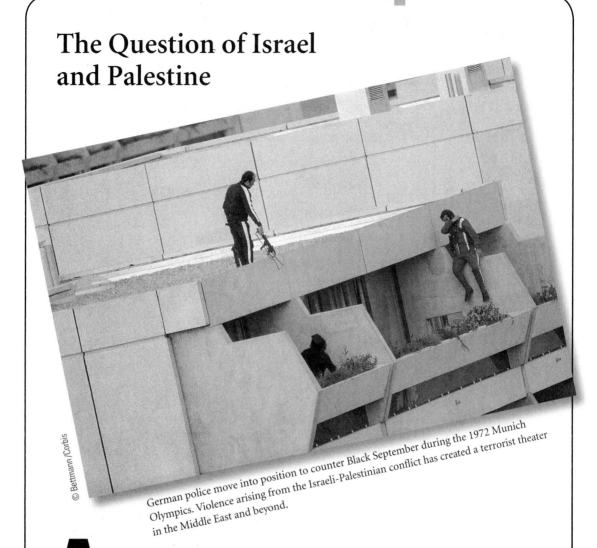

© Bettmann/Corbis

German police move into position to counter Black September during the 1972 Munich Olympics. Violence arising from the Israeli-Palestinian conflict has created a terrorist theater in the Middle East and beyond.

Although much of the world's attention has focused since 2001 on Jihadist networks, long-term conflict and terrorism in the Middle East continue. There is, in fact, a symbiotic relationship between the Jihadists and Middle Eastern terrorism; that is, they are separate yet interdependent, and they feed off one another. Most of the groups associated with the struggle over Israel and Palestine—with the notable exception of Hezbollah—have espoused relatively few international aspirations, although they maintain international Jihadist connections. This chapter explores the background of violence that has dominated the areas of Israel and Palestine for the past one hundred years.

Chapter Objectives

After reading this chapter, you should be able to:

1. Explain the origins of the Israeli-Palestinian conflict.
2. Describe the birth and development of the PLO.
3. Outline the rise and purpose of the group called Black September.
4. Describe how Palestinian terrorism influenced international terrorism.
5. Explain the effect of the 1982 Israeli invasion of Lebanon on the structure of Middle Eastern terrorism.
6. Summarize issues in the current Israeli-Palestinian conflict.
7. Define terms and issues associated with the Israeli-Palestinian conflict.

The Origins of the Conflict

Key Points and Questions:

1. How did the conflict between Zionists and Palestinians begin?
2. What promises did the British make to Arabs, Jews, and the French during World War I?
3. What happened to the Middle East between the wars?
4. How did Arabs in general respond to the creation of Israel?
5. Why did the Palestinians turn to terrorism?

Very few of the world's conflicts create as much emotion as the confrontation between Israel and the Palestinians and their allies. Both sides distort the position of the other, and efforts to bring moderates together are hampered by a continuing cycle of bombing and retaliation. If you speak of Palestinian rights, hard-line supporters of Israel may call you a terrorist. On the other hand, if you speak to Palestinians, Arabs, or even Muslims in general about Israel's right to exist, Israel's enemies may dismiss you as a **Zionist**, that is, a person favoring the creation of a Jewish state. Why is there such hatred? A brief overview of recent history explains the problems. (See Timeline 9.1.)

Yonah Alexander (1976, pp. 211–257) explains that the modern animosity began in the 1890s when European Jews began flocking to Palestine to create a Jewish state. The Palestinian Arabs welcomed the Jews because their land was controlled by the Turks, and the Arabs felt the Jews would assist in a revolt against the Turks. But this proved to be a sticky point. The Zionists were willing to remove the Turks, but they also wanted control of Palestine without interference from the Palestinians. The Zionists were also backed by a significant amount of money from the United Kingdom and the United States.

World War I (1914–1918) complicated the issue. The British, who were fighting the Turks, hinted that they would allow Arabs all through the region to unite in one government if the Arabs would revolt against the Turks. At the same time, they promised the Zionists they would recognize the creation of Israel. Unfortunately, Israel would have been located right in the center of the land the British seemed to promise

Timeline 9.1

The Israel-Palestine Conflict

1948	Many Palestinian Arabs flee Israel. General war results in Arab defeat.
1956	The Suez Crisis. Israel defeats Egypt.
1959	Fatah is created.
1964	The PLO is created in the Arab-occupied West Bank.
1965	Fatah launches its first attack.
1967	Six-Day War. All Arab nations are decisively defeated.
1968	Battle of Karamah.
1969–1970	The terrorist campaign increases.
1970	King Hussein of Jordan drives the PLO to Lebanon.
1970	Different PLO groups launch their own terrorist campaigns.
1972	Black September strikes the Munich Olympics.
1973	Egypt and Syria strike Israel, and Egypt wins an initial success. The Israelis counterattack and the United States intervenes to keep a surrounded Egyptian army from being destroyed.
1978	Camp David Peace Accords.
1981	Egyptian president Anwar Sadat assassinated by Egyptian Jihadists.
1982	Israel invades Lebanon; Hezbollah formed.
1987	The first Intifada begins; Hamas forms.
1988	Jordan gives up its claim to the West Bank; Arafat renounces terrorism and recognizes Israel.
1990	Iraq's leader Saddam Hussein embraces the PLO.
1992	Arafat and the Israelis begin a dialogue.
1993	Oslo Accords.
1995	Arafat and the Israelis conduct elections in the Occupied Territories.
1996	Hamas terrorism threatens peace; Arafat cracks down on terrorist groups.
1998	Palestinians and Israelis agree to the Wye Accords.
2000	Israel retreats from Lebanon; the PLO and Israel begin direct dialogues in Washington, D.C.
2000	Al Aqsa Intifada begins in November.
2004	Arafat dies.

the Arabs. The British, however, made another promise to the French—a promise to split the Middle East when the war was over. They kept that last promise, infuriating both the Arabs and the Jews (Becker, 1984, p. 9).

The British created the modern nations of the Middle East and supported local rulers of Arab tribes that had helped them during the war. They established a protective zone around Palestine and Jordan, hoping to keep a foothold in the area. Both the Arab Palestinians and the Jews fought British rule. Both sides used terrorism, and the Jews created two modern terrorist organizations, the **Irgun Zvai Leumi** and the **Stern Gang**. Fighting slowed in Palestine during the early stages of World War II (1939–1945), but terrorism reemerged before the end of the war.

After the war, Jews victimized by Nazi persecution flocked to Palestine, where they fought the British and sought to create an independent Jewish state. By 1948 the British were exhausted. With the strong support of the United States, the British supported the creation of the modern nation of **Israel**. Almost every nation in the world joined the effort, except the Arabs, and the United Nations recognized Israel in 1948. The Arabs felt completely powerless, but the new Israelis were overjoyed.

The Arabs decided to take matters into their own hands and attacked Israel in 1948. They were soundly defeated. Thousands of Palestinians found that they were no longer welcomed in the new country of Israel, and their Arab neighbors did little to help them. The Arabs fought the Israelis on and off for nearly forty years, and they were defeated each time.

After Egypt saved face in an offensive in 1973, it sought peace with Israel. Jordan also joined this peace process, but Syria and Iraq strongly rejected any peace, as well as Israel's right to exist. The militant Arabs who joined the Syrians and Iraqis called themselves the **Rejectionist Front** because they rejected the right of Israel to exist.

Many Palestinians continued to fight the Israelis, and they were supported by Arab nationalists and more conservative Arabs from Saudi Arabia and the Gulf states. Since the Palestinians were not strong enough to attack the **Israeli Defense Force (IDF)** directly, they used other tactics, referring to their actions as *military operations* and *commando tactics*. They bombed public places, attacked farms, and conducted open murder. Most Israelis and most of the people in the West called these actions terrorism.

The Rise of the PLO

In 1968, Cuba hosted a number of revolutionary groups in a training session outside Havana (History Channel, 2000). Several leftist and nationalist groups and individuals from around the world attended the event, including **Yasser Arafat**, leader of the **Palestine Liberation Organization (PLO)**. Arafat stated that revolution united all revolutionaries from the past to the present. He embraced other terrorists in the Cuban training camps and promised to join them in international revolution. It seemed to some that Arafat's organization could be part of an international conspiracy.

In reality, however, the PLO was an attempt to set up a quasi-government for displaced Palestinians. Some lived in Israel, some in Palestinian areas controlled by Israel, and some simply moved to other countries. In 1957, Arafat gathered groups of disgruntled Palestinians in Jordan, and in 1964, he formed the PLO. His purpose was to create a political organization to help form a multinational alliance against Israel. He hoped Arab governments would jointly launch a war against the European-created state.

After Israel's initial fight for independence in 1948, the IDF defeated its Arab foes in 1956, 1967, and 1973 (the *Arab-Israeli Wars*; see Another Perspective: Important Terms, Concepts, and People in the Middle East). Arab armies looked strong on paper, but they were torn with internal dissension and by officer corps more involved in internal politics than military proficiency (Bill and Leiden, 1984, p. 261). Their armies could not fight well against the IDF, and the 1967 war devastated Arab and Palestinian morale. As the Palestinians looked for a new military champion, Yasser Arafat stepped forward to assume the role. Joining a group of young Palestinians, Arafat formed a quasi-military organization called **Fatah** in 1959 and merged it into the PLO in 1964. After Arab defeats in 1967 and 1973, Fatah became stronger.

The self-made leader of the PLO proposed terrorizing unfortified civilian targets (Wallach and Wallach, 1992). Using a group of Fatah warriors known as **fedayeen**, Arafat and Kahlil Wazir (also known as Abu Jihad, killed by Israeli intelligence in April 1988) began to attack Israel. Fatah ran its first operation in 1965, blowing up an Israeli water pump. After the 1967 **Six-Day War**, Arafat began launching hit-and-run strikes against Israel from Jordan. The actions made Arafat a hero in the eyes of the defeated Arabs.

The reality of Fatah's power was less glamorous than Arafat's growing reputation. According to Walter Laqueur (1987, p. 216), Fatah was limited to three tactics: (1) sending small ambush teams from the Jordanian border, (2) planting bombs, and (3) shelling Israeli settlements from Jordan. Arafat called this guerrilla warfare; the Israelis called it terrorism.

The initial media coverage of Fatah's attacks caused the PLO's status to rise throughout the Arab world, and Arafat's fortunes rose along with it. All the conventional Arab armies were in disarray. Only the PLO had the courage and will to strike, and they were outnumbered and outgunned, and they did not even have a country. They had only the fedayeen. Their action was indirect, but the invincible IDF seemed to be incapable of combating the PLO's clandestine tactics.

Fatah after Karamah: A Legend Is Born

Edward Weisband and Damir Roguly (1976, pp. 261–262) say Fatah did not emerge as a significant fighting force until 1968, when it was forced to defend one of its base camps. On March 21, tired of raids from Jordanian-based PLO compounds, the Israelis launched a mechanized assault on the village of Karamah—one of Arafat's primary bases in Jordan. Both sides distorted the facts, but the battle affected the Arab world.

Jillian Becker's (1984, pp. 62–64) account of the raid on Karamah is extremely pro-Israeli, but it reflects the impact the raid had on the Arabs. According to Becker, the Israelis dropped leaflets two hours before the raid, telling Jordanians in the area to leave. The Jordanians dispatched a military force to resist the violation of their territory, and Fatah dug in at Karamah. The Israeli attack was ferocious, supported by

Important Terms, Concepts, and People in the Middle East

Arab-Israeli Wars   A generic terms for several wars:

1948, Israel's fight for independence

1956 Suez Crisis, when Britain, France, and Israel attack Egypt to keep the Suez Canal open; Israel takes the Gaza Strip

1967 Six-Day War, pitting Israel against its Arab neighbors; Israel takes Jerusalem, the West Bank, and other areas

1973 Yom Kippur War (Muslims frequently call it the Ramadan War) when Egypt and Syria strike Israel to regain occupied territories; Egypt is initially successful, but its major army was surrounded in a counterattack.

Arafat, Yasser   Leader of the Palestine Liberation Organization (PLO), later the Palestine National Authority (PNA), and later the Palestine National Council (PNC); widely recognized secular leader of the Palestinian movement.

Baalbek   Lebanese city in the Bekaa Valley; original headquarters of Hezbollah.

Camp David Peace Accords   1978 peace agreement between Egypt and Israel.

Dome of the Rock   The place where Muslims believe Abraham (Ibrahim) had a vision of God.

Eretz Israel   The land of Israel under King David; many Jewish fundamentalists feel God has called them to retake this land and expel the Arabs.

Fedayeen   Warriors who sacrifice.

Gaza Strip   Palestinian strip of land along the Mediterranean.

Golan Heights   Region in Syria overlooking Israel.

Gush Emunim   Literally, Bloc of the Faithful; Jewish group formed in 1974 that believes God literally promised Jews the Kingdom of David.

Habash, George   Christian founder of the Popular Front for the Liberation of Palestine.

Hawatmeh, Naiaf   One of the founders of the Popular Front for the Liberation of Palestine; later led the Democratic Front for the Liberation of Palestine.

Interim Agreement   Follow-up to 1993 Oslo Accords in 1995 to allow elections in Palestinian territory.

Intifada   1987–1993 uprising in Palestinian areas; al Aqsa Intifada began in 2000.

Jabril, Ahmed   Leader of the Popular Front for the Liberation of Palestine; later leader of the Popular Front for the Liberation of Palestine, General Command.

Jewish settlements   Legal and illegal settlements in Palestinians lands; in 2004 Prime Minister Ariel Sharon proposed withdrawing from the Jewish settlements.

Knesset   The Israeli parliament.

(*continued*)

Labor Party   The liberal Israeli political party.

Likud Party   The conservative Israeli political party.

Mossad   The Israeli intelligence service.

Mujahadeen   Holy warriors.

Muslim Brotherhood   An Islamic revivalist organization founded by Hasan al Banna in Cairo in 1928.

Occupied Territories   Palestinian territories under the post–World War I British division of Palestine that were occupied by Israel after the 1967 Six-Day War.

Palestinian diaspora   The displacement in 1948 of Palestinians living in Israel.

Palestine National Authority (PNA) Semiautonomous body established after the Oslo Accords.

Palestine National Council (PNC)   Representative body from the Occupied Territories, the Gaza Strip, and the Palestinian diaspora.

Peace process   Generic term used to describe efforts to create a lasting peace between Palestine and Israel as well as general peace in the area.

Rabin, Yitzak   Israeli Labor Party leader, politician, and prime minister; assassinated in 1995 by a Jewish extremist for brokering a peace plan.

Rejectionist Front   A grouping of individuals, political parties, and states that reject Israel's right to exist.

Roadmap for Peace   The term used by President George W. Bush while trying to bring peace to the Middle East starting in 2002.

Sharon, Ariel   Israeli military officer, defense minister, and prime minister; maintains a hard line against Palestinians.

South Lebanon Army   The security force established by Israel to control south Lebanon after the withdrawal of the Israeli Defense Force in 1985.

Sykes-Picot Pact   A 1916 agreement between Britain and France for control of the Middle East.

Tanzim   Fatah's militia.

Temple Mount   The site of the ancient Jewish Temple, a former Christian church, and the al Aqsa mosque.

Wailing Wall   The remaining western wall of the ancient Jewish Temple in Jerusalem.

West Bank   The West Bank of the Jordan River, formally controlled by Jordon. It was seized by Israel in the 1967 war.

Wye Accords   1998 Israeli-Palestinian agreement to abide by previous commitments.

Zion   The hill on which Jerusalem stands.

Zionist   In contemporary usage, a Jew wishing to reestablish the Jewish homeland; Arabs and many Muslims frequently use the term to refer to all Jews.

armor and helicopter gunships. After heavy fighting, Karamah held firm despite the odds against the Palestinians.

In the minds of Arabs, it was a victory for the PLO, more specifically for Fatah and Arafat. Becker claims this was ironic because it was the Jordanian army that stopped the Israeli armor; Arafat had already fled the scene. Others maintain Arafat was present throughout the fighting. Yet, as Weisband and Roguly point out, the PLO emerged from Karamah with the reputation of a fighting force, and Yasser Arafat became a bona fide hero.

After Karamah, the PLO began a terrorist campaign in earnest against Israel. Many other terrorist groups began to grow within the organization. Like Fatah, they were not strong enough to strike the IDF directly, but they could strike civilians. Terrorism was the only viable military tactic for a small group of relatively weak people who wanted to launch an offensive against a superior force. By attacking civilians, hijacking airplanes, and conducting assassinations, terrorist groups within the PLO could strike against the Israeli military indirectly. In Arafat's defense, the PLO adopted terrorism for the same reason the Irgun Zvai Leumi and the more radical Stern Gang had used it two decades earlier: It was the only tactical option available. The Irgun and Stern Gang targeted Arabs and British military forces in an effort to drive non-Jews from Palestine. Terrorism was a military convenience for Jewish militants, and it served the same purpose for militant groups splintering from Fatah in the PLO.

Arafat became aware that terrorist targets were receiving considerable worldwide media attention. Savage attacks resulted in television news features. Hijackings and hostage-taking incidents brought extended press coverage. They were made-for-TV dramas, and television used terrorists to keep viewers in front of the screen. Therefore, under Arafat's tutelage, the PLO campaign became increasingly dramatic and public. In the media, it appeared that the Palestinians were united in their struggle against Israel, and Arafat was willing to use the power of press to bring attention to the plight of the Palestinian people.

The PLO came to symbolize much more than the plight of the Palestinians in the realm of international terrorism. It emerged as a role model for terrorist groups in the Americas, Europe, and Asia. With the publicity the PLO gained from several airline hijackings, terrorists from other parts of the world went to the Middle East to train with them. Nationalistic militants from Ireland and the Basque region of Spain trained in PLO camps. The ideological left turned to the PLO, and European left-wing terrorists also flocked to PLO training centers. German leftists forged particularly strong links with the Palestinians. Cuba proclaimed that the PLO served as an example for South and Central American revolutionary groups. Arafat's reputation grew beyond the bounds of the Middle East.

In turn, terrorism became an expression of political unity for the PLO; nonetheless, the PLO splintered. When an organization uses terrorism, it must call on true-believing fanatics who do not readily make alliances or compromise with any form of leadership. Despite Arafat's attempt to keep the movement together, various terrorist groups within the PLO started to go their own way as early as 1970. These groups included the Democratic Front for the Liberation of Palestine and the Popular Front for the Liberation of Palestine; and later, individuals such as Abu Abbas, Abu Ibrahim, and Abu Nidal defected. Walter Laqueur (1987) says that when the history of the PLO is written, it will be a chronology of continuous splits among splinter groups.

Arab leaders in Syria and Iraq had long been rivals of Jordan's King Hussein, and they saw potential benefits in the splintering of the PLO. The rival **Ba'athists**, or pan-Arabic socialists, in Syria and Iraq began to view the PLO both as a potential instrument with which to achieve their foreign policy objectives, and as an ally against Jordan. The popularity of the PLO allowed it to act with more and more autonomy, and it joined with Syrian- and Iraqi-sponsored opposition parties in Jordan. This did not please the king of Jordan.

Palestinian Violence Expands

Key Points and Questions:

1. Why did King Hussein force the PLO from Jordan?
2. Where did the PLO flee after the Jordanian Army attacked?
3. How did this help terrorism to spread to Europe?
4. How did Black September seize the world's attention?

King Hussein of Jordan viewed the increasing strength of the PLO in his land with growing concern. He had entered the war against Israel with some reluctance and preferred to take a moderate stance in the pan-Arabic struggle. Closely identified with British culture and friendly with the West, Jordan did not endorse the radicalism of Syria and other militant Arab states. King Hussein was especially wary of Syrian and Iraqi expansionist dreams and was more concerned with the protection of Jordan than with a united Arab realm.

As the PLO grew, it identified more closely with militant Arab states, giving them a potential base in Jordan. Concerned with the growing influence of foreign nationals in his own land, in 1970 King Hussein ordered the PLO to stop attacking Israel. He was not trying to protect Israel but to stop the spread of rival influences in Jordan.

But the PLO was not about to quit its successful campaign against Israel. Radical elements in Iraq and Syria encouraged Arafat to defy Hussein's order. Members of the Ba'ath Party saw the PLO as a tool that could be used against the Israelis. More important, they came to view the organization as a weapon to help the cause of revolution and socialism among all Arabs. Arafat defied Hussein's order and stepped up operations against Israel.

Arafat continued training in Jordanian PLO camps and invited revolutionaries throughout the Middle East to participate. His exiled Palestinian government took no orders from its Jordanian host. A variety of PLO and foreign terrorist groups continued making raids against Israel, and Arafat's reputation as a revolutionary hero spread beyond the Middle East. This became too much for King Hussein. After Palestinian terrorists hijacked three airplanes and destroyed them in Jordan, the king decided to act. In September 1970, Hussein attacked the PLO.

Arafat and the PLO were taken completely by surprise. The PLO terrorist offensive against Israel had worked because the terrorists operated in base camps that, although subject to Israeli attack, were relatively immune from annihilation. This was not the case when King Hussein's Jordanian Army struck; the PLO had nowhere to run. As Jordanian regulars bombarded PLO camps and launched an all-out assault, Arafat fled to southern Lebanon.

Arafat could not control terrorists in the many PLO splinter groups, so he created a new group to strike at Israel, naming it **Black September** after King Hussein's September attack. With German terrorist help, Black September attacked in Munich at the 1972 Olympic Games. They took most of the Israeli Olympic team hostage, killing those who tried to escape. German police moved in, and the world watched a drawn-out siege. Black September terrorists negotiated transportation to Libya, but while they were moving to the aircraft designated to fly them from Germany, the German police launched a rescue operation. Unfortunately, plans went awry and the terrorists machine-gunned their hostages before the German police could take control. The Israelis and a German officer were killed. It was a terrorist victory, and European leftists and nationalists saw it as partially their triumph.

The PLO and the Changing Face of Middle Eastern Terrorism

Key Points and Questions:

1. Why did the Fatah segment of the PLO begin to split into various factions?
2. Describe the origins and growth of the Abu Nidal network.
3. How did other nations become involved in the Middle East conflict?
4. Why did Libya become involved in the Palestinian question?

In 1970, the expulsion of the PLO from Jordan marked a turning point in Middle Eastern terrorism. While Black September planned the attack at the 1972 Olympic Games, other Arab states realized the potential of the PLO's tactics for use in other conflicts. Fatah split from within because new leaders emerged to rival Arafat. A host of splinter groups rejected the path of the PLO, and they developed separate ideological paths. As various terrorist groups split off from Arafat's control, a host of Arab states offered support and assistance, causing further splits within Fatah. Strangely, some of the new groups were not overly interested in the Palestinian cause. In fact, the splintering PLO groups were often used as terrorist agents against rival Arab states.

The **Abu Nidal group**, also known as Black June, evolved as one of the most important splinter groups from Fatah. The group formed in the early 1970s when Sabri al-Banna, code named Abu Nidal, went to Baghdad to recruit fedayeen for Arafat's Fatah. When Abu Nidal arrived in the Iraqi capital, he was in a foul mood. Arafat had stated publicly that the PLO would recognize Israel's right to exist in return for a Palestinian homeland. Abu Nidal, a member of the Rejectionist Front, was incensed. Knowing Abu Nidal's frustration, Saddam Hussein, then Ba'athist vice president of Iraq, approached the terrorist with a proposition. Instead of working for Arafat, Saddam explained, Abu Nidal could develop his own organization, and the Iraqis would assist with funding. Abu Nidal accepted the offer and broke with Fatah (Melman, 1986, pp. 69–75; Seale, 1992, pp. 111–113, 123–124).

After accepting Saddam's monetary offer, Abu Nidal created a new type of terror network. In order to stifle internal dissension, he developed a rigid hierarchy and assumed absolute control of the new organization. He also created an internal committee, the Committee for Revolutionary Justice, a group of internal thugs that kept Abu Nidal's followers in line. Abu Nidal grew powerful, and his network moved with more efficiency than the other Fatah splinter groups. The Iraqis were pleased. They increased funding, asking Abu Nidal to conduct operations in support of the Ba'ath Party. These actions drew the attention of Syria.

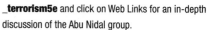

Go to **http://cj.wadsworth.com/white _terrorism5e** and click on Web Links for an in-depth discussion of the Abu Nidal group.

Syria was more interested in gaining power in Lebanon than supporting the rights of displaced Palestinians. It actively encouraged the PLO to splinter, and it promoted general anarchy in Lebanon. Syria also recruited some of the radical splinter groups from the PLO and prepared them for a variety of missions. Although Israel was always deemed to be the main enemy in the Middle East, the Syrians attacked Arab targets as well and saw an opportunity to use terrorism against any nation, including Palestinians and Arab states that opposed Syrian designs on Lebanon. Syria approached Abu Nidal with a proposition. They offered to fund Abu Nidal if he would conduct operations for Syria. Abu Nidal accepted.

Patrick Seale (1992) believes the Abu Nidal network transformed from an ideological terrorist group to a gang of mercenaries renting themselves out to the highest bidder. After accepting the Syrian offer, Abu Nidal went on to accept missions and payment from Libya and other Arab states. When his comrades complained, Abu Nidal eliminated them with the help of the Committee for Revolutionary Justice. As Abu Nidal's reputation spread, the Soviet Union sought to use his services. Using contacts in Poland, East Germany, and Albania, Communist agents helped Abu Nidal set up an infrastructure in Europe. In 1985 his terrorists attacked the Rome and Vienna airports. Seale concludes that Abu Nidal simply became a gun for hire.

In Libya, Colonel Moamar Khadaffy saw how effectively Iraq and Syria used the Abu Nidal network. Seeing himself as the leader of the Arabic world, Khadaffy sought to establish his own links with Abu Nidal. Financing terrorist operations and building a training camp for the Abu Nidal group, Khadaffy came to realize that Abu Nidal was too independent. Libya could not depend on Abu Nidal to do its bidding. Accordingly, Khadaffy reached out to the PLO and created his own terrorist group with the help of his intelligence service (Reese, 1986).

Fatah began as a movement to wage war against Israel, but it disintegrated into a variety of squabbling factions. Some groups remained loyal to Arafat, while others sought their own sponsors and new directions. Arafat created a new internal security section to protect himself from other Palestinian terrorist groups. By the late 1980s, when the Abu Nidal group reached its zenith, various Palestinian groups alternately fought each other or formed temporary alliances. They engaged in criminal activity, moving beyond the bounds of the Middle East into Europe. Groups laundered money, sold drugs, ran protection rackets, engaged in petty crimes, and also conducted terrorist operations against the West, the Israelis, and each other. It became very difficult to distinguish Fatah's splinter groups from organized crime gangs (Ehrenfeld, 2003, pp. 71–110).

Intifadas and Religious Revival

 Key Points and Questions:

1. What are the three questions that have defined terrorism in the Middle East?
2. Why did many Palestinians turn to the first Intifada?
3. What was Arafat's reaction to the Intifada?
4. Did the Oslo peace talks complicate or resolve efforts to make peace?
5. What was the immediate cause of the al Aqsa Intifada?

As Fatah split and states sponsored the creation of new terrorist groups, both Palestinians and other Arabs became disillusioned with the direction of the struggle against Israel. To understand this, it is helpful to look at three competing interests in Middle Eastern violence. The central issue focuses on Israel and the Palestinians: Who will govern and what areas will be governed? Related to these questions is the internal power struggle among Arab states. Most Arabs ideally believe that all the Arab nations should be united in one Islamic state. The problem again focuses on governance. The leader of each Arab state believes that he should lead a pan-Arabic nation. This results in internal rivalries among Arab states. Finally, militant Muslims, both Arabs and non-Arabs, came to believe that secular politics are doomed to failure. They preach revolutionary Islam, and their views currently dominate violence in the Middle East. The religious question also surfaced in the Israeli-Palestinian struggle.

On December 9, 1987, thousands of protesters marched in Jabiliya, a Palestinian refugee camp in the Gaza Strip, to protest the Israeli killing of four Palestinians. When the Israelis tried to stop the demonstration, a spontaneous riot broke out in Gaza. Within days it had spread through all the **Occupied Territories**, the areas controlled by Israel but claimed by Palestinians, and two dozen Palestinians had been killed. As resistance continued, the Palestinians called the uprising the **Intifada**, and it had a religious flavor.

By January 1988 the Palestinian branch of the Muslim Brotherhood, Hamas, formed to direct the new resistance. Arafat, exiled in Tunisia because of the Israeli invasion of Lebanon, formed his own organization in an attempt to gain control of the Intifada, but Hamas emerged as the stronger force. Young Palestinian boys gathered on street corners to throw rocks at Israeli soldiers and police officers. The Israelis responded with overwhelming force, but resistance increased. To many Palestinians, as well as to Arabs in North Africa and the Middle East, it seemed that where secular politics had failed religion might prevail. Hamas established a comprehensive organization to operate charities, hospitals, and schools and to provide other social services. Its military wing assisted with the Intifada and conducted direct strikes against the Israelis (Hiro, 1996, pp. 123–124).

The United States responded to the Intifada with a new peace proposal. Inviting representatives from the Israeli and Palestinian camps, the United States brokered a temporary peace agreement in September 1993. Known as the **Oslo Accords**, the peace agreement introduced a radical new concept to the long struggle: It defined a semiautonomous **Palestinian National Authority** (**PNA**) and hinted at the possible creation of a Palestinian state.

After years of fighting, cautious optimism spread through the area. Israeli forces partially retreated from the Occupied Territories, and the new PNA assumed limited responsibility for governance. Hamas rejected the Oslo Accords, giving Arafat increased stature among the majority of Palestinians. He assumed control of the new PNA and governance of major portions of the Occupied Territories. Unfortunately, the optimism surrounding the new direction was misplaced (Palmer and Palmer, 2004, p. 211).

Extremists on both sides abhorred the peace process. The Hamas Charter states that it will never accept the existence of Israel (Rubin and Rubin, 2002, pp. 54–59). Israel also struggled with the process, and many Israelis did not favor it. Extremist groups like the fanatic Gush Emunim and terrorist groups like Kach and Kahane Chai called for Israel to expand to its biblical borders and destroy the Arabs. Other Israelis took a less radical view but still maintained a hard line toward the Palestinians. The violent voices on both sides of the Israeli-Palestinian conflict dominated political activity. As Israeli prime minister Yitzak Rabin stood in the face of this opposition and worked for peace, he lost his life. In 1995, a Jewish religious extremist assassinated him, hoping to derail the peace process. His efforts proved to be successful as extremists in Palestine and Israel moved to the forefront (Palmer and Palmer, 2004, p. 212).

In May 1996, the conservative Israeli Likud Party came to power, indicating that it would not trade any land in the Occupied Territories for peace with the Palestinians. The Likud Party traditionally has emphasized strength and military power as Israel's best hope for peace. The new Likud government, under the direction of Benjamin Netanyahu, tried to back away from the Oslo Accords as it increased military action in Lebanon. This brought Hezbollah, Hamas, and other militants back to the streets, and the fragile peace threatened to evaporate. Suicide bombers began staging attacks against Israel.

By 1998, however, the Israelis and Palestinians signed a new agreement, the Wye Accords, and Arafat reasserted power over the PNA. Netanyahu lost a 1999 national election to Ehud Barak of the more centrist Labor Party, and Barak formed a government intent on bringing peace. If Arafat could have spoken for all Palestinians, he might have been able to agree to some type of permanent peace. Critics say, however, that he was too corrupt and too interested in conflict to do so. For his part, Barak ordered Israeli forces in Lebanon to withdraw, and with the help of President Bill Clinton, he tried to negotiate a peace settlement with Arafat during a retreat at Camp David. Unfortunately, efforts of the **Camp David Peace Accords** failed, and the Israeli-Palestinian conflict took a new direction in 2000.

The Likud Party campaigned against Barak in 2000, and its leader, former general and Israeli defense minister **Ariel Sharon**, upstaged his political rival in a show of bravado. In September 2000 he took a heavily armed group of Israelis to the site of the Wailing Wall, the remnant of the Jewish Temple that once stood in Jerusalem. The visit infuriated Palestinian Muslims because the area is also the site of a holy shrine in Islam, the al Aqsa mosque. Palestinians, encouraged by a number of religious groups, took to the streets in a second spontaneous uprising. The **al Aqsa Intifada** erupted all through the Occupied Territories. Sharon won the election and was reelected in 2003.

The current state of the Israeli-Palestinian conflict has been defined by years of ruthless terrorism and counterterrorism. It has sparked a wave of suicide bombings and counterstrikes, including targeted assassinations of Palestinian leaders. The United States has even been targeted as many Palestinians made their way from the new autonomous enclaves, the Occupied Territories, Lebanon, and Jordan to fight U.S. forces after the 2003 invasion of Iraq.

Yasser Arafat died in the fall of 2004. Many people believe his death may help to bring peace to the region, but extremists on both sides have the ability to compromise any treaty. In early 2005 Hamas and the militant Palestinian group Islamic Jihad stated they would suspend suicide strikes, pending the outcome of new peace negotiations. Hezbollah watches from the sidelines. Much of the struggle has turned to religion, and members of the Rejectionist Front maintain their hatred of Israel with passionate zeal. Israel, on the other hand, has produced its own brand of religious fanaticism. Moshe Amon (2004) argues that this strain of Judaism calls for the conquest and destruction of the Arab states surrounding Israel, and he believes this view increasingly influences the Israeli government. Terrorists and violent extremists do not compromise. Mainstream political leaders must be able to control violent political organizations in their own ranks if any type of peace is to prevail.

Summary of Main Points

1. The Israeli-Palestinian conflict began more than one hundred years ago and became more heated after the creation of Israel in 1948.

2. The first terrorist groups in the Middle East were Jewish. The Irgun Zvai Leumi and Stern Gang targeted Palestinians and British soldiers in the struggle to create Israel.

3. Terrorism reemerged in the Middle East after conventional wars proved disastrous for the Arabs.

4. Fatah joined the PLO under Arafat's leadership and took a leading role in the struggle against Israel after the 1967 war.

5. Fatah continually splintered. One of the strongest organizations to split from Fatah was the Abu Nidal organization. Abu Nidal abandoned the Palestinian cause, however, and became a gun for hire. Syria, Iraq, and Libya created Palestinian terrorist groups to serve their own interests.

6. The three questions that define terrorism in the Middle East concern the conflict between Israel and Palestine, which Arab leader will dominate the region, and the future of the Jihadists.

7. The peace process in the Middle East has been underway for several decades. It is constantly disrupted by each side striking to gain an advantage over the other.

Key Terms

Make sure you can define, explain, or identify the following people, ideas, organizations, or terms:

Zionist   144
Irgun Zvai Leumi   146
Stern Gang   146
Israel   146
Rejectionist Front   146
Israeli Defense Force (IDF)   146
Yasser Arafat   146
Palestine Liberation
   Organization (PLO)   146
Fatah   147
fedayeen   147

Six-Day War   147
Ba'athists   151
Black September   152
Abu Nidal group   152
Occupied Territories   154
Intifada   154
Oslo Accords   155
Palestinian National Authority (PNA)   155
Camp David Peace Accords   155
Ariel Sharon   155
al Aqsa Intifada   156

Suggested Readings

Now that you've been introduced to this topic, you can learn more by reading:

Anton LaGuardia's *War Without End*, a historical and political analysis of the conflict that criticizes both Israeli and Palestinian policies.

You may also want to read:

Karen Armstrong, in *Jerusalem*, examines the sacred city of three faiths.

Ahron Bergman's *Israel's War* summarizes Israel's military history since 1947.

Sami Hadawi, in *Bitter Harvest*, summarizes the plight of many Palestinians.

Web Resources

Go to *http://cj.wadsworth.com/white_terrorism5e* and click on Web Links to find:

- A history of the Israeli-Palestinian conflict on the MidEast Web
- A "primer" about the conflict at the Middle East Research and Information Project

The Companion Website for *Terrorism and Homeland Security*, Fifth Edition

http://cj.wadsworth.com/white_terrorism5e

At the Book Companion Website you can review chapter outlines, use the flash cards to test your terrorism vocabulary, and check out the many other study aids you'll find there. You'll find valuable data and resources at your fingertips to help you study for that big exam or write that important paper.

Terrorism Updates

**http://www.wadsworth.com/criminaljustice_d/special_features/ext/terrorism
_site090802/index.html**

Visit the *Terrorism: An Interdisciplinary Perspective* website to find the most current information about the fields of terrorism and homeland security. With a focus on domestic and international issues, this site explores the scope of terrorism in our world today. You'll find essays on important topics in terrorism and homeland security, critical thinking web activities, and InfoTrac College Edition keywords. Most importantly, the website is updated weekly with current news and research articles on domestic and international terrorism. You are invited to use these web resources to supplement your understanding of the topics covered in this chapter.

Current Perspectives: Readings from InfoTrac College Edition

Terrorism and Homeland Security

The sixteen articles in this reader offer a representative selection that helps you understand the important issues about terrorism and homeland security. It includes FREE access to InfoTrac College Edition and can also be bundled with the text for free.

Chapter 10

Middle Eastern Terrorism in Metamorphosis

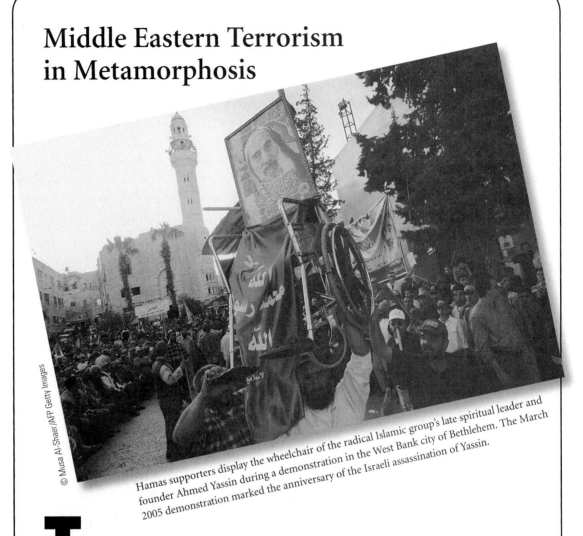

Hamas supporters display the wheelchair of the radical Islamic group's late spiritual leader and founder Ahmed Yassin during a demonstration in the West Bank city of Bethlehem. The March 2005 demonstration marked the anniversary of the Israeli assassination of Yassin.

© Musa Al-Shaer/AFP Getty Images

The Jihadist organizations are international by nature, although the nationalistic branch of Hezbollah is larger than its international component. Terrorism in Israel and Palestine has been a different matter. It has been localized, and its violence was not originally couched in religious language. The modern era (since the Six-Day War in 1967) began with a secular terrorist campaign that gradually evolved into religious violence. Unlike the other Jihadists, however, the Palestinian groups using religious language do not want to wait for an international Islamicist jihad. They hope to create an Islamic Palestine before a pan-Islamic state emerges. Their activities are also influenced by controversial counterterrorist policies. All of these factors threaten a fragile peace process, and since most Palestinians and their neighbors view the United States as an ally of Israel, Middle Eastern terrorists may bring their battle to the United States.

Chapter Objectives

After reading this chapter, you should be able to:

1. Discuss the origins of the Palestinian Islamic Jihad, its structure, and its operations.

2. Explain the confusion surrounding the term *Islamic Jihad*.

3. Describe the current operational capabilities of Hamas.

4. Explain the effect of the al Aqsa Intifada on Hamas.

5. Define shifts that may cause Hamas to target the United States.

6. Explain Fatah's gravitation toward the al Aqsa Martyrs Brigades.

7. Summarize the reasons for the expanded use of suicide bombers in the al Aqsa Intifada.

8. List and describe the activities of Jewish terrorist and extremist organizations.

9. Summarize controversial Israeli counterterrorist policies.

The Palestinian Islamic Jihad

Key Points and Questions:

1. What factors confuse discussions of the Palestinian Islamic Jihad (PIJ)?

2. How did the PIJ come to reflect militant Salafi philosophy?

3. Explain whether the PIJ have any connections with Hezbollah.

4. How does the U.S. State Department assess the PIJ?

5. Does the structure of the PIJ help it to operate?

6. What is the current status of the PIJ?

7. Does the PIJ have connections in the United States?

Discussions of the terrorist group **Palestinian Islamic Jihad (PIJ)** are sometimes confusing because a number of small groups operate under the name of *Islamic Jihad* (see Table 10.1). American intelligence sources believe that Hezbollah's umbrella included Islamic Jihad from 1982 until sometime around 1988. But Hezbollah officials deny this and claim no relation with Islamic Jihad (Harik, 2004, pp. 16–27, 164–175). Other groups also use the name Islamic Jihad and operate in other countries. Confusion increases because founders of the PIJ structured the organization in secret.

The PIJ emerged from Egypt. Its founders—Fathi Shekaki, Abdul Aziz, and Bashir Musa—were influenced by militant Salafism and disillusioned with the Muslim Brotherhood. While the Brothers spoke of education and peaceful change, the founders of the PIJ wanted to create an Islamic state using military action. They moved into the Gaza Strip in the late 1970s and eventually went to southern Lebanon. When they returned to the Occupied Territories, they believed that they could become the vanguard of a local Islamic revolution (Institute for Counter-Terrorism, 1996), and they began to create a new terrorist organization.

To understand this geographical and religious journey, it is necessary to look at the PIJ's first leader. **Fathi Shekaki** fell under the influence of the Muslim Brother-

Table 10.1

Islamic Jihads

Several groups operate under the name *Islamic Jihad*, maintaining offices in Damascus, Beirut, Khartoum, and Tehran. They also raise funds in the United States.

Group	Location
Islamic Jihad	Lebanon, 1982–1988
Islamic Jihad Organization	Jordan
Islamic Jihad	Jordan
Islamic Jihad Temple	Pro-Iranian
Islamic Jihad Organization, the al Aqsa Battalions	Israel
Islamic Jihad Squad	Egypt and Sudan
Islamic Jihad, Shekaki Faction	Syria, Lebanon, and Israel

hood in Egypt, but like Sayyid Qutb, he longed to take direct action against corrupt Muslim governments and the infidels who influenced them. He felt the Brothers were too patient, waiting for the Islamic world to awaken and create a pan-Islamic society. This was too idealistic for the practical Shekaki. Revolutions, he believed, started in localized geographical areas. In other words, ideas spread violently after a revolution had taken place, not gradually as an entire people became enlightened through education. As Shekaki championed Islamicist theories in 1978, much of the world's attention was focused on Iran. In the wake of the Iranian Revolution, the Ayatollah Khomeini created an Islamic government and talked of spreading the revolution. Nothing could have been closer to Shekaki's heart (Donovan, 2002).

Shekaki supported the Iranian Revolution, hailing it as a model for bringing Islamic law to the community of believers throughout the Islamic world. He left Egypt with Abdul Aziz and Bashir Musa to settle in the Gaza Strip in 1981. In the shadows of the occupied territory, the PIJ grew, espousing revolution as a means of action. Shekaki wanted no social program or general political movement. He felt his small group should be devoted to one thing: military action. Bombings and other terrorist tactics would serve as the vanguard of the Islamic revolution in the same manner that Khomeini's revolution in Iran toppled the shah (Military.com, 2004). Shekaki and his cohorts waited for a chance to strike.

His opportunity was not long in coming. In 1982 Israeli tanks rolled through the Shi'ite settlements of southern Lebanon, and as discussed in Chapter 8, Revolutionary Guards from Iran went to the area to fight the Israelis under the umbrella of Hezbollah. Shekaki and his newly formed PIJ also went to Lebanon. While there, he recruited terrorists and formed relations with local Shi'ites. These overtures brought the PIJ into contact with Iran and the spiritual leaders who had been trained in Najaf, including Hassan Fadlallah (Israeli Foreign Ministry, 4-11-96). Shekaki soon discovered that he and his Iranian allies had a similar vision.

Shekaki was also impressed with two of Hezbollah's innovations: the umbrella-styled organization and the suicide bomber. He copied both of them. The PIJ may have become one of the groups operating under Hezbollah's umbrella, or it might have remained autonomous. In either case, the PIJ soon became its own umbrella. Shekaki found that by letting his group split, he became virtually invisible to his enemies. The United States had never seen anything like the PIJ (Taubman, 1984). It was a "nongroup." Both Hezbollah and the PIJ took the West totally by surprise; their structures gave terrorism a new kind of power (Wright, 1986, pp. 84–86).

The U.S. Department of State (1996, 2004a) sees the structure of the PIJ as a pillar of strength. PIJ terrorists gained power through the group's hidden structure because it made them invisible. As Robin Wright (1996, p. 86) notes, the PIJ had no infrastructure or visible means of support. It was not concerned with claiming credit for operations, but it was concerned about killing. Shekaki's terrorists lived and died for one thing: to kill their enemies. Action, not slogans and ideas, caused revolution.

The group's invisibility was partially due to the growing number of groups claiming the name "Islamic Jihad." Shekaki's group had no concern about who called themselves Islamic Jihad as long as they killed PIJ enemies. Even a single action from a group would confuse investigators. After all, it seemed impossible to fight an organization that was not an organization. There was no place to launch a counterstrike.

When the first Intifada broke out in 1987, the PIJ increased political action and joined the battle in the streets. Shekaki was captured and deported from Gaza in 1988, but he returned in short order. When the 1993 Oslo Accords promised some hope for the end to violence, Shekaki joined a new Rejectionist Front. Allying with various other groups, including the other Islamic Jihads, Shekaki called for a wave of violence. The PIJ struck Israeli targets, assassinated soldiers, and perfected the tactic they copied from Hezbollah, suicide bombing. This was too much for the Israelis. If they could not figure out how to strike a nebulous network of groups, they could strike its figurehead. Shekaki was assassinated in Malta in 1995; most sources believe the Israelis were behind the attack.

Time magazine reporters interviewed Shekaki nine months before his death (*Time*, 1995). There would be no peace, he said, until Israel was destroyed. He also reiterated his willingness to use human-guided missiles—the suicide bombers. Unlike Hamas, he stated that Islamic Jihad was willing to accept a liberated Palestine even without a united Arab realm. The U.S. Department of State (1996) took such statements at face value, pointing to threats for an expanded suicide bombing campaign in 1995.

Shekaki's successor, **Ramadan Abdullah Sallah**, maintained the Shekaki philosophy. Raised in Gaza and educated in the United Kingdom, Sallah continued the campaign against Israel. He formed a loose alliance with Hamas and conducted joint PIJ-Hamas operations. True to its original design, the PIJ remained small, consisting of no more than a few dozen members (Donovan, 2002).

The September 2000 al Aqsa Intifada sent the PIJ into a frenzy of activity as the group launched a suicide bombing campaign. Divisions among the various factions narrowed, and the PIJ sought deeper ties to Hezbollah and Hamas. Yet the PIJ could not match the number of bombings from other terrorist groups during the early stages of the al Aqsa Intifada, so it tried to create more spectacular bombings. These actions included deadly strikes on civilian targets designed to kill and maim ordinary Israeli citizens. It also endorsed the use of women and children as suicide bombers.

The U.S. Department of Justice (2-20-03) believes that despite its nebulous infrastructure, the PIJ has an organized network of financial supporters around the world,

The U.S. Government's View of the Palestinian Islamic Jihad

The U.S. government has a dim view of the PIJ. The State Department lists the PIJ as a terrorist organization, and the Department of Justice actively prosecutes alleged PIJ members in the United States. This view is reflected in the following press release issued after the arrest of a university professor in Florida:

> WASHINGTON, D.C.—Attorney General John Ashcroft, Assistant Attorney General Michael Chertoff of the Criminal Division, U.S. Attorney Paul I. Perez of the Middle District of Florida, and James F. Jarboe, FBI Special Agent In Charge of the Tampa Field Office, today announced the arrest of four members of the Palestinian Islamic Jihad (PIJ), a designated foreign terrorist organization, following the return of a 50-count indictment by a federal grand jury in Tampa, Florida.
>
> The indictment, returned Feb. 19 and unsealed today, charges a total of eight defendants under RICO with operating a racketeering enterprise from 1984 until the present that engaged in a number of violent activities. In addition, the indictment charges conspiracy within the United States to kill and main persons abroad, conspiracy to provide material support and resources to PIJ, conspiracy to violate emergency economic sanctions, engaging in various acts of interstate extortion, perjury, obstruction of justice and immigration fraud. If convicted, the defendants face up to life in prison.
>
> "The individuals named in this indictment play a substantial role in international terrorism—they are 'material supporters' of foreign terrorist organizations. They finance, extol and assist acts of terror," said Attorney General John Ashcroft. "Our message to them is clear: We make no distinction between those who carry out terrorist attacks and those who knowingly finance, manage or supervise terrorist organizations. We will bring justice to the full network of terror."

Source: U.S. Department of Justice (2-20-03).

including in the United States. The U.S. government claims it has uncovered a PIJ financial and administrative network at a Florida university, and it has charged several alleged members. Steven Emerson (2002, pp. 112–124) claims that PIJ distributes literature and raises funds throughout the United States. The U.S. Department of State (2004a) still believes that some funds come through Iran and possibly Syria (see Another Perspective: The U.S. Government's View of the Palestinian Islamic Jihad).

Hamas

Key Points and Questions:

1. Where and why was Hamas created?
2. How is Hamas organized?
3. Describe Hamas's relationship with the PLO and Palestinian National Authority.
4. How did Hamas grow?
5. Define "inside" and "outside" leadership.
6. What was the impact of the al Aqsa Intifada on Hamas?
7. How might Hamas operations threaten the United States?

The story of Hamas is tied to the late **Sheik Ahmed Yassin**. Born in 1938, Yassin grew up in Gaza under the influence of the Muslim Brotherhood. He believed that Islam was the only path that could restore Palestine, and he preached reform and social welfare. Many Palestinians in Gaza began to follow Yassin's powerful call. When he told followers to secretly gather weapons in 1984, they obeyed, but it cost him his freedom. The Israelis discovered Yassin's plans and jailed him. He was released in 1986 and decided that in the future his organization would have a military wing. The Palestinian Muslim Brothers would become the nucleus of Hamas (Institute for Counter-Terrorism, 2004).

Hamas was formed in December 1987 at the beginning of the first Intifada (Isseroff, 2004). Yassin was disappointed with the secular direction of the PLO and wanted to steer the resistance movement along a religious course. Several technically trained university graduates, engineers, teachers, and Islamic scholars joined the movement. They published the **Hamas Charter** in 1988, declaring that Palestine was God-given land, from the Jordan River to the Mediterranean. There could be no compromise with the Israelis, and Israel could not be allowed to exist. Unlike Arafat's PLO, Hamas would fight Israel with religious zeal. Unlike the PIJ, Hamas would be much more than a military organization. It would be a Muslim government, the forerunner of a Palestinian Muslim state.

Hamas's organization reflects this original charter (Hamas, 1988), maintaining a political wing to oversee internal and foreign relations. Its largest unit, especially in Gaza, is its social wing. According to the third pillar of Islam, *Zakat*, Muslims are to give alms and share with the poor. Hamas runs charities, schools, hospitals, and other social service organizations in Gaza where employment is sometimes as high as 85 percent. These social services have made Hamas popular among the Palestinians. Hamas's military wing, the Izz el Din **al Qassam Brigades**, is named after a martyr during the period of the British occupation of Palestine and forms the military striking power of Hamas.

Hamas's relationship with the PLO and the Palestinian National Authority (PNA) has been shaky (Westcott, 10-19-00). The reason can be traced to its religious orientation. Although Yassin and his followers vowed never to use violence against fellow Palestinians, they have always opposed Arafat. When the Oslo Accords created the PNA in 1993, Hamas joined other groups in a new Rejectionist Front. This move resulted in a new wave of violence that almost doomed Hamas by the end of the decade.

After the first Intifada, Hamas faced an internal power struggle. Yassin was jailed from 1989 to 1997, and during that time, the American-educated **Musa Abu Marzuq** took over Hamas. His strategy was much more violent than Yassin's. He assembled a new leadership core and based it in Jordan. He also sought financial backing from Syria and Iran. His tenure became known as the **"outside" leadership** because he based Hamas outside of Palestinian territory. Yassin believed the struggle should remain inside Palestine; thus his leadership group became known as the **"inside" faction**.

Marzuq's leadership also caused a struggle with the PNA (Institute for Counter-Terrorism, 2004). In 1996 Marzuq authorized a campaign of suicide bombing inside Israel. The PIJ launched one at the same time, and both campaigns continued into 1997. They were especially savage, targeting civilians and public places. Bombs were designed to kill, cripple, and maim. Some bombs were even laced with rat poison to cause wounds to continue bleeding after treatment. Israel gave Arafat an ultimatum:

Crack down on Hamas or Israel would. The PNA arrested a number of Hamas's leaders, and Marzuq's offensive waned.

After Yassin was released from prison in 1997, he gradually reasserted control over Hamas, even though he remained under house arrest. He moved operations back to the Gaza Strip, and violence continued to 2000, but slowly decreased. Leaders of the al Qassam Brigades were incensed, claiming that both the inside and outside leadership were placing too much attention on political solutions (Arab Gateway, 2002). In the meantime, Jordanian officials closed Hamas operations in Amman, and the outsiders who could avoid arrest fled to Syria. By 2000 some observers believed a lasting peace might be at hand. Unfortunately, they were disappointed (Karmon, 2000; Wikas, 2002). The al Aqsa Intifada started in September.

It is hard to overstate the effect of the al Aqsa Intifada on Hamas. Quarreling between the al Qassam leaders and the political wing came to a standstill. Moderates and hard-liners drew closer together. As the Israeli Defense Force (IDF) swarmed into Palestinian areas, Arafat's makeshift government, the PNA, lost much of its power. Hamas, therefore, had the opportunity to assert its muscle. The distinction among the various Palestinian forces began to blur, and Hamas grew stronger by forming alliances with Hezbollah and the PIJ. It then joined the largest suicide bombing campaign the Middle East had ever seen.

In the summer of 2003 Palestinian prime minister Mahmud Abbas brokered a limited cease-fire, asking Hamas, the PIJ, and related groups to end their campaigns. But the peace effort ended in August after a suicide bombing on a bus in Jerusalem. The Israelis responded by renewing a policy of selective assassination, that is, they identified leaders of Hamas and systematically murdered them. Hamas passed another milestone in the campaign against Israel: It used a female suicide bomber in a joint operation with a newer group, the al Aqsa Martyrs Brigades (Stern, 12-18-03). Hamas had followed the lead of the Liberation Tigers of Tamil Eelam (LTTE), the Kurdish Workers' Party, and the Chechnyan rebels, who have also used female suicide bombers.

The future of Hamas may take an interesting turn because of circumstances outside the Middle East. In March 2004 Yassin was leaving a mosque in Gaza when Israeli helicopters appeared and fired three missiles at him. Like other Hamas leaders before him (see Table 10.2), he was killed instantly. Hamas announced his replacement, Abdel Aziz Rantisi, an old member of the group of the inside faction. However, the Israelis assassinated Rantisi in the same manner shortly after he took office. A new leader was appointed, but Hamas kept his identity secret (Oliver, 5-23-04; Keinon, 5-21-04).

Some analysts believe the new leader is **Khalid Mashal**, an outsider operating from Damascus. If this is true, Hamas may develop an international orientation and present a threat to the United States (Lake, 4-29-04). Reuven Paz (2004) senses a shift in Hamas thinking. In August 2004 U.S. and Iraqi forces battled the Shi'ite militia of Maqtada al Sadr in Najaf, Iraq. Paz points out that Hamas issued two very interesting communiqués in the wake of this battle. The first one condemned the United States for fighting around **Najaf**, the site of a Shi'ite holy shrine, and it called on all Iraqi people to band together to defeat America. The second statement was different, and Paz notes that it looked like a correction. The new release called upon Iraqis to support the militia of Maqtada al Sadr.

Table 10.2

Assassination of Hamas Leaders
Israel has targeted Hamas leaders throughout the al Aqsa Intifada.

Person	Position	Israeli Action
Riyad Abu Zayd	Military commander	Ambush, February 2003
Ibrahim Maqadah	Military commander	Helicopter attack, May 2003
Abdullah Qawasmah	Suicide bomb commander	Ambush, June 2003
Ismail Shanab	Political leader	Bomb strike, August 2003
Sheik Ahmed Yassin	Head of Hamas	Helicopter attack, March 2004
Abdel Aziz Rantisi	Replaced Yassin	Helicopter attack, April 2004

Paz concludes that Hamas is shifting targets and focus. Hamas began as a strong Sunni organization, a Palestinian extension of the Muslim Brotherhood, influenced by militant Salafi puritanism. Much of its monetary support came from Saudi sympathizers, and Sheik Yassin and the inside group kept Hamas in the Salafi camp. Even though the outsiders operated in other countries, Hamas remained focused on Israel. The jihad was not international; it belonged to Hamas, the Islamic resistance movement in Palestine. The assassinations of Yassin and Rantisi, however, may have changed the equation.

Paz points to Hamas's two communiqués as evidence. The first was addressed to the Iraqi people. Logically, it expresses Sunni concern for U.S. intervention in the area and calls for unification. The second version, the *corrected version* according to Paz, asks for support of a junior Shi'ite scholar in defense of a Shi'ite holy site. Al Sadr is not a senior scholar; he is a young radical confronting the senior Shi'ite scholars of Iraq. He is also a disciple of the Ayatollah Khomeini. A Sunni Salafi militant would not be concerned with the defense of a holy mosque in Najaf or an Iranian-styled Shi'ite scholar, Paz argues, but a member of Hezbollah would be.

Paz comes to an interesting conclusion. He believes that leadership has passed to Khalid Mashal or someone very close to him in the outsider Damascus group. Mashal and his followers are abandoning the "Palestine first" philosophy of Hamas and drawing closer to the revolutionary Shi'ite views of Hezbollah and Iran. Hamas condemned the Wahhabi-supported al Qaeda violence of the Tawhid of Abu Musab al Zarqawi and its allied group Ansar al Islam (Dakroub, 5-14-04). This is ironic because militant Salafis and Wahhabis are engaged as allies in a global jihad. Paz believes that by voicing support for Iranian-styled Shi'ites and not Shi'ites in general, Hamas is falling into Hezbollah's orbit. If this is true, the organization will move closer to Syria and Iran, both on the U.S. State Department's list of nations supporting terrorism. Hamas may well end up becoming an enemy of the United States, targeting Americans and American interests.

The Al Aqsa Martyrs Brigades

Key Points and Questions:

1. Why did the al Aqsa Martyrs Brigades form?

2. How does it differ from other local Palestinian groups?

3. What tactics do the Brigades use?

4. Define the two differing positions on leadership in the Brigades.

5. How are the Brigades organized?

6. Why was the Fatah General Council formed?

Suicide bombing became the most important tactic of all the Palestinian terrorist groups at the beginning of the al Aqsa Intifada. Hezbollah, Hamas, and the PIJ were in the forefront, giving leadership to local religious groups (see Expanding the Concept: Who's Who among Palestinian Groups of the Al Aqsa Intifada). Fatah also became involved, but it continued its secular orientation. Its two main forces were the politically oriented Force 17 and the Tanzim Brigade. Other Fatah splinter groups joined, and while they resisted Arafat's control, they also steered clear of religion. This became a problem because the local Jihadists were dominating the fight. If Fatah wanted to play a leading role, it had to move from the secular to the religious realm. Religious terrorists dominate the al Aqsa Intifada (Shahar, 2002).

BBC News (7-1-03) says Fatah's new-found religious appearance came from the grass roots of Palestinian society. Formed to put Fatah at the center of the new Intifada, the group called itself the **al Aqsa Martyrs Brigades** (or the Brigades). The Brigades began as a secular group, but they increasingly used Jihadist rhetoric. They were also the first secular Palestinian group to use suicide tactics. Hezbollah, Hamas, and the PIJ do not recognize Israel's right to exist. This is not so with the Brigades. They claim their purpose is limited: Their goal is to stop Israeli incursions and attacks in Palestinian areas, and they intend to punish Israel for each attack. Whether this explanation is accepted or not, one thing is clear: The Brigades have become the most potent Palestinian force in the al Aqsa Intifada.

The Council on Foreign Relations (2004) believes the tactics of the al Aqsa Martyrs Brigades have made them particularly deadly against the Israelis. At first, shadowy spokespeople said they would strike Israeli military targets only inside Palestinian territory. This practice was soon abandoned, however, and attacks moved into Israel proper. The Brigades' primary tactics have been drive-by shootings, snipers, ambushes, and kidnap-murders. Yet, as with so many other terrorist groups, their most devastating tactic has been the use of suicide bombers.

Yael Shahar (2002) says the al Aqsa Martyrs Brigades suicide bombers were frightening for two reasons: They were secular, and they sought out crowded civilian targets. They delivered human bombs filled with antipersonnel material designed to inflict the maximum amount of casualties. Their purpose was to kill and maim as many victims as possible in the most public way possible. Furthermore, as mentioned above, they used the first female suicide bomber in the Middle East on January 27, 2002, in conjunction with Hamas. They expanded their targets and their casualties

Expanding the Concept

Who's Who among Palestinian Groups of the Al Aqsa Intifada

Al Aqsa Martyrs Brigades   The al Aqsa Martyrs Brigades are based on the West Bank in refugee camps. Formed after the beginning of the al Aqsa Intifada, the Brigades appear to be Fatah's answer to the Jihadists. Some members are motivated by Hezbollah, suggesting to some analysts that the Brigades have Shi'ite elements. Other analysts think that the Brigades are Fatah's attempt to take the Intifada's leadership away from Hamas and the PIJ. The Brigades are organized along military lines and became one of the first secular groups in the Middle East to use suicide bombers. Many experts believe that Arafat either directly controls the Brigades or that they operate with his approval. A command council is responsible for leadership, and terrorist operations are divided into six geographical areas. If Yasser Arafat controls the Brigades, members have directly violated his orders on several occasions. The division commanders control the rank-and-file members, not the command council.

Black September   Named after the September 1970 Jordanian offensive against Palestinian refuges in western Jordan, Black September was the infamous group that attacked the Israeli athletic team at the 1972 Munich Olympics. Israel spent years hunting down and killing the members of Black September. The 1972 attack also prompted the Germans to create a new elite counterterrorist group, Federal Border Guard Group 9 (GSG-9), headed by Ulrich Wegener.

Democratic Front for the Liberation of Palestine (DFLP)   A Christian, Naiaf Hawatmeh, created the DFLP in 1969 when he broke away from the PDFLP (see p. 170). This Marxist-Leninist group seeks a socialist Palestine and was closely associated with the former Soviet Union. In 2000 the group joined Arafat in Washington, D.C., to negotiate with Israeli Prime Minister Ehud Barak. As a reward, the U.S. Department of State took the DFLP off its list of terrorist groups. The DFLP currently limits its attacks to the Israeli Defense Force.

Fatah   Fatah began as the military wing of the former Palestine Liberation Organization (PLO) and was Yasser Arafat's strongest military muscle. Formed in the early stages of the PLO, Fatah was part of an underground organization formed in 1959. It emerged in the open in 1965 after beginning initial terrorist attacks against Israel in 1964. Fatah rose to prominence after the 1967 Six-Day War because it became the only means of attacking Israel. Fatah fought the Jordanians for ten days in September 1970 and regrouped in Lebanon. It joined the Lebanese Civil War (1975–1990) and was eventually expelled to Tunisia. In the first Intifada (1987–1993), Fatah Hawks, political militants in the PLO, organized street demonstrations and disturbances, but emerging religious groups threatened Fatah's leadership among the militant Palestinian groups. Fatah went to the bargaining table in Oslo in 1993 and joined the peace process. It currently holds the majority of seats in the Palestinian government. Although it is now a political party, many analysts associate it with the al Aqsa Martyrs Brigades. The Tanzim Brigade and Force 17 (see p. 170) come from the ranks of Fatah, and it has traditionally championed Palestinian nationalism over ideology or religion.

Force 17   Officially known as Presidential Security, Force 17 is an arm of Fatah. It operated as Yasser Arafat's security unit.

(continued)

Hamas In December 1987, a few days after the first Intifada began, the Islamic Resistance Movement (Harakat al Muqawama al Islamiyya, or Hamas) formed. It was composed of the Palestinian wing of the Muslim Brotherhood. The Brothers advocated an international Islamic movement, and most of them did not support violence. Hamas differs from the Brothers' position in that it has localized the Islamic struggle and accepts violence as a norm. Hamas is organized as a large political union, and its primary mission is to oppose the PLO; today it represents an alternative to the Palestine National Council. Its military wing is called the Izz el Din al Qassam Brigade, named for a martyr in the 1936 Arab Revolt against the British in Palestine. In 2004 Israel assassinated Hamas's spiritual leader, Sheik Ahmed Yassin. As soon as Hamas appointed a new leader, the Israelis killed him, too. Hamas is a large organization, but its terrorist wing is rather small. Frequently allied with Islamic Jihad, Hamas competes with other Fatah organizations.

Hezbollah Hezbollah is the Iranian-backed Party of God operating from southern Lebanon. The local branch of the group forms alliances of convenience with other organizations participating in the al Aqsa Intifada. The international branch is believed to run the most effective terrorist network in the world. (See Chapter 8.)

Palestinian Islamic Jihad (PIJ) A small group emerging from the Muslim Brotherhood in Egypt in 1979. While the Brothers spoke of an international Islamic awakening, the PIJ felt the struggle could be nationalized and had to become violent. PIJ leaders were enamored with the 1979 Iranian Revolution, and even though they were Sunnis, they sought contact with Iran's revolutionary Shi'ites. The PIJ operates out of the Gaza Strip and forms alliances of convenience with other organizations. It has grown closer to Hamas since the al Aqsa Intifada. The PIJ seeks to destroy Israel and establish an Islamic state in Palestine. The group has strong links to the United States, allegedly in Florida, and it is one of the groups that has mastered suicide bombing.

Palestine Liberation Front (PLF) Three different groups call themselves the Palestine Liberation Front: The Abu Abbas faction based in Iran supports the old-style leadership used by Arafat, the Abdal Fatah Ghanem faction supports Libya, and the Talat Yaqub faction favors Syria. The name of the group comes from Ahmed Jabril, a former Syrian Army captain, who formed the first PLF in 1961. After the Six-Day War in June 1967, the PLF merged with two small radical groups to form the Popular Front for the Liberation of Palestine, but Jabril broke away and formed the Popular Front for the Liberation of Palestine–General Command (see p. 170). The PFLP-GC split in 1977 after Syria backed Lebanese Christians in the Lebanese Civil War (1975–1990), and the anti-Syrians formed a new group, reviving the PLF name. The PLF had yet another internal war in 1984, and Abu Abbas, a militant leader who rebelled against Syria, returned one faction to Arafat, expelling all Syrian influence. Abdal Fatah Ghanem broke from Abbas and sided with Syria. His group remained active in Lebanon. Talat Yaqub tried to remain neutral. After he died of a heart attack, his faction gravitated toward Libyan support. All three factions of the PLF seek to destroy Israel. The PLF's most notorious action was the hijacking of an Italian luxury liner, the *Achille Lauro* in 1985. American forces captured the hijackers, but Abu Abbas was released. He went to the Gaza Strip

(*continued on page 170*)

and eventually to Iraq. He was captured during the U.S. invasion of Iraq in 2003 and died in captivity.

Popular Democratic Front for the Liberation of Palestine (PDFLP)   The PDFLP is the military wing of the DFLP (see p. 168).

Popular Front for the Liberation of Palestine (PFLP)   The PFLP is a Marxist-Leninist Arab nationalist group that emerged after the June 1967 Six-Day War. Egypt initially supported the PFLP but withdrew finances in 1968 when PFLP leaders criticized the Egyptian president. Operating in Lebanon under the command of Wadi Hadad, the PFLP began attacking Israeli airliners in 1968. In 1970 the group staged four hijackings in a six-day period; three of the planes were destroyed in the Jordanian desert in front of international media. Since the PFLP was closely linked to Arafat's Fatah, the Jordanians drove Arafat from their territory in September 1970. In 1975 it allied with Carlos the Jackal, a Latin American terrorist, and the Red Army Faction, a left-wing terrorist group from Germany, to attack an oil minister's conference in Vienna. Although the PFLP has been successful at times, it has been riddled with factionalism. The first splits came in 1968 and 1969 when Ahmed Jabril and George Habash broke from the PFLP. Wadi Hadad left the organization in 1976 when the Palestine National Council disavowed the use of terrorism outside the vicinity of Israel and the territories it occupied. He formed the Popular Front for the Liberation of Palestine–General Command, but died in 1978. Habash returned to the PFLP in 1976 and directed the campaign against Israel. He eventually reconciled with Fatah and handed leadership over to Abu Ali Mustafa in 2000. Mustafa was assassinated by the Israelis in August 2001. Ahmed Sadat, his successor, retaliated by killing an Israeli official. The PFLP has grown in stature since the al Aqsa Intifada.

Popular Front for the Liberation of Palestine–General Command (PFLP-GC)   The PFLP formed in 1967 when George Habash agreed to ally with Ahmed Jabril's PLF. Habash, a Christian, assumed leadership of the group, but he soon clashed with the Syrian-oriented Jabril. Syria continued to court Jabril, and he broke from Habash in 1968 to form the PFLP-GC. The PFLP-GC advocates armed struggle with Israel, and it became one of the most technically sophisticated organizations in the area. It originally operated from southern Lebanon with support from Syria. By the late 1980s, the PFLP-GC followed the lead of the Abu Nidal organization and rented its services to various governments. Some analysts believe the group was behind various international airline bombings. The PFLP-GC has been eclipsed by suicide bombers since 2000, but Jabril is increasingly emphasizing religion. This places the PFLP-GC closer to Jihadist groups, but it still remains one of the most technically sophisticated terrorist organizations in the area. Jabril has always favored military action over sensationalized terrorist events.

Tanzim Brigade   Not directly involved in terrorism, the Tanzim Brigade is the militia wing of Fatah.

increased; after allowing the PIJ and Hamas initially to play the leading role in the rebellion, the Brigades moved to the forefront of the rebellion.

Leadership of the Brigades is a controversial topic. They seem to be directly associated with their parent group, Fatah, but it is unclear how their operations are directed and from where. One school of thought maintains that Arafat led and paid for the Brigades. Israeli intelligence claims they have proof of Arafat's involvement. Shahar (2002) says that IDF forces raided Arafat's headquarters in Ramallah in 2002 and captured PNA documents that show payments to various factions inside the Brigades, payments personally approved by Arafat. The Israelis say that Arafat may not have determined targeting and timing, but he paid the expenses and set the agenda.

Other investigations point to another conclusion. The Council on Foreign Relations (2004) believes Arafat may have run the Brigades but admits there may be another source of leadership. A BBC News (7-1-03) investigation points to Marwan Barghouti as the commander. (Ironically, Barghouti is currently in Israeli custody.) A Palestinian spokesman, Hassan Abdel Rahman, says the documents Israel seized in 2002 are false and claims the Israelis planted them (Rothem, 2002). Arafat claimed he knew nothing about the Brigades.

PBS's *Frontline* (2002) conducted an interview with a Palestinian leader code named Jihad Ja'Aire at the height of the first bombing campaign. Ja'Aire claimed that he and all the other Brigade commanders were under Arafat's control. Arafat provided the direction, Ja'Aire said, and all the members obeyed him. This does not condemn Arafat, Ja'Aire pointed out, because the group operates with a different philosophy. The al Aqsa Martyrs Brigades will accept a negotiated peace. If Israel had accepted the 1967 borders, that is, the borders before Israel added the West Bank and Gaza Strip after the Six-Day War, and stopped incursions into Palestinian areas, Arafat could have called off the attacks.

Whether Arafat had direct control of the Brigades remains a subject of debate, partly because of the way the Brigades are organized. Taking a cue from the international Jihadist groups, the al Aqsa Martyrs Brigades have little centralized structure. Their administration has been pushed down to the lowest operational level so that they may function almost autonomously. Cells exist in several Palestinian communities, and leaders are empowered to take action on their own without approval from a hierarchy. In addition, Israel has targeted the Brigades' leadership for selective assassination, but the organization continues.

No matter where leadership authority lies, the managerial relations within the Brigades remain a paradox, even to the Palestinians. In June 2004 some of the leading figures in the Palestinian territories formed the **Fatah General Council** for the purpose of investigating the al Aqsa Martyrs Brigades and Arafat's relation to them. This enraged some of the Brigades, and they took action against Arafat. Claiming that Arafat had abandoned them, they surrounded his house and threatened him. If Arafat controlled the Brigades, his hold may not have been very tight (Algazy, 5-27-04).

As of this writing, no obvious leadership struggle has occurred within the Brigades since Arafat's death. This could indicate that Arafat exercised control; a more likely reason is that the Palestinians are awaiting the outcome of elections and the possibility of peace. If the al Aqsa Martyrs Brigades are really willing to accept a negotiated compromise with Israel, they may be the first group to accept a long-term cease-fire.

Jewish Fundamentalist Groups in Israel and Palestine

Key Points and Questions:

1. What is the basis of militant Judaism?
2. Who created Kach and why did he create it?
3. What happened to Kach's founder?
4. What is Kahane Chai?
5. Who was Baruch Goldstein?
6. What is the Gush Emunim?
7. Summarize Hanauer's view of Jewish fundamentalism.
8. Does Amon agree with Hanauer's view?

Religious violence in the Middle East is not limited to militant Islam. Jewish groups have also been involved in terrorist violence, and some of them have direct links to the United States. Militant Judaism is based on the biblical notion that God has promised to restore the state of Israel. The theology is racist, eschatological, and linked to the conquest and possession of territory. No other groups are permitted to control sacred territory, according to militant Judaism, and the Messiah can appear only when the state of Israel has been restored. Such thinking has produced deadly results.

One militant group is called **Kach** (Thus!). It was created by Rabbi Meir Kahane, an American Jewish cleric who immigrated to Israel in 1971. Serving synagogues in New York City in the early 1960s, Kahane's descriptions of religion and the superiority of Jews began to grow more militant. In 1968, he created the Jewish Defense League, a group that was involved in several terrorist incidents in the United States. Moving to Israel in 1971, Kahane combined politics and biblical literalism to demand that all Arabs be expelled from territories occupied by Israel. He called for the militant creation of "Greater Israel," the ancient Israel of King David. He was assassinated in 1990 in the United States.

Kahane's son, Benjamin, created a new group, **Kahane Chai** (Kahane Lives), shortly after Kahane's assassination. According to the U.S. Department of State (1999), both groups have been involved in harassing and threatening Palestinians, and they have threatened to attack Arabs and Israeli officials who seek peace. Baruch Goldstein, a member of Kach, killed nearly two dozen Muslims as they worshipped in the al Aqsa mosque in 1994. When Kach and Kahane Chai issued statements in support of Goldstein's terrorism, the Israeli government declared both groups to be terrorist organizations. President Clinton signed an executive order in 1995 prohibiting Americans from involvement in the groups. Kach and Kahane Chai are committed to stopping any peace proposal that recognizes the territorial rights of Palestinians.

Laurence Hanauer (1995) states that Kach and Kahane Chai have defined God's biblical promises in terms of territory. In the Hebrew Bible, God makes a covenant with Abraham and his descendents. (Muslims have the same story in the Koran and believe they are also Abraham's children.) Hanauer argues that militant Judaism takes the focus away from a covenant with people and focuses it on conquering new lands. This creates a climate for increased terrorism.

The leaders of these ethnocentric movements are sophisticated and socially connected. While Kach and Kahane Chai alienate most Israelis because of their violent rhetoric, other movements with the same views have grown. **Gush Emunim**, a fundamentalist Israeli settlement in Palestinian territory, is one such movement (Hanauer, 1995). Gush Emunim has the same set of beliefs as the violent fundamentalists, but their rhetoric appears normative compared with the violent rhetoric of the other groups. This has generated political support for Gush Emunim inside Israel.

Hanauer sees several problems with Jewish militant extremism and the prospects for peace. First, the extremists denounce the existing social order because it is not racially pure. All social, economic, and political problems are blamed on the failure to ascend to the moral high ground of Jewish biblical literalism. Second, the extremists claim the exclusive right to determine the truth. Third, they advocate an ideal order, and Gush Emunim and Kach claim that the Messiah can only return once the existing order is purified. Fourth, the national identity of Israel and its political legitimacy can only be determined through religion. Finally, all current events are defined within a narrow set of beliefs that define a limited worldview and identify only a few people as being chosen by God.

Hanauer believes such extremism may result in increased terrorist violence. Extremists do not answer to democratic ideals; they answer directly to their concept of God. The land of Israel is deified in their theology, so any attempt to achieve a land settlement is demonized. Jewish extremism leads to violence. Hanauer concludes that Baruch Goldstein, the terrorist who murdered the Muslim worshippers in 1994, was not a loner who simply snapped. He was the product of a Jewish extremism rooted in territorialism. Hanauer believes this structure will produce more religious terrorism.

Moshe Amon (2004) agrees with Hanauer and takes the argument further. He believes that Israel was founded on secular principles but that Jewish Orthodox extremists gained control over government policy (see Another Perspective: David's Kingdom and Israeli Settlements). This is suicidal, Amon argues, because the only chance of peace is negotiation with the Palestinians and the Arab nations. If Israeli extremists prevent the government from negotiating some type of settlement with their Arab neighbors, militant Arabs will win control of Arab

Another Perspective

David's Kingdom and Israeli Settlements

Many supporters of Israel and a good number of Israeli peace activists do not favor expansion into Palestinian areas. Moshe Amon (2004) writes that although Israel is a secular democracy, it is being influenced by religious extremists. Ultra-orthodox rabbis, he maintains, seek to conquer the biblical Kingdom of David. Jewish extremists, with the support of the state, have moved into Palestinian areas to establish permanent settlements. Many militants believe that when David's kingdom is restored, every person on earth will follow the teachings of the God of Israel. Amon says some of the militants fight Israeli soldiers, while some of their leaders call for the murder of non-Jews. Amon believes this behavior not only threatens Israel's moral character, but its very survival.

foreign policy. A time will come when Israel cannot stand against them or when the entire area will be destroyed with weapons of mass destruction. To create the opportunity for some type of peaceful settlement, Amon believes, all religious extremism must come to an end.

Controversial Counterterrorist Policies

Key Points and Questions:

1. What is the difference between a tactical approach to an incident and a counterterrorist policy?
2. What is the purpose of *bulldozing*?
3. Why did Operation Grapes of Wrath backfire?
4. How did the world respond to the idea of a security fence?
5. Does selective assassination work?

Many Israeli police and military units have established excellent reputations in counterterrorist operations. Mossad, the Israeli intelligence service, is known for its expertise. Shin Beth, the domestic Israeli security service, is one of the most effective secret police forces in the world. The IDF is an excellent fighting machine. Not to be left out, the Israeli police know how to handle bombs, snipers, kidnappings, and a variety of normative nonterrorist events. The tactical operations of these units are second to none.

Tactical operations, however, differ from policies. Governments decide the broad philosophy and practice of a policy, and tactical operations take place within the guidelines of long-term political goals. Policy involves a strategic view of a problem and the means to settle it. Unlike Israel's excellent tactical record, its counterterrorist policies have stirred international controversy (see Another Perspective: Controversial Tactics).

When Israel first faced suicide bombings, the government implemented a controversial policy called **bulldozing** whose purpose was to destroy the family homes of suicide bombers. If militant charities and governments compensated families of martyrs, the Israelis reasoned, bulldozing homes would be more painful than the pleasure of economic reward. The pattern continued. Soon, not only the homes of families were bulldozed, but suspected leaders in militant groups and others were targeted. In 2004 farms and other areas were bulldozed. The policy expanded to include clearing ground for military

Another Perspective

Controversial Tactics

Israel has engaged in tactics that have enraged the Palestinians and many others. Critics call these tactics Israeli terrorism. Defenders say that Israel has a right to protect itself. The United States almost always supports Israel, frequently using its veto power in the U.N. Security Council to keep the United Nations from condemning Israeli actions. Controversial tactics include

- Destroying the homes of suicide bomber families
- Selective assassination of Palestinian leaders
- Killing innocents when striking militants
- Excessive use of force
- Commando raids in neighboring countries

reasons and clearing space to build a **security fence**, that is, a wall separating Israel from Palestinian areas (*Palestine Monitor*, 4-29-04; *New York Times*, International, 7-29-04). Critics maintain that bulldozing takes place to further Israel's self-interests.

Judith Harik (2004, pp. 117–124) describes another controversial policy: punishing Lebanon for the sins of Hezbollah. In 1993 Israel launched a limited offensive in Lebanon to disrupt Hezbollah operations. They destroyed bridges, power plants, and other infrastructure targets in **Operation Grapes of Wrath**. Dozens of innocent Lebanese were killed in the process. Israel hoped to drive a wedge between the Lebanese and Hezbollah. Like bulldozing, the theory was based on punishment. The Israelis wanted to hurt Lebanon to force its government to clamp down on Hezbollah. The policy was not only controversial, it backfired. Harik believes the attack brought the Lebanese closer to Hezbollah and strengthened Syria's hand in Lebanese affairs. She thinks Israel's offense was an abysmal failure.

In an effort to stop Palestinian attacks, the government of Ariel Sharon proposed an idea that dated back to Hadrian of the Roman Empire. The Israelis began constructing a massive wall. On the surface, this might seem to be an uncontroversial issue, but the path of the wall grabbed the attention of the world. The concrete and barbed-wire barrier snaked through Palestinian areas, often putting water and other resources in the hands of the Israelis. It also separated people from services, jobs, and their families. Much of the international community condemned the wall (Black, 11-18-03).

The most controversial aspect of Israel's counterterrorism policy is **selective assassination**. Israel has maintained a consistent policy against terrorism. When it is struck, it hits back hard. Israeli commandos and IDF units have allegedly killed opposition leaders in the past, such as Abu Jihad of the PLO and Fathi Shekaki of the PIJ, but the policy expanded during the al Aqsa Intifada when Israel began the wholesale assassination of Hamas's leadership.

Reuven Paz (2004) questions the effectiveness of this policy, suggesting that it might internationalize the conflict. Left-wing political leaders in Israel deplore the policy, calling such assassinations "gangster murders" (Kafala, 8-1-01). Human rights groups have condemned the policy and challenged it in Israeli courts (BBC News, 1-24-02). Nations all over the world have condemned Israel for these targeted assassinations as well.

Charles Krauthammer (7-16-04) reflects the feelings of those who support these controversial policies. Israel is under attack, he writes. Although the United Nations, for instance, condemned the security fence, he says its construction reduced suicide attacks. Many Israelis feel that harsh policies must be implemented to deter terrorism (Kafala, 8-1-01). Furthermore, the United States repeatedly has taken the position that Israel cannot be condemned for harsh measures until the international community also denounces Palestinian terrorism.

Although supporters claim that Israel should be allowed to take the steps necessary for self-defense, the policies remain controversial. The important question to try to answer is, Do harsh policies reduce terrorism or increase the cycle of violence? Thus far, the question remains unanswered, and violence continues from both sides of the fence.

Summary of Main Points

1. The PIJ originated in Egypt and moved to Gaza. Its sole purpose is to engage in military operations against Israel. Many groups, some of which are allied with the PIJ, use the name *Islamic Jihad*.

2. Hamas grew from the first Intifada. It opposed the PLO and Yasser Arafat. The al Aqsa Intifada transformed Hamas.

3. The PIJ, Hamas, and other groups have copied Hezbollah tactics with suicide bombings. This became the most popular method of mass attack against Israel during the al Aqsa Intifada.

4. The al Aqsa Martyrs Brigades emerged from Fatah. The Brigades have taken much of the limelight away from other Palestinian terrorist groups. Unlike the religious groups, the Brigades might accept a negotiated settlement with Israel.

5. The al Aqsa Intifada has blurred the divisions among many Palestinian terrorist groups.

6. Jewish extremist groups believe that the biblical Kingdom of David belongs to the Jews. Many have used terrorist tactics against Arabs. Some of the settlers in Palestinian areas attack Israeli soldiers.

7. Israel has targeted terrorism and violence with harsh policies. The families of suspected and known terrorists suffer group punishment.

Key Terms

Make sure you can define, explain, or identify the following people, ideas, organizations, or terms:

Palestinian Islamic Jihad (PIJ)   160
Fathi Shekaki   160
Ramadan Abdullah Sallah   162
Sheik Ahmed Yassin   163
Hamas Charter   164
al Qassam Brigades   164
Musa Abu Marzuq   164
"outside" leadership   164
"inside" faction   164
Khalid Mashal   165

Najaf   165
al Aqsa Martyrs Brigades   167
Fatah General Council   171
Kach   172
Kahane Chai   172
Gush Emunim   173
bulldozing   174
security fence   175
Operation Grapes of Wrath   175
selective assassination   175

Suggested Readings

Now that you've been introduced to this topic, you can learn more by reading:

David Horovitz, *Still Life with Bombers*, presents a series of interviews with Israelis and Palestinians who are victimized by violence. He argues that Israel is partially to blame for the situation in the Middle East but condemns the Palestinians, especially Yasser Arafat.

You may also want to read:

Andrea Nusse, in *Muslim Palestine: The Ideology of Hamas*, takes a detailed look at Hamas.

Yonah Alexander has written two background works, *Palestinian Religious Terrorism* and *Palestinian Secular Terrorism*, that provide a current, comprehensive synopsis of violence in the region.

Avraham Sela and Shaul Mishal present a sympathetic view of Hamas in *The Palestinian Hamas: Vision, Violence, and Co-existence*. Arguing that the media have demonized Hamas, they point to its social, health, and educational roles.

Web Resources

Go to *http://cj.wadsworth.com/white_terrorism5e* and click on Web Links to find:

- Stories about Israel and Palestine from PBS's *Frontline World* website
- Australia's position on the Palestinian Islamic Jihad (PIJ)
- A research guide on the Middle East from the University of Delaware library

The Companion Website for *Terrorism and Homeland Security*, Fifth Edition

http://cj.wadsworth.com/white_terrorism5e

At the Book Companion Website you can review chapter outlines, use the flash cards to test your terrorism vocabulary, and check out the many other study aids you'll find there. You'll find valuable data and resources at your fingertips to help you study for that big exam or write that important paper.

Terrorism Updates

http://www.wadsworth.com/criminaljustice_d/special_features/ext/terrorism _site090802/index.html

Visit the *Terrorism: An Interdisciplinary Perspective* website to find the most current information about the fields of terrorism and homeland security. With a focus on domestic and international issues, this site explores the scope of terrorism in our world today. You'll find essays on important topics in terrorism and homeland security, critical thinking web activities, and InfoTrac College Edition keywords. Most importantly, the website is updated weekly with current news and research articles on domestic and international terrorism. You are invited to use these web resources to supplement your understanding of the topics covered in this chapter.

Current Perspectives: Readings from InfoTrac College Edition
Terrorism and Homeland Security

The sixteen articles in this reader offer a representative selection that helps you understand the important issues about terrorism and homeland security. It includes FREE access to InfoTrac College Edition and can also be bundled with the text for free.

Chapter 11

Nationalistic and Ethnic Terrorism

A citizen walks down the street as British soldiers take positions in Derry (Londonderry), North Ireland, in 1971. Nationalistic violence embraces many of the tactics of ideological terrorism but is based in ethnic identity and the desire for political autonomy.

© Darde/AFP/Getty Images

Despite the influence of religion on modern terrorism, other forms of terror continue to exist. National and ethnic struggles still dominate certain regions of the world. For many years, analysts of terrorism examined nationalist terrorists within the same framework as older left-wing terrorist groups. Robert Trundle Jr. (1996) questions this approach, saying that because the structure of ethnic violence has changed, the old models are no longer applicable. At one time, this process may have worked, but it is currently obscuring the understanding of ethnic violence. Trundle has a point. Ethnic terrorism is still a factor in some areas of the world, but it has been less popular since the growth of Jihadist terrorism.

Chapter Objectives

After reading this chapter, you should be able to:

1. Summarize Byman's argument about the logic of ethnic terrorism.
2. Describe the development of terrorism in the Basque region of Spain.
3. Outline the operations and status of the PKK.
4. Describe the issues surrounding terrorism in Sri Lanka.
5. Outline the history of violence in Ireland from the Viking incursion to the Protestant Reformation.
6. Summarize Anglo-Irish relations from the Plantation of Ulster to the potato famine.
7. Explain the logic of Republic violence.
8. Summarize the history of the IRA from the Easter Rebellion to the present.

The Logic of Ethnic Terrorism

Key Points and Questions:

1. What is Byman's central argument about ethnic terrorism?
2. How do ethnic terrorists try to forge their identity?
3. What role does violence play in ethnic terrorism?
4. Why is fear a special weapon for ethnic terrorists?
5. Describe the audiences of ethnic terrorists.
6. What is Byman's approach to counterterrorism?

Daniel Byman (1998) of the RAND Corporation advances a thesis on the structure and logic of ethnic terrorism. He says ethnic terrorism differs from terrorism carried out in the name of ideology, religion, or economic gain. He acknowledges the growing influence of religion on terrorism, but he believes **ethnic terrorism** is a unique entity, even though the line between ethnic and religious violence is blurred. Ethnic terrorists are usually more nationalistic than their religious counterparts. He uses evidence from the Liberation Tigers of Tamil Eelam (LTTE), the Kurdish Workers' Party (PKK), the Provisional Irish Republican Army (PIRA), and the Basque Nation and Liberty (ETA) as evidence for his thesis.

Ethnic terrorists try to forge national identity. Their primary purpose is to mobilize a community, and they do so by appealing to the nationalistic background of a particular ethnic group. Byman says terrorist activity is used to make a statement about the group's identity. When the inevitable government persecution follows terrorist actions, it draws attention to the group and allows the terrorists to present themselves as victims. This process may increase public awareness of ethnic or nationalistic grievances and it may lead to new sources of support. Terrorism also polarizes other ethnic groups and forces them to either ally with the terrorists or oppose them.

Violence plays a special role in ethnic terrorism. Whereas political terrorists use violence in a symbolic manner and religious extremists use it to make a theological statement, violence is the raison d'être of ethnic terrorism. It keeps an idea alive. As long as a bomb goes off or a police officer is murdered, the identity and existence of ethnic differences cannot be denied. Violence sustains the conflict, even when political objectives are far out of reach. The fear created by violence serves ethnic interests. Violence also serves to undermine moderates who seek peaceful solutions.

Fear is also a special tool of ethnic terrorists. Political terrorists direct fear toward an external audience in the hopes of creating an illusion that the government's sociopolitical structure cannot work. Violent ethnic terrorists use fear to polarize various constituencies. The government, for example, is told that it is not welcomed in the ethnic enclave. Violence declares the government illegitimate. Other ethnic groups are told to avoid the terrorists' areas. Fear polarizes cultural differences, forcing greater identification with one's own group. Fear also keeps a group from developing alternative identities.

Byman argues that governments are limited in their response to such fear. They can enter the game and try to promote rival identities. They can also engage in group punishment, but this usually backfires and only drives moderates to the terrorist camp. They can try to gain the cooperation of moderates, but moderates usually lack the strength to control the terrorists. Finally, they can open the doors to political participation. Many governments are reluctant to do this, however, because it seems as though they are rewarding political violence. In essence, fear is a powerful weapon for ethnic terrorists.

Ethnic terrorists have a built-in audience. Ideological terrorists must focus on the whole political spectrum, and violent religious extremists must address a broad theological audience. Ethnic terrorists simply tell their constituency that they are part of the group. Byman says there is no room for converts, nor is there a place for mass appeal. Either you are in, or you are out.

Most analysts focus on the outcomes of a terrorist campaign. They ask, What do the terrorists hope to achieve? They measure the success of the campaign and the response of security forces to assess the effectiveness of counterterrorist actions. Byman argues that this technique is not applicable to ethnic terrorism. Violence is the form of terrorist communication, and success is measured in the continuing threat of violence. Any target outside the ethnic enclave will suffice because there is no such thing as an innocent bystander. Anyone not in the group is an enemy, and violent action against the enemy is the measure of success.

Unlike ideological terrorists, ethnic terrorist organizations tend to be long-lasting. They can build logistical structures much more easily than ideological terrorists because they appeal to an ethnic group, and they can hide in a ready-made population. For example, guerrillas and terrorists in the Russian-controlled province of Chechnya call on Chechnyan nationalism in a struggle for autonomy. Jihadist ideologues have not been able to create a large base of support for the cause, but Chechnyan nationalists have many followers because of their appeal to patriotism (see Timeline 11.1). Some groups suffer as an ideological entity but become stronger when they abandon political beliefs for their ethnic core. For example, Byman argues that Hezbollah is

Timeline 11.1

Chechnya as a Nationalist Revolt

Chapter 8 examined the war in Chechnya as part of the Jihadist struggle. Many Jihadists have flocked to the Trans-Caucasus region, thinking it to be another Afghanistan. However, if you look at the history of the area, you can see how this is also an ethnic or nationalistic rebellion.

1830	Imperial Russia expands into the Caucasus region.
1859	Russia annexes Caucasus, including Dagestan and Chechnya.
1917–1923	Dagestan and Chechnya declare independence.
1923	The Communists conquer Caucasus, adding Dagestan and Chechen-Ingush to the USSR.
1944	Stalin purges the Caucasus area, fearing Chechens and others were influenced by Germany.
1991	The USSR falls; Chechens declare independence, but Russia rejects the claim.
1994–1996	Russia invades Chechnya; agrees to a cease-fire after severe casualties.
1997	Chechens launch bombing campaign in Russia; rebels enter Dagestan.
1999	Russia renews the war, takes Dagestan and launches devastating strikes on Chechnya.
2002	The Moscow theater takeover.
2004	The Breslan school takeover.

Sources: Walker (10-29-01); Lynch (2004); Johnson and Brunner (2004).

much stronger as a Palestinian group than it was as the "Party of God." This implies that security forces need to handle ethnic terrorists differently. In Byman's words, the tried-and-true methods of counterterrorism do not work against ethnic violence.

What does he suggest as an alternative? Moral outrage has no place in countering ethnic terrorism because it will only lead to group cohesion. A government must persuade the leaders of the ethnic group in question that it has a vested interest in maintaining the social structure and it can achieve its goals by working within the current system. Byman suggests three methods for government policy: Empowering the ethnic community, winning over moderates to the political system, and encouraging self-policing.

Byman's approach to ethnic and nationalistic terrorism is correct. When the ethnic community becomes a partner with the prevailing authority, violence and terrorism can be reduced. Governments that have used these strategies have been successful in reducing violence in areas such as Ireland, Turkey, Spain, and Sri Lanka. Yet the situation is always volatile, and there has been no attempt, for instance, to include moderates in Chechnya. India's endemic terrorism is more complicated because ethnicity is tied to differing religions. Just when it appears that security forces are making gains, terrorist violence can frequently be used to derail attempts to bring peace.

The Basque Nation and Liberty

Key Points and Questions:

1. Where is the Basque region?
2. Why do some Basques support a separatist movement in Spain?
3. How is the ETA organized?
4. How do the majority of Basques view the terrorist campaign?
5. What are the chances for peace?

In March 2004 a series of bombs exploded in the central train station of Madrid, Spain, killing nearly two hundred people. Although the plot was eventually tied to Jihadists, the first response from Spain and the international media pointed to the group **Euskadi ta Askatasuna (ETA, or Basque Nation and Liberty)**. The ETA has waged a campaign of violence since 1959 that has killed more than eight hundred people (see Expanding the Concept: The Basque Conflict). They have specialized in car bombings and assassinations, and they have targeted Spain's number one industry, tourism. The ETA's goal is to establish an autonomous homeland in northern Spain and southern France (Foreign Policy Association, 2004; Council on Foreign Relations, 2002; Goodman, 2003).

The Basque region of France and Spain has long been a source for major nationalist terrorism in Europe. Primarily located in Spain, the Basque region extends over the Pyrenees into France (see Figure 11.1). **Basque separatists** believe they should be allowed to develop a homeland in Spain, and since the 1950s, Basque separatism has been an important issue in Spanish politics. Many Americans are not aware of the Basque lands because they are unaware of the evolutionary nature of many European

Figure 11.1
Basque Region

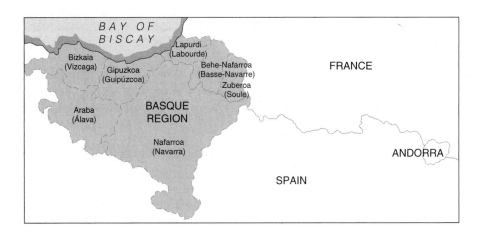

Expanding the Concept

The Basque Conflict

The Issue   Basque separatists want a homeland completely independent of Spain. The nationalists control a semiautonomous Basque parliament, but they are divided in their desire for autonomy. A substantial minority of Basques wants to remain united with Spain.

The Group   Although the Basque region has never been independent, it has its own language and culture. Francisco Franco, the Spanish dictator, tried to crush Basque culture and force the Basques to become Spanish.

The Campaign   The Basque Nation and Liberty (ETA) began a campaign against Spain in 1959. The group was responsible for assassinating Franco's probable successor and many other officials. They agreed to a cease-fire in 1998 but broke the treaty a year later. The Spanish government has given the Basques regional governing authority, and Basques use their own language and run their own schools. The majority of Spaniards believe the ETA to be the most important issue in Spain, and both Basques and Spaniards are tired of ETA violence. Spain also has a strong Jihadist movement, but there is no connection between the Jihadists and the ETA.

The Future   The ETA released a statement in October 2004 stating that it wished to achieve freedom through dialogue with France and Spain. In the past, radicals in the ETA have returned to violence after suggesting peace.

Sources: Goodman (2003); Agence France Presse (10-28-04).

nations. The Basque region of Spain has always had its own language and culture (Clark, 1979), and even though it had not existed as an independent kingdom since 1035, it had maintained its own culture. This changed when Francisco Franco, the fascist Spanish dictator (1939–1975), forcibly campaigned against Basque national identity. A resurgence of Basque nationalism during the 1950s reflected a centuries-old tradition of unique language and culture.

Edward Moxon-Browne (1987) examines the Basque separatist movement and its relation to terrorism. Moxon-Browne maintains that current problems are the result of a gradual loss of national identity that began in the nineteenth century when Madrid assumed greater control of the region, and accelerated in the early twentieth century because of industrialization. After the Spanish Civil War (1936–1939), Franco completely incorporated the Basque region into Spain, banning its language and expressions of national culture. Regaining them became the focus of the modern struggle.

Terrorism grew out of the nationalist movement. The ETA formed as an offshoot of a nationalist political party in 1959. Composed of young, frustrated nationalists who wanted regional autonomy, the ETA was not originally violent, but its members turned to violence when Franco tried to repress the movement. In 1966, the ETA voted to follow the example of the Third World and engage in armed revolution. In 1968, the group started a terrorist campaign. A more militant group, the ETA-M, broke away from the ETA in 1974. ETA-M described itself as the military wing of the ETA and, according to Moxon-Browne, was responsible for the worst atrocities of the 1970s and 1980s.

Both the ETA and the ETA-M have waged a campaign under the name ETA. Violence reached its zenith between 1977 and 1980 and declined steadily throughout the 1980s. The ETA conducted a sporadic campaign during the 1990s, agreeing to a short cease-fire in 1998. In 1999 the ETA broke the cease-fire with a car bomb. In 2001 the ETA was responsible for murdering thirty foreign tourists, and it has tried to conduct major bombings, including an attempt to bring down one of Spain's largest buildings.

Robert Clark (1984) has studied the characteristics of Basque terrorists, and Moxon-Browne uses this as a basis to describe the characteristics of the ETA. Membership matches the composition of the local population, although most terrorists are males. The ETA is primarily a working-class movement, as are many nationalist terrorist groups. Its members were not necessarily raised in a Basque family, but they were raised in Basque enclaves and feel a strong ethnic identity. The overwhelming majority feel they are fighting for all the members of their community.

One of the most interesting characteristics of the ETA is that its members did not view terrorism as a full-time activity. According to Moxon-Browne's research, they maintained some type of employment while serving in the ETA. In addition, most members engaged in terrorism for only about three years. After this, they returned to their full-time occupations.

Clark (1984) says the eventual goal of Basque terrorism is regional independence. In this sense, the ETA is very similar to the IRA. Another parallel is that the majority of Basques do not support the terrorist campaign, even though most support nationalism and some form of independence. Given these circumstances, one of the prime tasks of the Spanish government has been opening the political system to the Basques while allowing them to maintain their cultural heritage. This strategy has served to delegitimize terrorism.

In the late 1980s, the Spanish government began to further delegitimize the ETA by fostering democracy in the Basque region. Although this did not limit nationalistic desire, it gave nationalists a peaceful outlet for their views. They became participants in the control of their destiny. Steven Greer (1995) points to the national police force as evidence of the effects of democratization. It turned the tables on the ETA. By opening peaceful avenues, such as self-policing, both the Spanish and the Basques were able to denounce violence. The ETA found it harder to operate.

Francisco Llora, Joseph Mata, and Cynthia Irvin (1993) point to another change in the ETA. As Spanish authorities opened opportunities for democracy and national expression, the ETA transformed itself into a social movement. Only hard-core militants were left to preach violence, and faced with a growing lack of support in Spain, they began seeking sanctuary in France. The French government, however, began taking actions of its own; although the government has been traditionally sympathetic to Basque nationalism, French prosecutors reversed their position, charging more than seventy ETA members with terrorism in 1994 and convicting more than sixty members by 1995. The base of ETA support appears to be eroding.

Michel Wieviorka (1993) believes that Spain's attempt to open the political system will eventually deter the ETA. In the past, he says, the ETA has claimed to represent the Basque people. Now that the Basques have their own school system, government institutions, and local parliament, the ETA can no longer make that claim. In the end, Wieviorka says, the struggle was twofold: cultural and political. When the political system opened, the desire for ethnic cultural identity was not strong enough to support violence. Repressive policies created the tension, and when they were removed, the support for fighting eroded. If Wieviorka's thesis is correct, ETA actions will eventually be limited to sporadic violence, or the group may even disappear. At this time, however, the ETA still engages in terrorist violence.

Siamik Khatami (1997) summarizes the situation well, and his thesis reflects Byman's conclusions about the logic of ethnic terror. Khatami says that since the fall of the Soviet Union, the ETA and its political wing have become more entrenched in a working-class ideology. They believe the economic structure of the Basque region provides its ethnic identity. Khatami believes the ETA will not compromise on ethnic identity. This gives Spanish authorities a solid opportunity to open the doors of political participation to middle-class Basque moderates. Khatami believes this will become the best weapon against ETA violence.

The PKK and Its Alter Egos

Key Points and Questions:

1. What was the main focus of the PKK?
2. How did the PKK become involved in Middle Eastern terrorism?
3. How did many Kurds respond to PKK terrorist tactics?
4. What was the effect of the capture of Ocalan?
5. What is the long-term future of the PKK?

Turkey is currently facing a wave of religious terrorism, but for the past three decades its major problem came from **Kurds**, an ethic group inhabiting parts of southern Turkey, northern Iraq, and northern Iran (see Expanding the Concept: The Kurdish Conflict). The **Kurdish Workers' Party (PKK)** is a Marxist-Leninist terrorist organization composed of Turkish Kurds. Officially changing its name to Kurdistan Freedom and Democracy (KADEK) in 2002 (see sidebar Another Perspective: The PKK by Any Other Name), it operates in Turkey and Europe, targeting Europeans, Turks, rival Kurds, and supporters of the Turkish government. It represents the same ruthless brand of Maoism as the Peruvian guerrilla organization Shining Path, murdering residents of entire villages who fail to follow its dictates. The PKK/KADEK has developed chameleon-like characteristics. Although it started as a revolutionary Marxist group, since 1990, it has employed the language of nationalism. Even more startling, since 1995, it has also used the verbiage of religion.

The PKK was founded in 1974 to fight for an independent Kurdistan (Criss 1995). Unlike other Kurdish groups, the PKK wanted to establish a Marxist-Leninist

The Kurdish Conflict

The Issue   The Kurds are an ethnic group inhabiting northern Iraq, southern Turkey, and northern Iran. When other groups received national sovereignty at the end of the World War I, the Kurds remained divided among the three nations. The Treaty of Sevres (1920) created an independent Kurdistan, but it was never implemented. About 12 million Kurds live in Turkey.

The Group   The Kurdistan Workers' Party (PKK) formed in 1978 as a Marxist-Leninist group. Its goal was to create an independent socialist Kurdistan.

The Campaign   After training in Syria, the PKK launched a guerrilla campaign in Turkey. By the early 1990s, the PKK turned to urban terrorism, targeting Turks throughout Europe and in Turkey. After its leader, Abdullah Ocalan, was captured in 1999, the PKK pledged to work for a peaceful solution; however, it maintained various militant organizations operating under a variety of names. The PKK maintains links with other revolutionary groups in Turkey and with some international terrorist groups.

The Future   Turkey is being considered for admission to the European Union. The EU, NATO, and the United States list the various entities of the PKK as terrorist organizations. In October 2003 the United States agreed to crack down on the PKK in northern Iraq, and a solution to the Kurdish question might result from negotiation among the United States, the Kurds, and the Turks.

Sources: Dymond (10-2-04); Council on Foreign Relations (2004); U.S. Department of State (2004).

The PKK by Any Other Name

The PKK operates under a variety of names. According to the U.S. Department of State these include

- Freedom and Democracy Congress of Kurdistan
- Kurdistan Peoples' Congress (KHK)
- Peoples' Congress of Kurdistan
- Liberation Units of Kurdistan (HRK)
- Kurdish Peoples' Liberation Army (ARGK)
- National Liberation Front of Kurdistan (ERNK)
- Kurdistan Freedom and Democracy Congress (KADEK)
- Kongra-Gel (KGK)

The PKK officially changed its name to KADEK in April 2002 and to Kongra-Gel in 2003.

Source: U.S. Department of State (2004).

state. Although the PKK targeted Turkey, the Kurds claim a highland region spanning southeast Turkey, northeast Iraq, and northwest Iran (see Figure 11.2). Taking advantage of Kurdish nationalism, the PKK began operations in 1978, hoping to launch a guerrilla war.

The plans for revolution, however, proved too grandiose. There was sentiment for fighting the Iraqis, Iranians, and Turks, but not enough support for the Communists. Most Kurds wanted autonomy, not Communism. The PKK was not strong enough to wage a guerrilla war without some type of support, and its political orientation prevented them from allying with other Kurdish groups. The PKK had two choices: It could either wage a propaganda campaign or throw itself into terrorism. Its leadership chose the path of terror.

PKK leaders increased their efforts to build a terrorist organization by moving into Lebanon's Bekaa Valley in September 1980. While training

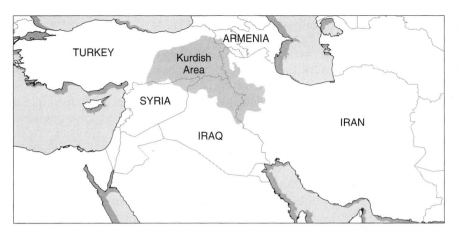

Figure 11.2
Kurdish Region: Turkey, Iraq, and Iran

there, they met some of the most accomplished terrorists in the world, and after the 1982 Israeli invasion of Lebanon, they quickly found allies in the Syrian camp. For the next two years, the group trained and purged its internal leadership. In the meantime, some PKK members cultivated sympathy among several villages in southern Turkey. By 1984 a number of trainees had moved through camps in Lebanon, and the PKK moved to its bases of support for a campaign against Turkey.

Support turned out to be the key factor. Moving from base to base in Turkey, the PKK also received money and weapons from Syria. The relatively weak group of 1978 emerged as a guerrilla force in 1984, and it ruthlessly used terrorism against the Turks and any number of their allies. Civilians bore the brunt of PKK atrocities, and within a few years, the PKK had murdered more than ten thousand people. The majority of these murders came as a result of village massacres (Criss 1995). Turkey responded by isolating the PKK from their support bases and counterattacking PKK groups. Turkish security forces operated with a heavy hand.

The tactics had a negative effect on the Kurds. Although they were ready to fight for independence, they were not willing to condone massacres and terrorist attacks. The PKK responded in 1990 by redirecting offensive operations. Rather than focusing on the civilian population, the PKK began limiting its attacks to security forces and economic targets. Having expanded into Western Europe a few years earlier, PKK leaders stated they would strike only "legitimate" Turkish targets. The PKK also modified its Marxist-Leninist rhetoric and began to speak of nationalism.

In a 1995 interview (Korn, 1995), PKK leader **Abdullah Ocalan** reiterated the new PKK position. When asked whether he was a Marxist, Ocalan stated that he believed in "scientific socialism." Ocalan said this would become a new path because the Muslim population and the Kurds in particular had suffered at the hands of Marxist-Leninists. He cast his statements in anti-imperialist format, stating that Kurdistan was only resisting imperialist powers.

In October 1995, Ocalan asked the United States to mediate between the PKK and Turkey, saying the PKK was willing to settle for a federation instead of complete autonomy. U.S. officials immediately rejected the terrorist's rhetoric, which was nothing new. The PKK had started speaking of federal status in 1990 (Criss 1995). Irrespective of the form of government, Ocalan wanted semiautonomy. In the October 1995 letter to the United States, Ocalan asked for federal status "like the United States." Earlier that year, he had asked for the same thing, "like the Russian Federation" (Korn, 1995). The most dramatic announcement came later. By December, the PKK was using the rhetoric of Islam, citing religious texts instead of Marxist-Leninist ideology. Ocalan appealed to Muslim Kurds, in the name of God, to revolt against the so-called secular Turkish government.

At first it might sound surprising to hear the Marxists of the PKK using religious language, but it is politically understandable. The PKK shifted its position to achieve the greatest amount of support. Ocalan had been moving in an anti-Western direction for many years. His terrorists attacked a NATO base in 1986, and they kidnapped nineteen Western tourists in 1993. As Jihadist rhetoric grew against the West, Ocalan simply copied the verbiage. Additionally, there was something more. In June 1996, an Islamic religious government came to power in secular Turkey. Ocalan wanted to prove he was not an ogre who massacred civilians in their villages, but that he was simply a good Muslim.

Ocalan's shift to religion gave the PKK new life. Leftist movements in Turkey followed the path of their European counterparts: They went into hibernation. When Ocalan proclaimed a doctrine of Marxist Islam, the PKK managed to survive. A unilateral cease-fire in December 1995 placed Turkey in an awkward position. According to Nur Bilge Criss (1995), Ocalan's religious rhetoric played well not only among Kurds, but also throughout the Middle East. Writing before the 1996 election, Criss predicted Turkey would move closer to the Islamic world to counter this threat. He also said the supreme irony is that Turkey may be drawn away from NATO to an alliance with Iraq or Iran in an effort to counterbalance the Kurds and the Syrians. His predictions turned out to be incorrect.

The PKK represents the pejorative nature of terrorism. When the terrorist label is applied to a group like the PKK, the whole movement is questioned. Kurds have long suffered at the hands of their neighbors. The Iranians have slaughtered them, Saddam Hussein used rockets and poison gas to destroy entire Kurdish villages, and the Turks have repressed them. The PKK is a terrorist organization, but expressing Kurdish nationalism is not a terrorist act. Many thousands of Kurds were victimized by state terrorism long before the PKK unsheathed its sword.

Turkish authorities captured Abdullah Ocalan in Kenya in February 1999, and a security court sentenced him to death in June. Ocalan offered to chart a new course for the PKK a few weeks later. Since Turkey was lobbying to join the European Union (EU), it delayed and eventually reversed the death sentence. (Members of the EU may not invoke capital punishment.) It appeared as if there might be a window for peace.

The question of ethnic violence remains open, and the problem has increased since the U.S.-led invasion of Iraq. Turkey casts a wary eye on the Kurds, and many Kurdish guerrillas would actively fight Turkey and Iran for an autonomous homeland. Today, the PKK has thousands of supporters in Turkey and in Europe, but the United States agreed to crack down on the organization in northern Iraq in late 2003 (Dymond, 10-02-04). This may create new possibilities for a negotiated peace between the Turks and the Kurds.

The Liberation Tigers of Tamil Eelam

Key Points and Questions:

1. How did the conflict in Sri Lanka originate?
2. What issues pit the Tamils against the Sinhalese?
3. Why did the LTTE emerge?
4. How did LTTE tactics evolve?

The **Liberation Tigers of Tamil Eelam (LTTE, or Tamil Tigers)**, have been fighting for an independent homeland for nearly 3 million **Tamils** in northern and eastern Sri Lanka (see Figure 11.3). The LTTE has waged a guerrilla campaign using terrorism as both a prelude to guerrilla warfare and a way to support uniformed guerrillas in the field. They have killed thousands and assassinated prominent political figures, such as Indian prime minister Rajiv Gandhi and President Ranasinghe Premadasa of Sri Lanka. They also continue to attack moderate Tamils who oppose their cause. The basis of ethnic conflict is exacerbated by struggles between Hindus and Muslims. The struggle for Sri Lanka has been a long, dirty, and terrible war (see Expanding the Concept: The Sri Lankan Conflict and Timeline 11.2).

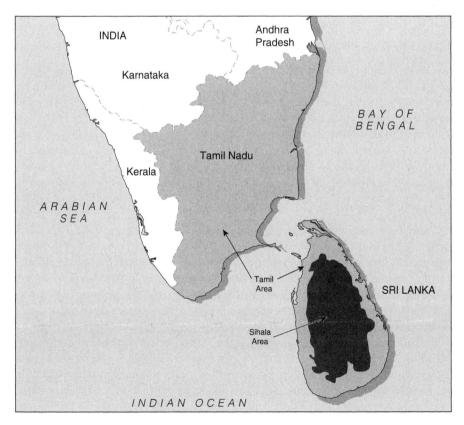

Figure 11.3
Sinhalese and Tamil Areas in Sri Lanka; Tamil Areas in India

Expanding the Concept

The Sri Lankan Conflict

The Issue   In 1948 the British granted Sri Lanka independence. The island was inhabited by the dominant Sinhalese and the Tamils. Although the constitution granted Tamils representation in the government and civil service, by 1955 they felt they were being systematically excluded from Sri Lanka's economic life.

The Group   As ethnic tensions increased, some Tamils turned to violence. The Liberation Tigers of Tamil Eelam (LTTE, or Tamil Tigers) formed in 1976 to fight for the Tamil minority.

The Campaign   The Tigers began a campaign against the Sri Lankan Army, and they targeted India when the Indian prime minister tried to bring peace by deploying security forces. The LTTE is known for kidnapping young children and socializing them in LTTE camps. The Tigers also became masters of assassination and suicide bombings. The LTTE was the first modern secular group to use suicide bombers. Many members live in a virtual death cult, and the Black Tigers, the suicide wing of the LTTE, are known for carrying cyanide capsules around their necks when they attack.

The Future   The LTTE agreed to a cease-fire in December 2001 and began peace negotiations in 2002. Although occasional outbreaks of violence have occurred, many experts believe the LTTE is suffering from a lack of resources.

Source: Council on Foreign Relations (2004).

Manoj Joshi (1996) traces the struggle's origins to the autonomy India gained at the end of World War II. As India sought to bring internal peace among Hindus and Muslims, the island of Sri Lanka (formerly known as Ceylon) faced a similar problem. In addition to religious differences, the Tamil minority in Sri Lanka was concerned about maintaining its ethnic identity. Tamils along the southeastern coast of India supported the Sri Lankan Tamils in this quest. As the Sri Lankan government was formed, the Tamils found themselves in positions of authority. Although they accounted for only 17 percent of Sri Lanka's population (the Sinhalese account for the majority), the Tamils were well-represented in the bureaucracy. This changed in 1955.

Claiming that Tamils dominated the Sri Lankan government, the Sinhalese majority forced the government to adopt a "Sinhalese-only" policy. Tamils began to grumble, and some spoke of violence. A Tamil assassin killed the Sinhalese leader in 1959, setting the stage for further violence. Seeking sanctuary in the Tamil region of India, militant Tamils filtered across the short expanse of ocean to wage a low-level terrorist campaign through 1975. Spurred by their successes, they began larger operations.

The Tamil experience was similar to the situation in Ireland. Buoyed by religious differences and ethnic support, Tamil separatists could begin a guerrilla campaign by waging terrorist war. Their ethnic support base gave them the opportunity to do so. In 1975, **Velupillai Pirabhakaran**, a young Tamil militant, took advantage of the situation and formed the LTTE. (*Eelam* means homeland.) Pirabhakaran faced prob-

Timeline 11.2

The Sri Lankan Civil War

1972	New constitution favors Buddhist Sinhalese.
1983	Anti-Tamil riots; Tamils hunted and killed.
1987	First LTTE suicide bombing.
1991	Indian Prime Minister Rajiv Gandhi killed by a suicide bomber.
1996	Suicide bomber kills ninety-one people at Colombo Central Bank.
2002	Government and Tamil Tigers sign a cease-fire.
2004	Cease-fire threatened when a tsunami kills thousands.

Source: *Wall Street Journal* Research Staff (1-11-05).

lems similar to those of other terrorists. He had to raise money, which he did through bank robberies and assassinations, and he needed to eliminate rival terrorists to claim leadership of the movement.

The LTTE eventually emerged as the leading revolutionary group and launched Sri Lanka into a full-blown terrorist campaign. The Tigers were not satisfied with this, however, wanting to build a guerrilla force and eventually a conventional army. The Sinhalese majority reacted violently in 1983. Ignoring the government, Sinhalese protesters flocked to the streets of Colombo, Sri Lanka's capital, in a series of anti-Tamil riots. Many Tamils fled to India, and the LTTE returned to terrorism.

Reactions to the riots were a turning point for the LTTE. Unable to foment the revolution from above, the group established contacts with the Popular Front for the Liberation of Palestine. Since that time, the Tamil Tigers have mounted three on-again, off-again terrorist campaigns. At first, India responded by forming a joint peacekeeping force with Sri Lanka. India's primary purpose was to keep violence from spilling over into the mainland. India reevaluated its policy after a number of assassinations and violent encounters, and the government has vowed never to send troops to Sri Lanka again.

The LTTE has incorporated a variety of tactics since 1984. Their ability to operate is directly correlated to the amount of political support they enjoy during any particular period. In 1988 and 1992, they sought to control geographic areas, and they moved using standard guerrilla tactics, forming uniformed units. They even created an ad hoc navy. In weaker times, they relied on bank robberies, bombings, and murder. In the weakest times, they have also employed suicide bombers. They used suicide attacks in 1995 on land and at sea.

Before 1983, Joshi estimates that the LTTE had only forty followers. The anti-Tamil riots were a catalyst to growth, as links were formed in the Middle East. Terrorist training camps appeared in the Tamil region of India in 1984 and 1985, and the training cadre included foreign terrorists. India responded by signing a joint peace agreement with Sri Lanka, and soon found itself under attack from a highly organized terrorist group, numbering between ten thousand and sixteen thousand.

When not attacking India, the Tamil Tigers launched operations in Sri Lanka. Although they had once struggled to be recognized as the leaders of the independence movement, the Tigers ruthlessly wiped out their opponents and terrorized their own ethnic group into providing support. Yet security forces enjoyed several successes, and by 1987, the Tamil Tigers were in retreat.

According to Joshi, this was a very dangerous period for the group. In fact, it was almost wiped out. Retreating to the jungle, the Tamil Tigers abandoned the new-found position of power and practiced terrorism from jungle hideaways. They increased contact with Tamil bases in India, using India for logistical support. Politically adept, the LTTE asked for a cease-fire in 1989, giving India a chance to withdraw from the joint security force. No sooner had the Indians left than the LTTE renewed its attack on the Sri Lankans.

In 1990, the LTTE expanded its operations by converting a fishing fleet into a makeshift navy. Suicide boats and other seaborne operations threatened the waters between Sri Lanka and India. By 1991, India was once again targeted by Tamil terrorists, and the Indian Navy was forced to respond to the growing threat. Not only did the LTTE fight small-scale sea battles with the Indians, but its terrorists also succeeded in assassinating Prime Minister Gandhi on May 21, 1991. When Indian authorities cracked down on Tamil bases, the Tamil Tigers increased their terrorist attacks against India.

From 1994 to 1995, the Tamil Tigers waged another bombing and assassination campaign, and although their bases in India were limited, they had geographic strongholds on Sri Lanka. They did what no other terrorist group has been able to do. Supported by guerrilla strongholds, Tamil Tigers appeared in uniforms in 1994 and fought pitched battles with the Sri Lankan security forces. Suicide bombings increased during the same time. Faced with open revolution, the Sri Lankan government signed a peace agreement in January 1995.

Joshi's research ended in the summer of 1995. The peace accord broke down, and the Sri Lankan Army went on the offensive. The LTTE suffered several setbacks, but the group made headlines in 1996 with suicide bombings in Colombo. In the spring of 1996, Sri Lankan security forces launched an all-out assault on Tamil strongholds on the northern portion of the island. Some commentators (de Silva, 5-5-96; Berthelsen, 5-9-96) believed this would be the end of the LTTE. They were wrong.

Rohan Gunaratna (1998) argues that the LTTE is in a unique position because it has such a large guerrilla base. The guerrillas are perfectly capable of fighting a protracted war against security forces, and if defeated, the LTTE can revert to terrorism. Indeed, this has been the LTTE's tactic. In the wake of new fighting, the LTTE has followed the path of suicide bombing. Although the guerrilla campaign subsided a bit in 1999, suicide bombings increased in 2000. The hardcore LTTE is a long way from any negotiated settlement. The hope of the Sri Lankan government is to attract moderate Tamils into a coalition government and deprive the Tamil Tigers of their ethnic and guerrilla support.

In December 2001 the LTTE agreed to a cease-fire with the government of Sri Lanka. Although the Tigers still threaten violence, their resources may be depleting. The Council on Foreign Relations (2004) believes that the international community's efforts to thwart terrorism after September 11 are responsible for this situation. Arms shipments have been virtually eliminated, and expatriate Tamil communities in Australia, Canada, and the United States are no longer allowed to gather and ship resources to Sri Lanka. The largest hit was economic. LTTE assets were frozen in the wake of September 11. The Council on Foreign Relations believes the LTTE may no longer be able to fight.

The Tamil Eelam Web homepage (2005) suggests that negotiations may work. The Tamils believe that Sri Lanka is the home of two sovereign peoples: the Tamils and the Sinhalese. They argue that the island can be divided into two sovereign areas and that both groups can live together, albeit separately. They also believe they are operating their own governmental, economic, and educational systems. According to the homepage, the LTTE is not a terrorist organization; it is the army of the Tamil people. It may well be that the Sinhalese and Tamils are able to negotiate peace from the recent cease-fire, but most of the world would not agree with this assessment of the Tigers. The leaders who conscript children and foster suicide bombings are and will remain terrorists in the eyes of most people.

The Origins and Development of the Anglo-Irish Conflict

Key Points and Questions:

1. What impact did the Vikings and Normans have on Ireland?
2. How did the Protestant Reformation affect ethnic struggles in Ireland?
3. Summarize revolts and independence from the time of the Plantation of Ulster to the potato famine of 1845–1848.
4. Explain the rationale for Home Rule.
5. Why did the Ulster Protestants and many British military officers oppose Home Rule?

Irish culture originated with Celtic invasions three centuries before Jesus (Costigan, 1980). The Irish settled in tribal groups, and government was maintained through kinship and clans. No Celtic ruler or political authority ever united Ireland as a single entity. In about C.E. 500, the Irish were introduced to Christianity and became some of the most fervent converts in the world. The medieval church played a large role in uniting Ireland, but the traditional Gaelic tribal groups still remained separate. They submitted to a central religion, not a central political system.

The relations among Gaelic tribes became important when Viking raiders began to attack Ireland around C.E. 800. The divided Irish were dominated by their Viking rulers, and the Norsemen used Ireland as a trading base and center of commerce. The Vikings built several Irish cities, including Dublin.

Viking rule of Ireland was challenged in 1014, when a tribal chieftain, Brian Boru, was declared high king of Ireland. He led a united tribal army against the Vikings and defeated them at Clontarf. Fate ruled against the Irish, however. At the end of the battle as King Brian knelt in prayer, he was assassinated. Dreams of a united Ireland crumbled with Brian Boru's death, and the clans and tribes soon divided leadership again.

Costigan (1980) believes this paved the way for a gradual Norman invasion of Ireland. The Normans were the descendants of William the Conqueror and had ambitions for extending their domains. With the Irish divided and the Viking influence limited, Normans began to stake out territorial claims on the island with the permission of the Norman king. The Normans were particularly successful in Ireland because they used new methods of warfare. By 1172, the Norman king of England had assumed the rule of Ireland.

The Normans and the Irish struggled in a way unlike modern fighting. The Normans could not maintain the field force necessary to control the Irish peasants, and the Irish did not have the technology that would allow them to attack smaller Norman forces barricaded in castles. Therefore, the Normans built castles to control Irish cities, and Irish peasants generally dominated rural areas. This situation continued until the sixteenth century.

The Protestant Reformation of the 1500s had a tremendous effect on Ireland. Wanting to free himself from the ecclesiastical shackles of Rome, the English king, Henry VIII, created an independent Church of England. He also created a similar church in Ireland, but the Irish Catholics rejected this move and began to rebel against the English king. The troubles created by the Reformation have literally continued into the twenty-first century in Ireland.

The problems of the early Reformation were magnified by Henry's daughter Elizabeth. Not content with merely ruling Ireland, Elizabeth I carved out the most prosperous agrarian section—the Plantation of Ulster—and gave it to her subjects to colonize. English and Scottish Protestants eventually settled there, displacing many of the original Irish inhabitants. This created an ethnic division in Ireland fueled by religious differences and animosities.

According to Costigan (1980), the 1600s in Ireland were dominated by three major issues. First, the Plantation of Ulster was expanded, and Irish peasants were systematically displaced. Many of them perished. Second, Oliver Cromwell came to Ireland to quell a revolt and stop Catholic attacks on Protestants. He massacred thousands of Irish Catholics, thanking God for granting him the opportunity to kill such a large number of his enemies. Cromwell's name still stirs hatred as a result.

The third issue of the 1600s also involved Catholic and Protestant struggles, and the image of the conflict is still celebrated in ceremonies today. From 1689 to 1691, James II, the Catholic pretender to the British throne, used Ireland as a base from which to revolt against William of Orange, the English king. In August 1689, Irish Protestant skilled workers, called Apprentice Boys, were relieved by the English after defending Derry through a long siege by the pretender. The following year William defeated James at the battle of the Boyne River.

The revolt was over, but the Protestants were now forever in the camp of the House of Orange. Protestants have flaunted these victories in the face of Catholics since 1690. Each year they gather to militantly celebrate the Battle of the Boyne and the Apprentice Boys with parades and demonstrations. These celebrations fuel the fire of hatred in Northern Ireland and demonstrate the continuing division between Protestants and Catholics. In fact, the current troubles started in 1969, when riots broke out in Londonderry and Belfast after the annual Apprentice Boys parade.

The 1700s and early 1800s in Ireland were characterized by waves of revolt, starvation, and emigration. Irish nationalists rose to challenge English rule, but they were always soundly defeated. Each generation seemed to bring a new series of martyrs willing to give their lives in the struggle against the English.

Among the best-known revolutionaries was Thomas Wolfe Tone. From 1796 to 1798, Wolfe Tone led a revolt based on Irish nationalism. He tried to appeal to both

Protestants and Catholics in an attempt to form a unified front against Great Britain. Wolfe Tone argued that Irish independence was more important than religious differences. In the end, his revolt failed, but he had created a basis for appealing to nationalism over religion.

Despite the efforts of people like Wolfe Tone, religious animosity did not die in Ireland. During the late 1700s, Protestants and Catholics began to form paramilitary organizations. Divided along religious lines, these defense organizations began violently to confront one another. The Orange Orders were born during this period. Taking their name from William of Orange, these Protestant organizations vowed to remain unified with Great Britain. The Orange Lodges soon grew to dominate the political and social life of Northern Ireland.

The early 1800s brought a new level of political struggle to Ireland. In 1801, the British Parliament passed the Act of Union, designed to incorporate Ireland into the United Kingdom. Struggle over the act began to dominate Irish politics. Unionists, primarily the **Orange** Protestants in the north, supported the act, whereas Republicans, who became known as **Greens**, argued for a constitutional government and an independent Ireland. Daniel O'Connell led the Republican movement in the early part of the century, and Charles Stewart Parnell, a Protestant, created a democratic Irish party to support the cause in the late 1800s.

The struggle for Republicanism accompanied one of the saddest periods in Irish history. Displaced from the land, Irish peasants were poor and susceptible to economic and agricultural fluctuations, especially because they began to rely on the potato as their main crop. In 1845, the crop failed, and agricultural production came to a standstill until 1848. Nearly 1 million Irish peasants starved while wealthy farms in the north exported other crops for cash (Woodham-Smith, 1962).

The 1845–1848 potato famine devastated Ireland. Its effects were felt primarily among the poor, especially among the Irish Catholics. During an era in which other industrialized nations were experiencing a tremendous rise in population, Ireland's census dropped by 25 percent. As famine and disease took their toll, thousands of Irish people emigrated to other parts of the world. During this period, Unionists in the north consolidated their hold on Ulster.

In the years following the famine, some members of the British Parliament sought to free Ireland from British control. They introduced a series of Home Rule acts designed to give Ireland independence. Charles Stewart Parnell and other Republicans supported Home Rule, but they faced fierce opposition from Unionists, who were afraid Home Rule would shift the balance of economic power in the north. They believed continued union with Great Britain was their only option for economic success. Unionists were supported in British military circles because army officers accepted the Ulster Protestants as British citizens and viewed the Catholic Republicans as colonial subjects. In the minds of some members of the British Army, Irish Catholics simply amounted to another native tribe revolting against the British empire.

Even though Parnell was Protestant, most Republicans were Catholics living in the southern part of Ireland. Unionists tended to be Protestant skilled laborers, industrialists, and landlords in the north. The religious aspect of the conflict remained and was augmented by deep economic divisions.

It should be noted that by the nineteenth century, both Unionists and Republicans were fully Irish; that is, Catholics and the Protestants, despite all political differences, identified themselves as citizens of the Emerald Isle. Unionist Protestants in the north had lived in Ireland for generations, and they were as Irish as their Catholic counterparts. The Unionists were able to call on Britain for help, but the struggle in Ireland began to take on the earmarks of an intra-Irish conflict. Irish Unionists, usually Protestant, dominated the north, and Irish Republicans, primarily Catholics, controlled the south.

The Early History of the Irish Republican Army

Key Points and Questions:

1. How did the Irish Republican Brotherhood form?
2. Why did the IRB gravitate toward violence?
3. What factors caused the conflict between Republicans and the police?
4. How did Feinian ideology influence Patrick Pearse?

By the twentieth century, the struggle in Ireland mainly had become a matter of the divisions between Unionists and Republicans. The Unionists often had the upper hand because they could call on support from the British-sponsored police and military forces. The Republicans had no such luxury, and they searched for an alternative.

Costigan (1980) believes that the Republican military solution to the Irish conflict was born in New York City in 1857. Irish Catholics had emigrated from their homeland to America, Australia, Canada, and New Zealand, but they never forgot the people they left behind. Irish immigrants in New York City created the Irish Republican Brotherhood (IRB) as a financial relief organization for relatives in Ireland. After the American Civil War, some Irish soldiers returning from the U.S. Army decided to take the struggle for emancipation back to Ireland. Rationalizing that they had fought for the North to free the slaves, they believed they should continue the struggle and free Ireland. The IRB gradually evolved into a revolutionary organization.

J. Bowyer Bell (1974), who has written the definitive treatise on the origins and development of the **Irish Republican Army (IRA)**, says that the IRA began with a campaign of violence sponsored by the IRB in the late 1800s. Spurred on by increased Irish nationalist feeling in the homeland and the hope of Home Rule, the IRB waged a campaign of bombing and assassination from 1870 until 1916. Its primary targets were Unionists and British forces supporting the Unionist cause. Among their greatest adversaries was the British-backed police force in Ireland, the Royal Irish Constabulary (RIC).

The activities of the IRB frightened Irish citizens who wanted to remain united with Great Britain. For the most part, these Irish people were Protestant and middle class, and they lived in the north. They gravitated toward their trade unions and Orange Lodges to counter growing IRB sympathy and power. They enjoyed the sympathy of the British Army's officer corps, and they also controlled the RIC.

The Fenians (named after the mythical Irish hero Finn McCool) of the IRB remained undaunted by Unionist sentiment. Although Unionists seemed in control, the IRB had two trumps. First, IRB leadership was dominated by men who believed each generation had to produce warriors who would fight for independence. Some of these leaders, as well as their followers, were quite willing to be martyred to keep Republicanism alive. In addition, the IRB had an organization. It not only threatened British power, but it also provided the basis for the resurgence of Irish culture.

At the turn of the century, no person embodied Irish culture more than Patrick Pearse. The headmaster of an Irish school, Pearse was an inspirational romantic who could move crowds to patriotism and inspire resistance to British policies. He was a hero among Irish Americans, and they sent hundreds of thousands of dollars to support his cause. He told young Irish boys and girls about their heritage, he taught them the old Irish language of Gaelic, and he inspired them to be militantly proud of being Irish. He was also a member of the Supreme Council of the IRB. When the concept of Home Rule was defeated in the British Parliament, Republican eyes turned to Pearse.

The 1916 Easter Rebellion

Key Points and Questions:

1. What caused the Easter Rebellion?
2. How did the IRB transform into the IRA?
3. Why did Patrick Pearse and James Connolly differ about political orientation?
4. Describe the outcome of the Easter Rebellion.

By 1916, the situation in Ireland had changed. The British had promised Home Rule when World War I came to an end in 1918. Most people in Ireland believed the British, but Unionists and Republicans secretly armed for a civil war between the north and south. They believed a fight was inevitable if the British granted Home Rule, and each side was determined to dominate the government of a newly independent Ireland.

Some forces, however, were not willing to wait for Home Rule. With British attention focused on Germany, leaders of the IRB believed it was time for a strike against the Unionists and their British supporters. At Easter in 1916, Patrick Pearse and James Connolly led a revolt in Dublin. Pearse felt the revolt was doomed from the start but believed it was necessary to sacrifice his life to keep the Republican spirit alive. Connolly was a more pragmatic socialist who fought because he believed a coming civil war was inevitable.

The **1916 Easter Rebellion** enjoyed local success because it surprised everyone. Pearse and Connolly took over several key points in Dublin with a few thousand armed followers. From the halls of the General Post Office, Pearse announced that the revolutionaries had formed an Irish Republic and asked the Irish to follow him. The British, outraged by what they deemed to be treachery in the midst of a larger war, also came to Dublin. The city was engulfed in a week of heavy fighting.

Whereas Pearse and Connolly intended to start a popular revolution, the British intended to fight a war. In a few days, British artillery devastated Dublin. Pearse recognized the futility of the situation and asked for terms. J. Bowyer Bell (1974) points out the interesting way Pearse chose to approach the British: He sent a message to the general in charge of British forces using a new title—commanding general of the Irish Republican Army. The IRB had transformed itself into an army: the IRA.

Transformations continued in the political arena, and, ironically, what Pearse and Connolly could not achieve in life, they could achieve in death. Irish opinion was solidly against the IRA, and most Irish people held Pearse and Connolly responsible for the destruction of Dublin. The British, however, failed to capitalize on this sentiment. Rather than listen to public opinion, they cracked down on all expressions of Republicanism. Dozens of Republicans, including Pearse and the wounded Connolly, were executed, and thousands were sentenced to prison. The British promise of Home Rule seemed forgotten. Most Irish people were appalled by the harsh British reaction, and the ghosts of Pearse and Connolly held power within the IRA. Irish political opinion shifted to favor revolution.

Independence and Separation

 Key Points and Questions:

1. How did Sinn Fein keep the IRA alive?
2. What caused the Tan War?
3. Why did the peace treaty separate Eamon de Valera and Michael Collins?
4. How did Ireland split between the Republic and Ulster?
5. Why did the British form the Royal Ulster Constabulary?

Sinn Fein, the political party of Republicanism, continued its activities despite the failure of the Easter Rebellion. When World War I ended, many of the jailed Republicans were released. Eamon de Valera emerged as the leader of Sinn Fein, and Michael Collins came to the forefront of the IRA. Together, de Valera and Collins began to fight for Irish independence in 1919.

As discussed in Chapter 2, Michael Collins had studied the tactics of the Russian People's Will and the writings of earlier anarchists and terrorists. He used these studies as an inspiration for strategy and launched a guerrilla war against the British. After obtaining a list of British and loyalist Irish police and intelligence officers, Collins sent IRA terrorists to their homes and killed them. He attacked police stations and symbols of British authority. A master of terrorist strategy, Collins continued a campaign of terror against Unionists and the RIC.

The British responded by sending a hastily recruited military force, called the Black and Tans because of their mismatched uniforms, and Ireland became the arena for a dreadful war. Both sides accused the other of atrocities, but murder and mayhem were the tactics of each party. The conflict became popularly known as the Tan War or the Black and Tan War.

Meanwhile, Home Rule had not been forgotten by more moderate groups. Politicians in Britain and Ireland sought to bring an end to the violence by formulating the steps to grant Irish independence. The main stumbling block was the north, where Protestant Unionists were afraid of being abandoned by the British. In 1921, the situation was temporarily solved by a treaty between Britain and Ireland. Under the terms of the treaty, Ireland would be granted independence while the northern section around Ulster would remain under British protection until it could peacefully be integrated into Ireland. Southern Ireland became the free state—the Republic of

Ireland. The majority of people in Ireland accepted the treaty, as did Michael Collins. But the IRA did not.

When the treaty between Ireland and Britain was ratified in 1921, a civil war broke out in the newly formed republic. Michael Collins led the Irish Army, while de Valera took the helm of the IRA. The IRA fought Irish government forces, claiming that Irish independence had to extend to all Irish people. They rejected British control of the north. De Valera campaigned against his former colleagues and eventually orchestrated the murder of Michael Collins.

For their part, the British wanted nothing to do with the civil war in the southern areas. They tightened their hold on Northern Ireland and bolstered its strength with a new police force, the **Royal Ulster Constabulary** (RUC). The northern Unionists were delighted when the British established a semiautonomous government in Northern Ireland and gave it special powers to combat the IRA. The Unionists used this power to gain control of Northern Ireland and lock themselves into the British orbit. Ireland became a divided country. (See Figure 11.4.)

Figure 11.4
Northern Ireland

Trends in the IRA: 1930–1985

Key Points and Questions:

1. Explain the split in IRA ranks.

2. Why did the civil rights movement replace IRA violence?

3. What was the reaction to the manner in which the British responded to civil rights violence?

4. How did various fragments of the IRA reemerge?

In 1932, de Valera was elected prime minister of the Irish Free State. Although he passed several anti-British measures, he was soon at odds with the IRA. Two important trends emerged. J. Bowyer Bell (1974) records the first by pointing to the split in IRA ranks. By the 1930s, some members of the IRA wanted to follow the lead of their political party, Sinn Fein. They felt the IRA should express itself through peaceful political idealism and they should begin working for a united socialist Ireland in the spirit of James Connolly.

Another group of IRA members rejected this philosophy. They believed the purpose of the IRA was to fight for Republicanism. They would never be at peace with the British or the Unionists until the north was united with the south. They vowed to carry on the fight. They broke with the de Valera government and formed a provisional wing of the IRA during the 1930s. The Provisional IRA vowed to keep up the fight. De Valera turned on them and silenced them for a number of years. They launched an ineffective terrorist campaign in Northern Ireland from 1956 to 1962, and they fell out of favor with Irish Republicans. Just when it seemed that the Provisional IRA was defunct, a Catholic civil rights campaign engulfed Northern Ireland in 1969. The failure of the civil rights movement in Northern Ireland can be directly linked to modern Irish terrorism and the rebirth of the IRA.

Alfred McClung Lee (1983, pp. 59–97) discusses another trend in Ireland. Internally, the IRA split into a traditional official branch (the **Officials**) and a more militant provisional wing (the **Provisionals**). He notes that externally the economic situation in Northern Ireland consolidated in favor of the Protestant Unionists. From 1922 to 1966, the government in Northern Ireland systematically reduced the civil rights of Catholics living in the north. During the same period, the economic power of the Unionists increased.

According to Lee, the political and economic conditions in Northern Ireland provided the rationale for a major civil rights movement among the Catholics. Although the movement had Republican overtones, it was primarily aimed at achieving adequate housing and education among Ulster's Catholic population in an attempt to improve economic growth. The civil rights movement was supported by both Protestants and Catholics, but the actions of the Northern Irish government began to polarize the issue. Increasingly, the confrontation became recognized as a Unionist-Republican one, and the old battle lines between Protestants and Catholics were redrawn. By 1969, the civil rights movement and the reaction to it had become violent.

The IRA had not been dormant throughout the civil rights movement, but it had failed to play a major role. For the most part, the leaders of the civil rights movement were peaceful Republicans. The IRA could not entice the civil rights leaders into a guerrilla war, and it had virtually destroyed itself in an earlier campaign against the government of Northern Ireland. In 1969, the Provisional IRA was popular in song and legend, but it held little sway in day-to-day Irish politics. Some type of miracle would be needed to rejuvenate the IRA.

The reason for IRA impotence can be found in the second generation of Provisionals. Wanting to follow in the footsteps of their forebears, the Provisionals began to wage a campaign against the RUC in Northern Ireland in the late 1950s. They established support bases in the Republic and slipped across the border for terrorist activities. Although they initially enjoyed support among Republican enclaves in the north, most Irish people, Unionists and Republicans alike, were appalled by IRA violence. Even the Officials criticized the military attacks of the Provisionals. Faced with a lack of public support, the Provisional IRA called off its offensive in the north. By 1962, almost all of its activities had ceased. Some Provisionals joined the civil rights movement; others rejoined former colleagues in the Official wing. Most members, however, remained in a secret infrastructure and prayed for a miracle to restore their ranks and prestige. In 1969, their prayers were answered.

The government in Northern Ireland reacted with a heavy hand against the civil rights workers and demonstrators, and this repression was the answer to IRA prayers. Peaceful attempts to work for equal rights were stymied by northern Irish militancy (Hastings, 1970, pp. 40–56). Catholics were not allowed to demonstrate for better housing and education; if they tried to do so, they were attacked by the RUC and its reserve force, known as B-Specials. At the same time, no attempts were made to stop Protestant demonstrations. The Catholics believed the RUC and B-Specials were in league with the other anti-Catholic Unionists in the north.

Issues intensified in the summer of 1969. Civil rights demonstrators planned a long, peaceful march from Londonderry to Belfast, but they were gassed and beaten by the RUC and B-Specials. On August 15, 1969, the Protestants assembled for their traditional Apprentice Boys celebration. Just a few days before, the RUC had enthusiastically attacked Catholic demonstrators, but on August 15 it welcomed the Protestant Apprentice Boys with open arms. The Catholics were not surprised: Many B-Specials had taken off their reservist uniforms to don orange sashes and march with the Protestants.

Protestant marchers in Londonderry and Belfast armed themselves with gasoline bombs, rocks, and sticks. They not only wished to celebrate the seventeenth-century victory in Derry, but they were also thrilled by the recent dispersal of the civil rights marchers and hoped to reinforce their political status by bombarding Catholic neighborhoods as they marched by. When the Protestants began taunting Catholics, violence broke out. By nightfall, Belfast and Londonderry were in flames. Three days later, Britain sent the British Army in as a peacekeeping force. Ironically, the British Army became the miracle that the IRA so desperately needed.

According to most analysts and observers, the early policies and tactics of the British Army played an important role in the rebirth of the IRA. In an article on military policy, J. Bowyer Bell (1976, pp. 65–88) criticizes the British Army for its initial response. He says the army went to Ulster with little or no appreciation of the historical circumstances behind the conflict. According to Bell, when the army arrived in 1969, its commanders believed they were in the midst of a colonial war.

They evaluated the situation and concluded there were two "tribes." One tribe flew the Irish tricolor and spoke with deep-seated hatred of the British; the other flew the Union Jack and claimed to be ultrapatriotic subjects of the British Empire. It seemed logical to ally with friends who identified themselves as subjects.

Bell believes this policy was fatal. Far from being a conflict to preserve British influence in a colony, the struggle in Northern Ireland was a fight between two groups of Irish citizens. Neither side was "British," no matter what their slogans and banners claimed. The British Army should have become a peaceful, neutral force, but it mistakenly allied itself with one of the extremist positions in the conflict. That mistake became the answer to IRA prayers.

Bell argues that the reaction of Republican Catholics fully demonstrates the mistake the British Army made. The Unionists greeted the army with open arms, but this was to be expected. Historically, the British Army had rallied to the Unionist cause. Surprisingly, however, the Republicans also welcomed the army. They believed that the RUC and B-Specials were the instruments of their repression and that the British Army would not continue such restrictive measures. It was not the British Army of the past. In Republican eyes, it was a peacekeeping force. The Republicans believed the British Army would protect them from the Unionists and the police.

Such beliefs were short-lived. As the British Army made its presence felt in Ulster, Republicans and Catholics were subjected to the increasing oppression of army measures. Military forces searching for subversives surrounded and gassed Catholic neighborhoods, and soldiers began working as a direct extension of the RUC. Londonderry and Belfast were military targets, and rebels fighting against the government were to be subdued. As confrontations became more deadly, Republican support for the British Army vanished.

Feeling oppressed by all sides, Catholics and Republicans looked for help. They found it, partly, in the form of the IRA. The Officials and Provisionals were still split during the 1969 riots, and the IRA was generally an impotent organization. According to Iain Hamilton (1971), the IRA pushed its internal squabbles aside, and the Officials and Provisionals focused on their new common enemy, the British Army. The new IRA policy emphasized the elimination of British soldiers from Irish soil and brushed aside internal political differences.

Robert Moss (1972, pp. 16–18) remarks that the British Army found itself in the middle of the conflict it had hoped to forestall. Alienated nationalists offered support for the growing ranks of the IRA. Each time the British Army overreacted, as it tended to do when faced with civil disobedience, the Republican cause was strengthened.

Reporter Simon Winchester (1974, pp. 171–180) notes another outcome of the conflict: As IRA ranks grew, Orange extremist organizations also began to swell. While crackdowns by British Army patrols and incidents of alleged torture by intelligence services increased the ranks of the IRA, Unionist paramilitary organizations grew in response. The British Army also began taking action against the Unionist organizations and then truly found itself in the midst of a terrorist conflict.

Go to **http://cj.wadsworth.com/white
_terrorism5e** and click on Web Links for an in-depth discussion of counterterrorist tactics and a discussion of Unionist terrorism in Ireland.

In 1972, the British government issued a report on the violence in Northern Ireland. Headed by Leslie Scarman (1972), the investigation concluded that tensions inside the community were so great, once they had been unleashed, little could be done to stop them. The policies of the police and the British Army had done much to set those hostile forces in motion. The report concluded that normative democracy could not return until the people in Northern Ireland had faith in all government institutions, including the security forces. The report indicated that a legal method was needed to resolve the violence.

The Peace Accord and Peace Process in Ireland

Key Points and Questions:

1. What is the Anglo-Irish Peace Accord?
2. Describe differing views on prospects for peace in Ireland.
3. What is the current trend in the IRA?

In 1985, the United Kingdom and the Republic of Ireland signed a peace accord regarding the governance of Northern Ireland. Known as the **Anglo-Irish Peace Accord**, the agreement seeks to bring an end to terrorism by establishing a joint system of government for the troubled area. Seamus Dunn and Valerie Morgan (1995) believe many Protestant groups feel betrayed by this agreement. They surmise such groups may resort to violence if they feel they have no voice in the political system, and they believe that all groups must feel they have a vested interest in peace if the process is to work. It took militant Protestants and Catholics nearly ten years to lay down the weapons of terrorism, and sporadic outbursts of violence still occur.

J. Bowyer Bell (1998) describes the problem of peace in Ireland as a long ending to a lengthy process. The IRA declared a cease-fire in 1994 but broke it in 1996. Trying to bring life into the Anglo-Irish Peace Accord, British prime minister Tony Blair invited the most militant Irish nationalists to the peace table in 1998 and continued negotiations. This brought the ethnic Irish party Sinn Fein to the table, but more militant Irish Republicans broke ranks. This led to the birth of the Real Irish Republican Army or the True Irish Republican Army, as well as several other Orange and Green terrorist organizations. These groups renewed a campaign of violence in 1998, hoping to destroy the Anglo-Irish peace initiatives.

Bell is not optimistic about the ability of any political entity—government or otherwise—to bring peace to the island nation by avoiding every avenue of conflict. Bell says there are too many agendas and too many people served by ethnic violence. Protestant violence may also increase because many Protestants believe the British government has abandoned them (Dunn and Morgan, 1995). The growth of Orange organizations like the Red Hand Defenders and Orange Volunteers, two new terrorist groups that have disavowed the peace accords, reinforce these conclusions.

More recent research (Monaghan, 2004; Hughes and Donnelly, 2004; Carmichael and Knox, 2004) suggests that although low-level violence may continue, the amount of terrorism is decreasing. For example, paramilitary shootings on both the Unionist and Republican sides have been reduced. Radical parties are using rhetoric inside the political process. Although still using the nationalistic and ethnic rhetoric of the past, they tend to operate peacefully. In addition, people who were jailed for terrorism and violent political activity have seemed to be more concerned with reintegrating into their families and communities after their incarceration than with carrying on the struggle.

By 2005 the road to peace seemed more secure. Ironically, the Irish Republic Republican Party has seemed less interested in Green issues than it has in organized crime. It has been associated with armed robbery, including a major bank robbery, and in late 2004 several IRA members allegedly murdered Robert McCartney in a Belfast bar fight. The murderers were particularly brutal, and IRA terrorists threatened to kill anybody who testified against them. When McCartney's sisters took the threats to the press, officials from the IRA offered to kill the offenders. This resulted in the marginalization of the IRA and Sinn Fein. Several U.S. politicians shunned Sinn Fein's leadership during the 2005 Saint Patrick's Day celebrations, and Senator Ted Kennedy and President G. W. Bush condemned the IRA (BBC, 3-9-05). At long last, the people of Ireland seem to be tired of radical violence.

Summary of Main Points

1. Byman believes ethnic terrorism differs from other forms of terror. It requires different policies and countertactics.

2. The Basque region of Spain has been subjected to a campaign of ethnic and nationalistic terrorism since the 1950s. Today, hardcore ETA militants have retreated into their ethnic identity and target all those who oppose them, even middle-class Basques.

3. The PKK was a Kurdish terrorist group. Its leader has been arrested, but supporters in Europe and Turkey number in the thousands.

4. The LTTE emerged from the Tamil population in Sri Lanka. It became so strong that it was able to move from terrorism to guerrilla warfare. In 1995, the LTTE began a campaign of suicide bombing. Today, a fragile peace is threatened by ethnic divisions.

5. Ireland has a long history of struggles with foreign incursion and occupation. The process began with Viking raids and continued with Norman invasions.

6. The Protestant Reformation created fierce religious differences in Ireland. These differences were exacerbated by Oliver Cromwell's raids into Ireland, the Plantation of Ulster, and British settlements of Protestants in Catholic lands.

7. Irish Republicans have a long tradition of rebellion against the British. From the 1690s to the present, each generation of Republicans has had its own set of rebellious heroes.

8. The Irish Republican Army grew from the violence of the 1916 Easter Rebellion. Although it split into factions, it first waged a campaign against the United Kingdom, and then it attacked anyone, including fellow Irish people, who accepted the division of Ireland.

9. The current situation in Ireland had its beginnings in 1969 when the IRA reemerged in the face of repressive British policies. Both the governments of Ireland and the United Kingdom tried to control violence, and they joined in a peace accord in 1985. By 2005, even the extremists seemed to be tiring of terrorism.

10. The IRA currently behaves more like a criminal group than an organization of political terrorists.

Key Terms

Make sure you can define, explain, or identify the following people, ideas, organizations, or terms:

ethnic terrorism   179

Euskadi ta Askatasuna (ETA, or Basque
    Nation and Liberty)   182

Basque separatists   182

Kurds   185

Kurdish Workers' Party (PKK)   185

Abdullah Ocalan   187

Liberation Tigers of Tamil Eelam (LTTE,
    or Tamil Tigers)   189

Tamils   189

Velupillai Pirabhakaran   190

Orange   195

Green   195

Irish Republican Army (IRA)   196

1916 Easter Rebellion   197

Sinn Fein   198

Royal Ulster Constabulary   199

Officials   200

Provisionals   200

Anglo-Irish Peace Accord   203

Suggested Readings

Now that you've been introduced to this topic, you can learn more by reading:

Peace in the Midst of Wars: Preventing and Managing International Ethnic Conflicts, edited by David Carment, Patrick James, and Donald Puchala, examines the problems of regional ethnic conflict now that the Cold War has ended. It discusses strategies for preventing conflict and explores for ways for making peacekeeping operations more effective.

You may also want to read:

Robert Clark explores the Basque situation in two books, *The Basques* and *The Basque Insurgents.*

J. Bowyer Bell's *The Secret Army* is a history of the IRA from 1916 to 1970.

M. R. Narayan Swamy explores the Tamil Tigers in *Tigers of Lanka: From Boys to Guerillas.*

Web Resources

Go to *http://cj.wadsworth.com/white_terrorism5e* and click on Web Links to find:

- "Reasons behind Terrorism" and other articles from the World Conflict Quarterly
- A conservative view of the effect of the PKK from Michael Rubin
- "A Terrorist's Bitter End," an article from Time.com on the arrest of Abdullah Ocalan
- A variety of information about Northern Ireland, including about its criminal justice agencies
- A history of the Royal Ulster Constabulary (RUC)
- Information about the Police Service of Northern Ireland (homepage)
- Information about Tamil Eelam (homepage)

The Companion Website for *Terrorism and Homeland Security,* **Fifth Edition**

http://cj.wadsworth.com/white_terrorism5e

At the Book Companion Website you can review chapter outlines, use the flash cards to test your terrorism vocabulary, and check out the many other study aids you'll find there. You'll find valuable data and resources at your fingertips to help you study for that big exam or write that important paper.

Terrorism Updates

**http://www.wadsworth.com/criminaljustice_d/special_features/ext/terrorism
_site090802/index.html**

Visit the *Terrorism: An Interdisciplinary Perspective* website to find the most current information about the fields of terrorism and homeland security. With a focus on domestic and international issues, this site explores the scope of terrorism in our world today. You'll find essays on important topics in terrorism and homeland security, critical thinking web activities, and InfoTrac College Edition keywords. Most importantly, the website is updated weekly with current news and research articles on domestic and international terrorism. You are invited to use these web resources to supplement your understanding of the topics covered in this chapter.

Current Perspectives: Readings from InfoTrac College Edition
Terrorism and Homeland Security

The sixteen articles in this reader offer a representative selection that helps you understand the important issues about terrorism and homeland security. It includes FREE access to InfoTrac College Edition and can also be bundled with the text for free.

Chapter 12

Ideological Terrorism

AP/Wide World Photos

Ideological groups fight to impose their political will. Here FBI Agents engage in the 1996 standoff against the Freemen of Montana, several members of which were eventually arrested for circulating millions of dollars in bogus checks and threatening to kill a federal judge. The Freemen believe that all forms of organized government are illegitimate and have no right to collect taxes or even require auto tags; that the Freemen can defy foreclosure actions; that they can issue arrest warrants and hold trials of government officials; and that they can act as their own central bank and defraud the government, financial institutions, and merchants.

Although the world is experiencing a wave of religious terrorism, ideological terror lies under its surface. In addition, the theoretical roots of modern terrorism were developed during periods when anticolonial revolutions and ideological terrorists dominated the world of subnational violence. Before we move to domestic terrorism, it will be helpful to consider the ideological roots of terror and the role of ideology in terrorist violence. It is resurfacing in single issues around the world and in insurgencies like the violence in Iraq. This chapter examines the theory of ideological revolution, the status of important campaigns, and the transformation of ideology in guerrilla warfare and state-sponsored terrorism.

Chapter Objectives

After reading this chapter, you should be able to:

1. Describe the current status of ideological terrorism.
2. Discuss the theory of urban terrorism described by Marighella.
3. Summarize the relationship between terrorism and guerrilla warfare.
4. Give an overview of Western Europe's experience with left-wing terrorism.
5. Explain the demise of left-wing terrorist movements in Europe.
6. Cite examples of ideological terrorism in Asia and the Middle East.
7. Describe the new form of ideological terrorism.
8. Debate the nature of the insurrection in Iraq.

The Status of Ideological Terrorism

Key Points and Questions:

1. What is ideological terrorism?
2. Where did it develop?
3. How does the recent shift to religious terrorism affect ideological violence?
4. How has ideological violence transformed in the past decade?
5. Discuss the relationship between ideology and state-sponsored terrorism.

Ideological terrorism refers to small groups who terrorize for the purpose of imposing their political ideals on others. The term was first used to describe left-wing, anarchist, and Communist revolutionaries. Small groups in Europe and South and North America fought to impose a new social order from about 1960 to 1985. They found economic and governmental systems to be oppressive, and they sought to replace them with an ideal form of socialism. Around 1980 resurgent right-wing groups began to grow in Europe and the United States. These groups wanted to turn back the clock and restore an ideal form of patriotism and strength. Around 1995 left- and right-wing groups started drawing closer together, but the majority of ideological violence has been based around single issues in the early years of the twenty-first century (see Expanding the Concept: Ideology as a Surrogate Religion: Aum Shinrikyo). **Single-issue terrorists** embrace a single cause such as antiglobalism, animal rights, ecology, abortion, or anarchism.

Like other forms of violence, ideological terrorism was not created in a vacuum; it developed from theories of revolution and was closely tied to models of **guerrilla warfare.** Yet, guerrillas differ from terrorists. A model of guerrilla revolution spread from Latin America, especially after the 1959 Cuban Revolution, but the small groups of violent ideologues were far removed from the massive and popular guerrilla forces in Cuba, El Salvador, Colombia, and other Latin American countries. Groups of students and true-believing adults joined left-wing revolutionary movements without any real chance of toppling a government. Right-wing extremists followed, and then single-issue terrorists emerged. Regardless of the type of political

Ideology as a Surrogate Religion: Aum Shinrikyo

On March 20, 1995, Tokyo was subjected to a technological terrorist attack from a radical religious sect. Members of Aum Shinrikyo (Japanese for Supreme Truth) released a poisonous gas into the crowded subway system. The terrorists were not individuals seeking social release or some nebulous form of political revenge; they were members of an organized religious group trying to destroy the Japanese government.

According to the U.S. Department of State (1996), the poison gas attack in the Tokyo subway was the first large-scale use of chemical agents by terrorists. Diplomatic officials estimated that cult members hoped to destabilize the Japanese government and seize power in the confusion. Aum Shinrikyo terrorists struck five subway trains simultaneously, killing twelve people and sending approximately fifty-five hundred to hospitals for treatment. Subsequent investigations by Japanese police linked Aum Shinrikyo to a previous gas attack in 1994, which killed seven and injured five hundred people (Muir, 1999).

The group's charismatic leader, Shoko Asahara, planned murders and dress rehearsals before the subway attack and developed a mechanism for funding, developing, and supporting a program of weapons of mass destruction (Brackett, 1996). All of this came not from a nation-state but from a cultlike terrorist group whose members included technicians and scientists.

The technology behind the attack was frightening. The terrorists used sarin gas, a deadly, odorless, colorless gas developed by Nazi researchers during World War II. They carried containers of chemicals that would produce the gas when exposed to air and placed their innocent-looking packets under their subway seats. Each terrorist punctured the lethal container just before 8:00 a.m., and sarin gas clouds began working their way through the subway cars with immediate results.

Aum Shinrikyo committed terrorist acts, but it functioned like a cult. Other such groups still exist; it is possible they will form the next wave of ideological terrorism.

---

extremism, ideological terrorists tried to violently impose their political ideals on others (Dyson, 2000).

The recent shift to religious violence had several effects on ideological terrorists. First, most of the groups lost state sponsors when the Soviet Union collapsed (Hoffman, 1999). Second, right-wing groups modified their politics with tailor-made religions, especially in the United States (Berlet and Lyons, 2000, pp. 247–264). Third, as death and violence increased with the advent of religious terrorism, many ideologues renounced violence (Stern, 2003b, pp. 11–12; Napoleoni, 2003, pp. xix–xxiii). Finally, the nations that continued to support terrorism did so under the new rules of the game. They either endorsed religion or let the issue driving violence become a **surrogate religion** expressed in absolutist terms. Either way, as Bruce Hoffman (1999) points out, terrorism became more lethal.

In some instances, groups use ideology as a surrogate religion, that is, the group replaces religious behavior with an ideology that has the power of religion. Such groups may create elaborate rituals and hierarchy of religious-like masters in the organization. Followers may give the group's leader the status of an earthly deity or believe that the leader has special powers to contact a deity. In other situations the leader's authority is so absolute that it cannot be questioned. Members of the group frequently pass through various initiation rites, and they accept punishment and authority from the leader. When violence is internalized, that is, focused on its own members, the group can become a religious cult. If the group targets victims in the outside world, it frequently behaves like a religious terrorist organization. The Japanese Red Army and Aum Shinrikyo, for instance, disciplined their own members with violent rituals while launching terrorist attacks on the outside world (see Expanding the Concept: The Japanese Red Army).

Today, much of the violence associated with ideology is not terrorism. It is expressed in protest movements and violent street demonstrations. Anarchists, for ex-

Expanding the Concept

The Japanese Red Army

Europe harbored several left-wing terrorists organizations, but ideological groups grew in other areas, too. None was more unique than the Japanese Red Army, which intertwined leftist ideology with Japanese nationalism. The Red Army forged relations with terrorist groups all over the world. Ironically, it was a Japanese leftist group, but its most active cell would operate in Lebanon, fighting in the Palestinian cause.

The Red Army was one of the most unique terrorist groups to emerge from the 1960s because it embraced many differing issues, ranging from left-wing political action to recapturing Japan's historical nation-of-warriors society. It can be classified as a left-wing group in the Western tradition (that is, in the Western economic tradition), but it exhibited some cultic characteristics as it engaged in ritualized behavior designed to subjugate members to a particular leader. The Red Army emerged from the second generation of post–World War II dissatisfaction in Japan. After World War II, Japanese youth suffered an identity crisis that eventually transformed into growing university unrest and the beginning of academic radicalism.

The Red Army was spawned during the turmoil of 1969. It conducted its first operation in 1970, hijacking an airplane to North Korea. The North Korean Intelligence Service accepted the young Communists with open arms and offered support for the movement. Members soon drew away from the student movement (although they still encouraged rioting and violent confrontations) to engage in violent revolution. Solidifying their relationship with the North Korean Intelligence Service, the group engaged in confrontational street violence, armed robberies, bombings, and assassinations. Yet, just as the group was in the process of initiating a an urban campaign in Japan, it did a very strange thing. The Red Army split into two different orientations: One group stayed in Japan and was eventually destroyed by infighting. The other migrated to the Middle East and formed an alliance with the Popular Front for the Liberation of Palestine. Part of the Japanese faction internalized violence, while other members sought connections with Asian Communists. The Middle Eastern faction continued to identify itself as the Japanese Red Army, but it became consumed with the Palestinian cause. Some members in the Middle East eventually evolved into mercenaries, hiring themselves to the highest bidder. The name remains, but the Japanese Red Army tried to take too many directions to remain viable in the twenty-first century.

Source: Farrell (1990).

ample, roam the world to protest economic summits. These actions are disruptive and violent, but they are not terrorism. In other areas, ideology has motivated guerrilla forces. Nations fighting guerrillas frequently call their enemies "terrorists," but guerrillas emerge from the general population and fight. Although they use clandestine tactics, they attack only military and security forces rather than randomly murder people.

State-sponsored terrorism is terrorism supported by a nation-state, complicating the issues surrounding terrorism in general. Each year the U.S. Department of State issues a list of nations that support terrorism. Libya has been working hard to win its way back into American graces, but North Korea remains on the list because it is committed to fighting for Stalinist ideology by supporting terrorist groups, exporting weapons, and using its intelligence service in acts of terrorism. States such as Syria and Iran also remain on the list because they believe they have a right to support resistance to Israel (Harik, 2004, pp. 165–174). Michael Hirsh (2002) argues in an article in *Foreign Affairs* that most of the world does not understand America's approach to state-sponsored terrorism, believing that the United States condemns it when convenient and ignores it when it serves U.S. foreign policy.

To be sure, ideology is related to state-sponsored terrorism, but ideological terrorism has been transformed since the fall of the Soviet Union. Today, the ideology that supports terrorism tends to come from the passion surrounding an issue, not state sponsorship. Amir Taheri (7-21-04) summarizes this well. Ideological terrorists are driven by a single overriding cause that dominates life. State sponsorship may occur on the fringes, but a single ideology drives the violence.

Ideology and Marighella's Urban Model

Key Points and Questions:

1. Why did Fanon call people of the Third World to revolution?
2. How does the rural model of guerrilla warfare differ from the urban model of terrorism?
3. What was the purpose of terrorism in Fanon's mind?
4. Which of Fanon's ideas did Marighella import for South America?
5. What was the purpose of violence for Marighella?
6. How did Moss summarize Marighella's process?

Ideologically driven terrorism emerged from anticolonialism. The model for such terrorism was based on the idea of the **urban guerrilla** and **urban terrorism**. Initially, these ideas were intellectually championed by **Frantz Fanon**, a psychiatrist who worked in Algeria during the war against the French (1954–1962). Fanon believed the pressures caused by exploitive imperialism were the primary causes for mental illness in Algeria. He produced two works, *The Wretched of the Earth* and *A Dying Colonialism*, as a result of his Algerian experiences. He died of cancer in 1961, a year before the French-Algerian War ended, unable to play a leading role in revolutions; his thought, however, remained strongly imprinted on revolutionary minds in Africa, Asia, and Latin America.

In *The Wretched of the Earth*, Fanon writes that Western powers have dehumanized non-Western people by destroying their cultures and replacing them with Western values. Even when Westerners are not present, they are represented by a native middle class that embraces Western values and turns its back on the general population. The middle class forgets the native culture and replaces native intellectualism with Western traditions. The masses end up suffering a perpetual identity crisis: To succeed, they are forced to deny their heritage. Fanon argues that the natives can follow only one course of action: revolution.

He claimed decolonization was destined to be a violent process because it involved replacing one group of powerful people with another group. No group would willingly surrender power. Therefore, according to Fanon, achieving freedom was inherently violent. Political action and peaceful efforts toward change were useless. Only when oppressed people recognized that violence was their only alternative would they be assured of victory.

Fanon advocated rural guerrilla warfare as the primary method of revolution. Third World revolutionaries could not mount direct, conventional campaigns at the beginning of their struggles. If guerrillas gathered in the countryside, however, they could strike at their European enemies and flee to the safety of rural areas. Terrorism was a tool for the city and agricultural areas controlled by Europeans. It was designed to support the rural guerrillas by attacking European security forces, colonists, and native sympathizers.

Terrorism had a specific purpose: to terrorize Westerners and their followers into submission. Guerrilla terrorists were to murder and mutilate their victims to frighten white settlers out of the country and leave natives too scared to serve colonial masters. Urban terror was to create mayhem, and all terrorism was to be excessively brutal to communicate fear. This would bring on government repression, but repression would encourage more natives to flock to the terrorist cause. Fanon's guerrilla model thus uses terrorism as a strategy and deviates from typical guerrillas who try to build a military force.

Popular throughout the Third World, Fanon's ideas flourished in Latin America. Beginning in Brazil, some revolutionaries believed the city would be the focus of Latin American revolution, and they embraced Fanon's idea of terrorism by moving it from the countryside into town. They felt revolutionaries could create an environment in which the population would rise to take power without centralized leadership. Directly reflecting Fanon, these revolutionaries believed terrorism was a method for communicating zeal, a way to infuse people with a spirit of revolt. The foremost proponent of this idea in Latin America was **Carlos Marighella** (see Expanding the Concept: Urban Terrorists vs. Rural Guerrillas).

Marighella was a Brazilian legislator, a leader of the nationalist Communist party, and eventually a fiery revolutionary terrorist. He was killed by Brazilian police in an ambush in São Paulo in 1969. In two major works, *For the Liberation of Brazil* and *The Minimanual of the Urban Guerrilla*, Marighella designed and presented practical guides for terrorism. These books have had more influence on recent ideological terrorism than any other set of theories. Marighella is to ideological terrorists what Sayyid Qutb is to Jihadists (see Chapter 7).

The **Marighella model** was apolitical although his call to terrorism was politically motivated. He wanted to move violence from the countryside to the city and

Urban Terrorists vs. Rural Guerrillas

Carlos Marighella developed the idea of urban terrorism under the influence of Frantz Fanon. The purpose was simply to kill victims, attack institutions, and disrupt normal life. This would bring government repression, but the people would not tolerate the crackdown for long. Marighella believed they would engage in a spontaneous massive uprising and overthrow the government.

Ernesto "Che" Guevara was a leader in the Cuban Revolution. His approach was the opposite of Marighella's. Guevara believed that rural guerrillas should create bases in the countryside where they could train and from which they could recruit and get supplies. They could also use the countryside to hide from military forces.

Each time a base was created, Guevara advocated building up the local guerrilla force until it could be used as a column, which would be the equivalent of several military companies or a battalion. A column could directly engage government forces. Eventually, columns would join to form a guerrilla army. When sufficient strength had been gathered, the guerrillas would transform into a regular army and operate under military principles to defeat the government army and institute a new political order.

Marighella believed that violence would cause the revolution; Guevara believed that the revolution should use violence for political ends. Guevara's methods have worked in Ireland, China, Algeria, Cuba, and other locations. Marighella's model, on the other had, has never worked although his methods have resulted in thousands of deaths.

designed a method for organizing a campaign of terror that, for the past fifty years, has been used by groups ranging across the political spectrum—from the Japanese Red Army to the Freemen of Montana (see Another Perspective: Groups Influenced by Carlos Marighella).

Marighella believed the basis of revolution was violence, which created a situation in which revolution could flourish. Any type of violence was acceptable because it contributed to a general feeling of panic and frustration among the ruling classes and their protectors. It need not be structured, and efforts among groups need not be coordinated. Marighella's most original concept was that all violence could be urban-based and controlled by a small group of urban guerrillas. This concept of revolution spread from Brazil throughout the world.

Robert Moss (1972, pp. 70–72) provides an excellent synopsis of Marighella's writings in a four-stage model. Urban terrorism was to begin with two distinct phases, one designed to bring about actual violence, and the other designed to give that violence meaning. The violent portion of the revolution was to be a campaign employing armed revolutionary cells to carry out the most deplorable acts of violence. Targets were to have symbolic significance, and although violence was designed to be frightening, its logic would remain clear with regard to the overall revolution. That is, those who supported the revolution need not fear terrorist violence.

The terror campaign was to be accompanied by a **psychological offensive**, that is, a mass movement of revolutionary sympathizers, to provide peripheral support

Another Perspective

Groups Influenced by Carlos Marighella

The *Tupamaros* operated from 1963 to 1972 in Montevideo, Uruguay. Members killed, kidnapped, and bombed their way through a decade, trying to destroy the government. In 1972 Uruguay declared martial law, and the police and military went on a rampage, executing ten thousand people in a six-month period and destroying the Tupamaros.

The *Red Army Faction* of Germany was influenced by the Tupamaros. Supported by the former Soviet Union through East Germany, the Red Army Faction made international headlines but never evolved to much more than a criminal gang.

The *Shining Path* of Peru fell under Marighella's influence but formed a hybrid terrorist model. The guerrillas operated in the countryside, freely using terrorist tactics against the local population. They took ground, held territory, and even taxed local villages. Rural peasants who submitted to the Shining Path were brutalized by the Peruvian military when government forces retook areas from the terrorists.

Italy's *Red Brigades* created a variety of separate organizations in several cities throughout Italy, foreshadowing the umbrella organizations of the twenty-first century. They proved to be effective, kidnapping several prominent government leaders, including a prime minister and a U.S. general. They killed some of their victims, including Prime Minister Aldo Moro.

Direct Action of France believed that European leftist groups were too diverse, so the group tried to unite all revolutionary terrorist groups into a single organization. They failed because the groups were too weak to unite.

Several groups influenced by Marighella operated in the United States. Revolutionary groups like the *New World Liberation Front* and *Weather Underground* read and believed in Marighella's *Minimanual of the Urban Guerrilla*. Ironically, the extremist right would model reactionary groups after Marighella's firing team. Before Louis Beam coined the term "leaderless resistance," Marighella advocated the tactic for South America.

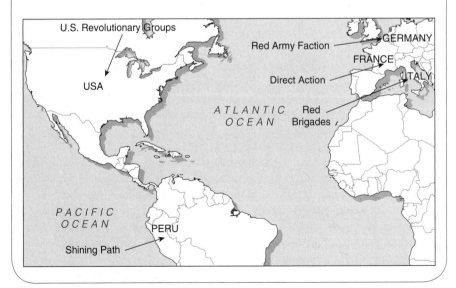

for terrorists. Not only would the psychological offensive join students and workers in low-level challenges to governmental authority, but it would also be used to create a network of safe houses, logistical stores, and medical units. In essence, the supporting activities would carry out standard military-support functions.

A campaign of revolutionary terrorism in an urban setting could be used to destabilize government power. A psychological assault would persuade the government and the people that the status quo no longer held. They would come to feel that the terrorists were in control. When this situation developed, Marighella believed, the government would be forced to show its true colors. With its authority challenged and the economic stability of the elite eroded, the government would be forced to declare some form of martial law. This would not be a defeat for terrorism, but rather exactly what the terrorists and their supporters wanted. Governmental repression was the goal of terrorism at this stage.

This view might appear to be contradictory, but there was a method to Marighella's madness. Marighella believed that the public supported government policies because they did not recognize the repressive nature of the state. A terrorist campaign would force the government to reveal that repressive nature, thereby alienating the public. With no place to turn, the public would turn to the terrorists, and the terrorists would be waiting with open arms. As the ranks of the urban guerrillas grew with the rush of public support, Marighella believed, the revolutionaries would gradually abandon their terrorist campaign. Their efforts would focus more and more on the construction of a general urban army, an army that could seize key government control points on cue. When the urban army had reached sufficient strength, all its forces would be launched in a general strike.

Marighella's model has spawned violence throughout the world and has helped several terrorist groups organize murder in a variety of contexts. The reason is that the promise of revolution comes only with violence. Followers of Marighella do not need to build a logical organization to establish power. The purpose of the urban guerrilla is to shoot. The job of the **firing team**, Marighella's basic unit, is to kill. Violence creates the revolution. This belief makes such a model popular among small, violent extremist groups that have no chance of implementing a political agenda.

The firing team is composed of four to five terrorists. Several firing teams are needed to construct a terrorist organization, but the team can exist on its own. Teams can join together as needed to concentrate their power, but their small size ensures both mobility and secrecy. For Marighella, the firing team is the basic weapon of the urban guerrilla. When groups are motivated by Marighella, whether the Red Brigades in Milan (discussed p. 218–219) or Christian patriots in Montana (see Chapter 14), they need no further justification for action. Violence will create a revolution. (Note how closely this model matches the theory behind the chain organizations described by Arquilla, Ronfeldt, and Zanini [1999]; see Chapter 3.)

This model of urban terrorism and revolution would be an excellent theory for revolutionaries if it were functional. Unfortunately for terrorists, it does not work. It causes terrorism and disrupts systems, but it does not topple governments. And unfortunately for the rest of the world, many small groups nonetheless use the model to justify murder. Innocent people are killed until security forces either arrest or destroy the members of the firing team. Most ideological terrorist groups have followed the path of Marighella. They cannot become strong enough to create a new order, but they can terrorize a community or country.

The Demise of Left-Wing Ideology in Europe

 Key Points and Questions:

1. According to Corrado and Evans, why did ideological terrorism emerge in Europe?
2. Why did left-wing terrorism decline?
3. What was Pluchinsky's fear about future terrorism?
4. Why did left-wing terrorist groups try to band together?
5. Which left-wing groups failed?
6. What type of terrorism replaced left-wing violence?

A group taking action under the name of the Red Brigades set several fires and conducted a bombing in Italy in 2004, but few analysts of terrorism were overly alarmed. The Red Brigades had not been very active since 1995, although they had carried out one or two minor events every year. Analysts were instead more concerned with single-issue terrorism. Europe has experienced a pattern of declining left-wing revolutionary terrorism and its reemergence into single-issue violence. A brief overview explains the reason.

Raymond Corrado and Rebecca Evans (1988, pp. 373–444) examine Western European terrorism and conclude that it has developed into a variety of forms with few common threads. Dormant after World War II, terrorism among indigenous native groups began to reemerge during the 1960s. Corrado and Evans believe this renewed growth was a response to Western European modernization and industrialization. The ideological terrorists of the 1960s, on both the left and the right, were expressing their frustration with the social structures imposed by a modern industrial society.

Nationalistic violence remained, but ideological terrorism could not maintain a base of support. Corrado and Evans argue that the fundamental difference between ideological and nationalist terrorists can be found in their goals. Ideological terrorists in Europe reject the economic and social structure of industrial capitalism; they want a new order. Despite ideological division, both the left and the right fight for this goal. Nationalists, on the other hand, frequently embrace capitalism and fight for ethnic self-determination. They desire economic opportunity within the context of a strong national identity. Nationalism stays, ideology does not.

By 1988, Corrado and Evans conclude, the popularity of nationalistic and left-wing terrorism was changing. They suggest that the pluralism of Western democracies opened the door to peaceful participation in the political system and offered opportunities for change. Violence no longer seemed an attractive method for groups to express their grievances. As pluralistic governments worked to relieve frustration, the attractiveness of terrorism waned, and terrorists lost their support base. Corrado and Evans assumed that terrorist violence would fade away, only reappearing in a few sporadic incidents. Had the political structure of Europe remained constant since their writing, they would have been correct: Left-wing terrorism was out of vogue, and nationalist terrorism was on the decline.

Few analysts of terrorism—indeed, few scholars, politicians, soothsayers, or prophets—predicted three key events that changed the political destiny of Europe and the world. In 1989, the Berlin Wall came down, leading to the reunification of Germany. To the south, new nations emerging from the former Yugoslavia took up arms and resumed a centuries-old struggle. But the greatest change of all came in the East. The Soviet Union dissolved, along with the authoritarian rule of the Communist Party in the republics of the former Soviet Union and Eastern Europe. These three changes occurred at a time when Western Europeans were taking bold steps toward economic and political unity.

Dennis Pluchinsky (1982, pp. 40–78) saw potential changes a decade before they occurred. The left might decline, but he feared Europe would become a terrorist battleground. Pluchinsky also believed international and state-sponsored terrorism would grow in Europe, and a greater threat was posed by what he called **supraindigenous terrorism**. By this, Pluchinsky meant that local terrorist activities would extend beyond local boundaries. Each time a government brings one variety of terrorism into check, Pluchinsky argued, a new strain appears. Unfortunately, no analyst of terrorism was more correct. Middle Eastern religious terrorism spilled into Europe, and murderous **ethnic cleansing**, that is, killing or driving out ethnic or religious groups inhabiting an area, dominated the Balkan Peninsula.

As the structure of Europe and the world changed from 1989 to 1992, European terrorism also changed, just as Pluchinsky had predicted. Ideological terrorism swung from left to right, changing its structure as it moved. Nationalistic terrorism remained, but conflict rose in the form of ethnic violence. Ethnic violence grew into open warfare in the Balkans. New criminal organizations appeared, and old ones were revitalized. The threat of Jihadist terrorism replaced threats from the left, and Europe experienced new strains of terrorism.

After an unprecedented growth since 1968, left-wing terrorism began to decline by 1986. Whereas Corrado and Evans correctly saw the demise of the left as evidence of eroding political support for terrorism, other analysts believed it was a prelude to a new leftist campaign. Pointing to the unification of left-wing terrorist groups, these analysts feared conspiracy was at its zenith around 1985. They believed all the radical groups in Europe were forming to create a single superterrorist network. They warned that a new terror campaign would be worse than anything the West had experienced.

Stephen Segaller (1987, pp. 36–40) had another suggestion. Direct Action in France, the Communist Combat Cells of Belgium, the Red Army Faction of Germany, the Red Brigades in Italy, and other groups were all uniting, but the reason for unification was exactly the opposite of what many analysts thought. The leftists were seeking unity out of *weakness*, not strength. The political assumptions Corrado and Evans made were correct. Left-wing extremism had run its course. The very societies the terrorists were trying to undermine had won the struggle. How had this happened?

Segaller had the answer, and it matched the Corrado-Evans thesis. Modern European terrorism emerged in the 1960s as an extreme reflection of left-wing activism. Fueled by the Vietnam War, European leftists were influenced by events in Latin America, as well as by revolutionary leaders such as Carlos Marighella. The Red Army Faction (also known as the Baader-Meinhof Gang in its early days) began a campaign in Germany, followed by copycat groups and more long-term terrorist organizations in other countries.

By 1970, most left-wing groups and the resurgent nationalist groups modeled themselves after the Marighella model. Segaller said that although European terrorists longed for a Marighella-style revolution, they never achieved it because they were too weak. In 1985, they faced their weakness and tried to form a confederation to gain momentum.

The left-wing coalition was an effort to pool dwindling resources and support. Members of the Communist Combat Cells of Belgium went to Paris searching for the French terrorist group Direct Action. Shortly afterward, the leadership of Italy's Red Brigades also made overtures to Direct Action. West Germany's Red Army Faction (RAF) expressed an ideological union with these groups, and Direct Action responded by publishing several communiqués, claiming that a new left-wing unified terrorist movement had formed. In reality, the left-wing terrorist groups were sounding a retreat, possibly even a death knell.

Some authors like Claire Sterling (1986) and Benjamin Netanyahu (1986, 1997) have argued that this represented an organized international campaign of terrorism against the West. A closer scholarly analysis suggests this is not the case, however. Once again, Pluchinsky (1993) gives the reason. The left had played out. No longer supported by the Soviet Union, the groups simply could not stand alone. West European leftists lacked the support and the appeal to remain operational. He points to Germany's RAF to demonstrate the point.

On May 28, 1998, the RAF issued a communiqué stating that it was ceasing operations. Christoph Rojahn (1998) says the RAF mirrored the demise of the European leftists, but they were responsible for Germany's massive security apparatus. In addition, mainstream left-wing politicians had limited effect while the RAF was in the streets. The RAF ceased operations because it was a miserable failure. Although it had maintained a campaign of violence for decades, it was never able to link with a mainstream issue. The group could not attract the support of the radical left, with the exception of the following in its own narrow circle. Rojahn concludes that the 1998 declaration of peace was the group's recognition of its failure.

Southern Europe has experienced a similar decline in left-wing terrorism, and Xavier Raufer (1993) looks at Italy's Red Brigades as another example of the weaknesses in the left. When the Red Brigades approached Direct Action in 1985, they were already rapidly fading from their glory days of headline-grabbing murders. Raufer believed the Red Brigades would soon follow the unilateral peace declaration of the RAF.

Vittorfranco Pisano (1987) identifies nearly three hundred left-wing groups in Italy appearing between 1967 and 1985, and most of them had a Marxist-Leninist orientation. The best-known group was the Red Brigades, which formed in Milan after Renato Curio broke away from a left-wing working-class political organization.

Leaders gathered more militant followers and announced plans for a terrorist campaign in 1970. Margherita Cago joined Curio and later became his wife. The future militants called their organization the Red Brigades, and Curio's 1970 group of militants became known as the Historical Nucleus.

The Red Brigades' violent Communist ideology made no mystery of its strategy for revolution (Pisano, 1987). Curio and Cago sought to make the cities unsafe for any government official or sympathizer. They believed a climate of violence would help bring about a revolution in Italy and eventually in all of Europe. Members of the Brigades saw themselves as the vanguard of a worldwide Communist revolution. They believed sensational violence would be their key to the future. The group taking action in the early part of the twenty-first century, however, has little resemblance to the Red Brigades of the past.

The organization of the **Red Brigades** was unique in European terrorism. They came closer to matching the Marighella model than did any other group in Europe. They were bound in a loose confederation, with a central committee meeting periodically to devise a grand strategy. A key difference, however, was that whereas the Tupamaros operated only in Montevideo, the Red Brigades had a variety of urban centers. Each unit, therefore, became a fairly autonomous organization within its own area. The Red Brigades managed to establish independent headquarters in several major Italian cities.

Currently, left-wing terrorism in Europe is out of vogue. Only three groups remained active in the mid-1990s: Dev Sol in Turkey, GRAPO in Spain, and 17N in Greece (Pluchinsky, 1993). Raymond Corrado and Rebecca Evans were correct: The ideological basis for left-wing terrorism has been eliminated. Yet, Pluchinsky's earlier prediction has also proved to be correct. Single-issue terrorism is in its infancy in Europe. It centers on issues surrounding globalism, the environment, genetic engineering, animal rights, and the power of multinational corporations. The bigger threat comes from international Jihadists, who have targeted Germany, Belgium, the Netherlands, France, Spain, and the United Kingdom. Cultlike groups, such as Aum Shinrikyo, also threaten to become involved in the next wave of ideological terrorism. As Pluchinsky suggests, new strains replace the old.

Iraq Insurgency: Guerrillas or Terrorists, Ethnic or Ideological?

Key Points and Questions:

1. What were the official reasons for the U.S.-led invasion of Iraq?
2. List various names used to describe the insurgents in Iraq.
3. What are the three types of groups fighting for power in Iran?
4. How do Muslim cultural views of family relationships fit into the insurrection?
5. Discuss the levels of conflict that can be seen in the Iraq insurgency.

In March 2003 U.S.-led forces launched an invasion of Iraq. There were several official objectives. First and foremost the United States sought to enforce a mandate from the United Nations to end the production and possession of weapons of mass destruction in Iraq. The United States also wanted to end the reign of **Saddam Hussein** and implement a democratically elected government. Finally, the stated purpose was to end collusion between Saddam Hussein and al Qaeda. The U.S.-led offensive rolled through Iraq, and opposition dissolved. On May 1, 2003, President George W. Bush landed on an aircraft carrier and dramatically announced the end of major combat operations. Neither he nor most Americans understood that major combat operations were only beginning (for a variety of views, see Simon and Stevenson, 2004; Lopez and Coright, 2004; Diamond, 2004; and Dobbins, 2005).

After the major offensive, the campaign of violence against the United States and its allies was horrendous. Hostages were savagely beheaded, and suicide bombers killed indiscriminately. American soldiers were murdered while roaming through areas thought to be safe. Innocent Iraqis were killed by targeting and accidental strikes, or sometimes they were simply caught in the crossfire. Iraqi prisoners were abused by American military personnel, while tremendous battles occurred around suspected insurgent strongholds. Democratic elections took place in Iraq in January of 2005, but the **Iraq insurgency** continued (Benjamin and Simon, 9-1-03; Diamond, 2004).

President Bush and many other government officials referred to the insurgents as terrorists. Media outlets vacillated among several names, including "terrorists," "fighters," "suicide bombers," "homicide bombers," "outlawed militiamen," and "followers" of various leaders. They identified Tahwid and Ansar al Islam as two of the terrorist organizations fighting Americans and claimed that al Qaeda allies had come to Iraq. There seemed to be no clear enemy (Benjamin and Simon, 9-1-03).

There are terrorist organizations in Iraq, and there are terrorists who kidnap and murder soldiers, diplomats, journalists, and businesspeople from several nations. Yet, the counterinsurgency in Iraq is not simply a fight against terrorism. The most helpful way to think about the insurgency is to look at different categories of groups opposing the occupation and the Iraqi government and to consider the differences in cultures (U.S. Army, 2003).

The United States and allied forces are not engaged in a battle against Iraqis in general or against one group of Iraqis in particular. There are three main insurgent groups. The first is composed of displaced Ba'athists who were part of Saddam Hussein's regime (Benjamin and Simon, 9-1-03). Although some of these people have been incorporated in the new Iraqi government, others remain outside. Many Ba'athists believe they can reclaim power. At times they use terrorist tactics—car bombs and murder—but they see themselves engaged in a guerrilla campaign in the style of Frantz Fanon.

The second group of insurgents is composed of Iraqis who want the United States to leave their country. Sunni militants who do not belong to the Ba'athists generally fight along tribal lines. Militant Shi'ites want to make Iraq an Islamic republic like Iran. The most noted militant Shi'ite leader is Maqtada al Sadr with his **Mahdi Army**. Al Sadr is a product of the Najaf seminary, where many Hezbollah and Iranian Islamic scholars were trained. Al Sadr is not overly popular among the upper classes, but his name is revered among the poor. Many Shi'ites oppose his brand of Islam and do not want to see an Islamic republic (Raman, 3-3-04). Others think he is a renegade. The Iranians approve of al Sadr and sent him support. For the most part, al Sadr's followers avoid terrorist tactics, and he wants to build political legitimacy. This second group of insurgents also includes Iraqi criminals who do not care about the country's leadership and engage in crime to make a profit.

The third group of insurgents is composed of Jihadists who have come to Iraq to fight the United States. There are two classes of Jihadists. Some flock from surrounding areas to fight as guerrillas. If they use terrorism, it is highly selective and its purpose is to kill Americans and their supporters. The other group is composed of terrorists within an al Qaeda–style umbrella. Some, such as Abu Musab al Zarqawi, were trained in al Qaeda camps (Thompson, 10-16-03). Others have an ideological link to al Qaeda and affiliated groups, but they exist on their own. Terrorism is the primary tactic of the Jihadists, and they are behind many of the murderous kidnappings and suicide bombings. America's confrontation with this second group of terrorists is a fight against terrorism (Cronin, 5-23-03).

The three insurgent groups do not share a common vision for the future of Iraq and they are frequently at odds with each other (Paz 2004). The Shi'ite organizations have condemned al Zarqawi's kidnap-murders, and al Sadr has intervened in other kidnappings to have hostages freed. Several power struggles are occurring in Iraq among several different groups.

The cultural factor in the reasons behind the violence in Iraq becomes extremely important. The boundaries of Iraq, and most parts of the Middle East, are the product of European boundary settlements at the end of World War I. The lines remain somewhat artificial today, and they frequently cross a more important boundary— the one delineating tribes. Families and extended family groups are one of the most important aspects of Arab culture (Nydell, 2002, pp. 91–99).

Raphael Patai (2002, pp. 78–100) says that ideally Arabs see their ancestors as one of two great tribes in Arabia, one from the north and the other from the south. Although this idea is part of the Arab myth or sacred story, it is a practical part of the situation in Iraq today. Relations begin within the immediate family and reach out to extended families, clans, and tribes. These family ties are so crucial that when a U.S.-dominated coalition of non-Arab nations invades an Arab country, tribal loyalties will come to the forefront. An old Arab folk saying illustrates the overriding importance of family ties in Arab culture and the response to "the stranger": "I and my brothers against my cousins; I and my cousins against the stranger" (Patai, 2002, p. 22).

When such cultural aspects combine with the various ideologies motivating insurgent groups, it is possible to see that a major portion of the insurrection does not involve terrorism. At the same time, many of the actions against Americans and their allies do involve terrorism. Fighting takes place on multiple levels. The tactics that work against terrorists do not work against guerrillas or conventional militias. If the United States is to end major combat operations in Iraq, it will need to implement a strategy that addresses the major issues that insurgents and terrorist groups use to justify violence. Not all of the enemies can be combined into a simple category, and the battle is not merely a war against terrorism. Failure to make such distinctions may lead to defeat (Hoffman, 1-13-03; Wheeler, 12-20-03).

Summary of Main Points

1. Terrorism waged in the name of a political ideology is in a state of change. Nations have shied away from supporting ideological issues, but some states support Jihadists.

2. Most ideological terrorists followed the philosophy of Carlos Marighella. Single-issue terrorists may also follow this path.

3. Guerrilla warfare differs from terrorism, but guerrillas who were inspired by Frantz Fanon abandoned guerrilla tactics for terrorism.

4. Western European left- and right-wing terrorism is in decline. It is being replaced by single-issue and religious terrorism.

5. Single-issue groups often disrupt society, but many do not practice terrorism. The groups that do engage in terrorist violence are centered on multinational corporations, animal rights, and ecological issues.

6. There are many forms of violence in Iraq, including conventional guerrilla fighting and terrorism. Each group is motivated by separate issues.

Key Terms

Make sure you can define, explain, or identify the following people, ideas, organizations, or terms:

ideological terrorism 208	Marighella model 212
single-issue terrorists 208	psychological offensive 213
guerrilla warfare 208	firing team 215
surrogate religion 209	supraindigenous terrorists 217
state-sponsored terrorism 211	ethnic cleansing 217
urban guerrilla 211	Red Brigades 219
urban terrorism 211	Saddam Hussein 220
Frantz Fanon 211	Iraq insurgency 220
Carlos Marighella 212	Mahdi Army 220

Suggested Readings

Now that you've been introduced to this topic, you can learn more by reading:

Andrew Heywood, in *Political Ideologies: An Introduction*, explains the background of several ideologies, including those that spawn terrorism and political violence.

You may also want to read:

Martha Crenshaw's collection of essays *Terrorism in Context* looks at shifting ideas through cases studies.

Walter Reich and Walter Laqueur's edited work *Origins of Terrorism* contains essays from several distinguished scholars.

Kim Cragin and Sara Daly analyze shifting terrorist ideologies in *The Dynamic Terrorist Threat*.

Web Resources

Go to *http://cj.wadsworth.com/white_terrorism5e* and click on Web Links to find:

- An analysis of the future of terrorism and ideological terrorism at the Terrorism Research Center
- 1995 comments from the Canadian Security Intelligence Service about the motivations and causes of terrorism
- Carlos Marighella's "Minimanual of the Urban Guerrilla"
- A detailed Iraq timeline from the BBC

The Companion Website for *Terrorism and Homeland Security*, Fifth Edition

http://cj.wadsworth.com/white_terrorism5e

At the Book Companion Website you can review chapter outlines, use the flash cards to test your terrorism vocabulary, and check out the many other study aids you'll find there. You'll find valuable data and resources at your fingertips to help you study for that big exam or write that important paper.

Terrorism Updates

http://www.wadsworth.com/criminaljustice_d/special_features/ext/terrorism _site090802/index.html

Visit the *Terrorism: An Interdisciplinary Perspective* website to find the most current information about the fields of terrorism and homeland security. With a focus on domestic and international issues, this site explores the scope of terrorism in our world today. You'll find essays on important topics in terrorism and homeland security, critical thinking web activities, and InfoTrac College Edition keywords. Most importantly, the website is updated weekly with current news and research articles on domestic and international terrorism. You are invited to use these web resources to supplement your understanding of the topics covered in this chapter.

Current Perspectives: Readings from InfoTrac College Edition
Terrorism and Homeland Security

The sixteen articles in this reader offer a representative selection that helps you understand the important issues about terrorism and homeland security. It includes FREE access to InfoTrac College Edition and can also be bundled with the text for free.

Part Three DOMESTIC
TERRORISM

Conceptualizing Terrorism in America

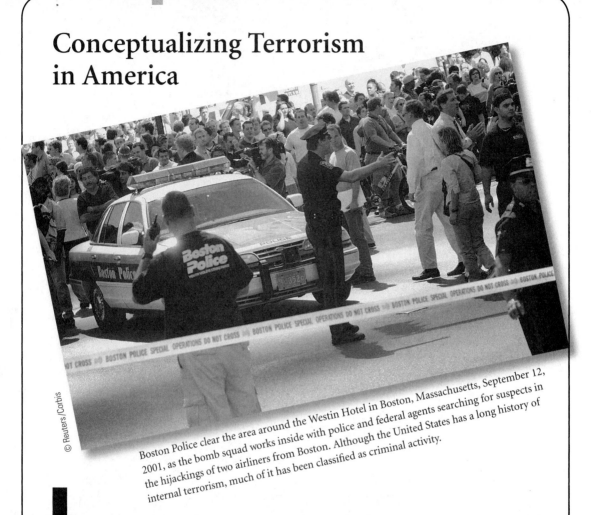

Boston Police clear the area around the Westin Hotel in Boston, Massachusetts, September 12, 2001, as the bomb squad works inside with police and federal agents searching for suspects in the hijackings of two airliners from Boston. Although the United States has a long history of internal terrorism, much of it has been classified as criminal activity.

It is difficult to find a common way to think about domestic terrorism. Although Brent Smith (1994) has characterized terrorism in America as "pipe bombs and pipe dreams," the country has experienced several forms of terrorism in recent years. Even given the deadly bombing in Oklahoma City in April 1995 and the attacks of September 11, 2001, America's recent experience with terrorism has been limited. Small ideological groups, violent activists, political extremists, and actions by foreign nationals have accounted for the bulk of domestic terror. And although the United States was suddenly thrust into a Jihadist conflict on September 11, it still experiences problems from homegrown violent extremists. Several noted scholars, law enforcement agencies, and bureaucratic organizations have tried to come to grips with this problem. This chapter will introduce attempts to understand terrorism in the United States, and Chapter 14 will discuss movements in more detail.

Chapter Objectives

After reading this chapter, you should be able to:

1. Outline the ideas of the early studies of domestic terrorism.
2. Discuss the problems surrounding the conceptualization of domestic terrorism.
3. List and define several classification systems for terrorism in the United States.
4. Describe the conceptual framework the FBI used after September 11.
5. Define three methods for defining domestic terrorism and explain the relationships among them.
6. Summarize Brent Smith's analysis of terrorism in the United States.
7. Summarize Emerson's findings on Jihadist activities in America.
8. Explain the different positions regarding the Jihadist debate in the United States.

Early Studies of Domestic Terrorism

Key Points and Questions:

1. What was the purpose of the National Advisory Commission Task Force on Disorders and Terrorism?
2. Which of the Task Force's recommendations remain valid?
3. List the historical precedents for recent domestic terrorism.
4. From where do models for domestic terrorism derive?
5. What are the two caveats Bell and Gurr issue regarding their research?
6. What are vigilante, insurgent, and transnational terrorism?

The United States has a long history of political violence, but until recently, few scholars characterized this experience as "terrorism." Three exceptions to this rule were H. H. A. Cooper, J. Bowyer Bell, and Ted Robert Gurr, all three of whom initiated work before it was popular to speak of domestic terrorism. Cooper directed the preparation of the report on terrorism by the National Advisory Commission on Criminal Justice Standards and Goals. Bell is a leading authority on terrorism, and he has conducted the best-known scholarly work on the Irish Republican Army. Gurr is a political scientist and an expert on domestic political violence. Cooper and the National Advisory Commission provided the conceptual framework for domestic terrorism, and Bell and Gurr placed terrorist violence within the perspective of the American political experience.

Cooper and coauthors (1976) produced the presidential report on the political context of domestic terrorism. Combining the examination with work on civil disorders, Cooper and colleagues demonstrated the need to prepare law enforcement departments and other supporting agencies for emergencies. They presented a series of recommendations for emergency response. Although the Report of the **Task Force on Disorders and Terrorism** is thirty years old, the standards of performance it suggests remain valid.

Cooper's team developed a pragmatic emergency response planning model, whereas Gurr placed terrorism within its historical context. In an article written with J. Bowyer Bell (Bell and Gurr, 1979), Gurr argues that terrorism is a tactic used by the weak to intimidate the strong and, in turn, used by the strong to repress the weak. In this sense, America's history is filled with terrorist activities. Various political movements have used forms of terrorism to seek political gains. At the same time, industrial giants and those holding power have historically used terrorism to maintain control over workers and unions.

Bell and Gurr begin their review by looking at the late 1800s. Despite the American paranoia about radicals at that time, terrorism in the nineteenth century was primarily aimed at protecting the status quo and the economic environment. The actions of company security police and private corporations were often terroristic in nature, designed to keep workers from disrupting production. Labor radicals, however, also behaved violently; the labor movement of the late nineteenth century was replete with violence. Bell and Gurr call all these actions a form of terrorism.

Labor violence was not the only source of early U.S. terrorism. The frontier had its own special form of violence. As people moved west, the laws of the United States trailed far behind. Settlers developed their own brand of makeshift justice. At times, this type of justice spilled over into vigilante activities. Bell and Gurr believe that some vigilante actions equaled terrorism. In more recent times, the actions of the Ku Klux Klan are an example.

Although America has a long history of political violence, Bell and Gurr separate modern American terrorism from its historical precedents. In the 1960s, they argue, the character of domestic terrorism began to change, becoming rooted in radical politics, nationalism, and the international community's experience with terrorism. The use of terrorism to maintain social order was forgotten in the modern setting, and domestic terrorism was defined as a radical phenomenon.

Bell and Gurr believe the shift toward left-wing violence was derived from foreign models. Both political revolutionary groups and nationalistic groups in the United States took their ideas from terrorists in the Middle East and Asia. In this sense, both types of groups saw themselves as being involved in a broader struggle of international proportions.

Their logic had a catch, however. Bell and Gurr note that American terrorist groups did not have the same impact as their foreign counterparts. The American public rejected the violence of the revolutionary groups, and popularity was never fully achieved, even among their most sympathetic audiences. Revolutionary terrorists in the United States ended up as small bands of social misfits who had very little effect on the political system. As a result, the United States has been spared the excesses of revolutionary terrorism.

Bell and Gurr issue two caveats with their conclusion. First, even though the United States has avoided significant domestic terrorism, both criminals and political activists have used terrorist tactics on a local level, particularly the tactics of bombing and hostage-taking. Second, nationalistic terrorists from Puerto Rico have been far more successful than revolutionaries at launching terrorist campaigns because they have an indigenous base of support. Although they have not had a major impact, Puerto Rican terrorists have enjoyed more success than revolutionary terrorists because of this support.

In a later work, Gurr (1988a) updates some of these ideas about domestic terrorism and outlines three types of terrorism: (1) vigilante terrorism, (2) insurgent terrorism, and (3) transnational terrorism.

Vigilante Terrorism   The growth of right-wing extremists is indicative of **vigilante terrorism**. The purpose of vigilantes is to defend the status quo or return to the status quo of an earlier period. Gurr points to the Ku Klux Klan, the Christian Identity movement, and other white supremacy organizations as examples of vigilante terrorism that rely on right-wing rhetorical traditions.

Insurgent Terrorism   Gurr describes insurgent terrorists in revolutionary terms. Black militants, white revolutionaries, and Puerto Rican nationalists fall into this category. **Insurgent terrorism** aims to change political policies through direct threats or action against the government. It is the political antithesis of vigilante terrorism because it attacks the status quo.

Transnational Terrorism   **Transnational terrorism** occurs when nonindigenous terrorists cross national borders. Gurr identifies several sources of transnational terror in the United States. Some foreign nationals have carried their fights onto U.S. soil, and some domestic groups have been inspired by foreign events. In other cases, foreign countries may have begun to target Americans at home. However, Gurr does not think the threat of transnational terrorism has been as great as has been popularly believed. Of course, he was writing before the bombing of the World Trade Center in 1993 and the Jihadist movement inside the United States.

The Problem of Conceptualizing Terrorism in the United States

Key Points and Questions:

1. Give examples of counterterrorism efforts in some U.S. police agencies.
2. How does the localized orientation of law enforcement affect the way law enforcement officers conceive of terrorism?
3. Describe U.S. law enforcement experiences with terrorism.
4. How do hate crimes confuse law enforcement responses to terrorism?

Some American police agencies have gone to great lengths to prepare for terrorism. Chief Roger Bragdon of the Spokane (Washington) Police Department has monitored extremist activity and prepared his officers for domestic and international terrorism for a number of years. Deputy Chief John Miller of the Los Angeles Police Department created a local antiterrorism unit, just as Commissioner Raymond Kelly did for New York City. Chief Edward Lohn of Cleveland insisted that his commanders and investigators were prepared for terrorism. Las Vegas created one of the best law intelligence units in the country, while executives in Philadelphia, Detroit, Washington, D.C., Chicago, and many other major jurisdictions also looked for ways to stop terrorism. But these agencies were exceptions, and many police departments have not followed their lead. There are reasons for this situation.

First and foremost, American police officers do not spend a lot of time thinking about terrorism. Even in the wake of standoffs with domestic religious extremists, the Oklahoma City bombing, and al Qaeda's attacks, a number of U.S. law enforcement agencies remain focused on local issues. Most police managers do not think in the abstract and pride themselves on localized pragmatism. City councils and county commissioners look at local crime and the immediate concerns of their constituents. They rarely ask their police executives to apply critical thought in hypothetical exercises. Many people believe terrorism happens somewhere else (NBC/*The Wall Street Journal*, 8-23/25-04). Terrorism is simply too exotic for most agencies until gun-toting students shoot their way through a local high school or a Jihadist sleeper cell is caught running live-fire exercises.

Another problem is that although U.S. law enforcement officers routinely deal with terrorism, they call it something else. Even the FBI labels the majority of domestic terrorist activities under the common titles of crime in the Uniform Crime Report, an annual standard measure of criminal activity in the United States. In addition, the FBI's reports on domestic terrorism do not classify many terrorists' acts as "terrorism"; they are classified as regular crimes. Nonetheless, in the 1980s, the FBI's practical methods for countering terrorism were recognized throughout the world, and they became the only agency that could coordinate thousands of local U.S. police departments in a counterterrorist direction. The irony of their efforts was that the FBI simply did not call much of their work counterterrorism. In addition, when terrorists are successful, as in Oklahoma City in 1995 or in New York City and Washington, D.C., in 2001, Congress is quick to point a finger at the FBI, forgetting about past successes (see Federal Bureau of Investigation, 2002).

Closely related to this problem is the simple fact that even after September 11 most domestic terrorism goes unnoticed. William Dyson (2004) tracks terrorist incidents in the United States and has identified nearly three hundred between September 11, 2001, and December 2004. Most of these incidents were limited to threats or extensive property damage, and none of them involved massive deaths. These are probably the reasons most Americans fail to notice terrorist activity. Bombing serves as an excellent example. According to a *New York Times* News Service (8-25-96) analysis, domestic bombings tripled between 1985 and 1994, from 1,103 to 3,163. Large explosions capture the world's attention, but the overwhelming number of bombings in the United States deal with individual criminal vendettas and single-issue terrorism. Mere property damage does not, and should not, garner the same attention as murder.

Another reason for the lack of concern is that recent terrorism developed slowly in America. Terrorism grew with radical groups beginning about 1965, and although there were some sensational activities, terrorists did not routinely target the United States until 1982. Before then, most American terrorist movements died for lack of support. Since 1982, however, terrorists have produced an increasing number of victims in the United States. Even though the majority of incidents still involve low-level criminal activity, Americans have sadly learned that they cannot automatically dismiss terrorism as something that happens somewhere else.

Finally, the term *hate crime* is frequently used with terrorism, confusing the issue even more. **Hate crime** is a new term defined by federal law and dozens of state statutes. It is a legal definition, not a manifestation of terrorism. Mark Hamm (1994, 1996) says that a hate crime is an illegal act designed to target a particular social group. With Hamm's definition in mind, it is possible to see that terrorists may use hate crimes just as they use other types of crime, but hate crime is a specific violation of law. It is not terrorism.

Classifying Terrorism in Criminal Justice

Key Points and Questions:

1. Where do criminologists and police officers differ on crime classification methods?
2. How does a tactical typology of terrorism assist law enforcement?
3. How did the National Advisory Commission on Criminal Justice Standards and Goals classify terrorism?
4. In what way does Harris's classification system reinforce this position?
5. Describe Smith's approach to classification systems.
6. How does Smith relate to the FBI position after September 11?

There is a great deal of tension between theoretical criminologists and practical analysts who look for an immediate solution to a specific problem. Classical criminologists look for an explanation of social phenomena, and they search for theories to explain crime or behavior in general. This crucial work produces theories that guide policies. From a tactical perspective, however, an immediate response to crime does not depend on general explanations. It is more important to understand the nature of the immediate problem and possible practical solutions. The same goes for terrorism: A label appropriate for theoretical criminology will not always lead to a response that solves an immediate problem. U.S. police officers routinely handle terrorism even though they call it by a variety of names. It would be helpful if law enforcement officers had a practical framework that explained their counterterrorist role.

Tactically, police and security forces should keep two issues in mind. First, a beat police officer is usually the first responder to domestic terrorism. Second, the investigation techniques used in large, sensationalized terrorist incidents are the same techniques a local agency would use to investigate a stink bomb placed in the locker room of a high school football team. From a practical perspective, counterterrorism depends on the fundamentals. Good investigative skills, such as the collection and preservation of evidence and good interviewing techniques, are important, and it is also important for law enforcement officers to understand the context of the crimes they investigate.

A label can define the political response to an incident, and when the term *terrorism* is applied to a crime, public fears increase. Terrorism has a political meaning beyond the immediate crime, even though a terrorist incident may be nothing more than a localized crime (Cooper et al., 1976; Smith, 1994). Most governments allow security forces greater latitude when dealing with terrorism and terrorists, and police in the United States need to be able to differentiate between tactical and political responses to terrorism. When used for tactical purposes, frameworks that classify terrorism may lead to effective prevention and response. If the same system is used in an emotionally charged atmosphere, the law enforcement response might have dire consequences for individual freedoms. The FBI may be justified by looking at criminal activity in the Uniform Crime Report instead of raising political alarms, yet on a tactical level, law enforcement needs to understand the scope of its counterterrorist mission.

Although this is not an optimistic thought, humans live in a constant state of conflict. Indeed, it is impossible to have a human social organization without conflict. Even in the most peaceful community, social organization is maintained because the controlling group can force people to join the organization and then force members to obey the organization's rules. The amount of force is subject to limitation, but the ability to coerce is real. Therefore, social organizations are never truly "at peace"; they are always "at war." The amount and level of conflict vary, but conflict is normative.

To illustrate this, consider a concept developed by the U.S. Army in the early 1970s. After the Vietnam War, the army realized that its mission was changing and it had to be prepared to fight any number of different styles of war. Conflict could range from low-level brushfire wars to nuclear devastation, and the meaning of war was nebulous at best. To clarify this situation, the U.S. Army spoke of a **spectrum of conflict** (see Expanding the Concept: Spectrum of Conflict and the front endpapers). The spectrum was a continuum that ranged from low-intensity conflict to full-scale war. This scale probably more correctly reflects the human condition than the belief that we can either be at war or at peace. It also helps us understand terrorism.

Over the past few years, I have used a typology to train military and police personnel in counterterrorism. Police and military officers have told me that it has helped them conceptualize their counterterrorist mission. The three parallel lines in the model symbolize three different measures that roughly correlate with each other. The first measure shows the level of activity. It is fairly simple to grasp: Incidents on the low end equal low activity, and the high end represents increasing rates of violence. The second line represents the type of activity. The line itself indicates the size of the terrorist group. On the extreme left, directly correlated with low activity on the activity continuum, is a single individual. Size increases as you move to the right. In terrorism, the level of activity is generally correlated with the size of a group. Generally, the larger a group, the greater its potential for terrorist violence.

Go to **http://cj.wadsworth.com/white_terrorism5e** and click on Web Links to view the Tactical Typology of Terrorism.

Notice that the second line is divided by a nebulous border separating criminal and political terrorism. This border is intentionally open because terrorists are free to move between the criminal and political boundaries. The openness is designed to illustrate the movement of political violence. Some criminal groups can become so large that they may act like terrorist groups. Small terrorist groups can become so focused on crime that they become nothing more than criminal gangs. Examples of these types of groups appear underneath the line.

The final continuum illustrates the type of response. Most criminal terrorism and a good share of political terrorism is a law enforcement responsibility. This means that when nonpolice units assist police agencies as part of a security force, they must think as the police do. For example, deadly force is always the last alternative in police operations. Additionally, legal procedures and an emphasis on individual rights guide each phase of a law enforcement response and investigation.

Law enforcement officers can apply a practical tactical typology to terrorism because applied analysts have been working toward a practical classification system of terrorism for a number of years. One of the early attempts to classify domestic ter-

Spectrum of Conflict

Because humans live in a perpetual state of conflict and conflict management, civil coercive power has a place on the spectrum of conflict. Even before conflict rises to a military level, civil authorities routinely face challenges that must be met by implied or direct force. At the lowest level of organization, informal norms and mores enforce compliance, and if they fail, stronger coercive force is applied. In modern Western society, this may be civil or criminal law, whereas a more passive social group might use expulsion or shunning. Regardless, social groups always have the potential to exhibit coercive force to enforce behavior.

Terrorism is a form of violent civil disobedience, and it can be placed on a spectrum of conflict. At the most basic governmental level, the state faces low-level challenges with *ordinary crime.* This increases with *group violence*, then *rioting* and wider disorders, and finally *terrorism.* At this point, military options may be used as the continuum moves to guerrilla war, low-level war, conventional war, technological war, wars of ecological destruction, and wars of oblivion.

Ethicists may correctly argue that we must always move to minimize conflict by using the least amount of force, but morality is not the issue here. Terrorism is simply a form of conflict among social organizations that accept conflict as normal. And as a form of conflict, its tactics can be modeled.

rorism came from the National Advisory Commission on Criminal Justice Standards and Goals, Task Force on Disorders and Terrorism (Cooper et al., 1976, pp. 3–7). The report cites several types of terrorism. Political terrorism is described as violent criminal behavior designed to produce fear for political outcomes. Nonpolitical terrorism is designed simply to produce fear; quasi-terrorism involves nonpolitical terrorist activities during the commission of crimes. The report also describes limited terrorism violence aimed at changing government policy, and it talks about state repression.

The FBI has also produced a workable tactical typology. Officially, the FBI defines terrorism by the way it is recorded in the annual report on terrorism called *Terrorism in the United States.* John Harris (1987, pp. 5–13) summarizes the FBI view by examining five types of groups responsible for domestic terrorism in the 1980s: (1) white leftists, (2) Puerto Rican leftists, (3) black militants, (4) right-wing extremists, and (5) Jewish extremists. Like the FBI reports on domestic terrorism, Harris does not include criminal incidents involving terrorist tactics, and he limits his topic to the problem of political terrorism.

According to Harris, all domestic terrorist groups, with the exception of Puerto Rican nationalists, lack an indigenous base, and they tend to have localized ideological bases. Types of groups are generally defined by location. For example, white supremacy groups tend to be rural, and revolutionary groups are generally urban. Because it tends to be geographically confined, American terrorism does not affect all local police agencies in the same manner. Although twenty years old, this typology still guides the way terrorist incidents are reported.

The unofficial typology the FBI uses is much more pragmatic and effective. It guides agents on a day-to-day basis and is used to coordinate activities with local police departments. According to publicly released information (Federal Bureau of Investigation, 10-12-04), two categories cover the classification system: Domestic Terrorism (DT) and International Terrorism (IT). DT involves violent political extremism, single-issue terrorism, and lone wolf or berserker activities (see Chapter 3). IT is defined as threats that originate outside the United States. The FBI defines activities on the basis of origin. In 2002 its Joint Terrorism Task Force (JTTF) arrested six suspects near Buffalo, New York, for supporting Jihadists. The JTTF called this DT because the activities originated in the United States. The attacks of September 11 are called IT because they originated outside U.S. borders (see Federal Bureau of Investigation, 2002).

Although not defined by the official categories of the Uniform Crime Report, this FBI system for defining terrorism provides a format for guiding investigations. For DT, political extremism involves violent left- and right-wing extremists. Single issues include violent activities associated with debates over abortion, ecoterrorism, animal rights, and genetic engineering. Lone wolves are included in the category when their actions are politically motivated. IT is composed of three subsets: state-sponsored terrorism, clearly defined autonomous groups, and Jihadists. The FBI focuses attention on the most active categories, so in the past five years emphasis has been placed on single-issue terrorists and Jihadists.

Closely related to this type of summary is a classification system developed by Brent Smith (1994). Using FBI data, Smith places terrorist groups into three broad categories: (1) right-wing extremists, (2) left-wing and single-issue terrorists, and (3) international terrorists. Smith believes that right-wing groups form a category by themselves, but that left-wing groups are different. Single-issue groups, criminal gangs, ecologists, and old-style leftists fit neatly into the left-wing extremist category. International terrorists form the remaining group.

Smith's Analysis of Domestic Terrorism

Key Points and Questions:

1. What important findings can be derived from Smith's research?
2. What does Smith have to say about the characteristics of terrorists?
3. How can categories be used to classify left- and right-wing terrorism?
4. Using examples, explain the characteristics of domestic terrorists.
5. How does Smith summarize the research problems he encountered?
6. How did Smith overcome these problems?

Using data from official sources, Brent Smith (1994; Smith et al., 2004) presents one of the best factual summaries of recent terrorism in the United States and a criminological analysis of domestic terrorism. The factor separating the average criminal from the average terrorist is *motivation*. According to Smith, terrorists remain criminals, but they are motivated by ideology, religion, or a political cause. Smith does not examine criminal terrorism as a tactical typology—it would have been difficult to do this because he uses FBI data, and the FBI does not measure criminal terrorism—but he provides a practical framework for approaching counterterrorism. By focusing on motivation, Smith has developed a promising model that may reveal patterns of behavior among types of terrorists (see Another Perspective: Brent Smith's Approach to Domestic Terrorism).

Smith's research reveals several important findings. American terrorism grew increasingly to a high level about 1985, just at the time the government was improving its counterterrorist tactics. Better government efficiency led to a series of arrests that decimated terrorist groups by the late 1980s. Right-wing groups tried to reemerge, but the left-wing groups did not. Left-wing terrorism remained a viable entity, however, because left-wing extremists were typically more loyal to their causes than were their right-wing counterparts. The left-wing groups also remained supported by Puerto Rican nationalists and single-issue groups such as ecological terrorists. In fact, Smith believes ecological terrorists have a great potential for violence in the future.

Many analysts have tried to profile terrorists, but since terrorism is a fairly infrequent crime and most often handled as a normative violation of criminal law, Smith says it is difficult to conduct research on domestic terrorism because the database is so small. Smith takes two methodological steps that give a better picture of American terrorists: He lists the characteristics of domestic terrorists, and he compares left-wing and right-wing extremists. His findings indicate that American terrorists differ from their international counterparts. Native-born U.S. terrorists tend to be older than international terrorists, and foreign operatives working in the United States follow that trend. Many domestic terrorists are older than thirty, whereas international terrorists in the United States tend to be older than the young extremists in other parts of the world.

Although ideological groups differ in their beliefs, Smith notes that those on both the left and the right tend to fund themselves through armed robberies. Despite this similarity, the left and right actually differ quite a bit. Smith compares left- and right-wing terrorists in five categories: (1) ideology and beliefs about human nature, (2) economic views, (3) geographic bases of support, (4) tactics, and (5) selection of targets. Left-wing terrorists favor Marxism, target the economic status quo, base themselves in urban environments, and select symbolic targets of capitalism. Right-wing terrorists are vehemently anti-Marxist and very religious. In addition, they support the economic system without supporting the distribution of wealth, base themselves in rural areas, and focus attacks on symbols of governmental authority. Although their ideology differs, both groups use similar terrorist tactics.

Smith offers several ideas for further examination. For example, he points out that left-wing terrorists were more active in the 1980s than right-wing terrorists. Official data show the truth of this, but it possibly is the case because of the way official

Another Perspective

Brent Smith's Approach to Domestic Terrorism

Although there are several classification systems for terrorism, Brent Smith has developed a simple and effective approach. He classifies terrorism as

1. Violent left-wing activities (including revolutionary nationalists and single-issue violence)
2. Violent right-wing activities
3. Foreign terrorism

Source: Smith (1994).

data are reported. Many right-wing terrorist activities, such as assaults, arsons, bombings, and robberies, are reported as regular crimes. Would the levels of left-wing and right-wing activity be the same if the FBI counted all possible terrorist incidents as terrorist activities?

In another comparison, Smith notes that left-wing groups tend to follow the Marighella model of revolution (see Chapter 12), whereas right-wing groups stay in fortresses in rural areas. Again, the data demonstrate this is correct. But is this a difference in philosophy or geography? Right-wing groups frequently barricade themselves, but other activities, such as Louis Beam's "leaderless resistance," are straight from Carlos Marighella. Perhaps the fortress mentality of right-wing groups is primarily due to geographic factors, particularly their favoring of rural locations.

In terms of the extremist right, Smith traces the resurgence of right-wing terrorism during the 1980s. He believes the right-wing groups began the decade on a high note but fell apart by 1984. Although they formed several organizations to try to rejuvenate the movement, Smith believes they failed.

Smith says left-wing terrorists have undergone no major transformation, remaining essentially the same from the 1960s to the present. Several protest groups began conglomerating around anti–Vietnam War movements after 1967, and by the end of the decade, some of them had become violent revolutionaries. After 1970, left-wing groups began acting in concert and frequently joined with Puerto Rican nationalists. When the Macheteros, a violent Puerto Rican nationalist group, emerged in 1979, they soon found allies among violent leftists. Smith says left-wing groups tended to act in a coordinated fashion, and evidence indicated they were linked internally. He also says Puerto Rican terrorists were supported by Cuba. Smith's research confirms earlier findings of others (Stinson, 1984).

According to Smith, the May 19 Communist Organization (M19CO) was one of the more recent successful left-wing terrorist groups. Emerging from elements of the SDS, Black Panther Party, and Student Non-Violent Coordinating Committee, the M19CO united several violent leftists under a common umbrella. The group formed in 1977, taking the "May 19" in its name from the birthdays of the North Vietnamese Communist leader Ho Chi Minh and American Muslim leader Malcolm X. The M19CO was racially mixed, and approximately half of the members were women. A few months after its formation, members of the group launched a campaign to free "political" prisoners and attack capitalism.

The M19CO was most active from 1980 to 1984. The group conducted several robberies, planted bombs at military installations and private businesses, and murdered some of its victims. It attracted members of many other left-wing groups, and Smith found that it spawned temporary splinter groups under a variety of names. Its most infamous activity occurred in 1981, when M19CO members robbed an armored car, killing a guard and wounding another, and then murdered two New York police officers who were deployed at a roadblock.

In 1984, the group's luck began to run out. Several members were indicted for a myriad of crimes, while others were on the run. Some members were incarcerated on simple charges to give the government time to investigate more serious offenses. The Joint Terrorism Task Force, managed by the FBI, the New York City Police Department, and the New York State Police, proved successful against the M19CO. By 1989, all members of the M19CO either were in prison or were hiding. (The task force would demonstrate its worth again in the successful investigation and prosecution of the 1993 World Trade Center bombing.)

Another left-wing group operating in the 1980s was the United Freedom Front (UFF). The UFF was composed mainly of anti–Vietnam War activists and protesters. Although not as active as the M19CO, the UFF became infamous for its ability to bomb American businesses. Members of the UFF and its clone group, the Armed Resistance Unit, were captured and jailed after the murder of a New Jersey state trooper. Despite some attempted activities through the late 1980s, left-wing terrorists virtually disappeared after 1990.

In Smith's analysis, ecological terrorists represent a trend similar to the actions of the older left-wing groups. In the past several years, ecological terrorists have manifested their movement in two areas. First, some groups, such as the Evan Mecham Eco-Terrorist International Conspiracy (EMETIC), have focused on environmental and land-use issues, attacking developers and loggers. A second type of group, illustrated by the Animal Liberation Front, protests the use of animals in scientific experimentation. Both groups mirror the characteristics of left-wing terrorists, and members are fanatically dedicated to their causes. Smith believes such groups may lead domestic terrorist activities in the twenty-first century.

Smith also focuses on international terrorism in the United States, stating that since 1985, the country has experienced foreign terrorism as surrogate warfare. Although the issue is fully discussed in the next section, Smith raises an interesting point about American policy. When terrorists attack the United States, law enforcement agencies frequently need the help of the military and intelligence communities. This creates the possibility that military forces will be used to fight political crimes by using American law. The internment of al Qaeda suspects in Cuba would seem to indicate that Smith's predictions were correct. In addition, in response to international terrorism, the United States has given its law enforcement agents the power to arrest terrorists on foreign soil.

Smith's work concludes with a criminological analysis of domestic terrorism. He finds that laws regarding terrorism in the United States are exceptionally vague. International terrorists tend to plead guilty more frequently than right-wing and left-wing terrorists. Left-wing terrorists fare the best in court, whereas few right-wing cases are dismissed. Smith says there are insufficient data for determining whether sentences differ. Although the public may think that terrorists are not punished harshly enough, limited data indicate terrorists receive substantially longer sentences than traditional criminals. Finally, terrorism is a matter of attitude. Smith believes a person is not a terrorist until the government applies the label. And that label can have long-term effects.

Smith (2004) has assembled a nationwide research team, the American Terrorism Project, that will reveal even more information about domestic terrorism. Relying on some of the best known criminal justice scholars in the country, Smith's team is examining every recent case in which terrorists have been brought to trial and convicted. The team is trying to discover common behavioral characteristics surrounding terrorist events. The findings will enhance criminological knowledge about individual terrorists and their groups.

Steven Emerson's View of Jihad and His Critics

 Key Points and Questions:

1. How did Jihadist organizations take root in the United States?
2. What role did charities play in financing Jihadist operations?
3. How does Revell assess the effect of Jihadist organizations?
4. Explain the relationship between the Alkifah Refugee Center and the 1993 World Trade Center bombing.
5. Who were the leading suspects in Emerson's investigation?
6. What is the Investigative Project?
7. How do critics respond to Emerson?

Another conceptual problem in analyzing American terrorism comes from international terrorism inside U.S. borders. In the wake of September 11, Jihadist terror dominated America's media and political institutions. It also spawned controversy. The debate started in 1994 after Steven Emerson, an investigative journalist who spent several years covering the Middle East, produced a PBS program titled **"Jihad in America"** (Emerson 1994). Emerson was already known for his analysis of Iraq (Emerson and Del Sesto, 1991), and his program touched off a heated debate between his supporters and his critics. Emerson stayed at the center of the controversy by creating a research group called the Investigative Project. Although his critics are infuriated, this group has gathered more information about Jihadists than most other organizations.

According to "Jihad in America," Jihadist organizations took root in the United States during the Soviet-Afghan War. Undeterred by U.S. intelligence agencies, mujahadeen traveled through the country to raise funds and established charitable organizations (see Chapter 5 for a more thorough look at how terrorism is funded). When the war ended in 1989, many mujahadeen and their fundraising mechanisms remained in the country, giving Jihadists a base in the United States. Unfortunately, their wrath turned on the United States. For instance, Emerson linked the 1993 World Trade Center bombing to the domestic terrorist networks before the government convicted some of their members.

Former associate deputy FBI director Oliver B. (Buck) Revell, interviewed on Emerson's PBS program, stated that once the mujahadeen and their associates came to the United States, they found a hospitable environment. They could raise money, film

Expanding the Concept

The Charlotte Hezbollah Cell

A deputy sheriff moonlighting as a security guard in Charlotte, North Carolina, noticed a group of people buying cigarettes at a discount tobacco store. He noticed them because they were buying hundreds of cigarette cartons and loading them into vans. The deputy assumed it was a cigarette smuggling operation and called the Bureau of Alcohol, Tobacco, and Firearms (ATF). Buying cigarettes in one state and then selling them in another can be criminally profitable because of varying state tobacco laws and tax systems. When the ATF agents starting investigating, they were surprised at what they found. The FBI, CIA, and many other agencies were also interested in the case.

Hezbollah was operating in Charlotte.

In this case the suspects purchased cigarettes in North Carolina and ran them to Michigan. North Carolina had a tax of five cents per pack on the cigarettes and a charge of fifty cents per carton. Michigan, however, taxed cigarettes at seventy-five cents per pack and $7.50 per carton. North Carolina did not require a tax stamp, but Michigan did. Smugglers transported the cigarettes from North Carolina to Michigan, stamped them with Michigan tax stamps, and then sold them at regular prices without paying taxes.

The U.S. attorney for western North Carolina, Robert Conrad, assumed the suspects were smuggling North Carolina cigarettes to Michigan and profiting by not paying tax. This turned out to be the base of the investigation, as the smugglers kept some of the money, but other illegal profits took a strange path. Conrad followed some money to Vancouver, Canada, and other profits went overseas. Conrad's office traced the money to Lebanon. Far from a simple cigarette scheme, the smuggling operation turned out to be an operation to support Hezbollah. The Charlotte Hezbollah cell, as it came to be known, was broken because investigators and prosecutors looked beyond the surface.

Source: *United States v. Mohamad Hammoud, et al.* (2002).

---

videos, run printing presses, and eventually attack the very country whose freedoms they enjoyed. For the first time in its history, the United States housed a terrorist infrastructure that stretched from the American heartland all the way through the Middle East to Southeast Asia. According to Revell, it is the most global network of terrorists the United States has ever faced.

Emerson credits Abdullah Azzam, one of the founders of al Qaeda, with the construction of the financial network. Azzam understood the vast amount of support available in the United States after helping to establish the **Alkifah Refugee Center** in New York City. According to Emerson, U.S. officials did not realize that the center was the front for another organization that called for jihad. In fact, the Alkifah Refugee Center's Arabic letterhead called for holy war.

Azzam spread his Jihadist network through thirty-eight states, with multiple bases in Pennsylvania, Michigan, California, Texas, and New England (see Expanding the Concept: The Charlotte Hezbollah Cell). Azzam returned to Pakistan in 1989, only to be killed by an assassin, but his work was completed by several supporters, including his cousin Fayiz Azzam.

Emerson names several prominent officials working in various radical groups in the domestic jihad. **Tamim al-Adnani** is the most vigorous recruiter and successful fundraiser among all the leaders. Emerson says al-Adnani has assisted in domestic terrorist incidents, including the 1993 World Trade Center bombing. Fayiz Azzam gives speeches calling for blood and holy war. **Elsayyid Nossair**, who was charged with the murder of militant Rabbi Meir Kahane and convicted of lesser offenses, maintained a clearinghouse for terrorist literature before his arrest. Even in prison, Emerson says, Nossair helped plan the World Trade Center bombing.

Emerson says the most important holy warrior operating in the United States was Sheik **Omar Abdel Rahman**. Before being charged with acts of terrorism in the United States, Rahman had been expelled from Egypt for conspiracy in the 1981 assassination of Egyptian president Anwar Sadat. Moving to New York City, members of Rahman's group helped plan the assassination of Rabbi Kahane while recruiting terrorists for a holy war against the United States. Emerson's PBS program caught Rahman in Detroit in 1991 calling for conquest of the infidel's land. Rahman has since been indicted for acts of terrorism, including complicity in the 1993 World Trade Center bombing. Emerson states that Sheik Abdul Wali Zindani, who has been involved in assassinations and bombings around the world, has taken Rahman's place.

Emerson also says well-known terrorist groups have established bases in the United States. He claims the Islamic Association for Palestine (IAP) is Hamas's chief propaganda arm in the United States. Under the name Aqsa Vision, the IAP produces many films, including military training videos. Based in Richardson, Texas, the IAP is one of several organizations with links to Hamas. Palestinian Islamic Jihad (PIJ) has a base in Tampa, Florida. Hezbollah also has a network in the country.

Emerson claims to have found more than thirty radical Middle Eastern groups in the United States, adding that the FBI has confirmed that terrorist groups have command centers in California, Nevada, Texas, Florida, Illinois, and New Jersey. Oliver Revell says the intention of these groups is to harm the United States and prevent it from being able to take international action.

Emerson followed "Jihad in America" with two major endeavors. First, he assembled a research team and founded the Investigative Project. Scouring media outlets and other sources, the Investigative Project produces an anthology of news articles about terrorism from around the world and conducts its own research. Second, Emerson (2002) followed the PBS broadcast with the book *American Jihad*, which documents his charges. The findings of both efforts point to a network of terrorist cells, false charities, and training camps in the United States. The results are shared with both the public and U.S. law enforcement. (See Another Perspective: Some of Emerson's Conclusions.)

Emerson's research has stirred controversy in several communities (see Another Perspective: The Critics Attack Emerson). Some journalists ignore his conclusions. John Sugg (1999) wrote a scathing diatribe against Emerson, claiming that he is sloppy with facts and arrives at incorrect conclusions after major terrorist incidents.

For example, Sugg says, Emerson initially blamed the wrong group for the 1993 World Trade Center bombing. In 1995, Sugg writes, Emerson blamed Jihadists for the Oklahoma City bombing. He also criticizes Emerson for alleging PIJ connections in Florida without proper evidence.

A journal on terrorism that features Emerson's work responded to Sugg's allegations with a press release that refuted Sugg's positions. Sugg's publisher responded by saying that the journal's press release contained errors and misstated facts consistent with Emerson's inaccurate reporting (FAIR, 2-2-99). In essence, Sugg believes that Emerson's conclusions about terrorism are painfully incorrect, but the Investigative Project can point to the arrest of alleged PIJ members in southern Florida as evidence of success.

Ibrahim Hooper (11-15-00), a representative from a Muslim organization known as the Council on American-Islamic Relations (CAIR), believes that Emerson is overly critical of Islam. Responding to an editorial opinion Emerson expressed in the *Wall Street Journal*, Hooper said that Emerson is an attack dog of the American pro-Israeli lobby. He claimed that Emerson is "Islamophobic" and his purpose is to smear the image of Islam. *The Wall Street Journal* did not print Hooper's response.

Nihad Awad (9-10-03), the head of CAIR, attacked Emerson's research in written testimony to the Senate Subcommittee on Terrorism, Technology, and Homeland Security. Awad says Emerson is a self-appointed terrorism expert who began making false charges in 1991; he agrees with Hooper's charge of "Islamophobia." He criticizes "Jihad in America," saying that it places every Muslim institution in America under a general terrorist umbrella.

Another Perspective

Some of Emerson's Conclusions

- ■ Al Qaeda is recruiting in American prisons.
- ■ Saudi contributors fund Jihadists in America and elsewhere.
- ■ Wahhabism, or the puritanical movement in Arabia associated with Mohammed ibn Abdul Wahhab, leads to attacks on non-Muslims and moderate Muslims.
- ■ Radical Islamic schools promote violent actions against Jews.
- ■ Many charities are fronts for Jihadists.
- ■ Hamas and al Qaeda may have established links.

Sources: Emerson and Levin (2003); "Countdown with Keith Olberman" (5-5-04); Fesperman (8-25-04).

Another Perspective

The Critics Attack Emerson

Steven Emerson has been the recipient of a storm of criticism. Some of his critics allege that he

- ■ Attacks Muslims
- ■ Lumps all Islamic groups under one umbrella
- ■ Distorts information
- ■ Does not report facts
- ■ Is part of a pro-Israeli movement
- ■ Acts as an intelligence agent for Israel

Sources: Awad (9-10-03); Hooper (11-15-00); FAIR (2-2-99); Sugg (1999).

The controversy surrounding Emerson's work is indicative of the final conceptual problem in domestic terrorism. It is difficult to conduct inquiries when a specific ethnic or religious group stands threatened to be painted with a broad brush and given an incorrect label. Some people may call Jihadists dangerous heretics, but they are *Muslim* heretics. Some of the institutions with which they associate also claim to be Islamic. This necessitates contacts between Islamic groups and researchers, journalists, and law enforcement personnel. It will always be a delicate situation at best.

Summary of Main Points

1. Cooper, Bell, and Gurr provided the first summaries of domestic terrorism by focusing on differing forms of social violence; the nature of terrorism began to change by the time of Cooper's report.

2. Conceptualizing domestic terrorism is challenging because many law enforcement agencies do not deal well with the problem; terrorism is reported a number of different ways, and there are different classification systems for defining terrorism and terrorists. Smith points to several research difficulties, and Emerson's research shows the difficulty of isolating Jihadist terrorism.

3. A tactical typology of terrorism can provide law enforcement agencies and other security forces with a practical method for conceptualizing terrorism.

4. The FBI system for classifying domestic terrorism is similar to Smith's. It focuses on international terrorists in America, left- and right-wing terrorism, lone wolf violence, and single-issue terrorism.

5. Smith finds declining levels of ideological terrorism and increasing threats from single-issue terrorists.

6. Emerson's research supports the existence of a network of Jihadist terrorist organizations in the United States. Critics believe that he has categorized too many Muslims as terrorists. Regardless, Emerson's research group, the Investigative Project, has assembled an array of reports, many of which point to a Jihadist network inside America's borders.

Key Terms

Make sure you can define, explain, or identify the following people, ideas, organizations, or terms:

Task Force Report on Disorders and Terrorism   227
vigilante terrorism   229
insurgent terrorism   229
transnational terrorism   229
hate crime   230

spectrum of conflict   232
"Jihad in America"   238
Alkifah Refugee Center   239
Tamim al-Adnani   240
Elsayyid Nossair   240
Omar Abdel Rahman   240

Suggested Readings

Now that you've been introduced to this topic, you can learn more by reading:

Brent Smith's book *Terrorism in America: Pipe Bombs and Pipe Dreams* takes readers through a twisting web of conspiracy theorists, nationalists, and foreign terrorists.

You may also want to read:

Steven Emerson's *American Jihad* offers a detailed synopsis of his research.

Lyman Sargent has edited a book of readings called *Extremism in America* to help readers conceptualize extremist views that lead to political violence.

The RAND Corporation has a report by Kevin Riley and Bruce Hoffman called "Domestic Terrorism."

Web Resources

Go to *http://cj.wadsworth.com/white_terrorism5e* and click on Web Links to find:

- An analysis of the future of terrorism and ideological terrorism at the Terrorism Research Center
- The Terrorism Knowledge Base from the National Memorial Institute for the Prevention of Terrorism (MIPT)
- Steven Emerson's 2004 testimony before Congress and opposition to it

The Companion Website for *Terrorism and Homeland Security*, Fifth Edition

http://cj.wadsworth.com/white_terrorism5e

At the Book Companion Website you can review chapter outlines, use the flash cards to test your terrorism vocabulary, and check out the many other study aids you'll find there. You'll find valuable data and resources at your fingertips to help you study for that big exam or write that important paper.

Terrorism Updates

http://www.wadsworth.com/criminaljustice_d/special_features/ext/terrorism _site090802/index.html

Visit the *Terrorism: An Interdisciplinary Perspective* website to find the most current information about the fields of terrorism and homeland security. With a focus on domestic and international issues, this site explores the scope of terrorism in our world today. You'll find essays on important topics in terrorism and homeland security, critical thinking web activities, and InfoTrac College Edition keywords. Most importantly, the website is updated weekly with current news and research articles on domestic and international terrorism. You are invited to use these web resources to supplement your understanding of the topics covered in this chapter.

Current Perspectives: Readings from InfoTrac College Edition
Terrorism and Homeland Security

The sixteen articles in this reader offer a representative selection that helps you understand the important issues about terrorism and homeland security. It includes FREE access to InfoTrac College Edition and can also be bundled with the text for free.

Chapter 14

Terrorism in the United States

Although many Americans still do not understand the scope of domestic terrorism, violence from terrorism has occurred throughout the history of the United States. Theorists and policymakers have various definitions and frameworks to describe the subject, but domestic terrorism is a social reality. Now that conceptual frameworks have been examined, this chapter will follow Brent Smith's model of domestic terrorism by looking at nationalistic terrorism, right- and left-wing political violence, and single-issue terrorism. Many of these events involve crimes reported under categories of the FBI's Uniform Crime Report, and others are based on tax evasion, weapons possession, and violations of the Racketeer Influenced and Corrupt Organizations (RICO) Act. Even though these events are prosecuted under a variety of state and federal laws, they constitute the bulk of domestic terrorism.

© Ralf-Finn Hestoft /Corbis

Three weary rescue workers lean on a car after attempting to find survivors of the Oklahoma City bombing. On April 19, 1995, a fuel-and-fertilizer truck bomb exploded in front of the Alfred P. Murrah Federal Building, killing 168 people. Although extremist ideology and violent political behavior are not new in the United States, this bombing brought the issues of domestic terrorism to the forefront.

Chapter Objectives

After reading this chapter, you should be able to:

1. Summarize the issues regarding and identify groups in the Puerto Rican nationalist movement.

2. Outline the history of right-wing extremism in the United States.

3. Explain white supremacy and Christian patriotism.

4. Summarize right-wing extremist tactics.

5. Explain the demise of left-wing terrorism and the rise of single issues.

6. Discuss antiabortion attacks.

7. Describe violence in the animal rights, ecological, and anti–genetic engineering movements.

8. Explain Black Hebrew Israelism.

Nationalistic Separatism: The Case of Puerto Rico

Key Points and Questions:

1. How did the United States become involved with Puerto Rico?

2. Describe three positions on Puerto Rico's relations with the United States.

3. How did violent groups originate?

4. Why did nationalist groups ally with the left?

5. What is the status of nationalistic terrorism?

Ronald Fernandez (1987) explores the reasons for terrorism conducted by Puerto Rican nationalists in the United States. Puerto Rico was colonized by the Spanish shortly after the European discovery of America, and the Spanish ruled the island for nearly three centuries. This changed in 1898, when the United States captured Puerto Rico in the Spanish-American War.

At first, the Puerto Ricans welcomed the United States as liberators, believing they were going to be granted independence, but they were disappointed. Instead of freeing the island, the United States granted Puerto Rico commonwealth status. Its special relationship to the United States grew with the increasing military importance of the island. Currently, the population is divided by three opinions. Some desire Puerto Rican statehood. Others want to create an independent country, and some of these people favor a Marxist government. A third constituency wants to maintain commonwealth status. This leaves the United States with a paradox: No matter which group is satisfied, two other groups will be disappointed.

Violent revolutionaries in Puerto Rico appeared more than fifty years ago. Puerto Rican nationalists tried to assassinate President Harry Truman in 1950 and entered the chambers of the House of Representatives in 1954, shooting at members of Congress on the floor. Holes from the bullets remain on some desks in the House Chambers today. Like their nationalistic counterparts in Europe, revolutionary groups merged with left-wing organizations around 1970 through roughly 1980.

Puerto Rican groups were able to continue operating despite the decline in left-wing terrorism (Smith, 1994).

A number of revolutionary organizations embraced the nationalist terrorist campaign. The Armed Forces of National Liberation (FALN) began operating in the United States after 1945, and they were joined by other Puerto Rican terrorists in following decades. One of the most notorious groups was the Macheteros. Other groups included the Volunteers for the Puerto Rican Revolution (OVRP), the Armed Forces of Liberation (FARP), the Guerrilla Forces of Liberation (GEL), and the Pedro Albizu Campos Revolutionary Forces (PACRF). Before the decline of the left, Puerto Rican terrorists routinely joined left-wing operations.

Smith (1994) notes that the Puerto Rican groups were the only domestic terrorists with strong international links during the 1980s. He believes Puerto Rican revolutionary support comes primarily from Cuba, and many members are in hiding there. Aside from carrying out the largest armored car robbery in the history of United States in 1983, Puerto Rican groups have conducted several bombings, assassinations, and even a rocket attack against FBI headquarters in San Juan. They have selectively murdered U.S. citizens, especially targeting U.S. military personnel stationed in Puerto Rico.

Since the fall of the Soviet Union, Puerto Rican terrorists have been less active, but their infrastructure remains intact. According to Fernandez (1987), terrorism has become one means of revolution. Smith believes the problem of Puerto Rican violence will not simply evaporate. Law enforcement officers must continue to respond to Puerto Rican terrorism, but at some point, American policymakers need to resolve the status of Puerto Rico to the satisfaction of its people. In 1998 the House of Representatives asked for a binding vote to determine Puerto Rico's status, but the vote failed to alter the future. Forty-six percent of Puerto Rican voters wanted statehood, and only 3 percent wanted independence. Fifty percent of voters said they did not want to accept statehood, commonwealth status, or independence, but they did not say what they did want (Rivera, 2005). The future of Puerto Rico remains uncertain although terrorist violence decreased in the first decade of the twenty-first century.

The Development of Right-Wing Violence

Key Points and Questions:

1. Where did right-wing extremism originate?
2. How did it develop in the 1800s?
3. What are the phases of development of the Ku Klux Klan?
4. What type of religious beliefs accompanied right-wing extremism?
5. What are Anglo-Israelism and Christian Identity?

On the morning of April 19, 1995, television and radio special-news reports indicated that some type of explosion had occurred in Oklahoma City in or near the federal building. These reports were quickly amended, and reports of the size and extent of damage increased with each moment. By noon it was apparent that the United States had suffered a devastating terrorist attack.

As scenes of the injured and dead, including children, and smoldering wreckage dominated the nation's television screens, attention turned toward the Middle East. Conventional wisdom placed blame for the incident on some militant Islamic sect. Many Arab Americans were harassed, and some were openly attacked. The country was shocked when a young white man with a crew cut was arrested for the bombing. It was hard to believe that the United States had produced terrorists from its own heartland.

Although many people were surprised, even a cursory history of right-wing extremism in the United States reveals that extremist ideology and violent political behavior is nothing new (White, 2001). The first incident of antifederal behavior came shortly after the American Revolutionary War (1775–1783). In 1791, the federal government levied an excise tax on the production of whiskey. Farmers in western Pennsylvania, a top whiskey-producing area in the country, were incensed. The unpopular tax provoked riots and created general disorder. In October 1794, President George Washington mobilized the National Guard of several states and sent the troops to Pennsylvania. The **Whiskey Rebellion** quickly ended, but not the resentment against the federal government (Phillips, 1999, pp. 332–334).

Antifederal attitudes were common in some circles in the early 1800s. The so-called **Know-Nothings** operated in the eastern United States before the Civil War (1861–1865). Organizing under such names as the Order of the Sons of America and the Sons of the Star Spangled Banner, these groups were anti-Catholic, anti-Irish, and anti-immigration. They felt Catholic immigrants were destroying American democracy. When confronted by authority, party members would claim to "know nothing," hence, their name (McPherson, 1988, pp. 135–143).

Although the Civil War had many causes—slavery, farming versus industry, and sectionalism—one of the greatest was disagreement over the power of the federal government. Southerners questioned the legitimacy of the federal government, and they believed Congress was taking the powers reserved for the states. Most Southerners were not fighting to preserve slavery; they were fighting to keep the power of local governments. When the Confederacy was defeated in 1865, the issue did not die (McPherson, 1988, pp. 858–859; Foote, 1986a, pp. 35–40; Foote 1986b, p. 1042).

Agrarian failures and depressions spawned radical economic theories during the 1870s and 1880s. These rural movements were complemented by labor violence and the introduction of anarchism from the left. Businesses and local and state governments frequently repressed both left-wing and right-wing versions of extremism. After the turn of the century, though, mainstream Americans came to believe that the left posed a greater threat to democracy. This attitude increased after 1919, when a wave of left-wing terrorism swept the country. As a result, right-wing extremist organizations grew. They popularized extremist views and claimed judges, elected officials, and police officers in their ranks. Right-wing extremists also turned to an organization that had been created in the wake of the Civil War, the **Ku Klux Klan (KKK)**.

The KKK had been the brainchild of Confederate cavalry genius General **Nathan Bedford Forrest** (Berlet and Lyons, 2000, pp. 58–62). Forrest had intended to create an antiunionist organization that would preserve Southern culture and traditions. When the newly formed KKK began terrorizing freed slaves, Forrest tried to disband the organization. But it was too late, and the KKK began a campaign of hate. By the early twentieth century, the organization had nearly died, but it revived in the extremist atmosphere after World War I (1914–1918).

The KKK has operated in three distinct phases through history (Berlet and Lyons, 2000, pp. 58, 85–103, 265–286). Shortly after the Civil War, hooded **Knight Riders**, as they were called, terrorized African Americans to frighten them into political and social submission. This aspect of the Klan faded by the end of the century. The second phase of the Klan came in the 1920s as it sought political legitimacy. During this period, the KKK became popular, political, and respectable. But it collapsed in the wake of a criminal scandal. The modern KKK grew after World War II (1939–1945), becoming, up to the present day, fragmented, decentralized, and dominated by hate-filled rhetoric.

The development of the modern Klan parallels the growth of right-wing extremism from the 1930s to the present. Michael Barkun (1997) describes the growth of extremism from a religious view. Barkun says that a new religion, Christian Identity, grew from the extremist perspective (discussed more below). Starting with a concept called **Anglo-Israelism** or British Israelism, American right-wing extremists saw white Americans as the representatives of the lost tribes of Israel. Wesley Swift preached this message in a radio ministry from California beginning in the late 1940s. Two of his disciples were William Potter Gale and Richard Butler. Gale went on to form several right-wing associations, including Posse Comitatus. Butler retired from an engineering career, moved to Idaho, and formed the **Aryan Nations**. Gale and Butler preached Swift's message of Christian Identity.

Christian Identity is a strange blend of Jewish and Christian biblical passages and is based on the premise that God was white (White, 1997; 2001). Since Adam and Eve were created in the image of God, they were also white. Nonwhites, or "mud races," evolved from animals and eventually produced the Jews, who try to destroy God's white race and establish a kingdom of the devil. Jesus, who is the ultimate white man, came to help the white Israelites in their struggles, but the Jews crucified him. God intervened, promising that a militant resurrected Jesus would return to reclaim the world for white people. White Israelites eventually migrated to Europe, and each white tribe founded one of the countries in the northern and western parts of the continent. These became the Aryan Nations.

Identity theology is based on a story of conflict and hate. According to this theology, Jews have gained control of the United States by conspiring to create the Federal Reserve System. The struggle between whites and Jews will continue until whites ultimately achieve victory with God's help. At that point, the purpose of creation will be fulfilled. Such theological perversions are necessary when converting a religion of love into a doctrine of hate (see Chapter 4).

Barkun points out that Christian Identity helped to provide the basis for violence among the extremists. Before the Christian Identity movement, American extremism was characterized by ethnocentrism and localized violence. Christian Identity gave a new twist to the extremist movement: It was used to demonize Jews. Christian Identity provided a theological base for stating that white people originated with God and Jews came from the devil. Such eschatological presumptions are deadly (see Stanton, 1991, p. 36).

Contemporary Right-Wing Behavior, Beliefs, and Tactics

 Key Points and Questions:

1. What issues hold right-wing extremism together?

2. Does hysteria play a role in the movement?

3. How extensive is violence from right-wing extremists?

4. Describe Sapp's threefold approach to understanding right-wing orientation.

5. In what ways has right-wing violence shifted in the past decade?

The appearance of modern right-wing extremism came to fruition around 1984 and has remained active since that time. According to personal research (White, 1997, 2000, 2002), several issues hold the movement together. First, the right wing tends to follow one of the forms of extremist religions. The name of God is universally invoked, even by leaders who disavow theism (a belief in God). Second, the movement is dominated by a belief in conspiracy and **conspiracy theories**. Followers feel they are losing economic status because sinister forces are conspiring to swindle them out of the American dream. The primary conspiratorial force was Communism, but after the fall of the Soviet Union, it became the United Nations. The extremist right believes a conspiracy of Jewish bankers works with the United Nations to create a **New World Order**, a belief that Jews control the international monetary system. Finally, right-wing extremists continue to embrace patriotism and guns. They want to arm themselves for a holy war (see Barkun, 1997; Berlet and Lyons, 2000, pp. 345–352).

In his popular historical work *Dreadnought: Britain, Germany and the Coming of the Great War*, Robert K. Massie (1991) points to the hysteria in Great Britain and Germany during the naval race before World War I. Both the British and the Germans demonized one another, and their national rivalries often gave way to irrational fears. In one of the more notable British reactions, the fear of German naval power gave rise to a particular genre (or style) of popular literature. These stories had a similar theme. Secret German agents would always land in the United Kingdom and destroy the British Empire through some type of subversive plot. Whether poisoning the water supply, destroying the schools, or infiltrating the economic system, the fictional Germans never attacked directly. They were mysteriously secretive, and they were everywhere.

The actions of right-wing extremists fit Massie's description of the hysterical fears in Britain. Extremists believe alien forces are conspiring to destroy the United States. Bill Stanton (1991, pp. 78–82) says that in 1978, the KKK led the way into the modern era when it emerged in Georgia and North Carolina as a paramilitary organization. Within a decade, many members of the extremist right had followed suit. Not only were they willing to accept conspiracy theories, but they were also ready to fight the hordes that they believed would destroy the American way of life.

Brent Smith (1994) paints a realistic picture of right-wing extremism, arguing that terrorism from the right wing is fairly limited. Groups are rural and tend to emerge from farm-based compounds. For example, Posse Comitatus formed as a tax protest group and engaged in violent resistance to local law enforcement. The most celebrated case dealt with Gordon Kahl, who killed three law enforcement officers in

North Dakota and Arkansas before being killed in a shoot-out. Another group, The Order, was a militant offshoot of the white supremacy movement. By 1987, however, The Order was defunct, and the right wing was fading.

Even while this was happening, most right-wing criminal activities were not labeled as terrorism, and even though the celebrated cases of violent right-wing extremism faded in 1987, the ideology that spawned them did not. So-called "hate crimes" increased, creating concern among criminal justice researchers (Hamm, 1994). Membership in extremist groups grew after their apparent collapse in 1987, and by 1994, the extremists were back in business. A look at the structure of the right-wing movement explains why.

According to Allen Sapp (1985), the right-wing movement had evolved into three distinctive trends by 1984. The first trend involved the **white supremacy movement**, with its three main branches of the Ku Klux Klan, neo-Nazis, and other white European or Aryan-based organizations. Sapp and other researchers (Holden, 1985, 1986; Wiggins, 1985, 1986; Coates, 1987) believe the Idaho-based Aryan Nations holds the key to the unification of the white supremacy movement. The late Richard Butler, former leader of the Aryan Nations, interacted with the leaders of several white supremacy movements and held an Aryan Congress each year to draw the white supremacists together.

Sapp says the second trend in extremism is **survivalism**. Survivalists withdraw from society, forming compounds in rural areas. Irwin Suall and David Lowe (1987) describe these groups as hybrids, combinations of old supremacy groups and more sophisticated modern hate groups. These groups typically establish themselves on a communal basis, rallying around a strong leader. Secluding themselves in armed compounds, they wait for the eventual collapse of government. The existence and philosophy of these groups are critically important to the change in right-wing extremism in the 1990s.

The final category in Sapp's typology deals with *religion*. Many right-wing extremists follow Christian Identity. American patriots, or *Christian patriots* in Christian Identity theology, stand willing to fight against their racial enemies. By moving into the realm of religion, violent right-wing extremists transform the white supremacy and survivalist movements into a holy war against Jews and non-whites.

Although such theories make sense to the extremists, they are so radical that few thinking people would follow them. As a result, extremist right-wing groups were waning by 1987. The late Richard Butler tried to compensate for declining numbers by inviting **Skinheads** (young people who shave their heads and profess white supremacy) to the Aryan Nations Congress in Hayden Lake, Idaho, to little avail. True believers remained loyal to the cause, but they were few and far between.

Things changed about 1991. Three issues rejuvenated the extremist right (Stern, 1996). First, the **Brady Bill** (named for President Reagan's press secretary, James Brady, who was disabled in an assassination attempt) caused many conservatives to fear federal gun-control legislation. The extremist right played to these fears, toning down issues like white supremacy and Christian Identity and claiming that the intrusive federal government was out to eliminate gun ownership. Extremists felt they had an issue that appealed to mainstream conservatives. By stressing the fear of gun control, right-wing extremists hoped to appear to be in the mainstream.

The second issue dealt with a botched U.S. Marshal's Office attempt to arrest Randy Weaver on a bench warrant at Ruby Ridge in the mountains of Idaho. A white supremacist and adherent of Christian Identity, Weaver was charged with selling illegal firearms to undercover agents from the Bureau of Alcohol, Tobacco, and Firearms (ATF). Weaver was arrested and released on bail. When he refused to appear for the assigned court date, U.S. marshals tried to bring him in. Tragically, U.S. Marshal William Degan and Weaver's young son, Sammy, were killed in the ensuing shootout. The FBI responded by laying siege to Weaver's mountain cabin. In the following days, an FBI sniper shot and killed Weaver's pregnant wife before he surrendered (Walter, 1995).

The **Ruby Ridge incident** had a strong symbolic impact on the extremist right. According to Stern (1996), **Bo Gritz**, a leading extremist figure, drew national attention to the siege when he came to negotiate surrender. Gritz is an articulate, charismatic individual who retired as a colonel from the U.S. Army Special Forces, and his voice and opinions carry far beyond the extremist right. He left Ruby Ridge saluting Skinhead demonstrators and calling for the formation of special resistance forces (SPIKE groups) to prevent further standoffs (Walter, 1995).

Closely related to Ruby Ridge, in the minds of the extremist right, was a third event: the federal siege of the Branch Davidian compound near Waco, Texas. In 1993, ATF agents attempted to serve a search warrant on the compound, but they were met with a hail of gunfire. Four agents were killed, and several were wounded. After a three-month siege, FBI agents moved in with tear gas. Unknown to the agents, the compound was laced with gasoline. When the FBI moved in, the Branch Davidians burned their fortress, killing more than seventy people, including several young children, inside the compound.

Stern says the **Waco siege** also became a symbol for the extremist right, even though it had very little to do with the right-wing movement. An ATF report (1995) said that in reality, the Waco siege involved a group of people led by a dismissed Seventh Day Adventist, Vernon Wayne Howell, who changed his name to **David Koresh**. Taking advantage of the weak and distraught, Koresh established the Branch Davidian compound outside Waco. According to the ATF, Koresh gathered illegal weapons and committed a variety of unlawful activities. He ruled his flock with messianic illusions, claiming that the end was near and he would save the world. In the end, he simply murdered his followers rather than admit his messianic failings, but he set the stage to be embraced by the extremist right. Although Koresh had nothing to do with right-wing extremists per se, he had the right formula: guns, a survivalist compound, and a belief in a Warrior God.

If Stern is correct, the Brady Bill, Ruby Ridge, and Waco gave new life to the fading right-wing movement, and a shift in the religious orientation of the extremist right helped to rejuvenate their ranks. Although many American Protestants would agree that the United States was the new chosen land, perhaps even a new Israel, few could stomach the blasphemy and hatred of Christian Identity. In the 1990s, however, the religious message changed. Patriotism and anti-Semitism proved to be as strong as the Christian Identity message.

Today, the situation has shifted again. If the movement was revitalized in the 1990s, it mutated after September 11, 2001. Violent members of the right-wing movement melted away from large organizations and began to congregate in small groups. Following the pattern of international terrorist groups, they organized chains or hubs, small groups operating autonomously. The days of large meetings seemed to fade as well. One Montana criminal intelligence commander told me he believed that the current leaders of the movement do not know how to arrange large rallies. As a result, he said, the movement in the Pacific Northwest, for instance, looks more like a conglomeration of terrorist cells. But they remain violent and anticipate some type of anti-Jewish awakening.

The irony is the existence of the smaller groups engaged in more individual violence. Additionally, these groups began to form linkages with single-issue groups, including anarchists and left-wingers. The future is currently unclear. The groups may be fading as the left-wing did in the 1980s, or they may be repositioning themselves. Militias tended to turn to patriotism and more normative behavior after September 11. The path of the violent offshoot groups remains undetermined.

The wild card is the vacuum in leadership. Richard Butler, leader of the defunct Aryan Nations, died in September 2004. No one had been able to unite the extremist right like Butler. Leaders are jockeying for power, but no single leader with Butler's charisma and organizational skills has moved to the forefront. A number of potential leaders are due for release from prison, so a leader may emerge. In the meantime, small groups dominated by Christian Identity theology and Christian patriotism engage in localized violence.

Conspiracies, Militias, and the Call to Arms

Key Points and Questions:

1. What are the variations of Christianity that appeared in the right-wing extremist movement?

2. Why do violent right-wing groups need conspiracy theories?

3. How is the militia movement violent?

4. What changes took place after September 11?

Christianity has undergone some strange transformations in the violent circles of right-wing extremism sometimes known as the **hate movement** (White, 1997, 2001). For example, some extremists adopted Norse mythology. Following Erich Luddendorff, a German general from World War I, extremists began preaching **Nordic**

Christianity in northern Germany. This belief system migrated to the United States and took root in Michigan, Wisconsin, Montana, and Idaho in the 1990s. Using ancient Norse rites, they claimed to worship the Triune Christian Deity, but they added Odin (Wotan) and Thor. Odin, the chief of the Norse gods, called Nordic warriors to racial purification from Valhalla, or the Viking heaven. Thor, the god of thunder, sounded the call with a hammer that shook the heavens.

In another religious derivation, **Creatorism** rejects Judaism and Christianity altogether (see Church of the Creator, 2005). Creatorists claim the Creator left humanity on its own, and each race must fend for itself. Embracing the urban Skinheads, Creatorists call for a racial holy war, or **RAHOWA**. They produce racially oriented comic books designed to appeal to alienated white youth. They also publish *The White Man's Bible*, which emphasizes racial purity. Creatorists argue that an intervening, loving God is nothing more than an idle lie. White people have been left on their own by a deistic Creator, and they are expected to fight for their survival. Essentially, Creatorism is a religion with more violent tendencies than Christian Identity.

If extremists were trying to achieve mainstream political acceptance through issues like gun control, taxation, and the New World Order, however, they could not merely appeal to Odin. The majority of right-wing extremists retreated to more conservative churches and relied on individual interpretations of scripture from lay preachers along the American frontier to justify antigovernment actions. This group can loosely be described as **Free-Wheeling Fundamentalists**.

Unlike the hate religions, the Free-Wheeling Fundamentalists do not believe the American government is part of a satanic conspiracy. They do believe, however, that the federal government and local governments are their enemies and that God will assist them in their confrontation with evil. Using antifederalist rhetoric, they boost their call to revolution with appeals to the Christian theology of frontier lay preachers. They call on a personal God—a self-defined concept of divinity usually not recognizable in the Hebrew, Muslim, or Christian scriptures. By 1995, this movement became popular in the rural West and Midwest, and it has set the stage for right-wing extremism into this century (see O'Conner, 11-2-04).

Free-Wheeling Fundamentalism affected the Christian patriot movement. While many Christian patriots believe that the United States is God's promised land, many of them are not willing to demonize other races or religions. Many Christian patriots believe that the government no longer serves average Americans, and they believe bankers and businesspeople work together against farmers and other rural Americans. They believe in God, America, and freedom, but they do not accept the hate-filled tenants of Identity theology and reject Nordic Christianity as a collection of heretical myths. They feel that the government will not defend the country against foreign enemies and that it favors the United Nations over the United States. As survivalist ideology grew in the 1980s, the Free-Wheeling Fundamentalists turned to a new idea—the **militia movement.**

Militias thrive on conspiracy theories. They believe the U.S. government is leading the country into a single world government controlled by the United Nations and that the New World Order is a continuation of a conspiracy outlined in **the Protocols of Zion**, a document written after World War I, claiming that Jews are out to control the world (Stern 1996). The militias play on conspiracy, fear of government, racism, antiabortion rhetoric, and anti-Semitism. In Stern's analysis, Bo Gritz, militia leader John Trochmann, and the white supremacy leaders are one and the same. Stern links the militia movement to Christian Identity (see Maise and Burgess, 2005).

Research conducted by the Strategic Intelligence Division of the ATF (1995) suggests that the militia movement is far from monolithic. ATF analysts believe militias tend to be issue oriented. Groups gather around taxes, abortion, gun control, and/or Christian Identity. Other research reflects the ATF findings (White, 1997, 2001). Militias are almost always religious, but few embrace Christian Identity, Nordic Christianity, or Creatorism. For justification, they rely on Free-Wheeling Fundamentalism and violent passages of Christian scripture quoted out of context. Most simply interlace their anti-tax, anti–gun control rhetoric with such biblical passages.

There is one more thing to say about the militia movement. Simply joining a militia group does not make a person a terrorist. Incidental observations have indicated that several people have joined the militias out of a sense of powerlessness. As a reporter from the *Toledo Blade* quipped to the author, these are folks who never quite made it. The reporter says the militia makes them feel important, and he is probably correct. Many militia members are frustrated, feel overwhelmed, and are socially unable to cope with the rapid pace of change in the modern world. They may be extremists, but they are not terrorists.

Paramilitary groups, or armed civilian militias that organize themselves in a military manner, operate on different levels. For example, the Arizona Vipers allegedly planned to blow up a number of federal installations in 1996, and many of them eventually pled guilty to possessing illegal explosives. Interviews of several prominent militia members indicate, however, that they had never heard of the Arizona Vipers. The Freemen of Montana represent another variation. They allegedly terrorized a small town, Jordan, Montana, by flaunting laws like an urban gang. When the federal government took action in 1996, creating another siege, militia members across the country expressed support but took steps to increase their ideological distance from the Freemen. Paramilitary groups come in a variety of shapes and sizes, and most of their action is rhetorical. The Arizona Vipers and the Freemen of Montana are exceptions. Rhetoric turns to violence when small, detached groups emerge from larger extremist groups.

A new trend emerged after the sieges of Ruby Ridge in 1992, Waco in 1993, and the Freemen standoff in Jordan, Montana. Old left-wing extremists and new right-wing extremists began to search for common ground. One philosophy, the **Third Position**, tried to unite both extremes. Radicals (left-wing) and reactionaries (right-wing) found that they shared some things in common. They hate the government, they have no use for large corporations, and they distrust the media. The Third Position serves to blur the line between left and right by uniting former enemies around common themes. This becomes more apparent when examining the newest form of domestic terrorism, ecological violence.

The small violent groups after September 11 began taking action without a centralized structure. In several areas two or three people began to operate without contacting other groups or conglomerating at large convocations. They planned bombings, chemical attacks, and spoke of a spontaneous revolution (CNN, 1-30-04; CBS News, 8-5-04). Embracing the ideas of Carlos Marighella (see Chapter 12), these unrelated groups felt that any act of violence would help to create the mayhem necessary to topple the government. The organization style was new, but the ideology that drove the groups had been planted earlier from the hills of West Virginia. It was contained in the philosophy of William Pierce.

Pierce's Blueprint for Revolution

 Key Points and Questions:

1. Who was William Pierce?
2. What was the premise of *The Turner Diaries*?
3. How might violent groups act on and model Pierce's ideas?
4. How does the novel *Hunter* complement *The Turner Diaries*?

William Pierce was a white supremacist with headquarters in rural West Virginia. He led an organization called the **National Alliance**, purchased Resistance Records, a recording label for Skinhead hate music. Pierce held a doctoral degree and worked as a college professor. Until his death in 2003 he drew the attention of watchdog groups, scholars, and law enforcement officers (Pitcavage, 1999a). Pierce wrote two novels that summarized his thought and provided a blueprint for revolution.

Pierce's most noted novel, **The Turner Diaries**, was written under the pseudonym Andrew MacDonald (1985) and is a fictionalized account of an international white revolution. The work begins as a scholarly flashback from "New Baltimore" in the "year 100," and it purports to introduce the diary of the protagonist, Earl Turner, during the "Great Revolution," a race war that mythically took place in the 1990s.

For the most part, *The Turner Diaries* is a diatribe against minorities and Jews. It is well-written and easy to read. The danger of the work is that from a technical standpoint, it is a how-to manual for low-level terrorism. Using a narrative or storytelling format, Pierce describes the proper methods for making bombs, constructing mortars, attacking targets, and launching other acts of terrorism. Anyone of average intelligence who reads *The Turner Diaries* will leave the book with an elementary idea of how to become a terrorist.

The second potential danger of *The Turner Diaries* is more subtle. The book could serve as a psychological inspiration for violence; that is, it could inspire copycat crimes. The frequent diatribes in and the philosophy behind the book justify murder and mayhem. Pierce presents the destruction of nonwhite races, minorities, and Jews as the only logical solution to social problems. Although he is not religious, he uses a general cosmic theology, presented in a "holy" work called The Book, to place Earl Turner on the side of an unknown deity.

Some extremists who read this book have taken action. Robert Matthews, for example, founded a terrorist group called the **Bruder Schweigen** (the Silent Brotherhood) or The Order based on Turner's fictional terrorist group. The Oklahoma City bomber Timothy McVeigh was arrested with a worn copy of *The Turner Diaries*.

Written in 1989, **Hunter** is another Pierce novel written under the pen name Andrew MacDonald. Although not as popular as *The Turner Diaries, Hunter* tells the story of a lone wolf named Hunter who decides to launch a one-person revolution. He stalks the streets to kill African Americans, interracial couples, and Jews. The book is dedicated to a real-life killer, and like *The Turner Diaries*, it could inspire copycat crimes. In 1999, two right-wing extremists went on killing sprees in Chicago and Los Angeles in a style reminiscent of the violence in *Hunter*.

Extremist literature is full of hate, instructions, and suggestions. Pierce has introduced nothing new in the literature of intolerance. However, he has popularized terrorism in two well-written novels. Unfortunately, they could also serve as a blueprint for violence.

The Decline of the Left

 Key Points and Questions:

1. When did left-wing terrorism dominate the United States?
2. What happened to left-wing groups in the United States?
3. How did intellectual elites interact with left-wing extremists?
4. Did Riley and Hoffman find growing concern about leftist violence among the police?
5. How was guilt a factor in the demise of the left?
6. Compare developments in the United States to the experience in Italy and Germany.

Left-wing terrorist groups dominated terrorism in the United States from about 1967 to 1985. Fueled by dissatisfaction with the Vietnam War, violent radicals broke away from student protest movements. Soon, various groups emerged, and they separated from the student movement to join ranks with nationalistic terrorists. Their favorite tactic was bombing, but unlike right-wing groups, they tried to avoid casualties. Various groups made headlines, but their influence faded. By the late 1980s, several leftist groups formed coalitions such as the Armed Resistance Unit, but they were forced to do so out of weakness rather than strength (Wolf, 1981, pp. 40–43).

Several things contributed to the demise of left-wing terrorism in the United States. One of the major problems was that intellectual elites controlled the movement (Serafino, 2002). During a time of student activism, leftist elites developed followings and sympathy across a broad spectrum of collegiate and highly educated people. Kevin J. Riley and Bruce Hoffman (1995) note that this gave the left a broad constituency. Yet, the movement lost its base when student activism began to disappear from American academic life. As the mood of the country shifted toward more conservative patterns of behavior, the left-wing terrorists had little sympathetic ideological support.

Riley and Hoffman surveyed several U.S. law enforcement agencies in the mid-1990s to determine their concern with domestic terrorism. Police departments were worried about terrorism, but left-wing groups were not at the top of their agenda. Only 25 percent of the urban agencies surveyed reported any left-wing activity; the responding departments reported much more activity from other types of groups. Riley and Hoffman say that the left-wing groups had engaged in symbolic violence.

Some identified with Marxist-Leninist ideology, while others worked against specific political issues such as U.S. military involvement in Central and South America. The collapse of the Soviet Union did not help left-wing popularity. In 1995 police perceived right-wing and Puerto Rican groups to be the greatest threats. The greatest concentration of left-wing groups was on the West Coast, but they were comparatively weak compared with other threats.

Loretta Napoleoni (2003, xix–xxiii) finds that guilt was a factor as left-wing terror faded in Europe. People who may have been sympathetic to the ideology of left-wing terrorists could not tolerate their violent activities as terrorism increased. This may have been a factor in American terrorism as well. Furthermore, left-wing violence waned with the fall of Communism, and police tactics improved with time, putting many terrorist groups on the defensive (Peacetalk, 2003).

The decline of American left-wing terrorism may reflect a similar trend in Europe. Xavier Raufer (1993) says German leftists failed when the government stole their agenda. The conservatives of the Reagan era certainly did not take the left-wing agenda, but they did take the country's heart. American mainstream interests turned from the extremist left. Donatella della Porta (1995) points to this process in Italy. The Red Brigades were able to attract a broad sympathetic audience, but the government and authorities came to understand this and turned the tables, winning the support of the public. Unfortunately, as their power based waned, the Red Brigades increased violence in an effort to gain new recruits. American groups were too weak to do this, although they grabbed headlines.

Left-wing terrorism did not disappear, however; it was transformed. Leftist movements became more specific, focusing not only on certain political behavior, but on particular causes. When the left faded, single-issue groups emerged to take their place. These new groups grew and began a campaign of individual harassment and property destruction.

Ecoterrorism, Animal Rights, and Genetic Engineering

 Key Points and Questions:

1. How did the ecoterrorism and animal rights movements begin?
2. What is monkey wrenching?
3. Ecoterrorists usually commit what type of crime?
4. Have some single-issue groups called for violence?
5. How can ELF be compared with ALF?
6. Who are some of the allied groups in the ecological movement?
7. How is genetic engineering related to ecological violence?

According to the FBI (Jarboe, 2-12-02), supporters of **ecoterrorism**, **animal rights**, and anti–**genetic engineering** came together in the United Kingdom in 1992. The new group called itself the **Earth Liberation Front (ELF)**. Composed of radicals from Earth First!, the Animal Liberation Front (ALF), and other disaffected environmentalists, the group migrated from Europe to the United States. The alliance has been responsible for more than six hundred criminal acts since 1996. Its tactics include sabotage, tree spiking, property damage, intimidation, and arson, resulting in tens of millions of dollars of damage. One ELF member recently called for violent action, even though both ELF and ALF deny this.

ELF was predated when radical ecologists began to sabotage road-working and construction machinery in the late 1970s. As was the case with the right wing, a novel inspired the ecoterrorists. **The Monkey Wrench Gang**, a 1975 novel by Edward Abbey, told the story of a group of ecologists who were fed up with industrial development in the West. Abbey, however, is an environmental activist rather than a hate-filled ideologue like William Pierce. His novel is a fictional account that has inspired others. In *The Monkey Wrench Gang*, the heroes drive through the western states sabotaging bulldozers, burning billboards, and damaging the property of people they deem to be destroying the environment. (This is the same type of low-level terrorism German leftists used in the mid-1990s.) Such **monkey wrenching** has become a key tactic of ecoterrorists.

Bryan Denson and James Long (1999) conducted a detailed study of ecological violence for the *Portland Oregonian*. They found that a shadowy conglomeration of violent ecologists were not willing to watch developers move into undeveloped areas. ELF had no hierarchy and was not associated with any particular location. They used a terrorist tactic long associated with the past, however: ELF targeted its victims with arson.

Denson and Long found that damage from ecoterrorism reached into the millions of dollars. They conducted a ten-month review and only considered crimes in excess of $50,000 damage. Cases that could not be linked to environmental groups were eliminated. They found one hundred cases with very few successful law enforcement investigations. ELF mastered firebombs and would not strike their targets when people were present. Their goal was to destroy property. Their firebombs grew increasingly sophisticated, and they placed bomb-making instructions on the Internet.

According to Denson and Long, most violence associated with ecoterrorism has taken place in the American West. From 1995 to 1999, damages totaled $28.8 million. Crimes included raids against farms, destruction of animal research laboratories at the University of California at Davis and Michigan State University, threats to individuals, sabotage against industrial equipment, and arson. ELF activities have increased each year since 1999 and have expanded throughout the country (Schabner, 1-30-04). At least some members want to take their actions in a new direction. In September 2002 an ELF communiqué stated that it would "no longer hesitate to pick up the gun" (Center for Consumer Freedom, 9-4-02).

In the past decade ecological and animal-rights extremists have united and are known by a variety of names with a myriad of extremist causes. For instance, ELF, Earth First!, and the Justice Department are interested in preserving the planet. The ALF, Animal Rights Militia, Band of Mercy, and Paint Panthers champion animal rights. Like their right-wing counterparts, many of these groups merely engage in rhetoric or disruptive behavior. The violent groups, such as ELF and ALF, advocate and engage in economic damage. They want to economically force land developers, ski lodges, farms, and research labs out of business.

Ecoterrorists are uncompromising, illogical extremists just like their right-wing counterparts. A review of their ideological literature shows they use ecology as a surrogate religion, that is, they are attached to their ideology in a manner that many religious people attach themselves to faith (White, 2000). Like all extremists, their positions are full of contradictions, but they brush these aside because they feel their cause is more important than contradictions.

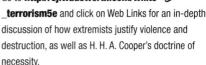

Go to **http://cj.wadsworth.com/white _terrorism5e** and click on Web Links for an in-depth discussion of how extremists justify violence and destruction, as well as H. H. A. Cooper's doctrine of necessity.

Antiabortion Violence

Key Points and Questions:

1. What tactics have violent antiabortion activists used?
2. How do they justify these actions?
3. What aspects of bombing is Nice trying to explain?
4. Do Nice's findings produce a theory of antiabortion violence?
5. Are Nice's findings applicable today?

For the past three decades the amount of violence against abortion clinics and personnel, or **antiabortion violence**, has risen. Violent antiabortionists began with bombing and arson attacks more than twenty years ago, and they have enhanced their tactics. Doctors and nurses have been assaulted when entering clinics. A gunman murdered Dr. David Gunn as he entered a clinic in Pensacola, Florida, in 1993. A year later the Reverend Paul Hill killed another doctor and his bodyguard when he entered the same clinic (Risen and Thomas, 1-26-98). Hill was executed in 2003. Dr. Barnett Slepian was killed at home in 1998 when a sniper shot through his window. Alleged bomber Eric Rudolph evaded federal authorities for years after bombings at the 1996 Olympics, a gay night club, and an abortion clinic in Birmingham, Alabama.

Abortion is a heated topic pitting pro-life and pro-choice advocates against one another. Most pro-life advocates abhor and denounce antiabortion violence because it is a contradiction of what they represent. Violent antiabortion advocates, however, justify their actions in the same manner as other political extremists. According to Risen and Thomas (1-26-98) both murderers in Pensacola felt a specific holy duty to kill the doctors they confronted. Paul Hill, for example, shot his victims five times, laid his gun down, and walked away. Michael Griffin, Gunn's murderer, felt that God gave him instructions to give Gunn one final warning. When Gunn ignored him, Griffin waited for five hours and then shot him three times in the back as he left the clinic. Accepting the status quo is worse than using violence to change behavior. It is the standard justification for terrorism.

Violence is not the only illegal action among those who break the law. The manual of the Army of God (n.d.) has four sections titled "99 Ways to Stop an Abortionist." It discusses low-level tactics such as gluing locks, shutting off water, and slashing tires. These are the tactics of radical ecologists in Germany (Horchem, 1985), but the manual does not credit a source or inspiration for the suggested tactics. The manual also describes methods for confronting workers and those seeking an abortion (see Another Perspective: Tactics in Violent Antiabortion Attacks).

David Nice (1988) attempts to build a theory of violence by examining trends in abortion clinic bombings. (Though done in 1988, Nice's research remains applicable today.) He notes that the literature reveals several explanations for violent political behavior. One theory suggests that social controls break down under stress and urbanization. Another theory says that violence increases when people are not satisfied with political outcomes. Violence can also be reinforced by social and cultural values. Finally, violence can stem from a group's strength or weakness, its lack of faith in the political system, or its frustration with economic conditions.

Nice matches trends in abortion clinic bombings against these theories of violence. His examination of thirty bombings during a three-year period revealed some patterns. First, bombings tended to be regionalized. Along with two in Washington, D.C., the bombings occurred in eight states, only three of which had more than four bombings. Nice compares the social factors in the detonation areas with the theories about violence.

Nice concludes that abortion clinic bombings are related to several social factors. Most of the bombings occurred in areas of rapidly expanding population and declining social controls. This means bombings tended to occur in urban areas. The slowest-growing states in the United States did not experience bombings, whereas half of the fastest-growing states did.

Bombings also reflected a method of communicating frustration with political processes and outcomes. Bombing is a means of taking direct action. Nice notes that most bombings took place where the ratio of abortions to live deliveries is relatively high. Abortion bombers feel compelled to action by social and political circumstances. They believe they are making a positive impact on the political situation. Nice also notes that bombings predictably occur more frequently in states that have a highly active militant antiabortion constituency.

States that experience bombings also exhibit a greater toleration for crimes against women. Clinic bombings are highest in areas where cultural and social violence against women is considered more "acceptable." States that have passed laws against domestic violence experience fewer bombings than states with no such laws.

Bombings are also a sign of weakness. Although seemingly paradoxical, areas having strong concentrations of antiabortion sentiment do not experience as much bombing. If an area experiences antiabortion activism, however, the bombing rate tends to be higher. In addition, Nice says that when high populations of Roman Catholics, Baptists, or Mormons are present, the number of bombings declines. When potential bombers feel outnumbered, however, they may take action because they feel weak.

In summary, Nice found that abortion clinic bombings were positively correlated with every theory of violence, except the theory of economic deprivation. There was no relation between abortion clinic bombings and economic conditions. Nice concludes that antiabortion violence appears in areas of rapid population growth where the abortion rate is high. As social controls decrease and the desire to substitute political controls increases, bombings develop into a form of political action.

Some of Nice's findings seem to be applicable to increased violence. According to Risen and Thomas (1-26-98), the murderers who killed abortion doctors felt the killings were necessary to make a political statement. Killing was a means of communication. Paul Hill was so excited by Gunn's murder that he successfully publicized it by appearing on *The Phil Donahue Show* and confronting Gunn's son. Activists were also prominent in the area where the shootings took place. It created the atmosphere in which the killers wished to make a stronger statement than actions taking place outside the clinic.

There is no easy solution to the abortion debate, as proponents of each side believe they are morally correct. The side favoring the right to choose an abortion feels it is defending constitutional rights. Those against abortion often believe they are following God's will. No matter which side dominates, the other side may react violently. The abortion debate represents a political issue in which the positions have been identified by militant extremes. As such, it is a perfect example of terrorism.

Black Hebrew Israelism: An Apocalyptic Single Issue

Key Points and Questions:

1. Why is the FBI concerned about Black Hebrew Israelism?
2. What is Black Hebrew Israelism?
3. How did its theology develop?
4. Who is Yahweh ben Yahweh?
5. What is Mitchell's Nation of Yahweh?
6. Explain the tactics of the Black Hebrew Israelists.

In the public version of the FBI's **Project Megiddo**, a report about possible religious and cult terrorism at the turn of the millennium, FBI analysts say that Black Hebrew Israelism has the potential to become a violent group. Some critics have scoffed at this suggestion, saying the FBI overreacted to a set of beliefs. Others believe the FBI has identified dangerous violent religious trends.

What is **Black Hebrew Israelism**? In a nutshell, it is Christian Identity with an African twist. According to Tory Thorpe (1996), Black Hebrew Israelites believe that the original Israelites were dark-skinned Africans. They migrated to Nigeria during the Jewish Diaspora and waited for God to fulfill promises to the Hebrews. The white slave trade interfered, however, and created a greater diaspora of black African Israelites.

The mythology of Black Hebrew Israelites and their beliefs dates back to the Civil War. In the latter part of the twentieth century, again like Christian Identity, the group developed an elaborate theology to explain the status of African Americans.

For example, according to **Yehuda ben Yisrael**, a proponent of Black Hebrew Israelism, whites conspired to cancel the relationship between Africa and God. Another source explains that curly hair is evidence of the divine origins of black skin. The *African Heritage Study Bible* is used to demonstrate that the Jews who Moses led out of Egypt were black.

The theology of Black Hebrew Israelism does not constitute a need for law enforcement investigation or even curiosity, so when any police agency inquires about the belief system, it is bound to create controversy. The First Amendment grants freedom of religion, so anyone is free to believe the tenets of Black Hebrew Israelism. This is the reason some people criticized the FBI for examining the group in Project Megiddo. But the FBI is not interested in religion; it is concerned with potential violence. Some segments of Black Hebrew Israelism have a history of cultic violence, and some have demonized non-African races. Like the potential violence in Christian Identity, this merits law enforcement's attention.

The most attention has been gained by the actions of Hulon Mitchell Jr. According to court records (U.S. Court of Appeals, 1996), Mitchell and Linda Gaines moved to Miami, Florida, in 1979 and laid the foundation for a Black Hebrew Israelite group known as the **Nation of Yahweh**. Mitchell told followers that God and Jesus were black and he, Mitchell, had been chosen to lead blacks back to Israel. By 1980, he ordered followers to abandon their given names and assume Hebrew identities. Gaines became Judith Israel and Mitchell took the name **Yahweh ben Yahweh**. (Yahweh is an anglicized version of the Hebrew tetragram YHWH, or the name of God.) Mitchell's new name could be translated as "God son of God."

By 1985, the Nation of Yahweh developed into a group of worshippers who focused their attention on Mitchell. He kept social order through violent discipline as members pledged their loyalty to him. Mitchell built the Temple of Love and stationed armed guards around its entrance. Gaines controlled the income of all temple members, while Mitchell ruled his followers with an iron hand. Mitchell began expanding his theology, teaching that whites were devils and his followers were to kill them in the name of God. He created an internal group called the **Brotherhood**, and one could obtain membership only by killing a white person.

When some members tried to leave the group, they were beaten and beheaded. Over the next few years, Mitchell dispatched **Death Angels** to kill whites in the Miami area. The Death Angels were ordered to bring victims' severed body parts back to Mitchell as proof that the murders had occurred. After a five-month trial, Mitchell, Gaines, and some of the other followers were convicted under federal organized crime statutes.

Black Hebrew Israelism is indicative of the tension between believing and acting, and it presents a dilemma for those charged with security. The theology of Black Hebrew Israelism is not violent, and most of its adherents would never follow in Hulon Mitchell's footsteps. The problem for those charged with preventing violence, however, is that when a belief system degrades or demonizes another group, violence often follows. Any time extremist beliefs are fused with hatred, the larger community may be at risk.

Summary of Main Points

1. Puerto Rican nationalist groups seek independence from the United States. This becomes complicated because many Puerto Ricans want to either keep commonwealth status or seek statehood.

2. Right-wing extremism can be traced to the Whiskey Rebellion of 1794. It continued through the next two centuries.

3. Contemporary right-wing extremism is based on Christian patriotism or similar movements, white supremacy, and types of survivalism. Frequently, an individual extremist belongs to more than one phase of the movement.

4. Right-wing tactics have been inspired by fiction and other glamorized segments of the movement. Violent offenders include defenders and attackers. Nonviolent offenses include disorderly conduct and other forms of civil disobedience.

5. Left-wing terrorism dwindled much in the way it did in Europe. Single-issue violent extremists dominate the left-wing movement today.

6. Radical ecologists and animal-rights activists primarily engage in property destruction in the name of their causes. Their goal is economic disruption. There are alliances among the groups today.

7. Antiabortion violence began with bombing and arson but moved into assault and murder. The same factors that spawned bombing seem to surround selective assault and murder.

8. Black Hebrew Israelism is an African-American version of Christian Identity. It claims that black Africans were the original Israelites. One violent group, the Nation of Yahweh, demonized whites and called for their destruction.

Key Terms

Make sure you can define, explain, or identify the following people, ideas, organizations, or terms:

Whiskey Rebellion   247
Know-Nothings   247
Ku Klux Klan (KKK)   247
Nathan Bedford Forrest   247
Knight Riders   248
Anglo-Israelism   248
Aryan Nations   248
Christian Identity   248
identity theology   248
conspiracy theories   249
New World Order   249
white supremacy movement   250
survivalism   250
Skinheads   250

Brady Bill   250
Ruby Ridge incident   251
Bo Gritz   251
Waco siege   251
David Koresh   251
hate movement   252
Nordic Christianity   252
Creatorism   253
RAHOWA   253
Free-Wheeling Fundamentalists   253
militia movement   253
the Protocols of Zion   253
paramilitary groups   254
Third Position   254

Suggested Readings

Now that you've been introduced to this topic, you can learn more by reading:

Michael Barkun's *Religion and the Racist Right* is a treatise on the Christian Identity movement. It contains historical information and political analysis.

You may also want to read:

John George and Laird M. Wilcox, *American Extremists*, is a book about extremist beliefs.

Complement George and Wilcox with a reader edited by Lyman Sargent, *Extremism in America*.

Chip Berlet and Matthew Lyons' *Right-Wing Populism in America* is an historical analysis of the right-wing movement.

The public, unclassified version of the FBI's Project Megiddo explains several violent domestic movements.

Former ELF spokesman Craig Rosebraugh provides a description of ELF in *Burning Rage for a Dying Planet*.

Carol Mason, in *Killing for Life*, examines violence in the pro-life movement.

Web Resources

Go to *http://cj.wadsworth.com/white_terrorism5e* and click on Web Links to find:

- A discussion of domestic terrorism
- A discussion of several forms of extremism from BeyondIntractability.org
- Single-issue extremists often deny that they encourage violence, but they often support it on websites. Type the name of a single-issue group in a Web search engine and see what happens.

The Companion Website for *Terrorism and Homeland Security*, Fifth Edition
http://cj.wadsworth.com/white_terrorism5e

At the Book Companion Website you can review chapter outlines, use the flash cards to test your terrorism vocabulary, and check out the many other study aids you'll find there. You'll find valuable data and resources at your fingertips to help you study for that big exam or write that important paper.

Terrorism Updates

http://www.wadsworth.com/criminaljustice_d/special_features/ext/terrorism_site090802/index.html

Visit the *Terrorism: An Interdisciplinary Perspective* website to find the most current information about the fields of terrorism and homeland security. With a focus on domestic and international issues, this site explores the scope of terrorism in our world today. You'll find essays on important topics in terrorism and homeland security, critical thinking web activities, and InfoTrac College Edition keywords. Most importantly, the website is updated weekly with current news and research articles on domestic and international terrorism. You are invited to use these web resources to supplement your understanding of the topics covered in this chapter.

Current Perspectives: Readings from InfoTrac College Edition
Terrorism and Homeland Security

The sixteen articles in this reader offer a representative selection that helps you understand the important issues about terrorism and homeland security. It includes FREE access to InfoTrac College Edition and can also be bundled with the text for free.

Part Four ISSUES IN HOMELAND SECURITY

Chapter 15

In Search of Homeland Security

© Alex Wong/Getty Images

The United States Coast Guard on patrol for the Department of Homeland Security. The demands of homeland security bring new roles for law enforcement, military, and other public agencies.

In the years since September 11, 2001, Americans routinely speak of *homeland security*, and the federal government has created a new cabinet-level department responsible for it. Despite these actions, there is an overriding irony: The country is not quite sure what it means by homeland security. It would seem to mean something less than a military action because the Department of Homeland Security (DHS) is separate from the Department of Defense, and more than half of the agencies that make up DHS have arrest power. By the same token, DHS leadership is full of retired military personnel, and DHS controls the U.S. Coast Guard, an organization that assumes a military role in wartime. The major impetus for forming DHS was the Jihadist attacks of September 11, but the DHS intelligence section coordinates domestic and international information. This does little to clarify the roles of the Department of Justice, the military, and the CIA. America will slowly come to grips with the meaning of homeland security as agencies and various levels of government and industry fashion new relationships, but the nation has a long way to go. This chapter introduces the complexities surrounding homeland security.

Chapter Objectives

After reading this chapter you should be able to:

1. Define *homeland security* and explain confusion surrounding the term.

2. Summarize war as envisioned by Clausewitz and Sun Tzu.

3. Explain the difference between the attack on Pearl Harbor and the attacks of September 11.

4. Outline the reasons for the changing nature of conflict.

5. Define the role of structures and symbols in homeland security.

6. Explain law enforcement's role in homeland security.

7. Describe experiences with domestic intelligence systems.

8. Discuss the role of planning in homeland security.

9. Summarize the need to share information.

10. Describe the intelligence reform spawned by the 9-11 Commission.

Defining Homeland Security

Key Points and Questions:

1. What is homeland security and why is it difficult to define?

2. Is there a difference between *mission* and *understanding*?

3. How does policy become involved in homeland security?

4. What is civil defense?

A leading figure from the Department of Defense spoke about homeland security at a workshop I attended in the autumn of 2004. He outlined the president's homeland security strategy, citing three major elements of the Bush administration's policy. The workshop was interesting not only because of the official's proximity to the heart of policy, but because other high-ranking officials had also addressed workshop members. One said there were five major elements to President Bush's policy, while another used the number four. When asked about the differing numbers of policy elements, the leading official admitted that different segments of the administration used different numbers, but he said there was a general understanding in the White House about the elements of homeland security.

There is a reason for this apparent confusion, and it is applicable in both political parties. America has no common definition of homeland security. Issues surrounding homeland security are confused because the country is dealing with a new concept, a new meaning of conflict, and a change in the procedures used to defend the United States. In the past, military forces protected the homeland, projecting power beyond U.S. borders, but the world changed with the end of the Cold War in 1991. Another reason for confusion lies in the fact that the new **Department of Homeland Security (DHS)** is responsible for protecting the borders and the country's interior. Coupled with this state of affairs are bureaucratic efforts to redefine relations among agencies. The situation is further complicated when state and local governments become involved. Finally, a host of private businesses, nonprofit organizations, and health care systems are involved in security efforts. It is therefore not easy to find a common definition for homeland security.

Despite the confusion, it is possible to come to grips with the concept. **Homeland security** simply means *keeping the country safe*. The concept formed in the wake of a Jihadist attack, but it has expanded beyond September 11. Basically, homeland security protects lives, property, and infrastructure. It is designed to secure the United States.

It might be more appropriate to move beyond definitions and look at missions and common understandings. Essentially, *mission* and *understanding* mean the same thing, but there are many different understandings of homeland security because many agencies have differing missions. For example, the Department of Energy (DOE) is responsible for protecting nuclear materials, power grids, and gas lines. DOE's understanding of homeland security is related to its mission. The Border Patrol, on the other hand, uses its agents to secure U.S. borders and points of entry. It has a law enforcement mission and defines homeland security within this context. Frankly, the Defense Department official at the workshop was quite correct in saying that there was a common understanding of homeland security. The elements of security expand or contract depending on an organization's mission.

There is confusion, to be sure, but it centers on policy, not mission. The policy guiding homeland security in the United States has not been fully developed, and executives are not quite sure of the way that all the missions of various agencies fit together. Several groups inside and outside of government are adjusting to new roles. The intelligence community has been criticized, and the 9-11 Commission and its supporters were successful in implementing their version of reform within the intelligence community. This leaves the roles of various intelligence groups in transition. The law enforcement and military communities are trying to find policies to define their roles. The functions of domestic and international laws have not been fully established. Various levels of government and private industry are trying to figure out where they interact. All of these maneuvers take time.

Homeland security also involves **civil defense**, that is, citizens engaged in homeland security. During the Cold War various organizations involved in civil defense gradually learned specific missions. After 1960 civil defense structures were to help government protect citizens in areas such as emergency communications through private and public broadcasting, direct assistance during emergencies, evacuation routes, and fallout shelters. Civil defense did not develop overnight; rather, it emerged slowly from civilian functions during World War II. The idea of "civil defense" will take on a new meaning in the coming years because the nature of conflict has changed. Homeland security is much more than the sum of agencies charged with protecting the United States. A major portion of security is a civic responsibility.

Clausewitz, Sun Tzu, and Views of War

Key Points and Questions:

1. How do Republicans and Democrats tend to view the war on terrorism?

2. What events began to blur the distinction between war and peace?

3. How did Clausewitz view war?

4. Does Hanson think the views of Clausewitz are applicable in the modern era?

5. How might Sun Tzu provide a broader framework for understanding the problems of homeland security?

6. Why will criminal justice and other civil forces play a role in national defense?

Just below the surface of jurisprudence, the practice of terrorism has blurred the distinction between war and peace. As described in Chapter 1, President Bush and his administration are fond of speaking of the *war on terrorism*. The Democratic Party might criticize the way the Republicans manage the war, but Democrats also refer to a war on terrorism. Although Republicans tend to see the issue as a military problem and Democrats frequently speak of terrorism as a criminal act, the public rhetoric of both sides focuses on bringing the enemy to justice. As Daniel Pipes (2003, pp. 242–257) says, it is one

Go to **http://cj.wadsworth.com/white _terrorism5e** and click on Web Links for an in-depth discussion of the philosophy of conflict and the way it applies to homeland security, as well as the Clausewitzian paradigm.

thing to define your enemies as "evil doers" and quite another to actually identify them. Can you "declare war" on "evil doers" and "bring them to justice?" he asks. Philosophers of war answered the question many years ago.

Before the time of growing terrorism, Americans thought they knew the meaning of conflict. War was an extension of politics fought within the legal framework of the Constitution. Quite simply, the Constitution states that only Congress has the power to declare war, and Congress declares whether America is in a state of war or of peace. However, the anticolonial struggles after World War II; the Vietnam War; and the battles in Somalia, Serbia, Afghanistan, and Iraq confused the issue. American troops fought limited wars in peacetime.

The situation grew more complex as violence spread in the homeland and abroad. Civil agencies faced standoffs with militant groups; a U.S. citizen bombed the federal building in Oklahoma City; two teenagers went on a shooting spree at their high school in Colorado (and many others throughout the country); the World Trade Center towers were destroyed and the Pentagon attacked on September 11. Clearly, the law enforcement and public service workers involved were not soldiers, but they were being called to restore order during military-style attacks. The FBI was empowered to seize suspects beyond territorial limits, and military forces joined them in the hunt. When suspects were identified, prosecutors issued arrest warrants, and when suspects were caught, they went to trial in U.S. courts. Terrorism is changing the nature of conflict. Law enforcement agencies, courts, and corrections joined in the battle, even though they are not constitutionally associated with military power.

The American concept of conflict has been deeply influenced by the Prussian general and military philosopher **Carl von Clausewitz** (1780–1831), who cut his teeth during the nationalistic wars against Napoleon (1795–1815). Joining the Prussian Army as a twelve-year-old drummer boy to fight against France, he came to believe that the French Revolution created a new type of war, and he began to study war as a philosophical problem (1984 [1831]; for critiques see Liddell Hart, 1967; Craig, 1968; Howard, 1988).

The strength of the French, Clausewitz reasoned, came from their ability to place the nation in arms, that is, to rally the people to the belief that all citizens of a nation are potential soldiers or supporters of the military. To defeat the French, Germany must become a nation-in-arms, unite under a democracy, and employ its own citizen soldiers. The proof of victory would come when Germany's political will could be imposed on France. Clausewitz joined a group of reformers and tried to modernize the Prussian Army. The Prussians were destroyed, however, in 1806 after the Battle of Jena-Auerstädt, and Clausewitz was carried off to Paris in captivity with a Prussian prince. He began writing, formulating a philosophy of national war.

Clausewitz's notions (see Another Perspective: Clausewitz and War in the Western Tradition) were derived from his study of history, especially the Thirty Years' War (1618–1648) and Frederick the Great (1740–1786). They were also influenced by his decision to join the Russian Army in 1812 to fight Napoleon and the German War of Liberation (1813–1814). Clausewitz's ideas come to us from a book published by his wife Maria the year after he died. *On War* is a philosophical treatise on the nature of total, nationalistic wars. It has also been one of the most influential works on military forces in the twentieth century. Clausewitz's understanding of the nation-in-arms clearly renders the meaning of war, but it may not help Americans who desire to bring terrorists to justice.

Victor Hanson (1989) criticizes Clausewitz and the Western way of battle, claiming the West is consumed with the way war was fought in ancient Greece. According to this line of thought, the purpose of military action is to seek a decisive engagement, and Clausewitz's philosophical treatise emphasizes this point. Terrorism, however, is designed to produce the opposite effect, seeking to avoid direct confrontation with force. In addition, since the emergence of professional, modern warfare in the West after the Peace of Westphalia (1648), the purpose of war has been to impose political will on the defeated party. American law enforcement does not seek a decisive battle with enemy forces, and its purpose can never be the imposition of political will. The goals of terrorism are to create panic and cause social systems to break. These goals mean that criminal justice and other civilian agencies will be involved in combating terrorism. America is neither at war nor at peace, and another paradigm for this situation may be more helpful.

Nearly two thousand years ago a Chinese philosopher, **Sun Tzu**, produced a treatise on the paradoxes of war (*The Art of War*, see Management Analytics and others, 1995). Rather than conceiving of times when a political realm is either at war or at peace, Sun Tzu saw war and peace as two sides of the same coin. War and politics were psychological forces held together by the belief in power. In Sun Tzu's philosophical structure, the highest form of military leadership comes in breaking the enemy's resistance without fighting. Leaders must be able to control their anger and project power. When military leadership is strong, the state will be strong and have less need to act. If the state appears to be weak, it is vulnerable despite its strength.

Terrorism is based on Sun Tzu's concept of strength-to-weakness, not the strength-to-strength battle as Clausewitz described (see Another Perspective: Sun Tzu and the Logic of Terrorism). In modern military parlance this is called **asymmetry**. Asymmetry simply means competing forces are out of balance; that is, a weak force fights a much stronger power. A good analogy is to think of a single angry hornet attacking a hiker in the woods. The hornet can sting the hiker, and if it is lucky, cause the hiker to panic or maybe induce a fatal allergic reaction. If the hiker stays calm, however, a single swat ends the attack. The odds are in the hiker's favor. Terrorists are much like the hornet with two exceptions: They tend to be true-believing fanatics who sacrifice lives, not an angry insect acting in defense of self or territory, and they are willing to attack while avoiding social conventions and societal norms. Hornets attack the same way under natural instincts, but terrorists fight outside the rules.

The reason terrorists fight outside the norms of society is revealed by the imbalance of power. The major powers hold all the cards in international trade, legal authority, and military power. It does no good to strike them in the open, but they are vulnerable when attacked outside the norms of standard international relations. The lesson is as old as terrorism: "If you can't kill their soldiers, kill their civilians." The purpose of terrorism is to give the impression that powerful economic, military, and political forces cannot protect ordinary people going about daily routines. Terrorists do not seek an open battle but want to show that the norms of civil society cannot protect the population of the superior force. Enemy forces prepared for combat are too strong, but police stations, off-duty military personnel, and schoolchildren make tempting targets.

Obviously, military forces must cope with this change, but criminal justice agencies become involved in homeland security precisely because terrorists fight outside the rules. They commit virtually every type of crime imaginable when preparing an attack. If they wore uniforms, struck military targets, and fought within recognized international conventions, they would not be terrorists (Crenshaw, 1983, pp. 14–32).

Another Perspective

Sun Tzu and the Logic of Terrorism

Compare the selected paraphrases of Sun Tzu with those of Clausewitz. Which statements are more applicable to conventional battles with front lines and uniformed soldiers? Which statements are more applicable to guerrilla warfare and terrorism?

- If you know yourself and your enemy, you will be successful. If you know yourself and do not know your enemy, you will fail many times. If you know neither yourself nor your enemy, you will never succeed.

- The worst way to take a town is to lay siege. The best way is to make the inhabitants believe they are beaten.

- A military leader who projects strength can settle a dispute without losing a soldier.

- The best leader subdues the enemy's troops without fighting.

- Reduce the enemy by creating problems, making trouble, and making them rush to any given point.

Of course, they will never do this because terrorists lack the military strength and political appeal to engage in such activities. This means they will be arrested, tried, and incarcerated. Since terrorists attack the homeland, all aspects of the criminal justice system will be involved in homeland security. It is a new role, but the world is fighting by Sun Tzu's rules.

Pearl Harbor and 9-11: Two Different Worlds

Key Points and Questions:

1. How does the attack on Pearl Harbor differ from the attacks of September 11?
2. How do the Jihadists view such a conflict?
3. Why are terrorists playing with a new set of rules?

December 7, 1941, is known as "a day that will live in infamy"; September 11, 2001, is certainly a day that burned into the hearts of Americans. Both events held common surprises. For example, both Pearl Harbor and the suicide strikes indicated that America was vulnerable to attack. Both events occurred with no formal declaration of war, and both involved civilian casualties. Pearl Harbor and September 11 also shook the soul of the United States.

Despite these similarities, September 11 differs significantly from Pearl Harbor. The purpose of the Japanese surprise attack was to destroy U.S. military capabilities in the Pacific. Japanese governmental and military officials knew the United States would go to war as soon as the surviving Zeros returned to their carriers. Their purposes were to temporarily destroy America's capacity to wage war, achieve political objectives with military might, and negotiate a truce from a position of strength. By contrast, the September 11 attacks were designed for drama. They were a tragedy performed on a subnational level, with the purpose of murdering thousands of people to create an aura of fear. There could be no negotiation because it is not permissible to negotiate with the devil. If the hijackers killed the enemies of evil, then God won. If they died in the process, God would replace them with future martyrs. Failure was out of the question, and victory was assured by God's promise (Lichtblau, 9-29-01; Juergensmeyer, 2000, pp. 143–155).

The goal of the September 11 terrorists was not one of conventional military strategy. Its purpose was to create so much fear that Western institutions would change their behavior. There was no grand offensive to follow the attacks and no notion of a rational, negotiated peace. The terrorists who targeted the United States wanted the West to believe that mass murder can happen at any time. In the words of Thomas Barnett (2004, pp. 18–34) the terrorists of September 11 were playing by a new set of rules. They were attacking globalization while America was defending state power.

If Barnett is correct, the September 11 attacks and the subsequent world of international terrorism have ushered in a new style of conflict. Jihadists are not attacking state power; they are attacking the idea of Western, and particularly American, culture. Their war is with a global system that they fear and hate, and they resist being included in an economic arrangement they resent. This logic is not only applicable to Jihadists. When the ideology of domestic terrorists is examined, similar types of concerns emerge. Modern terrorism is aimed at the infrastructure of everyday life and the symbols that define that structure (see Homer-Dixon, 2002; Stevenson, 2003).

Redefining Conflict, Defense, and Intelligence

Key Points and Questions:

1. Why is it necessary to rethink the position taken on Clausewitz?
2. What aspects of military affairs have been changed because of terrorism?
3. How do military forces operate "deeply" in society?
4. How has modern warfare changed, according to Crefeld?
5. Does the French-Algerian War reflect his thesis?

It is not enough to suggest that terrorism has affected criminal justice. The whole nature of military action has been changing since World War II. Clausewitz himself probably would have thought beyond his initial notions. He wrote during an age when states fielded armies and those armies faced each other. He quite naturally focused on state-to-state war, but Clausewitz pointed to two other factors. Sometimes wars are fought on frontiers against irregular armies. Clausewitz was familiar with this because of Prussia's partition of Poland with Russia and Austria. In addition, Clausewitz's most famous maxim was that *war is an extension of politics*. In other words, the only reason a nation fights is to win a political victory. It may be necessary to think beyond open field battles, but Clausewitz would have been the first to shift military efforts if it meant victory (see Cebrowsky and Gratska, 1998; Cebrowsky and Barnett, 2003).

The recent growth of terrorism has changed all aspects of military affairs, and the nation must be prepared to enter a new type of war. Thomas Barnett (2004, pp. 6–7) says the Pentagon prepared to fight state-to-state battles during the 1990s. They tried to stop enemy movement, waited for the chance to concentrate forces in a single effort, and secured bases and supply lines. Military forces must still be prepared to fight these battles, but their mission has been extended. Terrorists do not fight in field engagements; therefore, military forces must transform their structures to take the fight to terrorists. New capabilities must be developed to prevent violence, keep infrastructures operating, develop strategies that include the whole political spectrum, and defend the social structure. While not contained in Clausewitz's work, these transformations certainly reflect his thesis.

Retired Vice Admiral Arthur Cebrowsky (2004) says that U.S. armed forces need to develop the ability to operate "deeply" in society, that is, to fully understand, accept, and defend America with a complete comprehension of American culture combined with the willingness to completely understand any enemy society in depth. He believes that America needs to create a new defense culture that permeates all levels of society and that breaks down barriers between organizations. Military forces must be able to fight and defeat irregular forces, they must be able to find targets, and they must develop ways to avoid strategic surprise. This type of strategy involves **social immersion**, and military forces need to harness the power of higher education. The United States needs forces that thoroughly understand American culture and the cultures of our enemies and friends.

Martin van Crefeld (1991, pp. 142–156) presents the same idea a different way. War has changed, Crefeld argues, and it no longer reflects the rationality of Clausewitz. Most importantly, many communities outside the West feel their very existence is threatened. A war for existence changes the nature of conflict because the strategic rules of war and the rational extension of policy are thrown out the window. When a community fights to survive, fighting *is* the policy. Outbursts of violence are statements of existence as well as celebrations of being. In such circumstances, there can be no study of political purpose. Violence is the purpose. It demonstrates life.

Crefeld uses the French-Algerian War (1954–1962) as an example. It was not war in the classical sense. There were no front lines, the Algerians did not field an army, and their attacks on the French and other Westerners violated established codes of conflict and criminal law. The French responded with a Clausewitzian cost-benefit analysis. They looked at the cost of keeping Algeria and weighed it against the benefits. When they sent paratroopers and police officers to fight, they did so as a continuation of this policy. Their goal was to impose their political will on the Algerians. Crefeld said this is why they lost.

The Algerian nationalists of the National Liberation Front (FLN) approached the situation differently. They never conducted an analysis; they fought for the community's survival. As the war dragged on, survival became more important. In other words, violence justified violence. War brought more and more recruits to the ranks of the FLN. Crefeld notes that the ability of the Algerians to accept punishment was almost limitless. Estimates of Algerian casualties range to 1 million. The French, however, lost twenty-two thousand soldiers and three thousand civilians over eight years, less than they lost in traffic accidents over the same period. Fighting France became the FLN's policy. As long as they fought, they were succeeding.

Crefeld's theory reflects part of Barnett's thesis. Barnett (2004, p. 11) implies that military forces must change for future battles. In the future, they will develop "police-like" capabilities. The reason for this is clear. The nature of conflict has changed. If we combine these two ideas, it is logical to conclude that a force fighting to impose political will operates differently from a force fighting for existence. If military forces approach homeland security as a continuation of national policy, they will bring the wrong weapons to the wrong war. They will also fail to utilize their ultimate striking power: American citizens.

Barnett takes the concept much further. War as we know it has ended, he writes. The purpose of power is to create a new set of international rules in which all nations are included in economic development, prosperity, and peace. This, Barnett says, is a future worth creating. When nations are excluded, he argues, violent terrorists have no incentive to play within the rules. The purpose of preparing to fight is to create an environment where violence is nonrewarding. It is to extend opportunity and improve the human condition. This extends the meaning of war far beyond the realm of military force and gives new roles to a variety of governmental and private agencies.

The Role of Symbols and Structures

Key Points and Questions:

1. Why are symbols important in homeland security?
2. What are symbolic targets?
3. Why do terrorists attack them?
4. Where is America vulnerable in terms of symbols?

Asymmetrical war is waged against **symbolic targets**, and homeland security is designed to secure symbols. Just because a target has symbolic significance does not mean it lacks physical reality. The bombing of the Murrah Federal Building in Oklahoma City in 1995, for example, had symbolic value, but the casualties were horrific. Attacks against symbols disrupt support structures and can have a high human toll. Defensive measures are put in place to protect both the physical safety of people and property as well as the symbolic meaning of a target (see Juergensmeyer, 2000, pp. 155–163; Critical Incident Analysis Group, 2001, pp. 9–16).

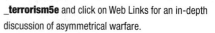

Go to **http://cj.wadsworth.com/white _terrorism5e** and click on Web Links for an in-depth discussion of asymmetrical warfare.

Grenville Byford (2002) points out that symbolic attack may simply be designed to inflict massive casualties; that is, killing people has a symbolic value. Killing civilians serves a political purpose for terrorists. American citizens contribute economically to the well-being of the country, and since they participate in a democracy, they ultimately control military policy. Targeting them, Byford argues, may have practical as well as symbolic value. Rather than engaging in political rhetoric about morality, Byford concludes, it is more productive to understand that Americans represent symbolic targets of military value. His conclusion reflects the alleged saying of nineteenth-century Prussian prime minister Otto von Bismarck: "Righteous indignation is no substitute for a good course of action." There is little to be gained by ranting about evil doers, but much can be accomplished by developing strategies to protect targets.

Strategies for protection should be grounded in the understanding of the problem. Ian Lesser (1999, pp. 85–144) outlines three forms of terrorism: symbolic, pragmatic, and systematic. **Symbolic terrorism** is a dramatic attack to show vulnerability; **pragmatic terrorism** involves a practical attempt to destroy political power; and **systematic terrorism** is waged over a period of time to change social conditions. Although identifying these three forms of terrorism, Lesser points to several examples in which symbolic factors enter into attacks. In other words, terrorists use symbolic attacks or attacks on symbols to achieve pragmatic or systematic results.

The University of Virginia's Critical Incident Analysis Group (CIAG) brought a number of law enforcement officials, business leaders, government administrators, and academics together to discuss America's vulnerability to symbolic attack (Critical Incident Analysis Group, 2001). Symbols can have literal and abstract meanings, such as the case of a capitol that serves literally and abstractly as the seat of government power. The key to security is to offer protection without destroying abstract meanings. For example, the words of one CIAG participant summed up the problem: We want to protect the Capitol building, he said, without making Washington, D.C., look like an armed camp.

Another Perspective

Community Threat Analysis

Examine the following considerations for defensive planning, or community threat analysis. What other items might be added?

- ■ Find networks in and among communities. Look at transportation, power grids and fuel storage, water supplies, industrial logistics and storage, and the flow of people.
- ■ Think like a terrorist. Which targets are vulnerable? Which targets would cause the most disruption? Which buildings are vulnerable? Where is private security ineffective?
- ■ Obtain architectural plans for all major buildings. Protect air intakes, power supplies, and possible points for evacuation.
- ■ Have detailed emergency information for each school.
- ■ Practice tactical operations in each school building after hours.
- ■ Prioritize. Assign a criticality rating to each target, assessing its importance, and rank targets according to comparative ratings.
- ■ Coordinate with health services.
- ■ Discuss triage and quarantine methods. Plan for biological, chemical, and radiological contamination.
- ■ Look at emergency plans for other communities and use the appropriate methods.
- ■ Prepare added security for special events.
- ■ Designate an emergency command post and roles for personnel from other agencies. Practice commanding mock attacks.
- ■ Study past emergencies and determine what law enforcement learned from its shortcomings.

Source: Management Analytics and others (1995).

All societies create symbols and American democracy is no different. In a time of asymmetrical war, American symbols demand protection. The key to security, the CIAG concludes, is to enhance protection while maintaining openness. The irony is that every added security measure increases the feeling of insecurity. The CIAG report cites metal detectors at county courthouses as an example. Simply going through the detector before entering a building gives a person the feeling that all things might fall apart. The key is to make symbolic targets as secure as possible while giving the illusion that very few security precautions need to be taken.

Law Enforcement's Special Role

Key Points and Questions:

1. What role does American law enforcement have in homeland security?
2. Should law enforcement move beyond reacting to events?
3. What will happen if American police think beyond reaction?
4. What police techniques would be effective against terrorism?

If military forces are to transform in a fashion suggested by Thomas Barnett (2004), law enforcement must seek and find new roles. More than half of the DHS agencies have police power, and state and local governments look to law enforcement for preventing attacks and responding to the unthinkable. Interestingly, federal, state, and local officers have taken the leading role in identifying and disrupting terrorism in the United States. Whether terrorists are homegrown or imported from foreign lands, police agencies are responsible for breaking some of America's most formidable terrorist cells. Law enforcement has a key function in homeland security (see Carter, 2004).

American law enforcement has a long tradition of *reactive patrol*, that is, responding to crimes and calls for assistance. With the advent of radio-dispatched motorized patrol, response time became the measure of police effectiveness. It was assumed that the sooner police arrived at the scene of a crime, the more likely they were to make an arrest. Like fire departments responding to smoke, police effectiveness was determined by its ability to respond quickly to crime.

The problem of terrorism brings the need for *preemptive, offensive policing* to a new level. If law enforcement simply responds, it will have little impact on the prevention of terrorism. Defensive reaction alone leaves the initiative with terrorist organizations. In addition, no government can afford to fortify all the potential targets in a jurisdiction. Even if all targets could be defended, the goal of asymmetrical warfare is not to destroy targets, but to show that security forces are not in charge. Terrorists are free to strike the least-defended symbolic target. Defensive thinking, like reactive patrol, cannot win a fight in the shadows.

If state and local agencies shift to offensive thinking and action, two results will inevitably develop. First, police contact with potential terrorists will increase, but as Sherry Colb (10-10-01) points out, the vast majority of any ethnic or social group is made up of people who abhor terrorism. This increases the possibility of negative stereotyping and the abuse of power. Second, proactive measures demand increased intelligence gathering, and much of the information will have no relation to criminal activity. If not properly monitored, such intelligence may be misused.

Another issue appears in the private sector. Kayyem and Howitt (2002) find that offensive action begins in the local community. The weakness in local systems occurs, however, because state and local police departments do not frequently think beyond their jurisdictions, and they do not routinely take advantage of potential partnerships inside their bailiwicks. Kayyem and Howitt believe partnerships are the key to community planning. One of the greatest potential allies is private security. Unfortunately, many law enforcement agencies frown upon private security and fail to create joint ventures with the private sector.

On the positive side of the debate, counterterrorism is not a mystical operation. It uses many of the skills already employed in preventive patrol, criminal investigation, and surveillance. With a few tweaks, police intelligence operations and drug enforcement units can add counterterrorism to their agendas, and patrol and investigative units can be trained to look for terrorist activities in the course of their normal duties. If properly managed, these activities need not present a threat to civil liberties. (See Chapter 16 for a broad discussion of this issue.)

Building Intelligence Systems

 Key Points and Questions:

1. Why is intelligence critical in homeland security?
2. Why is information gathering like academic research?
3. What happened to the intelligence community under President Carter?
4. How have law enforcement agencies constructed intelligence systems?
5. What is the danger when police collect noncriminal information?

Redirecting military and police forces is an essential part of developing a system to protect the homeland. The most important aspect of security, however, is the information that guides security forces. If policies and strategy are important to the overall effort, information is crucial for day-to-day operations. For example, Thomas Barnett's (2004) idea of creating an inclusive geopolitical economic policy in which everybody wins is a long-term strategy for reducing international violence. Somewhere between the current state of affairs and the outcome of such a policy is the everyday world of homeland security. This world is driven by intelligence, and security forces can be no more effective than their ability to gain information and process it into a meaningful guide (see Another Perspective: David Carter's Recommendations for Law Enforcement Intelligence).

Information gathering is akin to academic research. Before beginning, a researcher needs basic knowledge of a field and an understanding of subdisciplines. Much of this background information has no direct bearing on the actual question a researcher is trying to answer, but without background preparation, the researcher cannot address the question. Command of basic information allows the researcher to move toward applying results. Applied information, the specificity the researcher seeks, is divided into both in-depth knowledge about a specific topic and the latest information from the discipline. In the sciences and social sciences, this process leads a researcher from general concepts to applied ideas, from abstract principles to glimpses of reality.

While academic in nature, this process is directly applicable to gathering intelligence. Police intelligence systems can be modeled after academic research. Basic intelligence involves general information about a subject and its subdisciplines. Applied intelligence involves gathering basic information about a target and real-time information about current activities.

The practical application of this process comes through organizing structures aimed at collecting, analyzing, and forwarding information. Someone in every American law enforcement agency should be assigned to collect and forward terrorist intelligence. In small agencies this may mean assigning a person who represents several police and sheriff's departments, while in moderate-sized agencies the function could be performed in the detective bureau or the planning unit. Large metropolitan and state police agencies need full-time intelligence units. At the state and regional levels, efforts must be made to assemble, categorize, and analyze information and place it within national and international contexts (see Another Perspective: David Carter's Recommendations for Law Enforcement Intelligence).

Another Perspective

David Carter's Recommendations for Law Enforcement Intelligence

David Carter suggests refocusing law enforcement efforts. Police activity, he argues, should be led by intelligence. In order to accomplish this, police agencies should take an "R-cubed" approach: reassess, refocus, and reallocate.

1. Reassess the following:
   a. Calls for service
   b. Specialized units
   c. Need for new specializations
   d. Community resources
   e. Potential threats
   f. Current intelligence
   g. Political mandates from the community
2. Refocus
   a. Establish new priorities based on reassessment.
   b. Weigh priorities in terms of criticality.
   c. Actually implement changes.
3. Reallocate: Commit the resources needed to implement changes.

Law enforcement intelligence differs from intelligence gathered for national security. Law enforcement agencies must base their activities on a reasonable suspicion to believe that some criminal activity is taking place.

Source: Carter (2004).

Law enforcement and national defense intelligence came under difficult times during the administration of President Jimmy Carter (1976–1980). Carter was not seeking to dismantle intelligence operations; he wanted to protect Americans from their government. The president tried to correct the abuse of power and end the scandal of using covert operations against American citizens. The CIA had tested drugs and biological agents on unknowing citizens, while the FBI's counterintelligence program, **COINTELPRO**, exceeded the authority of law enforcement. In responding to such abuses, the government began to limit the power of intelligence operations, unintentionally hampering their effectiveness.

President Carter's reaction was understandable, but critics believe he went too far, and no other administration has been able to reconstitute effective intelligence organizations. A *Time* magazine article (Calabresi and Ratnesar, 3-11-02) states the issue succinctly: America needs to learn to spy again. National security intelligence is crucial, but law enforcement has a role, the *Time* authors argue. They also censure bureaucratic structures for failing to share information, and they condemn the system for relying too heavily on machine and electronic information. We need information from people, the *Time* authors state emphatically. Another weak point, the writers emphasize, is the inability to analyze information. Intelligence is fragmented and in-

Types of Intelligence

There are different types of intelligence gathering systems. The differences are crucial when dealing with civil rights (see Chapter 16), but each intelligence system has its own practical methods for assembling information.

Criminal intelligence is gathered by law enforcement agencies investigating illegal activity. State, local, and federal police agencies are not allowed to gather, store, and maintain record systems on general activities. Their information must be based on a reasonable suspicion that some sort of criminal activity is taking place. Certain FBI operations may gather noncriminal intelligence if agents are assigned to national security. They do not use this evidence in criminal prosecutions.

National defense or security intelligence is gathered by several organizations in the Department of Defense, National Security Agency, Department of Energy, Department of Homeland Security, FBI, and CIA. Defense or security intelligence is usually based on one or more of the following sources:

- HUMINT: Human intelligence from spies, informers, defectors, and other people
- IMINT: Imagery intelligence from satellites and aircraft
- SIGINT: Signal intelligence from communications
- MASINT: Measures and signatures intelligence from sensing devices

Defense or security intelligence can be gathered whether the targets are involved in a crime or not.

effective. Their opinion has been reflected in other studies (Best, 12-3-01; Betts, 2002; Wise, 6-2-02).

Unlike national defense or security intelligence gathering, police agencies are required to demonstrate a reasonable suspicion of criminal activity before they may collect information. As long as agencies reasonably suspect that the law is being broken, law enforcement departments may gather and store **criminal intelligence**. The USA Patriot Act (see Chapter 16) increases the ability of law enforcement and intelligence agencies to share information, but David Carter (2004), one of the foremost academic experts on law enforcement intelligence in the country, solemnly warns that the abuses of the past cannot be repeated if police agencies want to develop effective intelligence systems (see also Dreyfuss, 3-23-02). If police agencies improve their intelligence gathering operations, they will do so under more stringent rules than those required for national security.

Gathering information within the bounds of criminal intelligence need not bar the path to efficiency. Not only is it possible to build criminal intelligence systems within the letter and spirit of legal regulations, several agencies have an excellent track record in doing so. The New Jersey State Police (NJSP), for example, has an extensive intelligence gathering apparatus (New Jersey State Police, 2002). The NJSP Intelligence Service Section is made up of three main divisions. The Intelligence Bureau is the largest division, composed of six units. The Analytical Unit is responsible for reviewing data from organized crime families and street gangs. It synthesizes information to produce a broad picture of the entire state, and it also conducts threat assessments for major public events. The Casino Intelligence Unit collects information on gambling affiliations with traditional and nontraditional crimes. It also serves as the government's liaison for regulatory agencies and conducts background investigations on contractors working in the casino industry. The Electronic Surveillance Unit conducts court-authorized monitoring and assists federal agencies in national security investigations. Critical information is shared through the Liaison Computerized Services Unit, including the sharing of information with agencies outside New Jersey. The Services Unit also codifies and organizes intelligence reports. Finally, the Street Gang Unit collects information and works with local gang task forces. The NJSP system is a model for gathering, organizing, analyzing, and sharing criminal information.

Two other divisions complete the picture of the NJSP system, including a unit for terrorist intelligence. The Central Security Unit is responsible for New Jersey's counterterrorist mission. Its primary purpose is the prevention of terrorist activities through intelligence operations. In other words, it is a proactive organization designed to prevent terrorism through interdiction. According to its official public statement, the Central Security Unit is primarily concerned with maintaining civil peace, protecting dignitaries, and monitoring known hate groups.

The Solid Waste Unit, which gathers information about hazardous materials and keeps an eye on organized crime, and the Casino Bureau round out the organization of the NJSP Intelligence Service Section. The key to its organization and its preventive capabilities is the collection, analysis, and sharing of information. Recently, NJSP linked its intelligence service with federal law enforcement, giving it the potential for greater effectiveness.

The state of California also introduced a new concept in statewide intelligence systems, the California Anti-Terrorism Information Center (CATIC). Formed after September 11, this statewide intelligence system is designed to combat terrorism. The center links federal, state, and local information services in one system and divides operational zones into five administrative areas. Trained intelligence analysts operate within civil rights guidelines and utilize information in a secure communications system (California Department of Justice, 2002). Information is analyzed daily.

CATIC is unique in state and local law enforcement. It combines both machine intelligence, that is, the type of information that can be gathered by computers and other automated devices, with information coming from a variety of police agencies. The information is correlated and organized by analysts looking for trends. Future projections are made by looking at past indicators. Rather than simply operating as an information gathering unit, CATIC is a synthesizing process. It combines public information with data on criminal trends and possible terrorist activities. Processed intelligence is designed to produce threat assessments for each area and to project trends outside the jurisdiction. The CATIC system attempts to process multiple sources of information to predict threats. By centralizing the collection and analytical sections of a statewide system, California's Department of Justice may have developed a method for moving offensively against terrorism.

The New York City Police Department (NYPD) has taken the offensive spirit a step further. Police Commissioner Raymond Kelly created two new units, one for counterterrorism and one for intelligence. Retired Marine Corps general Frank Libutti heads the counterterrorism section, and a former high-ranking CIA official, David Cohen, was selected to head the intelligence section. Kelly stated that he wanted the NYPD to do a better job of intelligence analysis and to work more closely with the federal government. The International Association of Chiefs of Police (IACP) said the plan was appropriate for New York City (Johnson, 1-29-02).

Law enforcement agencies present their intelligence systems in a positive light, but there are some critics. The FBI and CIA have been criticized resoundingly for failing to gather information before the September 11 attacks and ineffectively analyzing the information they did have (Dillon, 10-4-01; Nordland, Yousafzi, and Dehghanpisheh, 8-19-02). The Bush administration and police agencies expressed disapproval of the FBI's information-sharing policies (Fields, 5-3-02). Civil liberties groups fear growing power in agencies associated with homeland security, while others express concern over expanding executive authority (Herman, 12-3-01).

Planning for Homeland Security

Key Points and Questions:

1. What is the purpose of planning?
2. Why does terrorism make planning complex?
3. What questions does the IACP suggest asking to protect communities?
4. How can noncriminal intelligence be forwarded?

Everyone knows that planning should take place before a problem emerges. Effective police planning incorporates a description of a goal and methods for achieving it (Hudzik and Cordner, 1983). Planning should be based on the assets available to an agency and a projection of resources needed to meet the goal. A good plan will show how different entities interrelate and may reveal unexpected consequences. Planning brings resources together in a complex environment to manage multiple consequences.

The complexities of terrorism can seem overwhelming, so planning is essential. It enhances the gathering, organizing, and analyzing of information (Bodrero, 2002). Police agencies have long been aware of the need to make reactionary plans. Emergency planning, for example, is a tool for dealing with weather disasters and industrial accidents. After riots in Dade County, Florida, in 1980, local agencies developed field force deployment plans similar to mutual aid pacts among firefighters. The tragedies of Oklahoma City and September 11 brought several plans to fruition, and successful efforts in planning can be transferred into offensive strategies.

The IACP (International Association of Chiefs of Police, 2001) believes planning can be guided by looking for threats inside local communities. Police agencies should constantly monitor communities to determine whether a terrorist threat is imminent. Indicators such as an increase in violent rhetoric, the appearance of extremist groups, and increases in certain types of crimes may demonstrate that a terrorist problem is on the horizon. Planning is based on the status of potential violence, and law enforcement can develop certain responses based on the threat. Prepared responses, the

IACP contends, are proactive (see Another Perspective: Information for Planning).

Richard Best (12-3-01) points to another aspect of planning. National security differs from law enforcement, Best argues. In police work, officers react to information provided voluntarily. Police actions are governed by the rules of evidence, and the ultimate purpose is to protect the rights of citizens, including those who have been arrested. **National security intelligence**, on the other hand, is used to anticipate threats. It uses aggressive methods to collect information, including, at times, operations in violation of the law. National security intelligence is ultimately designed to protect targets, not individual rights.

Best quotes former director of central intelligence Stansfield Turner to summarize the differences between national security and law enforcement. Give the FBI a task, Turner once said, and it will try to complete the mission within the constraints of the law. Give the CIA the same mission, and it tries to complete the task without concern for legality. This dilemma is indicative of a prime concern for law enforcement. It cannot abandon its public service role. Regardless of policy, the American police will lose public trust if they rely on covert operations. With Best's insight, law enforcement should plan and develop two channels for information.

One channel should be aimed at law enforcement intelligence, that is, the types of information police agencies collect. As Best (12-3-01) describes, this information is based on criminal activity and the protection of individual rights. It is governed by the rules of evidence. Yet, police agencies will inevitably come upon defense information, especially when monitoring community indicators.

Much of this intelligence will not be used in criminal investigation. At this point, state and local police agencies should be prepared to pass such information along to defense sources. These two paths for information, one for criminal investigation and one for national security, can serve as the basis for dealing with intelligence collected by state and local police agencies.

Another Perspective

Information for Planning

List the areas in the jurisdiction that make potential targets for terrorists.

- List available resources.
- Project potential attacks.
- Identify critical infrastructures.

Factors influencing plans, including

- Emergency command structures
- Coordination among agencies
- Mass casualties
- Victim and family support
- Preservation of evidence
- Crime scene management
- Media relations
- Costs
- Training and preincident exercises

Source: International Association of Chiefs of Police (2001).

Creating a Culture of Information Sharing

Key Points and Questions:

1. What is information sharing?
2. What systems exist for sharing information and how effective are they?
3. What is the National Criminal Intelligence Sharing Plan?
4. What did the 9-11 Commission recommend for both national defense and law enforcement intelligence?

The National Strategy for Homeland Security (Office of Homeland Security, 2002, p. 56, and U.S. Department of Homeland Security, 2004, pp. 3–34) calls for increased **information sharing** among law enforcement agencies. The reports say America will build a cooperative environment that enables sharing of essential information. It will be a "system of systems that can provide the right information to the right people at all times." This is an excellent idea in principle.

Some systems are already in place. The **Regional Information Sharing System (RISS)** is a six-part information network whose policies are controlled by its members (Bodrero, 2002). It is ideal for sharing intelligence. It has secure intranet, bulletin board, and conference capabilities. The High Intensity Drug Trafficking Areas (HIDTAs) system and the El Paso Intelligence Center (EPIC) are also sources for information sharing. Another is the International Association of Law Enforcement Intelligence Analysts (IALEIA). In addition, some states are looking to pool their resources in a common intelligence network.

Critics say these networks are underused. Robert Taylor (1987) finds two primary weaknesses in U.S. systems: Intelligence is not properly analyzed, and agencies do not coordinate information. Chad Nilson and Tod Burke (2002) claim law enforcement is the primary institution responsible for protecting America from terrorism by sharing information. Ironically, their finding is presented as a recommendation, not a description of current practices.

In 2003 the attorney general endorsed the **National Criminal Intelligence Sharing Plan**. Established with several standards, the purpose of the plan is not only to create a culture of sharing, but to generate the structures and communications systems to make it happen. In theory, all agencies will communicate in a single network. David Carter (2004) suggests a method for doing so while maintaining a criminal predicate for collecting information and sharing within the bounds of the law. The National Criminal Intelligence Sharing Plan and the guidelines proposed by Carter provide a method for criminal justice agencies to secure the homeland.

National security intelligence is another matter. The 9-11 Commission Report (2004, pp. 399–428) suggested several reforms for restructuring government in the wake of the September 11 attacks (see Another Perspective: 9-11 Commission Recommendations), and the recommendations became law in December 2004. The recommendations focused on defense, intelligence, information sharing, homeland security, and law enforcement. The most sweeping recommendation came with the creation of a national intelligence director. The commission argued that the government was structured to fight the Cold War, not to counter terrorism. The commissioners felt that reorganization of the intelligence community and elevation of a director to the presidential cabinet level would help safeguard America.

Members of the 9-11 Commission held meetings with citizens, lobbied Congress, appeared on television, and joined with the families of victims of the September 11 attacks to demand reform. Their campaign was emotional, and anyone who criticized the reforms they proposed seemed almost un-American. Yet criticism came.

Judge Richard A. Posner (8-29-04) argues that the 9-11 Commission Report presents two competing parts. The first, he writes, is an excellent step-by-step analysis of the events that led up to the attacks on September 11 and an explanation of actions after the terrorists struck. The second part of the report is a series of recommendations. Posner says that he paused when he encountered the recommendations because

9-11 Commission Recommendations

The 9-11 Commission suggested the following reforms:

1. Create a National Counterterrorism Center.
2. Create a director of national intelligence to oversee intelligence gathering and all the agencies involved in national defense intelligence.
3. Refocus the CIA. Reporting to the director of national intelligence, the CIA director should
   a. Build the analysis capability of the CIA
   b. Increase information gathered from people
   c. Develop extensive language capabilities
   d. Recruit from diverse groups in order to have agents who can blend with a variety of cultures
   e. Establish routine communications with other agencies
4. Paramilitary operations should move to Special Operations in the Defense Department.
   a. Covert operations should move to the Defense Department.
   b. Northern Command should assume responsibility for military threats against the United States.
5. Make the intelligence budget public.
6. Demand that agencies share information.
7. Streamline and strengthen congressional oversight of intelligence and homeland security.
8. Accelerate the appointment of national security administrators during presidential transitions.
9. Introduce new structures in the FBI.
   a. Create career paths for agents and others assigned to intelligence and national security.
   b. Create a culture of cross-fertilization between criminal justice and national defense.
   c. Restructure the budget to emphasize (1) intelligence, (2) counterterrorism and counter-intelligence, (3) law enforcement, and (4) criminal justice services.
10. The Department of Homeland Security should
    a. Assess threats
    b. Develop and test emergency plans
    c. Protect the critical infrastructure
    d. Create a system for response to threats and attacks

Source: 9-11 Commission Report (2004).

the policies and directions the commission suggested were not altogether consistent with the analysis of the first part of the report.

Posner suggests that the FBI's record of combating terrorism was poor, and there may be no reason to believe that restructuring will improve its capabilities. Combining fifteen different intelligence agencies designed to do everything from launching spy satellites to gathering criminal information is illogical, he says. The agencies exist for different reasons and are responsible for different tasks. The national intelligence director who is supposed to manage the new conglomerated menagerie of agencies will spend most of his or her time dealing with arguments among the intelligence community, the Department of Justice, and the secretary of defense. Posner writes that in the aftermath of September 11, governmental agencies have an incentive to work together, but restructuring bureaucracy will not automatically make the United States safer.

Congress mandated the 9-11 Commission's recommendations in an emotional atmosphere in December 2004. There are questions for the future, questions that deal with the nature of intelligence, democracy, and individual rights. The defense and intelligence establishments have the legal right and mission to collect information to protect the country. The central question for criminal justice focuses on the role of law enforcement. The 9-11 Commission recommends changes in the FBI, but the vast majority of law enforcement activities take place far from the federal criminal justice system. Other nations have models for collecting information while protecting individual rights, but the commission did not consider these models, assuming that an analysis of American activities was sufficient. The question of balancing security with freedom is delicate, and the new intelligence infrastructure has not dealt with all the issues.

Summary of Main Points

1. Americans define homeland security in several different ways. Its meaning is institutionally unclear.

2. Clausewitz viewed war as a rational political process between states. Sun Tzu viewed war as a psychological process at many different levels.

3. The difference between the ideas of Clausewitz and Sun Tzu can be illustrated by comparing Pearl Harbor with September 11. The former was a military attack rationally designed to obtain a political objective. The latter was a psychological attack designed to create an aura of fear.

4. The nature of conflict is changing because entire cultures fear for their existence. When threatened in this manner, they do not respond rationally.

5. Psychological attacks are aimed at structures and symbols of power.

6. Law enforcement has a leading role in homeland security because of its presence in communities and its ability to gather information.

7. Model systems for information gathering can be found in the New Jersey State Police, the California Anti-Terrorism Information Center, and the New York Police Department.

8. Planning should be designed to anticipate community needs, solve issues before they become problems, and respond to crises with adequate resources.

9. The crux of counterterrorism involves information sharing among all levels of government.

10. The reform recommendations of the 9-11 Commission became law in December 2004. The new law changes the structure of intelligence gathering and establishes a director of national intelligence.

Key Terms

Make sure you can define, explain, or identify the following people, ideas, organizations, or terms:

Department of Homeland Security
  (DHS) 269
homeland security 270
civil defense 270
Carl von Clausewitz 272
On War 272
Sun Tzu 273
asymmetry 273
social immersion 276
asymmetrical war 277
symbolic target 277

symbolic terrorism 277
pragmatic terrorism 277
systematic terrorism 277
COINTELPRO 281
criminal intelligence 282
national security intelligence 285
information sharing 286
Regional Informational Sharing System
  (RISS) 286
National Criminal Intelligence Sharing
  Plan 286

Suggested Readings

Now that you've been introduced to this topic, you can learn more by reading:

Thomas P. M. Barnett's *The Pentagon's New Map* explains the security environment in the post–Cold War era. He outlines a grand strategy for security in the modern world.

You may also want to read:

Martin van Crefeld, in *The Transformation of War*, analyzes the changes in modern conflict.

Lawrence Sulk's *Police Intelligence* discusses the practical aspects of information gathering.

Howard Safir summarizes homeland security in *Security: Policing Your Homeland, Your State, Your City.*

Web Resources

Go to *http://cj.wadsworth.com/white_terrorism5e* and click on Web Links to find:

- The Department of Homeland Security website
- A guide for law enforcement intelligence by David Carter
- The 9-11 Commission Report
- The text of the Intelligence Reform and Prevention of Terrorism Act of 2004

The Companion Website for *Terrorism and Homeland Security*, Fifth Edition
http://cj.wadsworth.com/white_terrorism5e

At the Book Companion Website you can review chapter outlines, use the flash cards to test your terrorism vocabulary, and check out the many other study aids you'll find there. You'll find valuable data and resources at your fingertips to help you study for that big exam or write that important paper.

Terrorism Updates

http://www.wadsworth.com/criminaljustice_d/special_features/ext/terrorism_site090802/index.html

Visit the *Terrorism: An Interdisciplinary Perspective* website to find the most current information about the fields of terrorism and homeland security. With a focus on domestic and international issues, this site explores the scope of terrorism in our world today. You'll find essays on important topics in terrorism and homeland security, critical thinking web activities, and InfoTrac College Edition keywords. Most importantly, the website is updated weekly with current news and research articles on domestic and international terrorism. You are invited to use these web resources to supplement your understanding of the topics covered in this chapter.

Current Perspectives: Readings from InfoTrac College Edition
Terrorism and Homeland Security

The sixteen articles in this reader offer a representative selection that helps you understand the important issues about terrorism and homeland security. It includes FREE access to InfoTrac College Edition and can also be bundled with the text for free.

Chapter 16

Protecting the Homeland and Protecting Civil Liberties

Police power on display in New York City during the Republican National Convention, August 2004. Some people fear that the freedoms sacrificed for security threaten civil liberties in the United States.

© Chris Hondros/Getty Images

September 11 changed the way America views terrorism. The wars in Afghanistan and Iraq claimed the lives of thousands while massive antiterrorist measures were taken at home. The USA Patriot Act, which made significant changes in the structure of federal law enforcement, was passed within weeks of the September attacks. The creation of the Department of Homeland Security was one of the largest reorganizations of the federal government in history. In 2004 the 9-11 Commission issued a report calling for the complete overhaul of the U.S. Intelligence system, and it became law in December 2004. All of these activities generated tremendous controversy, and the debates took place as America waged foreign wars against an enemy who projected no central front. As America's internal debates continued, terrorist events around the world became deadlier. Chapter 15 explored the way terrorism has transformed war. Now we will consider how changes in the manner of war affect the structure of civil society.

Chapter Objectives

After reading this chapter you should be able to:

1. Describe the relationship between the idea of defense in depth and civil liberties.
2. Summarize the USA Patriot Act.
3. Explain the views of supporters and critics of the Patriot Act.
4. List the constitutional issues that affect homeland security.
5. Cite arguments to support and criticize increasing executive power to combat terrorism.
6. Discuss the functions of national defense (or security) and criminal intelligence.
7. Describe the paradox when criminal justice systems are involved in national defense intelligence operations.
8. Discuss the dangers of militarizing police work.

Defense in Depth: Why Civil Liberties Interact with Civil Defense

Key Points and Questions:

1. How do communities behave when they feel their existence is threatened?
2. Define "defense in depth."
3. How does defense in depth interact with individual rights?

Changes in how war is fought affect the structure of civil society. For example, Jihadist communities feel that their very existence is threatened. To paraphrase their most important philosopher, Sayyid Qutb (1990), Jihadists are on the edge of a cliff and about to topple over. They are threatened by Muslims who do not accept the Jihadist philosophy and by the non-Muslim West. As a result, Jihadists believe they can use any method for disrupting their enemies' societies. Stated another way, the target of terrorism is social order. Terrorists fight against the way a group of people live. Therefore, combating terrorism is not simply a matter of taking a battle to an enemy. It involves the preservation and protection of social order.

The logic of conflict becomes clear when the method of fighting and targets of combat are placed together. Terrorism targets *civil* society and *civilian* targets. Defending against terrorism implies that military force must extend beyond the military. In other words, to defend against terrorism, a nation or culture must use *civil defense*. The idea of **defense in depth** implies that all levels of society must become involved in homeland security. Defense in depth is designed to protect a community fighting for its way of life (see Cebrowsky and Barnett, 2003; Barnett, 2004).

Homeland defense makes sense within this logic, but it raises a host of issues. This logic assumes that the community wants to fight for its existence. It implies that all members of the community are committed to preserving a similar goal. Approaching conflict in this manner may solve logical issues, but it asks a society to engage in great sacrifice to achieve its objectives. As Martin van Crefeld (1991, pp. 142–156) says, at some point violence serves to justify violence. This style of thought also asks members of a social group to be sufficiently ruthless with enemies and to have the political will for rigid self-examination. In short, defense in depth may require citizens to sacrifice the assumptions of everyday life. People may be asked to alter the way they live. For example, Americans have learned to tolerate increased security at airports and public schools.

The ideas of democracy and individual freedom have been developed in the West for the past thousand years. The United States, founded on these principles, struggles with the issues of democracy and civil rights. At the country's birth, property-holding males governed, women were noncitizens, and slavery was acceptable. The rights of citizenship have spread slowly for nearly 250 years, and the reality of individual freedom occurs in the tension between ideal freedom and state power. Defense in depth alters the balance by emphasizing state power. Laws, military behavior, police power, information gathering, and other aspects of civil existence are altered when an entire society engages in a conflict.

When homeland security is being discussed, the topic of individual rights usually becomes part of the discussion. To engage in a struggle against terrorism, Americans must examine themselves and honestly select a course of action they will accept. It cannot be imposed by legislative action, military force, or police power. It cannot be defined by self-appointed civil rights guardians. Attorneys and courts are fond of claiming this area for their exclusive jurisdiction, but the issue extends far beyond judicial logic. If Americans want to secure the homeland, they need to engage in a thorough self-examination and decide what they are willing to sacrifice and how they will maintain the most cherished aspects of social freedom (Cole and Dempsey, 2002, pp. 11–12).

This is not an abstract academic exercise. Many Jihadists are engaged in what they believe is a life-and-death cosmic struggle between good and evil. They believe they must not lose the battle for God and feel bound by no rules in the course of this holy war (Ruthven, 2000, p. 398). Killing their enemies—Muslims who disagree with the Jihadist philosophy and non-Muslims—is a sacramental act. Death is the ultimate expression of their religion, and killing is horrific and spectacular. If the Jihadists obtain weapons of mass destruction, they will use them. Americans will be better prepared to secure the homeland if they have engaged in a nationwide discussion of defense in depth and its impact on civil liberties before an attack. If the discussion takes place after a population center has been destroyed, emotions and reaction will guide the response. In that case, homeland security could become a threat to the American way of life.

The USA Patriot Act

Key Points and Questions:

1. What are the contents of Title I of the USA Patriot Act?
2. Why is Title II the most controversial aspect of the Patriot Act?
3. How do other sections of the Patriot Act affect criminal justice?
4. What is the Regional Information Sharing System and how does the Patriot Act affect it?
5. What do supporters of the Patriot Act believe?
6. What frightens critics of the Patriot Act?

An Overview of the USA Patriot Act

Critics of the USA Patriot Act say it infringes on civil liberties. Supporters believe it provides critical law enforcement tools. Here is an overview of the sections affecting law enforcement.

Title I, Designed to Enhance Domestic Security　Creates a counterterrorism fund, increases technical support for the FBI, allows law enforcement to request military assistance in certain emergencies, expands the National Electronic Task Force, and forbids discrimination against Muslims and Arabs.

Title II, Designed to Improve Surveillance　Grants authority to federal law enforcement agencies to intercept communication about terrorism, allows searches of computers, allows intelligence agencies to share information with criminal justice agencies, explains procedures for warrants, creates new definitions of intelligence, allows for roving wiretaps, and provides for expanding intelligence gathering. The USA Patriot Act has a sunset clause: If not renewed by Congress, it will automatically expire.

Title III, Designed to Stop Terrorism Finances　Grants expanded powers to law enforcement agencies to seize financial records, provides access to financial records, forces transactions to be disclosed, and expands investigative power in money laundering.

Title IV, Designed to Protect U.S. Borders　Outlines measures to protect the borders, tightens immigration procedures, allows foreigners to be photographed and fingerprinted, and gives benefits to victims of terrorism.

Title V, Enhances Investigative Powers　Provides a reward program, calls for sharing of investigative findings among law enforcement agencies, extends Secret Service jurisdiction, and forces educational institutions to release records of foreign students.

Title VI, Designed to Compensate the Families of Public Safety Officers Killed during a Terrorist Attack

Title VII, Designed to Expand the Information Sharing Network　Provides for the expansion of law enforcement's nationwide information exchange, the Regional Information Sharing System (RISS).

Title VIII, Strengthens Criminal Laws　Defines terrorist attacks, defines domestic terrorism, provides the basis for charging terrorists overseas, criminalizes support for terrorism, criminalizes cyberterrorism, allows investigation of terrorism as racketeering, and expands bioterrorism laws.

Title X, Contains Miscellaneous addenda

The Bush administration sponsored legislation in the weeks following September 11 that contains increased responsibilities for criminal justice and other agencies. The **USA Patriot Act** has ten sections, or titles, outlining new powers for government operations (for a summary, see Doyle, 2002) (see Expanding the Concept: An Overview of the USA Patriot Act). Title I is designed to enhance domestic security. It creates funding for counterterrorist activities, expands technical support for the FBI, expands electronic intelligence gathering research, and defines presidential authority in response to terrorism. This section of the law also forbids discrimination against Arab and Muslim Americans.

Some of the most controversial aspects of the Patriot Act appear in Title II. The purpose of this section is to improve the government's ability to gather electronic evidence. In other words, it allows police officials expanded authority to monitor communications. It also allows intelligence and federal law enforcement agencies to share noncriminal information with each other. In addition, it forces private corporations to share records and data with federal law enforcement departments during investigations and allows the FBI to seize material when it believes national security is jeopardized. Title II also contains a sunset clause, automatically ending the provisions of the Patriot Act unless it is renewed, and demands congressional oversight.

Other sections of the law affect law enforcement and the criminal justice system in a variety of ways. Title III empowers federal law enforcement to interact with banking regulators and provides arrest power outside U.S. borders for terrorist financing and money laundering. Title IV increases border patrols and monitoring of foreigners within the United States, while mandating detention of suspected terrorists. Title VII focuses on police information sharing, specifically targeting a nationwide police investigative network known as the Regional Information Sharing System (RISS). Before the Patriot Act, RISS was to be used only in criminal investigations.

Supporters of the Patriot Act believe it will increase federal law enforcement's ability to respond to terrorism and will create an intelligence conduit among local, state, and federal police agencies (U.S. Department of Justice, 2005). They believe counterterrorism will be strengthened by combining law enforcement and **national defense intelligence**. Opponents of the law argue that it goes too far in threatening civil liberties while expanding police powers (Cole and Dempsey, 2002, pp. 186–187) (see Expanding the Concept: Terrorism vs. the Constitution). Critics are especially

Expanding the Concept

Terrorism vs. the Constitution

David Cole and James Dempsey (2002) produced an argument after the 1996 antiterrorism law took affect in the wake of the 1995 Oklahoma City bombing, and they reiterated their cry with regard to the USA Patriot Act. Stated simply, they fear that federal law enforcement power is growing too strong in a wave of national hysteria. Their thesis is that antiterrorism legislation empowers law enforcement agencies to enforce political law. By contrast, terrorists must violate criminal laws to practice terrorism. Therefore, Cole and Dempsey argue, it is best to keep the police out of politics and focused on criminal violations. If terrorists are prosecuted under criminal law, the Constitution will be preserved.

Cole and Dempsey point to four cases that illustrate their fears:

1. In the late 1960s and early 1970s, the FBI trampled the rights of suspects and citizens through COINTELPRO, its counterintelligence program.
2. From 1981 to 1990, the FBI overreacted against U.S. citizens who expressed sympathy for revolutionaries in El Salvador. The FBI even designated friends of activists "guilty by association." (continued on page 296)

3. In the 1990s, Muslims and Palestinians were targeted by investigations without reasonable suspicion to believe they were involved in a crime.

4. Also during the 1990s, political investigations expanded against radical environmentalists and others.

Citing a group of law professors that petitioned Congress to limit political investigations, Cole and Dempsey argue that law enforcement should gather intelligence only when there is reason to suspect criminal activity. They worry that the 1996 antiterrorism legislation and the 2001 Patriot Act gives the police power to regulate political activity.

The real danger is not using reasonable efforts to fight terrorism, they say. There are certain instances when the intelligence community should share information with the criminal community. For example, when Osama bin Laden was charged in the bombings of Dar es Salaam and Nairobi, it would have been appropriate for the FBI and CIA to share information. Cole and Dempsey worry that Congress has handed over too much power to share without judicial review. The proper role of the courts, they argue, is to oversee the use of police power.

Their argument illustrates the passions involved in counterterrorism. The Cole-Dempsey thesis is endorsed by a host of jurists, self-appointed civil rights organizations, legal scholars, and die-hard conservatives that support many of the Bush administration's other efforts. There is even support for their position inside law enforcement, especially within the FBI. Yet, the situation is complicated by another factor: the American belief that a role of government is to protect life, liberty, and property. Do the victims of September 11 enjoy those rights, too?

As you consider this question, the balance between the need for security and the constitutional guarantees of freedom comes into focus. The answer literally centers on life-and-death issues, and dangers arise when the balance is tipped too far toward either side.

Source: Cole and Dempsey (2002).

concerned about sharing noncriminal intelligence during criminal investigations. The most pressing concern centers on the increased power of the government to monitor the activities of its own citizens.

Title II and the Debate about Intelligence Gathering

Key Points and Questions:

1. Why is intelligence gathering controversial?
2. Will intelligence gathering affect the balance of governmental power?
3. Where does homeland security intersect with the Constitution?
4. Will the Patriot Act change the role of criminal justice agencies?
5. Describe differing responses from the Patriot Act's critics and supporters.

The most controversial facets of counterterrorism are symbolized by the USA Patriot Act, and the most sensitive aspect of the law deals with intelligence gathering and sharing. Many diverse groups across the spectrum of American politics, from constitutional conservatives to civil libertarian activists, worry that the law will encroach on civil freedoms. The American government was founded on the idea of **civil liberties**. This means citizens are free from having their government infringe unreasonably on the freedoms guaranteed in the Constitution and the Bill of Rights. Stated simply, increasing the ability of the government to collect information increases executive power. Therefore, intelligence activities, or gathering information, symbolize the fears of critics. Supporters counter by saying that a nation cannot fight terrorism without gathering intelligence (for general comments on intelligence in U.S. law enforcement, see Carter, 2004).

When criminal justice and national security agencies gather information about organizations and people, they do so as an extension of the executive branch of government. Any effort to expand executive power will affect the other branches of government. The U.S. Constitution separates the powers of the three branches of government: executive, legislative, and judicial. This is known as the **separation of powers**, and these powers are also separated in the criminal justice system. Elected bodies of lawmakers (the legislative branch) pass laws, courts (the judicial branch) rule on them, and law enforcement and correctional agencies (executive branch) enforce them. This separation of power balances the amount of power wielded by each branch of government (Perl, 1998; Best, 12-3-01; Cole and Dempsey, 2002, pp. 15–16; Carter, 2004, pp. 8–17).

A quick overview of constitutional issues illustrates points where homeland security policies and the Constitution intersect. The main body of the Constitution separates powers and prescribes duties for each branch of government. It reserves powers not explicitly given to the federal government to the states, and through the *posse comitatus* **clause**, forbids the use of military power to enforce civilian law. The **Bill of Rights**, the first ten amendments to the Constitution, also comes into play by protecting free speech and assembly (First Amendment), preventing the government from illegal search and seizure (Fourth Amendment), and preventing self-incrimination (Fifth Amendment). The Sixth Amendment helps to protect these rights by ensuring that suspects have access to an attorney. The **Fourteenth Amendment**, the most important amendment for law enforcement after the Bill of Rights was added to the Constitution following the Civil War, ensures that suspects cannot lose their rights except by the due process of law. The interpretations of the Constitution and its amendments have protected American liberties for more than two centuries.

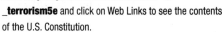

Go to **http://cj.wadsworth.com/white _terrorism5e** and click on Web Links to see the contents of the U.S. Constitution.

The Constitution guides the United States in war and peace, and it allows certain necessary actions in times of emergency—actions that would be prohibited if there were no emergency. This makes terrorism a constitutionally murky subject, a nebulous cloud fogging the boundary separating war and peace, because many people disagree about the nature of terrorism. Many legal scholars argue that terrorism is not a continuing emergency (Cole and Dempsey, 2002, pp. 189–201). For example, America's enemies of September 11 used terrorists trained in military-style camps to attack civilian targets and military forces engaged in peacetime activities. Logically, national security agencies, such as military forces and the CIA, try to prevent attacks as if they were engaged in a war. Criminal justice agencies do not take actions for war; they protect individual rights, and local, state, and federal courts are not charged with national defense (see del Carmen, 1991, pp. 73–176). Controversy arises when criminal systems and the defense establishment begin to blend activities.

National Public Radio (12-6-01) broadcasted a special report focusing on constitutional issues in December 2001, and matters quickly lined up along party lines. Former attorney general John Ashcroft called for the right to deport suspected terrorists in secret hearings, and Defense Secretary Donald Rumsfeld gave orders to detain accused al Qaeda terrorists without trial. Two of the detainees were U.S. citizens. Critics argued that such actions endangered the rights of Americans (National Public Radio, 12-6-01; Seelye, 6-23-02).

Former Senate Judiciary Committee chair Patrick Leahy (D-Vermont) said the executive orders coming from the Bush administration were disconcerting. According to Senator Leahy, President Bush's antiterrorist proposals threatened the system of checks and balances, giving the executive branch of government too much power. Attorney General John Ashcroft disagreed with Senator Leahy's conclusions, arguing that the proposed guidelines were solely for the purpose of protecting the country from terrorists. This constitutional theme runs through discussions of homeland security. One group is skeptical of increased executive power, and the other sees it as logically necessary to protect the country.

Several other issues come to the forefront with regard to civil liberties. Civil rights attorney Nancy Chang (2001) criticizes the Patriot Act on the basis of democracy. She points out that the act was rushed through the House and Senate, with no public hearings and no time for public debate. There were no conference or committee reports. No time was allowed for security needs to be examined; the legislation came quickly in the emotional tide of September 11. The most important aspect, she finds, is the increased ability of the government to look into the affairs of its own citizens. By allowing the government to blur the distinction between defense intelligence and criminal evidence, the Patriot Act tramples on reasonable expectations of privacy.

Others argue that the Patriot Act is an unreasonable attack on electronic communication (Electronic Frontier Foundation, 2001b). According to this line of thought, the government overreacted to September 11. Technological societies are open to attack by subnational groups or even deranged individuals, and protection requires thoughtful, reflective analysis and reaction. Instead, Congress rushed legislation, amending fifteen different statutes. The law gives federal law enforcement agencies the right to monitor Internet searches and to keep tabs on individual queries. The government is allowed to contact roving wiretaps without probable cause in the hope of obtaining information. For many, the provision in Title II forcing Internet service providers to give information to federal law enforcement agencies is not acceptable.

Not everyone believes the Patriot Act represents an attack on individual rights. For example, two senators with strong civil liberties records think criticism of the act is premature (Straub, 5-1-02). Senator Dianne Feinstein (D-California) believes we cannot rush to judgment. Time will show how the act is used in the real world. It may be necessary to revisit the law, but first we need to see how it is implemented. Senator Charles Schumer (D-New York) believes the law is balanced. It limits personal freedom while reasonably enhancing security. Both senators think it is necessary to balance civil liberties and social protection.

Championed by the Bush administration, the Patriot Act is a lightning rod in the debate pitting national security against civil liberties. Technological societies are vulnerable to technological attack, regardless of ideology. Whether this involves individuals engaged in a killing spree, criminal gangs, or terrorist conspiracies, a technological society is open to attack. The more sophisticated the attackers become, the greater the chances are for multiple deaths. September 11 exacerbated the issue, but America was vulnerable before the hijackings and remains vulnerable today. Supporters claim that the Patriot Act and other governmental actions are necessary for security. Critics believe security cannot come at the unreasonable expense of civil liberties. This debate continues, and the courts have yet to rule on the issues.

The Case for Increasing Executive Powers in the Face of Terrorism

Key Points and Questions:

1. How does the Fourth Amendment apply to homeland security?
2. Cite examples of unreasonableness within the context of the Fourth Amendment.
3. How does Colb view profiling?
4. What actions did the Bush administration take to increase executive power?
5. How do the cases of Hawdi and Padilla reflect these actions?

Several constitutional scholars have examined the issue of increasing executive powers to combat terrorism. Lewis Katz (11-24-01) believed in limited government before September 11, but he rethought his position in the wake of the attacks. His concerns center on diminishing the rights of Americans, and he finds an analogy in drug enforcement. America launched its "war on drugs" and soon discovered it could not thwart drug traffickers under constitutional rules of evidence. As a result, police power has been growing since 1971, Katz argues, and citizen protection under the Fourth Amendment has been decreasing (see Expanding the Concept: The War on Drugs as an Intelligence Model).

While leery of government, Katz says the real test of the Fourth Amendment is **reasonableness**. In normal times, police officers can be held to a higher standard of behavior than in times of emergency. September 11 constituted an emergency. It was not unreasonable to interview Middle Eastern immigrants, Katz concludes, nor was it unreasonable to increase electronic surveillance powers. A long-time opponent of a national identification system, Katz says such a system would not be unconstitutional, provided citizens were not ordered to produce identification without reasonable suspicion. Actions taken to prevent another September 11, he argues, do not violate the Fourth Amendment when they are reasonable.

Katz does believe some government actions are unreasonable. Eavesdropping on attorney-client conversations, for example, violates the Sixth Amendment, a suspect's right to counsel. Military tribunals deny the presumption of innocence. He argues that we cannot sacrifice the very liberties we are fighting to preserve. Katz's argu-

The War on Drugs as an Intelligence Model

The war on drugs has produced a national system of police intelligence gathering and dissemination. Combined federal, state, and local law enforcement agencies operate in conjunction to gather intelligence and conduct operations.

Proponents hail this process as a model of sharing resources and intelligence. They point to cooperation among agencies and investigative information-sharing systems as the answer to the intelligence problem (National Drug Intelligence Center, 2002). At the national level, drug intelligence reports are synthesized and disseminated to state and local agencies. On the surface, these multijurisdictional efforts seem to be an effective tool in countering drug traffickers.

Opponents have a different view. Many police administrators believe the systems are not effective, and they refuse to participate in them (Herman, 12-3-01). Other people outside law enforcement look at the intelligence network and claim it to be both a failure and an assault on the Fourth Amendment. Proponents of this position state that the war on drugs is ineffective, and the real loser in the process is civil liberty. Critics feel that trying to collect drug intelligence merely leads to labeling certain people or groups without making a dent in drug traffic.

ment indicates that the balance of powers is a dynamic entity vacillating according to circumstances. In other words, there is no blanket policy of reasonableness, and care must be taken to balance security with civil liberties.

Sherry Colb (10-10-01) of Rutgers University's School of Law also applies a doctrine of reasonableness. Examining the issue of racial profiling, Colb concedes that police in America are facing a new enemy. Racial profiling has not helped the police control drugs, she argues, and it violates the due process clause of the Fourteenth Amendment. Yet, the scope of September 11 calls previous assumptions about profiling—or targeting specific groups of people on the basis of race, ethnicity, religion, or other social factors—into question. As police agencies assemble profiles of terrorists, one of the characteristics may be race.

Colb believes any profiling system, including one having race as a factor, will yield many more investigative inquiries than apprehensions. The reason is that there is only a small number of terrorists in any group, regardless of their profile. The population of people matching the profile is greater than the population of terrorists in the profile group. By the same token, a number of terrorists may fall within a particular ethnic group, and the urgency of September 11 may require action. If a terrorist profile develops and it includes race as one of the characteristics, Colb suggests that some opponents of racial profiling may find they endorse it in the case of counterterrorism.

The Bush administration moved quickly in the wake of September 11 (Van Natta, 3-30-02). Wanting to do everything possible to catch terrorists, the Department of Justice scrapped the restrictions it placed on agents in earlier times. Issuing new guidelines, it freed the FBI from the requirement to rely on reasonable suspicion before launching an inquiry. Unless the courts rule otherwise or legislative bodies intervene, agents are free to search for indicators of illegal activity in open-source information, including the Internet. They can monitor chat rooms or engage in data mining.

Agents can go undercover in political or religious organizations to search for threats to security. No longer required to seek centralized approval, local FBI offices would be empowered to launch inquiries based on their own information and initiative.

New guidelines, executive orders, and military tribunals have created strange twists in the criminal justice system. Reporter Katherine Seelye (6-23-02) examines the summer of 2002 when two foreign-born terrorist suspects were arrested on the basis of probable cause and were sent to trial. At the same time, two U.S. citizens, Yasser Esam Hawdi and Jose Padilla, were held by military force without representation. Hawdi was fighting for al Qaeda when captured in Afghanistan in November 2001, and Padilla was arrested on May 8, 2002, for his alleged involvement in a plot to detonate a dirty bomb in the United States. Hawdi and Padilla, both of whom would have been criminally charged before September 11, were detained much like prisoners of war, while two alleged terrorists arrested on U.S. soil were afforded the rights of criminal suspects. Hawdi was released in September 2004.

Ruth Wedgwood (6-14-02), a former federal prosecutor who now teaches law, offers an explanation of the irony between Americans being detained militarily and foreigners being held under civilian arrest. She says al Qaeda attacked civilian targets, gaining an advantage in the U.S. criminal justice system. Al Qaeda, Wedgwood says, has learned it is best to recruit U.S. citizens for operations because citizens are not subject to arbitrary arrest. Pointing to Jose Padilla, Wedgwood states that his arrest represents a conundrum between reconciling public safety and the law. The issues surface in the difference between intelligence operations and law enforcement administration. In short, she says, going to trial means exposing intelligence sources for the sake of a criminal conviction.

Wedgwood presents the logic of the two situations. Common sense dictates that the detention of terrorists does not follow the pattern of criminal arrests. Terrorists are detained because no writ, no law, and no court order will stop them from attacking. They must be physically restrained, Wedgwood says. The purpose of detention, she argues, is not to engage in excessive punishment, but to keep terrorists from returning to society. She admits that the situation presents a public dilemma for a nation under the rule of law.

Wedgwood argues that indefinite detention by executive order is not the most suitable alternative. Terrorists could be given a military hearing to determine whether they continue to represent a threat. A panel of judges might rule on the danger of releasing suspected terrorists from custody. The Constitution is not a suicide pact, she says, citing a famous court decision. Common sense demands a reasonable solution to the apparent dichotomy between freedom and security.

E. V. Konotorovich (6-18-02) is not as concerned about executive orders as Wedgwood. The stakes are so high, he argues, that the United States must make all reasonable efforts to stop the next attack. Torture is out of the question in this country, but drugs are a viable alternative. Police are allowed to do body cavity searches for contraband in prison, Konotorovich argues, and the September 11 attacks make such searches pale in the face of massive terrorism. Drugs should not be used for prosecution, he says, but they are acceptable for gaining information. The threat is real, and legal arguments against obtaining information are illusory. Americans captured by al Qaeda have been quickly executed. Konotorovich believes Americans must take decisive actions against such terrorists.

The Case against Increasing Executive Powers in the Face of Terrorism

 Key Points and Questions:

1. Has the Patriot Act increased executive authority too greatly?
2. What type of court reviews warrants issued under the Foreign Intelligence Surveillance Act?
3. After the Patriot Act might FISA evidence be used in criminal investigations?
4. What concerns have civil libertarians voiced?

Susan Herman (12-3-01) of Brooklyn Law School vehemently urges a different approach to antiterrorism, believing the Patriot Act to be a law that throws the balance of powers out of kilter. She asserts that Congress has relinquished its power to the president, and Congress also failed to provide any room for judicial review. Congress, Herman argues, has chosen to fight terrorism by providing funding to the Bush administration, while simultaneously giving up its powers for control. Proposals coming from the administration complement congressional actions by increasing the executive power to take actions without judicial review. For Herman, the beginning of the "war on terrorism" translates to a "war on the balance of powers." Herman's argument is based in constitutional law. She compares the USA Patriot Act with two previous sweeping pieces of legislation: the 1968 Crime Control and Safe Streets Act and the 1978 Foreign Intelligence Surveillance Act (FISA). Both laws provide guidelines for domestic surveillance.

Title III of the Safe Streets Act mandates judicial review of police surveillance. Under Title III, criminal evidence cannot be gathered without prior approval from a federal court, and while a judge reviews a request for surveillance in secrecy, the police must prove that wiretaps or other means of electronic eavesdropping will lead to probable cause. FISA surveillance differs from Title III warrants. Under FISA, various forms of eavesdropping can be used to gather intelligence. A special judicial review is required before surveillance can be initiated, and any evidence gathered during the investigation cannot be used in a criminal prosecution.

The constitutional concern Herman voices partially focuses on judicial review. The courts have not been as vigilant in protecting individual rights during intelligence cases as they are in criminal trials. For example, she cites the record of FISA surveillance requests. Between 1978 and 2001 federal law enforcement officers applied for 4,275 FISA warrants. They were all granted.

In fairness to the judicial reviewers, you should remember that evidence gleaned from these warrants is not used in criminal prosecutions, but this is not the issue bothering Herman. She compares FISA warrants to the type of surveillance proposed under the Patriot Act and concludes that the Patriot Act allows the government to watch its own citizens with similar rules.

There is no guarantee that such surveillance will exclude evidence used in criminal prosecutions. The other part of Herman's argument focuses on the relationship between executive and legislative powers, and she feels the Patriot Act concentrates too much power in the executive branch. The act gives the attorney general power to detain and deport aliens with less judicial review than was required before September 11, and the attorney general is only required to have reason to believe the action is necessary. Courts, she states, would require a much higher standard of proof. The Patriot Act also gives the attorney general and the secretary of state the power to designate certain associations as terrorist groups, and they may take actions against people and organizations associated with these groups. Herman believes Congress has failed to aggressively seek a role in the Patriot Act. By increasing executive powers, the Constitution is threatened. Her primary fear, she concludes, is that increased executive powers will be used to mask an attack on civil liberties.

The American Civil Liberties Union (ACLU) (3-20-02) voices other concerns with civil liberties. Citing increased executive powers to detain immigrants, the ACLU charges the attorney general with trying to "gut" immigration courts. The ACLU expresses two concerns. First, after September 11 the attorney general ordered the detention of several hundred immigrants. He refused to openly charge most of the detainees and refused to make the list known for several months. In addition, Attorney General Ashcroft sought to have the rules for detaining and deporting immigrants streamlined. He wanted to make the process more efficient by decreasing the amount of judicial review involved in immigration and naturalization cases. These issues incensed the ACLU.

Tightening immigration laws, the ACLU argues, is a smoke screen for increasing executive powers at the expense of individual rights. The ACLU believes the attorney general will rely on political issues rather than the rules of evidence when deciding which cases to prosecute. With immigration courts streamlined, there will be no judicial body to oversee executive decisions. The ACLU also believes President Bush will appoint judges sympathetic to Attorney General Ashcroft's views. This process undermines civil liberties, the ACLU says, at the expense of the Constitution.

To demonstrate the point, the ACLU points to the post–September 11 case of Ali Maqtari. Married to a member of the armed forces, Maqtari was driving his wife to Fort Campbell, Kentucky, when police stopped him for questioning and detained him without probable cause to believe he had committed a crime. He was held for eight weeks without formal charges, according to the ACLU. After Maqtari was granted a hearing, a court ruled that the government's position was unjustified and he was released. Without effective judicial review, the ACLU says, Maqtari may not have been released. Coming to grips with terrorism should not involve scrapping personal freedoms protected by the Constitution.

The Debate Concerning Intelligence Gathering

Key Points and Questions:

1. Why does controversy erupt when state and local governments are used for national defense?

2. What type of intelligence is usually collected by state and local law enforcement agencies?

3. Does the police role change if agencies collect defense intelligence?

4. How does Best describe the function of state and local law enforcement?

Effective counterterrorism policy is based on intelligence. The 9-11 Commission Report (2004, pp. 339–348) criticizes federal agencies for failing to recognize and share intelligence. The Patriot Act, before the commission's findings, was designed to facilitate intelligence gathering and to ensure intelligence sharing. Although this remains controversial on the federal level, it is logical because the federal government is constitutionally responsible for national defense. The government can make the argument that *any* federal agency can assist in this process. The problem comes when the federal government requests assistance from state and local governments. When the federal government asks state agencies to collect and forward national defense intelligence, many people take notice.

Any attempt to use state and local law enforcement in intelligence gathering operations will have constitutional implications. The police may be used in homeland security, but there are passionate and logical positions against this and equally powerful arguments supporting it. Regardless, even when the executive branch proposes a course of action, police operations will be influenced by court decisions. Local law enforcement's role in homeland defense cannot be developed in a constitutional vacuum.

The criminal justice system collects *criminal* intelligence, not information regarding national security. It collects information when it has reasonable suspicion to believe people are involved in crimes. Although some people may argue about the type of criminal intelligence the police gather, no one questions their right to gather information about criminal activity (see Commission on Accreditation for Law Enforcement Agencies, 1990; Walker, 1992; Radelet and Carter, 2000; Carter, 2004, pp. 8–17).

The dilemma emerges because terrorism moves the police into a new intelligence realm (see Expanding the Concept: The Criminal Justice Dilemma). Criminals engage in crime for economic gain or psychological gratification. Terrorists are political actors using crime to strike their enemies. This causes terrorists to encounter the police, but not from the standpoint of traditional criminals. To gather counterterrorist intelligence, the police are forced to collect political information. If state and local law enforcement agencies are included in national defense, they will collect information having no relation to criminal investigations. No matter which position you might support, this is a dilemma for American democracy. The police are not designed to collect political information (Schmitt, 4-29-02).

While lacking a defined role, the police in the United States have traditionally been associated with crime control. They respond to crime, prevent crime, and engage in social-maintenance tasks, such as traffic control, inside local communities. Although not a formal role, the preoccupation with responding to and preventing crime has become the de facto purpose of American law enforcement. Local communities and states have empowered agencies to keep records to assist them in anticrime efforts, but many federal, state, and local laws, as well as a number of civil rights groups, have imposed limits on the type of information the police may gather and retain. Any move to include the police in an intelligence gathering system alters the expectations local communities have about law enforcement. Communities may decide to empower their police agencies to collect intelligence, but this means changing the focus of police work (see Manning, 1976).

The Criminal Justice Dilemma:
National Security or Crime Prevention and Response?

Among the controversies surrounding the USA Patriot Act is the role for criminal justice, especially law enforcement. The debate comes to a head when the role of intelligence is discussed. There are two general schools of thought about the role of the police in intelligence gathering. One position can be summarized as "eyes and ears." Advocates of this position believe that state and local law enforcement officers should be used as extensions of, or the eyes and ears of, America's intelligence agencies. They believe the police should collect information and forward it to the appropriate intelligence unit. Extreme proponents of this position would use special police units to collect information beyond potential evidence used in criminal investigations. The purpose of such units would be to monitor the activities of political groups that might engage in violence.

Another train of thought can be called traditional crime response and prevention. Supporters of this perspective fear police intelligence gathering activities will interfere with the traditional police missions of fighting crime and providing a social service. They believe that other agencies should gather intelligence. Some other people have a parallel view, fearing expanded police powers.

After September 11, the difference between these two positions became more than an academic debate. Local, state, and federal police agencies began to share information at an unprecedented level. State and local agencies expanded training activities in terrorism, and Attorney General John Ashcroft ordered the FBI to create more Joint Terrorism Task Forces (JTTFs). The attorney general also used his prosecutors, the U.S. attorneys who represent the government in the federal court system, creating Anti-Terrorism Task Forces (ATTFs) in all the nation's U.S. attorneys' offices. The name changed to Anti-Terrorist Information Coordinators (ATICs) in 2003. All the federal efforts were based on the assumption that local, state, and federal agencies would work together. The attorney general also called for a "seamless interface" between law enforcement and defense intelligence.

Terrorism, both domestic and international, poses a variety of problems; Richard Best (12-3-01) summarizes well the dilemma over the role for criminal justice. On the one hand, state and local law enforcement agencies are in a unique position to collect and analyze information from their communities. Corrections officials can perform the same role by both incarcerating terrorists and gaining information through "jailhouse intelligence." Law enforcement and correctional agencies can become the eyes and ears of domestic intelligence. On the other hand, when the criminal justice system has participated in national defense in the past, abuses have occurred. The primary question is, does criminal justice have a role in homeland security? The secondary questions become, do criminal justice agencies want to assume this role, and does the public they serve want them to assume it? There are no easy answers to these questions.

Militarization and Police Work

Key Points and Questions:

1. Have U.S. police agencies developed units that reflect military organizations?

2. What does *militarization* mean?

3. How does the International Association of Chiefs of Police view militarized police responses?

4. What trends seem to be evolving regarding the militarization of police work?

There are roles for law enforcement in homeland security, but there are questions about the necessity of developing these functions along military lines. Some policymakers have responded by increasing the military posturing of the police. In other words, some police agencies have developed units that appear more suited for military functions than police work. On the other hand, some administrators and critics stress the civilian aspect of law enforcement, and they lament the paramilitary approach to controlling social problems. The debate between these two approaches will become more intense as the police role in homeland defense is institutionalized over time.

Before discussing the issue, it is necessary to define **militarization**. Military forces are necessary for national defense, and they are organized along principles of rigid role structures, hierarchies, and discipline. A military posture prescribes unquestioning obedience to orders and aggressive action in the face of an enemy. In Clausewitz's sense (see Chapter 15), military forces are either at war or at peace, and when engaged in war, their efforts are targeted toward an enemy. Any bureaucracy can be militarized when it adopts military postures and attitudes, and the police are no exception. If the United States is engaged in a "war" against terrorism, some policymakers will inevitably want the police to look more and more like a military force, especially because the Constitution prevents the American armed forces from enforcing domestic law. In this context militarization refers to a process in which individual police units or entire agencies begin to approach specific problems with military values and attitudes. They adopt paramilitary dress, behave with military discipline, and, most importantly, prepare to make war with an enemy.

In 1967 the International Association of Chiefs of Police (IACP) discussed the problem of confronting violent demonstrators (International Association of Chiefs of Police, 1967, pp. 307–327). The late 1960s was a time of social change and violent confrontation, and state and local police frequently found themselves facing hostile crowds. In response, the police often imported military maneuvers to control violent demonstrations, and the tactics were successful. The IACP, however, was not quick to jump on a military bandwagon. The training manual instructs police officers to use minimal force to solve potential problems. The appearance of paramilitary force was a last resort, and it developed only when a situation had deteriorated. The IACP, America's largest association of state and local police executives, has traditionally favored the civil role of policing over a militaristic approach.

Terrorism may bring a change in attitudes. For example, since many forms of terrorism require resources beyond the capacity of local police agencies, law enforcement has been forced to turn to the military for assistance. State and local law enforcement agencies have few international resources compared with the defense and intelligence communities. Finally, terrorism demands a team approach. Law enforcement officers exercise quite a bit of individual discretion when operating on calls or initiating activities, and they generally work alone or in small groups of two and three. Terrorism, like special events, changes the equation, bringing hundreds of officers together in a single function. The temptation may be to militarize the police response to terrorism.

Two trends may be seen in this area. The first comes from violent demonstrations. The Metro-Dade Police Department in Florida developed a technique for responding to urban riots after a particularly bad riot in 1980. It was called the Field Force technique and it was effective. By 1995 hundreds of U.S. police agencies used the process, and it seems firmly established in the early years of the twenty-first century. The concept is based on responding to a growing disorderly crowd, a crowd that can become a precursor to a riot, with a massive show of organized police force. Officers assemble in an area away from the violent gathering; isolate the area, providing a route for the crowd to disperse; and then overwhelm it with military riot tactics. A Field Force exercise looks as though a small army has moved into an area utilizing nonlethal violence (see Christopher, 1999, pp. 398–407; Kraska and Kappeler, 1999, pp. 435–449).

A second source of militarization comes from police tactical units. These special operations units are called out to deal with barricaded gunmen, hostage situations, and some forms of terrorism. They are also frequently used on high-risk drug raids. Tactical units use military weapons, small-unit tactics, and recognized military small-unit command structures (see Cappel, 1979; Jacobs, 1983; Mattoon, 1987). In the past few years many of the units have abandoned the blue or brown tactical uniforms of police agencies for military camouflage, therefore making it virtually impossible to distinguish them from military combat units.

Peter Kraska (1996) takes exception to these trends in militarization. He argues that police in America have gradually assumed a more military posture since violent standoffs with domestic extremists, and he fears terrorism will lead to a further excuse to militarize. This will adversely affect democracy, Kraska argues, because it will lead police to picture their jurisdictions as war zones and their mission as military victory. If the problem of terrorism is militarized, other social problems will follow. Kraska's point is well taken. As Michael Howard (2002) states, calling our struggle with terrorism a "war" creates a variety of conceptual problems. In addition, Americans have become used to military metaphors for other social problems such as "wars" on drugs or poverty.

Most terrorist analysts believe terrorism is best left to the police whenever possible (see Wardlaw, 1982, pp. 87–102). The difficulty is that the growing devastation of single events sometimes takes the problem beyond local police control. In addition (Department of Defense, 1–9–01; Perl, 2001), military forces are often targeted, and they must develop forces to protect themselves. Some of the same principles guiding military force protection will eventually spill into American policing. As the future develops, state and local police may often find themselves in the midst of subtle social pressure to militarize the terrorist problem and respond to it with paramilitary force.

Summary of Main Points

1. Changes in the nature of conflict bring about a need to operate deeply in the social structure. This concept can be called *defense in depth*. Since it encompasses civil society, it is not possible to talk about such a concept with regards to homeland security without discussing civil rights.

2. The USA Patriot Act passed in 2001. Its purpose was to enhance the gathering and sharing of intelligence. It increased executive authority.

3. Supporters of the Patriot Act believe that its gives the government tools necessary for combating terrorism. Critics maintain that the Patriot Act threatens civil liberties.

4. The Patriot Act affects the doctrine of the separation of powers, *posse comitatus*, the Bill of Rights, and the Fourteenth Amendment.

5. An increase in executive powers makes criminal justice more effective, but it threatens civil liberties.

6. National defense intelligence protects the country from attack. Criminal intelligence provides information about illegal activities.

7. Criminal justice agencies protect individual civil rights. When they become involved in national defense intelligence, their focus changes.

8. Law enforcement remains a civilian entity. There is a danger when police work become militarized.

Key Terms

Make sure you can define, explain, or identify the following people, ideas, organizations, or terms:

defense in depth 292	*posse comitatus* clause 297
USA Patriot Act 294	Bill of Rights 297
national defense intelligence 295	Fourteenth Amendment 297
civil liberties 297	reasonableness 299
separation of powers 297	militarization 306

Suggested Readings

Now that you've been introduced to this topic, you can learn more by reading:

David Cole and James Dempsey, in *Terrorism and the Constitution*, compare reactions to the USA Patriot Act with overreactions in the past.

You may also want to read:

Ted Gottfried, in *Homeland Security versus Constitutional Rights*, examines both the need for security and the need for individual rights.

Bruce Schneier, in *Beyond Fear: Thinking about Security in an Uncertain World*, argues that all security involves tradeoffs, and we must realistically assess threats to focus on actual dangers.

Web Resources

Go to *http://cj.wadsworth.com/white_terrorism5e* and click on Web Links to find:

- The text of the USA Patriot Act provided by the Electronic Frontier Foundation, as well as discussions about speech, privacy, and electronic ownership
- A defense of the USA Patriot Act from the Department of Justice
- A CRS Report for Congress summarizing the USA Patriot Act
- An article from the *Christian Science Monitor* about the Patriot Act, with links to the views of supporters and opponents of the act

The Companion Website for *Terrorism and Homeland Security,* Fifth Edition

http://cj.wadsworth.com/white_terrorism5e

At the Book Companion Website you can review chapter outlines, use the flash cards to test your terrorism vocabulary, and check out the many other study aids you'll find there. You'll find valuable data and resources at your fingertips to help you study for that big exam or write that important paper.

Terrorism Updates

http://www.wadsworth.com/criminaljustice_d/special_features/ext/terrorism _site090802/index.html

Visit the *Terrorism: An Interdisciplinary Perspective* website to find the most current information about the fields of terrorism and homeland security. With a focus on domestic and international issues, this site explores the scope of terrorism in our world today. You'll find essays on important topics in terrorism and homeland security, critical thinking web activities, and InfoTrac College Edition keywords. Most importantly, the website is updated weekly with current news and research articles on domestic and international terrorism. You are invited to use these web resources to supplement your understanding of the topics covered in this chapter.

Current Perspectives: Readings from InfoTrac College Edition
Terrorism and Homeland Security

The sixteen articles in this reader offer a representative selection that helps you understand the important issues about terrorism and homeland security. It includes FREE access to InfoTrac College Edition and can also be bundled with the text for free.

Chapter 17

The Bureaucracy of Homeland Security

Homeland security not only faces the challenge of balancing civil liberties with protection, it must deal with another major obstacle: organization. The creation of the Department of Homeland Security (DHS) was one of the most massive reorganizations of government in American history. It combined several agencies ranging from the Secret Service to the Coast Guard. DHS is responsible for protecting almost every facet of American life in the homeland. It has its own intelligence analysts and is developing new capabilities. It coordinates activities with thousands of other bureaucracies on state and local levels as well as with private sector organizations; therefore, DHS must be able to relate to several differing levels of bureaucracy, and all these relationships must be negotiated.

© Matthew Staver / Bloomberg News / Landov

Bureaucracy increased after September 11, 2001. New organizations, such as the Transportation Security Administration (pictured), sprang to life, while other established agencies quickly reorganized. The creation of the Department of Homeland Security in 2002 involved a massive reorganization of federal bureaucracy. A new law transformed the command structure for the entire national security intelligence community in December 2004. Despite such sweeping changes, agencies still compete for bureaucratic power.

Chapter Objectives

After reading this chapter, you should be able to:

1. Describe the ideal bureaucracy as envisioned by Max Weber.
2. Explain the ways homeland security represents Weberian bureaucracy.
3. State the importance of law enforcement and intelligence in homeland security.
4. Outline the functions of the Department of Homeland Security.
5. Explain issues involved in border protection.
6. Define and describe infrastructure protection.
7. Describe law enforcement's relationship with DHS.
8. Explain the logic of reconstructing law enforcement on state and local levels.
9. Summarize factors that inhibit information sharing.
10. Outline Flynn's critique of homeland security.

Bureaucracy: The Weberian Ideal

Key Points and Questions:

1. What did Weber mean by *bureaucracy*?
2. How would an ideal bureaucracy work to solve a problem?
3. How do labor and management operate in an ideal bureaucracy?
4. What are the two competing views about the value of bureaucracy?
5. What two functions must be structured to meet this bureaucratic ideal?

If you have studied public administration, you have most likely encountered the classic works on bureaucracy. **Max Weber** (1864–1920), one of the founding masters of sociology, coined the term **bureaucracy** to describe professional, rational organizations. For Weber, every aspect of organizational structure was to be aimed at rationally producing a goal. In other words, people organize for a purpose and their organization should accomplish that purpose.

For example, if your purpose is to keep dirt from washing over a hill, you organize people who know how to keep dirt from washing away. You then select managers who know how to get people to accomplish the task. Managers impersonally direct the organization to build walls, dig trenches, and change drainage patterns. They do not favor friends, relatives, or tradition. They avoid people who attract others through charisma. The managers use only people who can accomplish assigned tasks. People who assist in managing are selected because they know how to manage people who can do the job. When the task is finished, dirt no longer washes over a hill. The process is rational: There is a problem, people organize to solve it, they work together, and the problem is solved. Weber believed that impersonal, professional human groups (bureaucracies) converge to solve the problems of society. Weber argued that bureaucracy should be designed to accomplish specific purposes.

In Weber's ideal, labor is to be divided into specific functions or bureaus, and all the bureaus or functions of the organization are to assemble logically to produce the whole. The bureaus work together and produce a logical outcome. Management in the organization is rationally oriented and devoid of friendship, family, or political influences. Modern bureaucratic management ideally comes from leaders who excel at leadership. There is no place for inherited leadership or popular, elected managers in Weber's bureaucracy. Every aspect of the organization centers on rational efficiency (Weber, 1947).

More than a century has passed since Weber first outlined the field that would become known as bureaucratic organizational theory. To be sure, hundreds of other scholars have filled volumes of books with organizational theories. These works range from highly theoretical psychological treatises to practical business administration guides. The sheer number of these tracts indicates the issue at hand. Running an organization is a complicated affair, and the larger and more complex the organization becomes, the more difficult it is to manage (for example, Downs, 1967; Warwick, 1975).

There are two views concerning expanded homeland security bureaucracy. Supporters of one position maintain that consolidating power is efficient. They argue that a large bureaucracy with a clear mission will empower the security forces to perform their mission. The decision to create DHS is based on this ideal (Office of Homeland Security, 2002). Proponents of a second position suggest that decentralizing power personalizes services and helps develop links to communities. They believe localized, informal offices are more adept at recognizing and handling problems. Support for this position can be found among those who seek to trim the homeland defense concept and those who favor limiting the involvement of state and local governments in a larger organization (see Another Perspective: Taking Aim at Bureaucracy). Although both ideas appear to be new in the wake of September 11, they are actually part of an ongoing issue.

Maureen Baginski: Shaking Bureaucracy

When FBI Director Robert Mueller was faced with the problem of information sharing, he looked for someone who could travel through the maze of governmental bureaucracies on several levels. He found that person in the Signals Security section of the National Security Agency. Maureen Baginski, assistant executive director for intelligence, came to the FBI in 2003 with the mandate to do something for which the Bureau was not known. She was to develop a method for sharing classified information with local police agencies.

She approached the assignment with vigor and looked for new ways of gathering and sharing information. Refusing to be hampered by federal laws protecting classified intelligence as well as agents who did not care to share information, Baginski began developing methods for FBI analysts to filter secure material while getting real-time facts to local law enforcement, facts that agencies could immediately use. She also sought to create career tracks for criminal analysts in the FBI.

General Richard Myers, chair of the Joint Chiefs of Staff, is fond of telling military people that the *need to know* has been replaced by the *need to share*. Few in government embody this notion more than Baginski. When critics maintain that bureaucracy simply cannot work, they need to look at the work of Maureen Baginski.

Sources: Author's private notes, Major City Chiefs Meeting, Washington, D.C., 4-5-04, and private discussion with Maureen Baginski at a meeting of the Bureau of Justice Assistance, Intelligence Working Group, Washington, D.C., 2004. See also Baginski (8-22-04).

The Role of Law Enforcement and Intelligence

Key Points and Questions:

1. How do intelligence agencies and law enforcement organizations deal with the issues surrounding bureaucracy?

2. How does homeland security involve intelligence and law enforcement?

3. What are the FBI's charges?

4. How does the CIA operate within this environment?

5. What is the role of DHS?

6. Do military forces have a role in the bureaucracy of homeland security?

The role of law enforcement and intelligence in homeland security is not exempted from the issues surrounding bureaucracy. Whether federal, state, or local, bureaucratic police work is a political process occurring in the context of official, routine procedures. Intelligence agencies, whether involved with the military or not, face the same problems. Both intelligence gathering and law enforcement organizations operate within the American political system. They reflect government power, and their actions have political ramifications. Internally, conflicts arise from personal rivalries, territorial fights, and power struggles. They are as much a part of these services as they are in any organization (Gaines and Cordner, 1999, pp. 179–180; see also Walker, 1992).

Homeland security involves the use of intelligence and law enforcement. The Bush administration argues that in foreign lands counterterrorism is a military problem. In the United States, however, the lead agency for counterterrorism is the FBI (Best, 12-3-01). The FBI has several charges in this realm. First, under Director Robert Mueller its charge is to prevent terrorism. Second, it is to coordinate intelligence gathering and sharing activities with the Border Patrol, Secret Service, and CIA. Third, it is to operate as partners with state and local law enforcement. Finally, since the FBI is in the Department of Justice, it is to coordinate activities with DHS and the Department of Defense (DOD). Under the intelligence reform law of 2004, all intelligence coordination must take place in the National Counterterrorism Center (NCTC) (U.S. Congress, 2004).

This face of homeland security involves a new role for the CIA. When it was originally established at the end of World War II, the CIA was supposed to be the agency that would coordinate all U.S. intelligence data, but the head of the agency, the director of central intelligence, never received the political authority to consolidate the information gathering power. In addition, the CIA was to operate apart from U.S. criminal law. It was not officially allowed to collect data on Americans inside the United States (Best, 12-3-01). Today, the situation is somewhat modified. Chastised by public outcries and the 9-11 Commission, and formally ordered by the president, the CIA is to cooperate fully with the FBI on counterterrorism intelligence (Office of Homeland Security, 2002; Baginski, 8-22-04). The FBI and CIA are to work jointly on intelligence gathering and sharing inside and outside of America's borders.

The Department of Homeland Security was created from the Office of Homeland Security in 2003. It is also charged with counterterrorism. DHS includes law enforcement agencies, such as the Secret Service, the Border Patrol, the new Immigration and Customs Enforcement, the U.S. Customs Service, and other agencies. It has its own military force, the U.S. Coast Guard, and the Coast Guard has limited law enforcement power. DHS is responsible for port security and transportation systems. It manages security in airports and the massive Transportation Security Administration. It has its own intelligence section, and it covers every special event in the United States, from political conventions to football games. It is clearly the largest organization involved in homeland security (Department of Homeland Security, 2004).

The **Department of Defense** has a limited but critical role in homeland security. It augments civilian defense, provides special operations capabilities, and interdicts terrorists before they arrive in the United States. In some cases military intelligence can also be used in counter-narcotics operations. Military forces can be used to protect the borders, and the president or Congress can request that the limitations of *posse comitatus* be suspended under the Fourth Amendment when temporarily dictated by emergency and necessity. Currently, the main military role in counterterrorism is to project American power overseas. DOD's military forces take the fight to terrorists in other lands, rather than letting terrorists become a problem within America's borders (Barnett, 2004, pp. 299–303).

This is an impressive array of American power. In theory, led by the FBI and the CIA, multiple agencies will work together to gain information, analyze it together, and share the results with every bureaucracy concerned with homeland security. *Cooperation* and *sharing* are the two passwords of the day. Not only is this a charge to federal bureaucracies, but the FBI and CIA are to create a cooperative, sharing atmosphere with thousands of state and local law enforcement agencies. And cooperation does not stop there. DHS calls on the entire system of homeland security bureaucracies to form relations with local communities and private industry. On paper this is a massive force designed to stop terrorism and protect the United States of America.

The bureaucratic problem involves a multitude of agencies. Many questions remain. The NCTC is to synthesize threat information every day. What role does each intelligence agency play? Do the analysts assigned to the NCTC report to their agencies or the NCTC? The national intelligence director is responsible for federal responses, and none of the director's agencies can force state and local law enforcement

to participate in intelligence operations. If state and local officers do participate, how do they legally gather and forward information? Do they need a criminal predicate to collect information? DHS coordinates the information network. What incentives exist for state and local law enforcement and private industry to participate in this system?

These questions can be addressed, but they are not answered in the reorganization of either government or the intelligence community. It will take imaginative, forceful leadership to coordinate this bureaucracy of bureaucracies.

Protecting the Borders

Key Points and Questions:

1. What department and agencies are responsible for border protection?
2. Where are U.S. borders vulnerable?
3. How does DHS utilize cooperation and technology?
4. What internal criticism has been leveled at border security?
5. How have local governments responded to border security?

Aside from the myriad of law enforcement– and intelligence-related functions, the federal government has another major goal: to protect America's borders. The responsibility falls on the DHS and a grouping of agencies contained within it. The main agencies include the Secret Service, the Coast Guard, Customs and Border Protection, Immigration and Customs Enforcement, the Federal Law Enforcement Training Center, the Office of Domestic Preparedness, and the Transportation Security Administration. Many of the agencies coordinate their efforts with local units of government, and many DHS personnel are armed and carry arrest power.

American borders are vulnerable in several areas. First, long stretches of unprotected areas along the northern and southern borders are open to infiltration. Second, more than three hundred seaports must be secured. Third, the DHS has agencies responsible for securing entry into the United States at airports, and it is responsible for protecting air travel once the entry points are protected. Fourth, border agents are responsible for staffing entry points along the northern and southern borders. This activity is augmented by efforts by the Coast Guard as it patrols the ocean shores and Great Lakes. Finally, another DHS agency has the task of accounting for noncitizens within U.S. borders (U.S. Department of Homeland Security, 2005).

The scope of activities is daunting, even for an agency as large as DHS, and the problems are multiplied because of the variety of functions. In some cases, such as keeping track of noncitizens, DHS cooperates with the FBI and CIA. In another case, DHS has increased the number of people who patrol the border, and it has tried to shift agents to the least secure areas. DHS also uses technology, such as **biometric measuring**—that is, identification systems based on body characteristics such as fingerprints, facial patterns, or DNA—to maintain records on aliens (U.S. Department of Homeland Security, 2005).

These functions have not come without problems. Critics say that DHS activities, broad as they may be, are not altogether effective (Flynn, 2004a, 2004b). A union representing DHS employees surveyed five hundred border patrol agents and five hundred immigration inspectors from the Border Protection and U.S. Customs divisions. The union president stated that old bureaucratic procedures leave borders unprotected, and members of the union agreed. Only 16 percent were satisfied with DHS's efforts. The majority of respondents complained of low morale. DHS administrators complained that the survey was conducted among line-level personnel (Alonso, 8-29-04).

Some DHS policies have not been popular with other countries. For example, DHS implemented a policy of fingerprinting and photographing visitors from some other countries; some of America's closest allies were exempted from the process. This policy met with a storm of criticism from nation after nation. Brazil even retaliated, requiring photographs and fingerprints from U.S. visitors to its land. DHS has also tried more advanced methods of biometric measuring, hoping to create a database of body types. Some have complained that the process was ahead of its time (CNN, 1-29-04).

Local governments have been asked to assist with **border protection**, but some of them have balked at the idea. Many local governments feel they need the trust and cooperation of foreigners living in their areas. If aliens look upon the actions of local governments with distrust, several governmental functions may be hampered. The education system will be disrupted, aliens will not seek health care, and law enforcement officials can neither get information nor serve people in the jurisdiction (National Immigration Forum, 2004).

The 9-11 Commission Report (2004, pp. 400–407) addressed the issue of border security and suggested sweeping reforms. The commission said that more than 500 million people cross U.S. borders each year, and 330 million of them are foreigners. Bureaucratic reform is essential if these crossings are to be monitored because the system before September 11 was unable to provide security or monitor foreigners in the United States. A single agency, the commission recommended, should screen crossings with a single format. In addition, an investigative agency should be established to monitor all aliens in the United States. The commission also recommended gathering intelligence on the way terrorists travel and combining intelligence and law enforcement activities to hamper their mobility. The commission suggested a standardized method for obtaining identification and wanted passports using biometric measures. In essence, the commission recommended standardizing the bureaucratic response for monitoring the entry of foreign nationals.

Infrastructure Protection

Key Points and Questions:

1. What types of bureaucracies must interact to protect the nation's infrastructure?
2. How do critics feel about efforts to protect the infrastructure?
3. How does Clarke view infrastructure protection?
4. What bureaucracy should play the leading role in infrastructure protection?

Another area concerning bureaucracy is **infrastructure protection**. Information, energy, communication, transportation, and economic systems are vulnerable to terrorist attack. Their vulnerability requires all levels of government to develop new capabilities to provide protection. The Department of Homeland Security (Office of Homeland Security, 2002, pp. xi–xii) states that law enforcement agencies will need to develop cooperative links with public and private bureaucracies, including private security organizations, educational institutions, and health care systems. Fortunately, state and local police agencies are not starting in a vacuum. The International Association of Chiefs of Police (IACP, 2001) issued guidelines to provide cooperation among all levels of government and private industry. The purpose was to identify threats to the infrastructure and defend against them (see Another Perspective: Infrastructure Protection).

Just because some units of government and private industry realize that the infrastructure needs to be protected does not mean that bureaucracies will jump to action. Critics feel too little is being done. Jeanne Cummings (8-13-02) points to two primary weaknesses. Even a year after September 11, the federal government had failed to release resources to state and local governments. State emergency planners complain they received little federal direction and no federal money. Cummings says the problem is even worse in the private security industry. Through a survey of security at America's largest shopping mall in Minnesota, Cummings concludes that federal law enforcement does little to assist private security. Keeping Americans safe, Cummings says, depends on state and local efforts outside Washington.

Richard Clarke, a former special advisor to the president with an impressive bipartisan service record, testified before the Senate Subcommittee on the Judiciary on February 13, 2002 (Clarke, 2002). He outlined many of the threats facing

Infrastructure Protection

President Clinton issued a directive declaring law enforcement to be part of the nation's critical infrastructure. Shortly after taking office, the Bush administration published a report based on the directive. Among its points are the following:

- Each law enforcement agency is responsible for the protection of its own infrastructure. The U.S. government mandates federal agencies to develop plans and encourages local agencies to do so.
- Local plans should be flexible, based on the recommended model but applicable to individual needs.
- Because police agencies use information systems, each department is asked to review its infrastructure and assess vulnerabilities. Factors recommended for the threat assessment include evaluating critical missions and capabilities, critical assets, critical interdependent relations, types of threats, and vulnerability to attack.
- Planning for protection should be based on a prioritized listing of critical services and vulnerabilities.

Source: Vatis (1999).

the nation's infrastructure, painting a grim picture. Most computer systems are vulnerable to viruses, Clarke believes, because customers will not pay for proper protection. The government has opened more communication channels with users and vendors, but more protection is needed. Clarke says the nation's power system and technological organizations that support it are vulnerable to disruptions. The Internet and computer networks that support these systems are also vulnerable to attack. Pointing to the railroad industry as an example, Clarke shows how many "low-tech" organizations have imported "high-tech" support systems. Shut down electrical grids and computers, Clarke maintains, and you'll shut down transportation and communication.

As Clarke stated in his testimony, the FBI should not have been the lead agency for infrastructure protection; the role is more suited to technological specialists. (On November 25, 2002, the Bush administration ordered the National Infrastructure Protection Center to move to DHS following Clarke's recommendation.) Extending Clarke's logic, it can also be argued that state and local law enforcement should not play the leading role in infrastructure protection. The key is to develop relationships so state and local police agencies can support security functions.

Protection of the infrastructure comes not with technical expertise equivalent to that of industrial specialists; it comes when specialists in crime fighting and protection establish critical links with the public and private organizations serving as America's infrastructure. Linkages should be developed in two crucial areas. First, the police should be linked to the security forces already associated with infrastructure functions. The American Society of Industrial Security (Azano, 2003) has made great strides in this area, and more needs to be accomplished. Second, state and local law enforcement agencies must establish formal and informal networks with the organizations in their jurisdictions, and these networks should expand to a cooperative federal system.

Michael Vatis (1999) points to another area: **cybersecurity**. Police agencies need to become involved in the protection of their own information infrastructures (see Another Perspective: Recommendations for Cybersecurity). Following the trend in most American organizations, police agencies integrate electronic management and records systems in everyday routines. If these systems are disrupted, police agencies could lose their ability to function. Surveying major agencies throughout the country, Vatis argues that infrastructure defense begins at home. He worries that law enforcement agencies are not only unprepared to defend community infrastructures, they cannot protect their own support systems.

Another Perspective

Recommendations for Cybersecurity

The Institute for Security Technology Studies at Dartmouth College recommends following the "best practices" of security in the computer industry. Best practices include the following:

▮ Update software.
▮ Enforce rigid password security.
▮ Disable unnecessary services.
▮ Scan for viruses and use virus protection.
▮ Utilize intrusion detection systems.
▮ Maintain firewalls.

Source: Vatis (2001, p. 19).

DHS, Security, and Police Work

Key Points and Questions:

1. What role do local communities and law enforcement agencies play in DHS's strategic plan?

2. What are the two categories of emergency response planning?

3. How would the addition of homeland security operations affect local law enforcement?

4. What new academic skills will be required for law enforcement officers engaged in homeland security?

One of the most important aspects of DHS's operations is communicating with local communities, law enforcement agencies, and private industries as they relate to intelligence gathering activities and infrastructure protection. DHS (2004) says that local efforts are essential to successful security plans. The International Association of Chiefs of Police (2001) believes that local law enforcement agencies will become the hinge on which all local efforts pivot. It will be the job of local law enforcement, the IACP says, to coordinate activities from a host of agencies throughout local jurisdictions all through the United States.

As envisioned by federal bureaucracy, homeland security entails coordinating efforts from several local organizations, including private industry, public service, health care systems, and law enforcement. Emergency response planning falls in two broad categories: prevention and reaction (Cilluffo, Cardash, and Lederman, 2001). State and local agencies assume expanded roles in this concept because they are the obvious choice for prevention, and they will be among the first to respond to a domestic attack. If local agencies assume such a role, law enforcement officers will be forced to rethink the ways they do business.

As discussed in Chapter 16, national defense intelligence is a function of the federal government. As local agencies become involved in homeland security, they will need to think beyond criminal intelligence. Two new functions become apparent. They must become involved in assessing threats in their jurisdictions. They must also learn to recognize possible items that may add to national defense intelligence and develop routines to forward such information. This creates a legal problem because law enforcement agencies need to have a reasonable suspicion that criminal activity is taking place before they can collect information (see Carter, 2004; O'Conner, 11-2-04).

If engaged in homeland security, state and local police agencies will need to expand the role of traditional law enforcement. On the most rudimentary level, officers could be assigned to security tasks and trained to look for information beyond the violation of criminal law. On a more sophisticated level, police intelligence units could be established to gather and pass on intelligence information. The most effective initial practice would be to train patrol officers, investigators, and narcotics officers to look for indicators of terrorism during their daily activities. This would be an effective method of enhancing intelligence, but critics fear government infringement on civil liberties (see Chapter 16, and Cole and Dempsey, 2002, pp. 186–187).

Assuming that local law enforcement agencies will collect information only within the context of criminal investigations, bureaucratic problems remain. The process of gathering defense intelligence is not readily apparent in American policing. Most law enforcement officers did not enter police ranks thinking that they were joining an army or aspiring to be part of DHS. Their motivation generally focuses on the elimination of crime, not national defense. In addition, local police policies and employment incentives reinforce their original notions. Officers are encouraged to maintain a local view, and police managers reinforce pragmatic actions while discouraging abstract thinking. Police work is extremely political, and law enforcement officers think locally. To paraphrase former speaker of the House Tip O'Neill's maxim, "All law enforcement politics are local." The goal is not to alienate constituencies, but to develop deep community ties to help keep information flowing. Information about suspects, crimes, and criminal activity translates into power and successful individual performance with police agencies, and it solves crimes (Manning, 1976, p. 35).

State and local officers are not rewarded for thinking in terms of international issues or national security. Chiefs and sheriffs do not usually praise abstract reasoning. In an early critique of collegiate criminal justice programs, Lawrence Sherman (1978) claims that higher education has done little to help this situation. Criminal justice programs do not produce abstract, critical thinkers for law enforcement, Sherman believes; they impart skills. According to a recent survey by *Police: The Law Enforcement Magazine*, graduates steeped in academic preparation are not as welcome in law enforcement agencies as recruits with military experience (July 2002). Discipline and the willingness to obey orders are more important than individual thinking and creativity.

Modern terrorism is an abstract, nebulous concept fluctuating according to historical and political circumstances. To combat terrorism, security forces require groups of people with abstract reasoning skills, knowledge of international politics and history, and specialized expertise in particular regions (Betts, 2002). If the police are to participate as full partners in this process, they must bring skilled specialists to the table. The ethos behind policing, however, rejects this logic. American law enforcement relishes pragmatic information with immediate applicability on the beat.

Localized attitudes bring contempt from intelligence agencies. Unlike analysts in defense intelligence, state and local police officers frequently exhibit no concern for in-depth background information, the kind of information needed to understand intelligence. As a result, intelligence bureaucracies frequently question police competence. In-

Another Perspective

New Approaches to Mission

If state and local law enforcement officers were to begin looking for signs of terrorism, they would need to frame basic questions about potential adversaries. For example, in addition to criminal briefings before patrol or investigative tours, officers would need to think of questions such as the following:

- What is the M.O. of our enemy?
- How does the enemy's organization function?
- What types of tactics will the enemy use?
- What types of weapons will the enemy use?
- How can information be gathered while protecting the source?
- What activities in the community might indicate that terrorists may be operating in a jurisdiction?
- How can information be shared securely with other agencies?

telligence analysts know information is not usually valuable until it is categorized and placed within social and political contexts. If police agencies are unable to engage in this type of examination, intelligence organizations are hesitant to form partnerships with them. These factors present enormous problems as the DHS tries to create a network of information.

Possible Approaches for Homeland Security Bureaucracies

Key Points and Questions:

1. How might law enforcement become involved in homeland security?
2. Why are Joint Terrorism Task Forces applicable to state and local law enforcement?
3. Who might object to using local law enforcement in homeland security?
4. Have other nations used law enforcement in this manner?

The organizational processes inhibiting law enforcement intelligence gathering and sharing do not eliminate police participation in homeland defense. Many alternatives can be developed within legal guidelines. Critics like Cole and Dempsey (2002) believe that gathering security information in the course of criminal investigations is both legal and effective. Intelligence specialists like David Carter (2004) approach from the other side of the spectrum, but they reach a similar conclusion. For example, rather than bringing police officers into the intelligence process as full partners, police officers could be trained to look for indicators of terrorism in the course of normal operations and to pass the information along. Trained police officers may expand their efforts by creating public and private partnerships through community policing efforts.

Another alternative for state and local agencies is to combine training in alertness with specialized training for selected officers. Rather than bringing an entire department into intelligence gathering operations, select units could engage in counterterrorist activities. This is the logic behind the FBI's **Joint Terrorism Task Force (JTTF)**. These units combine local, state, and various federal police officers, as well as corrections officials and prosecutors, in regional units designed to combat terrorism. Local and state officers are given federal authority, while the presence of such officers gives federal agents the ability to act in local jurisdictions. The JTTFs have been effective in many cases (Watson, 2002).

On the surface JTTFs seem tailored to the needs of state and local law enforcement, but in some cases they meet opposition. Local governments have refused to allow their police forces to assist in counterterrorist activities, and some jurisdictions refuse to share criminal intelligence with federal law enforcement. Civil libertarians sometimes see the formation of a JTTF as too great of a consolidation of government power. In addition, although academics and government officials are fond of using the phrase "criminal justice system," the courts are not part of the system because they do not belong to the executive branch. State and federal courts may well limit the role of local agencies in homeland security, especially in intelligence gathering activities.

On the other hand, police are in a perfect position to engage in intelligence gathering activities and expand their role in national defense. Other Western democracies have done this quite successfully, including France and Germany. The Canadians and British accomplished the same thing while keeping more of a public service model than the French or the Germans. The security role can be formalized, but many factors inhibit the process.

Bureaucratic Inhibitors

Key Points and Questions:

1. List the organizational factors that must be overcome before local agencies can be used in homeland security.

2. Does the FBI always have good relations with local law enforcement?

3. Do various federal law enforcement agencies compete with each other?

4. What is the vested political interest in local governmental control?

5. What is "the bureaucracy problem"?

Unlike the ideal rational organizations envisioned by Weber, public service organizations have foibles that emerge in the everyday social construction of reality. Personalities are important, varying levels of competency limit or expand effectiveness, and organizations tend to act in their own interests.

If all the organizations involved in homeland security agree to pool their efforts, several bureaucratic hurdles need to be cleared (see Swanson, Territo, and Taylor, 2001, pp. 643–644; Best, 12-3-01; Bodrero, 2002; Mitchell and Hulse, 6-27-02). Some of the important issues include the following.

FBI versus Police and Sheriff's Departments

In October 2001, FBI Director Robert Mueller attended the IACP meeting in Toronto, Ontario. According to police chiefs who attended the meeting, it was not a pleasant experience. State and local law enforcement executives criticized Mueller for failing to share information. According to several private comments from FBI agents, Mueller vowed this would never happen again. American law enforcement would witness a new FBI. Despite the intentions of the most forceful bureaucratic leaders, however, orders do not always go as planned. There have been success stories with information sharing, but there have also been tales of woe. Many American police executives are not convinced that the FBI is in partnership with efforts to stop terrorism (Levitt, 1-28-02).

The purpose here is not to condemn the FBI, but to acknowledge a bureaucratic issue. Many state and local police executives do not trust the FBI, and the attitude extends down through the ranks of law enforcement agencies. If police in America are to become part of homeland defense, the relationship between the FBI and state and local law enforcement must improve (Riordan and Zegart, 7-5-02).

Federal Law Enforcement Rivalries

Unfortunately, federal law enforcement agencies mistrust one another at times, and their failure to cooperate in some circumstances influences local police relationships. Many federal law enforcement agencies openly resent the FBI, and this attitude is frequently reciprocated. In addition, the creation of new bureaucracies such as the Transportation Security Administration exacerbates rivalries. In the real world of bureaucracy, organizations on every level frequently act out of self-interest rather than concern with an overall mission (Valburn, 2-4-02).

Advocates of Local Control

Some people feel cooperation between state and local law enforcement will result in the de facto concentration of police power. This attitude was alive and well at the turn of the twentieth century when state police agencies were forming. Many local governments believed that state police forces had too much power, and many states limited these agencies to patrolling state highways. Civil libertarians believe that consolidated police power will erode civil rights. Local government officials worry that their agendas will be lost in federalization. The bureaucratic arguments extend beyond these interest groups (Hitt and Cloud, 6-10-02).

The Problem of Legal Bureaucracy

Another factor inhibiting police cooperation is the legal bureaucracy of criminal justice. Samuel Walker (1985) points out that the criminal justice system is actually not a system at all, but a multifaceted bureaucracy with intersecting layers. Drawing on earlier research, he refers to the process quite humorously as the "wedding cake model." Rather than a smooth flow among police, courts, and corrections, Walker sees a model based on plea bargaining, celebrated cases, and long-term punishment for the worst offenders.

Each entity in the criminal justice system is independent, although it interacts with the other parts. There is no overall leader, and law enforcement, courts, and correctional agencies refuse to accept single management. From the Constitution's perspective, the courts are hardly designed to fit into a criminal justice system. While police and correctional institutions represent the executive branch of government, the courts autonomously belong to the judicial branch (del Carmen, 1991, pp. 275–277). Efforts to increase the efficiency of homeland defense will not change these relationships.

The Bureaucracy Problem

The federal government cannot assume that the reforms will carry over into state and local governments. The states may cooperate with the federal government, but they are not mandated to do so. The states and their local governments have entrenched bureaucracies with their own managerial structures and agendas. These organizations will not suddenly change methods of operation simply because centralized executive authority has mandated new policies for homeland defense. In a nutshell, this is the epitome of the "bureaucracy problem," yet it does not imply that state and local governments will automatically reject chances to participate. Change can happen, and may even be welcome, if federal agencies enter into cooperative relationships with their local counterparts (Liptak, 5-31-02; see also Downs, 1967; Warwick, 1975).

Some advocates believe federal reform has pointed the way. A 1995 attempt to reduce paperwork in federal government is one example. An earlier effort came in the 1978 Civil Service Reform Act where special executives were given managerial authority and placed in performance-based positions.

Yet, managing homeland security will still require attention to the issues raised in this chapter. Large organizations are difficult to manage, and problems increase rapidly when organizational effectiveness requires cooperation on several levels. Homeland security calls for new alliances among federal agencies and cooperative relations among local, state, and federal levels of government.

If the DHS can create effective partnerships with intelligence and law enforcement agencies on the federal level, it could focus attention on these issues. However, homeland security becomes a problem much larger than gathering and analyzing information. In addition, there is a problem beyond the scope of this chapter: responding to an event. Response involves massive coordination among agencies. Fortunately, all levels of government have extensive experience in this realm. The problem appears in *preventing* terrorism, and prevention requires bureaucratic change. Powerful bureaucrats and bureaucratic procedures do not change easily.

Stephen Flynn's Critique of the Ideal

Key Points and Questions:

1. According to Flynn, what are two reasons America is squandering opportunities for defense?
2. How does Flynn view national security and homeland security?
3. What evidence does he cite to show we are not protecting the infrastructure?
4. How is private industry involved in securing the homeland?
5. How do Jihadists view economic attacks?
6. What benefits does Flynn see from a real security system?

Stephen Flynn, a senior fellow in national security studies at the Council on Foreign Relations (2002, 2004a, 2004b), believes the goals of homeland security are crucial but that America's bureaucracies and leadership are squandering the opportunity to really defend the United States. Flynn says America has made two crucial mistakes. First, homeland security has been separated from national security. Second, the infrastructure is vulnerable to attack. Although all of the rhetoric is in place for homeland security, the reality is that the United States has not organized its resources for defense.

Flynn vehemently argues that homeland security should be part of a national strategy to defend the United States. America needs to be able to strike a blow as well as to take one. Although both parties speak of the war on terrorism, the problem is not something that can be destroyed only by fighting in other areas of the world. There is no central front, Flynn argues, and America cannot always project its power to fight elsewhere. The United States has prepared to fight overseas while neglecting to protect the home front.

To illustrate the point, Flynn points to the use of weapons of mass destruction. According to the CIA, the most likely scenario for smuggling weapons of mass destruction into the United States is by sea. It is difficult to inspect all of the cargo containers in seaports; therefore, the oceans represent an opportunity for terrorists. Flynn points out that the Bush administration has done very little to protect the nation's 361 seaports. All of the rhetoric is there, but there is not sufficient action. He is incredulous because in 2004 the United States spent more money every three days to fight the war in Iraq than it has in three years of protecting seaports.

The nation's critical infrastructure remains open to attack, Flynn says. In the 2005 military budget, the Department of Defense was allotted $7.6 billion to enhance the fortifications of its bases. In the same budget, the infrastructure for the *entire* nation will receive only $2.6 billion. Dirty bombs and chemical threats can be

Another Perspective

Infrastructure Problems in the DOE

"60 Minutes" reporter Ed Bradley examined the Department of Energy and its nuclear facilities. It has many problems, including the following concerns:

■ Stolen keys to secure facilities that were not replaced for three years.

■ Guards were sleeping on duty.

■ Facilities were penetrated during mock terrorist attacks.

Bradley's report concluded that America's nuclear facilities are protected on paper but that DOE has not implemented real security measures.

Source: Bradley (8-29-04).

developed from hazardous material, yet over the past three years funds have been drastically reduced to secure the disposal of such material. Police and firefighters have been cut even though they are crucial for security.

Flynn also sees a problem in strategic thinking in DHS and other agencies. For example, the scientific and medical communities are essential elements of homeland security. Nearly 50 percent of the scientific and medical personnel employed by the federal government will retire before 2010. Currently, they are not being replaced quickly enough. The colleges and universities that would produce them are underfunded. In addition, the federal government has virtually ignored private industry, claiming that it is responsible for protecting its own infrastructure. However, Flynn finds that private industry is not doing this.

Although the United States needs enhanced border security, increased border protection will not protect America against terrorist attack. Security is a dynamic process that combines intelligence, military, and law enforcement power. It requires coordination and cooperation internationally. Attacks are planned overseas and it is possible to infiltrate and build infrastructures. Flynn says America needs an integrated system for defense.

Flynn believes that Jihadists are fully aware of vulnerabilities in the infrastructure. They will not simply let the United States bring the fight to them; they intend to strike, and the safest and most effective way to hit America is to strike the infrastructure. Jihadists understand the economic effect of their actions. For example, Flynn says that if terrorists managed to shut down America's closed container operations for just three weeks, the whole world could be thrown into an economic recession.

Flynn urges policymakers to reinvent homeland security. Defense at home is as important as the ability to wage military action overseas. DHS and other federal bureaucracies should think of security from a broad perspective. There are many benefits for doing so. Flynn argues that developing an integrated system against terrorism would reduce the drug trade, contraband smuggling, and theft. These are residual benefits for a strategic program, he believes.

The best current model for homeland security is the air industry. Although it experiences horrific periodic disasters, people continue to fly. Flynn believes this is because of the faith people have in the air transportation system. They know that failures, while inevitable, are an aberration. They continue to use the system because they *believe* it is safe. Flynn says homeland security should have the same goal. In a system of civil defense, people have a civic responsibility to maintain the system. When bureaucracies recover from failure, people will *believe* in their own safety and continue to function. This is the goal of bureaucracy, Flynn argues. Americans must be able to absorb a major attack and continue to function.

Summary of Main Points

1. Max Weber's ideal bureaucracy rationally organized people under goal-oriented leaders. Workers and managers were selected for their abilities only.

2. Most American governmental organizations, the military, and some private industry base their structures on the Weberian ideal of bureaucracy.

3. Many bureaucracies are involved in homeland security, and their most important functions center around law enforcement and activities related to intelligence.

4. DHS has assumed many roles in homeland security. It coordinates activities with DOD, the FBI, and the CIA. It must also work with state and local agencies.

5. Border protection involves ports of entry, seaports, border checkpoints, ocean shores, and vast expanses of land on the northern and southern borders.

6. Infrastructure protection refers to security provided for the underpinnings of social life, such as roadways, computer networks, bridges, electrical grids, and pipelines.

7. If state and local law enforcement agencies are to take part in homeland security, the mission needs to be reconceived. Making the needed changes seems to make sense, but several factors work against change.

8. Flynn maintains that the focus on homeland security is misplaced. People and products coming into the country need to be checked and monitored. America needs to become resilient to recover from terrorist strikes.

Key Terms

Make sure you can define, explain, or identify the following people, ideas, organizations, or terms:

Max Weber   311
bureaucracy   311
Department of Defense   314
biometric measuring   316
border protection   316

infrastructure protection   317
Richard Clarke   317
cybersecurity   319
Joint Terrorism Task Force
  (JTTF)   322

Suggested Readings

Now that you've been introduced to this topic, you can learn more by reading:

Stephen Flynn's *America the Vulnerable* is a hard-hitting, no-nonsense overview of the problems facing homeland security. A retired Coast Guard officer, Flynn thoroughly examines security risks and infrastructure vulnerabilities. He makes several recommendations for organizing America's bureaucracies. This is one of the most important books in the field.

You may also want to read:

Anthony Cordesman's *Terrorism, Asymmetric Warfare, and Weapons of Mass Destruction* gives an integrated view from military and civil defense perspectives.

The 9-11 Commission Report assessed several organizational issues involved in homeland security.

To understand how bureaucracies function and the way they distribute power, see *Bureaucracy: What Government Agencies Do and Why They Do It*, by James Q. Wilson.

Web Resources

Go to *http://cj.wadsworth.com/white_terrorism5e* and click on Web Links to find:

- An article from the Committee on Government Reform titled "What's the Hold Up?: A Review of Security Clearance Backlog and Reciprocity Issues Plaguing Today's Government and Private Sector Workforce"
- A report on Border Transportation and Security from the Congressional Research Service (CRS), as well as a complete listing of CRS reports
- The position of the Department of Homeland Security on securing the country's borders
- A critique of the DHS role in intelligence from Justin Rood of the *Congressional Quarterly*

The Companion Website for *Terrorism and Homeland Security*, Fifth Edition

http://cj.wadsworth.com/white_terrorism5e

At the Book Companion Website you can review chapter outlines, use the flash cards to test your terrorism vocabulary, and check out the many other study aids you'll find there. You'll find valuable data and resources at your fingertips to help you study for that big exam or write that important paper.

Terrorism Updates

http://www.wadsworth.com/criminaljustice_d/special_features/ext/terrorism _site090802/index.html

Visit the *Terrorism: An Interdisciplinary Perspective* website to find the most current information about the fields of terrorism and homeland security. With a focus on domestic and international issues, this site explores the scope of terrorism in our world today. You'll find essays on important topics in terrorism and homeland security, critical thinking web activities, and InfoTrac College Edition keywords. Most importantly, the website is updated weekly with current news and research articles on domestic and international terrorism. You are invited to use these web resources to supplement your understanding of the topics covered in this chapter.

Current Perspectives: Readings from InfoTrac College Edition
Terrorism and Homeland Security

The sixteen articles in this reader offer a representative selection that helps you understand the important issues about terrorism and homeland security. It includes FREE access to InfoTrac College Edition and can also be bundled with the text for free.

Chapter 18

The Media: Affecting Terrorism and Homeland Security

© Mario Tama/Getty Images

Reporters look over transcripts of emergency calls made at the World Trade Center on September 11, 2001, released by the Port Authority of New York and New Jersey, August 2003, in New York City. The media dominates most impressions of terrorism through dramatic stories created for television.

The scene became all too familiar in 2004: A man stood behind a blindfolded and rope-bound hostage, reading a religious proclamation about both the hostage and the symbol he represented. Although the doomed hostage was the real victim, the terrorist and his colleagues portrayed themselves as the casualties of an unjust world. They believed themselves to be victims throughout all history, and the murder they were about to commit would partially atone for this injustice. After the proclamation was complete, the terrorist kicked his hostage to the floor, pulled out a long knife, and beheaded the hostage while crying out, "God is great!" Scenes like this played out time and time again on a powerful force multiplier: the Internet. An Algerian Jihadist once said that he would rather kill one European in front of a camera than kill a hundred in the desert. Modern terrorism is a media phenomenon, and its power can help or hinder homeland security.

Chapter Objectives

After reading this chapter you should be able to:

1. Discuss the relationship between terrorism and television.
2. Explain the media as a force multiplier.
3. List the ways terrorists, security forces, and governments try to use the media as a weapon.
4. Describe the effects of growing international media and the Internet on terrorism.
5. Explain the tension between security forces and the media.
6. Discuss the contagion effect of media coverage.
7. Debate the issues of freedom of the press and censorship.

Television and Terrorism: A Cozy Relationship

Key Points and Questions:

1. Why is television related to terrorism?
2. How has twenty-four-hour news coverage changed terrorism?
3. How does TV reporting try to create perpetual drama?
4. Is there a pattern for reporting drama?
5. What is the Infotainment Telesector?
6. How does the Infotainment Telesector threaten homeland security?

Over the years, several studies have pointed to the close relationship between terrorism and television. H. H. A. Cooper (1977a) was one of the first analysts to point to the issues, explaining that terroristic acts were made-for-TV dramas. Abraham Miller (1982) published one of the first books on the subject, pointing out that television brought terrorist events into our homes. More recently, Yassen Zassoursky (2002) says that television and the Internet give terrorists an immediate international audience. Gadt Wolfsfeld (2001) says terrorist acts have become so graphic and sensational that they cannot help but grab media attention. Alex Schmid and Janny de Graaf (1982) say that the relationship between terrorism and the media is so powerful that Western democracies may need to take drastic actions to limit unrestricted media coverage of terrorist events and even implement **censorship**. Recently, Ted Koppel of ABC News summed the situation by stating television and terrorism go together (Smith, 2005).

The media are powerful tools, especially television and its twenty-four-hour news stations. They have changed the nature of terrorism because one of their goals is to increase the number of viewers. News programming provides information, but it is also designed to keep audiences watching. Viewers attract the companies that will spend money for advertising and thereby generate television's profits. Accordingly, Levin (2003) says that one of the purposes of television news coverage is to keep the audience primed with emotion and excitement. The next exciting event is always just around the corner. Of course, the report will come after a series of commercials, but it will include a breath-taking, on-the-scene interview with the reporter covering the story. Terrorism is perfect for this scenario because it is so dramatic. The story need not be about terrorism, however; any drama will do.

Bad weather, for example, is a gift to television, and the pattern used to cover storms is the same as that used to report dramatically about terrorism (see Another Perspective: TV News Drama Patterns). You can see these similarities in an example of how a local TV station covered a recent change in the weather. One spring day in West Michigan the sky grew grayer than usual, the wind kicked up, and thunderclouds spilled down buckets of rain. Although the weather was nothing out of the ordinary for the time of the year, a local television station interrupted programming, announcing a thunderstorm warning.

A meteorologist sat confidently behind a desk, calmly walking the audience through the Doppler radar display and explaining that the rain would continue for at least half an hour. He frequently shifted to on-the-scene reporters in surrounding communities. As the camera beamed in, the meteorologist asked the reporters what the weather was like. Each reporter stood in the rain, holding a microphone in one hand and an umbrella in the other. They reported that it was raining. One reporter suggested that such weather could lead to a tornado watch. Back in the studio the meteorologist expressed concern but reassured the audience that this was merely a thunderstorm. The National Weather Service had issued no tornado watch. Nevertheless, one on-the-scene reporter retorted, we could not be too careful, and if there was a tornado watch, this station would be the first to report it. The audience should stay tuned for further developments.

Examine how the reporting events unfolded and look for a pattern common to other kinds of reporting. You may be able to see the structure of **TV news drama patterns**. The central theme was weather, the essence of the drama. The reporters provided news, and they packaged the story in a manner to persuade their audience of its importance. Viewers were encouraged to "stay tuned" because the drama was constantly unfolding. The station provided the expert interpreter, the meteorologist—a scientist who alone was qualified to explain the drama. He was supported by a cast of information gatherers standing in the rain.

Other issues were present. The report gave the illusion that somehow the audience could be in control of the situation if they would only absorb the information provided by the meteorologist and his supporting cast. The meteorologist, the prime reporter or anchor, calmly organized the facts and arranged them in an entertaining manner. Whether the weather, Monday Night Football, or terrorism is being reported, these are basic elements in the pattern of television drama. Any subject will suffice if it generates an audience.

David Levin (2003) examines this process, drawing on the work of earlier sociologists. He says that such reporting patterns are packaged in segments called **news frames**. The purpose of a news frame is to assemble words and pictures to create a pattern surrounding an event. The news becomes a symbolic representation of an event in which the audience is allowed to participate from a distance. Television and other media "spin" the event so that it can be translated into the understanding of popular culture. They use rhetoric and popular images to set the agenda, and drama becomes the hook to attract an audience. H. H. A. Cooper (1977a) was one of the first scholars to demonstrate that terrorism matched this pattern perfectly.

Cooper says that terrorism fits the pattern so well because it is made for television. Its life-and-death drama unfolds in ways that demand attention, and television reporters gravitate toward it. Before being too critical of the media, however, the reason that television is so quick to pounce on a terrorist event is that its audiences want to watch it. It is perpetual drama that draws attention. Audiences like the drama and watch it.

Douglas Kellner (2002) knows that terrorism attracts attention, but he is critical of America's typical news frame. After September 11, Kellner says, American television presented only one news frame: The attack was a clash of civilizations, and only a military response would stop future attacks. He says that Jihadists also recreated the same simplistic pattern. Television beat the war drum and called in a variety of terrorism experts who reflected the single view. Radio was even worse, Kellner argues, engaging in sensationalistic right-wing propaganda. (Note that many media personalities would say that academia offers its own propaganda from the other side of the political spectrum.)

Benjamin Barber (1996, pp. 76–83) analyzes the problems of news frames and popular mind-sets in *Jihad vs. McWorld*. The title suggests that he is examining the world of the Jihadists, but he is really looking at global economic inequities and the resulting ideologies that drive people into different systems. Instead of moving people to discuss solutions to problems, Barber believes, the media flourish on one overriding factor: entertainment. He humorously calls the news networks the **Infotainment Telesector**.

The Infotainment Telesector is not geared for depth; it is designed to create revenue. "News" becomes banter between a news anchor and a guest, and debates evolve into shouting matches between controversial representatives of particular positions. Issues are rarely discussed with the support of data or public policy analysis. Hosts perpetually interrupt their guests, or they provide their own answers to the questions they ask, using pithy justifications for their rudeness like "no spin zone" or "hardball." Many shows are driven by pleasing personalities who do not explore topics in depth. Morning news shows are full of interviewers who reveal common knowledge, and reporters often interview other reporters about information, rather than doing an in-depth analysis of an event from differing perspectives (see Expanding the Concept: Attracting the Lowest Common Denominator). Some networks even play emotional music when showing scenes from the news frame (see Franklin, 3-31-03).

The nature of the Infotainment Telesector and the desire of networks to beat other networks have a negative effect on homeland security. Competing news outlets may leak documents, unveil confidential plans, and expose vulnerabilities. Although the media try not to cooperate with terrorists, terrorists continually increase the dramatic violence to attract coverage. When the drama is compelling, news footage is constantly replayed, giving the illusion that attacks are repeated over and over. (As an example, consider the number of times during the weeks following September 11 you saw the World Trade Center towers crumble.) News hosts spend time interviewing reporters from the field who speculate on the facts surrounding an event. This leads to a dilemma for policymakers. Freedom of the press is guaranteed by the First Amendment, but television coverage frequently becomes part of the story it is covering.

The Media as a Force Multiplier

Key Points and Questions:

1. What happened to the Western monopoly on mass media communication?
2. How has this loss changed perceptions of U.S. foreign policy?
3. How did Hezbollah learn to use television?
4. How has television affected the al Aqsa Intifada?
5. In what ways can movies and the Internet become force multipliers?

When television news coverage first started, the West—the United States in particular—not only enjoyed an edge in mass media broadcasts, it had a virtual monopoly. America broadcasted its versions of truth both domestically and abroad, and American news has always been self-absorbed. As communication venues expanded, other countries began to present news from other perspectives, and nations outside the West viewed the world much differently from the way Americans did. In the 1990s a new Arab television network, **al Jazeera**, began broadcasting news from an Arab perspective (National Public Radio, 7-9-04). Terrorists found they could use the expansion of the mass media to reach audiences in new ways.

At first, terrorists reached audiences with drama. The Popular Front for the Liberation of Palestine hijacked four airliners in 1970. They destroyed three of them with explosives in the Jordanian desert and detonated the other one in Cairo as television cameras covered the explosions. As time went on, terrorists realized that hostage dramas were made for television. In 1985 Lebanese associated with Hezbollah hijacked a TWA flight with 145 passengers. The media not only covered the event, one American television network even broadcasted the arrival of U.S. commandos, causing terrorist to disperse hostages from the aircraft throughout Beirut.

Terrorists in Asia used hostages in a similar manner, and media coverage in hostage incidents often had the effect of placing security forces on the defensive. If terrorists could successfully manipulate the situation, they could portray both hostages and themselves as victims while police and military forces appeared to be aggressors (Wilkinson, 1997). In 1999 hijackers of an Indian airliner put the concept into practice, using press coverage as leverage to pressure the Indian government. As the West lost its monopoly on the electronic media, other networks began covering events from different perspectives (Harsono and Eriyanto, 3-3-03).

The growth of media outlets and competing perspectives on the news has had a huge effect on the way the United States is viewed around the world, and this effect extends to perceptions of terrorism and America's foreign policy. For example, the Mid East Forum (2004) made note of a program dealing with the Clinton administration's embargo on Iraq during the 1990s. When asked whether Iraqi citizens suffered under the embargo, Secretary of State Madeleine Albright admitted that they did. She also said that children were particularly affected, but the gains against Saddam Hussein justified the suffering of innocent children. The Forum points out that this statement was played once in the United States, and most Americans agreed that the embargo was worth it, wanting to keep weapons of mass destruction out of Saddam Hussein's grasp. The same message played dozens of times in the Middle East, however, where it was commonly believed that hundreds of thousands of Iraqi children were starving to death. The Forum concludes that one program changed the way many Arabs viewed the United States.

A point of view presented from various perspectives changed the way U.S. foreign policy was perceived, but the power of the media goes further than this. Organizations have learned they can manipulate the media to get their message across. For instance, Hezbollah projected a positive image on **al Manar**, Lebanese national television, as the Israelis withdrew from Lebanon and again during the al Aqsa Intifada (Harik, 2004, pp. 160–161, 189).

Al Manar television presented a sympathetic view of the al Aqsa uprising, and Hezbollah was quick to take advantage of al Manar's twenty-four-hour coverage. The method of reporting was the key to success. The news was interspersed with inspirational religious messages. Hezbollah was able to get al Manar to focus on its role in the Intifada and to run programs on Hezbollah's former glories. In an effort to demoralize the Israelis, al Manar broadcasted pictures of Israeli casualties and ended with the question, Who will be next?

Power came to Hezbollah in the form of visual images. Judith Harik (2004) believes al Manar television helped to elevate Hezbollah to heroic status. She cites one example that swept through Lebanon. Faced with heavy fighting in a West Bank village, Israeli forces withdrew, but the Israeli Defense Force (IDF), through Israeli mass media, denied that it had abandoned the village. Al Manar presented another view. When the Israelis withdrew, Hezbollah fighters entered the village along with Palestinian mujahadeen. Hezbollah raised its flag over the village, and someone took a picture. As the IDF was denying it had retreated, al Manar showed the village with the Hezbollah flag flying high overhead. Hezbollah achieved a media victory.

Gadt Wolfsfeld (2001) says that such media victories are crucial. During the al Aqsa Intifada both sides tried to use the media, and Wolfsfeld believes there are lessons to be learned from this experience. Struggles for the way a battle is reported are as important as combat on the battlefield. Neither side wants to be portrayed as the aggressor. The Palestinians know that sensational television coverage presents one of their best chances to receive outside intervention, while Israel practices damage control. Both sides have structures for capturing media attention and presenting their respective views (see Another Perspective: Fighting for the Media).

Wolfsfeld also believes the media are the primary tools for demonizing the enemy, and the most powerful tool is the way television reports casualties. Both sides use the same pattern. One side presents its own casualties in compassionate and horrific terms, while casualties on the other side are described as mere statistics. Although radio and print media are important, television takes center stage because it can show bloody images. The worst images are shown many times over on the twenty-four-hour networks.

The media make conflict worse in a subtle way, Wolfsfeld believes, because drama dwindles when news organizations report peace efforts. Most reports about peace efforts are stories of breakdowns and failures. When an explosion threatens peace talks or terrorists behead a hostage after fighting has ended, television, radio, and newspaper reporters flood the world with gruesome stories. Negotiations during the al Aqsa Intifada are not dramatic, Wolfsfeld notes, but explosions and machine gun fire are riveting. The only time peace becomes dramatic is when heads of state sign major treaties. Unfortunately, violence is more frequent.

The Internet is one of the most important force multipliers easily available to terrorists. Natalya Krasnoboka (2002) says that research shows the electorate in most countries is gravitating to online reporting and discussion. Many people think the Internet will make countries more democratic, while other media analysts believe it will have no more effect than traditional news sources. Krasnoboka says that empirical evidence presents a different conclusion. The Internet does not have an overwhelming effect in democratic countries, but it is a powerful tool for opposition forces in authoritarian regimes.

Krasnoboka says the Internet is gaining the attention of security forces. When the media is heavily controlled, online communication brings the only measure of freedom, and it is emerging as a major source of information. By extending Krasnoboka's logic, it would seem that when two sides engage one another, they would see the Internet as a propaganda tool. Indeed, Krasnoboka concludes, this is exactly what happens under authoritarian regimes. Governments try to control the Internet for their own purposes. They see its potential as a weapon for opposition and revolution.

Terrorists understand the power of the Internet and its potential as a force multiplier. They run their own websites, and they sometimes hack into existing sites to broadcast propaganda videos. They also imbed pixels in legitimate websites to transmit secret communications. Yassen Zassoursky (2002) says these abilities enhance the power of terrorist groups, and he believes that the Internet's communication capabilities allow terrorist groups an opportunity to attack the global community. Sonia Liff and Anne Sofie Laegren (2003) reinforce Zassoursky's thesis by pointing to Internet cafés, which they say enhance the Internet's striking power because they make communication untraceable.

The cinema is another venue for both assisting terrorism and distorting issues. Medhi Semati (2002) points out that movies create popular images that can be used for the purposes of propaganda. The American image of a terrorist is generally a cinematic picture, and terrorists use the same medium in other parts of the world to project their own image. Fouzi Slisli (2000) says that any such image is grounded in simplicity and cultural stereotypes (see Another Perspective: Stereotypes and Media Reports). In the final analysis, movies are responsible for strong emotional projections. Unlike the news, they can be completely grounded in fiction. Mock documentaries even give the illusion that a propaganda film is an objective news analysis.

No matter what the means of communication, the mass media are part of terrorism. Wolfsfeld (2001) concludes that it is necessary to accept the fact that both the media and security forces will fight to control media images and that bias in the media is misunderstood. Slanted news and political bias are taken for granted, given the orientation of a media outlet. The actual bias comes from the media's endless quest for sensational violence. The mass media compete for the most dramatic, bloody imagery. Wolfsfeld does not hold the media responsible for terrorism, but he concludes that it is part of the story, noting wryly that Roman gladiators kept one eye on the opponent and one eye on the crowd.

Security Forces vs. Reporters

Key Points and Questions:

1. Why do security forces conflict with the media?
2. Cite the media's two conflicting goals.
3. How do drama and symbiosis affect the coverage of terrorism?
4. How do reporters collude with terrorists or governments?
5. Discuss the ways security forces and governments use the media as a force multiplier.

Paul Wilkinson (1997) argues that some form of media will always be used to communicate the message of terrorism, whether it is by tavern gossip in the Middle Ages or today's electronic global network (see Another Perspective: Wilkinson's Analysis of the Media). Terrorists want to use the media as a psychological weapon, while governments seek to harness the power of the media for social control. For example, coverage of hostage situations tends to make security forces look as though they are responsible for the victims. Reporters often do not realize this because they are under tremendous pressure to be first with the story. As a result, Wilkinson concludes, law enforcement and military goals conflict directly with the needs of the media. His findings are supported by two decades of study.

Within the ranks of everyday police or military operations, it is not uncommon to hear many statements criticizing the media. Chiefs of police and military commanders generally do not respect media figures and reporters, and their attitudes are reflected by line personnel. Specialized command units are often created in police agencies to portray a favorable image to reporters, and U.S. military forces have been assigned to public relations.

Reporters, newspapers, and television news teams are generally not trusted. Police and security forces officially represent the social order, and they are charged with the maintenance of stability. They see themselves as servants of the public interest in the United States and other Western democracies. Additionally, they believe they make decisions for the public good. They perceive themselves to be the forceful extension of democracy. Officially, they recognize the media's right to report information, but they develop elaborate plans to control reporting (U.S. Department of Homeland Security, 5-11-04).

Richard Schaffert (1992) concludes that democracies can lower the amount of terrorism by implementing some form of media control, and he argues that such actions do not endanger democracy. He points to the United Kingdom, Germany, and Italy as examples of countries that have exerted some form of media control while maintaining democracies and individual rights for citizens. The United States has two problems with this approach: Many Americans see terrorism as a distant problem that does not require such measures as censorship, and most Americans abhor the idea of censorship. Critics of media control would not accept limited government censorship. The United Kingdom, Germany, and Italy do not have a First Amendment.

Aside from the issue of governmental regulation, media organizations have two competing and often contradictory roles: They control the flow of information while simultaneously making the news entertaining enough to "sell." Although this appears to be a new development, experts concerned with the competing roles of the media raised the issue long ago. M. Cherif Bassiouni (1981) points out the potential conflict these competing purposes bring to terrorist scenarios. The police or security forces are charged with bringing a situation to a "successful" conclusion that includes preserving order and protecting lives. The press, however, has the job of transmitting information while making the story interesting to the consumer. During live coverage, the media must also facilitate interaction between the scene and the audience.

Bassiouni (1982) argues that the police must respond to terrorist situations by *lessening* their drama and psychological impact. News producers, however, see the drama of terrorism as the perfect attention grabber. Bassiouni notes that terrorism defies security force goals while catering to media goals. The issue of terrorism heightens the animosity between the police and the media, reflecting a deeper conflict between those in government and those in the media.

More recent research reinforces Bassiouni's conclusions. Government officials seldom enjoy having their decisions analyzed and criticized by journalists for the benefit of a mass audience, but this is one of the major functions of media presentations. Tensions run high in terrorist situations, especially when the event is ongoing or when hostages are involved. Television and newspaper reporters usually arrive at the scene of a terrorist incident within minutes of security forces. Distrust and distaste often dominate their interactions from the start. As a result, officials in democratic governments often try to manipulate the story by claiming that the government's version represents the public interests. News organizations tend to look for evidence of a government's position, rather than accepting claims about the public interest at face value (Council on Foreign Relations, 2004).

This predicament gives rise to three points of view about terrorism and the media. First, some members and supporters of the press see the media as a quasi-constitutional force keeping the government in check. A second group wants to limit press coverage during terrorist events. These people see the media as terrorism's ally. A third faction feels the opposite is true: The media may exploit terrorism, but they rarely convey messages favorable to terrorists.

Members of the media, of course, do not purposefully intend to endanger lives or escalate terrorism (Perl, 1997; Dvorkin, 2003). Once again, this issue was raised in earlier studies of the media and terrorism. Abraham Miller (1982, pp. 133–147) points to internal codes of conduct controlling journalistic practices and guidelines for helping reporters to behave responsibly. Under no circumstances are they to interfere with security forces or to help terrorists, even inadvertently.

Journalists, interestingly enough, seem to fear manipulation by terrorists as much as they do government control. The media claim to have the right to have access to and report all findings. Some analysts and government officials feel this right hampers governmental decision making. Reporters have defended their position by saying that in a democracy, all the people have a right to influence decision making. They can only do this, some media defenders have claimed, when they are given unrestricted information (Dvorkin, 11-12-03; Rasul, 10-7-04).

Several analysts of terrorism vehemently disagree with the position taken by some members of the media. Terrorism is a new type of struggle, and terrorists have made the media their ally. Modern terrorists view communication as a potential weapon, and they seek to exploit it by eliciting media exposure. Reporting gives the illusion that terrorists are extremely powerful, and over-reporting causes widespread anxiety. In areas where ethnic or religious tensions run high, such as India and Indonesia, dramatic reporting of terrorist incidents has led to widespread violence. Willingly or unwillingly, the media have become a tool of terrorists (Alexander, 1984, pp. 135–150; Dobkin, 1992, p. 103; Astraatmadja, 3-3-03; Bowden, 2004; Smith, 2005).

The recent history of media research suggests that terrorists and the media have a symbiotic relationship. For example, Norman Podhoretz (1981) says modern reporters are in subtle, informal collusion with terrorists, in business together for mutual benefits. The media do not consciously conspire with terrorists, but they play to each other's needs. Yoel Cohen (1983) shares this view, pointing out that the PLO would not exist if it were not for media coverage and media sympathy. And reporting on PLO violence, in turn, helps the media make their profits.

J. Bowyer Bell (1978a) and H. H. A. Cooper (1977a, pp. 140–156) agree that the media have produced what they call **terrorist theater**—it is filled with action and is entertaining. In this sense, Bell and Cooper would agree with Alexander's position that the press has become an ally of terrorism. Yet they question the effectiveness of this relationship. Subsequent research has indicated that the coverage of terrorism is not helpful to terrorist groups. For instance, Gabriel Weimann (1983) found that reporting terrorist events increases the public's knowledge about terrorism but builds little sympathy for terrorists. Michael Kelly and Thomas Mitchell (1981) documented that news reports focus mainly on violence, which paints a negative picture of terrorism. L. John Martin (1985) agrees, implying that a negative media image causes terrorist propaganda efforts to backfire.

More recent research reinforces earlier findings. Paul Marsden (2000, 2001) argues that when terrorist events are reported, they can create a mental epidemic of anxiety. It spreads, he says, in the same pattern as a disease. Reporting can also give "how-to" instructions to would-be terrorists. Alexei Venediktov, an editor for a prominent Moscow radio station in the Russian Federation, argues that the modern mass media have lost touch with their audience. Drawn by the fascination of violence, the Russian media have focused on sensationalized reports in Chechnya, rather than seeking a deeper political analysis of the problem (Rosbaltnews, 6-6-04). Most recent studies of the media and terrorism conclude that the press and terrorism are locked in a kind of symbiosis (Lockyer, 2003).

While governments and security forces are quick to point out the shortcomings of the media, there is another issue. Some analysts and scholars maintain that the media serves the interests of governments. In other words, these studies suggest that reporting works as a force multiplier for those who control political power. For example, David Paletz, Peter Fozzard, and John Ayanian (Paletz, Ayanian, and Fozzard, 1982; Paletz, Fozzard, and Ayanian, 1982) conducted two studies on the way the media handles terrorism. They examined coverage of the Red Brigades, the Irish Republican Army (IRA), and the Armed Forces of National Liberation (FALN) by both television and newspapers. In their television study, the researchers focused on the three major American network nightly news programs. They searched for the method of reporting, as well as any biases, and concluded that television generally ignores the motivations for violence, focusing instead on the violence itself.

The method of coverage network television used was found to have a negative effect on terrorism. The purpose of terrorism is to communicate a message about its goals and objectives. Network television does not do this. In fact, the audience is appalled by terrorist violence. Paletz and colleagues conclude that television engenders no sympathy for terrorists because coverage clearly portrays terrorism as an illegitimate form of violence.

Paletz et al. approached newspapers in a similar manner. In an analysis of the *New York Times*, they found a coverage pattern similar to that of television. Although the newspaper provided greater depth in covering the issues surrounding a terrorist event, the coverage generally delegitimized the acts of terrorism and the terrorists, while legitimizing the government.

Far from being a tool for terrorism, the media served the interests of the government, Paletz's team found. They claim the perspectives of news stories depend on the source, and in the majority of terrorist stories examined, governments were the source. Reporters are under pressure to produce quickly, so more than 75 percent of their stories came from government sources. This meant reporters also picked up the labels that government sources applied to the terrorists. The terrorists seldom fared well.

Pippa Norris, Montague Kern, and Marion Just (2003) reach a similar conclusion when examining the events of September 11. While journalists may err on the side of terrorists, they argue, the media often interpret events in favor of governments. The media created a cultural shift after September 11 by using news frames that changed American perceptions of terrorism. Although the actual dangers of international terrorism were decreasing, according to U.S. State Department data, reporting after September 11 increased American fears, suggesting that terrorism was increasing dramatically. The news frames were crucial to the cultural shift because they reduced extremely complex situations to predictable and understandable contexts. Americans constructed a new social reality, a view that they must go to war with terrorism, as a result of news frames.

Elements of the news frame exacerbate the problem. Reporters not only report the drama, they are drawn to the language of terrorism because it increases the drama. When governments respond, reporters most frequently lapse into the rhetoric of the voices of political authority, using pejorative words to become the rhetorical advocates of government policy. For example, news reporters frequently talk about "the war on terrorism," "rouge states," "continuous war," and "homicide bombers" at the prompting of government officials. This gives the illusion that the conflict is bipolarized. Simple rhetoric claims that the struggle is between the forces of good, counterterrorists, and the agents of evil, terrorists (Lockyer, 2003).

Does Reporting Make Terrorism Contagious?

Key Points and Questions:

1. Does evidence from bomb threats suggest they are contagious?
2. How do police-media relationships affect contagion?
3. How does Schlesinger respond to arguments about contagion?
4. How do more recent studies affect findings on contagion theory?

One of the older questions about modern terrorism is, Does extensive news coverage lead to more terrorism? In other words, is terrorism contagious? Some analysts believe in this **contagion theory** and it has been a hotly debated issue for nearly thirty years.

Allan Mazur (1982) is convinced that media reports have a suggestive effect on violent behavior. His study compares bomb threats in the nuclear industry with the amount of press coverage nuclear power plants received. He begins by noting that news reports of suicides increase the number of suicides, and he wonders whether he might find a similar pattern in the nuclear industry.

Mazur examined bomb threats against nuclear power facilities from 1969 to 1980, comparing them with the amount of coverage devoted to nuclear power on television and in newspapers. He found the number of threats proportionately matched the number of news stories. When coverage increased, bomb threats increased; when coverage decreased, bomb threats decreased.

Mazur concludes that the media can affect public behavior through suggestion. Coverage of problems in the nuclear industry seems to suggest there is a need for a general public response. Some people choose to make their statements violently. He is not sure whether the media alone causes the response or whether their reports combine with other factors. He is positive about the contagion effect, however.

M. Cherif Bassiouni (1981) believes media coverage has several contagious effects. Media reports promote fear and magnify the threat in the public mind. That fear spreads. The media also influence the way terrorists select their targets; to spread violence, terrorists select targets for maximum publicity. The media have become the vehicle for maximizing the psychological impact of terrorism. From this standpoint, terrorism is contagious: Media-reported terrorism causes more terrorism.

Bassiouni applies the contagion hypothesis to criminal and political terrorism. He believes researchers have not derived any conclusive data, but the contagion theory is popularly accepted, especially in law enforcement circles. Although the evidence remains inconclusive, Bassiouni decides that there must be some basis to the contagion theory.

Philip Schlesinger (1981) is not willing to go quite so far. He believes the contagion theory is merely a hypothesis of terrorist researchers. Schlesinger does not reject the notion that terrorism can be contagious, but he denies that evidence proves the point. Schlesinger argues that contagion theory is used to support the case for censorship and that analysts who subscribe to it are merely trying to force their opinions on those who can control the media.

The early debates have continued. The Council on Foreign Relations (2004) argues that terrorism spreads through media coverage. Terrorists learned to adapt their methods and messages on the basis of media coverage. Hijacking became a problem when satellite television coverage allowed news networks to cover events in real time, and hijackings increased as a result. Al Qaeda learned that it could create greater insecurity when the world was saturated with news coverage, if it maintained anonymity. Other terrorist organizations followed. The growth of the World Wide Web and new cable networks such as al Jazeera brought about other changes. Terrorism is not only contagious, it evolves with changes in media technology.

The Internet also adds to the contagion effect, according to some analysts. Terrorist organizations set up websites by purchasing several potential sites from a host. Knowing that intelligence and law enforcement agencies will attack the sites, terrorist organizations continually move the product from one website to another. The psychological result inspires would-be terrorists to follow suit (Hosenball, 4-4-05). Contagion is magnified when rumors are spread through e-mails and websites (Council on Foreign Relations, 2004).

The greatest proponents of contagion theory argue that media reporting, especially television, leads to a copycat effect. These analysts cite data about the rise in violent activity any time it is covered extensively on television. Furthermore, proponents of this belief contend that coverage of suicide terrorism results in more suicide terrorism. The reason copycat terrorism occurs is that media reports encourage people to transform dark thoughts into reality. All people have thoughts of violence and homicide, but they do not always act on them, accepting such negative thoughts as disturbing fantasies, not reality. When a suicide bomber attacks and the event is repeatedly broadcasted, mental images are transformed into reality. By copying the media reality in daily life, the copycat changes thought into action (Marsden, 2001).

The contagion effect is debated hotly because of its impact on the freedom of the press. If terrorism is contagious and the media serve as the method of dispersing the contagion, then the public has a right to expect that the media be placed under some form of control. People who believe that the contagion effect is overemphasized fear control of the press. Proponents of the contagion effect tend to believe that some form of media regulation is necessary for public safety.

Censorship Debates

Key Points and Questions:

1. What are three choices governments face when it comes to freedom of the press and terrorism?

2. Does freedom of speech mean that the media are free to report any information?

3. How do tort laws become a passive system of regulation?

4. Summarize arguments for and against censorship.

5. How might media coverage in the twenty-first century end the debate about censorship?

Paul Wilkinson (1997) believes that governments face three choices when it comes to freedom of the press and terrorism. A popular position is to assume a laissez-faire, or hands-off, attitude. This approach assumes that all the interested parties will reach an effective method for responsible media coverage of terrorism. A second choice is censorship. In this case some government agency would have veto power over news reports. A final choice is self-regulation. Wilkinson says that many times reporters would not behave in an irresponsible manner if they knew what they could do to avoid serving terrorists and their causes. He notes that governments and security forces seldom provide direction for news organizations. Again, this debate is not new.

Schmid and de Graaf (1982) argue that the original purpose of free speech was to allow a person to present a view. With the rise of capitalism in the 1800s and the late nineteenth century's corporate consolidation of the media, newspapers and eventually television news assumed the responsibility for protecting individual freedom of speech. Freedom from censorship came to equal the media's right to report the news.

Juanita Jones and Abraham Miller (1979) suggest that government restrictions on dissemination of news do not violate the press's rights during emergency conditions. They compare hostage situations against the backdrop of the First Amendment and view the problem through case-law history. They argue this is not an abstract problem; lives hang in the balance during hostage crises. They believe reporting and the freedom to report are not the only critical concerns in such crises: The impact of the media on the event and media interference with police operations have also become central issues.

Jones and Miller say the press could legally be excluded from certain areas during hostage situations, especially when police procedures call for secrecy in an attempt to save lives. However, the U.S. Supreme Court will not allow blanket denial through a set of preconditions. Limitations to access are supported only when they are justified by the circumstances. A total or standard ban on news access is not acceptable.

Hostage situations especially bear out the point. Jones and Miller say the police have a right to place restrictions on the press. The media's behavior at a hostage incident is a matter of conduct, not speech. Denial of access and specific regulations for the protection of hostages are acceptable, and such actions have been upheld in the courts. It is a form of censorship acceptable under the First Amendment, and it denies neither free speech nor a free press.

Jones and Miller demonstrate that they are not trying to stop reporting. Miller's (1982) additional work provides further evidence of this. The researchers believe the police only want the media to behave in a responsible manner. The police can help encourage this by providing the media with realistic and timely information. If the police and media could come to an understanding of each other's positions, Jones and Miller believe many confrontations could be mollified.

Taking a different view, Philip Schlesinger (1981) argues that the media in Western democracies favor government stability. Schlesinger centers his argument on the concept of *legitimization*. The media have worked to delegitimize terrorist violence. Schlesinger examines the role of security forces in Northern Ireland and concludes that the British press has acted "responsibly" in terms of covering the government's position. That is, the press has supported the government while condemning anti-government violence. He feels such actions only reflect "responsibility" as defined by the government.

Schlesinger argues that the media approach terrorism on official and unofficial levels. Language is crucial, because it can serve to either support or deny the legitimate right of a political position to exist. Officially, media language is used to criminalize terrorism. Unofficially, it can serve to criminalize the issue that motivates terrorists.

The language of news reporting has become secondary to the way in which the media have portrayed governments. Schlesinger says that when the first incidents of modern terrorism started to break out in Northern Ireland, reporters tried to print and broadcast "objective" reports. Such reports were often as critical of government policy as they were of terrorists. This enraged the government, especially the security forces engaged in dangerous activities.

These debates have continued. Shane Kingston (1995) vehemently disagrees with Schlesinger, arguing that terrorism caters to the media. In the early days of modern terrorism, about 1965 to 1985, it was fairly easy for terrorists to manipulate television because any event was an unfolding drama. Television producers, however, became more sophisticated and countered terrorist manipulations by refusing to air terrorist propaganda without editing or comment. Yet, Kingston says, the terrorists also became more adept at using the press. Using Ireland as a case study, Kingston says the IRA presented itself positively in the 1990s.

Despite the decades-long debate about media censorship and terrorism, changes in the structure of the mass media may lead to the end of the controversy. The reason is that there are many new forms of media coverage, and no single government is strong enough to impose censorship on all of them. For example, *The Economist*

(3-26-05, p. 48) reports that the struggle for Israel and Palestine has moved from the battlefield to the television station. Both sides realize that military victory cannot be achieved without winning a media victory. There are two aspects to a media strategy. First, a press office has to spin events favorably so that actions can be presented to the world's press in a positive light. The Israelis have a tremendous advantage in this area, according to *The Economist*. The second step involves soliciting support from media outlets that have already taken sides. The logical conclusion from the article is that censorship has little to do with news coverage. In the first instance political information competes for its view in the world's media. In the second, the media serves as a propaganda machine.

Another reason censorship is losing its appeal is that the press has truly developed an international flavor. The Arab television network al Jazeera, for example, covers events from its own perspective, and it will not be dominated by appeals or threats from the West. In addition, many countries outside the United States became angry with the American press after September 11. They complained that Americans covered every story from a "U.S.-centric" bias. Muslims, in particular, believed that Islam was stereotyped on American television. When U.S. politicians pressured foreign governments to rein in their own press, it created further resentment. Non-Western countries believe the world's media have been controlled by Western biases, and their emerging news organizations are not about to subject themselves to any form of Western censorship (World Economic Forum, 2002; Harsono and Eriyanto, 3-3-03; Dvorkin, 11-12-03).

Finally, the World Wide Web has changed the censorship argument. Assume for a moment that an international treaty produced a situation in which the entire world agreed to censor reporting on terrorism. Although this is virtually an impossible scenario, assume that all the world's media outlets agreed to cooperate by implementing voluntary restrictions to enhance censorship. Even in such an unlikely scenario, a terrorist group with a video camera and a laptop computer has access to the Web. Technology has rendered debates about censorship moot, except when a single nation seeks to keep its own media outlets under tight control. Even in this case, that nation's citizens can flip on a computer or smuggle a signal from a satellite dish.

Summary of Main Points

1. Television and terrorism are closely related. Terrorists feed television's need for drama, and television gives terrorists a means of communication.

2. The mass media become a force multiplier because reporting can increase the psychological aura surrounding terrorist events.

3. Terrorists use the media as a weapon by enhancing the power of attacks, using it to broadcast a political message, gaining publicity for a violent political movement, and hiding messages in regular transmissions.

4. The Internet has increased terrorism's power, but not in ways that are fully understood. The greatest threat seems to be the ability to conduct anonymous communication.

5. Members of the media and security forces often seem to be at odds when responding to terrorist events. Security forces want to restore the scene, inves-

tigate, and eliminate terrorism. Media sources want to tell the story, and they function in a highly competitive environment. Sensational drama increases the attraction of the story to readers and viewers.

6. Some researchers believe media reporting of terrorism encourages people to join the violence. This is known as contagion theory; it means these researchers believe terrorist violence is contagious.

7. Censorship is the most controversial area of media relations. It may have been possible to invoke some internal control in an earlier time, but such methods were controversial because they foster private media cooperation with the government. Today, technology and the growth of international news organizations make censorship difficult.

Key Terms

Make sure you can define, explain, or identify the following people, ideas, organizations, or terms:

censorship   330
TV news drama patterns   332
news frames   332
Infotainment Telesector   333

al Jazeera   334
al Manar   335
terrorist theater   339
contagion theory   341

Suggested Readings

Now that you've been introduced to this topic, you can learn more by reading:

Brigitte Nacos, in *Mass-Mediated Terrorism: The Central Role of the Media in Terrorism and Counterterrorism*, examines the way the media covers terrorism around the world. She argues that terrorists know how to use the global media as a force multiplier and that violence is often conducted to publicize a cause. She also looks at the role the media have on counterterrorist policies.

You may also want to read:

Nancy Palmer's *Terrorism, War, and the Media* presents a series of articles on the power of the media in times of conflict.

Two early studies are Alex P. Schmid and Janny F. A. de Graaf's *Violence as Communication*, and Abraham Miller's *Terrorism, the Media, and the Law*.

Richard W. Schaffert, in *Media Coverage and Political Terrorists: Quantitative Analysis*, provides an examination of empirical information.

Pippa Norris, Mantague Kern, and Marion Just present a collection on news frames in *Framing Terrorism: The News Media, the Government, and the Public*.

Web Resources

Go to *http://cj.wadsworth.com/white_terrorism5e* and click on Web Links to find:

▪ The website of the Joan Schorenstein Center on the Press, Politics, and Public Policy
▪ An interview from National Public Radio on the way violence is portrayed in different nations
▪ An article from the *New Yorker* on real-time reporting during the war in Iraq

The Companion Website for *Terrorism and Homeland Security,* **Fifth Edition**

http://cj.wadsworth.com/white_terrorism5e

At the Book Companion Website you can review chapter outlines, use the flash cards to test your terrorism vocabulary, and check out the many other study aids you'll find there. You'll find valuable data and resources at your fingertips to help you study for that big exam or write that important paper.

Terrorism Updates

**http://www.wadsworth.com/criminaljustice_d/special_features/ext/terrorism
_site090802/index.html**

Visit the *Terrorism: An Interdisciplinary Perspective* website to find the most current information about the fields of terrorism and homeland security. With a focus on domestic and international issues, this site explores the scope of terrorism in our world today. You'll find essays on important topics in terrorism and homeland security, critical thinking web activities, and InfoTrac College Edition keywords. Most importantly, the website is updated weekly with current news and research articles on domestic and international terrorism. You are invited to use these web resources to supplement your understanding of the topics covered in this chapter.

Current Perspectives: Readings from InfoTrac College Edition
Terrorism and Homeland Security

The sixteen articles in this reader offer a representative selection that helps you understand the important issues about terrorism and homeland security. It includes FREE access to InfoTrac College Edition and can also be bundled with the text for free.

Glossary

The purpose of this glossary is to provide a quick introduction to the key terms and concepts used in the text. For a more in-depth introduction, check the material in the text. When you feel that you have mastered the concepts from the textbook information, see the suggested readings and websites for greater detail.

Go to **http://cj.wadsworth.com/white_terrorism5e** and click on Web Links for comprehensive lists developed by the U.S. Department of State ("Patterns of Global Terrorism, 2003"), the Council on Foreign Relations, the Terrorism Research Center ("Terrorist Group Profiles"), and the International Policy Institute for Counter-Terrorism.

Abu Nidal group   Also known as Black June, this group evolved as one of the most important splinter groups from Fatah. The group formed in the early 1970s when Sabri al-Banna, code named Abu Nidal, went to Baghdad to recruit fedayeen for Arafat's Fatah. Saddam Hussein, then Ba'athist vice president of Iraq, approached the terrorist with a proposition. Instead of working for Arafat, Abu Nidal could develop his own organization, and the Iraqis would assist with funding. Abu Nidal accepted the offer and broke with Fatah.

Academic consensus definition (of terrorism)   Developed by Alex Schmid, this definition combines elements of more than thirty other definitions. It is the most comprehensive definition used by both governments and scholars.

Active cadre   In a pyramid ideological or ethnic terrorist group, the active cadre are the people who actually carry out terrorist acts.

Active supporters   In a pyramid ideological or ethnic terrorist group, the active supporters (or director supporters) take action to sustain the actual terrorists (active cadre).

Al Aqsa Intifada   The Intifada that erupted after Ariel Sharon's visit to the al Aqsa mosque in Jerusalem in September 2000.

Al Aqsa Martyrs Brigades   Formed to put Fatah at the center of the new Intifada, the group also calls itself the Brigades. Began as a secular group, but they increasingly used Jihadist rhetoric. They were also the first secular Palestinian group to use suicide tactics. They claim their purpose is limited: Their goal is to stop Israeli incursions and attacks in Palestinian areas, and they intend to punish Israel for each attack. The Brigades have become the most potent Palestinian force in the al Aqsa Intifada.

Al Jazeera   The independent twenty-four-hour Arab television news network broadcasting from Qatar.

Al Manar   A twenty-four-hour Lebanese television news network.

Al Qaeda 2.0   Peter Bergen uses this term to describe al Qaeda's transformation into a grouping of autonomous Jihadist movements.

Al Qassam Brigades   The military wing of Hamas.

Al Turabi, Hasan   An Islamicist leader, government official, and spokesman in Sudan who welcomed Osama bin Laden when he was driven from Saudi Arabia for criticizing the Saudi family during Operation Desert Shield.

Al Zawahiri, Ayman   An Egyptian physician and leader of Jihadists in Egypt, Zawahiri joined Osama bin Laden in Afghanistan in 1986. He helped found al Qaeda with bin Laden and Abdullah Azzam.

Al-Adnani, Tamim   One of the most vigorous fundraisers for Jihadist causes in the United States before the 1993 World Trade Center bombing.

Algerian Civil War   From 1992 to 2002 Algerian governmental forces fought Jihadists in a deadly civil war. The war started when Algerian military forces voided an election that brought Islamicists to power.

Alkifah Refugee Center   A worship center in New York City where many Jihadists congregated.

Anarchism   A philosophy that champions individual freedom and refuses to acknowledge centralized authority.

Anglo-Irish Peace Accord of 1985 A negotiated attempt to bring peace to Northern Ireland. President Bill Clinton was able to assist with the expansion of the agreement during his administration (1992–2000).

Anglo-Israelism The belief that the lost tribes of Israel settled in Western Europe. God's ancient promises to the Hebrews become promises to the United Kingdom, according to this belief. Anglo-Israelism predated Christian Identity and is the basis for most Christian Identity beliefs.

Anthrax A natural bacterial toxin that has been enhanced by weapons programs (weaponized). People can be infected by eating contaminated food (gastrointestinal anthrax), being exposed through the skin (cutaneous anthrax), and inhaling spores (inhalation anthrax). Inhalation anthrax is the most deadly form.

Antiabortion violence Violence targeting abortion clinics or workers. Such violence has taken place in the form of bombings designed to destroy property or kill workers, arsons, murder, threats, and false biological attacks.

Apocalyptic eschatology A belief that God will bring an end to time and space while creating a new order. Most followers of this form of eschatology believe that God will destroy the world and bring humankind to final judgment.

Arafat, Yasser (1929–2004) Leader of the Palestine Liberation Organization (PLO) and later the Palestine Authority. After the formation of Israel, Arafat was one of the founders of Fatah in 1959, which began raids in Israel after the 1967 war. Arafat eventually renounced terrorism in the hope of creating a Palestinian state. He received a Nobel Peace Prize in 1994. He was elected president of the Palestinian Authority in 1996 and held the position until his death.

Aryan Nations An American anti-government, ultra-right, anti-Semitic White supremacist group. It was founded in the 1970s by Richard Girnt Butler as an arm of the Christian Identity group Church of Jesus Christ-Christian. The group promotes the message of Christian Identity.

Ascetic eschatology A form of eschatology where adherents practice self-discipline and denial in the hope of creating a closer link with a Deity.

Asymmetrical war Wars in which the warring sides are grossly unequal. The less powerful side does not fight the more powerful side under the conventional rules of war because it cannot win by using these tactics. The weaker side uses unconventional methods of fighting.

Asymmetry A term used in guerrilla warfare and terrorism to describe the manner in which a small, weak force fights a stronger power.

Ayatollah Khomeini One of the grand ayatollahs of Shi'ite Islam, Khomeini was the driving force behind Iran's 1979 revolution and was leader of the country's first theocratic government. He ruled from 1979 to 1989.

Azzam, Abdullah A Palestinian intellectual and professor, Azzam went to Afghanistan to join the mujahadeen. He created al Qaeda with Osama bin Laden and Ayman al Zawahiri. He was assassinated with a car bomb in 1989. Some people believe bin Laden was behind the assassination.

Ba'athist A pan-Arabic socialist movement. It was particularly popular in Hafaz Assad's Syria and Saddam Hussein's Iraq.

Bakunin, Mikhail (1814–1876) A Russian revolutionary who fought the Tsar. He formed an alliance with Sergey Nechaev. His revolutionary views were primarily rhetorical, but they inspired later generations.

Barnett's logic Thomas P. M. Barnett explains that the rules of conflict changed at the end of the Cold War. Nations existing in a secure economic structure are prepared to fight within the rules of state-to-state war. Terrorists, on the other hand, do not have a vested interest in maintaining economic and political structures because they do not benefit from them. Therefore, *they fight outside the rules.*

Basque separatists Ethnic Basques who seek to form an independent country in the Basque region in France and Spain. Militant separatists practice terrorism.

Beam, Louis An American right-wing extremist leader involved in the Ku Klux Klan and other white supremacy groups. Beam coined the term *leaderless resistance* to describe small autonomous cells or individuals that take action on their own.

Berserker An individual terrorist taking action without a leader or hierarchy. See Lone wolf avenger.

Bin Laden, Osama The founder of al Qaeda, with Abdullah Azzam and Ayman al Zawahiri. As of 2005, some intelligence sources believe he is dead or severely wounded. Others believe he still functions along the border between Pakistan and Afghanistan.

Biological weapons Weapons made from live bacterial, viral, or other microorganisms. Biological weapons are hardened, or *weaponized*, so that they can survive in unfriendly environments. This process also makes them more deadly. The major weakness of biological weapons is that they cannot be controlled. For example, if terrorists were to release a weaponized strain of smallpox, the disease might spread to the terrorist group and their allies.

Biometric measuring   Identification systems based on body characteristics such as fingerprints, facial patterns, or DNA.

Black Hebrew Israelism   An African-American version of Christian Identity. Followers maintain that God is black and the original Hebrews were black Africans. The idea is nearly two hundred years old, and most followers are nonviolent. In extreme forms, whites and Jews are demonized. In one extreme version, Death Angels were dispatched to kill white people.

Black September   A new group created by Arafat to strike at Israel, named after King Hussein's September attack. With German terrorist help, Black September attacked in Munich at the 1972 Olympic Games. They took most of the Israeli Olympic team hostage, killing those who tried to escape. Black September terrorists negotiated transportation to Libya, but while they were moving to the aircraft designated to fly them from Germany, the German police launched a rescue operation. Unfortunately, plans went awry and the terrorists machine-gunned their hostages before the German police could take control.

Border protection   Refers to the security of America's borders and other ports of entry.

Botulism   A bacterial agent ingested in the human body. A botulin agent can be weaponized.

British Israelism   See Anglo-Israelism.

Brotherhood   An internal secretive group in the Nation of Yahweh. One could only be admitted by killing a white person.

Bruder Schweigen   German for *silent brothers*. The late Robert Miles, leader of the Mountain Church of Jesus in Michigan, penned an article about the struggle for white supremacy, entitling it "When All of the Brothers Struggle." It also served as the name of two violent right-wing extremist groups, Bruder Schweigen and Bruder Schweigen Strike Force II.

Bulldozing   Israel's policy of destroying the homes of suicide bomber families. It also refers to Israel's destruction of Palestinian homes to secure its borders.

Bureaucracy   A term used by sociologist Max Weber to describe rational organizations.

Camp David Peace Accords   President Jimmy Carter brought Egypt's Anwar Sadat and Israel's Menachim Begin to Camp David and successfully negotiated a peace treaty between the two countries in 1978. Jihadists assassinated Sadat three years later in retaliation.

Capone discovery   A term used by James Adams to describe the Irish Republican Army's realization that it could raise funds for terrorism by engaging in organized crime.

Cell   The basic structure of a terrorist group, a cell is a small unit of people who have joined for combat.

Censorship   As used in this text, an argument for controlling the way media cover terrorism. Advocates believe that terrorists manipulate the media and favor controlling the news. Opponents fear that censorship denies free speech.

Centralized hubs   Centralized terrorist organizations that supply and cooperate with separate cells that attach themselves to the hub. It is similar to an umbrella organization.

Chain organization   A grouping of autonomous terrorist organizations that agree to cooperate for specific periods of time or for certain operations.

Chemical agents   Four basic varieties: nerve agents, which enter the body through ingestion, respiration, or contact; blood and choking agents, which are usually absorbed through the respiratory system; and blistering agents, which burn the skin and internal tissue areas upon contact.

Christian Identity   An American extremist religion proclaiming white supremacy. Adherents believe that white Protestants of Western European origins are the true descendants of the ancient Israelites. Believers contend that Jews were spawned by Satan and that nonwhites evolved from animals. According to this belief, white men and women are the only people created in the image of God.

Civil defense   Refers to citizens engaged in homeland security.

Civil liberties   Individual rights granted to citizens under the U.S. Constitution.

Clarke, Richard   A government official with an expertise in government security and counterterrorism. Clarke served several administrations, both Republican and Democrat. He became controversial after leaving the Bush administration and claiming publicly that President George W. Bush and his advisors were mishandling counterterrorism.

Clash of civilizations   The term used by Samuel Huntington to describe conflict in the post–Cold War era. Huntington believes cultures will clash with other cultures. Religion is one of the most important concepts in defining a culture or civilization.

Clausewitz, Carl von   Prussian field marshal and philosopher of war. His book *On War* shaped military doctrine in the twentieth century.

COINTELPRO An infamous FBI counterintelligence program started in 1956. Agents involved in COINTELPRO violated constitutional limitations on domestic intelligence gathering, and the program came under congressional criticism in the early 1970s. The FBI's abuse of power eventually resulted in restrictive rules on the FBI.

Collins, Michael (1890–1922) An Irish revolutionary, Collins employed terrorist tactics against the British and their Irish supporters. He signed a treaty with the British in 1922 that resulted in the Free State of Ireland but left Northern Ireland under the control of the United Kingdom. Many members of the Irish Republican Army (IRA) rejected the treaty, and Ireland became engulfed in a civil war between pro-treaty and anti-treaty forces. Collins was assassinated by the IRA in August 1922. His methods inspired guerrilla and terrorist leaders throughout the twentieth century.

Column The guerilla equivalent of a military battalion, a column is composed of several cells. Terrorists use the term to designate combinations of cells.

Computer virus A biological metaphor for a human-made program introduced into a computer or computer system. Viruses typically copy themselves and move through systems. The purpose of a virus is to disrupt a computer or computer network. A *worm* is a virus that uses a computer's memory, but it does not affect other programs.

Conspiracy theories As used in this text, any number of extremist right-wing theories claiming that sinister forces are plotting to overthrow the American government and enslave its people.

Contagion theory States that copycat criminals are inspired by reports of terrorist strikes. The thesis is that terrorism spreads like a disease.

Cosmic struggle As used in this text, a concept from Mark Juergensmeyer contending that terrorists must resist their enemies because their struggle represents a fight between God and the devil. If God loses the fight, the purpose of creation is destroyed. Terrorists, therefore, feel they cannot lose a cosmic battle or they will fail God.

Creatorism The deistic religion of Ben Klausen's Church of the Creator. It claims that white people must struggle to defeat Jews and nonwhite races.

Criminal intelligence Information based on the reasonable suspicion that a criminal activity is occurring or about to occur. It is collected by law enforcement agencies in the course of their preventive and investigative functions. It is shared on information networks such as the Regional Information Sharing System (RISS) Net. Unlike national defense intelligence, criminal intelligence is based only in criminal law. Agencies must suspect some violation of criminal law before they can collect intelligence.

Cybersecurity Protection of individual computers and networks or defense of the computer infrastructure.

Cyberterrorism Targeting computer networks or using computers as a weapon in a terrorist attack.

De facto campaign A cluster of activities from unrelated individuals and/or groups focusing on a common issue or cause. For example, a single environmental terrorist might sabotage a piece of farm equiptment. A second action, conducted by a small group, might involve arson in a real estate development, while a third group vandalizes the home of a mining executive. The effect for law enforcement is like that of a unified campaign.

Death Angels Select members of the Brotherhood in the Nation of Yahweh. They were sent to murder white people in the Miami area.

Defense in depth The idea that all levels of society must become involved in homeland security. Defense in depth is designed to protect a community fighting for its way of life. Retired Vice Admiral Arthur Cebrowsky believes that counterterrorist units must operate deeply in society. Cultural awareness, language skills, and nation building are part of defense in depth.

Deified terrorism The belief that terrorist violence is justified by God. It is holy terror.

Demonization Refers to a process by which certain groups are blamed for the evils of society. Members of the demonized group are viewed as something less than human and held accountable because they conspire with evil forces.

Department of Defense (DOD) Headed by the secretary of defense, it is composed of America's armed forces. DOD has civilian undersecretaries for the Army, Navy, and Air Force. (The Marines are part of the Navy and the Coast Guard serves in the Department of Homeland Security.) A military chief of staff commands each of the armed forces, and they report to a military chair. A commandant commands the Marine Corps. In the past decades a Special Operations Command, which deals with offensive actions against terrorism, has grown increasingly autonomous.

Department of Homeland Security (DHS) Created by Congress from the Office of Homeland Security after the attacks of September 11, 2001. DHS came into being in 2003 under Secretary Thomas Ridge.

Desert Shield An allied coalition assembled by President George H. W. Bush to protect the Persian Gulf region after Iraq invaded Kuwait in 1990.

Desert Storm The February 1991 counterattack by coalition forces to drive Iraqi forces from Kuwait. Headed by U.S. General Norman Schwartzkopf.

Dirty bomb Radioactive material placed around a conventional explosive. The purpose of the explosive is to spread radioactive (dirty) material around a large area.

Document fraud As used in this text, forging documents to hide the identity of terrorists or selling phony documents to raise money for terrorism.

Domestic intelligence systems Law enforcement networks gather criminal intelligence within America's borders. The FBI was responsible for gathering national security information under the Foreign Intelligence Surveillance Act until the USA Patriot Act. Law enforcement currently is encouraged to share both criminal and suspected national defense intelligence with other agencies. This move is extremely controversial, and some jurisdictions have refused to allow local police agencies to participate in the process. The departments of defense, justice, and homeland security and several other executive branch agencies collect domestic intelligence. In 2004 all federal intelligence systems were mandated to serve under a national director.

Earth Liberation Front (ELF) Supporters of ecoterrorism, animal rights, and anti-genetic engineering came together in the United Kingdom in 1992 to form this new group. Composed of radicals from Earth First!, the Animal Liberation Front (ALF), and other disaffected environmentalists, the group migrated from Europe to the United States. The alliance has been responsible for more than six hundred criminal acts since 1996. Its tactics include sabotage, tree spiking, property damage, intimidation, and arson, resulting in tens of millions of dollars of damage.

Ecoterrorism Terrorism against alleged environmental abusers.

Eschatology The study of the end of all time.

Ethical eschatology Viewing the world through a new moral lens and acting within the guidelines of a new moral code.

Ethnic cleansing Killing or driving out ethnic or religious groups inhabiting an area. For example, during the breakup of Yugoslavia from 1992 to 1995 Serbian forces sought to cleanse Bosnia of indigenous Muslims. They killed thousands of people, raped and tortured females, and drove entire villages away with the threat of murder and pillage. Samuel Huntington believes that ethnic cleansing will become a common form of conflict in the clash of civilizations.

Ethnic terrorism Terrorism based on ethnic or nationalistic identity.

Euskadi ta Askatasuna (ETA, or Basque Nation and Liberty) Formed as an offshoot of a Spanish nationalist political party in 1959. Composed of young, frustrated nationalists who wanted regional autonomy, the ETA was not originally violent, but its members turned to violence when Franco tried to repress the movement. In 1966, the ETA voted to follow the example of the Third World and engage in armed revolution. In 1968, the group started a terrorist campaign. They have specialized in car bombings and assassinations, and they have targeted Spain's number one industry, tourism. The ETA's goal is to establish an autonomous homeland in northern Spain and southern France.

Fadlallah, Hassan A spiritual leader of Hezbollah and a member of its governing council.

Failed state A state that cannot govern itself. Unofficial organizations evolve and exert rule in certain areas of the state.

Fanon, Frantz (1925–1961) A psychiatrist from Martinique whose theory of terrorism was particularly powerful during the heyday of left-wing terrorism in the United States and Western Europe.

Fatah The military wing of the Palestine Liberation Organization (PLO).

Fatah General Council The governing council of Fatah.

Fatwa A religious proclamation issued by an Islamic religious scholar.

Fedayeen Warriors who sacrifice. The fedayeen are the soldiers of Fatah.

Firing team According to Carlos Marighella, the basic unit of urban guerrillas.

Force multiplier Increasing striking power without increasing personnel. Terrorists use the media, transnational support, technology, and religion as force multipliers.

Forrest, Nathan Bedford (1821–1877) A famed and gifted Confederate cavalry commander and founder of the Ku Klux Klan in Pulaski, Tennessee. Forrest tried to disband the KKK when he saw the violent path that it was taking.

Fourteenth Amendment Grants the right of due process. A citizen cannot forfeit rights guaranteed by the

Constitution unless the government has convicted the person of a crime following proper legal procedures. The proper procedures are the due process of law.

Free-Wheeling Fundamentalists   White supremacists or Christian patriots who either selectively use Bible passages or create their own religion to protect the patriot agenda.

Guerrilla warfare   The type of conflict in which irregular soldiers fight conventional forces with no specific front line. As defined by Ernesto (Che) Guevara, guerrilla warfare joins indigenous rebels with professional revolutionaries. They slowly build columns and work to build a conventional army. Guerrillas use terrorism as a selective tactic. They are careful not to target local populations because their purpose is to win sympathy and support.

Gush Emunim   A fundamentalist Israeli settlement in Palestinian territory that has the same set of beliefs as the violent Israeli fundamentalists, but their rhetoric appears normative compared with the violent rhetoric of the other groups.

Hamas   **(Islamic Resistance Movement)** The Palestinian wing of the Muslim Brotherhood, created during the First Intifada in opposition to the secular policies of the PLO. Formed in 1987, Hamas established social services networks, schools, and hospitals in the Gaza strip and the West Bank. It also administered an effective military wing known as the al Qassam Brigades and sponsored several deadly suicide bombings during the al Asqa Intifada. The United States lists Hamas as a terrorist organization, but supporters claim it legitimately resists Israel. Since the death of Arafat in 2004, Hamas has played an increased political role among the Palestinians. Hamas limits its attacks to Israel and the occupied territories. Israel waged a campaign of assassination against Hamas leadership during the al Asqa Intifada.

Hamas Charter   The guiding document for Hamas. It rejects Israel's right to exist.

Hate crime   A crime motivated by race, ethnicity, or other categories defined as a protected status by federal law.

Hate Movement   An American white supremacy philosophy that demonizes Jews and people of color.

Hawala   An ancient system for moving vast sums of money without actually exchanging funds over international borders or within the banking system.

Heinzen, Karl (1809–1880)   A radical German democrat who embraced anarchy. He came to the United States after the 1848 revolutions failed in Europe. He

is best known for his tract on murder, and his ideas were publicized by the German-American Johann Most.

Hemorrhagic fever   A variety of related infections that usually involve digestive disruptions, fever, and extensive bleeding.

Hezbollah   A Syrian- and Iranian-backed Shi'ite group, also called the Party of God. The group was spawned in Lebanon after the Iranian Revolution, which culminated in the overthrow of the secular shah of Iran. Hezbollah's purpose is to spread the Islamic law of Shi'ite Islam. Although it is most frequently associated with violence in Lebanon and Israel, Hezbollah has an international Jihadist wing. It also created the organizational style that groups like the Egyptian Islamic Group, Ansar al Islam, the Egyptian Islamic Jihad, the GIA, the Palestinian Islamic Jihad, and al Qaeda would use.

Hezbollah International   A separate international group in the security wing of Hezbollah, managed by master international terrorist Imad Mugniyah. Is a shadowy group, and the Supreme Council denies its existence. The international section has cells in several different countries, including the United States, and maintains an extensive international finance ring partially based on smuggling, drugs, and other crimes. Its leader keeps close ties with operatives in the Tri-Border Region and Ciudad del Este and also runs a terrorist training camp off the coast of Venezuela.

Homeland security   The term used after the September 11, 2001, attacks to describe defense within American borders. It spawned the Office and later Department of Homeland Security. Officials used the term "security" to separate DHS's operations from the Department of Defense.

Homicide bomber   A term some people favor to describe suicide bombers. Proponents claim that suicide bombers murder people; therefore, they wish to use the term homicide bombers.

Hunter   Written by William Pierce under the pen name Andrew MacDonald, *Hunter* is a fictional book describing a white supremacist who goes on a killing spree targeting nonwhites, interracial couples, and Jews.

Hussein, Saddam   The Ba'athist leader of Iraq displaced by U.S. military forces in the second Gulf War.

Ibn Taymiyyah, Taqi (ca. 1269–1328)   An Islamic scholar who was forced to flee Baghdad in the face of invading Mongols. He believed that the Crusaders and Mongols defeated Islamic armies because Muslims had fallen away from the true practice of Islam. Emphasizing *tawhid,* or the oneness of God, ibn Taymiyyah attacked anything that threatened to come between humanity and God.

Identity theology A theology based on a story of conflict and hate. According to this theology, Jews have gained control of the United States by conspiring to create the Federal Reserve System. The struggle between whites and Jews will continue until whites ultimately achieve victory with God's help. At that point, the purpose of creation will be fulfilled. Such theological perversions are necessary when converting a religion of love into a doctrine of hate.

Ideological terrorism Refers to small groups who terrorize for the purpose of imposing their political ideals on others. The term was first used to describe left-wing, anarchist, and Communist revolutionaries.

Infrastructure protection Securing the underpinning structures of business, government, and other organizations, such as water systems, highway networks, fuel distribution pipelines, and electrical grids.

"Inside" faction The name of Sheik Ahmed Yassin's leadership group, because he believed the Hamas struggle should remain inside Palestine.

Insurgent terrorism Revolutionary terrorism directed against a government or government representatives.

Interservice Intelligence Agency (ISI) Pakistan's intelligence arm. It brokered U.S. funds for selected mujahadeen groups during the Soviet-Afghan War.

Intifada (First Intifada) A spontaneous Palestinian uprising in Gaza and the West Bank from 1987 to 1993. It resulted in the Oslo Accords and the promise of a Palestinian state.

Iranian Revolution The 1979 overthrow of Shah Mohammed Pahlavi that brought the Ayatollah Khomeini to power and a Shi'ite government to Iran.

Irgun Zvai Leumi A Jewish terrorist group in British Occupied Palestine that fought for the creation of a Zionist state.

Irish Republican Army (IRA) The name used with variations by a number of Republican terrorist groups. The IRA formed from revolutionary groups in the 1800s, and Patrick Pearse declared himself to be the commanding general of the Irish Republican Army during the 1916 Easter Rebellion. There have been many different branches of the IRA since 1916, and several Irish terrorist groups fight for the Republican cause but disavow the IRA.

Islam One of the world's three great monotheistic religions founded by the Prophet Mohammed. Muslims believe that the Archangel Gabriel (Jabril) revealed the nature of God over a period of twenty-two years to Mohammed. According to the faith, people are called into a loving relationship with God. All people will be judged at the end of time, but God's mercy will atone for those who repent and try to follow God's will. Muslims believe that God's true will—revealed imperfectly in the Hebrew and Christian Bibles—is contained in the Koran. There are several interpretations within Islam; the two major sects are the Sunnis and Shi'ites. Sunnis believe the prophetic power of Mohammed was transferred to the community of believers in 632, but Shi'ites contend that the Prophet's power remained in Mohammed's family. Most Shi'ites are "Twelvers," accepting twelve leaders, or imams, after Mohammed's death. While there are many interpretations of Islam, all Muslims believe five basic pillars or principles: (1) a confession of faith in God and acceptance of Mohammed as God's last and greatest prophet, (2) ritual prayers with the community, (3) giving alms, (4) fasting, especially during holy periods, and (5) making a pilgrimage to Mohammed's birthplace, Mecca. Many terrorists claim to act in the name of Islam, but most Islamic scholars believe terrorism is a violation of Islamic law.

"Islamic resistance" Hezbollah guerrillas who maintain that it is not a crime to resist the Israelis. They believe that fighting the Israelis is not an act of terrorism.

Islamicists Muslims who accept the theology of Taqi ibn Taymiyyah, Mohammed ibn Abdul Wahhab, and Sayyid Qutb. A militant Islamicist is a Jihadist, although some terrorism analysts use these terms interchangeably.

Israel An independent Jewish state created after World War II when Jews, victimized by Nazi persecution, flocked to Palestine, where they fought the British to create an independent state.

Israeli Defense Force (IDF) Israel's military forces.

Jamaat Islamiyya A sinister Jihadist group, formed with the purpose of placing Indonesia under strict Islamic law.

Jammu and Kashmir An area in northern India claimed by both India and Pakistan and the scene of a long-term struggle, including the infiltration of Jihadist groups. Disputes almost caused a nuclear war in late 2001 and early 2002.

Jihad A theological term in Islam with many meanings. It can be interpreted as struggling to overcome sin. Some Muslims use the term to describe work to improve the community. After the Battle of Badr in 624 when the Muslim community of Medina defeated a non-Muslim army from Mecca, Muslims increasingly used the term to describe defensive warfare to protect the community. Jihadists use the word to describe their attacks on unbelievers and Muslims who do not accept narrow Jihadist theology. Jihadists also seek to impose their brand of Islamic law on the community, although Mohammed stated that Muslims should never force people to become believers. In the Jihadist definition, it is permissible to attack and kill non-Muslims, women, children, and fellow Muslims. Most Islamic scholars reject and condemn this interpretation.

"Jihad in America" A controversial TV show that aired on PBS in 1994. It maintained that mujahadeen had established bases in America to wage a holy war on the United States. Critics claim the show is anti-Muslim; supporters believe it identifies the threat behind Jihadist terrorism.

Jihadists A generic term used to describe Muslims who have literalized the meaning of *jihad* (holy war), accepting it as a literal call to war against Muslims who do not accept their interpretation of faith and non-Muslims. Jihadists are sometimes known as Islamic radicals or Islamicists. They are also mistakenly called Islamic fundamentalists. Jihadists accept the puritanical philosophies of Taqi ibn Taymiyyah and Sayyid Qutb.

Joint Terrorism Task Force (JTTF) An operational concept in U.S. law enforcement. It combines law enforcement officers and intelligence personnel from several local, state, and federal agencies. Managed by local FBI offices, there are more than 130 JTTFs across the nation.

Justification for violence Anyone who engages in violent activity, whether it is legitimate or not, must feel that the actions are necessary and acceptable. Terrorists seek to justify their actions just like all other people.

Kach A Jewish militant group created by Rabbi Meir Kahane, an American Jewish cleric who immigrated to Israel in 1971.

Kahane Chai A Jewish militant group, created by Kahane's son, Benjamin, shortly after Kahane's assassination. The group name literally means "Kahane lives."

Killing religions Religions developed during the food-gathering cycles of pre-agrarian and early agricultural societies, based on the premise that a deity would help the community in times of crisis. In the killing religions, gods slaughtered enemies.

Koresh, David Name adopted by Vernon Wayne Howell, the leader of the Branch Davidians. He was killed when the FBI assaulted the Branch Davidian compound in 1993.

Ku Klux Klan Created in the wake of the Civil War, and the brainchild of Confederate cavalry genius General Nathan Bedford Forrest. Forrest intended to create an antiunionist organization that would preserve Southern culture and traditions. When the newly formed KKK began terrorizing freed slaves, Forrest tried to disband the organization. But it was too late, and the KKK began a campaign of hate. By the early twentieth century, the organization had nearly died, but it revived in the extremist atmosphere after World War I. The modern KKK grew after World War II, becoming, up to the present day, fragmented, decentralized, and dominated by hate-filled rhetoric.

Kurdish Workers' Party (PKK) A Marxist-Leninist terrorist organization composed of Turkish Kurds. Officially changed its name to Kurdistan Freedom and Democracy (KADEK) in 2002, it operates in Turkey and Europe, targeting Europeans, Turks, rival Kurds, and supporters of the Turkish government. It represents the same ruthless brand of Maoism as the Peruvian guerrilla organization Shining Path, murdering residents of entire villages who fail to follow its dictates. The PKK/KADEK has developed chameleon-like characteristics. Although it started as a revolutionary Marxist group, since 1990, it has employed the language of nationalism. Even more startling, since 1995, it has also used the verbiage of religion.

Kurds An ethic group inhabiting parts of southern Turkey, northern Iraq, and northern Iran.

Laqueur's views of terrorist profiling Walter Laqueur believes it is not possible to develop a profile of terrorists because there is no one terrorist personality. Terrorism changes with social, political, and psychological factors. It appears in history in different ways at different times.

Large group (of terrorists) Term defined by Ted Robert Gurr. Large terrorist groups are capable of conducting campaigns.

Lashkar Jihad A militant Jihadist group formed to fight Christians in eastern Indonesia.

Leaderless resistance A concept referring to individuals or autonomous cells that take action on their own. It is similar to chain organizations.

Lebanese Civil War From 1975 to 1990 various factions fought for control of Lebanon. The situation spawned an Israeli invasion in 1982 to drive the Palestine Liberation Organization (PLO) from Lebanon and indirect intervention from Syria and Iran with Hezbollah.

Legal definition (of terrorism) A definition provided by a government in legislation. A law outlawing terrorism defines the elements of the crime within a statute. The elements of the law define terrorism.

Liberation Tigers of Tamil Eelam (LTTE, or Tamil Tigers) Emerged as a leading revolutionary group in Sri Lanka in 1975, formed by Velupillai Pirabhakaran. The group has been fighting for an independent homeland for nearly 3 million Tamils in northern and eastern Sri Lanka. Has waged a guerrilla campaign using terrorism as both a prelude to guerrilla warfare and a way to support uniformed guerrillas in the field. They have killed thousands and assassinated prominent political figures. They also continue to attack moderate Tamils who oppose their cause.

Lone wolf avenger A lone wolf refers to an individual terrorist taking action without a leader or hierarchy. As used by Jessica Stern, it refers to a single terrorist acting inside an ideology without the support of a leader or group.

Luxor massacre In November 1997 Jihadists murdered more than fifty tourists visiting the Egyptian pyramids at Luxor.

Macroeconomic theory (of terrorism) Suggests that counterterrorism policies should be aimed at providing the world's people with economic stability, opportunity, and participation in the mainstream economy.

Mahdi Army A militia headed by the Iraqi Shi'ite leader Maqtada al Sadr.

Marighella, Carlos A Brazilian Communist legislator who turned to terrorism when the Brazilian Army disbanded the government in 1966. His two most influential works were *For the Liberation of Brazil* and *The Minimanual of the Urban Guerrilla*. Marighella belonged to two terrorist groups in Brazil and inspired the Tupamaros of Uruguay. He was killed in a police ambush in São Paulo, Brazil, in 1969.

Marighella model A model for guerrilla warfare in which terrorism is used as a tactic. From Ernesto (Che) Guevara. See Guerrilla warfare.

Marzuq, Musa Abu Took over the leadership of Hamas when Ahmed Yassin was imprisoned from 1989 to 1997. His strategy was much more violent than Yassin's. He assembled a new leadership core and based it in Jordan and sought financial backing from Syria and Iran. His tenure became known as the "outside" leadership because he based Hamas outside of Palestinian territory.

Mashal, Khalid A leader in Hamas. Some analysts believe Mashal, a member of the outside leadership, began directing Hamas operations from Damascus after the assassination of Abdul Aziz Rantisi.

Militarization A process in which individual police units or entire agencies begin to approach specific problems with military values and attitudes. They adopt paramilitary dress, behave with military discipline, and, most importantly, prepare to make war with an enemy.

Militia movement The political movement that gave rise to homegrown militias. Self-appointed groups of citizens claim they are part of the unorganized militia contained in the Second Amendment to the U.S. Constitution. Militias generally believe they have the right to carry weapons, conduct military training, and defend the country. There are many differing philosophies guiding the movement, but most militias tend to embrace some form of political extremism.

The Monkey Wrench Gang A novel by Edward Abbey that sometimes inspires ecoterrorists.

Monkey wrenching The sabotage of construction equipment or construction sites in the name of ecology. The term comes from the Edward Abbey novel *The Monkey Wrench Gang.*

Morozov, Nikolai (1855–1946) A Russian revolutionary who joined the People's Will in 1880. He wrote a tract on terrorism and was arrested and held in prison until 1905. He died in obscurity.

Most, Johann (1846–1906) Advocated terrorism from a New Jersey–based newspaper and called for "propaganda by the deed" and the "philosophy of the bomb." He believed violent action was the best form of propaganda.

Mujahadeen Holy warriors. The term is used in both mainstream and radical Islam. Radicals use the term to describe Jihadists.

Musawi, Abus A leading figure in Hezbollah, responsible for its links to Iran.

Muslim Brotherhood An organization founded by Hasan al Banna in 1928 in Cairo based of the reform principles of Salafiyya or Salafi movement. Al Banna believed that only pure religion could reunite the Islamic world and deliver it from modern heresies.

Najaf The site of a Shi'ite holy shrine and the burial spot of Alir, Mohammed's son-in-law.

Narcoterrorism Either using terrorist tactics to support drug operations or using drug trade profits to finance terrorism.

Nation of Yahweh A violent offshoot of Black Hebrew Israelism founded in Miami by Hulon Mitchell Jr., also known as Yahweh ben Yahweh. The group is best known for Mitchell's dispatching of Death Angels with instructions to kill whites.

National Alliance   The white supremacist organization founded by the late William Pierce and headquartered in Hillsboro, West Virginia.

National Commission on Terrorist Attacks upon the United States (9-11 Commission)   A bipartisan commission appointed by President George W. Bush to investigate the terrorist attacks of September 11, 2001. The committee issued a report analyzing the events that led up to the attack, and it made recommendations for changing government, especially the intelligence services, to prevent future attacks. Its recommendations were adopted in December 2004.

National Criminal Intelligence Sharing Plan   A plan to share criminal intelligence among the nation's law enforcement agencies. It suggests minimum standards for establishing and managing intelligence operations within police agencies.

National Cyber Alert System   Developed by the Department of Homeland Security in 2004 to protect the nation's computer networks.

National defense intelligence   A system of agencies and networks that gather information about threats to the country. Any threat or potential threat is examined under the auspices of national defense intelligence. Unlike criminal intelligence, people and agencies gathering defense information do not need to suspect any criminal activity. The FBI is empowered to gather defense intelligence.

Nationalistic terrorism   Terrorism rooted in national or ethnic identity.

Nechaev, Sergey (1847–1882)   A Russian revolutionary known for writing a revolutionary catechism and his friendship with Mikhail Bakunin. Although many scholars believe his activities were primarily rhetorical, he brutally murdered one of the members of his own organization.

New economy of terrorism   The term used by Loretta Napoleoni to describe the methods modern terrorist groups use to fund operations.

New World Liberation Front (NWLF)   Formed in 1970 by a small group of radicals in San Francisco and was responsible for thirty bombings over the next seven years. The group claimed to be a "moral" revolutionary group, and it attacked only "legitimate" targets symbolized by corporate capitalism. Utility companies were a favorite, although they also bombed two sheriff's vehicles in the San Francisco area. They were at war with the establishment.

New World Order   A phrase used by President George H. W. Bush to describe the world after the fall of the Soviet Union. Conspiracy theorists use the phrase to describe what they believe to be Jewish attempts to gain control of the international monetary system and subsequently to take over the U.S. government.

News frames   The way the news is "packaged" or presented in television, radio, and print media.

1948 War   Israel's war of independence against the surrounding Arab states.

1916 Easter Rebellion   Revolt in Dublin on Easter in 1916, led by Patrick Pearse and James Connolly. Pearse and Connolly took over several key points in Dublin with a few thousand armed followers. Pearse announced the formation of an Irish Republic. The British came to Ireland to fight. British artillery devastated Dublin. The rebellion ended, but the conflict led to the formation of the Irish Republican Army.

Nonkilling religions   Developed after the killing religions, they embraced enemies and developed elaborate theologies to justify violence as a last resort. The nonkilling religions appeared in order to try to transcend everyday experience.

Nonorganization   A governing council created to share ideas, plans, and money but designed to disappear and leave autonomous groups to carry out attacks under a variety of names.

Nordic Christianity   Nordic Christianity incorporates the ancient Norse gods in a hierarchy under the Christian triune deity. It is similar to Odinism, but does not completely abandon Christianity.

Nossair, Elsayyid   An American Jihadist associated with violence in New York City.

Ocalan, Abdullah   The leader of the Kurdish Workers' Party (PKK).

Officials   (The Official IRA) The branch of the Irish Republican Army (IRA) associated with socialism.

Operation Grapes of Wrath   A 1996 Israeli military operation in Lebanon to punish the Lebanese for allowing Hezbollah to operate there. Judith Harik and others suggest that these types of attacks backfired on the Israelis.

Operation Iraqi Freedom   The code name for the U.S.-led invasion of Iraq in 2003.

Orange   As used in this text, the traditional color for Protestantism in Ireland. It is derived from William of Orange, who saved the Protestant cause in the seventeenth century.

Ordinary and extraordinary worlds   Terms used by Mircea Eliade to describe everyday and mystical experiences. When humans have intuitive, mystical, or extraordinary feelings, they can only describe them in everyday language. This can lead to the belief that the extraordinary experience must be literally true.

Oslo Accords A peace agreement between the Palestinians and the Israelis negotiated in Oslo, Norway, in 1993. It brought hope for a Palestinian state and brought the first Intifada to an end.

"Outside" leadership Leaders of Hamas who gathered in Jordan and later Syria. They based the command structure outside of Palestinian territory. Musa Abu Marzuq assembled a new leadership core and financial backing from Syria and Iran.

Palestine Liberation Organization (PLO) Created from groups of disgruntled Palestinians in Jordan, and formed in 1964 by Arafat, with the purpose to create a political organization to help form a multinational alliance against Israel. He hoped Arab governments would jointly launch a war against the European-created state.

Palestinian Islamic Jihad (PIJ) A military group formed in Egypt and migrating to Gaza. PIJ believes that Israel must be defeated before Palestinians can form a government. While Hamas and Hezbollah maintain large social service, educational, and public health sections, PIJ only contains a military wing.

Palestinian National Authority (PNA) The legislative body created to govern Palestinian lands.

Paramilitary groups Armed civilian militias that organize themselves in a military manner, operating on different levels.

Passive supporters In a pyramid ideological terrorist group, the passive or indirect supporters inadvertently take actions to sustain the terrorist cause.

Peace process Any number of efforts from 1948 to the present trying to create a permanent peace between Israel and its neighbors.

Philosophy of the bomb An anarchist belief that society can be changed only through violence.

Pierce, William The late leader of the National Alliance and author of *The Turner Diaries* and *Hunter*. Pierce died in 2002.

Pirabhakaran, Velupillai The founder and leader of the Liberation Tigers of Tamil Eelam, or Tamil Tigers.

Political eschatology An attempt to apply political theory to the end of all time.

***Posse comitatus* clause** A doctrine in the second article of the Constitution that forbids the government to use military forces to enforce law. (Do not confuse this with the right-wing extremist group Posse Comitatus.)

Pragmatic terrorism Involves a practical attempt to destroy political power.

Professional terrorist As used by Jessica Stern, terrorists who have lost contact with their original causes. They engage in terrorism in the same way any worker would take a normal job.

Professionalization of leadership As used in this text, describes the emergence of the professional terrorist. Professional leaders manage groups and hire their services much like mercenaries.

Project Megiddo A 1999 FBI research project designed to assess potential domestic terrorism, especially from groups espousing eschatological violence.

Propaganda by the deed An issue popularized by Johann Most, who believed that propaganda was best spread through action rather than words.

The Protocols of Zion A forged document written in Tsarist Russia allegedly explaining a Jewish plot to control the world. It was popularized in the United States by Henry Ford. It is frequently cited by the patriot and white supremacy movements. Ironically, Jihadists also use it as evidence against Jews.

Proudhon, Pierre Joseph (1809–1865) One of the advocates of modern anarchism. His political activities eventually landed him in a French prison, but Proudhon was not a man of violence. He called for the extension of democracy to all classes, to be accomplished through the elimination of property and government. Property was to be commonly held, and families living in extended communes were to replace centralized government.

Provisionals The militant provisional wing of the Irish Republican Army (IRA).

Psychological offensive As defined by Marighella, a mass movement of revolutionary sympathizers, to provide peripheral support for terrorists.

Puerto Rican nationalists Puerto Ricans who want the island to be completely autonomous. Nationalists oppose those who seek statehood and those who want to maintain commonwealth status.

Puerto Rico commonwealth status The status Puerto Rico received after the Spanish-American War that made it possible for the island to participate in interstate commerce without trade tariffs or other barriers.

Pyramid The manner in which ideological, ethnic, and nationalistic groups arranged their organizations from about 1965 to 1985. An active cadre operated at the top, while direct supporters, indirect supporters, and sympathizers existed below the actual terrorists. Some groups, like the Provisional Irish Republican Army, still follow this model.

Qutb, Sayyid (1906–1966) Member of the Muslim Brotherhood, Qutb laid the groundwork for the modern Jihadist movement. His work *Milestones* contains the arguments most frequently cited by the Jihadists. Osama bin Laden studied under Qutb's brother, Mohammed. Arrested and tortured by the Egyptian government, Qutb was hanged for his actions and outspoken writings. His writings are immensely popular in the Islamic world, especially among young people. Some Muslim governments ban his works.

Radical democrats Western economic reformers of the early and mid-nineteenth century who believed that government and the economy should be subjected to the democratic constraints imposed by citizens. Some radical democrats believed in the use of violence.

Reasonableness The actions an average person would take when confronted with certain circumstances. This is a Fourth Amendment doctrine.

Red Brigades A Marxist-Leninist group, which formed in Milan after Renato Curio broke away from a left-wing working-class political organization. The group sought to make the cities unsafe for any government official or sympathizer. They believed a climate of violence would help bring about a revolution in Italy and eventually in all of Europe. Members of the Brigades saw themselves as the vanguard of a worldwide Communist revolution. They believed sensational violence would be their key to the future.

Red Terror Introduced by Bolshevik leadership, this movement involved rounding up real and potential opponents and executing them without trial. Suspected supporters of the old regime were slaughtered when Red Army units moved into a new area.

Regional Information Sharing System (RISS) A law enforcement network that allows law enforcement agencies to share information about criminal investigations.

Rejectionist Front As used in this text, the people who reject Israel's right to exist.

Revolution When power is transferred from one class to another.

Revolutionary Guards The striking arm of militant Iranian Shi'ites during the 1979 revolution. Revolutionary Guards seized the American embassy in Teheran and held the captives hostage for more than a year. U.S. intelligence sources believe many Revolutionary Guards went to Lebanon in 1982 to help form Hezbollah.

Revolutionary terrorism A campaign of subversive revolutionary violence.

Ruby Ridge incident A 1992 standoff between alleged survivalists and U.S. federal law enforcement officers in Idaho during which a U.S. marshal and survivalist Randy Weaver's wife and son were killed.

Sacred story As applied to terrorism, a term used by Jessica Stern to provide a myth for a terrorist group. The story emergences like a legend to justify conflict with an enemy.

Sacred terrorism When mythological traditions in culture are incorporated into the mythological structure of holy terror. Terrorists use myths as a story to explain a religious struggle, and these sacred stories of terrorist groups serve as an important source of motivation.

Salafiyya, or Salafi movement Literally, the elder movement, that is, limiting the practice of Islam to the theological interpretations of Mohammed and his first four successors. It originated in North Africa and is the puritanical force behind the Muslim Brotherhood. The theology was militarized by Sayyid Qutb.

Sallah, Ramadan Abdullah Took over leadership of the Palestinian Islamic Jihad after the death of Fathi Shekaki.

Samed A banking system established by the Palestine Liberation Organization (PLO).

Secular terror Type of terror that operates within a dominant political and cultural framework. Secular terrorists want to win, to beat the political system that is oppressing them. Their goal may be to destroy social structure, but they want to put something in its place. Secular terrorists would rather make allies than indiscriminately kill their enemies.

Security fence As used in this text, a fence Israel is building between Israeli and Palestinian territories to prevent the infiltration of Palestinian militants.

Selective assassination Israel's policy of individually killing Palestinian leaders.

Sharon, Ariel A retired Israeli general and former defense minister, Sharon was elected prime minister in 2001 after the al Aqsa Intifada erupted in 2000. He represented the Likud Party.

Shekaki, Fathi One of the founders and leaders of the Palestinian Islamic Jihad; assassinated in 1995. Many people believe the Israelis were behind Shekaki's death.

Shell state An illegitimate organization that takes control of an area in a weak or failed state.

Shi'ite A sect of Islam that dominates Iran, southern Iraq, southern Lebanon, and portions of Afghanistan and Pakistan. Followers believe that one of Mohammed's descendents must return before God judges humanity. They also believe that Mohammed's power flowed through his heirs. Most Shi'ites believe that Mohammed had twelve direct heirs, or *imams*, and that the last imam was taken directly into heaven. He will return as a prelude to final judgment, and until that time ayatollahs are given some of the characteristics of the Twelfth Imam.

Sikhs A religious minority in India that combines elements of Islam and Hinduism. The Sikhs have struggled with the Indian government, and some followers have joined terrorist groups.

Simple definition (of terrorism) States that terrorism is illegitimate violence or the threat of violence used against innocent people for political purposes.

Single-incident terrorists Groups or individuals that engage in only one act of terrorism.

Single-issue terrorists Embrace a single overriding cause or issue. In the United States single-issue terrorism usually originates from one of the following issues: abortion, animal rights, the environment, or genetic engineering.

Sinn Fein The political party of Irish Republicanism. It denies ties with terrorist groups.

Six-Day War A stunning Israeli victory over all of its Arab neighbors in June 1967.

Skinheads As used in this text, any number of young men who violently embrace race hatred and white supremacy.

Sleeper cell Terrorist cells, placed in various countries throughout the world, designed to "sleep," or to stay hidden, until the time they are called to action.

Small group (of terrorists) Term defined by Ted Robert Gurr for terrorist groups that cannot mount a campaign because of their size; their efforts usually fail, and campaigns usually last less than eighteen months.

Smallpox A highly contagious disease involving skin eruptions, fever, and frequently death. Smallpox was thought to be eliminated except for stores in two laboratories—one in the United States and one in Russia. Fears have arisen, however, that other nations may have acquired and weaponized smallpox for use in biological terrorism.

Social immersion When speaking of homeland security, the concept refers to understanding one's own society as completely as possible, while knowing the society of any adversary in the same manner.

Spectrum of conflict A continuum that ranged from low-intensity conflict to full-scale war. This scale probably more correctly reflects the human condition than the belief that we can either be at war or at peace. It also helps us understand terrorism.

"Stans" The lands (-*stan* means land) of Central Asia composed of Turkmenistan, Uzbekistan, Kyrgyzstan, Tajikistan, and Kazakhstan.

State-sponsored terrorism Terrorism supported by a nation-state. Nations that use surrogates try to manipulate terrorist groups to further their own state policies. They usually deny any connection with the terrorist group being sponsored.

Stern gang A militant offshoot of the Irgun Zvai Leumi led by Avraham Stern.

Suicide bomber A person who intends to die in a terrorist attack by intentionally committing suicide in order to kill others. The technique was introduced in 1983 by Hezbollah and the Liberation Tigers of Tamil Eelam (LTTE) in two terrorist campaigns.

Suicide terrorism Involves the intentional sacrifice of an attacker's life for the purpose of inflicting damage on an enemy. The attacker intends to die during the attack. Suicide terrorists most frequently use a bomb, and the phrase **"suicide bomber"** generally means the same thing as suicide terrorism in the popular press. Although suicide terrorism seems to be a relatively new tactic in modern terrorism, it has been used in military operations for centuries.

Sun Tzu An ancient Chinese philosopher of war who made little distinction between war and peace and focused on subtle expressions of power. Many counterterrorism analysts believe that Sun Tzu's approach to conflict is applicable for fighting terrorism.

Sunnis The major sect of Islam. Sunnis broke with Shi'ites over the selection of leaders for the Muslim community. Sunnis believe that the community is capable of selecting its leaders. They also feel that Mohammed and the entire Muslim community are equal before God and that everybody will be judged equally at the end of time. About 85 percent of Muslims are Sunnis.

Supraindigenous terrorists A term coined by Dennis Pluchinsky to describe local ethnic terrorists who have the ability to reach beyond their geographical boundaries.

Surrogate religion Created when a group replaces religious behavior with an ideology that has the power of religion. Such groups may create elaborate rituals and hierarchy of religious-like masters in the organization. Followers may give the group's leader the status of an earthly deity or believe that the leader has special powers to contact a deity. Members of the group frequently pass through various initiation rites, and they accept punishment and authority from the leader. When violence is internalized, that is, focused on its own members, the group can become a religious cult.

If the group targets victims in the outside world, it frequently behaves like a religious terrorist organization.

Survivalism   Type of right-wing extremism. Survivalists withdraw from society, forming compounds in rural areas. Groups are hybrids, combinations of old supremacy groups and more sophisticated modern hate groups. These groups typically establish themselves on a communal basis, rallying around a strong leader. Secluding themselves in armed compounds, they wait for the eventual collapse of government. The existence and philosophy of these groups were critically important to the change in right-wing extremism in the 1990s.

Symbolic target   A target that may have limited military or security value, but it represents the power of the state under attack. Terrorists seek symbolic targets to strike fear into society and to give a sense of power to the terrorist group. The power of the symbol also multiplies the effect of the attack.

Symbolic terrorism   A dramatic terrorist attack to show the vulnerability of a government. Terrorists cannot hope to defeat an army so they seek to destroy the symbols of a nation. The purpose is to make citizens believe that a government is incapable of providing protection.

Systematic terrorism   A terrorist attack waged over a period of time to change social conditions.

Tactics of terrorism   According to Brian Jenkins, the tactics are bombing, hijacking, arson, assault, kidnapping, and hostage-taking. Bombing is the most frequent tactic used in domestic and international terrorism.

Tamils   The minority Hindu ethnic group on Sri Lanka.

Tanzim or **Tanzim Brigade**   One of the military organizations in Fatah.

Targets for cyberterrorism   According to the Council on Foreign Relations, the three primary targets are computers, computer networks, and data storage and retrieval systems.

Task Force Report on Disorders and Terrorism   The report issued by the National Advisory Commission Task Force on Disorders and Terrorism, the first presidential commission to investigate terrorism. Formed under the order of President Richard Nixon, the task force was headed by H. H. A Cooper and was composed of some of the most noted terrorism analysts of the time.

Terrorist campaign   The ability of a terrorist group to mount attacks over an extended period of time. In the past, most terrorist campaigns have been limited. New styles of organization may change this pattern.

Terrorist group   The primary source of social reality for an individual terrorist. It provides social recognition and reinforcement for its members. Like soldiers, who undergo a similar bonding process during basic training, potential terrorists join groups for varied reasons: They may be sympathetic to the cause, or they may simply be social misfits. The terrorist group reshapes identities and can provide a ticket to social acceptance.

Terrorist theater   The drama surrounding a terrorist event. Terrorists play to a wider audience, and many analysts describe their actions as if they were a theatrical performance.

Transnational terrorism   Terrorism that crosses international borders.

Tri-Border Region   In South America the point where Paraguay, Argentina, and Brazil join. Several Middle Eastern terrorist groups reportedly operate in the area. It also serves as a point where terrorist and criminal groups join together for economic gain.

Trotsky, Leon (1897–1940)   A leader of the Bolshevik Revolution in 1917 Russia, Trotsky emerged as the political philosopher of state terror during the civil war (1918–1921). He understood that both Russian and foreign opponents to communism were frightened by the thought of terrorism. He was ruthless in the extermination of opponents of the revolution and posited a theory of internationalizing communism through subversion and terrorism. When Stalin took control of the Communist Party, he exiled Trotsky, who traveled to Mexico and continued to formulate theories of revolution. He also criticized Stalin and the direction of communism in the Soviet Union. Trotsky was murdered by a Spanish communist in Mexico City.

True believer   Term coined by Eric Hoffer, a person totally consumed by a cause. True believers act with similar behavioral characteristics no matter what cause they champion. They are willing to take extreme actions, including violence, to achieve the objectives of their cause, and they accept no criticism, dissent, or alternative philosophies. They believe that they cannot be wrong and that their philosophy explains all the realities of social life.

Tularemia   An infectious bacterial agent transmitted to humans through animals, particularly rodents. It causes high fever, breathing problems, and sometimes death. It can be weaponized for terrorist use.

The Turner Diaries   Written by William Pierce under the pen name of Andrew MacDonald, a fictional book describing a white supremacist revolution in the United States.

TV drama patterns   A method of organizing and broadcasting a variety of television programs such that the attention of viewers is held and they do not change stations during commercials. Terrorism is covered as a drama as news unfolds.

Umbrella organization   A centralized terrorist organization that operates with semiautonomous organizations. Smaller suborganizations gather under the financial and logistical umbrella of the centralized group, but they remain free to conduct their own operations. It is similar to a hub organization.

Underground economy   Economic exchanges apart from official, legal trade and commerce.

Urban guerrilla   The name terrorists favored in left-wing campaigns circa 1965–1975. See Urban terrorism.

Urban terrorism   A concept conceived and developed by Frantz Fanon and Carlos Marighella and based on the idea that a terrorist group could create a revolutionary movement. Unlike guerrilla warfare, urban terrorism is based on the belief that a population will join in a spontaneous uprising. Terrorism is a strategy.

USA Patriot Act   Passed in October 2001, the Patriot Act expands law enforcement's power to investigate and deter terrorism. Opponents claim that it adversely affects civil liberties; proponents claim that it introduces reasonable measures to protect the country against terrorists.

Vigilante terrorism   Terrorism to maintain the status quo.

Virtual organization   A temporary organization of terrorist groups in which members interact with one another for a specific operation or campaign.

Waco siege   Federal law enforcement officers were involved in a lengthy siege at the Branch Davidian compound of David Koresh in Waco, Texas, after his followers resisted a search warrant issued by the Bureau of Alcohol, Tobacco, and Firearms (ATF). Branch Davidians killed four ATF agents and wounded a dozen others. Koresh's compound was consumed by fire when federal agents ended the siege in April 1993. More than seventy people were killed, including dozens of children.

Wahhab, Mohammed ibn Abdul (1703–1792)   Led a purification movement in Arabia based on the theology of Ibn Taymiyyah. The Wahhabi movement, or Wahhabism, refers to the puritanical movement in Arabia associated with ibn Abdul Wahhab.

War on terrorism   A term used by President George W. Bush to describe America's counterterrorism efforts after September 11, 2001. Leading figures in both political parties use the phrase, and sometimes other governments use it, especially when dealing with the United States. Proponents believe the phrase is justified because it describes the new nature of conflict. Critics say that it misrepresents the nature of terrorism, distorts public perceptions of events, and confuses policy.

Weaponized   The process of modifying the structure of a biological agent, such as a bacterium or virus, and using the resulting product as a weapon.

Weapons of mass destruction   Although usually classified as nuclear, chemical, or biological weapons, weapons of mass destruction may be any weapon designed to produce mass casualties.

Weber, Max   One of the great theorists of sociology. Weber is known for his theory of bureaucracy, which emphasizes rational leadership, goal orientation, and meritorious selection and promotional standards.

White supremacy movement   A political philosophy claiming that white people are superior to all other racial groups.

Yahweh ben Yahweh   The name Hulon Mitchell Jr. used as leader of the Nation of Yahweh.

Yassin, Sheik Ahmed (1938–2004)   Early leader of Hamas. Yassin believed that Islam was the only path that could restore Palestine and preached reform, social concern, and social welfare. He was also a leader of the al Aqsa Intifada who endorsed suicide bombings. He was assassinated by the Israelis in March 2004.

Yisrael, Yehuda ben   A proponent of Black Hebrew Israelism, Yisrael claims that whites conspired to keep African Americans from learning of their divine origin.

Zionist   A person who supports Zionism, a movement originating in late nineteenth-century Europe for the purpose of creating a Jewish state. Detractors often label all Jews as Zionists.

Bibliography

Abbey, Edward. (1975). *The Monkey Wrench Gang.* Salt Lake City: Roaming the West.

ABC News. (5-25-04). "Al Qaeda Has 18,000 Militants for Raid—Think Tank." Online. http://abcnews.go.com/sections/world/Investigation/Insider_DTR_040525.html.

———. (1998). "John Miller Interview with Osama bin Laden." Online. http://abcnews.go.com/sections/world/DailyNews/terror_980612.html.

Abuza, Zachary. (2003). *Militant Islam in Southeast Asia: Crucible of Terror.* Boulder, CO: Lynne Rienner Press.

———. (2002). "Funding Terrorism in Southeast Asia: The Financial Network of al Qaeda and Jemaah Islamiya." *Contemporary Southeast Asia.* August, 25 (2): 169–200.

Accampo, Elinor. (2002). "Class and Gender." In Malcolm Cook (ed.), *A Short History of the French Revolution.* New York: Oxford University Press.

Adams, David. (2003). "Narcoterrorism Needs Attention." *St. Petersburg Times*, March 10. Online. http://www.sptimes.com/2003/03/10/columns/Narcoterrorism_need.shtml.

Adams, James. (1986). *The Financing of Terror.* New York: Simon & Schuster.

Agence France Presse. (10-28-04). "Basque ETA Separatists Call for Unconditional Dialogue." Online. http://www.elkarri.org/en/pdf/Agence_France_Pres_28_10_04.pdf.

Al Qaeda. (n.d.) The Al Qaeda Manual. Location unknown: al Qaeda.

Albright, Madeleine. (2003). "Bridges, Bombs, or Bluster." *Foreign Affairs* 82 (September/October): pp. 2–19.

Alexander, Yonah. (2003). *Palestinian Secular Terrorism.* Ardsley, NY: Transnational Publishers, Inc.

———. (2002). *Palestinian Religious Terrorism: Hamas and Islamic Jihad.* Ardsley, NY: Transnational Publishers, Inc.

———. (1984). "Terrorism, the Media, and the Police." In Henry Han (ed.), *Terrorism, Political Violence and World Order.* Landham, MD: University of America Press.

———. (1976). "From Terrorism to War: The Anatomy of the Birth of Israel." In Yonah Alexander (ed.), *International Terrorism.* New York: Praeger.

Algazy, Joseph. (5-27-04). "Amnesty: IDF Killed 100 Children Last Year." From OccupiedPalestine.org. Online. http://fromoccupiedpalestine.org/node.php?id=1291.

Ali, M. Amir. (2005 [accessed]). "Jihad Explained." The Institute of Islamic Information and Education. Online. http://www.iie.net/Brochure-18.html.

Alonso, Zaldivar. (8-29-04). "Border Guards Divided on Security Adequacy." *Los Angeles Times*, reported in *The Grand Rapids Press*, p. A5.

American Civil Liberties Union. (3-20-02). "ACLU Decries Ashcroft Scheme to Gut Immigration Courts." Online. http://www.aclu.org/ACLUPressRelease.

Amon, Moshe. (2004). "Can Israel Survive the West Bank Settlements?" *Terrorism and Political Violence* 16 (Spring): pp. 48–65.

Anarchy Archives. (3-13-96). "Anarchy Archives: An Online Research Center on the History and Theory of Anarchism." Online. http://dwardmac.pitzer.edu/Anarchist_Archives/.

Animal Liberation Front. (2000). Homepage. Online. http://www.nocompromise.org/alf/alf.html.

Appleby, R. Scott. (9-28-01). "Building Peace to Combat Religious Terror." *The Chronicle of Higher Education.* Online. http://chronicle.com/free/v48/i05/05b01003.htm.

Arab Gateway. (2002). "Hamas." Online. http://www.al-bab.com/arab/countries/palestine/orgs3.htm.

Armstrong, Karen. (2000). *Islam: A Short History.* New York: Random House, Modern Library Chronicles. (1997).

———. (1997). *Jerusalem: One City, Three Faiths.* New York: Ballantine Books.

Army of God. (n.d. [accessed 2004]). "The Army of God Manual." Online. http://www.armyofgod.com/AOGhistory.html.

Arquilla, John, and David Ronfeldt. (1999). "The Advent of Netwar: Analytic Background." *Studies in Conflict and Terrorism* 22: pp. 193–206.

Arquilla, John, David Ronfeldt, and Michele Zanini. (1999). "Networks, Netwar, and Information-Age Terrorism." In Ian O. Lesser, Bruce Hoffman, John Arquilla, David

Ronfeldt, Michele Zanini, and Brian Michael Jenkins (eds.), *Countering the New Terrorism*. Santa Monica, CA: RAND.

Astraatmadja, Atmakusumah. (3-3-03). "Media and Terrorism." Journalism Asia, Center for Media Freedom and Responsibility. Online. http://www.cmfr.com.ph/ja/2003/media%20and%20terrorism/astraatmadja.

Awad, Nihad. (9-10-03). "Written Testimony of Nihad Awad before the Senate Subcommittee on Terrorism, Technology, and Homeland Security." Online. http://www.anti-cair-net.org/awadTestimony2003.html.

Azano, Harry J. (2003). "Can Security Help with Civil Defense?" *Security Management* (February). Online. http://www.securitymagement.com/.

Baginski, Maureen. (8-22-04). "Statement of Maureen A. Baginski before the House of Representatives Select Committee on Homeland Security." Online. http:www.gov/congress/congress04baginsky081704.htm.

Ballard, James David. (2003). *Nuclear Waste Transportation*. Reno: State of Nevada. Also available Online. http://www.state.nv.us/nucwaste/news2003/pdf/nas_ballard.pdf.

Barber, Benjamin R. (1996). *Jihad vs. McWorld: How Globalism and Tribalism are Reshaping the World*. New York: Ballantine Books.

Barkun, Michael. (1997). *Religion and the Racist Right: The Origins of the Christian Identity Movement*. Chapel Hill: University of North Carolina Press.

Barnett, Thomas P. M. (2004). *The Pentagon's New Map: War and Peace in the Twenty-First Century*. New York: G. P. Putnam's Sons.

———. (2004 [accessed]). "Thomas P. M. Barnett Website." Online. http://www.thomaspmbarnett.com.

Bassiouni, M. Cherif. (1982). "Media Coverage of Terrorism." *Journal of Communication* 32: pp. 128–143.

———. (1981). "Terrorism and the Media." *Journal of Criminal Law and Criminology* 72: pp. 1–55.

BBC News. (3-9-05). "Murder Witnesses Facing Threats." Online. http://news.bbc.co.uk/1/hi/northern_ireland/4332747.stm.

———. (11-16-04). "Timeline: Iraq—A Chronology of Events." Online. http://news.bbc.co.uk/1/hi/world/middle_east/737483.stm.

———. (7-1-03). "Profile: Al Aqsa Martyrs' Brigades." BBC News World Edition. Online. http://news.bbc.co.uk/z/hi/middle_east/1760492.stm.

———. (1-24-02). "Challenge to Israel's Assassination Policy." Online. http://news.bbc.co.uk/1/hi/world/middle_east/1780051.stm.

Becker, Jillian. (1984). *The PLO*. New York: St. Martin's.

Bell, J. Bowyer. (1998). "Ireland: The Long End Game." *Studies in Conflict and Terrorism* 21: pp. 5–28.

———. (1995). "The Irish Republican Army Enters an End Game: An Overview." *Studies in Conflict and Terrorism* 18: pp. 153–174.

———. (1978). "Terrorist Scripts and Live Action Spectaculars." *Columbia Journalism Review* 17: pp. 47–50.

———. (1976). "Strategy, Tactics, and Terror: An Irish Perspective." In Yonah Alexander (ed.), *International Terrorism*. New York: Praeger.

———. (1974). *The Secret Army: A History of the IRA, 1916–1970*. Cambridge, MA: MIT Press.

Bell, J. Bowyer, and Ted Robert Gurr. (1979). "Terrorism and Revolution in America." In Hugh D. Graham and Ted Robert Gurr (eds.), *Violence in America*. Newbury Park, CA: Sage.

Benjamin, Daniel, and Steven Simon. (9-1-03). "The Real Worry: In Iraq We Have Created a New Field of Jihad." *Time* (162): p. 35.

———. (2002). *The Age of Sacred Terror*. New York: Random House.

Bergen, Peter L. (2001). *Holy War, Inc.: Inside the Secret World of Osama bin Laden*. New York. The Free Press.

Bergman, Ahron. (2002). *Israel's Wars: A History Since 1947*. London: Routledge.

Berlet, Chip, and Matthew N. Lyons. (2000). *Right-Wing Populism in America: Too Close for Comfort*. New York: The Guilford Press.

Berthelsen, John. (5-9-96). "Room with No View." *Far Eastern Economic Review*, p. 159.

Best, Richard A., Jr. (12-3-01). *Intelligence and Law Enforcement: Countering Transnational Threats to the U.S.* Congressional Reference Service. CRS Report for Congress. Online. http://www.fas.org/irp/crs/RL30252.pdf.

Betts, Richard K. (2002). "Fixing Intelligence." *Foreign Affairs* (81): pp. 43–59.

Bill, James A., and Carl Leiden. (1984). *Politics in the Middle East*. Boston: Little, Brown.

Black, Ian. (11-18-03). "EU Hits Out at Israeli Fence." *The Guardian*. Online. http://www.guardian.co.uk/israel/Story/0,2763,1087396,00.html.

Blank, Stephan. (10-29-03). "Testimony—Committee on International Relations, Subcommittee on the Middle East and Central Asia, U.S. House of Representatives: Terrorism in Asia and the Pacific." *Congressional Quarterly*. Online. http://homeland.cq.cm/hs/display.do?dockey=/usr/local/cqonline/docs/html.

Bodansky, Yoseff. (1999). *Bin Laden: The Man Who Declared War on America*. Rocklin, CA: Forum.

———. (1986). "Terrorism in America." Paper presented at EITWAT (Equalization on the War against Terrorism), September, New Orleans, LA.

Bodrero, D. Douglas. (2002). "Law Enforcement's New Challenge to Investigate, Interdict, and Prevent Terrorism." *The Police Chief* (February): pp. 41–48.

Bouchat, Clarence J. (1996). "A Fundamentalist Islamic Threat to the West." *Studies in Conflict and Terrorism* 19: pp. 339–352.

Bovard, James. (2003). *Terrorism and Tyranny: Trampling Freedom, Justice, and Peace to Rid the World of Evil.* New York: Palgrave Macmillan.

Bowden, Mark. (2004). "News Judgment and Jihad." (Letters.) *The Atlantic Monthly* 294 (5).

Bowers, Stephen R., and Kimberly R. Keys. (1998). "Technology and Terrorism: The New Threat for the Millennium." *Conflict Studies* (May).

Brackett, D. W. (1996). *Holy Terror: Armageddon in Tokyo.* New York: Weatherhill.

Bradley, Ed. (8-29-04). "60 Minutes." Aired on CBS Television.

Bright, John. (1981). *A History of Israel* (3rd ed.). Philadelphia: Westminster.

Britain at Your Finger Tips. (2005 [accessed]). "Northern Ireland." Online. http://www.britainusa.com/nireland/.

Bruce, Steve. (1995). "Paramilitaries, Peace, and Politics: Ulster Loyalists and the 1994 Truce." *Studies in Conflict and Terrorism* 18: pp. 187–202.

Bureau of Alcohol, Tobacco, and Firearms, U.S. Department of the Treasury. (1995). *Violent White Supremacist Groups.* Washington, DC: ATF.

Burgess, Mark. (8-23-04). "Explaining Religious Terrorism." Center for Defense Information. Online. http://www.cdi.org/friendlyversion/printversion .cfm?documentID=2384.

Burke, Jason. (1-18-04). "Al Qaeda Launches Online Terrorist Manual." *Guardian Unlimited.* Online. http://www.guardian.co.uk/alqaida/story/ 0,12469,1125879,00.html.

Burton, Anthony. (1976). *Urban Terrorism.* New York: Free Press.

Byford, Grenville. (2002). "The Wrong War." *Foreign Affairs* 81 (July/August): pp. 34–43.

Byman, Daniel. (2003). "Should Hezbollah Be Next?" *Foreign Affairs* 82 (November/December): pp. 54–66.

———. (1998). "The Logic of Ethnic Terrorism." *Studies in Conflict and Terrorism* 21: pp. 149–169.

Calabresi, Massimo, and Romesh Ratnesar. (3-11-02). "Can We Stop the Next Attack?" *Time*, pp. 24–37.

California Department of Justice. (2002). Office of the Attorney General. Anti-Terrorist Information Center.

Online. http://caag.state.ca.us/antiterrorism/ index.htm.

Campbell, Joseph. (1985). *The Inner Reaches of Outer Space: Metaphor as Myth and Religion.* New York: A. van der Marck.

———. (1949). *The Hero with a Thousand Faces.* New York: MJF Books.

Campbell, Joseph, with Bill Moyer. (1998). *The Power of Myth.* New York: Doubleday.

Cappel, Robert P. (1979). *S.W.A.T. Team Manual.* Boulder, CO: Paladin Press.

Carment, David, Patrick James, and Donald J. Puchala (eds.). (1998). *Peace in the Midst of Wars: Preventing and Managing International Ethnic Conflicts.* Columbia: University of South Carolina Press.

Carmichael, Paul, and Colin Knox. (2004). "Devolution, Governance, and the Peace Process." *Studies in Conflict and Terrorism* 16 (Autumn): pp. 593–621.

Carter, David. (2004). *Law Enforcement Intelligence: A Guide for State, Local, and Tribal Law Enforcement Agencies.* Washington, DC: Department of Justice. Also available online. http://www.cops.usdoj.gov/Default .asp?Item=1404.

———. (2003). "Cyberterrorism and Computer Crime." Tallahassee, FL: Institute for Intergovernmental Research.

Casteel, Steven W. (5-20-03). "Narco-Terrorism: International Drug Trafficking and Terrorism—A Dangerous Mix." Testimony, Committee on the Judiciary, U.S. Senate. Online. http://www.judiciary.senate.gov/ testimony.cfm?id=764&wit_id=2111.

Cavanaugh, Tim. (3-11-04). "Meet Hizbollah." *Reasononline.* Online. http://reason.com/interview/hizbollah .shtml.

CBS News. (8-5-04). "Chicago Bomb Plot Stopped." Online. http://www.cbsnews.com/stories/2004/08/ 05/terror/main634270.shtml.

Cebrowsky, Arthur. (2004). "Netwar." Unpublished speech at the Assistant Secretary of Defense Conference on Special Operations. September. Alexandria, VA.

Cebrowsky, Arthur, and Thomas P. M. Barnett. (2003). "The American Way of War." *Proceedings of the U.S. Naval Institute* (January): pp. 40–45.

Cebrowsky, Arthur, and John J. Gratska. (1998). "Network-Centric Warfare: Its Origins and Future." *Proceedings of the U.S. Naval Institute* (January): pp. 28–35.

Center for Consumer Freedom. (9-4-04). "Non-Violent Protests with Guns?" Online. http://www.consumer-freedom.com/news_detail.cfm/headline/1561.

Centers for Disease Control and Prevention. (2001a). "Basic Facts about Anthrax." Atlanta: CDC.

———. (2001b). "Basic Facts about Smallpox." Atlanta: CDC.

Center for Strategic and International Studies. (2004). *Cybercrime, Cyberterrorism, and Cyberwarfare.* Forward and Recommendations. Online. http://www.csis.org/pubs/cyberfor.html.

———. (2001). See Cilluffo, Cardash, and Lederman, 2001.

Chang, Nancy. (2001). "The USA Patriot Act: What's So Patriotic about Trampling on the Bill of Rights?" Center for Constitutional Rights. Online. http://www.ccr-ny.org/whatsnew/usa_patriot_act.asp.

Cheema, Shah. (10-3-01). "Hawala—Traditional Asian Remittance System." Online. http://www.moreloanshere.com/articles/61/hawala-banking.html.

Chouvy, Pierre-Arnaud. (3-25-04). "Narco-Terrorism in Afghanistan." *Terrorism Monitor: In-Depth Analysis of the War on Terror* II (6).

Christian Science Monitor. (2005 [accessed]). "Conflict in Chechnya: Background." Online. http://www.csmonitor.com/atcsmonitor/specials/chechnya/ch1.html.

Christopher, William. (1999). "Report of the Independent Commission on the Los Angeles Police Department." In Larry K. Gaines and Gary W. Cordner (eds.), *Policing Perspectives: An Anthology.* Los Angeles: Roxbury.

Church of the Creator. (2005 [accessed]). "Creativity World Wide." Online. http://www.creator.org/.

Cid, David. (2004). "Suicide Bombers." Tallahassee, FL: Institute for Intergovernmental Research.

Cilluffo, Frank J., Sharon L. Cardash, and Gordon N. Lederman. (2001). *Combating Chemical, Biological, Radiological, and Nuclear Terrorism: A Comprehensive Strategy: A Report of the CSIS Homeland Defense Project.* Washington, DC: Center for Strategic and International Studies.

Clark, Robert. (1984). *The Basque Insurgents.* Madison: University of Wisconsin Press.

———. (1979). *The Basques.* Reno: University of Nevada Press.

Clarke, Richard. (2002). Testimony on Cyberspace Security. U.S. Senate Subcommittee on the Judiciary. Washington, DC: U.S. Senate, recorded from C-Span, February 13.

Clausewitz, Carl von. (1984 [1831]). *On War.* Translated by Michael Howard and Peter Paret. Princeton, NJ: Princeton University Press.

Clutterbuck, Lindsay. (2004). "The Progenitors of Terrorism: Russian Revolutionaries or Extreme Irish Republicans?" *Terrorism and Political Violence* 16 (Spring): pp. 154–181.

Clutterbuck, Richard C. (1980). *Guerrillas and Terrorists.* Athens: Ohio University Press.

———. (1975). *Living with Terrorism.* London: Faber & Faber.

CNN. (1-30-04). "Cyanide, Arsenal Stirs Domestic Terror Fear." Online. http://www.cnn.com/2004/US/Southwest/01/30/cynaide.probe.ap/index.html.

———. (1-29-04). "Most Will Miss Biometric Passport Deadline." Online. http://www.cnn.com/2004/US/01/28/biometric.passports/.

Coates, James. (1987). *Armed and Dangerous: The Rise of the Survivalist Right.* New York: Hill & Wang.

Cohen, Ariel. (10-29-03). "Testimony—Committee on International Relations, Subcommittee on the Middle East and Central Asia, U.S. House of Representatives." *Congressional Quarterly.* "Terrorism in Asia and the Pacific." Online. http://homeland.cq.cm/hs/display.do?dockey=/usr/local/cqonline/docs/html.

Cohen, Yoel. (1983). "The PLO: Guardian Angels of the Media." *Midstream:* pp. 7–10.

Colb, Sherry F. (10-10-01). "The New Face of Racial Profiling: How Terrorism Affects the Debate." *Find Law's Legal Commentary.* Online. http://writ.news.findlaw.com/200111010.html.

Cole, David, and James X. Dempsey. (2002). *Terrorism and the Constitution: Sacrificing Civil Liberties in the Name of National Security.* New York: The Free Press.

Collin, Barry. (2004). "The Future of CyberTerrorism: Where the Physical and Virtual Worlds Converge." Online. http://afgen.com/terrorism1.html.

Collins, Aukai. (2002). *My Jihad: The True Story of an American Mujahid's Amazing Journey from Usama Bin Laden's Training Camps to Counterterrorism with the FBI and CIA.* Guilford, CN: The Lyons Press.

Commission on Accreditation for Law Enforcement Agencies. (1990). *Accreditation Program Overview.* Fairfax, VA: CALEA.

Cooley, John. (2002). *Unholy Wars: Afghanistan, America, and International Terrorism.* London: Pluto Press.

Cooper, H. H. A. (2001). "Terrorism: The Problem of Definition Revisited." *American Behavioral Scientist* 44 (February): pp. 881–893.

———. (1978). "Terrorism: The Problem of the Problem Definition." *Chitty's Law Journal* 26: pp. 105–108.

———. (1977a). "Terrorism and the Media." In Yonah Alexander and Seymour Finger (eds.), *Terrorism: Interdisciplinary Perspectives.* New York: John Jay.

———. (1977b). "What Is a Terrorist? A Psychological Perspective." *Legal Medical Quarterly* 1: pp. 8–18.

Cooper, H. H. A., et al. (eds.) (1976). *Report of the Task Force on Disorders and Terrorism.* National Advisory

Committee on Criminal Justice Standards and Goals. Washington, DC: Government Printing Office.

Costigan, Giovanni. (1980). *A History of Modern Ireland.* Indianapolis, IN: Bobbs-Merrill.

Cordesman, Anthony H. H. (2001). *Terrorism, Asymmetric Warfare, and Weapons of Mass Destruction.* Westport, CT: Greenwood Publishing Group.

Corley, Felix. (3-4-04). "Ruslan Gelayev: Feared Chechen Rebel-Turned-Bandit." Independent News U.K. Online. http://news.independent.co.uk/people/obituaries/story.jsp?story=497568.

Cornwell, Bernard. (1997). *The Winter King: A Novel of Arthur.* New York: St. Martin's.

Corrado, Raymond, and Rebecca Evans. (1988). "Ethnic and Ideological Terrorism in Western Europe." In Michael Stohl (ed.), *The Politics of Terrorism.* New York: Dekker.

Council on Foreign Relations. (2004). "Terrorism: An Introduction." Online. http://www.terrorismanswers.com/terrorism/introduction/html. From http://www.cfrterrorism.org/index/, access the entire guide, including "Al-Aqsa Martyrs "Terrorism and the Media" (http://cfrterrorism.org/terrorism/media_print.html).

———. (2002). "Basque Fatherland and Liberty (ETA)." Online. http://cfrterrorism.org/groups/eta.html.

Countdown with Keith Olberman. (5-5-04). "Interview with Steven Emerson." Aired on MSNBC.

Covenant, the Sword, and the Arm of the Lord. (1982). *Defense Manual.* Zorapath-Horeb, AR: CSA.

Cragin, R. Kim, and Sara A. Daly. (2004). *The Dynamic Terrorist Threat: An Assessment of Group Motivations and Capabilities in a Changing World.* Santa Monica, CA: RAND. Also available online. http://www.rand.org/publications/MR/MR1782/MR1782.pdf.

Craig, Gordon A. (1968). *The Politics of the Prussian Army: 1640–1945.* New York: Oxford University Press.

Crefeld, Martin van. (1991). *The Transformation of War.* Cambridge, MA: Harvard University Press.

Crenshaw, Martha (ed.). (1995). *Terrorism in Context.* University Park: Pennsylvania State University Press.

———. (1983). *Terrorism, Legitimacy, and Power.* Middletown, CT: Wesleyan University Press.

Criss, Nur Bilge. (1995). "The Nature of PKK Terrorism in Turkey." *Studies in Conflict and Terrorism* 18: pp. 17–38.

Critical Incident Analysis Group. (2001). *Threats to Symbols of American Democracy.* Charlottesville: University of Virginia.

Cronin, Audrey Kurth. (2003). *Terrorist and Suicide Attacks.* Washington, DC: Congressional Reference Service. CRS Report for Congress. Online. http://www.fas.org/irp/crs/RL32058.pdf.

———. (5-23-03). "Al Qaeda after the Iraq Conflict." Congressional Reference Service. CRS Report for Congress, Order Code RS21529. Online. http://fpc.state.gov/documents/organization/21191.pdf.

Cronin, Audrey Kurth, and James M. Ludes. (2004). *Attacking Terrorism: Elements of a Grand Strategy.* Washington, DC: Georgetown University Press.

Crossan, John Dominic. (1999). *The Birth of Christianity: Discovering What Happened in the Years Immediately after the Execution of Jesus.* San Francisco: Harper San Francisco.

Cummings, Jeanne. (8-13-02). "States Mend Homeland Security Blanket." *Wall Street Journal,* p. A4.

Dakroub, Hussein. (5-14-04). "Beheading Condemned by Hamas and Hizbollah." *Independent News.* Online. http://news.independent.co.uk/world/middle_east/story.jsp?story=521094.

Danitz, Tiffany, and Warren P. Strobel. (1999). "The Internet's Impact on Activism: The Case of Burma." *Studies in Conflict and Terrorism* 22: pp. 257–269.

de Silva, Marik. (5-5-96). "Sunshine over Jaffna." *Far Eastern Economic Review:* p. 159.

DEA (Drug Enforcement Administration). (9-03). "Drug Intelligence Brief." Online. http://www.usdoj.gov/dea/pubs/intel/02039/02039.html.

del Carmen, Rolando. (1991). *Civil Liberties in American Policing: A Text for Law Enforcement Personnel.* Englewood Cliffs, NJ: Prentice-Hall.

Della Porta, Donatella. (1995). "Left-Wing Terrorism in Italy." In Martha Crenshaw (ed.), *Terrorism in Context.* State College: Pennsylvania State University.

Denson, Bryan, and James Long. (1999). "Ecoterrorism Sweeps the American West," *Portland Oregonian,* September 26; "Ideologues Drive the Violence," September 27; "Terrorist Acts Provoke Change in Research, Business, Society," September 28; "Can Sabotage Have a Place in a Democratic Community?" September 29. Online. http://www.oregonlive.com/cgi-bin/printer/printer.cgi.

Department of Defense. (1-9-01). "DOD USS *Cole* Commission Report." Online. http://www.defenselink.mil/pubs/cole20010109.html.

Department of Homeland Security. (5-11-04). "Homeland Security and the National Academies Highlight the Role of the Media in Terrorism Response." Online. http://www.dhs.gov/dhspublic/display?theme=43&content=3549&print=true.

Diamond, Larry. (2004). "What Went Wrong in Iraq." *Foreign Affairs* 83 (September/October): pp. 34–56.

Dillon, Sam. (10-4-01). "A Forum Recalls Unheeded Warning." *New York Times,* p. A16.

Dixon, Paul. (2004). "Peace within the Realms of the Possible? David Trimble, Unionist Ideology, and Theatrical Politics." *Terrorism and Political Violence* 16 (Autumn): pp. 462–482.

Dobbins, James. (2005). "Iraq: Winning the Unwinnable War." *Foreign Affairs* 84 (January/February): pp. 16–25.

Dobkin, Bethami A. (1992). *Tales of Terror: Television News and the Construction of the New Terrorist Threat.* New York: Praeger.

Donovan, Michael. (2002). "Palestinian Islamic Jihad." Center for Defense Information. Online. http://www .cdi.org/terrorism/pij.cfm.

Doran, Michael Scott. (2002). "Somebody Else's Civil War." *Foreign Affairs* 81 (January/February): pp. 22–42.

Downs, Anthony C. (1967). *Inside Bureaucracy.* Boston: Little, Brown.

Doyle, Charles. (2002). "The USA Patriot Act: A Sketch." Congressional Reference Service. CRS Report for Congress. Online. http://www.fas.org/irp/crs/RS21203.pdf.

Dreyfuss, Robert. (3-23-02). "The Cops are Watching You." Online. http://www.ccmep.org/hotnews2/cops_are _watching052302.htm.

Drug Enforcement Administration. (9-03). "Drug Intelligence Brief." DEA Online. http://www.usdoj.gov/dea/ pubs/intel/02039/02039.html.

Dunn, Seamus, and Valerie Morgan. (1995). "Protestant Alienation in Northern Ireland." *Studies in Conflict and Terrorism* 18: pp. 175–185.

Dvorkin, Jeffrey A. (2003). "Framing Terrorism." *Media Matters*, National Public Radio. Online. http://www.npr .org/yourturn/ombudsman/2003/031112.html.

Dymond, Jonny. (10-2-04). "U.S. and Turkey to Hit PKK." BBC News. Online. http://news.bbc.uk/2/hi/ europe/3158686.stm.

Dyson, William. (2004). "Incident Update." Tallahassee, FL: Institute for Intergovernmental Research. (Restricted distribution, unavailable for public review.)

———. (2000). "An Overview of Terrorism." Tallahassee, FL: Institute for Intergovernmental Research.

The Economist. (3-26-05). "The Battle for Public Relations." *The Economist*, p. 48.

———. (10-4-03). "Al Qaeda Operations are Rather Cheap." *The Economist*, p. 45.

Ehrenfeld, Rachel. (2003). *Funding Evil: How Terrorism Is Financed and How to Stop It.* Chicago: Bonus Books.

Electronic Frontier Foundation. (2001a). "USA PATRIOT Act as Passed by Congress." Online. http://www.eff. org/Privacy/Surveillance/Terrorism/20011025_hr3162 _usa_patriot_bill.html.

———. (2001b). "EFF Analysis of the Provisions of the USA Patriot Act." Online. http://www.eff.org/Privacy/ Surveillance/Terrorism_militias/20011031_eff_usa _Patriot_analysis.html

Eliade, Mircea. (1961). *Myths, Dreams, and Mysteries: The Encounter between Contemporary Faiths and Archaic Realities.* Translated by Philip Mairet. San Francisco: Harper.

Emerson, Steven. (2002). *American Jihad: The Terrorist Living among Us.* New York: Free Press.

———. (1994). "Jihad in America." Public Broadcasting System. Aired on PBS.

Emerson, Steven A., and Cristina del Sesto. (1991). *Terrorist: The Inside Story of the Highest Ranking Iraqi Terrorist Ever to Defect to the West.* New York: Villard.

Emerson, Steven, and Jonathan Levin. (2003). "Terrorism Financing: Origin, Organization, and Prevention: Saudi Arabia, Terrorist Financing and the War on Terror." Testimony, U.S. Senate, Committee on Governmental Affairs. July 31.

Enteshami, Anoushiravan. (1995). *After Khomeini: The Iranian Second Republic.* London: Routledge.

Esposito, John L. (2002). *Unholy War: Terror in the Name of Islam.* New York: Oxford University Press.

———. (1999). *The Islamic Threat: Myth or Reality.* New York: Oxford University Press.

———. (1998). *Islam: The Straight Path* (3rd ed). New York: Oxford University Press.

FAIR. (2-2-99). "Extra!'s Report on Steven Emerson: Setting the Record Straight." Fairness & Accuracy in Reporting. Online. http://www.fair.org/press-releases/emerson .html.

Fanon, Frantz. (1982). *The Wretched of the Earth.* New York: Grove.

———. (1980). *A Dying Colonialism.* London: Writers and Readers.

Farah, Caesar E. (2000). *Islam.* New York: Baron's Educational Series.

Farrell, William R. (1990). *Blood and Rage: The Story of the Japanese Red Army.* Lexington, MA: Lexington Books.

Federal Bureau of Investigation. (10-12-04 [accessed]). "Counterterrorism Website." Online. http://www.fbi .gov/terrorinfo/terrorism.htm.

———. (2002). "Terrorism in the United States." Online. http://www.fbi.gov/publications/terror/terror2000 _2001.htm.

———. (1999a). *Terrorism in the United States: Special Report—Thirty Years of Terrorism.* Washington, DC: FBI.

———. (1999b). *Project Megiddo.* Online. http:// permanent.access.gpo.gov/lps3578/www.fbi.gov/ library/megiddo/megiddo.pdf.

Fernandez, Ronald. (1987). *Los Macheteros: The Wells Fargo Robbery and the Violent Struggle for Puerto Rican Independence.* Upper Saddle River, NJ: Prentice Hall.

Ferrero, Mario. (2002). "Radicalization as a Reaction to Failure: An Economic Model of Islamic Extremism." Paper presented at the Economic Consequences of Global Terrorism conference. Berlin, June.

Fesperman, Dan. (8-25-04). "Link between Hamas, al-Qaida feared." *The Baltimore Sun.* Online. http://www.baltimoresun.com/news/local/bal-te.md.hamas25aug25,1,934840.story?coll=bal-local-headlines.

Fields, Gary. (5-3-02). "U.S. Probe of Intelligence Lapses to Go beyond CIA and FBI." *Wall Street Journal*, p. A4.

Financial Action Task Force on Money Laundering. (2-4-04). "Terrorist Financing." Online. http://www1.oecd.org/fatf/TerFinance_en.htm.

Findlay, Paul. (2001). *Silent No More: Confronting America's False Images of Islam.* Beltsville, MD: Amana Publications.

Finn, John E. (1987). "Public Support for Emergency (Anti-Terrorist) Legislation in Northern Ireland: A Preliminary Analysis." *Terrorism* 10: pp. 113–124.

Firestone, Reuven. (1999). *Jihad: The Origin of Holy War in Islam.* New York: Oxford University Press.

Flynn, Stephen. (2004a). *America the Vulnerable.* New York: Harper Collins.

———. (2004b). "The Neglected Home Front." *Foreign Affairs* 83 (September/October): pp. 20–33.

———. (2002). "America the Vulnerable". *Foreign Affairs* (81): pp. 60–74.

Foote, Shelby. (1986a). *The Civil War: A Narrative. Volume I: Fort Sumter to Perryville.* New York: Vintage Books.

———. (1986b). *The Civil War: A Narrative. Volume III: Red River to Appomattox.* New York: Vintage Books.

Foreign Policy Association. (2004). "Great Decisions Guides: Terrorism—The Basque ETA." Online. http://www.fpa.org/newsletter_info2478/newsletter_info_sub_list.htm?section=The%BasqueETA.

Franklin, Nancy. (3-31-03). "News under Fire: Real Time Reporting in the Fog of War." *The New Yorker.* Online. http://www.newyorker.com/critics/television/?030407crte_television.

Fraser, James, and Ian Fulton. (1984). *Terrorism Counteraction. FC 100-37.* Fort Leavenworth, KS: U.S. Army Command and General Staff College.

Friedman, Thomas L. (2004). "War of Ideas, Part 2." *The New York Times*, January 11, Section 4, p. 15.

Gaines, Larry K., and Gary W. Cordner. (1999). *Policing Perspectives: An Anthology.* Los Angeles: Roxbury.

Gambill, Gary C., and Ziad K. Abdelnour. (2002). "Hezbollah: Between Tehran and Damascus." Online. http://www.meib.org/articles/0202_l1.htm.

Gay, Oonagh. (1998). *The Northern Ireland Bill: Implementing the Belfast Agreement.* London: House of Commons Library.

George, John, and Laird M. Wilcox. (1996). *American Extremists: Militias, Supremacists, Klansmen, Communists, and Others.* Amherst, NY: Prometheus Books.

Gibson, James William. (1994). *Warrior Dreams: Paramilitary Culture in Post-Vietnam America.* New York: Hill & Wang.

Global Witness. (2003). *For a Few Dollars More: How al Qaeda Moved into the Diamond Trade.* London: Global Witness Ltd.

GlobalSecurity.org. (2004 [accessed]). "Weapons of Mass Destruction." Online. http://www.globalsecurity.org/wmd/.

Goldberg, Jeffrey. (2002). "In the Party of God: Hezbollah Sets up Operations in South America and the United States." *The New Yorker*, October 28.

Goodman, Al. (2003). "Basque Question: Spain's Pressing Problem." CNN. Online. http://www.cnn.com/SPECIALS/201/basque/stories/overview.html.

Gottfried, Ted. (2003). *Homeland Security versus Constitutional Rights.* New York: Lerner Books.

GPO Access. (2004). "Congressional Reports: H. Rpt. 108-796—Intelligence Reform and Terrorism Prevention Act of 2004." Online. http://www.gpoaccess.gov/serialset/creports/intel_reform.html.

Green, Joshua. (2002). "The Myth of Cyberterrorism: There Are Many Ways Terrorists Can Kill You, But Computers Aren't One of Them." *Washington Monthly* (November). Online. http://www.washingtonmonthly.com/features/2001/0211.green.html.

Greer, Steven. (1995). "De-centralised Policing in Spain: The Case of the Autonomous Basque Police." *Policing and Society* 5: pp. 15–36.

Grob-Fitzgibbon, Benjamin. (2004). "From the Dagger to the Bomb: Karl Heinzen and the Evolution of Political Terror." *Terrorism and Political Violence* 16 (Spring): pp. 97–115.

Grossman, Mark. (1999). "Cyberterrorism." Computer Law Tip of the Week. Online. http://www.mgrossmanlaw.com/articles/1999/cyberterrorism.htm.

Gunaratna, Rohan. (2002). *Inside al Qaeda: Global Network of Terror.* New York: Columbia University Press.

———. (2000). "Suicide Terrorism: A Global Threat." *Jane's Intelligence Review.* Online. http://www.janes.com/security/international_security/news/usscole/jir001020_1_n.shtml.

———. (1998). "International and Regional Implications of the Sri Lankan Tamil Insurgency." Institute for Counter-Terrorism. Online. http://www.ict.org.il/.

Gurr, Ted Robert. (1988). "Some Characteristics of Political Terrorism in the 1960s." In Michael Stohl (ed.), *The Politics of Terrorism.* New York: Dekker.

Hacker, Frederick J. (1976). *Crusaders, Criminals, and Crazies.* New York: Norton.

Hadawi, Sami. (1967). *Bitter Harvest: Palestine between 1914–1967.* New York: New World Press.

Haleem, Irm. (2004). "Micro Target, Macro Impact: The Resolution of the Kashmir Conflict as a Key to Shrinking al-Qaeda's International Terrorist Network." *Journal of Terrorism and Political Violence* 16 (Spring): pp. 18–47.

Hamas. (1988). "The Covenant of the Islamic Resistance Movement." Translated and copied by MidEastWeb. Online. http://www.mideastweb.org/hamas.htm.

Hambling, David. (3-21-04). "Experts Fear Terrorists Are Seeking Fuel-Air Bombs." *The New Scientist.* Online. http://www.newscientist.com/news/news.jsp?id=ns99994785.

Hamilton, Iain. (1971). "From Liberalism to Extremism." *Conflict Studies* 17: pp. 5–17.

Hamm, Mark. (1996). *American Skinheads: The Criminology and Control of Hate Crime.* New York: Praeger Paperbacks.

Hamm, Mark (ed.). (1994). *Hate Crime: International Perspectives on Causes and Control.* Cincinnati: Anderson.

Hanauer, Laurence S. (1995). "The Path to Redemption: Fundamentalist Judaism, Territory, and Jewish Settler Violence in the West Bank." *Studies in Conflict and Terrorism* 18: pp. 245–270.

Hanson, Victor Davis. (1989). *The Western Way of War: Infantry Battle in Ancient Greece.* New York: Alfred A. Knopf.

Harik, Judith Palmer. (2004). *Hezbollah: The Changing Face of Terrorism.* London: I. B. Taurus.

Harsono, Andreas, and Indonesia Eriyanto. (3-3-03). "Bali, Terrorism, and Indonesian Media." Journalism Asia, Center for Media Freedom and Responsibility. Online. http://wwwcmfr.com.ph/ja/2003/media%20and%20terrorism/harsono.html.

Harris, John W. (1987). "Domestic Terrorism in the 1980s." *FBI Law Enforcement Bulletin* 56: pp. 5–13.

Harris, Marvin. (1990). *Our Kind: Who We Are, Where We Came From, and Where We Are Going.* New York: Harper Collins.

Hastings, Max. (1970). *Barricades in Belfast.* New York: Taplinger.

Herman, Edward. (1983). *The Real Terror Network.* Boston: South End Press.

Herman, Susan. (12-3-01). "The USA Patriot Act and the U.S. Department of Justice: Losing Our Balances." *Jurist.* Online. http://jurist.law.pitt.edu/forum/forumnew40.htm.

Hewitt, Christopher. (1984). *The Effectiveness of Anti-Terrorist Policies.* Landham, MD: University Press of America.

Heywood, Andrew. (2003). *Political Ideologies: An Introduction.* New York: Palgrave Macmillan.

Hibbert, Christopher. (1999). *Days of the French Revolution.* New York: Morrow.

Higham, Nick. (2002). "America Keeps Its Blinkers On." *British Journalism Review* 13 (1): pp. 13–18. Also online. http://www.bjr.org.uk/data/2002/no1_higham.htm.

Hill, Fiona. (10-29-03). "Testimony—Committee on International Relations, Subcommittee on the Middle East and Central Asia, U.S. House of Representatives." *Congressional Quarterly.* "Terrorism in Asia and the Pacific." Online. http://homeland.cq.cm/hs/display.do?dockey=/usr/local/cqonline/docs/html.

Hill, Sean, and Richard Ward. (2002). *Extremist Groups: An International Compilation of Terrorist Organizations, Violent Political Groups, and Issue-Oriented Militant Movements.* Huntsville, TX: Sam Houston State University.

Hinton, Henry L., Jr. (1999). *Combating Terrorism: Observations on Biological Terrorism and Public Health Initiatives.* Washington, DC: General Accounting Office.

Hiro, Dilip. (1996). *Dictionary of the Middle East.* New York: St. Martin's Press.

———. (1987). *Iran under the Ayatollahs.* London: Routledge & Kegan Paul.

Hirsh, Michael. (2002). "Bush and the World." *Foreign Affairs* 81 (September/October): pp. 18–43.

History Channel. (2000). "100 Years of Terror." Four-part series. New York: A&E Television Networks.

Hitt, Greg, and David S. Cloud. (6-10-02). "Bush's Homeland Security Overhaul Faces Obstacles." *Wall Street Journal,* p. A4.

Hoffman, Bruce. (6-1-03). "The Logic of Suicide Terrorism." *Atlantic Monthly* (291): pp. 40–48.

———. (1999a). "Terrorism Trends and Prospects." In Ian Lesser, Bruce Hoffman, John Arquilla, David Ronfeldt, Michele Zanini, and Brian Michael Jenkins, *Countering the New Terrorism.* Santa Monica, CA: RAND.

———. (1999b). *Inside Terrorism.* New York: Columbia University Press.

———. (1998). "Old Madness, New Methods." Santa Monica, CA: RAND. Online. http://www.rand.org/publications/randreview/issues/rr.winter98.9/methods.html.

———. (1995). "Holy Terror: The Implications of Terrorism Motivated by a Religious Imperative." *Studies in Conflict and Terrorism* 18: pp. 271–284.

Hoffman, Bruce, et al. (Forthcoming). "Suicide Bombers." Santa Monica, CA: RAND.

Hoffman, Stanley. (1-13-03). "The High and the Mighty: Bush's National-Security Strategy and the New American Hubris." *The American Prospect* (13): pp. 28–32.

Holden, Richard. (1986). *Postmillennialism as a Justification for Right-Wing Violence.* Gaithersburg, MD: International Association of Chiefs of Police.

———. (1985). "Historical and International Perspectives on Right-Wing Militancy in the United States." Paper presented at the annual meeting of the Academy of Criminal Justice Sciences, March, Las Vegas, NV.

Homer-Dixon, Thomas. (2002). "The Rise of Complex Terrorism." *Foreign Affairs* 81 (January/February): pp. 52–62.

Hooper, Ibrahim. (11-15-00). "WSJ Rejects Muslim Reply to Steven Emerson." Council on American-Islamic Relations. Online. http://www.musalman.com/islamnews/amj-wsjrejectsmuslimreply.html.

Horchem, Hans-Josef. (1986). "Terrorism in West Germany." *Conflict Studies* 186.

———. (1985). "Political Terrorism: The German Perspective." In Ariel Merari (ed.), *On Terrorism and Combating Terrorism.* Frederick, MD: University of America Press.

Horovitz, David. (2004). *Still Life with Bombers: Israel in the Age of Terrorism.* New York: Knopf Publishing Group.

Hosenball, Mark. (4-4-05). "The Hunt for Zarqawi's Webmasters." *Newsweek*, p. 6.

Howard, Michael. (2002). "What's in a Name?: How to Fight Terrorism." *Foreign Affairs* 81 (January/February): pp. 43–59.

———. (1988). *Clausewitz.* New York: Oxford University Press.

Hudzik, John, and Gary Cordner. (1983). *Planning in Criminal Justice Organizations and Systems.* New York: Macmillan.

Hughes, Joanna, and Caitlin Donnelly. (2004). "Attitudes to Community Relations in Northern Ireland: Signs of Optimism in the Post Cease Fire Period?" *Terrorism and Political Violence* 16: pp. 567–592.

Huntington, Samuel P. (1996). *The Clash of Civilizations and the Remaking of World Order.* New York: Simon & Schuster.

———. (1993). "The Clash of Civilizations?" *Foreign Affairs* 72: pp. 22–49.

Institute for Counter-Terrorism. (2004). "Hamas." Online. http://www.ict.org.il/inter_ter/orgdet.cfm?orgid=13.

———. (2001). *Countering Suicide Terrorism.* Herzliya, Israel: Institute for Counter-Terrorism.

———. (1996). "Palestinian Islamic Jihad." Online. http://www.ict.org.il/inter_ter/orgdet.cfm?orgid=28.

Institute for Intergovernmental Research. (2004). "International Terrorism in Transition." Tallahassee, FL: IIR.

International Association of Chiefs of Police. (2001). *Terrorism Response.* Alexandria, VA: IACP.

———. (1967). *The Patrol Operation.* Alexandria, VA: IACP.

International Crisis Group. (2002). "Al Qaeda in Southeast Asia: The Case of the 'Ngruki Network in Indonesia." Online. www.crisisweb.org.

Isikoff, Michael, and Mark Hosenball. (3-12-04). "Paying for Terror." Newsweek Web Exclusive. Online. http://www.msnbc.msn.com/id/4963025/.

Israeli Foreign Ministry. (1998). "Iran and Hizbullah." Online. http://www.ict.org.il/_home.htm.

———. (1996). "Hizbullah." Online. http://www.israel-mfa.gov.il.

Israeli, Raphael. (2004). "Palestinian Women: The Quest for a Voice in the Public Square through 'Islamikaze Martyrdom.'" *Terrorism and Political Violence* (16): pp. 66–96.

Isseroff, Ami. (2004). "A History of the Hamas Movement." MidEastWeb. Online. http://www.mideastweb.org/hamashistory.htm.

Jaber, Hala. (1997). *Hezbollah: Born with a Vengeance.* New York: Columbia University Press.

Jacobs, Jeffrie. (1983). *S.W.A.T. Tactics.* Boulder, CO: Paladin Press.

Janke, Peter. (1983). *Guerrilla and Terrorist Organizations.* New York: Macmillan.

Jarboe, James. (2-12-02). Testimony before the U.S. House of Representatives, House Resource Committee, Subcommittee on Forests and Forest Health. Reproduced from "FBI Testifies to House Ecoterror Hearing." Online. http://www.furcommission.com/news/newsF04f.htm.

Jenkins, Brian Michael. (2004a). "The Operational Code of the Jihadists." Unpublished briefing prepared for the Army Science Board: RAND. April 1.

———. (2004b [accessed]). "Where I Draw the Line." *The Christian Science Monitor.* Online. http://www.csmonitor.com/specials/terrorism/lite/expert.html.

———. (2002). *Countering al Qaeda: An Appreciation of the Situation and Suggestions for a Strategy.* RAND. Online. http://www.rand.org/publications/MR/MR1620/index.html.

———. (1987). "Will Terrorists Go Nuclear?" In Walter Laqueur and Yonah Alexander (eds.), *The Terrorism Reader.* New York: Meridian.

———. (1984). "The Who, What, When, Where, How, and Why of Terrorism." Paper presented at the Detroit Police Department Conference on "Urban Terrorism: Planning or Chaos?," November, Detroit.

Jensen, Richard Bach. (2004). "Daggers, Rifles, and Dynamite: Anarchist Terrorism in Nineteenth Century Europe." *Terrorism and Political Violence* (16): pp. 116–153.

Johnson, David, and Borgna Brunner. (2004). "Timeline of Key Events in Chechnya, 1830–2004." Online. http://www.infoplease.com/spot/chechnyatime1.html.

Johnson, Kevin. (1-29-02). "NYPD adds CIA, military experts." *USA Today.* Online. http://www.usatoday.

Joll, James. (1980). *The Anarchists.* Cambridge, MA: Harvard University Press.

Jones, Juanita, and Abraham Miller. (1979). "The Media and Terrorist Activity: Resolving the First Amendment Dilemma." *Ohio Northern University Law Review* 6: pp. 70–81.

Joshi, Manoj. (1996). "On the Razor's Edge: The Liberation Tigers of Tamil Eelam." *Studies in Conflict and Terrorism* 19: pp. 19–42.

Joyner Library. (2004). "War on Terrorism." Joyner Academic Research Services, East Carolina University. Online. http://www.lib.ecu.edu/govdoc/terrorism.html.

Juergensmeyer, Mark. (2000). *Terror in the Mind of God: The Global Rise of Religious Violence.* Berkeley: University of California Press.

———. (1988). "The Logic of Religious Violence." In David C. Rapoport (ed.), *Inside Terrorist Organizations.* New York: Columbia University Press.

Kafala, Tarik. (8-1-01). "Israel's Assassination Policy." BBC News. Online. http://news.bbc.co.uk/1/hi/world/middle_east/1258187.stm.

Kagan, Robert. (2004). "America's Crisis of Legitimacy." *Foreign Affairs* 83 (March/April): pp. 65–87.

Kaplan, David E. (12-15-03). "The Saudi Connection: How Billions in Oil Money Spawned a Global Terror Network. *U.S. News and World Report.* Online. http://www.usnews/issue/031215/usnews/15terror.htm.

Karmon, Ely. (2000). "Hamas' Terrorism Strategy: Operational Limitations and Political Constraints." *Middle East Review of International Affairs* 4 (March). Online. http://meria.idc.ac.il/journal/2000/issue1/jv4n1a7.html.

———. (2001). "Osama bin Laden: Speculations on Possible State Sponsorship." Institute for Counter-Terrorism. Online. http://www.ict.org.il/

Katz, Lewis R. (11-24-01). "Anti-Terrorism Laws: Too Much of a Good Thing." *Jurist.* Online. http://jurist.law.pitt.edu/forum/forumnew39.htm.

Kayyem, Juliette, and Arnold M. Howitt (eds.). (2002). *Beyond the Beltway: Focusing on Hometown Security.* Cambridge, MA: Harvard University.

Keinon, Herb. (5-21-04). "Israel Preparing for Wave of Terror." *Jerusalem Post.*

Kelley, Kevin. (1982). *The Longest War.* Westport, CT: Hill.

Kellner, Douglas. (2002). "September 11, the Media, and War Fever Television." *New Media* 3 (May): pp. 143–151.

Kelly, Michael J., and Thomas H. Mitchell. (1981). "Transnational Terrorism and the Western Press Elite." *Political Communication and Persuasion* 1: pp. 269–296.

Kelsay, John. (1993). *Islam and War: A Study in Comparative Ethics.* Louisville, KY: John Knox Press.

Kepel, Gilles. (2002). *Jihad: The Trail of Political Islam.* Cambridge, MA: The Belknap Press of Harvard University.

Ketcham, Christine C., and Harvey J. McGeorge. (1986). "Terrorist Violence: Its Mechanics and Countermeasures." In Neil C. Livingstone and Terrell E. Arnold (eds.), *Fighting Back.* Lexington, MA: Heath.

Khatami, Siamak. (1997). "Between Class and Nation: Ideology and Radical Basque Ethnonationalism." *Studies in Conflict and Terrorism* 20: pp. 395–417.

Kibble, David. G. (1996). "The Threat of Militant Islam: A Fundamental Reappraisal." *Studies in Conflict and Terrorism* 19: pp. 353–364.

Kingston, Shane. (1995). "Terrorism, the Media, and the Northern Ireland Conflict." *Studies in Conflict and Terrorism* 18: pp. 203–227.

Kittel, G. (1964). *The Theological Dictionary of the New Testament,* Vol. II, *Delta–Eta.* Grand Rapids, MI: Eerdmans.

Konotorovich, E. V. (6-18-02). "Make Them Talk." *Wall Street Journal,* p. A12.

Korn, David A. (1995). *Interview with Abdullah Ocalan.* Online. http://kurdstruggle.org/index.shtml.

Kraska, Peter B. (1996). "Enjoying Militarism: Political/Personal Dilemmas in Studying U.S. Police Paramilitary Units." *Justice Quarterly* (13): pp. 405–429.

Kraska, Peter, and Victor Kappeler. (1999). "Militarizing American Police: The Rise and Normalization of Paramilitary Units." In Larry K. Gaines and Gary W. Cordner (eds.), *Policing Perspectives: An Anthology.* Los Angeles: Roxbury.

Krasna, Joshua S. (1997). "Narcotics and the National Security Producer States." *Texas Law Review.* Online. http://www.lib.unb.ca/Texts/JCS/s96/articles/krasna.html.

Krasnoboka, Natalya. (2002). "Real Journalism Goes Underground: The Internet Underground." *The International Journal for Communications Studies* 64 (5): pp. 479–499.

Krauthammer, Charles. (7-16-04). "U.N. Will Go to Any Length to Condemn Israel." *Jewish World Review.* Online. http://www.io.com/~freeman/updates/950.htm.

Kurz, Anat. (1994). "Palestinian Terrorism—The Violent Aspect of a Political Struggle." In Yonah Alexander (ed.), *Middle Eastern Terrorism: Current Threats and Future Prospects.* New York: Hall.

Kushner, Harvey W., and Benjamin Jacobson. (1998). "Financing Terrorist Activities through Coupon Fraud and Counterfeiting." *Counterterrorism and Security International* 5 (Summer): pp. 10–12.

Labeviere, Richard. (2000). *Dollars for Terror: The United States and Islam.* New York: Algora.

LaGuardia, Anton. (2003). *War without End: Israelis, Palestinians, and the Struggle for a Promised Land.* New York: St. Martin's Press.

Lake, Eli. (4-29-04). "Hamas Agents May Be Lurking in U.S.: Fears Rantisi's Vow to Attack May Awaken Operatives Here." *The New York Sun.*

Laqueur, Walter. (1999). *The New Terrorism: Fanaticism and the Arms of Mass Destruction.* New York: Oxford University Press.

———. (1987). *The Age of Terrorism.* Boston: Little, Brown.

Laqueur, Walter, and Yonah Alexander (eds.). (1987). *The Terrorism Reader.* New York: Meridian.

Lee, Alfred McClung. (1983). *Terrorism in Northern Ireland.* New York: General Hull.

LeFebre, Georges. (1967). *The Coming of the French Revolution.* Princeton, NJ: Princeton University Press.

Lesser, Ian. (1999). "Changing Terrorism in a Changing World." In Ian O. Lesser, Bruce Hoffman, John Arquilla, David Ronfeldt, Michele Zanini, and Brian Michael Jenkins (eds.), *Countering the New Terrorism.* Santa Monica, CA: RAND.

Levin, David. (2003). "Structure of News Coverage of a Peace Process." *Press/Politics* 8 (4): pp. 27–53.

Levitt, Leonard. (1-28-02). "A Fed-Friendly NYPD? Not Yet." *News Day.* Online. http://newsday.com/news/columnists/nynyplaz22256708jan28.

Lewy, Gunther. (1974). *Religion and Revolution.* New York: Oxford University Press.

Lichtblau, Eric. (9-29-01). "Impassioned Letter Left Behind by Hijackers Urges Them to Stay the Course in Return for Paradise." *Los Angeles Times.* Online. http://www.latimes.com/news/nation world/nation/la-092901letter.story.

Liddell Hart, Basil H. (1967). *Strategy.* New York: Praeger.

Liff, Sonia, and Anne Sofie Laegren. (2003). "Cybercafes: Debating the Meeting and Significance of Internet Access in a Café Environment." *New Media & Society* 5 (3): pp. 307–312.

Liptak, Adam. (5-31-02). "Changing the Standard." *New York Times.* Online. http://nytimes.com/2002/05/31/national/31ASSE.html.

Livingstone, Neil C., and David Halevy. (4-29-88). "Terrorist Operations Expensive." *National Review,* p. 28.

Llora, Francisco, Joseph M. Mata, and Cynthia L. Irvin. (1993). "ETA: From Secret Army to Social Movement: The Post-Franco Schism of the Basque Nationalist Movement." *Terrorism and Political Violence* 5: pp. 106–134.

Lockyer, Adam. (2003). "The Relationship between the Media and Terrorism." The Australian National University. Online. http://rspas.anu.edu.au/papers/sdsc/viewpoint/paper_030818.pdfnline.

Lopez, George A., and David Coright. (2004). "Containing Iraq: Sanctions Worked." *Foreign Affairs* 83 (July/August): pp. 90–103.

Luft, Gal, and Anne Korin. (2004). "Terrorism Goes to Sea." *Foreign Affairs* 83 (November/December): pp. 61–71.

Lynch, Dov. (2004). *Engaging Eurasia's Separatist States: Unresolved Conflicts and De Facto States.* Washington, DC: The United States Institute of Peace.

Lynch, Marc. (2003). "Taking the Arabs Seriously." *Foreign Affairs* 82 (September/October): pp. 81–94.

MacDonald, Andrew. (William Pierce). (1989). *Hunter: A Novel.* Hillsboro, WV: National Alliance.

———. (1985). *The Turner Diaries.* Arlington, VA: National Vanguard.

Maier, Timothy. (11-10-03). "Counterfeit Goods Pose Real Threat." *Insight on the News,* p. 21.

Maise, Michelle, and Heidi Burgess. (2005 [accessed]). "Extremist/Spoilers." BeyondIntractability.org. Online. http://www.intractableconflict.org/m/extremists.jsp.

Makarenko, Tamara. (2002). "Terrorism and Transnational Organized Crime: The Emerging News." In Paul Smith (ed.), *Transnational Violence and Seams of Lawlessness in the Asia-Pacific: Linkages to Global Terrorism.* Hawaii: Asia Pacific Centre for Security Studies.

Management Analytics and others. (1995). "Sun Tzu: The Art of War." Online. http://www.all.net.books/tzu/html.

Mannes, Aaron. (2004). *Profiles in Terror: A Guide to Middle East Terrorist Organizations.* New York: Rowman & Littlefield.

Manning, Peter K. (1976). *Police Work: The Social Organization of Policing.* Cambridge, MA: MIT Press.

Manuel, Marlon. (2000). "Center Closing as Hunt for Rudolph Scales Down." *Atlanta Journal-Constitution,* March 21.

Marighella, Carlos. (1971). *For the Liberation of Brazil.* Translated by John Butt and Rosemary Sheed. Harmondsworth, UK: Pelican.

———. (1969). *The Minimanual of the Urban Guerrilla.* Unpublished copy of the U.S. Army Military Intelligence School. Also online at http://www.marxists.org/archive/marighella-carlos/1969/06/minimanual-urban-guerrilla/.

Marsden, Paul. (2001). "Letter: Copycat Terrorism: Fanning the Fire." Online. http://jom-emit.cfpm.org/2001/vol5/marsden_p_let.html.

———. (10-4-01). "Psychologist Warns of Risk of Copycat Terrorist Attacks." University of Sussex. Online. http://www.sussex.ac.uk/press_office/media/media175.shtml.

Martin, L. John. (1985). "The Media's Role in International Terrorism." *Terrorism* 8: pp. 44–58.

Mason, Carol. (2002). *Killing for Life: The Apocalyptic Narrative of Pro-Life Politics.* New York: Cornell University Press.

Massie, Robert K. (1991). *Dreadnought: Britain, Germany and the Coming of the Great War.* New York: Random House.

Mattoon, Steven. (1987). *S.W.A.T. Training and Deployment.* Boulder, CO: Paladin Press.

Mazur, Allan. (1982). "Bomb Threats and the Mass Media: Evidence for a Theory of Suggestion." *American Sociological Review* 47: pp. 407–410.

McPherson, James M. (1988). *Battle Cry of Freedom: The Civil War Era.* New York: Ballantine Books.

Mehrota, O. N. (2000). "Ethnic Strife in Sri Lanka." Institute for Defence Studies and Analyses, India. Online. http://www.ict.org.il/home.htm.

Melman, Yossi. (1986). *The Master Terrorist.* New York: Avon.

Memorial Institute for the Prevention of Terrorism. (12-30-04). "Terrorism Information Center." Online. http://www.mipt.org/.

Michigan State University. (2004 [accessed]). "Criminal Justice Resources: Emergency Management." Online. http://www.lib.msu.edu/harris23/crimjust/emerman.htm.

Mid East Forum. (2004). "Perceptions of the United States in the Middle East." Aired on C-Span 2, February 14.

Middle East Research and Information Project. (2005 [accessed]). "Palestine, Israel and the Arab-Israeli Conflict: A Primer." Online. http://www.merip.org/palestine-israel_primer/toc-pal-isr-primer.html.

MidEast Web. (2005 [accessed]). "Israel and Palestine: A Brief History." Online. http://www.mideastweb.org/briefhistory.htm.

Military.com. (2004). "Palestinian Islamic Jihad." Online. http://www.military.com/Resources/ResourceFileView?file=PIJ-Organization.htm.

Miller, Abraham. (1982). *Terrorism, the Media, and the Law.* New York: Transnational.

Miller, John, Michael Stone, and Chris Mitchell. (2003). *The Cell: Inside the 9/11 Plot, and Why the FBI and CIA Failed to Stop It.* New York: Hyperion.

Miller, Judith, Stephen Engelberg, and William Broad. (2001). *Germs: Biological Weapons and America's Secret War.* New York: Simon & Schuster.

Mitchell, Alison, and Carl Hulse. (6-27-02). "Accountability Concern Is Raised over Security Department." *The New York Times.* Online. http://www.nytimes.com/2002/06/27/national/27RIDG.html.

Monaghan, Rachel. (2004). "An Imperfect Peace: Paramilitary Punishments in Northern Ireland." *Terrorism and Political Violence* 16: pp. 439–461.

Moss, Robert. (1972). *Urban Guerrillas.* London: Temple Smith.

Moxon-Browne, Edward. (1987). "Spain and the ETA." *Conflict Studies* 201.

Muir, Angus M. (1999). "Terrorism and Weapons of Mass Destruction: The Case of Aum Shinrikyo." *Studies in Conflict and Terrorism* 22: pp. 79–91.

Mullendore, Kristine, and Jonathan R. White. (1996). "Legislating Terrorism: Justice Issues and the Public Forum." Paper presented at the Academy of Criminal Justice Sciences Annual Meeting, March, Las Vegas, NV.

Murphy, Kim. (2-4-2004). "Chechnya Suicide Bombers." *The Los Angeles Times.* Online. http://www.latimes.com.

Nacos, Brigitte L. (2002). *Mass-Mediated Terrorism: The Central Role of the Media in Terrorism and Counterterrorism.* New York: Rowman & Littlefield.

Napoleoni, Loretta. (2003). *Modern Jihad: Tracing the Dollars behind the Terror Networks.* London: Pluto.

National Advisory Committee on Criminal Justice Standards and Goals. (1976). See H. H. A. Cooper et al. (eds.) (1976).

National Commission on Terrorist Attacks upon the United States. (2004). *The 9/11 Commission Report: Final Report of the National Commission on Terrorist Attacks upon the United States.* New York: W. W. Norton & Company. Also available online. http://www.9-11commission.gov/report/911Report.pdf.

National Conference of State Legislatures. (2003). "Cyberterrorism." Online. http://www.ncsl.org/programs/lis/CIP/cyberterrorism.htm.

National Immigration Forum. (2004). "State and Local Police Enforcement: Backgrounder: Immigration

Law Enforcement by State and Local Police." Online. http://www.immigrationforum.org/DesktopDefault .aspx?tabid=572.

National Public Radio. (7-9-04). "Outrage? Not So Much." *On the Media from NPR*. Online. http://www .onthemedia.org/transcripts/transcripts_070904 _outrage.html.

———. (12-6-01). "Liberty vs. Security: An NPR Special Report." Online. http://www.npr.org/programs/ specials/liberties/index.html.

NBC/*The Wall Street Journal*. (8-23/25-04). "War on Terrorism." PollingReport.com. Online. http:// www.pollingreport.com/terror.htm.

Netanyahu, Benjamin. (1986). *Terrorism: How the West Can Win*. New York: Avon. (Revised editions published 1995 and 1997.)

New Jersey State Police. (2002). Intelligence Service Section. Online. http://www.state.nj.us/lps/njsp/about/intel .html.

New York Times, International. (7-29-04). "World Briefing: Middle East." Online. http://www.nytimes .com/2004/07/29/international/29brie.html?ex= 1093752000&en=2ddc52a32376a2a2&ei=5070 &pagewanted=all.

New York Times News Service. (8-25-96). "American Terrorist: Just an Average Joe with a Bomb." Reported in the *Grand Rapids Press*.

Nice, David C. (1988). "Abortion Clinic Bombings as Political Violence." *American Journal of Political Science* 32: pp. 178–195.

Nilson, Chad, and Tod Burke. (2002). "Environmental Extremists and the Eco-Terrorism Movement." *ACJS Today* (24): pp. 1–6.

9-11 Commission Report. See National Commission on Terrorist Attacks upon the United States.

Nordland, Rod, Sami Yousafzi, and Babak Dehghanpisheh. (8-19-02). "How al Qaeda Slipped Away." *Newsweek*, pp. 34–41.

Norris, Pippa, Montague Kern, and Marion Just (eds.). (2003). *Framing Terrorism: The News Media, the Government, and the Public*. London: Routledge.

Nusse, Andrea. (1999). *Muslim Palestine: The Ideology of Hamas*. London: Harwood Academic Publications.

Nydell (Omar), Margaret K. (2002). *Understanding Arabs: A Guide for Westerners*. Yarmouth, ME: Intercultural Press.

O'Callaghan, Sean. (1998). *The Informer*. London: Bantam Press.

O'Conner, Tom. (11-2-04). "Civil Liberties and Domestic Terrorism." North Carolina Wesleyan College. Online. http://faculty.ncwc.edu/toconnor/429/429lect19.htm.

Office of Homeland Security. (2002). *National Strategy for Homeland Security*. Washington, DC: Office of Homeland Security.

Oliver, Haneef James. (2002). *The Wahabbi Myth: Dispelling Prevalent Fallacies and the Fictitious Link with bin Laden*. Birmingham, UK: Salafi Publications.

Oliver, Mark. (5-23-04). "Israel Targeting Entire Hamas Leadership." *The Guardian*. Online. http://www .guardian.co.uk/israel/Story/0,2763,1175986,00.html.

Organization for the Prohibition of Chemical Weapons. (2000). "Nerve Agents: Lethal Organo-Phosphorus Compounds Inhibiting Cholonest-erase." Online. http://www.opcw.nl/chemhaz/nerve.htm.

Osterholm, Michael T., and John Schwartz. (2000). *Living Terrors*. New York: Delta.

Ostovsky, Simon, Dmitry Beliakov, and Mark Franchetti. (9-29-04). "Death of Mercy." *Sunday Times (London)*. Features Section, pp. 14–16.

Palestine Monitor. (4-29-04). "Israel Emptying Jerusalem of Palestinians by Bulldozing Their Homes." Online. http://www.palestinemonitor.org/updates/israel _emptying_jerusalem_of_palestinians.htm.

Paletz, David L., John Z. Ayanian, and Peter A. Fozzard. (1982). "Terrorism on Television News: The IRA, the FALN, and the Red Brigades." In William C. Adams (ed.), *Television Coverage of International Affairs*. Norwood, NJ: Ablex.

Paletz, David L., Peter A. Fozzard, and John Z. Ayanian. (1982). "The IRA, the Red Brigades, and the FALN in the *New York Times*." *Journal of Communication* 32: pp. 162–171.

Palmer, Monte, and Princess Palmer. (2004). *At the Heart of Terror: Islam, Jihadists, and America's War on Terror*. Lanham, MD: Rowman and Littlefield.

Palmer, Nancy (ed). (2003). *Terrorism, War, and the Press*. Cambridge, MA: Joan Shorenstein Center.

Pape, Robert A. (2003). "Dying to Kill: The Strategic Logic of Suicide Bombers." *International Herald Tribune*, September 23.

Parker, Laura. (1-23-02). "A Frenzied Race for Answers, Antibiotics." *USA Today*, p. 6A.

Parliamentary Joint Committee on Terrorism. (2004). "The Listing of Palestinian Islamic Jihad. Australian Government. Online. http://www.aph.gov.au/house/ committee/pjcaad/pij/report/chapter3.pdf.

Patai, Raphael. (2002). *The Arab Mind*. New York: Hetherleigh Press.

Paz, Reuven. (2004). "Hamas' Solidarity with Muqtada al-Sadr: Does the Movement Fall under the Control of Hizbollah and Iran?" Herzliya, Israel: PRISM Series of Special Dispatches on Global Jihad, No. 4/2.

———. (2001). "The Islamic Legitimacy of Suicide Bombing." In Institute for Counter-Terrorism, *Countering Suicide Terrorism*. Herzliya, Israel: Institute for Counter-Terrorism.

———. (2000). "Abu Nidal: Coming in from the Cold?" Institute for Counter-Terrorism. Online. http://www.ict.org.il/.

PBS *Frontline*. (2003). "Israel/Palestine Territories—In the Line of Fire. Online. http://www.pbs.org/frontlineworld/stories/israel.palestine/.

———. (2002). "Interview: Jihad Ja'Aire, Al Aqsa Martyrs Brigade Leader." From OccupiedPalestine.org. Online. http://www.fromoccupiedpalestine.org/node.php?id=745.

———. (1999). "Hunting bin Laden." Online. http://www.pbs.org/wgbh/pages/frontline/shows/binladen/.

Peacetalk. (2003). "Politics and Markets." Online. http://www.peaktalk.com/archives/2003_07.php.

Perl, Raphael F. (2001). *National Commission on Terrorism: Background and Issues for Congress*. February 6. Online. http://www.maurizioturco.it/National_Security_Achive/Terrorism_and_US_Policy/crs20010206.pdf.

———. (1998). *Terrorism: U.S. Response to Bombings in Kenya and Tanzania: A New Policy Direction?* Congressional Reference Service. CRS Report for Congress. Online. http://usinfo.state.gov/topical/pol/terror/crs96091.htm.

———. (1997). "Terrorism, the Media, and the Government: Perspectives, Trends, and Options for Policymakers." Online. http://www.au.af.mil/au/awc/awcgate/state/crs-terror-media.htm.

Phillips, Kevin. (1999). *The Cousins' War: Religion, Politics, and the Triumph of Anglo-America*. New York: Basic Books.

Pierce, William. See Andrew MacDonald.

Pipes, Daniel. (2003). *Militant Islam Reaches America*. New York: Norton.

———. (1983). *In the Path of God: Islam and Political Power*. New York: Basic Books.

Pisano, Vittorfranco S. (1987). *The Dynamics of Subversion and Violence in Contemporary Italy*. Stanford, CA: The Hoover Institute.

Pitcavage, Mark. (2000). *Right-Wing Scams*. Tallahassee, FL: Institute for Intergovernmental Research.

———. (1999a). "Anti-Government Extremism: Origins, Ideology, and Tactics." Tallahassee, FL: Institute for Intergovernmental Research.

———. (1999b). "Current Activities and Trends." Tallahassee, FL: Institute for Intergovernmental Research.

———. (11-8-99). "Old Wine, New Bottles: Paper Terrorism, Paper Scams, and Paper Redemption." *Militia Watch Dog*. Online. http://www.adl.org/mwd/redemption/asp.

———. (4-7-99). "Trusts and the Untrustworthy: Pure Trusts and Patriots for Profit." *Militia Watch Dog*. Online. http://www.adl.org/mwd/puretrust.asp.

Plet, Barbara. (5-13-99). "World: bin Laden behind Luxor Massacre." BBC News. Online. http://news.bbc.co.uk/1/hi/world/middle_east/343207.stm.

Pluchinsky, Dennis. (1993). "Germany's Red Army Faction: An Obituary." *Studies in Conflict and Terrorism* 16: pp. 135–157.

———. (1986). "Middle Eastern Terrorist Activity in Western Europe: A Diagnosis and Prognosis." *Conflict Quarterly* 3: pp. 5–26.

———. (1982). "Political Terrorism in Western Europe: Some Themes and Variations." In Yonah Alexander and Kenneth A. Myers (eds.), *Terrorism in Europe*. New York: St. Martin's.

Podhoretz, Norman. (1981). "The Subtle Collusion." *Political Communication and Persuasion* 1: pp. 84–89.

Police Service of Northern Ireland. (2005 [accessed]). Homepage. Online. http://www.psni.police.uk/index/about_psni.htm.

Pollard, Neal. (10-31-04). "TRC Analysis: The Future of Terrorism." The Terrorism Research Center. Online. http://www.terrorism.com/modules.php?op=modload&name=News&file=article&sid=5658.

Posner, Richard A. (8-29-04). "The 9-11 Report: A Dissent." *The New York Times*. Online. http://www.nytimes.com/2004/08/29/books/review/29POSNERL.html?ex=1094787860&ei=1&en=b755f3ccc383aefd.

Post, Jerrold M. (1987). "Rewarding Fire with Fire: Effects of Retaliation on Terrorist Group Dynamics." *Terrorism* 10: pp. 23–36.

Qutb, Sayyid. (1990). *Milestones*. Indianapolis: American Trust Publications.

Radelet, Louis, and David Carter. (2000). *Police and the Community* (7th ed.). New York: Macmillan.

Raman, B. (12-3-04). "Suicide and Suicide Terrorism." South Asia Analysis Group. Online. http://www.saag.org/papers10/paper947.html.

———. (3-3-04). "Massacres of Shias in Iraq and Pakistan—The Background." South Asia Analysis Group. Online. http://www.saag.org/papers10/paper941.html.

———. (11-22-03). "Istanbul: The Enemy Within." *Asia Times*. Online. http://www.atimes.com/atimes/Middle_East/EK22Ak01.html.

———. (3-10-02). "Islamic Terrorism in India: The Hydra-Headed Monster." South Asia Analysis Group. Online. http://www.saag.org/papers6/paper526.html.

Randal, Jonathan. (2004). *Osama: The Making of a Terrorist*. New York: Knopf.

———. (1984). *Going All the Way*. New York: Vintage.

Ranstorp, Magnus. (1998). "Interpreting the Broader Context and Meaning of Bin-Laden's Fatwa." *Studies in Conflict and Terrorism* 21: pp. 321–330.

———. (1996). *Hizb'Allah in Lebanon: The Politics of the Western Hostage Crisis*. New York: St. Martin's Press.

———. (1994). "Hizbollah's Command Leadership: Its Structure, Decision-Making Relationship with Iranian Clergy and Institutions." *Terrorism and Political Violence* 6 (Autumn). Also available online at http://www.st-andrews.ac.uk/academic/intrel/research/cstpv/pages/terrorism.html.

Rapoport, David C. (2004). "Modern Terror: The Four Waves." In Audrey Kurth Cronin and James M. Ludes (eds.), *Attacking Terrorism: Elements of a Grand Strategy*. Washington, DC: Georgetown University Press.

Rashid, Ahmed. (2002). *Jihad: The Rise of Militant Islam in Central Asia*. New Haven, CN: Yale University Press.

Rasul, Azmat. (10-7-04). "Terrorism and Freedom of Information." Asia Media. Online. http://www.asiamedia.ucla.edu/print.asp?parentid=15686.

Rauf, Feisal Abdul. (2004). *What's Right with Islam: A New Vision for Muslims*. San Francisco: Harper.

Raufer, Xavier. (1993). "The Red Brigades: Farewell to Arms." *Studies in Conflict and Terrorism* 16: pp. 313–325.

Reese, John. (1986, September). Unpublished briefing presented at EITWAT (Equalization in the War Against Terrorism), New Orleans.

Reeve, Simon. (1999). *The New Jackals: Ramzi Yousef, Osama bin Laden, and the Future of Terrorism*. York, PA: Maple Press.

Regan, Tom. (7-14-04). "New Skirmishes in the Patriot Act Battle: Ashcroft Praises It, but Opponents Call the Report Suspect." *The Christian Science Monitor*. Online. http://www.csmonitor.com/2004/0714/dailyUpdate.html.

Reich, Walter, and Walter Laqueur (eds.). (1998). *Origins of Terrorism: Psychologies, Ideologies, Theologies, States of Mind*. Princeton: Woodrow Wilson Center.

Reuters. (4-21-96). "Israeli Intervention in Lebanon Is Latest of Many." Online. http://www.nando.net/newsroom/nt/421many.html.

———. (4-12-96). "Israel Arch Foe Hizbollah Tough Nut to Crack." Online. http://www.nando.net/newsroom/nt/412/r/whoiz.html.

Reuters, UK. (2-8-04). "Paper Says al Qaeda Has Nukes." Online. http://www.reuters.co.uk/newsPackageArticle.jhtml?type=topNews&storyID=454465&section=news.

Richardson, Louise. (2003). "Global Rebels: Terrorist Organizations as Trans-National Actors." In Russell D. Howard and Reid L. Sawyer, (eds.), *Terrorism and Counterterrorism: Understanding the New Security Environment*. New York: Dushkin/McGraw Hill.

Riley, Kevin Jack, and Bruce Hoffman. (1995). *Domestic Terrorism*. Santa Monica, CA: RAND. Also available online at http://www.rand.org/publications/MR/MR505/MR505.pdf.

Riordan, Richard J., and Amy B. Zegart. (7-5-02). "City Hall Goes to War." *New York Times*. Online. http://www.nytimes.com/2002/07/05/opinion/05RIOR.html.

Risen, James, and Judy L. Thomas. (1-26-98). "Pro-Life Turns Deadly: The Impact of Violence on America's Anti-Abortion Movement." Online. http://www.rickross.com/reference/a-abortion/a-abortion2.html.

Rivera, Magaly. (2005 [accessed]). "Welcome to Puerto Rico: History." Online. http://welcometopuertorico.org/history6.shtml.

Roberts, Adam. (8-27-02). "The Changing Faces of Terrorism." BBC Online. http://www.bbc.co.uk/history/war/sept_11/changing_faces_01.shtml.

Rojahn, Christoph. (1998). "Left-Wing Terrorism in Germany: The Aftermath of Ideological Violence." *Conflict Studies* (October).

Rood, Justin. (12-31-04). "Memo to New DHS Secretary: With Intel, Smaller is Better." *Page Fifteen: Congressional Quarterly*. Online. http://page15.com/2004/12/memo-to-new-dhs-secretary-with-intel.html.

Rosbaltnews. (6-6-04). "The Media and Terrorism." Online. http://www.rosbaltnews.com/print/print?cn=66803.

Rosebraugh, Craig. (2004). *Burning Rage for a Dying Planet: Speaking for the Earth Liberation Front*. New York: Lantern Books.

Ross, Jeffery Ian. (1999). "Beyond the Conceptualization of Terrorism: A Psychological-Structural Model of the Causes of This Activity." In Craig Summers and Eric Markusen (eds.), *Collective Violence: Harmful Behavior in Groups and Governments*. New York: Rowman & Littlefield.

Rothem, Dan. (2002). "In the Spotlight: al-Aqsa Martyrs Brigades." Center for Defense Information. Online. http://www.cdi.org/terrorism/Aqsa.cfm.

Royal Ulster Constabulary. (2001). "The Royal Ulster Constabulary." Online. http://www.royalulsterconstabulary.org/.

Rubenstein, Richard E. (1987). *Alchemists of Revolution*. New York: Basic Books.

Rubin, Barry, and Judith Colp Rubin (eds.). (2002). *Anti-American Terrorism and the Middle East: A Documentary Reader.* New York: Oxford University Press.

Rubin, James. (2003). "Stumbling into War." *Foreign Affairs* 82 (September/October): pp. 46–66.

Rubin, Michael. (8-5-04). "The PKK Factor." *National Review Online.* Online. http://www.nationalreview.com/rubin/rubin200408051220.asp.

Ruthven, Malise. (2000). *Islam in the World* (2nd ed.). London: Oxford University Press.

Saad-Ghorayeb, Amal. (2002). *Hizbu'llah: Politics and Religion.* London: Pluto Press.

Saeed, Abdullah, and Hassan Saeed. (2004). *Freedom of Religion, Apostasy, and Islam.* Aldershot, UK: Ashgate Publishing.

Safir, Howard. (2003). *Security: Policing Your Homeland, Your State, Your City.* New York: St. Martin's.

Sanction, Thomas. (3-1-99). "A Terrorist's Bitter End." CNN.com and Time.com. Online. http://www.time.com/time/daily/special/ocalan/bitterend.html.

Sapp, Allen. (1985). "Basic Ideologies of Right-Wing Extremist Groups in America." Paper presented at the annual meeting of the Academy of Criminal Justice Sciences, March, Las Vegas, NV.

Saradzhyan, Simon. (2-4-04). "Cult of the Black Widows." *The Moscow Times.* Online. http://www.themoscowtimes.com/stories/2004/02/04/011.html.

Sargent, Lyman Towed (ed.). (1995). *Extremism in America.* New York: New York University Press.

Scarman, Leslie. (1972). *Violence and Civil Disturbance in Northern Ireland in 1969.* Belfast: Her Majesty's Stationery Office.

Schabner, Dean. (1-30-04). "ELF Making Good on Threat." ABCNews.com. Online. http://abcnews.go.com/sections/us/DailyNews/elf010130.html.

Schaffert, Richard W. (1992). *Media Coverage and Political Terrorists: A Quantitative Analysis.* New York: Praeger.

Schevill, Ferdinand. (1922). *The History of the Balkan Peninsula: From the Earliest Times to the Present.* New York: Harcourt, Brace, and Co.

Schlesinger, Philip. (1981). "Terrorism, the Media and the Liberal-Democratic State: A Critique of Orthodoxy." *Social Research* 48: pp. 74–99.

Schmid, Alex. (1988, 2004). "Academic Consensus Definition." United Nations Office on Drugs and Crime. Online. http://www.unodc.org/unodc/terrorism_definitions.html.

———. (1983). *Political Terrorism: A Research Guide to Concepts, Theories, Data Bases, and Literature.* New Brunswick, CT: Transaction.

Schmid, Alex P., and Janny F. A. de Graaf. (1982). *Violence as Communication.* Newbury Park, CA: Sage.

Schmitt, Eric. (4-29-02). "Administration Split on Local Role in Terror Fight." *New York Times.* Online. http://www.nytimes.com/2002/04/29/politics/29IMMI.html.

Schneider, Friedrich. (2002). "Money Supply for Terrorism—The Hidden Financial Flows of Islamic Terrorist Organisations: Some Preliminary Results from an Economic Perspective." Paper presented at the Economic Consequences of Global Terrorism conference. Berlin, June.

Schneier, Bruce. (2003). *Beyond Fear: Thinking about Security in an Uncertain World.* New York: Springer-Verlag.

Schoof, Mark, and Gary Fields. (3-25-02). "Anthrax Attack Summary." *Wall Street Journal,* p. A20.

Schramm, Matthias, and Markus Taube. (2002). "The Institution Foundations of al Qaida's Global Financial System." Related papers not presented at the conference, The Economic Consequences of Global Terrorism. Berlin, June.

Scott-Joynt, Jeremy. (10-15-2003). "Charities in Terror Fund Spotlight." BBC News. Online. http://news.bbc.co.uk/2/hi/business/3186840.

Seale, Patrick. (1992). *Abu Nidal: A Gun for Hire.* New York: Random House.

Seelye, Katherine Q. (6-23-02). "War on Terror Makes for Odd Twists in Justice System." *New York Times.* Online. http://www.nytimes.com/2002/06/29/national/23SUSP.html.

Segaller, Stephen. (1987). *Invisible Armies: Terrorism into the 1990s.* San Diego: Harcourt Brace Jovanovich.

Sela, Avraham, and Shaul Mishal. (2000). *The Palestinian Hamas: Vision, Violence, and Co-existence.* New York: Columbia University Press.

Semati, Mehdi. (2002). "Imagine the Terror Television." *New Media* 13 (May): pp. 213–218.

Seper, Jerry. (2-11-04). "Sleeper Cells of al Qaeda in U.S. Despite War." *The Washington Times,* p. 6.

Serafino, Nina M. (2002). "Combating Terrorism: Are There Lessons to Be Learned from Foreign Experiences?" Congressional Reference Service. Online. http://fpc.state.gov/documents/organization/7957.pdf.

Shahar, Yael. (2002). "The al-Aqsa Martyrs Brigades: A Political Tool with an Edge." Institute for Counter-Terrorism. Online. http://www.ict.org.il/articles/articledef.cfm?articleid=430.

———. (1998). "Osama bin Ladin: Marketing Terrorism." Institute for Counter-Terrorism. http://www.ict.org.il/articles/articledet.cfm?articleid=42.

———. (1997). "Information Warfare." Institute for

Counter-Terrorism. Online. http://www.ict.org.il/
_articles/articledet.cfm?articleid=13.

Shay, Saul. (2002). *The Endless Jihad: The Mujahidin, the Taliban, and Bin Laden*. Herzliya, Israel: Institute for Counter-Terrorism.

Sherman, Lawrence W. (1978). *The Quality of Police Education*. San Francisco: Josey-Bass.

Simon, Steven, and Jonathan Stevenson. (2004). "The Road to Damascus." *Foreign Affairs* 83 (May/June): pp. 110–119.

Simpson, Glenn R., David Crawford, and Keith Johnson. (4-14-04). "Crime Pays, Terrorist Finds. *The Wall Street Journal*, p. 4.

Slisli, Fouzi. (2000). "The Western Media and the Algerian Crisis." *Race and Class* 41 (3): pp. 43–57.

Smith, Brent L. (1994). *Terrorism in America: Pipe Bombs and Pipe Dreams*. Albany: State University of New York Press.

Smith, Brent, et al. (2004). "The MIPT Terrorism Knowledge Base." University of Arkansas. Online. http://www.tkb.org/tkb.html.

Smith, Gordon. (2005). "Media and Terrorism." University for Peace: Institute for Media, Peace, and Security. Online. http://mediapeace.org/smith/htm.

Soussi, Alasdair. (6-14-04). "The Enigma That Is Lebanese Hezbollah." *World Press Review Online*. Online. http://www.worldpress.org/Mideast/1873.cfm.

Spechard, Anne, Nadeja Tarabrina, Valery Krasnov, and Khapta Akhmedova. (2004). "Research Note: Observations of Suicidal Terrorists in Action." *Terrorism and Political Violence* 16: pp. 305–327.

Stanton, Bill. (1991). *Klanwatch: Bringing the Ku Klux Klan to Justice*. New York: Grove Weidenfeld.

Sterling, Claire. (1986). *The Terror Network*. New York: Dell.

Stern, Jessica. (2003a). "The Protean Enemy." *Foreign Affairs* 82 (July/August): pp. 27–40.

———. (2003b). *Terror in the Name of God: Why Religious Militants Kill*. New York: Harper Collins.

———. (12-18-03). "When Bombers Are Women." Original in *The Washington Post*. Reprinted by Harvard University, John F. Kennedy School of Government. Online. http://www.ksg.harvard.edu/news/opeds/2003/stern_women_bombers_wp1121803.htm.

Stern, Kenneth S. (1996). *A Force on the Plain: The American Militia Movement and the Politics of Hate*. New York: Simon & Schuster.

Stevenson, Jonathan. (2003). "How Europe and America Defend Themselves." *Foreign Affairs* 82 (March/April): pp. 75–90.

Stinson, James. (1984). "Assessing Terrorist Tactics and Security Measures." Paper presented at the Detroit Police Department conference "Urban Terrorism: Planning or Chaos?" November, Detroit. (See also James Stinson [1981]. "Unconventional Threat Assessment: The Role of Behavioral Sciences in Physical Security." DNA-TR-83-32. Washington, DC: Defense Nuclear Agency.

Stohl, Michael (ed.). (1988). *The Politics of Terrorism* (3rd ed.). New York: Dekker.

Straub, Noelle. (5-1-02). "USA Patriot Act Powers Prompt Second Look." *The Hill*. Online. http://www.thehill.com/050102/patriot.shtm.

Suall, Irwin, and David Lowe. (1987). "Special Report: The Hate Movement Today: A Chronicle of Violence and Disarray." *Terrorism* 10: pp. 345–364.

Sud, Hari. (1-26-04). "End Muslim Terrorism by Ending Wahhabi Influence in Saudi Arabia." South Asia Analysis Group. Online. http://www.saag.org/papers10/paper903.html.

Sugg, John F. (1999). "Steven Emerson's Crusade: Why Is a Journalist Pushing Questionable Sources behind the Scene?" *Extra!* Online. http://www.fair.org/extra/9901/emerson.html.

Sulc, Lawrence B. (1996). *Law Enforcement Counterintelligence*. Shawnee Mission, KS: Varno Press.

Swamy, M. R. Narayan. (1994). *Tigers of Lanka: From Boys to Guerrillas*. Columbia, MO: South Asia Books.

Swanson, Charles R., Leonard Territo, and Robert W. Taylor. (2001). *Police Administration: Structures, Processes, and Behavior* (5th ed.). Upper Saddle River, NJ: Prentice-Hall.

Taheri, Amir. (7-21-04). "Terrorism Is a Double Edged Sword—It Cuts Both Ways." *Gulf News*. Online. http://www.benadorassociates.com/article/6058.

———. (1987). *Holy Terror*. Bethesda, MD: Adler & Allen.

Talkleft. (8-20-03). "Victory Act: Redefining Drug Crimes as Terrorism." Online. http://www.w3c.org/TR1999/REC-html1401-19991224/loose.dtd.

Tamil Eelam Homepage. (2005 [accessed]). Tamil Eelam Homepage. Online. http://www.eelam.com/.

Taubman, Philip. (1984). "U.S. Said to Know Little about Group Despite Intelligence Efforts." September 21, *New York Times*, p. A13.

Taylor, Eric R. (1998). *Lethal Mists: An Introduction to the Natural and Military Sciences of Chemical, Biological Warfare and Terrorism*. Commack, NY: Nova Science Publishers.

Taylor, Jerry. (2004). "The Suicide Bomber." Tallahassee, FL: Institute for Intergovernmental Research.

Taylor, Robert W. (1987). "Terrorism and Intelligence." *Defense Analysis* (3): pp. 165–175.

Thompson, Derek. (10-16-03). "Target: Zarqawi," ABC News. Online. http://abcnews.go.com/sections/world/WorldNewsTonight/zarqawi_030224.html.

Thorpe, Tory. (1996). "Black Hebrew Israelites." Online. http://www.blackomahaonline.com/blkheb.htm.

Thorton, Thomas P. (1964). "Terror as a Weapon of Political Agitation." In H. Eckstein (ed.), *Internal War*. New York: Free Press.

Tilby, Charles. (2003). "Anarchist and Left-Wing Terrorism." Tallahassee, FL: Institute for Intergovernmental Research.

Tillich, Paul. (1957). *The Dynamics of Faith*. New York: Harper Torch.

Time magazine. (1995). "Interview with a Fanatic" (Fathi Shekaki). February 6.

Times of India. (11-19-03.) "Dawood, Osama Share Smuggling Routes." Online. http://timesofindia.indiatimes.com/cms.dll/html/uncomp/articleshow?msid=291478.

Trundle, Robert C., Jr. (1996). "Has Global Ethnic Conflict Superseded Cold War Ideology?" *Studies in Conflict and Terrorism* 19: pp. 93–107.

Turks.US. (2-29-04). "Chechnya's Fighting Not Terror: U.S. Ambassador." Online. http://www.turks.us/article.php?story=20040229232835832.

Turvey, Brent E., Diana Tamlyn, and W. Jerry Chisum. (1999). *Criminal Profiling: An Introduction to Behavioral Evidence Analysis*. San Diego: Academic Press.

U.S. Army. (2003). "Cultural Guide to Iraq." Fort Riley, KS: U.S. Army, First Infantry Division.

U.S. Congress. (December 2004). "Intelligence Reform and Prevention of Terrorism Act of 2004." Online. http://www.congress.org/congressorg/webreturn/?url=http://thomas.loc.gov/cgi-bin/query/z?c108:S.2845.

U.S. Congress, House of Representatives. (5-18-04). "Testimony of Steven Emerson, Executive Director of the Investigative Project, before the House Financial Services Committee, Subcommittee on Oversight and Investigations." Online. http://financialservices.house.gov/media/pdf/051804se.pdf.

U.S. Congress, Office of Technology Assessment. (1995). *Environmental Monitoring for Nuclear Safeguards*. Washington, DC: Government Printing Office.

U.S. Court of Appeals (1996). Eleventh Circuit, No. 92-4473. *United States of America, Plaintiff-Appellee v. Robert Louis Beasley et al*. Online. http://www.law.emory.edu.11circuit/jan96/92-4773.man.html.

U.S. Department of Homeland Security. (2005 [accessed]). "Border and Transportation Security: Securing Our Borders." Online. http://www.dhs.gov/dhspublic/display?theme=50&content=875.

———. (2004). *Securing Our Homeland*. Online. http://www.dhs.gov/interweb/assetlibrary/DHS_StratPlan_FINAL_spread.pdf.

U.S. Department of Justice. (2005 [accessed]). "Preserving Life and Liberty." Online. http://www.lifeandliberty.gov/.

———. (2-20-03). "Members of the Palestinian Islamic Jihad Arrested, Charged with Racketeering and Conspiracy to Provide Support for Terrorists." Press Release. Online. http://www.usdoj.gov/opa/pr/2003/February/03_crm_099.htm.

U.S. Department of State. (2004a). "The Washington File—MIDEAST." Online. http://usinfo.state.gov/usinfo/products/washfile.html.

———. (2004b). *Patterns of Global Terrorism 2003."* Online. http://www.state.gov/s/ct/rls/pgtrpt/2003/.

———. (8-4-04). "Helsinki Groups Issue Three Reports on Human Rights Violations in Russia." Online. http://usinfo.state.gov/xarchives/display.html?p=washfile-english&y=2004&m=August&x=200408041344401CJsamohT0.2353632&t=livefeeds/wf-latest.html.

———. (1999). *Patterns of Global Terrorism: 1999*. Online. http://www.state.gov/www/global/terrorism/1999report/appb.html.

———. (1996). *Patterns of Global Terrorism 1995*. Washington, DC: Government Printing Office.

U.S. House of Representatives. (2005 [accessed]). "The United States Constitution." Online. http://www.house.gov/Constitution/Constitution.html.

———. (5-6-04). "A Review of Security Clearance Backlog and Reciprocity Issues Plaguing Today's Government and Private Sector Workforce." Committee on Government Reform. Online. http://reform.house.gov/GovReform/Hearings/EventSingle.aspx?EventID=970.

U.S. Marshals Service. (1988). Unpublished circular for domestic terrorism briefing.

United Nations. (5-17-04). "Definitions of Terrorism." Office on Drugs and Crime. Online. http://unodc.org/unodc/terrorism_definitions.html.

United States of America v. Mousa Mohammed Abu Marzook, et al. (2003). U.S. District Court, Northern District of Illinois, Eastern Division. Docket No. 03 CR 978.

United States v. Mohamad Hammoud, et al. (2002). United States District Court, Western District of North Carolina, Charlotte Division. Docket No. 3:00CR147-MU.

University of Delaware Library. (2005 [accessed]). "Middle East: A Research Guide." Online. http://www2.lib.udel.edu/subj/pols/resguide/mideast.htm.

Valburn, Marjorie. (2-4-02). "Air Marshal Program Drains Other Agencies." *Wall Street Journal*, p. A18.

Van Natta, Don, Jr. (3-30-02). "Government Will Ease Limits on Domestic Spying." *New York Times*. Online. http://www.nytimes.com/2002/03/30.html.

Vatis, Michael A. (2001). *Cyber Attacks during the War on Terrorism: A Predictive Analysis.* Hanover, NH: Institute for Security Technology Studies, Dartmouth College.

———. (1999). *Emergency Law Enforcement Services Vulnerability Survey.* Quantico, VA: Federal Bureau of Investigation.

Vice President's Task Force on Terrorism. (1986). *Public Report of the Vice President's Task Force on Combating Terrorism.* Online. http://www.population-security.org/bush_and_terror.pdf.

Walker, Edward W. (10-29-01). "Roots of Rage: Militant Islam in Central Asia." University of California, Berkeley. Online. http://ist-socrates.berkeley.edu/~bsp/caucasus/articles/walker_2001-1029.pdf.

Walker, Samuel. (1992). *The Police in America.* New York: McGraw Hill.

———. (1985). *Sense and Nonsense about Crime: A Policy Guide.* Pacific Grove, CA: Brooks/Cole.

Wall Street Journal Research Staff. (1-11-05). "A Chronology of Violence." *Wall Street Journal*, p. A16.

Wallach, Janet, and John Wallach. (1992). *Arafat in the Eyes of the Beholder.* Rocklin, CA: Prima.

Walter, Jess. (1995). *Every Knee Shall Bow: The Truth and Tragedy of Ruby Ridge and the Randy Weaver Family.* New York: HarperCollins.

Walter, John P. (5-2-02). "National Drug Control Strategy: Combating Narcoterrorism." Online. http://fpc.state.gov/9908.htm.

Wardlaw, Grant. (1982). *Political Terrorism: Theory, Tactics, and Counter-Measures.* London: Cambridge University Press.

Warwick, Donald P. (1975). *A Theory of Public Bureaucracy: Politics, Personality, and Organization in the State Department.* Cambridge, MA: Harvard University Press.

Watson, Dale L. (2002). *The Terrorist Threat Confronting the United States.* Washington, DC: Federal Bureau of Investigation, www.fbi.gov.

Waxman, Dov. (1998a). "The Islamic Republic of Iran: Between Revolution and Realpolitik." *Conflict Studies* (April).

———. (1998b). "Turkey's Identity Crises: Domestic Discord and Foreign Policy." *Conflict Studies* (August).

Weber, Max. (1947). *The Theory of Social and Economic Organization.* New York: The Free Press.

Wedgwood, Ruth. (6-14-02). "The Enemy Within." *Wall Street Journal*, p. A12.

Wege, Carl Anthony. (1994). "Hizbollah Organization." *Studies in Conflict and Terrorism* (17): pp. 151–164.

Weimann, Gabriel. (1983). "Theater of Terror: Effects of Press Coverage." *Journal of Communication* 33: pp. 38–45.

Weinberg, Leonard, Ami Pedahzur, and Sivan Hirsch-Hoefler. (2004). "The Challenges of Conceptualizing Terrorism." *Terrorism and Political Violence* 16 (Winter): 777–794.

Weisband, Edward, and Damir Roguly. (1976). "Palestinian Terrorism: Violence, Verbal Strategy, and Legitimacy." In Yonah Alexander (ed.), *International Terrorism.* New York: Praeger.

Westcott, Kathryn. (10-19-00). "Who Are Hamas?" BBC News Online. Online. http://news.bbc.co.uk/1/hi/world/middle_east/978626.stm.

Wheeler, W. (12-20-03). "Second End to Major Hostilities." Center for Defense Information. Online. http://www.cdi.org/program/document.cfm?DocumentID=1967&StartRow=1&ListRows=10&appendURL=&Orderby=D.DateLastUpdated&ProgramID=39&from_page=index.cfm.

Whine, Michael. (1999). "Cyberspace: A New Medium for Communication, Command, and Control by Extremists." Online. Institute for Counter-Terrorism. http://www.ict.org.il/articles/articledet.cfm?articleid=76.

White House. (9-11-2003). "Progress Report on the Global War on Terrorism." Online. http://usinfo.state.gov/xarchives/display.html?p=washfile-english&y=2003&m=September&x=20030911,84825ynnedd0.9592859&t=usinfo/wf-latest.html.

White, Jonathan. R. (2004). "International Terrorism in Transition." Tallahassee, FL: Institute for Intergovernmental Research.

———. (2002). "Political Violence." Tallahassee, FL: Institute for Intergovernmental Research.

———. (2001). "Political Eschatology: A Theology of Antigovernment Extremism." *American Behavioral Scientist* 44: pp. 937–956.

———. (2000). "The Religious Roots of Criminal Behavior." Tallahassee, FL: Institute for Intergovernmental Research.

———. (1997). "Militia Madness: Extremist Interpretations of Christian Doctrine." *Perspectives: A Journal of Reformed Thought* 12: pp. 8–12.

Wieviorka, Michel. (1993). *The Making of Terrorism.* Chicago: University of Chicago Press.

Wiggins, Michael E. (1986). "The Turner Diaries: Blueprint for Right-Wing Extremist Violence." Paper presented at the annual meeting of the Academy of Criminal Justice Sciences, March, Orlando, FL.

———. (1985). "The Relationship of Extreme Right-Wing Ideologies and Geographical Distribution of Select Right-Wing Groups." Paper presented at the annual meeting of the Academy of Criminal Justice Sciences, March, Las Vegas, NV.

Wikas, Seth. (2002). "The Hamas Ceasefire: Historical Background, Future Foretold?" Peacewatch. Online. http://www.washingtoninstitute.org/watch/Peacewatch/peacewatch2002/357.htm.

Wilkinson, Paul. (1997). "The Media and Terrorism: A Reassessment." *Terrorism and Political Violence* 9 (Summer): pp. 51–64.

———. (1995). "Terrorism: Motivations and Causes." Canadian Security Intelligence Service. Online. http://www.csis-scrs.gc.ca/eng/comment/com53_e.html.

Wilson, James Q. (1991). *Bureaucracy: What Government Agencies Do and Why They Do It.* New York: Basic Books.

Winchester, Simon. (1974). *Northern Ireland in Crisis.* New York: Holmes and Meier.

Windrem, Robert, and Charlene Gubash. (3-11-04). "Many Signs Point to al-Qaida." MSNBC News. Online. http://msnbc.msn.com/id/4507855/.

Wise, David. (6-2-02). "Spy Game: Changing the Rules So the Good Guys Win." *New York Times.* Online. http://www.nytimes.com/2002/06/02/weekinreview/02WISEhtml.

Wolf, John B. (1981). *Fear of Fear.* New York: Plenum.

Wolfowitz, Paul. (2004). "Ask the White House." The White House. Online. http://www.whitehouse.gov/ask/20040625.html.

Wolfsfeld, Gadt. (2001). "The News Media and the Second Intifada: Some Initial Lessons." *Press/Politics* 6 (4): pp. 113–118.

Woodham-Smith, Cecil. (1962). *The Great Hunger.* New York: Harper & Row.

World Economic Forum. (2002). "Media and Terrorism: Changing the Grand Rules." Annual Meeting 2002. Online. http://www.weforum.org/site/knowledgenavigator.nsf/Content/_S5980?open&topic_id=.

Worldnet Daily. (10-6-05). "U.S. Terror Allies Raise Millions." Online. http://www.worldnetdaily.com/news/articles.asp?ARTICLE_ID=34938.

Wright, Robin. (1989). *In the Name of God: The Khomeini Decade.* New York: Simon & Schuster.

———. (1986). *Sacred Rage.* New York: Touchstone.

Young, John A. T., and R. John Collier. (2002). "Attacking Anthrax." *Scientific American* (March): pp. 48–59.

Zassoursky, Yassen N. (2002). "Media and Communications as the Vehicle of the Open Society." *The International Journal for Communication Studies* 64 (5): pp. 425–432.

Zurawik, David. (9-12-01). "Television Served to Bring Us Together." *The Baltimore Sun.* Online. http://www.baltimoresun.com/news/custom/attack/bal-to.attacktv12sep12,1,6629769.story?ctrack=1&cset=true.

Index

Bold page numbers indicate material in tables or figures.

"Cybernotes" website, 86
cybersecurity, 319
cyberterrorism, 83–86
    countering in state and local government, 86
    cyber attacks and, 84
    cybersecurity and, 319
    defined, 83
    targets for, 83–84

Dagestan, **126**
Dakroub, Hussein, 166
Dar es Salaam, Tanzania, U.S. embassy in, al
        Qaeda attack, 88, 112, 115, 116, 295
Daschle, Tom, 93
David (king of ancient Israel), 172, 173
DEA (Drug Enforcement Administration),
        77, 78
Death Angels, 262
decentralization, terrorist group security
        and, 41
de facto campaign, 39
defense in depth, 292–293
Defense Intelligence Agency, terrorism defined
        by, 6
Degan, William, 251
de Graaf, Janny F. A., 330, 343
Dehghanpisheh, Babak, 284
deified terrorism, 50–51
del Carmen, Rolando, 298, 324
della Porta, Donatella, 257
Del Sesto, Cristina, 238
democracy, revolution and, 18
Democratic Front for the Liberation of
        Palestine (DFLP), 150, 168
demonization, 51
Dempsey, James X., 293, 295–296, 297, 320,
        321
Denson, Bryan, 258
Desert Shield, 110
Desert Storm, 110, 111
de Silva, Marik, 192
de Valera, Eamon, 198, 199, 200
Dev Sol (Turkey), 219
DFLP (Democratic Front for the Liberation of
        Palestine), 150, 168
Diamond, Larry, 220
"diamonds, conflict," 72
Dillon, Sam, 284
Direct Action (France), 214, 217, 218
direct logistical network, terrorists' need for,
        42
dirty bomb, 95, 96, 325–326
Dixon, Paul, 36
Dobbins, James, 220
Dobkin, Bethami A., 339
document fraud, 68, 69–70
domestic terrorism, 226–265, 244–265
    analysis by Brent L. Smith, 234–237
    classifying, 232–233
    conceptualizing, 226–243
        problem of, 229–231
    early studies of, 227–229
    growth in, 235
    labor violence and, 228
    vigilante actions and, 228, 229
Donnelly, Caitlin, 203
Donovan, Michael, 161, 162
Doran, Michael, 116
Downs, Anthony C., 312, 324

Doyle, Charles, 294
*Dreadnought: Britain, Germany and the Com-
        ing of the Great War* (Massie), 249
Dreyfuss, Robert, 282
Drug Enforcement Administration (DEA),
        77, 78
drug trafficking, 75, 77
    narcoterrorism and, 76–79
due process of law, 297, 300
Dunn, Seamus, 36, 203
Dvorkin, Jeffrey A., 339, 345
A Dying Colonialism (Fanon), 211
dynamite, 20, 82
Dyson, William, 26, 83, 208, 230

Earth First! 257, 258
Earth Liberation Front (ELF), 257–258
Easter Rebellion of 1916, 17, 25, 197–198
East Germany, Red Army Faction supported
        by, 214
Ebola virus, 91
The Economist, 68, 344–345
ecoterrorism, 235, 237, 257–259
Egypt
    bin Laden sent terrorists to fight in, 114
    Jihadist movements in, 129
    Qutb imprisoned by, 105
    radical groups of Islamicists in, 61
Egyptian Islamic Group, 130
    suicide bombings and, 89
Egyptian Islamic Jihad, 109, 110, 115, 130
Ehrenfeld, Rachel, 69, 70, 77, 154
Eliade, Mircea, 53, 54, 56
Elizabeth I (queen of England), 194
El Paso Intelligence Center (EPIC), 286
El Salvador
    guerrillas in, 208
    revolutionaries in, 295
Emerson, Steven, 70, 103, 163
    critics of, 240–241
    on Hamas, 238
    jihad as viewed by, 238–241
    "Jihad in America" program and, 238, 240
EMETIC (Evan Mecham Eco-Terrorist Inter-
        national Conspiracy), 237
Engelberg, Stephen, 91–92, 94
Engels, Friedrich, 21
England, Protestantism takes hold in, 25
Enteshami, Anoushiravan, 134
EPIC (El Paso Intelligence Center), 286
Eriyanto, Indonesia, 334, 345
eschatology, 59–60
Esposito, John, 62, 104, 129
    clash within civilizations theory and, 58, 59
    disagreement with Huntington's thesis
        and, 48
ethical eschatology, 59
ethnic cleansing, 217
ethnic terrorism, 178
    logic of, 179–182
Europe
    left-wing ideology in, demise of, 216–219
    religious terrorism spilled from Middle East
        into, 217
    states in, Abu Nidal sponsored by, 37
European Union (EU), Turkey being consid-
        ered for membership in, 186, 188
Evan Mecham Eco-Terrorist International
        Conspiracy (EMETIC), 237

Evans, Rebecca, 216–218, 219
executive powers, increasing in face of
        terrorism
    case against, 302–303
    case for, 299–301

Fadlallah, Sheik Mohammed Hassan, 134,
        138–139, 161
failed states, 74, 75
FAIR (Fairness & Accuracy in Reporting), 241
Fairness & Accuracy in Reporting (FAIR), 241
Fanon, Frantz, 211–212, 213, 220
Farah, Caesar E., 104
FARC (Popular Armed Forces of Colombia),
        75, 77
FARP (Armed Forces of Liberation), 246
Fatah, 170, 171
    attack on Israel and, 147, 150
    disintegration of, 153
    formation of, 147, 168
    after Karamah, 147, 150
    merger with PLO and, 147
    profile of, 168
    suicide bombing and, 167
Fatima, 131
fatwa, 115
FBI (Federal Bureau of Investigation)
    attack on San Juan headquarters of, 246
    Behavioral Science Unit of, 13
    counterintelligence program
        (COINTELPRO), 281, 295
    counterterrorism and, 230, 281, 295, 314
    criticism regarding September 11, 2001,
        attacks and, 284
    Freemen of Montana and, 207
    information sharing and, 295, 313, 314, 323
    Infrastructure Protection Center of, 86
    intelligence gathering and, 282, 284, 314
    keeping track of noncitizens and, 316
    9-11 Commission recommendations
        regarding, 288
    Posner on, 287
    powers of, after September 11, 2001, 271,
        300
    Project Megiddo and, 261, 262
    resented by other agencies, 323
    rivalries with other agencies and, 323
    Ruby Ridge incident and, 251
    terrorism defined by, 6, 233
    Terrorism in the United States and, 233
    Turner on, 285
    typology used by, 234
    underground economy and, 68
    Uniform Crime Report and, 230, 231–232,
        234, 244
    Waco siege and, 251
fear, terrorism and, 96
fedayeen, 147
Federal Border Guard Group 9, 168
Federal Law Enforcement Training Center, 315
Federal Reserve System, 248
Feinstein, Dianne, 298
Feng Chin, 69
Fenians, 196
Fernandez, Ronald, 245, 246
Ferrero, Mario, 76
field force exercise, 307
Fields, Gary, 284
Fifth Amendment, 297

fighters, media referred to al Qaeda members as, 101

The Financing of Terror (Adams), 66

Findlay, Paul, 103

firebombs, 258

Firestone, Reuven, 104

firing team, 215

First Amendment, 262, 297, 334, 338, 343–344

FISA (Foreign Intelligence Surveillance Act) of 1978, 302

FLN (National Liberation Front), 276

Flynn, Stephen, 316
critique on homeland security and, 325–326

Fneish, Mohammed, 138, 139

food poisoning, 92

Foote, Shelby, 247

force, 17, 167, 168

force multipliers, 9–10, 34, 40, 334–337

Foreign Intelligence Surveillance Act (FISA) of 1978, 302

Foreign Policy Association, 182

"Forlorn Hope," 86

Forrest, Nathan Bedford, 247–248

For the Liberation of Brazil (Marighella), 212

Fourteenth Amendment, 297, 300

Fourth Amendment, 297, 299, 314

Fox's O'Reilly Factor, 333

Fozzard, Peter, 340

France
attack on French Army by Hezbollah and, 134, 138
Basque region of, **182**
democracy in, 18
development of Jihadist networks and, 100, 106
Direct Action in, 214, 217, 218
French Revolution and, 17, 18, 22, 57, 272
police engage in intelligence gathering in, 322
potential al Qaeda attack in thwarted, 116
targeted by international Jihadists, 219
war and
French-Algerian War and, 211, 276
French Revolution and, 17, 18, 22, 57, 272
with Germany, 272
in Indochina, 74–75
Napoleonic Wars and, 25, 272

Franco, Francisco, 183

Franklin, Nancy, 333

Fraser, James, 35–37, 41

Frederick the Great, 272

Freedom (Freiheit), 21

freedom of religion, 262

Freemen of Montana, 207, 213, 254

Free-Wheeling Fundamentalists, 253, 254

Freiheit (Freedom), 21

French-Algerian War, 211, 276

French Revolution, 17, 18, 22, 57, 272

Friedman, Thomas, 8

Frontline, 111, 114, 171

Fulton, Ian, 35–37, 41

fundamentalist, 102

Furrow, Buford, 45

Gaines, Larry K., 314

Gaines, Linda, 262

Gale, William Potter, 248

Gambill, Gary C., 134, 138

Gandhi, Rajiv, 189, 192

Gaza, violence in, Saudi money traced to, 78

GEL (Guerrilla Forces of Liberation), 246

genetic engineering, 257–259

German Red Army, 35, 170, 217, 218
influenced by Tupamaros, 214

German War of Liberation, 272

Germany
counterterrorism group of, 168
Federal Border Guard Group 9 and, 168
Green Party extremists in, 44
Lenin and, 23
media control in, 338
naval race before World War I and, 249
Nazi
democracy's struggle against totalitarian-ism and, 8
extremist movements in, 12
Jews victimized by, 146
sarin gas developed by, 209
Nordic Christianity in, 252–253
police engage in intelligence gathering in, 322
radical ecologists in, 259
Red Army Faction and, 35, 170, 214, 217, 218
reunification of, 217
targeted by international Jihadists, 219
terrorism outlawed in, 5
war with France and, 272

Ghandour, Mohammed, 140

Ghanem, Abdal Fatah, 169

GIA (Algerian Armed Islamic Group), 129, 130

Gibson, James William, 12

global economy, 74

globalism, 73, 74

Global Watch, 73

Global Witness, 72

Goldberg, Jeffrey, 10, 110, 136, 137, 140

Goldman, Emma, 21

Goldstein, Baruch, 172, 173

Goodman, Al, 182

government repression, 20

GRAPO (Spain), 219

Gratska, John J., 275

Great Britain
creation of Jewish state and, 144, 146
democracy evolved in, 18
forces of, in Iraq and Kuwait, 110
Napoleonic Wars and, 25
naval race before World War I and, 249
origins and development of conflict with Ireland and, 193–196
police engage in intelligence gathering in, 322
Protestantism takes hold in, 25

Greece, 55
ancient, war in, 272
17N in, 219

Green, Joshua, 85–86

Green Party extremists in Germany, 44

Greens (Republicans)(Catholics), 38, 195–196, 197, 200, 201, 202, 203–204

Greer, Steven, 184

Griffin, Michael, 259

Gritz, Bo, 251, 254

Grob-Fitzgibbon, Benjamin, 20–21

Grossman, Mark, 83

group violence, 233

Gubash, Charlene, 102

Guerrilla Forces of Liberation (GEL), 246

guerrillas, 138
rural, 213

terrorists versus, 136, 208, 211, 213, 221
urban, 211, 215

guerrilla warfare, 208
Clausewitz and, 273
rural, 212, 213
Sun Tzu and, 273

Guevara, Ernesto "Che," 213

Gunaratna, Rohan, 87, 89–90, 106–107, 110, 111, 116, 125, 192

gun control, 250, 253, 254

Gunn, David, 259, 261

Gurr, Ted Robert, 32–33, 34, 227, 228, 229

Gush Emunim, 155, 173

Habash, George, 148, 170

Hacker, Frederick J., 13

Hadad, Wadi, 170

Hadrian (Roman emperor), 175

Haguenau, France, military cemetery in, 48

Haleem, Irm, 117

Halevy, David, 68

Hamas, 154, 163–166
Charter of, Israel's right to exist not recog-nized by, 155, 164, 167
founding of, 164, 169
fund raising and, 77, 78, 164
criminal activities in United States and, 238
Hezbollah alliance with, 140, 165
"inside" faction and, 164
Islamic Association for Palestine (IAP) and, 240
organization of, organization of Abu Nidal and, 37
Osama bin Laden and, 116
"outside" leadership and, 164
PIJ and, 162, 165
PIJ versus, 164
PLO versus, 164
PNA and, 164
profile of, 169
suicide bombings and, 87, 88, 89, 155, 164, 167
with female bomber, 165, 167
on Zarqawi's murdering young American, 11, 166

Hamilton, Iain, 202

Hamm, Mark, 230–231, 250

Hanauer, Laurence, 173

Hanson, Victor, 272

Harik, Judith, 132, 135, 160, 175, 211, 335

Harris, John, 233

Harris, Marvin, 54

Harsono, Andreas, 334, 345

Hastings, Max, 36, 201

hate crime, 230–231, 250

hate movement, 252

hate religions, 253

Hawala system, 69, **70**, 73

Hawatmeh, Naiaf, 148, 168

Hawdi, Yasser Esam, 300

Heinzen, Karl, 20–21

hemorrhagic fevers, 91

Henry VIII (king of England), 194

Herman, Edward, 5

Herman, Susan, 284, 301, 302–303

Hewitt, Christopher, 34

Hezbollah (Party of God)
attacks against United States by, 134–135
beginning of, 33, 130, 132